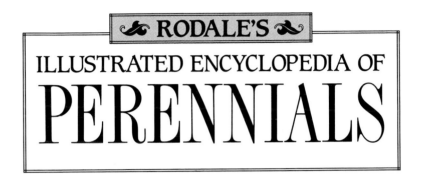

RODALE'S
ILLUSTRATED ENCYCLOPEDIA OF
PERENNIALS

RODALE'S

ILLUSTRATED ENCYCLOPEDIA OF
PERENNIALS

Ellen Phillips & C. Colston Burrell

Rodale Press, Emmaus, Pennsylvania

Our Mission

We publish books that empower people's lives.

RODALE BOOKS

Printed in the United States of America on recycled paper

Executive Editor: Margaret Lydic Balitas
Senior Editor: Barbara W. Ellis
Editor: Ellen Phillips
Contributing Editor: Nancy J. Ondra
Production Editor: Joan Benjamin
Associate Editor: Jean M. A. Nick
Copy Manager: Dolores Plikaitis
Copy Editor: Laura Stevens
Photo Editor: Heidi A. Stonehill
Editorial assistance: Susan L. Nickol
Office Manager: Karen Earl-Braymer
Indexer: Andrea Chesman
Book design: Darlene Schneck, Acey Lee, Lisa Nawaz
Art Director: Anita G. Patterson
Cover design: Linda Jacopetti

If you have any questions or comments concerning this book, please write:

Rodale Press
Book Readers' Service
33 East Minor Street
Emmaus, PA 18098

Library of Congress Cataloging-in-Publication Data

Phillips, Ellen.
    Rodale's illustrated encyclopedia of perennials / Ellen Phillips and C. Colston Burrell.
        p.   cm.
    Includes bibliographical references and index.
    ISBN 0-87596-570-9 hardcover
    1. Perennials.   2. Perennials—Encyclopedias.
    I. Burrell, C. Colston.   II. Rodale Press.   III. Title.
    SB434.P48   1993
    635.9'32—dc20   92-30109
                                          CIP

Distributed in the book trade by St. Martin's Press

8 10 9   hardcover

Contents

Acknowledgments

This book was made possible because of the support, enthusiasm, and inspiration of fellow perennial gardeners, designers, and writers. We would particularly like to thank Mary Ann McGourty, Stephanie Cohen, and Edith Eddleman for their wonderful designs; Pam Harper for her patience and encouragement; and Frank Fretz and Elayne Sears, whose fine illustrations speak for themselves. Special thanks to Edith, for being herself in times of need.

Thanks also to Dale Hendricks, whose extensive knowledge of perennial propagation helped us out on chapter 9; to Allan Armitage, whose contributions to the field have been invaluable; to Allen Bush, for the use of his nursery; to Mike Heger, for our initiation into northern gardening; to Sarah Price, for useful suggestions; and to the members of the Perennial Plant Association, for their encouragement and ideas.

The superb team of editors and designers that put and held this book together deserve every reader's thanks as well as ours. To all of you—especially Barbara Ellis, Nancy Ondra, Darlene Schneck, Acey Lee, and Heidi Stonehill—we couldn't have done it without you. Finally, to all of the backyard gardeners who told us they couldn't wait to get their hands on this book, thank you for your enthusiasm.

Credits

Writers

Ellen Phillips is a horticultural writer and editor at Rodale Press. She has a master's degree in creative writing from Indiana University and a master's degree in horticulture from the University of Kentucky. She is a former senior editor of *Organic Gardening* magazine. A lifelong gardener, naturalist, and poet, Ellen's specialties are ornamentals and garden history; her favorite garden activity is weeding.

C. Colston Burrell is a garden designer, writer, and photographer whose Minnesota-based design business, Native Landscapes, specializes in landscape restoration and the innovative use of native plants and perennials in garden design. He is the former curator of native plants at the U.S. National Arboretum and former curator of plants at the Minnesota Landscape Arboretum. Author of *Perennial Portraits 1991* and contributor to *Rodale's All-New Encyclopedia of Organic Gardening* and *Landscaping with Nature,* Cole's articles and photographs have appeared in many gardening publications. His lifelong interest in gardening, birding, and natural history has led to a penchant for veering into ditches while sighting rare warblers and outstanding native plants.

Garden Designers

Stephanie Cohen is a lecturer, teacher, and freelance garden writer. She teaches courses in herbaceous plants at Temple University and the Barnes Arboretum. Stephanie is education director at Waterloo Gardens in Exton and Devon, Pennsylvania. She is co-designer of the perennial border at River Farm in Virginia, headquarters of the American Horticultural Society, and she designed the herb garden at Temple University.

Edith R. Eddleman is a garden designer, writer, lecturer, photographer, and long-time plant enthusiast living in Durham, North Carolina. She studied garden design in England with John Brookes and at North Carolina State University (NCSU). Edith designed and implemented the NCSU Arboretum's perennial borders in 1982 and has served since that time as volunteer co-curator. Edith's articles have appeared in *Fine Gardening* and the Brooklyn Botanic Garden handbooks. Her designs have been featured in Pam Harper's *Designing with Perennials* and *Perennial Portraits 1991.*

Mary Ann McGourty is the proprietor of Hillside Gardens in Norfolk, Connecticut, a nursery specializing in uncommon perennials and perennial garden design and installation. She is the editor of *Taylor's Guide to Ground Covers, Vines & Grasses,* and she also contributed to *Taylor's Guide to Perennials.* Mary Ann and her husband, Fred, grow over 700 perennial species and cultivars in their garden.

Photographers

C. Colston Burrell: pages 35, 37, 44–45, 52, 150, 160, 295, 304–6, 309, 324, 341, 353, 357–58, 365, 367, 369, 380, 382 (top), 383–84, 392, 394, 400, 430, 435, 438, 443, 459 (top), 482–84.

David Cavagnaro: back cover (inset), pages 18, 28, 36, 41, 48 (top), 51, 53, 58, 62 (top), 70 (bottom), 159, 162–63.

Crandall & Crandall: pages 23, 56, 161.

Barbara W. Ellis: pages 331 (bottom), 464 (bottom).

T. L. Gettings/Rodale Stock Images: front cover, back cover (top), pages ii–iii, x, 1, 40.

Pamela Harper: pages 4, 7, 11–12, 19–21, 26, 31, 33–34, 38–39, 42, 49, 54–55, 59, 62 (bottom), 63, 282–94, 296–303, 307, 310–23, 325–30, 331 (top), 332–40, 342–44, 346–52, 354–55, 359–64, 366, 368, 370–79, 382 (bottom), 385–91, 393, 395–98, 401–10, 412–14, 416–28, 431–34, 436–37, 439–42, 444–58, 459 (bottom), 460–63, 464 (top), 465–81, 485–92.

Horticultural Photography™: pages 10, 14, 16, 43, 154.

Jerry Pavia: pages 3, 17, 24, 67–68, 71, 73.

Joanne Pavia: pages 60, 81, 280–81.

Susan A. Roth: pages 8–9, 13, 15, 25, 27, 32, 48 (bottom), 70 (top), 151.

Illustrators

Frank Fretz: pages 46, 78–80, 181, 186, 193, 195, 199, 202, 204, 206–8, 214, 218–20, 223, 227–29, 242–43, 246, 249, 271, 275, 278–79, 493–95.

Elayne Sears: pages 84, 86–89, 94, 96–99, 104, 106, 108–9, 114, 116, 118–19, 122, 124, 126–27, 132, 134, 136–40, 142, 144–45.

How to Use This Book

Whether you're a beginning gardener or a pro, *Rodale's Illustrated Encyclopedia of Perennials* offers everything you need to create the perennial garden of your dreams. In the pages that follow, you'll find the right mix of information and inspiration to take your garden from concept to reality. Unlike other perennial encyclopedias, this book tells you how to grow and use perennials. It also provides a complete encyclopedia of hundreds of great garden plants. You'll find a wealth of practical information and gorgeous garden designs, plus beautiful color photos and illustrations for the home garden.

Rodale's Illustrated Encyclopedia of Perennials is organized in three parts to make it easy to use. Part 1, "Designing the Perennial Garden," which begins on page 1, takes the guesswork out of garden design. You'll find straightforward advice on using color, bloom season, and other aspects of design to create the garden you want.

In Part 2, "Growing Perennials," which begins on page 162, we take you from plans to planting. Here you'll find all of the how-to information you need to grow a great garden, whether you're soil building or seed starting.

Part 3, the "Perennial Encyclopedia," which begins on page 280, lets you look up individual plants. Entries are listed by genus. For each genus, you'll find botanical and common names; descriptions of the species and best cultivars; planting, maintenance, and propagation information; and a section on how to use the plants. You'll also find at least one color photo for each entry.

There's more to this book than its three parts, though. We've also included a special section, "Basic Botany and Nomenclature" on page 493, that explains everything you need to know about botanical names, cultivars, and other plant-identification mysteries in clear, simple language. If you find other words you're not familiar with as you read the text, turn to "Key Words" on page 498 for an explanation. You'll find an overview of mail-order sources of perennial plants and seeds, as well as related periodicals and plant societies, in "Resources" on page 500. And "Suggested Reading" on page 502 will give you more sources of information on perennials and perennial gardening. We've written this book especially for you and your garden. Enjoy it!

*A good design is the first step toward a beautiful garden. Here, the slender spikes of 'East Friesland' violet sage (*Salvia × superba *'East Friesland') form a striking contrast to the 'Enchantment' lily (*Lilium *Asiatic Hybrid 'Enchantment') and the soft-pink hollyhock mallow (*Malva alcea *'Fastigiata') in the background. In this section, you'll learn perennial design basics so you can create your own garden with confidence.*

PART ONE

DESIGNING THE PERENNIAL GARDEN

CHAPTER ONE

Garden Design Basics

W hen you look at a beautiful perennial garden, you may find yourself wondering how the gardeners did it. How did they know which plants to choose? What made them combine blue, gray, and chartreuse, or put the ornamental grass behind the clump of black-eyed Susans? A garden can look as complicated as a jigsaw puzzle, where plants fit together like pieces to form a beautiful picture.

But even the most intricate puzzle has a key, and once you have the key, all the pieces fall into place. This chapter will give you the background to make the right design decisions based on your own taste and needs. We've broken the design puzzle into a few easy pieces.

WHAT DO YOU WANT YOUR GARDEN TO DO?

The most important design question may also be the simplest. What do you want your garden to do? If you're honest with yourself,

your answer will also lead to the best garden you've ever had. If you've never gotten too excited about your perennial garden, it may be because its style and function don't meet your needs. Remember that gardening is as much about simple enjoyment—sitting with friends and appreciating the view, or walking down a path and smelling the plants as they brush against you—as it is about chores.

Suppose you have a lovely formal border of pastel double peonies. At least, other people tell you it's lovely, but to you it's just a nuisance that blooms for a couple of weeks but has to be mowed around all year. That may be because your idea of a flower garden is a mix of plant sizes and bright colors that create a glorious show from June through August. Or a sedate row of peonies may just not look right with your house. A few peonies planted in a bed with other perennials may work better for you than a row.

If you clarify what you want from perennials, you'll stand the best chance of getting it. Ask yourself the following ten questions.

Perennial beauty. Most gardeners dream of creating a gorgeous perennial garden like this in their own backyards. Perennials add color, fragrance, and texture to the landscape, but they can also be used to transform an otherwise dull yard into an alluring place you'll want to visit again and again. Just witness how much richness and serenity this garden adds to the yard. In this chapter, you'll learn how to make your own garden dream a reality.

1. Do I want a big garden, or will one or two small beds suit my needs better?

2. Do I want to make my garden a major feature, or use it as the foreground for a wall, patio, walk, or foundation?

3. Do I want my garden to showcase individual plants, or is the overview of the entire garden more important to me?

4. Do I want a big show of bloom for one specific season, or a smaller show that continues from spring through fall?

5. What times of year do I most enjoy being out in the garden?

6. Are there times of year I'm likely to be away from home for a few weeks?

7. How much time do I want to spend tending to the garden?

8. Do I have a favorite color scheme, or do I like a mix of colors?

9. If I want a mix, would I rather see bright colors, pastels, or some of each?

10. Do I want lots of flowers to cut for fresh or dried arrangements, or will I mainly enjoy them outside?

Keep these questions—and your answers—in mind as you read through Part 1. They'll keep you focused on your own needs, so it will be easier to decide which ideas and techniques you need right now, which ones don't

Framing a living space. A garden is more than a group of plants—it's also the room you make to enjoy the show. When you're planning a garden, consider what kind of space you want your planting to create. The purple blooms of showy geranium (*Geranium* × *magnificum*), pink and white foxglove (*Digitalis purpurea*), and pinks (*Dianthus* spp.) entice visitors to explore the space, while the heady fragrance of roses encourages them to linger.

suit your needs, and which ones you might want to try later. You'll find out more about garden size and function later in this chapter. Color schemes and bloom season are covered in chapter 2. And if you enjoy arranging flowers, you'll learn which ones to grow, as well as how to use them, in chapter 11. But before you start exploring the possibilities, try a few easy exercises out in your yard.

TAKING AN INVENTORY OF YOUR LANDSCAPE NEEDS

Once you've started thinking about your garden and what you want it to do, it's time to get out your garden journal. You'll find that keeping all your records in a journal is invaluable as you make plans and review the progress of your garden. Don't worry if your journal gets cluttered and messy as time goes on; as long as you can still read it and find things in it, you will be able to get what you need from it.

Review the "Landscape-Needs Checklist" on this page and write down the parts that apply to your situation. As you review the checklist, make sure you look at your yard from every perspective: Look out at the yard from inside the house, including the upstairs windows. Look at it from the street, from down the street, from the front door, from the sides, from the back door, and from the back boundary line. Look back at the house from the yard. Date your list; you might want to add or change things later.

ASSESSING YOUR SITE

Now that you've looked at what *isn't* on your property, it's time to take stock of what is. Look over the "Site Inventory Checklist" on

Landscape-Needs Checklist

Here's an inventory of ways to use a garden to enhance your landscape. Run down the list and note in your garden journal all that apply to your situation. By reviewing what you've listed, you'll get a better idea of what you want from your garden—including how big to make it and where to put it. As you look at each entry in the checklist, ask yourself, "Do I want my perennial garden to do this?"

❑ Hide a bare foundation, or transform a dull or ugly foundation planting
❑ Soften a wall or fence
❑ Add color under shade trees
❑ Add interest along the front of the yard
❑ Soften a driveway
❑ Add color to a dooryard
❑ Surround a terrace, patio, or deck
❑ Soften the edges of a pool
❑ Beautify a lamppost or mailbox
❑ Create a boundary
❑ Hide an unattractive view or element (like a utility pole or laundry line)
❑ Add splashes of color in the lawn
❑ Fill a bare spot
❑ Create a place to walk to in the yard
❑ Beautify a garage or outbuilding
❑ Surround a bench, trellis, or arbor
❑ Soften the outlines of a raised porch
❑ Give a new home a more finished look
❑ Create a period look for the home
❑ Fill raised beds where vegetables once grew

page 6, then go out in your yard and look around. Write down the inventory items that apply to your own yard in your garden journal. Add any features that aren't on the checklist, then date your customized list. By reviewing your site inventory, you can see at a glance

Site Inventory Checklist

You may think you know everything about your yard, but once you start really looking at it, you may be surprised at how many details you've forgotten. As you read through this list, use a page in your garden journal to write down all the features that are in your yard. Note what part of the yard they're in. If you can add specific information, you'll customize your list even more (for example, by adding "brick" after patio, or "Norway maple" after specimen tree). When you're finished, you'll have a much clearer idea of where you could put a garden or gardens in your yard.

Boundaries

- ❏ Solid fence
- ❏ Open fence
- ❏ Wall
- ❏ Hedges, evergreen (formal or informal)
- ❏ Hedges, deciduous (formal or informal)
- ❏ Row of trees (evergreen or deciduous)

Paths, Walkways, and Driveways

- ❏ Walk
- ❏ Path
- ❏ Sidewalk
- ❏ Driveway (straight, circular, or curved)
- ❏ Plantings of annuals, perennials, or shrubs bordering any of the above

Water Features

- ❏ Swimming pool
- ❏ Pond
- ❏ Water garden
- ❏ Stream
- ❏ Birdbath
- ❏ Fountain

Entertainment Areas

- ❏ Play areas (such as a swingset)
- ❏ Lawn areas

- ❏ Terrace, patio, porch, or deck
- ❏ Bench or picnic table
- ❏ Gazebo or arbor

Utility Areas

- ❏ Garage
- ❏ Greenhouse
- ❏ Toolshed or other outbuilding
- ❏ Permanent clothesline
- ❏ Utility pole
- ❏ Central air-conditioning box
- ❏ Compost pile or bin

Other Features

- ❏ Trellis
- ❏ Gate
- ❏ Steps
- ❏ Dog house/dog run

Existing Plantings

- ❏ Specimen trees or shrubs (evergreen, deciduous, or mixed)
- ❏ Clumps of trees or shrubs (evergreen, deciduous, or mixed)
- ❏ Fruit trees
- ❏ Foundation plantings
- ❏ Groundcover plantings
- ❏ Flower beds, borders, or island beds (perennial, annual, or mixed)
- ❏ Vegetable garden
- ❏ Herb garden
- ❏ Berry plantings

Land Features

- ❏ Low areas
- ❏ Slopes or flat areas
- ❏ Berms
- ❏ Meadow areas
- ❏ Woodland areas
- ❏ Marshy areas

what's in your yard. Taking a careful look at your yard will make it easier to decide where to locate your perennial garden.

FITTING THE GARDEN TO THE YARD AND HOUSE

There's a garden for every size of yard and every style of house, but the same garden won't work in every situation. The huge, lush perennial borders that look so stunning on a tranquil estate would be impossible to fit in a small backyard, and the moisture-loving perennials they feature wouldn't grow in a dryland area. However, you can create the feel of a grand border even if you live in a row home or if your yard is in the desert. The trick is to match the scale and size of your garden to your yard and house.

Sizing Up Your Yard

First, look at your yard. Just as a tiny cottage-style flower bed would look out of place in front of a palatial villa, a small raised bed can get lost in a large yard. Suit the scale of your garden to the size of your yard, just as you try to suit it to your house.

A sunny site. It's important to match the perennials you choose to your site if you want them to thrive. A sunny site is perfect for most perennials, including garden phlox (*Phlox paniculata*) and globe thistle (*Echinops ritro*), shown here.

You can also grow striking yellow 'The Rocket' ligularia (*Ligularia stenocephala* 'The Rocket') in a sunny site if it gets afternoon shade and humus-rich soil that is constantly moist.

A walk in the woods. A wooded lot may have too much shade for sun-loving perennials like peonies and irises, but it's the ideal setting for a woodland garden like the one pictured here. Flowering trees provide the perfect backdrop for shade-loving perennials. Here a blooming kousa dogwood (*Cornus kousa*) sets off the hostas and astilbe (*Astilbe × arendsii*) lining the path, while fringed bleeding heart (*Dicentra eximia*) carpets the ground on the other side. Bright-yellow sundrops (*Oenothera fruticosa*) add a glowing contrast to the soft greens and pastels of foliage and flowers.

A small garden can have a big impact in a tiny yard; but the larger the yard, the bigger or brighter your garden must be to have the same effect. If you have a large yard but don't want a big garden, remember that you can often substitute boldness—such as bright color or a few large plants—for garden size. Also, a large yard with lots of elements—groups of trees and shrubs, an arbor, paths, an outbuilding—can set off a small garden better than the same-size yard with little more than a giant lawn. For simple techniques to determine garden size, see "Garden Size: A Realistic Assessment" on page 22.

This Old (or New) House

Before you set your heart on a particular garden style, you should take a hard look at your house. What kind of house do you have? Is it Colonial, Victorian, a thirties cottage, a ranch house, a stucco mission-style, or a contemporary with lots of unpainted wood and glass? If you can recognize a particular style, you can have a lot of fun deciding whether or not to match at least some elements of your garden to the house. For ideas, you might want to look at magazines like *Colonial Home, Victoria,* and *HG* to see what owners of similar houses are doing with their gardens. Check at your library for lifestyle garden books like *The American Woman's Garden* and books on garden history.

If your house doesn't fit any particular style or era, there are still several ways you can get a good garden match. One way is to find out when it was built—say, the twenties—and read up on what people were planting then. Another way is simply to size your house up visually, and match your garden to what you see. Does your house look formal or homey to you? Is it dark or light? Tall or long? Cottage-size or imposing? Look around your town at similar houses and examine their gardens. If you like what you see, or are attracted to a few elements of someone's design, jot down notes and try to visualize the scene back in your yard.

Some garden styles have become so popular that they've transcended their original period. If you enjoy colonial or cottage gardens, see "Garden Style" on page 22 for ideas on how to adapt these styles to your own garden.

SUITING SHAPE TO SITE

The best-looking gardens look as if they evolved naturally on their site. That's because the gardener chose the size and shape of the garden to fit the size and contours of the land. Use the land as your guide when you think about the size and shape of your garden—don't try to impose a garden on a site if it looks awkward or artificial. For example, a formal rectangular border plopped in the middle of a rolling landscape that's accented with informal clumps of shrubs and small

Perennials for dry sun. Try Mediterranean and meadow perennials for dry, sunny sites. These stone steps are softened with clumps of lavender cotton (*Santolina chamaecyparissus*), lavender (*Lavandula angustifolia*), and annual Dahlberg daisy (*Dyssodia tenuiloba*)—plus the pink blooms of 'The Fairy' rose.

Beautifying a boggy site. Wet areas don't have to be a drawback, as this gorgeous garden shows. The colorful mix of magenta, yellow, and red Japanese primrose (*Primula japonica*) and blue-flowered Siberian iris (*Iris sibirica*) backed by shrubs would make most gardeners envy the owner of this "difficult" site.

trees will never look as effective as one that's fitted to the natural contours of the site.

One way to make sure your garden looks right is to think about the space it defines rather than the space it takes up. To do this, consider the space that will surround or set off your border and the area from which you'll enjoy your perennials. In most cases, that will be a lawn—or perhaps a patio. The border will define and frame the lawn, and from a design standpoint, the shape of the lawn is more important than the shape of the border. That's because the lawn is uniform in color and texture and thus creates a stronger shape on the landscape. The flat green surface of the lawn provides the floor you'll walk or sit on to

see and enjoy the garden. Large beds of groundcovers, patios, or other areas covered with a uniform surface (such as paving or mulch) function the same way in a design.

So, when you are designing your garden, first decide what size and shape of lawn would be pleasing and provide enough room for your needs. Then design the perennial beds to define the shape you've created with the lawn. Use smooth curves or straight lines to form the edges of your beds—you want the lawn to be a restful counterpoint to the exciting color and texture of the flowers. Scalloped or wavy edges trick the eye into seeing motion, which will counteract the restful feeling you're trying to achieve. Furthermore, you want visitors to look at your perennials, not notice the shape of the edge you've created. Complex, wavy edges are also much harder to maintain than straight or smooth ones because they require more hand-trimming.

When your bed or border surrounds a patio or terrace, use the same principles. But remember, you're actually creating two spaces from which to enjoy your perennials: You'll view them from inside the patio as well as the larger lawn beyond the beds. For this reason, you'll need to take into account the shapes of both patio and lawn when you design the shape of your bed or border. If you're planning to put beds around a patio or terrace, you'll

find a lovely design in "A Bed for a Shaded Terrace" on page 122.

There are three basic kinds of perennial gardens—islands, beds, and borders or mixed borders. Each type of perennial garden serves a different function in the yard. When you look at your property, you should be able to see easily whether you'll want one, two, or all three types in different areas. But don't get too caught up in definitions. Although these are convenient ways to refer to perennial gardens, what you call your garden is much less important than how it looks.

Again, let the landscape define your needs. If you have a large lawn or a new home

Anchoring a large, open yard. The big, bold perennial garden in this photo creates a transition between the house and the yard, anchoring the house so it doesn't seem to be drifting aimlessly in a sea of lawn. Matching the yard and garden sizes creates a balanced look. If you have a large yard, you'll need a sizable border—or one that features very bold plants or bright colors—to make an impression. Plan for size from the start: A small bed often gets lost in a large yard.

Bold color for big effect. Small gardens planted with bright, bold perennials can have a big impact, as this grouping of colorful yellow and purple coneflowers (*Rudbeckia* and *Echinacea* spp.) demonstrates. The cool-white blooms of the orange-eye butterfly bush (*Buddleia davidii*) in the background make the hotter colors of the coneflowers seem even brighter.

perennial islands and borders are meant to be seen most often from a distance—across the lawn, from the road or driveway, or from the house. You or your guests might stroll across to take a closer look, but the major impact of these gardens comes with the long look. A perennial bed, on the other hand, is designed to be seen close up, since it's usually sited close to the house and family activity.

What this means in design terms is that structure and bold color—the things you can see from afar—are more important in perennial islands and borders. Subtler color schemes, textures, and fragrances—the things you appreciate up close—play a larger role in perennial beds. In a perennial bed, for example, you could enjoy the individual characteristics of each plant in a group of different cultivars of pinks (*Dianthus* spp.), since you'd be looking down from practically on top of them. Their differences would blur in a border seen from yards away.

Perennial Islands

Perennial island beds, as their name implies, are islands of flowers in a sea of lawn. These are freestanding and often free-form. They can be large if your lawn is large, or smaller if your lawn is more moderately sized. If your yard is sizeable, consider putting in several island beds. On the other hand, if your lawn is small, you probably shouldn't break it up with an island. A central area of lawn surrounded by gardens will make a small yard seem larger.

Perennial islands should look like natural features. Think of them as water pooling on the lawn, and try to give them the soothing oval or curving shapes that water would make if a pond formed there. Avoid circular islands, which look artificial, unless you're planting around a pole.

on a featureless lawn, without trees or shrubs, consider perennial islands, also called island beds. If there are places around your yard, especially near your house, where a planting of perennials would be attractive—in front of the house, on the side of a deck or patio, next to a pool—you need perennial beds. And if you'd like a long planting to edge a driveway, face a wall or fence, or surround one or more sides of your property, a perennial border is for you.

Another thing that separates these garden types is the way you look at them. Both

Replacing a shady lawn. Why have a sparse lawn in a shady spot, where lawn grasses don't grow well, when you can replace it with a lush perennial garden like this one? Bright blue Siberian iris (*Iris sibirica*) provides a bold splash of form and color in the foreground. The striking textured leaves of hostas combine with blue flax (*Linum perenne*), columbine (*Aquilegia* sp.), and buttercup (*Ranunculus* sp.) to add interest closer to the house. The softly undulating edge of the perennial garden makes the path to the house more inviting.

Perennial islands can look wonderful, breaking up featureless expanses of lawn or adding color under trees. They can also look terrible, like technicolor whales that have washed up on the lawn. Use the checklist below to make sure your yard is the right place for an island bed before you start removing sod. If you look at your yard, then run through the checklist and can't find a good place for a perennial island, try a perennial bed or border instead. They're usually easy to site. Here are some good places for perennial island beds.

▶ If you have a new house with a bare yard, an island bed can add color and height while you wait for trees or shrubs to mature.

▶ Try a small island bed around a mailbox or lamppost. These are places where a circular bed looks great. Keep the bed small, so it's in scale with the post, and connect it to the vertical structure by planting a clematis or other delicate vine to grow up the post.

▶ A great place for an island bed is under trees in the lawn. Grass grows poorly under trees, but you can choose shallow-rooted perennials that prefer partial to deep shade for your bed, or simplify and grow groundcover islands. You can connect several trees with one island bed, giving your yard a flowing, unified look.

▶ If your lawn dips or rises, go with the flow. Think about water pooling in the dip or collecting at the base of the rise, and shape your bed or beds accordingly.

▶ If you already have a berm on your property, you can turn it into an island bed. If the berm is at the edge of the property, planting it with perennials and ornamental grasses will add height and provide privacy. And no matter where a berm is, perennials will make it more attractive.

Since you can walk around a perennial island and view it from all sides, you must plant it carefully so that all sides are attractive.

A basic rule is to put the taller plants near the center of the island, with progressively lower-growing plants spreading out toward the sides and the lowest perennials along the edges. To keep your island bed looking natural, vary this rule a little by placing a few taller plants closer to the edges, as though they had spread out from the center.

If you want to look over the island to the other side of the lawn, choose lower-growing perennials; if, on the other hand, you want your island bed to provide some privacy or a sense of enclosure, choose tall plants like Japanese silver grass (*Miscanthus sinensis*) or Joe-Pye weed (*Eupatorium purpureum*) for the center. Make sure the island is large enough to balance the height of the tallest plants—you don't want them towering over the

Turning lawn into flowers. These gardeners decided to abandon their lawn altogether, replacing it with raised beds bursting with a colorful mix of annuals and perennials. These beds provide months of pleasure and take less time to maintain than a conventional lawn. If you're building a new house and haven't seeded the lawn, consider making part of your lawn a flower bed right from the start.

A sunny island bed. Island beds are a great way to add interest to a treeless expanse of lawn. Make sure you choose perennials that grow well in full sun. This island bed features bee balm (*Monarda didyma*), 'Zagreb' threadleaf coreopsis (*Coreopsis verticillata* 'Zagreb'), gooseneck loosestrife (*Lysimachia clethroides*), Carpathian harebell (*Campanula carpatica*), snakeweed (*Polygonum bistorta* 'Superbum'), and lamb's-ears (*Stachys byzantina*).

other perennials. For a great example of a large perennial island bed that provides year-round interest, see the design in "A Four-Season Perennial Garden" on page 84.

Perennial Beds

Perennial beds are different from perennial islands because they are most often placed at the edge of the lawn or along a building or patio, while island beds are placed in the lawn. Perennial flower beds often have clearly defined edges, and the beds can be raised, with low sides of brick, stone, or boards. But like island beds, perennial beds are usually meant to be seen from all sides.

Because perennial beds are meant to be viewed and appreciated from nearby, they're a plant lover's delight. A perennial bed is the perfect place for a plant collection—of fragrant plants, silver-leaved plants, cultivars of a species, rock garden plants, succulents, or whatever suits your fancy. A perennial bed is the perfect garden for the detail-oriented: Each nuance of leaf shape, variegation, or flower color comes into its own. You'll be close enough to your plants to enjoy them on an intimate basis.

Perennial foundations. The standard shrubs that are used for foundation plantings tend to be dark and uninviting. They also often overgrow the foundation, requiring repeated pruning. Perennials are a colorful solution to the foundation-planting puzzle—they stay in bounds, soften the outline of the house, and encourage visitors to come closer. Here, delphiniums, lilies, and poppies issue a bright and irresistible invitation.

Perennial beds are also the most popular of the three garden types since they represent the ultimate in suit-yourself planting. They can be delightfully informal, bursting with perennials of every description, or as formal as you like, edged with dwarf boxwood or lavender and grouped in a classic arrangement with paths between. They can also be as large as a lawn or as small as a barrel planter.

Since perennial beds are generally close to the house, it's important to think carefully about how they'll look through the seasons as you plan them. If you want a small bed, you might need to concentrate on your favorite bloom season—say, spring. Plant spring-blooming perennials with an eye toward how the foliage will look when the plants stop blooming. (Luckily, many spring bloomers, including peonies, Siberian irises, baptisias, and gas plants, have extremely handsome foliage.) You can add summer bloom by overseeding long-blooming annuals or tucking in some bright annual bedding plants.

If summer is your top season, plant your summer-blooming perennials with spring-blooming bulbs to extend the show. Ornamental grasses and perennials like yarrows and coneflowers that dry well in place can carry garden interest through fall and winter.

If your bed is in shade, you can have a lovely assortment of shade-tolerant perennials like Solomon's seals (*Polygonatum* spp.) and astilbes (*Astilbe* spp.), and add hostas, ferns, and other shade-loving foliage plants to extend seasonal interest. You'll find more ideas for shade in the design in "A Shady Wildflower Garden" on page 114.

Of course, if you have a larger bed, you can design a garden with perennials that will bloom in succession for season-long color, and still mix in bulbs and foliage plants for additional interest. You'll find dozens of design ideas for mixing other herbaceous plants with your perennials in "Enriching Your Plant Palette" on page 55.

An important point to keep in mind about perennial beds is that you and your guests will most likely enjoy them up close. So if your beds aren't in top-notch form, the wilting plants, dying flowers, and dog-eared foliage will be right in front of you. For this reason, it's best to choose plants that will stay attractive with little help from you. Look for perennials that are drought-tolerant and pest- and disease-resistant, and that don't need staking, dead-heading, and so on. Or if you have your heart set on prized plants that demand attention, plan on giving them the time and care they deserve. Part 2 will give you all the tips and techniques you need to keep your perennial flower beds looking great.

Perennial Borders

Perennial borders, also called mixed borders, are longer than flower beds and are generally designed to edge or frame another garden feature. They may run along one or more boundaries of the yard, edge a driveway or walk, or be used in front of a fence, hedge, or building. Borders may be rectangular, but usually they complement the

Connecting hedge and path. If the small strip between this hedge and path were lawn, it would be wasted space—and difficult to mow as well. Instead, it has been converted to a colorful mix of perennials, including lady's-mantle (*Alchemilla mollis*), pinks (*Dianthus* sp.), and yellow loosestrife (*Lysimachia punctata*).

garden feature they are near, echoing its shape. Often the edges are rounded off or the border undulates in a serpentine fashion.

The classic perennial gardens in English garden books and in botanical and other public gardens are usually borders. If you have a long space for a flower garden, as well as the budget to plant it and the time to tend it, few sights are as lovely as a beautiful perennial border.

Another good place for a border is along one or both sides of a driveway or walk. In this case, you'll be able to see the border from both

Edging a walkway. The colorful perennials edging this walkway add loads of personality and charm to an area that otherwise might be an uninteresting corridor of lawn. The prairielike garden includes daylilies, garden phlox, and ornamental grasses, along with coreopsis and purple coneflower (*Echinacea purpurea*).

Framing with flowers. This gorgeous perennial border frames the yard, marking the end of the lawn and creating a colorful transition between trees and grass. The gardener has used hardy, low-maintenance perennials like daylilies, artemisia (*Artemisia ludoviciana* 'Silver King'), catmint (*Nepeta* × *faassenii* 'Dropmore'), and loosestrife (*Lythrum virgatum* 'Morden Pink') to create the sophisticated look, while keeping maintenance to a minimum.

sides, so use the same planting scheme you would with an island bed: tallest plants in the middle, scaling down on either side to the ground. Make sure the plants you choose are in scale with the size of the walk or drive. Avoid very tall plants unless your driveway or walk is extremely wide, or the border will seem to close in on you, towering over your car or guests and creating an uninviting tunnel. Usually, you'll want a clear view over the border to the lawn.

Designing a border can seem intimidating because of its size, but it's really easier than many smaller gardens because you're designing for one view rather than two, three, or four, as with an island bed. You'll find all the design how-to you need to put a perennial border together (or a perennial island or bed, for that matter) in chapter 2. Turn to the design in "A Sunny Perennial Border" on page 94 for some instant inspiration, or think about using several repetitions of your favorite color theme from the design in "A Color Theme Garden" on page 132.

Making a Mixed Border

A border of perennials and other herbaceous plants like ornamental grasses and foliage plants is lovely during the growing season, but it can look bare from late fall

Jazzing up the driveway. Driveways can be boring, but this one is as beautiful as it is functional. Perennials create an attractive entryway by adding height, texture, and color to what would otherwise be a flat grass strip. An open fence forms a backdrop for the border. Featured perennials include Russian sage (*Perovskia atriplicifolia*), yellow torch lily (*Kniphofia* 'Primrose Beauty'), 'Morden Pink' loosestrife (*Lythrum virgatum* 'Morden Pink'), 'Little Miss Muffet' Shasta daisies, and 'Autumn Joy' sedum. A Jackman clematis vine clambers on the fence.

through early spring. Leaving some of the more structural plants—like ornamental grasses and coneflowers—standing until late winter is one way to increase the late-season interest. But to create a garden of lasting beauty, consider mixing woody plants like shrubs and small trees in with your perennials.

Trees and shrubs, with their trunks and branches, provide an enduring framework for the border. If they're deciduous, you can choose species with brilliant fall color, interesting bark, or showy, persistent berries for fall and winter interest. If they're evergreen, they'll provide fresh green color year-round, an especially welcome sight in winter.

To enhance the border during the growing season, choose shrubs or small trees with beautiful, and preferably fragrant, flowers. Select species that bloom when the rest of the garden is dragging, or choose trees and shrubs with a long bloom season. Trees and shrubs with variegated foliage or unusual foliage colors like gold, chartreuse, and purple are useful, too. You can match foliage and flower color to your predominant color scheme, or use the restful green of tree and shrub foliage as a backdrop for your perennials.

Mix shrubs and small trees into your

A classic border. A bench invites you to sit in the shade and enjoy the beauty of this sunny border. Lavender and garden phlox dominate the border in summer, creating a colorful counterpoint to the cool green of the lawn.

border the same way as you would any large plants: Use them individually to anchor the ends of the border, as repeating elements to tie the border together, or in groups in a very large border. Make sure the border is wide enough to look attractive with the shrubs or trees you have in mind; the shrubs and trees should look like part of the border, not like the border is skirting them. Trees and shrubs usually work best in a large border, where they're in scale with the size of the planting. Mixed borders are especially handsome along the boundary of a property where they can frame part or all of the yard.

GARDEN SIZE: A REALISTIC ASSESSMENT

You can get some idea of the size garden you'll need by marking the space out on the ground with garden hose. After you've laid out the hose, though, you may find that you need a more three-dimensional view to really tell how the space would look. In that case, try filling the area inside the hose boundary with cardboard boxes, half-filled leaf bags, or other bulky but fairly low objects. They'll help you visualize the impact your perennial planting will eventually have.

If you're planning either a larger perennial border that's backed by a hedge, wall, or fence, or a border that runs along a path, driveway, or road, you can see how long it should be without using a hose. The trick with a border is deciding how wide it should be. Again, one easy way to do this is to take leaf bags or other bulky objects and line them out from the fence or back boundary of the border. Set out a number of bags in lines spaced along the length of the border so you can really get a good idea of the width.

The longer the border, the wider it should be—to a point. Remember that you need to reach the back of the border to take care of it. You can't comfortably reach across more than about 4 feet to weed, plant, and do all the other routine chores that gardens need. If your border is open on both sides, with a path or drive in front and lawn behind, it can be wider because you'll have access from both front and back. But if your border is backed by a road or barrier like a fence and you want a wider garden, add a maintenance path between the border and the barrier. Make the path wide enough to kneel on comfortably—at least 2½ feet—or wider if you plan to take a wheelbarrow with you. The path not only gives you access to the plants but also allows better air circulation, which benefits both your perennials and any plants growing behind them.

GARDEN STYLE

Garden style is a matter of taste, not rules. Your garden should express your personal style—exuberant or restrained, classic or ultramodern, colorful or quiet. It should be as individual as you want to make it, whether that means adding your signature pink flamingo or a formal topiary. Use your own preferences to make your garden something you'll really enjoy.

Of course, you have to have a starting place. One good way to start thinking about your garden's style is to decide whether you prefer a formal or informal garden.

Formal or Informal?

Most gardens can be called formal or informal, no matter what their individual style is. These categories are so big that they cover knot gardens (formal), cottage gardens (informal), borders (usually formal), wildflower meadows (informal), and about every other garden style you can think of. Sets of specific characteristics make it easy to tell if you're looking at a formal or informal garden, although some gardens blur the distinctions or have characteristics of both. It's fun to look at gardens and see if you can place them in the appropriate category.

The Formal Garden

Formal gardens are often sparse in their use of elements, but are strong on the classic design principles of balance, repetition, and proportion. The gardener may have chosen to use 10 species rather than 50, but those 10 will be used to maximum effect. Below are some telltale clues that reveal the presence of the formal garden.

Structure. Formal gardens usually have a strong visible structure—brick, stone, or gravel walks; edged beds; stone or brick walls or austere fences. Geometrically shaped hedges and sheared evergreen trees or shrubs often serve as structural elements as well. Even without any perennials, you'd have a strong sense of a formal garden's shape and features.

Balance. Formal gardens tend to be symmetrically balanced, so no element looks isolated or out of place. A shrub on one side of the garden will have a partner shrub of the same species, or at least the same size and shape, on the other side; two or four beds of the same size and shape will echo each other in the courtyard or in front of the house. The geometric shapes of the various elements reinforce the formal garden's symmetry. Flower beds, lawns, and pools appear as squares, rectangles, triangles, circles, or ovals. Paths usually run in straight lines, while high walls may have straight or undulating edges.

Repetition. Formal gardens use repeating elements to emphasize balance, maximize impact, and rest the eye. If lavender is used to

Accenting a formal wall. The stiff foliage and upright flower spikes of wood hyacinth (*Scilla campanulata*) reinforce the formality of the brick wall and edged walk. Often, simple forms and a limited choice of plants are all you need to create a formal garden.

edge a bed, you can confidently expect lavender—or another low plant—to edge every other bed in the garden. If brick is used for one walk, brick will probably be used for the others, as well as for most of the other structural elements like walls and terraces. This makes the garden logical to the viewer. You don't expect any surprises, so your eyes can relax instead of jump from place to place. It also makes the garden easy to take in: You see at a glance the straight line of the border punctuated with repeated groups of plants or colors.

Proportion. Formal gardens are in proportion, so they look graceful and peaceful,

A formal garden. The pastel colors and rounded shapes of this perennial border soften the orderly effect of the clipped evergreen hedge and stone wall. Notice how the yellow plants on the right seem to flow downhill, from the thistle-like tufts of globe centaurea (*Centaurea macrocephala*) at the back to the rounded heads of 'Moonshine' yarrow (*Achillea* × 'Moonshine') and the spreading mats of sedum spilling over the rocks.

not jarring. All the elements are in scale with each other and with the rest of the yard and house. You'll find a large house, high hedge, large beds, wide paths, broad gates, and tall trees and shrubs. Or you'll see a small house with a low hedge, modest beds, narrower paths, a small pool, and so on. You won't find small beds and a narrow path leading to a massive bench, or a 150-foot-long border of 2- to 3-foot-tall perennials with one 10-foot-tall clump. Again, the effect is restful because you know what to expect. A garden that's out of proportion can make you jumpy because you instinctively know something is "wrong."

Classic details. Formal gardens tend toward classic details—lead statuary, bronze sundials, stone urns, wrought-iron gates. A lion-head fountain reinforces the formality of a rectangular water feature. Topiary—herbs or shrubs trained or pruned into geometric shapes, globes, corkscrews, and the like—can also be a feature of the formal garden. So can potted shrubs or small trees placed at strategic points between beds or along paths. Simplicity and restraint are the key words: If you want topiary, grow several in the same shape rather than trying for one of each shape.

The Informal Garden

Informal gardens are more relaxed in their approach, but often are more dynamic in their look. Unlike the formal garden, they can use many elements and play fast-and-loose with balance, repetition, and proportion. Sometimes details alone can make the difference—a formal patio with nicely clustered matching chairs can become cheerfully informal when a jumble of different chairs replaces the neatly ordered matching set. This mix-and-match attitude is typical of the informal gardens, but often design principles lurk below the seemingly disordered surface. Below are some clues to the character of the informal garden.

Lack of Structure. Informal gardens often are unstructured, with few "hard" elements to mark their existence. A rustic fence or bark-chip path may be their only features. Without any perennials, you might have a hard time finding the informal garden—that is, unless it features mixed plantings of trees and shrubs.

Asymmetrical Balance. Informal gardens tend to be asymmetrically balanced—a small bed may provide punctuation for a larger one, or a single hosta may be used as a counterpoint to a group of three. If an informal garden is symmetrically balanced, the effect is subtle rather than obvious as it is in the formal

Casual color. Oriental poppies blaze around this rustic fence in glowing tones of orange, pink, and scarlet, creating an informal but powerful effect. The foliage of Siberian and bearded irises (shown blooming with the poppies) and the flat, green seedpods of honesty (*Lunaria annua*) will add structural interest after the poppy foliage dies back in summer.

garden. Clumps of peonies will blend into the beds rather than standing out as major elements. Beds will be the same size but contain different plants. Shapes are usually more natural or organic than geometric—you'll find an amoeba-shaped water garden rather than a rectangle or circle, or a softly shaped (or unshaped) hedge rather than one that's been rigidly trimmed upright. Paths may wind or wander rather than running straight. But although the informal garden's balance is sometimes not as apparent as the formal

Informal exuberance. The delightful jumble of perennials in this cottage garden creates a lush, informal feeling. Differences in plant height and form add excitement and interest. Garden phlox, white-flowered nettle-leaved mullein (*Verbascum chaixii* 'Album'), catmint (*Nepeta* × *faassenii* 'Six Hills Giant'*), tree mallow (*Lavatera thuringiaca* 'Barnsley'), and purple elder (*Sambucus nigra* 'Purpurea') provide a wealth of textures within a carefully limited color scheme. The foliage of goldenrod (*Solidago* sp.) and the inviting bench both promise pleasures to come.

garden's, if you see an appealing informal garden, you can bet that it's balanced.

Lack of Repetition. Informal gardens don't necessarily use repeating elements; if they do, they usually don't use them consistently. Paths, fences, and other structural elements may vary in design and materials; beds may be different shapes and sizes; a plant may be used only once. This brings the feeling of change and movement to the garden. You can't count on a logical order. You expect surprises—anything could be around that bend in the path. This sense of the unexpected creates mystery and excitement, invit-

ing the viewer to explore the garden. It also makes the garden difficult to take in at a glance: Paths wind in and out, parts of the garden are hidden behind shrubs, a bed curves out of sight. You never know what's next.

Proportion. Most informal gardens are in proportion, so their elements are in scale with each other and with the rest of the yard and house. This is not always the case, though: A narrow path may wind through a large cottage garden, forcing you to brush the fragrant plants as you pass. A tiny bed may add jewel-like color to a corner of a large house, functioning as a single stately plant would in a formal garden. Or a giant arbor at the end of a small yard may be covered with climbing roses, grapes, and clematis, making you feel a tropical luxuriance when you sit on the bench beneath. But when they're successful, gardens that aren't in proportion are as carefully designed as those that are; they're not haphazard.

Whimsical details. Informal gardens are great places for whimsy—gazing balls, bee skeps, "found" treasures of all kinds, lawn art animals. You can get away with murder in an informal garden (that's part of the fun)—if it looks good, do it. You can also use rustic materials to set off your garden, like a terra-cotta birdbath or a half-barrel water garden. Elements that are normally formal can become whimsical with a twist—a rooster topiary rather than a globe, or a frog fountain instead of a lion's head. Enjoy yourself, but avoid excess: Five cute birdhouses are fun, but 50 are exhausting. However informal, your garden should still look attractive.

Two garden styles that represent the best in formal and informal gardens are the colonial and cottage gardens. Colonial gardens look especially attractive with colonial houses and wooden contemporaries. Cottage gardens are delightful with Cape Cod–style cottages, small houses, and rural properties. But these versatile styles adapt well, so if you want one, try it. Chances are that the results will be very satisfying.

The Colonial Look

Colonial gardens can be very formal, or you can soften the formality with cheerful, old-fashioned plants. You can have a formal knot garden with a boxwood edging, a peony border, or a mixed bed of lavenders, yarrows, irises, and old roses. Most colonial gardens were designed as groups of beds in a court-yard outside the house or enclosed with a low wall, fence, or boxwood hedge.

If you want your garden to look colonial, just give it a few classic touches. Boxwood and brick were both very popular in colonial times; even a few boxwoods at the corners of your garden will add a flavor of authenticity. If possible, use brick for your walks and walls; if the cost is prohibitive, a simple packed-earth path is the next best choice. A sundial or mill-stone will provide a central focal point and add a handsome touch. Both herbaceous and tree peonies were much admired by the colo-

Colonial style. This popular style has been adapted to many contemporary houses as well as colonial buildings. It relies on simplicity, as in the plain fence; repeating elements, like a boxwood edging; and a limited plant palette, emphasizing classic perennials like the irises, blue false indigo (*Baptisia australis*), and yellow bachelor's button (*Ranunculus acris*) shown here.

nists; don't forget them in your garden plans.

Remember that Jefferson, Washington, and other prominent colonists were avid gardeners and plant enthusiasts. It's fun to explore their garden diaries and notebooks for ideas for your own garden. The Thomas Jefferson Center for Historic Plants at Monticello (P.O. Box 316, Charlottesville, VA 22902) is a wonderful resource; they can supply period plant lists, and they also sell seed.

The Cottage Garden

Cottage gardens originated when people had small dooryard gardens and wanted to

A colorful cottage garden. The spirit of the cottage garden is alive and well in this yard, where pink, peony-flowered poppy (*Papaver somniferum*) mixes with gloriosa daisy (*Rudbeckia hirta* 'Gloriosa Daisy'), rose campion (*Lychnis coronaria*), and yarrow.

cram as many favorite plants into them as possible. At first these were kitchen gardens, and the plants were mostly edible, medicinal, or for dyeing. Flowers were an incidental benefit. But as edibles became commercially available and medicine moved to the realm of specialists, more and more flowers began cropping up in these dooryard gardens until they became the cottage gardens we all recognize—bursting with old roses and cheerful flowers like primroses (*Primula* spp.) and cottage pinks (*Dianthus plumarius*).

A cottage garden is a delightful mix of color, size, and fragrance. Annuals, biennials, and herbs mix freely with perennials, while vines roam over adjacent fences and trellises, and roses and other fragrant shrubs mingle with abandon. The cottage garden exemplifies freedom and joy. It's the perfect place for perennials and annuals that self-sow.

When you plan your cottage garden, remember its rustic roots. Consider siting it outside the back door, where you can step outside and enjoy the color and fragrance. A picket or other simple wooden fence sets off a cottage garden nicely, whether you enclose the entire garden or site it along a side of the fence. Wherever you put it, give your cottage garden a place in full sun. Both you and your garden will enjoy the bright location. For more inspiration, see the beautiful design in "A Fragrant Cottage Garden" on page 104.

By now you should have good ideas of the size and style of garden you want, but you still need to know how to pick the right plants and combine them to create a beautiful, satisfying bed or border. In chapter 2, you'll learn how to use color, size, texture, and seasonality, how to mix perennials with other plants, how to narrow the selection to the plants that suit your needs, and how to draw your own design. You'll be well on your way to your own dream garden!

CHAPTER TWO

Designing with Perennials

Two things tend to intimidate gardeners when they're thinking about putting in a perennial garden: the number of perennials to choose from, and the mystique that surrounds garden design. You may want to throw up your hands and say, "I'm not an expert! What do I know about designing gardens?" In this chapter, we'll tell you how to decide which perennials will meet your needs. And we'll take the mystery out of garden design. By breaking it down into simple steps that are easy to follow and fun to think about, we'll have you doing garden design in no time. And you'll love the way your new garden looks!

WAYS TO APPROACH DESIGN

Think of garden design as a series of plant combinations. When you're combining plants, there are two sets of considerations you need to think about. The first set relates to the appearance of the plants: when they bloom, what color they are (flower color *and* foliage color), how big they get, and what they look like—the form and texture of their foliage and flowers. The second set relates to the habits of the plants: what conditions they prefer (sun or shade, a wet or well-drained site, very fertile or average soil), how fast they grow, how long they live, and how much ongoing maintenance they require.

For a garden design to look good, you have to use plants that grow well together and that will grow well in your site. Stunted, dying, or unkempt plants will ruin a design no matter how gorgeous it looked on paper. If you have a site in full sun with good drainage, choose classic border perennials like peonies, irises, daylilies, and delphiniums. If you want to put a perennial garden under shade trees, choose woodland wildflowers and shade-tolerant plants like hostas. Don't try to force peonies to thrive in deep shade, or woodland phlox to flourish in full sun—they won't, and your garden's

29

appearance will suffer as much as the plants you're trying to grow.

This book makes it easy to find out which growing conditions perennials prefer. The plant entries in the encyclopedia section beginning on page 280 each include a "How to Grow" section that provides concise information on sun and shade, moisture and fertility, and other preferred conditions. (For quick reference, you can also use the perennial culture table on page 251. Just skim down the columns looking for plants that suit your site.)

When you put together lists of plants you'd like to use, check the encyclopedia entries to make sure they'll grow well together. The entries also discuss how fast the plants grow, if they're especially long- or short-lived, and how much maintenance (like staking, division, and deadheading) they need.

What slows down most gardeners is the first set of considerations—when the plants bloom, what color they are, how big they get, and what they look like. In this chapter, we'll deal with each of these in detail, so you can choose and combine plants with confidence.

DESIGNING BY BLOOM SEASON

One of your first considerations should be bloom season. When do you want your flowers to bloom? If you're home from the last spring frost to the first frost of fall, you'll probably want your garden to provide enjoyment during the entire growing season. But there are reasons you might want to focus your garden's show on one or two seasons.

If you love one season best, you could design your garden so the flowers will peak during that season. A lush display in spring, followed by more modest color through summer and fall, might be exactly right for the person for whom "garden" and "spring" are nearly the same word.

If you're at home in spring and fall but gone for part of the summer, you'll want to design a garden that blooms when you're there and requires minimum maintenance when you're not. Or if you live in a climate where summers are searing (or extremely humid), you might not want to be out in the garden until temperatures drop again in fall. On the other hand, a northern or West Coast garden can really come into its glory in summer, and you might want to focus your bloom peak so it falls during the hotter months.

Another reason to focus your attention on one or two seasons is if your garden is small. When you don't have a lot of space, a lush display in one season may look better than one or two plants in bloom at any given time. Remember that there are tricks you can use to extend bloom or color into other seasons, like planting spring-blooming bulbs with later-blooming perennials or adding some ornamental grasses for fall and winter color. You'll find more ideas for making the most of your garden, whatever its size, in "Enriching Your Plant Palette" on page 55.

As you think about seasonality, look at the garden designs in chapter 3. Five of the designs are shown in their two best seasons, so you can find lots of inspiration, whether you want a garden for spring, summer, fall, or all year round.

Spring Flowers

Spring is the most welcome season to many gardeners because the garden returns to life after its winter rest. We're eager to see any color—even green looks fresh and new—and the first blooms take on the excitement of an event. Now is the time for the little bulbs—snowdrops, species irises, glory-of-the-

Doing design right. Creating a beautiful perennial garden means choosing plants that look attractive and grow well together. In this autumn scene, a feathery clump of purple-flowered 'Hella Lacy' aster (*Aster novae-angliae* 'Hella Lacy') towers over the spiky foliage of 'Ivory' yucca (*Yucca* 'Ivory') and a rosy-pink-flowered cultivar of portulaca (*Portulaca oleracea*). The foliage of the yucca contrasts with the massed forms of the aster and portulaca.

snow, crocuses—and the hellebores, the Christmas and Lenten roses (*Helleborus niger* and *H. orientalis*), with their beautiful deep-green, fingered foliage. (For more on small bulbs, see "Bulbs for a Brighter Garden" on page 56.)

After the first flush of color from the bulbs, spring-blooming perennials take over. Some front-of-the-border perennials that bloom as brightly as bulbs are perennial candytuft (*Iberis sempervirens*), rock cresses (*Arabis* spp.), basket-of-gold (*Aurinia saxatilis*), and moss pink (*Phlox subulata*), offering matlike form and an almost electric range of white, purple, sulfur-yellow, pink, blue, and lavender. These plants like full sun and good drainage, making them excellent candidates for rock gardens.

As the larger bulbs—tulips, daffodils, fritillarias, and bulbous irises—signal the end of late frosts and the start of the vegetable growing season, mid-spring perennials come into their own. Bleeding heart (*Dicentra spectabilis*) bears sprays of pink-and-white or all-white heart-shaped flowers over equally graceful blue-green foliage. Columbines (*Aquilegia* spp.) produce ferny foliage and wiry stems that hold trembling clusters of spurred flowers in every color. Alumroots (*Heuchera* spp.) send up airy sprays of tiny pink, white, green, or red flowers; some, like 'Palace Purple' heuchera (*H. micrantha* var. *diversifolia* 'Palace Purple'), are grown for their showy foliage alone.

Grecian windflower (*Anemone blanda*) and poppy anemone (*A. coronaria*) start the anemone season with bursts of color in white,

Signs of spring. The delicate blooms of glory-of-the-snow (*Chionodoxa luciliae*) are tougher than they appear, for they are among the first small bulbs to bloom. Their pale-blue flowers signal the end of winter. For early color in your garden, plant them with species crocuses, Grecian windflower (*Anemone blanda*), snowdrops (*Galanthus* spp.), and bulbous irises.

Spring in bloom. Lush new growth is the hallmark of the spring garden—greens seem fresher, colors brighter. Each bloom is a cause for celebration after a long winter. Here, a clump of pasque flower (*Anemone pulsatilla*) is surrounded by forget-me-not (*Myosotis sylvestris*), pansies, and other spring-blooming flowers.

pink, blue, violet, and scarlet; other species will bloom in summer and fall. And alliums (*Allium* spp.) bear their cheerful globes or flat heads of star-shaped white, pink, lavender, rose, purple, or yellow flowers on sturdy stems over strap-shaped or tubular green foliage.

As spring moves toward summer, many of our most loved perennials come into their own. Bearded, Siberian, and Japanese irises bloom in every color of the rainbow except true red. Their foliage adds structural interest to the garden even when they're not blooming, and Siberian iris (*Iris sibirica*) also has handsome seedpods. Single, semidouble, and double peonies in white, red, pink, and coral

bloom on elegant shrubby plants; their foliage often turns an attractive copper or burgundy in fall.

Baptisias (*Baptisia* spp.) bear sprays of blue, cream, or white pealike flowers and beautiful blue-green foliage like a locust's. Baptisias also have attractive blue-black seedpods. Late spring is also the beginning of astilbe season. Astilbes (*Astilbe × arendsii*) are wonderful perennials for partially shaded sites with moist soil; their ferny foliage and red, pink, white, peach, or cream plumes mix well with hostas (*Hosta* spp.) and true ferns.

The delightful low-growing pinks (*Dianthus* spp.) produce flat single or double, often fragrant flowers over mats of blue- or gray-green foliage. Pinks are perfect for the front of the border in a well-drained, sunny site; they're also great for rock gardens. Many of them have petals with fringed edges, as though they had been cut with pinking shears; this gives them their common name, though in fact many are also pink in color (others are white, red, coral, or maroon). And don't forget oriental poppies, with huge papery blooms in shades of red, scarlet, orange, peach, pink, and white. Plant poppies where other plants can fill in when their foliage dies back in summer. Choose any or all of these classic perennials to carry your garden show into early summer.

Summer Splendor

Make sure your garden can take the heat and not look tired after the excitement of spring—include these reliable perennials for nonstop color all summer long. Daylilies bloom in every color except white and blue. Choose a selection of daylilies to bloom from June through August, or plant reblooming cultivars like 'Happy Returns' and 'Stella de Oro' for bloom from June through October.

Garden phlox (*Phlox paniculata*) is a mainstay of the summer border, blooming in white, orange, pink, lavender, red, and violet, often with a contrasting eye. Yarrows are also

Moving toward summer. Bearded irises are favorite perennials for late spring and early summer. Their fragrance and range of colors are hard to resist. In this colorful garden, deep-purple bearded irises are planted with pink snapdrag-ons and a variety of rock garden plants, including maiden pinks (*Dianthus deltoides*), white perennial candytuft (*Iberis sempervirens*), and diminutive, blue-flowered lithodora (*Lithodora diffusa*).

Waves of summer color. The perennials in this showy border are just a few of the many plants that will add summer color and excitement to the garden. This border is designed with waves of color, starting with magenta garden phlox, followed by fernleaf yarrow (*Achillea filipendulina*), globe thistle (*Echinops ritro*), and perennial sunflower (*Helianthus* sp.). Note how the deep-green of the shrubs and trees sets off the colorful flowers.

superb summer perennials, with ferny foliage and showy flat-topped blooms in white, cream, buff, yellow, pink, salmon, and cherry-red.

Coneflowers (*Rudbeckia* spp. and *Echinacea* spp.) are showy, reliable summer-blooming perennials, bearing big daisy flowers in shades of orange, yellow, mauve, and white. If you want more summer daisies, try the sturdy, yellow-flowered, lance-leaved coreopsis (*Coreopsis lanceolata*), feathery primrose-yellow *Coreopsis verticillata* 'Moonbeam', or pink-flowered *Coreopsis rosea*. Add more white to your daisy palette with Shasta daisy (*Chry-santhemum* × *superbum*) and feverfew (*Chrysanthemum parthenium*).

For a cooler look, choose lavender (*Lavandula angustifolia*), catmint (*Nepeta* spp.), and Russian sage (*Perovskia atriplicifolia*). The bushy forms, blue to lavender colors, and spiky flowerstalks of this summer-blooming trio contrast beautifully with the daisies. The large, showy Frikart's aster (*Aster* × *frikartii*) continues the lavender-blue theme with its prolific flowering and long bloom period.

Give your summer garden some height with the majestic spires of delphiniums and foxgloves (*Digitalis* spp.). Delphiniums bear blue, white, lavender, and violet flowers, while foxgloves are pink, mauve, yellow, cream, and white. And don't forget the tall, lovable hollyhocks (*Alcea rosea*), synonymous for many gardeners with childhood summers. You can choose single or double-flowering cultivars in every color but blue and green.

Closer to the ground, butterfly weed (*Asclepias tuberosa*) and crocosmia (*Crocosmia* × *crocosmiiflora*) make a fiery summer show in shades of red, scarlet, orange, and yellow. Two plants that are handsome enough to be grown for their foliage alone—hostas (*Hosta* spp.) and cranesbills (*Geranium* spp.)—are also summer bloomers. The spires of hostas bear lilac or white bell-shaped flowers, some of which are fragrant, while the cranesbills produce numerous single flowers in sometimes startling shades of pink, violet, blue-violet, maroon, and magenta.

Many of the sages also bloom in summer, with showy spikes of blue, white, red, lavender, and violet. And don't neglect the beautiful bellflowers (*Campanula* spp.), verbenas (*Verbena* spp.), speedwells (*Veronica* spp.), and balloon flower (*Platycodon grandiflorus*). There are dozens of others that make summer a glorious season in your perennial garden. Summer bulbs like glads (*Gladiolus* spp.),

The colors of summer. Here's a picture any gardener would like to see at home—the blooms of delphiniums and daylilies create a vibrant contrast of both color and form. These plants showcase the extremes of perennial gardening, too: Both like full sun and well-drained soil, but daylilies are tough, long-lived plants, whereas finicky delphiniums are short-lived and disease-prone.

Summer contrasts. A good plant combination like this one can capture the cheerful colors of summer. Here, the bright blooms of black-eyed Susan (*Rudbeckia hirta*) add sparkle to a sunny site, while sun-tolerant bracken (*Pteridium aquilinum*) creates a cool, shady feeling.

canna (*Canna* × *generalis*), and dahlias (*Dahlia pinnata* hybrids) are garden staples. The problem isn't finding something that will bloom in summer, but choosing from the wealth of summer-blooming perennials that are available.

An Autumn Blaze

Fall is one of the great highlights in the gardening year. For many gardeners, it is the high point of the year—the air feels crisp and bracing after summer's heat and humidity, and the sky is such a clear blue it looks azure. Other colors seem more intense, too—the beige of grasses and deep-green of evergreens set off the brilliant reds, scarlets, oranges, and yellows of deciduous trees and shrubs. In the perennial garden, you can echo these colors.

Mix in lilac, violet, and blue to cool the blaze.

The autumn show really begins in late summer, when the green buds of sedums like 'Autumn Joy' (*Sedum* × 'Autumn Joy') and 'Vera Jameson' (*S.* × 'Vera Jameson') open to reveal cotton-candy-pink flowers. Boltonias (*Boltonia asteroides*) are covered with hundreds of tiny white or pink daisies. Garden mums (*Chrysanthemum* × *morifolium*) begin their long bloom season, presenting a wealth of single, semidouble, and double daisylike flowers in every color but blue and green. Bonesets (*Eupatorium* spp.) bear large, airy clusters of red-violet flowers on bold shrubby plants that can reach 7 feet tall. And many species of aster join Frikart's aster (*Aster* × *frikartii*) in a collage of lilac, violet, pink, white, and cherry-red.

As temperatures drop, fall-blooming anemones produce bright but delicate-looking white, pink, rose, or mauve flowers on tall, wiry stems. Choose Japanese anemones (*Anemone* × *hybrida* and *A. tomentosa*) for autumn bloom; their foliage is unusually handsome, holding its own in the garden in spring and summer. (This is also true of chrysanthemum foliage—mums make beautiful green cushions, competing with peonies for the "Best Perennial Foliage Award.")

Fall bloom continues with the goldenrods (*Solidago* spp.), which add bright-yellow flames to the garden; their height and upright blooms contrast nicely with the daisy flowers and mounded forms of mums and asters. (There are also low-growing cultivars for the front of the border.) Another pleasant front-of-the-border plant is calamint (*Calamintha*

nepeta), which covers itself with tiny bluish white flowers and has minty foliage as a bonus.

Don't overlook the pleasure of foliage in the autumn garden. As the season progresses, many peony cultivars turn bronze or wine-red; evening primrose (*Oenothera* spp.) foliage also turns brilliant colors, from hot-pink through maroon; and some alumroots (*Heuchera* spp.) develop red patterns on their foliage.

Ornamental grasses are stars of the autumn garden; many bear spectacular flower heads that remain showy on the plant well into winter. Grasses also add structure to the garden, contrasting with the compact mounds of other autumn bloomers. You'll find more on grasses in "Adding Ornamental Grasses" on page 60. Round out your fall display with crocuses, autumn crocus (*Colchicum autumn-*

Flowers for fall. As autumn temperatures drop, many gardeners discover fall is one of the most enjoyable times in the garden. Savor the season with a sunny combination like the one shown here, which includes 'Gold Plate' fernleaf yarrow (*Achillea filipendulina* 'Gold Plate'), an orange-flowered cultivar of common sneezeweed (*Helenium autumnale*), perennial sunflower (*Helianthus* × *multiflorus*), and 'Herbstsonne' shining coneflower (*Rudbeckia nitida* 'Herbstsonne').

Adding late interest. To add interest to your garden through fall and into winter, plant fall-blooming perennials and ornamental grasses. This classic autumn combination features fountain grass (*Pennisetum alopecuroides*), 'Autumn Joy' sedum, and a fall-blooming aster (*Aster grandiflorus*), all of which offer late-season color and texture. You can leave the sedum and grass standing until late winter or early spring for an ongoing show.

ale), and other small fall-blooming bulbs; you'll find several to choose from in "Bulbs for a Brighter Garden" on page 56.

Winter Interest

For gardeners in most of the country, winter is a rest period—the garden rests, dormant under mulch or snow, and we rest, taking a break from outdoor gardening. In those parts of the Deep South and West Coast where the growing season continues from fall through spring, gardening goes on as usual, and garden beauty takes care of itself. But for those of us in areas that have winter freezes, it takes planning to give a garden winter interest. After all, just because we're not working in the garden doesn't mean we can't see it. A tidy mound of mulch might not look too bad, but a little forethought can assure a more pleasing vista for us and some needed nourishment for overwintering birds.

Three things take on new prominence in the winter garden: seed heads, stems, and foliage. The seed heads and stems of ornamental grasses are often brightly colored—yellow, orange, red, or purple—as winter begins, bleaching to a range of beiges, wheat, and off-white as the season progresses. Grasses add structure to the winter garden—a structure they're more likely to keep if you stake or tie them upright before winter arrives. You'll find more on grasses in "Adding Ornamental Grasses" on page 60.

There are also a number of perennials that will hold their showy seed heads well into winter if you don't "tidy up" and cut them off. Keep your pruners away from yarrows, baptisias (*Baptisia* spp.), Siberian iris (*Iris sibirica*), blackberry lily (*Belamcanda chinensis*), grape leaf anemone (*Anemone vitifolia*), purple coneflower (*Echinacea purpurea*), and cone-

flowers (*Rudbeckia* spp.). It's surprising how much the silhouettes of these perennials can add to a winter bed.

Winter interest is even easier in a mixed border. You can use open-growing trees with interesting bark like 'Heritage' river birch (*Betula nigra* 'Heritage') along with shrubs like Siberian dogwood (*Cornus alba* 'Siberica'), which has red twigs, and winterberry (*Ilex verticillata*) which is covered with bright-red fruit in fall and winter. Evergreens like dwarf mugo pine (*Pinus mugo* var. *mugo*) and boxwood (*Buxus* spp.) are also valuable for adding structure, color, and texture.

Bursting with color. Color is the first thing most of us notice in a garden, and it's the main reason many of us grow perennials. This lively border combines colors casually for a pleasing look, including magenta garden phlox, orange daylilies, yellow threadleaf coreopsis (*Coreopsis verticillata*), blue balloon flower (*Platycodon grandiflorus*), pale-pink coneflower (*Echinacea purpurea*), and white feverfew (*Chrysanthemum parthenium*).

COLOR CONSIDERATIONS

The first thing most gardeners ask about a new perennial is "What color is it?" Color catalogs are so popular because they let you see exactly what you're getting (if the catalog color is printed well). As you peruse the encyclopedia section of this book, you'll probably find yourself looking at the photos and taking away an impression of color.

Fragrance may be more memorable, but color is more important to most gardeners— and most of the general population as well. Given how central color is in our lives, and how much of it we see every day, it's surprising how intimidated people are by it. How many times have you heard or even said, "I'm just no good with color"? This is usually untrue; there aren't that many people whose wardrobes make us cringe. But there are definitely some people who seem to have a flair for choosing and mixing colors. These lucky gardeners can create eye-catching combinations time after time; they seem to have an instinctive appreciation of color harmony.

Your color sense may not be instinctive, but here's a secret: You can learn to combine colors just as beautifully. There are a few simple color techniques that are easy to learn and easy to use. Read the next few pages, play with the color wheel, then take your wheel and turn to the encyclopedia section on page 280. Choose a color combination, and flip through until you find photos of perennials with those flower colors. A little practice will give you a lot of confidence. Then take your show on the road. The next time you're passing a garden and see a color combination

Hot color combo. Hot colors — red, orange, yellow, hot-pink, and red-violet — combine well in the garden. Turning up the heat in this grouping are 'Violet Queen' bee balm (*Monarda didyma* 'Violet Queen') and an orangy-yellow heliopsis (*Heliopsis* sp.).

you like, try to decide why the colors work. If you can't think on the spot, note down the colors and review "Using the Color Wheel" on page 46. Don't forget to jot down foliage colors—they can be the key that makes the combination work.

A Color Glossary

What's the difference between a hue, shade, tint, and tone? What are hot, cool, and neutral colors? Before we start talking about how to use color, let's review what these terms mean. Then you can mix shades of blue with the best of them.

Hue. Hue is simply another word for color. Red, blue, and green are hues.

Shade. A shade is a color that has been darkened by adding black. Olive-green is a shade of green; mustard is a shade of yellow;

indigo is a shade of blue.

Tint. A tint is a color that has been lightened by adding white. Sea-green is a tint of green; primrose-yellow is a tint of yellow; sky-blue is a tint of blue.

Tone. A tone is a color that has been dulled by adding gray. The "country colors" are good examples: colonial-blue, old-rose, putty. Dull doesn't mean boring in this context; it means less bright.

Color temperature. Colors convey a feeling of temperature: Fire colors—red, orange, and yellow—are warm, while water colors— blue, green, and violet—are cool. Hot-pink is also considered a warm color, while pale-pink and gray are considered cool colors. To remember the difference between warm and cool colors, think of fall foliage (warm) and Easter pastels (cool).

Neutral color. Cream, beige, black,

A cool combination. Cool colors include blue, gray-green, white, silver, lavender, and green. This lovely combination of cool colors places lamb's-ears (*Stachys byzantina*), with its fuzzy silver leaves, in front of pale-blue flax (*Linum perenne* 'Sapphire') and a yarrow just coming into bud.

Using hot colors. The temperature seems to rise as you look at this colorful composition of yellow threadleaf coreopsis (*Coreopsis verticillata*), hot-pink garden phlox, and pale-orange daylilies. The yellow spikes of rocket ligularia (*Ligularia stenocephala* 'The Rocket') and wand loosestrife (*Lythrum virgatum*) bring up the rear. The bold colors and forms of these perennials raise the garden's excitement level, too.

tan, brown, silver, and gray, in their many tints, shades, and tones, are considered neutral colors. They are not "true" or rainbow colors from the color wheel, but peacemakers that "go with everything" and unify clashing colors. In the garden, green can also function as a neutral color.

Combining Colors

When you combine colors in the garden, you have to create a balance between unity and boredom. The fewer colors you use, the more unified the garden looks, but the more likely it is that it will end up looking uninteresting. The more colors you use, on the other hand, the harder it is to give the garden any feeling of unity or restfulness. Fortunately, there are ways you can balance both these extremes to create a pleasing color scheme that's both exciting and unified.

If you're not using many flower colors—if, for example, you're designing a color theme garden like the ones on page 134, or you want a garden that combines blue, yellow, and pink flowers—you can add color through foliage. Plants with purple, gray-green, silver, or variegated leaves can perk up the color scheme with-

Cooling things down. Here's a restful, cool color combination — a clump of white-striped bulbous oat grass (*Arrhenatherum elatius* var. *bulbosum* 'Variegatum') next to a clump of lavender-flowered garden chives (*Allium schoenoprasum*).

The blue spires of 'East Friesland' violet sage (*Salvia* × *superba* 'East Friesland') and the feathery foliage of fernleaf yarrow (*Achillea filipendulina*) provide an attractive backdrop. Cool colors draw the eye back into the garden.

out drawing attention away from the flowers.

You can also work with hot and cool colors very effectively in a limited-color garden. If you're using cool colors, like blue and lavender, add sparks of excitement with a hot color like peach; if you're using hot colors, like scarlet, orange, and yellow, add a few bursts of azure or sky-blue. You'll be surprised at how easily this technique can put the life back into a border.

If you want to use a lot of different flower colors, you run the risk of providing so many points of interest that it's impossible to see the garden as a whole—it has lost its focus. Keep this from happening by tying the bed or border together with clumps of repeating color—it will separate the groups of mixed colors so they're easier to take in, and give the eye something to rest on between bursts of color.

If you want to shift colors or combine clashing colors like orange and purple, you can do this most effectively by separating them with neutral colors. To do this, you can use plants with gray-green, green, or silver foliage, or ones with cream or chartreuse flowers. White is also technically neutral, but a pure-white works in the garden as a primary color—it's bold, bright, and dominant. Use pure-white to make a cool color impact, but use an off-white like cream to work as a neutral in the garden.

Designers' Color Tips

Garden designers have quite a few color tricks up their sleeve. Here are some tried-and-true techniques you can use to create pleasing effects and give your garden a more unified, less haphazard look:

▶ If you want to make part of a garden bed (or the entire bed) appear closer, fool the eye by using warm colors, which seem to advance toward the viewer; if you want it to look farther away, choose cool colors, which seem to recede.

▶ Gertrude Jekyll, who popularized the British perennial border, liked to use the full color spectrum in her designs. She'd begin a border with restful, cool colors, lead up to exciting, warm colors, then end with cool colors to balance the border and the viewing experience.

A green border. This striking perennial border won't always be all green. The broccoli-like buds of 'Autumn Joy' sedum will open to a clear-pink, then age to rusty-red as summer turns to autumn, and the tickseed (*Bidens* sp.) behind the sedum will bear yellow flowers. But for now, green provides all the interest, with clumps of variegated Japanese silver grass (*Miscanthus sinensis* 'Variegatus') and feathery wormwood (*Artemisia absinthium*) adding variations on the theme.

Using the Color Wheel

Use the color wheel to create fool-proof color combinations in your own garden. Match flower (or foliage) colors to the colors on the wheel, then combine them in one or more of the ways suggested below. Remember to choose perennials that will be in bloom at the same time.

Trace the color wheel and shapes below, or use a photocopier to enlarge them. Then, using the wheel and shapes, try all of the following ways to come up with winning combinations.

▶ Choose a color on the wheel, then look at the colors on either side of it. Blue, blue-green, and blue-violet are adjacent colors. You can use them together or add more variety by extending the color range to the next two colors as well—in this case, green and violet.

▶ If you put a ruler across the middle of a color block on the color wheel, it will also cross the center of the color on the opposite side of the wheel. These are complementary colors: Blue and orange,

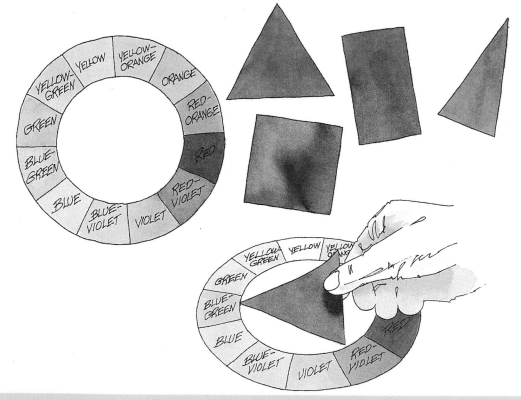

The color wheel. Use the color wheel to find color combinations that work well together. If you want to take more of the guesswork out of this process, trace or copy the color wheel and use markers, crayons, or colored pencils to fill in each section with the appropriate color. Then cut out a square, rectangle, equilateral triangle, and isosceles triangle—in the same scale as your color wheel. Place the shapes in the middle of the wheel and rotate them to see which colors they connect. Pick out the color combinations you like best.

red and green, and blue-violet and yellow-orange are examples. Combinations using these colors are vibrant and exciting—in fact, the pure colors in combination can almost seem to pulsate. You can enjoy this effect but tone down the brightness by using variations of the colors—peach and blue instead of orange and blue, for example. Or you can use a whole range of blues and oranges to add interest and variety.

▶ Draw an equilateral triangle or position a triangle cutout in the center of the color wheel, and the three colors it connects form a triad—green, orange, and violet, or blue-green, yellow-orange, and red-violet, for example. Watch what happens when you add small quantities of an adjacent color (like adding blue to the second triad).

▶ Draw an isosceles triangle or position an isosceles triangle cutout on the color wheel to form another kind of triad. By putting the top point of your isosceles triangle on yellow, you'll see that the two bottom points fall on blue-violet and red-violet. Turn to page 280 to see this very color combination using 'Moonshine' yarrow (*Achillea* × 'Moonshine'), 'Johnson's Blue' cranesbill (*Geranium* × 'Johnson's Blue'), and red valerian (*Centranthus ruber*).

▶ Draw a square or position a square cutout in the center of the color wheel, and the four colors it connects form a tetrad—one is green, yellow-orange, blue-violet, and red. Tetrads are pleasing in themselves, and you can add light and dark variations of the four colors for more diversity.

▶ Draw a rectangle or position a rectangular cutout on the color wheel, and it will connect two sets of complementary colors—like yellow and violet, with orange and blue. Rotate the rectangle for more harmonious combinations.

▶ Include plants in your border that bloom at different times but in the same color. You'll have a color echo through the bloom season to remind you of what was in bloom earlier and what's still to come.

▶ Instead of toning down a strong color with a neutral, use a softer tint of the same color; for example, try using the soft primrose-yellow of 'Moonbeam' coreopsis (*Coreopsis verticillata* 'Moonbeam') to tone down the clear, primary yellow of sundrops (*Oenothera fruticosa*).

Color Drifts

Color drifts are a natural concept: Nature tends to plant in groups. You seldom see a single black-eyed Susan by a roadside or just one oxeye daisy in a field. Instead, you'll find groups of daisies or a whole drift of trout lilies or violets under the trees. Garden designers have taken this concept out of the wild and moved it into the garden.

Using color in drifts is a concept that artists employ, too—especially when they create abstract paintings, simplifying a scene until it is entirely shape and color. You can try this technique for yourself. Put tracing paper over the cover photo of this book (or any of the photos of borders), and fill in the areas where each species is planted as drifts of color: white for the spires of delphiniums, green for the ornamental grasses, magenta for the low spires of lythrum, yellow-green for the lady's-mantle, and so on until the entire picture is filled in. You'll have a clear idea from the resulting "art" of how these colors work together; you can also see if you'd prefer a smaller block of red or magenta, or a different combination.

Planting in drifts unifies a perennial garden by reducing the hodgepodge effect of many different individual plants. It's especially

The many shades of green. Gardeners often overlook the dominant color in any garden—green. But as this combination shows, green doesn't have to take a background role: You can create a lovely combination by playing on its many variations. Here, variegated yellow archangel (*Lamiastrum galeobdolon* 'Herman's Pride') carpets the ground under the foliage of chartreuse-leaved 'Citation' hosta.

Focus on white. White plays a starring role in this lovely combination of lilies, baby's-breaths, and Shasta daisy (*Chrysanthemum* × *superbum*). As this garden illustrates, white is actually a strong color, able to hold its own against brighter colors such as the double yellow coreopsis (*Coreopsis* sp.) in the background.

effective in large borders, where individual plants might get lost. But if you have a small garden or are a plant collector at heart, consider planting in clumps rather than drifts—groups of three, five, or seven of the same perennial. You'll get some of the benefits of drift planting, like unified blocks of color and form, without sacrificing diversity.

STRUCTURING THE GARDEN

Structure is what gives a garden its shape. From the fall, when your perennials go dormant, until they're well up in spring, your garden's structure comes from things like the fence in back of the border, the path, the bricks edging your raised beds, or the trunk and branches of the Japanese maple or the old boxwood at one end of the border. These permanent elements are effective all year. They mark the shape of your garden. In discussions of design, they are often called the bones of the garden. Like the bones of a skeleton, they provide a framework for the plants that flesh out the garden in the growing season.

Structure also keeps the garden interesting when your perennials aren't blooming. If your garden is snow-covered most of the winter, it could blend into the lawn from fall to spring. But if snowfall in your area is sporadic or nonexistent, you'll just have a mulch-covered mound during the dormant months unless you plan for some structural elements. A fence or wall will define the garden, as will an edging to your bed. A path keeps the eye moving past the empty beds.

Evergreen and deciduous trees and shrubs will add color and interesting branch shapes and bark texture. If you choose carefully, you can grow some trees and shrubs with brilliant fall and winter berries, as well as some that

A color theme border. Bright-red 'Cambridge Scarlet' bee balm (*Monarda didyma* 'Cambridge Scarlet') and rocket larkspurs (*Consolida ambigua*) dominate this red, white, and blue border. But the owners had more than patriotism in mind when they designed it, as you can see from the hummingbird feeder tucked discreetly in one side of the border. This garden attracts butterflies as well as hummingbirds—and it's a great backdrop for Fourth of July picnics.

flower early in spring when the garden show is just beginning. (For a good selection, see "Shrubs and Small Trees for Mixed Borders" on page 72.)

If you have a mixed border, you can put shrubs and small trees in the border itself, but if your border or bed isn't big enough, you can still work them in. Plant a large shrub, small tree, or group of small shrubs at one or both ends of the bed or behind it. Or site your border next to or in front of an existing tree or shrub to add a visual framework for your garden. If you do decide to plant trees or shrubs, make sure their mature size won't be too large for your needs. Consider mature spread as well as height. Don't let your trees or shrubs cast your once-sunny border into gloom.

You can also add structure to a winter garden with herbaceous plants that keep last year's stems, seed heads, or foliage through the winter. Ornamental grasses and some perennials, including coneflowers (*Rudbeckia* and *Echinacea* spp.), will stand over winter. (For a list of others, see "Winter Interest" on page 39.)

Garden Structures

You can add structure to your garden with permanent or semipermanent accessories, too. A bench or table helps define the garden area. So does an arbor, gate, or trellis. A fountain, sculpture, or sundial—even a gazing ball—lets you and your visitors know that they are in your garden. These accessories provide visual cues that remind anyone who sees them of gardens, just like a wheelbarrow and watering can would. And most of them remain in the garden year-round, continuing to provide these cues even when the plants themselves are invisible.

Suit your accessories to your site—keep them in scale with your garden size. Don't put a giant park bench beside a tiny bed or use a small statue to anchor a 100-foot border. (Small garden art can be included in a large border to provide interest and surprise, but then it functions more like a plant than a structure.) And unless you're designing a sculpture garden, a few accessories are enough; keep your focus on your plants.

Don't forget that the most important

piece in any garden is a bench or chair. Make sure you have a comfortable seat in easy view of your perennials. The closer the seat, the more likely that you can enjoy the garden's fragrance and the butterflies and other visitors that share your appreciation of it. You won't be working in the garden all the time (although the seat also provides a convenient resting place between weeding bouts); part of the time, you should just be looking.

By giving yourself a good vantage point, you can think about design and plant combinations at your leisure—what looks good now, what you'd like to move or try next season, or what might perk up the color scheme in one part of the planting. And of course, a bench or old-fashioned swing is the perfect place to show off your garden to friends and family.

Form and Height

Once your perennials are up, they add structure to the garden with their forms and heights. The shrubby form of a peony or upright form of a bearded iris shapes the garden. So do the tall spires of a delphinium or black snakeroot (*Cimicifuga racemosa*), or the spiny bulk of bear's-breeches (*Acanthus* spp.).

Unlike most trees and shrubs, a perennial's form and height can change when it blooms: Plants that grow in low rosettes like foxgloves (*Digitalis* spp.) or mulleins (*Verbascum* spp.) can send up very tall bloom spikes; grasslike plants like alliums (*Allium* spp.) can suddenly produce huge globes of starry blooms like a display of fireworks. A lily, which is tall and thin in bloom, may suddenly become quite short when you deadhead it after its flowers fade.

Some perennials, like bleeding hearts (*Dicentra spectabilis*) and oriental poppies (*Papaver orientale*), have a great presence in the garden when they bloom in spring, then go dormant in summer and disappear completely. Learn the growth habits of perennials you're considering for your garden by looking them up in the encyclopedia section.

Working with Form

Think about the basic forms of perennials as you consider using them. What would this form look attractive with? Where should you use it? How many plants do you need for the form to make an impact? Perennials can have these basic forms: creeping or prostrate, mounded, weeping, round, vase-shaped, oval upright, pyramidal, upright, and columnar. These shapes provide design keys when you think about combining plants in your garden.

You can use a plant with a distinctive form to tie a border together by repeating the plant, or groups of the plant, along the length of the border. Siberian iris (*Iris sibirica*) produces attractive grasslike clumps of narrow sword-shaped leaves, for example, and its distinctive form would help hold a border together if clumps were repeated along the length of the border. You can also echo the shape of one perennial with another that has a similar form, or provide contrast by using a perennial of different but complementary form—intersperse clumps of ornamental grasses with the Siberian irises, for example. You can also change the form of a plant by pruning, shearing, or staking. Pruning can reduce overall height and ranginess, shearing can create a more compact, rounded shape, and staking can hold up plants that would normally weave through their neighbors.

Working with Height

How you use height in your garden depends on the shape of your bed or border and whether you can see it from the front only

or from both front and back. If you can see the bed or border from the front only (for example, if it's planted in front of a wall or hedge), place the tallest perennials in back, the next tallest in the middle, short perennials in the front, and prostrate perennials as an edging.

If you can see the back as well as the front (for example, in an island bed or one that borders a driveway with lawn on the other side), plant the tallest perennials in the center of the border, with plants of descending height on either side. Whether you can see one or

Combining heights and textures. There's more to creating a great garden than mixing colors—the best gardens use height and texture to provide season-long interest and excitement. Here, the tall, spiky whorls of lily foliage and flowers contrast wonderfully with the broad, corduroy-ribbed foliage of the hostas and the airy chartreuse lady's-mantle flowers (*Alchemilla mollis*).

Making the most of foliage texture. The bold texture of this variegated hosta is a perfect foil for the feathery fronds of maidenhair fern (*Adiantum pedatum*). Both of these plants grow well in shaded areas.

both sides, don't be too rigid about these height gradations, or you'll end up with a row planting. For a more relaxed look, pull some taller plants out toward the middle of the border and some mid-height perennials toward the edges.

Some perennials are tall but airy, creating a see-through effect in the garden. Plants like Japanese anemone (*Anemone × hybrida*) and Brazilian vervain (*Verbena bonariensis*) have slender bloom stalks that give a clear view of the plants behind them. Treat these plants as if they were shorter—put them in the middle of the border so you'll have plants behind them to form a backdrop. And here's a final height trick: In places in the bed or border where you see a sudden need for a taller plant, you can add quick height with tall annuals like spider flower (*Cleome hasslerana*).

TEXTURE IN THE GARDEN

Texture means several things in the garden. One is the effect foliage and flower shape and size have on the way a plant looks—is it bold-, medium-, or fine-textured? If a plant has large, solid leaves like hostas (*Hosta* spp.) or ligularias (*Ligularia* spp.), it's usually bold-textured. Plants with intermediate foliage like Siberian iris (*Iris sibirica*) or evening primroses (*Oenothera* spp.) are medium-textured. And plants with delicate, ferny or threadlike foliage like columbines (*Aquilegia* spp.) and pinks (*Dianthus* spp.) are fine-textured.

Flower shape and size can change the texture of a plant while it's in bloom. The graceful sprays of alumroots (*Heuchera* spp.)

Spotlighting flower texture. Panicles of purple moor grass (*Molinia caerulea*) arch gracefully over the bright, brash blooms of purple coneflower (*Echinacea purpurea*). Both these plants prefer full sun, and both will provide structural interest well into fall. You can cut both to enjoy indoors in arrangements, too.

A study in contrasts. You couldn't imagine more different foliage textures than the succulent reddish leaves of baby's-toes (*Sedum rubrotinctum*) and the felted silvery foliage of lamb's-ears (*Stachys byzantina*), but both evolved for the same purpose — to protect the plants from drought. These sun lovers make an ideal combination for a hot, dry site.

are fine-textured, while the foliage is medium-textured; the thimble-shaped blooms of fox-gloves (*Digitalis* spp.) are medium-textured, while the foliage is bold-textured. Plant habit can also affect overall texture. While the individual leaves of hardy cranesbills are fine- to medium-textured, the effect of their dense, matlike clumps is bold.

Surface Texture

Texture also refers to the appearance of leaf, flower, and stem surfaces. Are the leaves shiny like those of peonies, felted like lamb's-ears (*Stachys byzantina*), or matte (a dull, powdered finish) like 'Autumn Joy' sedum (*Sedum* × 'Autumn Joy')? Leaves can be veined like alumroots (*Heuchera* spp.), smooth like irises, or ribbed like hostas. And flower

petals can be shiny like those of evening primroses (*Oenothera* spp.), satiny like day-lilies, or papery like poppies.

When you're combining perennials, vary the textures of foliage and flowers. The eye quickly tires of many shiny-leaved plants together, refusing to take in differences between individual plants unless their colors are very different. The same is true of felted leaves, papery petals, and so on. The same look repeated over and over again becomes boring. Just as you contrast height and form to make a pleasing border, use textures to make your garden more interesting and inviting. The exception is when you're using perennials as an architectural feature, like a row of peonies or hostas. In that case, you want to create an overall impression and don't want individual plants calling attention to themselves.

Advanced Texture Techniques

Try these tips for putting texture to work in your garden. Color can create an impression of texture—the darker the color, the heavier or bolder the texture; the paler the color, the lighter or finer the texture. You can see this for yourself with a white, pale-blue, or pale-yellow bearded iris cultivar and a dark-violet, navy, or burgundy cultivar. Or look at a plant of purple-leaved ajuga (*Ajuga reptans* 'Atropurpurea') next to silver-variegated 'Silver Beauty' ajuga (*A. reptans* 'Silver Beauty').

If you put a perennial with bold texture in front of one with finer texture, you'll create an illusion of depth in your garden, since bold textures look closer, while fine textures look farther away. If your border is narrow, you can make it look deeper by using this technique.

ENRICHING YOUR PLANT PALETTE

This is a book about perennials and perennial gardening. But that doesn't mean you should plant only perennial flowers. You can create better designs with a wider range of color and form, extend seasonal interest, add

A foliage bonanza. Although the white plumes of rodgersias (*Rodgersia* spp.) add interest, it's the bold foliage that really draws the eye to this wet garden. If you have a large, boggy site, consider combining bronzeleaf rodgersia (*Rodgersia podophylla*) with ferns. Here, the delicate fronds of sensitive fern (*Onoclea sensibilis*) and ostrich fern (*Matteuccia struthiopteris*) contrast nicely with the broad, palmately lobed leaves of the rodgersias.

Getting the right mix. There's no reason to limit your garden to perennials. This colorful border mixes roses, which are really shrubs, and yellow snapdragons, which are tender perennials grown as annuals, with the azure wands of Italian bugloss (*Anchusa azurea*), a true perennial. Shrubs add height and texture to plantings, while annuals offer nonstop color until frost. Mixed borders work well if you remember that the plants in them have different needs.

fragrance, or cover gaps in a planting by extending the range of plants you include in your garden. Bulbs, annuals, ornamental grasses, groundcovers, herbs, foliage plants, trees, and shrubs all have their place. We'll discuss each of these groups of plants, review how to use them in perennial gardens, and suggest some of the best for mixing with perennials.

Bulbs for a Brighter Garden

Bulbs belong in the perennial garden—after all, they *are* perennials, and they're grown like other perennials. It's hard to imagine a sunny perennial bed without daffodils, tulips, crocuses, glads, and lilies. But even the "minor" bulbs—grape hyacinths (*Muscari* spp.), glory-of-the-snow (*Chionodoxa* spp.), snowdrops (*Galanthus* spp.), snowflakes (*Leucojum* spp.), stars-of-Bethlehem (*Ornithogalum* spp.), and squills (*Scilla* spp.)—can have a major impact on the garden, adding bright splashes of color in early spring, when they're most welcome.

Species bulbs are often very attractive and are becoming more widely available. They are lovely in the border and in rock gardens. But many species bulbs—even species tulips, crocuses, and daffodils—are dug illegally from the wild and imported for sale. Make sure the bulbs you buy are guaranteed to be nursery-propagated so you don't contribute to the endangerment of native populations. Cultivars of species bulbs are always nursery-propagated; if you buy *Tulipa praestans* 'Fusilier' instead of *T. praestans,* you'll know you're safe. (You'll find more about how to avoid wild-collected plants in "Wild-Collected Plants: A Conservation Issue" on page 75.)

Bulbs also brighten the garden in summer and fall. Besides glads and lilies, montbretias (*Crocosmia* spp.), dahlias (*Dahlia pinnata* hybrids), canna (*Canna* × *generalis*), calla lily (*Zantedeschia aethiopica*), tuberous begonias (*Begonia* Tuberhybrida Hybrids),

and caladium (*Caladium* × *hortulanum*) are summer staples. Many of the summer bulbs are tender perennials and must be dug and stored over winter or treated as annuals. But there are hardy summer- and fall-blooming bulbs, too: Saffron crocus (*Crocus sativus*) and autumn crocuses (*Colchicum* spp.), cyclamen (*Cyclamen* spp.), and spider lilies (*Lycoris* spp.) add jewel-like touches to the autumn garden, providing a welcome break from the goldenrods, asters, and chrysanthemums while echoing their colors.

Bulbs are generally easy to grow, asking little in return for their yearly display. But there are a few things you can do to make bulbs more effective in your garden. First, grow them

Best Bulbs for Perennial Gardens

Add sparkle to your garden with these care-free bulbs. Plant groups of the same species and color for greatest impact. If you'd like an assortment of colors, using mixed crocuses for instance, plant clusters or wedges of white, yellow, purple, and striped rather than one white, one yellow, and so on. Remember to include bulbs for summer and fall as well as spring interest.

Anemone spp. (anemones): fragile, 2–3-inch white, pink, red, blue, or purple blooms
Chionodoxa spp. (glory-of-the-snow): 1-inch, star-shaped blue, white, or pink flowers
Crocus spp. (crocuses): 1½–2-inch, cupped, white, yellow, or purple blooms in spring
Eranthis hyemalis (winter aconite): 1-inch-wide yellow blooms in winter or spring
Galanthus spp. (snowdrops): 1–1½-inch-long white and green bell flowers in early spring; one flower per stalk
Hyacinthoides hispanicus (Spanish bluebell): clusters of 1-inch-long blue flowers shaped like bells; pink- and white-flowered

forms are also available
Iris danfordiae (Danford iris): 1½-inch-wide yellow flowers in late winter
Leucojum aestivum (summer snowflake): ½–¾-inch-long white bell-shaped flowers
Lycoris spp. (spider lilies): clusters of 2–3-inch-long pink or red flowers
Muscari spp. (grape hyacinths): fragrant clusters of blue or white bell flowers
Narcissus spp. (daffodils): ⅓–4-inch-long flowers, usually white and/or yellow with trumpet centers; often fragrant
Ornithogalum spp. (stars-of-Bethlehem): 1–2-inch-wide white star-shaped flowers in spring or summer
Scilla spp. (squills): ½-inch-wide blue, purple, or white star- or bell-shaped flowers in spring; narrow or strap-shaped leaves
Tulipa spp. (tulips): star-shaped to cuplike spring flowers in single or double forms, 1 to several inches long, in all colors but blue; some fragrant

in well-drained soil. If voles eat your bulbs, there are two lines of defense: Plant them in gravel-lined holes, or plant them in buried wire cages. If squirrels or chipmunks are the problem, discourage them by planting bulbs in a dense groundcover. (For great groundcover suggestions, see "Perennial Groundcovers" on page 63.)

Bulbs need a complete food like other perennials, not just bonemeal as is often recommended. Give them a topdressing of compost or a good organic fertilizer in spring. And let their foliage ripen after bloom—don't mow or cut it down as soon as bloom fades. Growing bulbs among other perennials or in a groundcover will hide the foliage as it yellows. (Daffodils and hostas are a classic low-maintenance combination: By the time the daffodils have faded, the hosta foliage has grown up to cover them.) When bulb foliage has completely yellowed, it has served its purpose, and you can cut it off.

A Place for Annuals

Put annuals to work in your perennial garden. They'll provide nonstop color from early summer to frost, bridging gaps between your perennials' bloom times. Annuals fill in quickly, giving a finished look to a new

Filling in with annuals. Annuals can be lifesavers in the garden. Add them to provide summer-long bloom, bridge the gap between flowering perennials, make a new garden look mature, or fill in a critical color, height, or shape. Here, rose-pink flowering tobacco (*Nicotiana alata*) adds a complementary color to this perennial grouping of Carpathian harebell (*Campanula carpatica* 'Blue Clips'), 'Blue Spruce' sedum, and 'Golden Chimes' daylilies.

Making the most of annual color. Annuals such as these 'Sea Shells' cosmos can state your color theme with a summer-long show of bloom. They also fill in gaps where perennials have died back or are not yet established. Here, the cosmos blooms complement the colors and shapes of 'Pink Beauty' boltonia (*Boltonia asteroides* 'Pink Beauty') and the cherry-red 'Alma Potschke' aster (*Aster novae-angliae* 'Alma Potschke') in the background.

perennial garden in its first season. And they're perfect for planting with perennials like oriental poppies and Virginia bluebell (*Mertensia virginica*); these perennials die back after flowering, and the annuals will fill in the bare spots.

Use colorful low-growing annuals like petunias, wax begonias, marigolds, dusty miller (*Senecio cineraria*), annual candytuft (*Iberis umbellata*), and sweet alyssum (*Lobularia maritima*) to edge your perennial beds. Fill in missing colors with the wide range of snapdragon (*Antirrhinum majus*), annual statice

(*Limonium sinuatum*), and flowering tobacco (*Nicotiana alata*) cultivars available. Add height, striking form, and stunning bloom with spider flower (*Cleome hasslerana*). Globe amaranth (*Gomphrena globosa*) and 'Redform' fennel (*Foeniculum vulgare* 'Redform') are other popular choices for the perennial garden.

Annuals also come into their own in the shade, where spring-blooming bulbs and perennials put on an early show and then go green for the rest of the season. Shade-tolerant annuals like impatiens (*Impatiens wallerana*) and caladium (*Caladium* × *hortulanum*) add sparkle and a range of colors until they're nipped by a killing frost. And don't forget containers—set pots or urns of annuals at key points in the garden, or plant cheerful window boxes above a perennial foundation planting. Attractive container choices include pansies, petunias, zonal and ivy geraniums, edging lobelia (*Lobelia erinus*), browallia (*Browallia speciosa*), and garden nasturtium (*Tropaeolum majus*).

Adding Ornamental Grasses

Ornamental grasses are great plants for adding four-season interest to the perennial garden—they produce clumps of vertical or fountainlike foliage in spring, bloom in summer, set attractive seed heads and turn color in fall, and hold their form throughout the winter. Many have handsome white, cream, or yellow stripes, which contrast beautifully with the rounded or oval variegated foliage of perennials like hostas and Bethlehem sage (*Pulmonaria saccharata*). Others have steel-blue or red foliage.

Because ornamental grasses range in height from creeping (as low as 2 inches tall) to towering (some are over 10 feet tall), they can fill every garden niche from groundcover to large "shrub." Use them in the front, middle,

Mixing in ornamental grasses. Clump-forming ornamental grasses are perfect companions for perennials. Here, a clump of white-striped ribbon grass (*Phalaris arundinacea* var. *picta*) sets off the 'Moonshine' yarrow (*Achillea* × 'Moonshine') behind it. The white stripes of the grass also echo the white slats of the fence.

Ornamental Grasses for Your Garden

Because the foliage and flowers of ornamental grasses contrast so strongly with most perennials, grasses are excellent complements in the garden. Place them where they'll catch the light—and the breeze—to show off their finest qualities. Many grasses have striking foliage colors during the growing season and in autumn.

Carex spp. (sedges): clumps of narrow, arching leaves; to 2 feet tall; *C. elata* 'Bowles Golden' has green-edged, yellow foliage, *C. morrowii* 'Goldband' has yellow-edged leaves

Calamagrostis spp. (reed grass): tight 2–4-foot clumps; reddish, purple, or cream flowers; *C. arundinacea* 'Karl Foerster' has reddish green flowers in summer that turn gold in fall

Festuca spp. (blue fescue): fine-leaved clumps, height varies; *F. cinerea* 'Elijah Blue' has 8-inch soft-blue leaves; 2–3-foot

F. mairei has gray-green leaves

Miscanthus spp. (maiden grass): tall, clump-forming; large, plumelike blooms; *M. sinensis* 'Morning Light' grows 4–5 feet tall, light-green leaf blades edged with white look silvery; *M. sinensis* var. *strictus* grows 4–6 feet; yellow horizontal bands run across the green leaf blades

Panicum spp. (switchgrass): clump-forming, upright, dark-green to gray-green leaves, to 6 feet tall, airy flowers; *P. virgatum* 'Haense Herms' grows to 3½ feet, reddish fall color; *P. virgatum* 'Heavy Metal' has blue foliage, yellow in fall, 3½ feet

Pennisetum spp. (fountain grass): bottle-brush flowers, arching clumps, height varies; *P. alopecuroides* 'Hameln' has white flowers, dark-green leaves, 12–20 inches tall; *P. alopecuroides* 'Moudry' reaches 26 inches, black flowers, yellow-orange fall color

and back of the perennial border to add sparkle and contrast. Or site a tall grass like Japanese silver grass (*Miscanthus sinensis*) or switchgrass (*Panicum virgatum*) in the center of an island bed or at the ends of a border to anchor the planting.

Besides providing forms and textures that work well with perennials, ornamental grasses have two very desirable traits that make them valuable in perennial gardens: They catch the light, which seems to shine through the foliage and flower heads, making them glow; and they shimmer in the breeze, moving with every air current. Use these features to add excitement to your garden.

Remember to choose clumping grasses like the fountain grasses (*Pennisetum* spp.) or

feather reed grass (*Calamagrostis arundinacea*) rather than running grasses when you include ornamental grasses in a perennial garden. As their name implies, clumping grasses form increasingly larger clumps but stay in one place, while running grasses send out creeping stems or roots, which spread like weeds all over the garden (think of crabgrass). If you want to include a running grass like 'Feesey's Form' ribbon grass (*Phalaris arundinacea* 'Feesey's Form') because its pink, white, and green variegations are so beautiful, plant it in a deep, sunken bucket with the bottom cut out, or sink a wide metal edging around it to control its spread.

Although most ornamental grasses grow best in a sunny site, there are a number of

Left

Grasses with bold appeal. The boldly striped foliage, upright form, and stately height of zebra grass (*Miscanthus sinensis* 'Zebrinus') make it an excellent accent for a large island bed or perennial border. Zebra grass can grow 7' tall and makes a striking specimen plant in a sunny site.

Below

Ferns for the shady garden. Some perennials are excellent groundcovers for shade, like sweet woodruff (*Galium odoratum*), with its whorled leaves and starry white flowers. Imagine this wooded path with just the trees and woodruff; then notice how much lovelier this garden looks when you add ostrich fern (*Matteuccia struthiopteris*) to provide a contrasting texture and to bridge the height gap between groundcover and trees. Ferns are handsome, low-maintenance perennials — don't forget them when you design your garden.

stunning grasses that grow beautifully in shade. If you want to light up a shady garden, try golden-variegated hakone grass (*Hakonechloa macra* var. *aureola*) or one of the many variegated sedges (*Carex* spp.). There are also some lovely annual grasses for the perennial garden, including feathertop (*Pennisetum villosum*) and hare's-tail grass (*Lagurus ovatus*). These grasses have very showy flower heads and are among the best for dried arrangements.

Perennial Groundcovers

Most traditional groundcovers are perennial, including English ivy (*Hedera helix*), pachysandra (*Pachysandra* spp.), and common periwinkle (*Vinca minor*). But some perennials, used mostly in garden settings, also make great groundcovers. These plants are attractive in and of themselves, but they have the classic groundcover traits: They're low-growing, they spread quickly, and they form a dense cover that resists weeds. These perennials include ajuga (*Ajuga reptans*), spotted lamium (*Lamium maculatum*), and yellow archangel (*Lamiastrum galeobdolon*), all of which have cultivars with variegated foliage; ajuga also has bronze- and purple-leaved cultivars.

Some of the most delightful perennial groundcovers grow best where you need them most—in the shade under trees. These include the wild gingers (*Asarum* spp.), with their beautiful matte or glossy green foliage; sweet woodruff (*Galium odoratum*), with whorled leaves; green and gold (*Chrysogonum virginianum*), with bright-yellow flowers; delightfully fragrant lily-of-the-valley (*Convallaria*

Choosing plants for a wet site. A low, boggy part of your yard may be an ugly duckling waiting to be transformed into a swan. This gardener planted colorful Japanese primrose (*Primula japonica*), then mixed in foliage plants — sensitive fern (*Onoclea sensibilis*) and skunk cabbage (*Symplocarpus foetidus*) — to provide interest both before and after the primroses have bloomed.

majalis); and violets (*Viola* spp.), with their characteristic heart-shaped foliage.

Variegated bishop's weed (*Aegopodium podagraria* 'Variegatum') grows vigorously in sun or shade; make sure it can't invade your perennial border. If you need plant cover between stepping stones or in a sunny, rocky site, try one of the creeping thymes like the soft, silvery woolly thyme (*Thymus pseudo-lanuginosus*), or fragrant chamomile (*Chamae-melum nobile*). Other perennial groundcovers that like sun are the woolly white lamb's-ears (*Stachys byzantina*); cranesbills (*Geranium* spp.), with wonderful palmate foliage and

colorful flowers; and leadwort (*Ceratostigma plumbaginoides*), with bright-blue flowers and leaves that flush red in fall.

Because most perennial groundcovers have showy flowers as well as handsome foliage, they add color and life to dark areas as well as making sunny areas more interesting. But as with all groundcovers, you usually need many plants to make a visual impact. That makes perennial groundcovers ideal candidates for the nursery bed—an area that's been set aside specifically for propagating and growing young plants. You can grow seedlings in the well-prepared soil of this protected

More Perennial Groundcovers

These versatile groundcovers look lovely in the perennial garden, but they can also stand on their own. Use them along a walk to soften the straight edges, under trees to brighten a shady area, around a pool, or anywhere you don't want the high mainte-nance lawn grass requires. Descriptions and preferred growing conditions follow each plant name.

Arctostaphylos uva-ursi (bearberry): small, glossy, evergreen leaves on low, spreading plants; pink, bell-shaped flowers in spring; sun or partial shade

Asarum europaeum (European wild gin-ger): glossy, kidney-shaped leaves; 7 inches tall; shade

Convallaria majalis (lily-of-the-valley): fra-grant white or pink, bell-shaped blooms in spring; sun or shade

Cornus canadensis (bunchberry): white flowers in spring above whorls of leaves; 6 inches tall; shade

Epimedium spp. (epimediums): dainty heart-shaped leaflets; flowers in spring; shade

Helleborus spp. (hellebores): divided leaves;

evergreen; to 24 inches tall; green, white, pink or purplish flowers in winter or spring

Houttuynia cordata (houttuynia): red, pink, and white variegated or solid-green heart-shaped leaves; 1½–2 feet tall; sun or shade

Hypericum calycinum (St.-John's-wort): medium-green foliage turns red in fall; yellow flowers; sun

Liriope spp. (lilyturf): clumps of grass-like leaves; white or purple flowers; 1–1½ feet tall; sun or shade

Lysimachia nummularia (creeping Jenny): creeping plant for moist soil, 2–4 inches tall; small rounded leaves; yellow flowers; sun or partial shade

Sedum spp. (sedums): 2–24 inches tall; thick, succulent leaves; flowers in white, yellow, pink, or red; sun or partial shade

Tiarella cordifolia (Allegheny foamflower): heart-shaped leaves; white, fluffy flowers

Waldsteinia spp. (barren strawberries): evergreen, strawberry-like leaves; yellow flowers; 8–12 inches tall; sun or shade

area, or buy and establish stock or mother plants in the nursery bed, then take cuttings or root runners. For more on how to set up your own nursery bed, see "The Nursery Bed" on page 156.

Herbs for the Perennial Garden

Herbs were among the first cultivated plants but are often the last plants people think of including in the perennial garden. Don't leave them out of your garden—they add fragrance, flowers, and outstanding foliage, and they even provide seasonings for salads.

Of course, some herbs have such attractive flowers that they are now thought of as perennials in their own right, grown for beauty rather than use. These include lavenders (*Lavandula* spp.), catmint (*Nepeta* spp.), bee balm (*Monarda didyma*), calamint (*Calamintha nepeta*), and feverfew (*Chrysanthemum parthenium*). Medicinal herbs like foxglove (*Digitalis purpurea*) and purple coneflower (*Echinacea purpurea*) have also taken their place in the perennial garden.

Some of the best perennials for foliage interest, the artemisias, are also herbs. Artemisias are sun- and drought-proof, with ferny silver, white, or gray-green foliage and a shrubby or mounding habit. Try wormwood (*Artemisia absinthium*), 'Powis Castle' (*A.* × 'Powis Castle'), 'Silver King' (*A. ludoviciana* 'Silver King'), and silvermound artemisia (*A. schmidtiana*) in your garden. Artemisia foliage is aromatic and easy to dry for wreaths and arrangements. In hot, humid areas, mounding artemisias may lodge, or fall open, creating a circle of foliage around a dark, hollow center. If your plants lodge, consider replacing them with the more upright artemisias.

Other perennial herbs with fragrant foliage are lavender cotton (*Santolina chamaecyparissus*), which has feathery gray-green evergreen foliage; rosemary (*Rosmarinus officinalis*), with thick, intensely fragrant, needle-like evergreen foliage; and lemon balm (*Melissa officinalis*), with green or chartreuse (for the cultivar 'All Gold') mintlike leaves. An annual herb that has become popular for perennial gardens is bronze fennel (*Foeniculum vulgare* var. *purpureum*). It bears a cloud of very fine purple-bronze foliage and has a characteristic licorice fragrance when its leaves are rubbed.

Two herbs that look great in and out of bloom are chives (*Allium schoenoprasum*) and garlic chives (*A. tuberosum*). The upright clumps of tubular green foliage and perky globes of mauve flowers make chives a handsome plant for the front of the border, and, of course, a few clipped leaves are a welcome addition to a salad. Garlic chives have blue-green straplike leaves and showy flat heads of fragrant, white, starry flowers. The show continues with ornamental seed heads, but cut them before the seeds drop, or you'll be weeding out seedlings the following year.

Mat-forming herbs like thyme (*Thymus* spp.), pennyroyal (*Mentha pulegium*), and Corsican mint (*Mentha requienii*) are delightfully fragrant edgings for perennial beds. Lemon thyme (*Thymus* × *citriodorus*) is one of the best of the many species and cultivars, and it has a yellow-variegated cultivar, 'Gold Edge'. Thymes grow best in well-drained soil in full sun; cut them back to keep them from getting woody. The mints need well-drained but moist soil in full sun to partial shade. Plant these aromatic herbs where visitors will brush against them as they pass.

Herbs are a natural choice for the cottage garden, where they can cheerfully rub shoulders with annuals, perennials, and even vegetables. (For a delightful example of a cottage garden that uses herbs, see "A Fragrant Cottage

Choice Herbs for Perennial Gardens

Include perennial herbs in your garden for their strong form, attractive foliage color, delightful fragrance, or culinary uses. Herbs are the ultimate hands-on plants—you can often only appreciate their highly fragrant foliage if you run your hands over it or brush against it. They're a must for the cottage garden, but will enrich your garden, whatever its style. Descriptions and some possible uses follow plant names.

Alchemilla mollis (lady's-mantle): clumps of fan-shaped leaves with scalloped edges

Asarum spp. (wild ginger): heart or kidney-shaped leaves; some mottled; spicy scent

Asclepias tuberosa (butterfly weed): bright-orange flowers attract butterflies

Chamaemelum nobile (chamomile): low, spreading plant; sweet-scented fine, ferny leaves; yellow button flowers

Foeniculum vulgare (fennel): bluish green feathery leaves; yellow flowers; anise-scented; edible seeds, stems, and leaves

Galium odoratum (sweet woodruff): low whorls of sweet-scented green leaves; airy, white flowers

Lavendula angustifolia (lavender): lavender-scented leaves and flower spikes; dry purple flowers for sachets

Mentha spp. (mints): fragrant but invasive; scents include apple, pineapple, peppermint; used to flavor tea and vegetables

Poterium sanguisorba (salad burnet): rosette of blue-green, cucumber-flavored leaves

Rosmarinus officinalis (rosemary): bushy plant; narrow, gray-green, strongly scented leaves; excellent seasoning for meat

Ruta graveolens (rue): rounded plants with blue-green, pungent foliage

Salvia elegans (pineapple sage): red flowers attract butterflies; flavor drinks with pineapple-scented leaves

Salvia officinalis (garden sage): rough-textured, oblong leaves; purple, green, gold, and tricolored cultivars; seasoning

Tagetes lucida (sweet marigold): single yellow flowers above anise-scented leaves

Tanacetum vulgare (tansy): fernlike leaves; clusters of small, yellow button flowers

Garden" on page 104.) But herbs have traditionally had more formal uses as well—lavender rather than dwarf boxwood as an edging around a formal bed, and lavender or catmint (*Nepeta* spp.) as an underplanting with roses, for example. Low-growing herbs like thymes and chives are excellent for rock gardens, where they mix well with other perennials that demand full sun and good drainage.

Fundamental Foliage Plants

From one perspective, foliage is the most important thing in the perennial garden—it's there before, during, and after flowering; it creates textural depth and contrast; and it ties together any color scheme you choose, blending flower colors by providing a green backdrop. So don't overlook foliage when you're choosing perennials for your garden.

Some perennials are grown primarily for their foliage. Blue lilyturf (*Liriope muscari*), with its elegant straplike foliage, is handsome as an edging in a formal garden or along a path or patio; try one of its variegated cultivars for a brighter touch. Lamb's-ears (*Stachys byzantina*), beloved for its fuzzy silver-green leaves, is also an excellent edging plant for full sun. However, its flowers detract from the neat edging effect and attract bees; if you're allergic to bees or just don't like the flowers, cut off the bloom spikes before the flowers open. Many low-growing perennials with showy foliage are grown as groundcovers; you'll find them in "Perennial Groundcovers" on page 63.

Hostas are one of the premiere foliage perennials, with species and cultivars in every size from 3-inch groundcovers to 4-foot giants. The deeply ribbed texture of their spoon-shaped foliage makes hostas stand out in the garden. And the many color variations—from glossy dark-green to matte steel-blue to a chartreuse that's almost primrose-yellow, as well as almost endless variegations—make hostas quite versatile. The distinctive leaf shapes and wide color range of hostas make it easy to combine them with other perennials.

Some species and cultivars of alumroots (*Heuchera* spp.) are also grown primarily for their beautiful ivylike foliage. These include the red-purple 'Palace Purple' (*Heuchera micrantha* var. *diversifolia* 'Palace Purple'), red-centered 'Garnet' (*H. villosa* 'Garnet'), and silver-etched 'Dale's Strain' (*H. americana* 'Dale's Strain'). And the lovely soft, scalloped, clear-green leaves of lady's-mantle (*Alchemilla mollis*) make it a wonderful plant for the front of the border, where visitors can appreciate the way rainwater beads and glitters on the foliage like diamonds.

Other perennials have such handsome foliage that they function as foliage plants until their flowers steal the show. These include irises and daylilies, with architectural sword-shaped fans or straplike leaves; peonies, with glossy dark foliage and shrubby form; astilbes (*Astilbe* spp.) and bleeding hearts (*Dicentra* spp.), with ferny foliage; and the giant great

Mix 'n' match foliage. Except for the maidenhair fern (*Adiantum pedatum*), all the plants in this shady corner bloom. But foliage is the main feature of this woodland grouping, which includes hostas and fragrant Solomon's seal (*Polygonatum odoratum*). When you choose perennials, remember that you'll see their foliage all season — make sure it's worth looking at.

A bold combination for shade. The straplike foliage of golden-variegated Hakonechloa grass (*Hakonechloa macra* 'Aureola'), an ornamental grass for shade, and graceful fronds of maidenhair fern (*Adiantum pedatum*) soften the bold foliage of rodgersia (*Rodgersia sambucifolia*) and Japanese meadowsweet (*Filipendula purpurea*) in this highly textured mixed planting. Contrasting leaf colors, shapes, and forms provide lively interest.

coneflower (*Rudbeckia maxima*), with huge gray-green leaves.

Of course, some of the best foliage plants are ferns. Ferns, with their open texture and durable grace, make a wonderful counterpoint to flowering perennials. They are especially important in the shade garden, where many perennials are spring ephemerals, dying back after spring bloom. But there are also ferns that grow well in sunny gardens, including polypody ferns (*Polypodium* spp.), interrupted fern (*Osmunda claytoniana*), and cinnamon fern (*O. cinnamomea*). And don't overlook the handsome foliage of ornamental grasses, available in a wide variety of sizes, shapes, and colors. For more on grasses, see "Adding Ornamental Grasses" on page 60.

Trees and Shrubs for Larger Gardens

If you choose them carefully, trees and shrubs are some of the smartest additions you can make to a large perennial garden. They'll add height, color, and texture all year. You can select evergreens to anchor the border, or choose shrubs that bloom when your garden needs color most. Whatever you choose, woody

Choose These Perennials for Foliage

Foliage takes center stage often in a perennial garden, where limited bloom time and restrained bloom mass make foliage stand out. You can add more interest to your garden by mixing in some plants that are grown primarily for their foliage. Here are some of the best.

Achillea spp. (yarrows): aromatic, ferny leaves; white, pink, red, or yellow flowers

Armeria maritima (thrift): 2–4-inch-tall tufts of grasslike foliage; round flowers

Artemisia spp. (artemisias): mounded or upright, silvery foliage; fragrant

Astilbe spp. (astilbes): divided leaves; red, white, pink, or purple, feathery flowers

Belamcanda chinensis (blackberry lily): iris foliage; orange flowers on 3–4-foot stems; blackberry-like seed clusters

Bergenia cordifolia (heart-leaved bergenia): rounded, glossy leaves; 10–14 inches tall; pink flowers

Chrysanthemum pacificum (gold-and-silver chrysanthemum): green mum leaves edged with white; 1 foot tall; yellow button flowers

Iris pallida 'Variegata' (variegated sweet iris): gray-green and cream leaves; lavender flowers

Lamium maculatum cultivars (spotted lamium): gold-, white-, or silver-variegated leaves; 6–12 inches tall

Ligularia spp. (ligularias): broad, heart- or kidney-shaped leaves; yellow or orange flowers; 4–5 feet tall in bloom

Opuntia humifusa (prickly pear): thick, oval, spiny, leaflike stems; 4–6 inches tall

Pachysandra procumbens (Allegheny pachysandra): spreading, purple-and-green-mottled leaves; 9–12 inches tall

Polemonium caeruleum (Jacob's ladder): divided leaves; blue flowers; to 2 feet tall

Pulmonaria saccharata (Bethlehem sage): silver-spotted leaves; 18-inch-tall plant

Santolina chamaecyparissus (lavender cotton): white-woolly, aromatic leaves; plants form 1–2-foot mounds

plants will contrast beautifully with your perennials. And the best trees and shrubs for perennial gardens are also very low maintenance.

Butterfly bushes (*Buddleia* spp.) are wonderful shrubs for the butterfly garden. They bear long, showy flower spikes in summer and early fall. Try a dwarf fothergilla (*Fothergilla gardenii*) for fragrant puffs of spring flowers and knockout fall foliage color. Purple-leaved Japanese barberries, including *Berberis thunbergii* 'Atropurpurea' and the smaller *B. thunbergii* 'Crimson Pygmy', add bright color all year and can be sheared into formal shapes.

Boxwoods (*Buxus* spp.) are dense, slow-growing shrubs that take well to formal pruning; you can choose a low-growing cultivar for edging a bed, midsize plants for accents in the border, or large cultivars for anchoring the bed or adding focal points to the garden. Heavenly bamboo (*Nandina domestica*), really an open shrub rather than a bamboo, makes a lovely addition to southern gardens, with its upright stems, willowy foliage, large, showy white flower panicles, and stunning scarlet berries. The leaves of some cultivars turn attractive red or purplish shades in fall and winter.

Some shrubs show to best advantage in the perennial garden if they're cut back to the ground in late winter or early spring before growth starts. These include shrubs that bloom on new wood, like buddleias and

Above

Dwarf conifers for the rock garden. These diminutive shrubs add year-round structure and texture to rock gardens, and they form an attractive backdrop to the small, jewel-like plants that are often grown there. Like perennial rock garden plants, dwarf conifers enjoy full sun and good drainage. Some dwarf conifers will actually grow quite large. Try a few of the bigger ones in the perennial border for a rich effect.

Left

Using roses with perennials. Roses are beloved companions in the perennial garden. The shrubby form and abundant pink blooms of this rose contrast beautifully with the white flowers and low-growing gray foliage of snow-in-summer (*Cerastium tomentosum*).

Perennials under trees. Don't fight the losing battle to grow lawn under trees. Lawn grass grows sparsely under trees, often leaving bare, muddy gaps. And it's hard to mow over shallow tree roots and around trunks. Instead, grow a lush shade garden of woodland perennials like these western bleeding hearts (*Dicentra formosa*) and fringe cups (*Tellima grandiflora*). Notice how the rugged tree trunks add structure and texture to the herbaceous planting, too. Try a small tree in your next large border or island bed. Choose one with flowers, fall color, and attractive bark.

bluebeard (*Caryopteris* × *clandonensis*), named for its haze of clear-blue flowers in summer. Other shrubs lose their showy stem or foliage color if they're not cut back. This is the case with red-osier dogwood (*Cornus sericea*), which has bright-red twigs—a wonderful spring and winter feature—and some handsome cultivars with cream-variegated foliage, as well. Purple smoke tree (*Cotinus coggygria* 'Royal Purple'), with its branches of rubbery, oval, red-purple leaves, responds the same way. Cut it to the ground in late winter.

Not every favorite shrub or tree is appropriate for the perennial garden, since any shrub or tree you plant there will be showcased all year long. Choose plants that can take the limelight. Don't plant the following shrubs with your perennials: border forsythia (*Forsythia* × *intermedia*), which looks great in bloom but nondescript the rest of the year; common lilac (*Syringa vulgaris*), which will develop powdery mildew; deciduous azaleas (*Rhododendron* spp.), unless you have a shade garden; or old-fashioned weigela (*Weigela florida*), which matures at 10 feet tall and wide. Find another site for these shrubs, where they won't be front and center all year and will have plenty of room.

Shrubs and Small Trees for Mixed Borders

Woody plants add drama and sophistication to a perennial garden. They also anchor the garden, giving it a sense of permanence. Choose trees and shrubs that will mature at a size that fits your garden. Trees with a loose, open branching habit are less likely to shade out your garden as they mature—reserve large trees with dense canopies for the yard.

Aesculus parviflora (bottlebrush buckeye): 8–12-foot-tall shrub; white flowers

Buddleia spp. (butterfly bushes): shrubs with arching branches; purple, pink, yellow, or white flowers attract butterflies

Cercis canadensis (eastern redbud): small tree, 30–40 feet tall; reddish flowers in spring; heart-shaped leaves

Chionanthus virginicus (white fringe tree): shrub or small tree; white, fragrant flowers

Cornus kousa (kousa dogwood): 20–30-foot tree; white flowers; raspberry-like fruits

Hamamelis × *intermedia* (witch hazel): 15–20-foot shrub; yellow, orange, or red flowers in winter and spring

Hydrangea quercifolia (oakleaf hydrangea): 4–6-foot shrub; red in fall; white flowers

Hypericum spp. (St.-John's-worts): bushy shrubs; 1½–5 feet tall; striking yellow flowers

Ilex verticillata (winterberry): 6–10-foot shrub; red fruit in fall and winter

Koelreuteria paniculata (golden-rain tree): 30–40-foot tree; sprays of yellow flowers

Myrica spp. (bayberries): scented leaves and fruit; 10 feet tall and wide

Rhododendron catawbiense (Catawba rhododendron): broad-leaved evergreen shrub; 6–10 feet tall; lavender flowers

Spiraea × *bumalda* cultivars (Bumald spirea): 2–3-foot shrub; white or pink flowers in summer

Vaccinium spp. (blueberries): shrubs with red fall color; exfoliating bark

Viburnum spp. (viburnums): 4–15-foot shrubs, flowers usually white, some fragrant; red or bluish black fruit

---

Choose small trees with the same criteria in mind. Trees that have slender trunks and a fairly high, open canopy are ideal; if their bark is showy, like 'Heritage' river birch (*Betula nigra* 'Heritage'), you'll create added interest in your garden. A saucer magnolia (*Magnolia* × *soulangiana*) can make a lovely focal point in a perennial garden—especially against a wall—if pruned hard to control its size. Or choose a small cultivar of Japanese maple (*Acer palmatum*) for graceful form and elegant foliage.

Don't Forget Fragrance

Perfumes are often described as "unforgettable." That's because fragrance (or any smell) is the strongest memory-trigger. If you don't already know this, give yourself a quick test: How often have you walked into a store or home and smelled a soap, perfume, drink, tobacco, aftershave, or even mouthwash, and thought of a person? Have you ever smelled a flower and been magically transported back to your grandma's garden—or to a neighbor's? Does a specific smell (like a shampoo or freshly washed clothes) always remind you of a certain event in your life? Does the aroma of certain foods—say, a freshly cut watermelon or fried chicken—remind you of a particular place?

Make room for your favorite floral "triggers" in your garden, and add other fragrant plants to create new triggers for yourself, friends, and relations. It's nice to think that someone will remember you when they smell a certain peony or a fragrant iris. But it's even nicer to enjoy those delightful scents when you're working or strolling in the garden. Taking a deep breath of a fragrant daylily may help to remind you why you enjoy gardening.

Some excellent choices for perennial fragrance include bulbs like daffodils, tulips, and lilies. Herbs and other perennials with fragrant foliage, like calamint (*Calamintha nepeta*), catmints (*Nepeta* spp.), yarrows, artemisias, and chrysanthemums, are invalu-

able. Though they're small, sweet violet (*Viola odorata*) and lily-of-the-valley (*Convallaria majalis*) are highly perfumed.

Look for fragrant species and cultivars of iris, daylily, and hosta (like *Hosta plantaginea* and its cultivars); they're well worth the search. Fragrance is not something to take for granted, either: It's not a simple matter of there or not there. Some fragrances leave much to be desired, like the skunky aroma of fritillaries (*Fritillaria* spp.) and patrinia (*Patrinia scabiosifolia*). Plant these perennials where you and your guests can admire them from afar.

A garden with everything. This garden demonstrates how successful and attractive a well-planned mixed border can be. The rich interplay of color, form, and texture is due to the mixture of plants. This border features trees, shrubs such as 'Rose Glow' barberry (*Berberis* 'Rose Glow') and 'Elegantissima' tatarian dogwood (*Cornus alba* 'Elegantissima'), ornamental grasses such as ribbon grass (*Phalaris arundinacea* var. *picta*), and, of course, perennials. Perennials include 'Valerie Finnis' artemisia, 'Autumn Joy' sedum, and blue false indigo (*Baptisia australis*).

NARROWING YOUR PLANT CHOICES

With such a wealth of plants to choose from, how do you narrow your selection to manageable proportions? A good place to start is with your garden journal. Think about where you plan to put your garden and about how big you want it to be. Will the garden get full sun, or is it in partial or full shade? Does the soil stay moist, or is it especially dry? Note down the answers to these questions. You'll have the most attractive, low-maintenance garden if you grow plants that are well-suited to your conditions. If you plan to site your garden in full sun, avoid plants that need shade, and vice versa.

Next, turn to the USDA Plant Hardiness Zone Map on page 169, and find your hardiness zone. If you live in Zone 4, you'll be wasting money if you buy plants that are only hardy as far north as Zone 6. Think about your garden's color scheme, too—if you're using a limited range of colors, you can narrow your choices to plants with those flower or foliage colors. And don't forget bloom season. If you want a garden that blooms in spring and fall, choose perennials with that in mind.

Go outside and look at the site where you'd like to have your garden. About how high would you like the tallest plants to grow? (This can vary widely, depending on whether you'd like to see over the border to the lawn, block a distracting view, or reach a certain point on a wall or fence.) Then you can limit your plant choices to ones that don't exceed your maximum height.

Finally, avoid plants you don't like. If you've never liked lilies, choose something else, even if lilies suit your conditions. You can always add them later if you grow to appreciate them.

How Books and Catalogs Can Help

When you've noted down the various criteria for narrowing your plant choices—light and moisture requirements, hardiness zone, color scheme, and height limit—you're ready for the next stage in the selection process. It's time to read about potential candidates for your garden, check out their descriptions and growth requirements, and look at color photos that show their flowers and habit.

If you have favorite perennials you'd like to include, start with them. Turn to the encyclopedia section of this book, beginning on page 280, and look up each plant. If it meets your criteria, add it to the list of "approved perennials" for your garden. If it fails, jot down why: Notes such as "must have moist shade" will serve as a reminder, and you won't have to look it up again later. This will also give you a record to refer to if you plan a second garden in an area with different conditions.

Then, skim over the other entries, adding plants that look promising. Don't get carried away—remember that most perennials look best in groups, so you'll need several of each. An initial list of 20 to 40 different plants should be an ample place to start; you'll probably narrow it down even more when you begin working with your design.

You can also use mail-order nursery catalogs as a starting place in the selection process, skimming through the photos and noting the most appealing. Catalogs let you compare what's available; they often carry different species and cultivars, so order several for a good selection. You'll find addresses for catalogs in "Resources" on page 500. You can also use catalogs when you finalize your garden design (see "Bringing Your Design to Life" on page 80 to learn how), and of course, you can use them when you're ready to buy plants, so don't be shy about sending for them.

Every book and magazine article that discusses perennials and perennial gardening can provide you with ideas for choice plants and for good designs and plant combinations. You'll find a selection of books that relate to perennials in "Suggested Reading" on page 502.

Avoiding Pitfalls

The best way to avoid mistakes when selecting plants is to use common sense. Stick to plants that are easy to grow and that suit your conditions; leave finicky perennials to the connoisseur. Start with colors that you like in combinations you find pleasing. (For example, you may enjoy purple flowers and white flowers, but a purple-and-white flower may be overwhelming.) Base your garden on what you know you'll love; then you can experiment with confidence, knowing that even if a plant turns out to be a disappointment, most of the garden will look great.

One common pitfall that's easy to avoid is ignoring duration of bloom. Make sure you take into account how long a perennial blooms and what it will look like before and after flowering. Many perennials have a relatively short bloom season—two or three weeks—but make up for their brevity with attractive buds, foliage, or seed heads. Others have a long bloom season, while still others bloom for a short time, then disappear completely until the following year.

By checking length of bloom, you won't end up planting a stand of oriental poppies, then watching in disappointment as the plants go dormant in summer. You can still enjoy your poppies, but you'll know to interplant them with other perennials that will fill the gaps or to overplant them with annuals that will bloom from summer to frost. If you have a small garden, you may need a long bloom season from your perennials, since you won't have room for a lot of plants that would provide a succession of bloom; make sure you choose long-blooming species and cultivars.

Wild-Collected Plants: A Conservation Issue

Because wildflowers and other native plants are enjoying renewed popularity in perennial gardens, some unscrupulous nurseries are digging plants up in the wild and offering them for sale. Some of these plants are endangered, and their sale is often illegal. Reputable nurseries propagate the wildflowers and other native plants they sell; and as a responsible gardener, you should buy only nursery-propagated plants. Here are some ways to tell the difference:

▶ Beware of the phrase "nursery-grown." It doesn't necessarily mean that a plant is nursery-propagated; instead, it may have been collected, then grown on in the nursery for a season or two.

▶ Wildflowers that take a long time to propagate, like trilliums, trout lilies, and other spring woodland wildflowers, are often wild-collected. Don't buy them unless you're sure they're nursery-propagated.

▶ You should expect to pay the same price for a nursery-propagated wildflower as you would for any other perennial; beware of inexpensive plants or quantity discounts on wildflowers.

▶ Don't buy wildflowers that look like they were just dug from the ground and stuck in pots. Watch for battered or wilted leaves and plants that are too big for their pots but not potbound.

COPING WITH INTRUSIVE ELEMENTS

One of the most annoying aspects of garden design is something you often can't do a lot about: What if the neighbor's clothesline is your garden's most prominent feature? It may be a telephone pole, or a convenience store across the street, or your own central air-conditioning unit. But whatever it is, it's an eyesore. Your eye tends to stray toward it, no matter how hard you're concentrating on the first crocus of spring. And you're sure everyone else is looking at it, too.

Don't let an ugly view drive you to distraction. Whether it's in your yard or a neighbor's, there are design tricks you can use to minimize its impact and return your attention to enjoying your garden. These tricks boil down to the three D's: Distract, Divert, and Disappear. You can distract the viewer with something more exciting or alluring; divert attention in another direction; or make the ugly view disappear by blocking it from sight.

Eyesores in Your Own Yard

Take your garden journal into your yard. Look around, and note down any utilities or other unattractive objects you wish either looked better or were invisible. (You can also look for the list of these "uglies" that you made in your "Site Inventory Checklist" on page 6.)

Before you consider landscape solutions, decide if a quick fix would turn your eyesore into an asset: Would a coat of paint or a new roof transform your toolshed? Can you replace your clothesline with one of the retractable types? Would building or buying a new doghouse or swingset make the backyard look less like a junkyard? If cost is not prohibitive,

renovate first; you may find that many of your landscape problems are solved before you begin to plant.

On the other hand, it's hard to renovate the central air-conditioning unit or an above-ground fuel-oil tank. And if your dog has turned his run into a mud strip, you'll probably fight a losing battle trying to return it to grass. That's when creative landscaping can come to your rescue.

The easiest way to cope with an eyesore is to conceal it—make it disappear. Attach latticework to the dog pen and grow lush but lightweight vines like clematis (*Clematis* cultivars) or morning glories (*Ipomoea tricolor*) on the lattice, with hardworking perennials like daylilies and perennial candytuft (*Iberis semper-virens*) at its base. Conceal your compost piles behind tall perennials or ornamental grasses, or make bins to match the garden fence.

Don't box in a utility like a central air-conditioning unit with a fence or tightly sheared shrub wall, though, or you'll call attention to it rather than concealing it. (It also won't work effectively; be sure to follow manufacturer's recommendations whenever you build or plant around an air-conditioning unit or heat pump.) Instead, plant loosely pruned evergreens and colorful perennials around it, and tie them to the rest of the landscape, so your concealed utility looks like a mixed border or island bed.

Sometimes the worst eyesore in your yard is the house itself. If you can't afford to paint, or if paint wouldn't be appropriate, put up trellises and grow climbing roses, honeysuckle, or other concealing vines to cover as much vertical surface as possible. If an exposed foundation is the problem, plant large ferns, low-growing shrubs, and an assortment of perennials to beautify the site. A yard that's alive with colorful plantings of trees, shrubs, and perennials will draw the eye away from the house, while a bare lawn will focus attention on the house as the yard's outstanding feature.

Eyesores in Your Neighbor's Yard

It's harder to make eyesores in your neighbors' yards disappear—you may not be able to put up a tall enough fence, or you may not want to box in your own yard. However, you can still use the other two tactics—distraction and diversion—for dealing with ugly views.

Distract yourself and visitors from the neighbor's collection of rusting auto parts with an inviting swing, bench, or arbor that faces the other way. Put a colorful or clever feature, such as a hot-color island bed or a gazing ball nesting under a clump of ornamental grass like an Easter egg, where it will draw viewers to come over and look down, not over at the neighbor's laundry swaying in the breeze.

Divert wandering friends from danger zones by creating routes that lead to more appealing destinations. For example, an inviting and well-defined wood-chip path could lure garden-goers toward your lovely water garden and away from a confrontation with the neighbor's dog. Block the way to parts of the yard that provide vantage points to ugly views—with a structure, a bench, shrubs, or even a large rock, trellis, or piece of fencing—while making it easy to get to parts with better scenery. This technique will make your yard more interesting while minimizing the neighbors' impact.

DRAWING YOUR OWN DESIGN

When you've considered your site and what you want to plant on it, it's time to start drawing a design. The first step is to draw a rough sketch of your yard and its major features, so you can experiment with different garden shapes, sizes, and placement.

Once you've decided on a location, size, and shape for your garden, decide if you want it to follow a recognized style—formal or informal, cottage or colonial—or if you'd just like a pleasing combination of perennials. (For more on garden styles, see "Garden Style" on page 22.)

The next step is to make a bubble diagram of the garden, drawing the bed to scale on graph paper and sketching in the shapes of the plants you've chosen. With your bubble diagram in hand, you can refine the plan until you think it's perfect. Then cut photos of the plants from catalogs and paste or tape them on the diagram to make sure your design will look as beautiful as you hope.

We'll take you through all these steps on the following pages. As you work, don't be afraid to revise your design as often as you want. After all, it's a lot easier to move plants with a pencil than with a shovel!

On-Site Design

Start your design process by taking your garden journal out in the yard. Draw a base map of your yard in the journal. First, sketch in the yard's shape, adding dimensions in feet for each side. (If you have an existing survey of your property, you might want to start with it. Just trace over the survey and use the traced copy to note the features of your property.) Indicate what surrounds the yard on each side (a road, neighbor's yard, creek, park, and so on). Draw an arrow pointing north, so you'll know which way your garden is facing. If you have a slope on your property, add arrows on that part of the map; the arrows should point toward the low spot, in the direction of the slope.

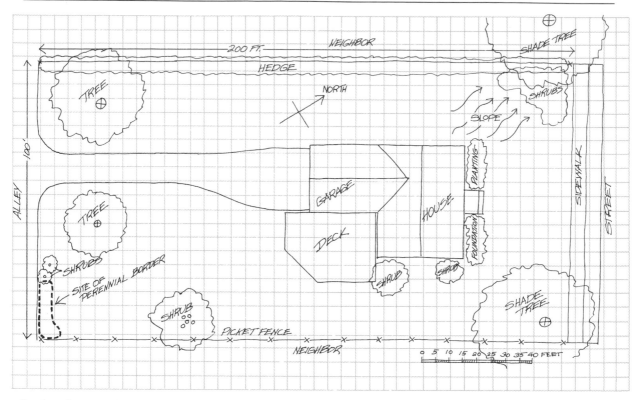

Drawing a base map. You'll find a simple base map of your property to be valuable every time you want to make a design change. Try to draw the elements to scale, starting with an outline of the yard and proceeding to the house and other major features. Add your yard's dimensions, any low or high points, a "North" arrow, and any other relevant information (wet areas, rocks, and so on). Then sketch in potential perennial beds or borders with a dashed line.

Next, fill in the yard's features. Start with the house, trying to draw it roughly to scale. (Rough is the key word for all these shapes— the size and position of these features are much more important than their appearance.) Add the garage and driveway next if you have them, then any paths and other outbuildings. Draw in patios, decks, large shade trees, water features, hedges, and other major features. Add existing gardens, shrubs, large clumps of flowers, and lawn furniture, including benches and arbors.

Once you think the map looks fairly accurate, make photocopies of it or use tracing paper to position perennial gardens. If you already have an idea of where you'd like the garden to go, sketch it to scale on a copy of your map and see how it looks. If you're unsure or want to experiment, try as many sizes, shapes, and positions as you feel like drawing.

When you've decided on a garden bed or border, take your garden map outside and check the sketch against the reality. If you want to get a more graphic view, lay a hose on the grass to outline the proposed bed or border, or cover it with a sheet of weighted black plastic to block out the space and shape. For a small garden, weighted newspapers would also work.

Don't forget exposure—have you sited your garden under trees, where the house or a neighbor's house or wall will shade it, or in the open, where it will have full sun all day? If *where* the garden is matters most to you, choose plants that will suit the exposure you've selected; if *what* you're planting matters more, site the garden where your favorite plants will get the exposure they prefer.

Making a Bubble Diagram

Once you know what size and shape you'd like your perennial garden to be, you can draw it as a bubble diagram. (It's called a bubble diagram because you draw in the plants as bubble-like blobs.) You'll need some graph paper and a list of the perennials you'd like to plant. First, draw the shape of your bed or border to scale on a piece of graph paper. A good scale to begin with is 1 inch on paper equals 1 foot of garden space. If you're planning a really large garden, use 1 inch equals 2 or 3 feet. Be sure to note on the graph paper what scale you're using.

Now you're ready to position your plants. To visualize your garden, refer to your list of plants. Read the descriptions of the plants in the encyclopedia section beginning on page 280, and note down the mature height, flower and foliage color, bloom season, and length of bloom for each plant. Think about which plants will look best together.

Using the description and height information for guidance, draw in rough circles for your plants. Use the same scale you did for the garden's dimensions (1 inch equals 1 foot, and so on). Position the largest plants first. Remember to put the tallest plants at the back of a bed or border, unless it's an island bed or can be seen from both sides, like a bed running along the driveway; in those cases, put the tall plants in the middle of the bed. Next, position the medium-size plants, then work in the smallest. Think about how big an area you would like each plant to cover. Many perennials will spread as wide as or wider than their height. Make your circles large enough to accommodate the plants' mature widths, unless you want to plant them closer and then move some to another site as they mature.

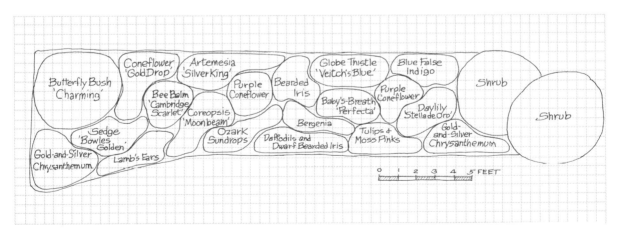

Making a bubble diagram. When you have an idea for the size and shape of your garden, draw its outline to scale on graph paper (1 inch on paper to 1 foot of ground is a good scale for most gardens). Use a pencil so you can "move" things around easily, and don't be afraid to make changes. Then draw in circles or "bubbles" to represent your perennials, making the scale of each bubble match the mature width of the plant. Write in the plant name, color, and bloom season in each bubble if you have room, so you can see at a glance how good the combinations are likely to look.

A design reality check. To make sure your paper garden really works, put a sheet of tracing paper over your bubble diagram. Using the bubbles as a guide, draw in the shapes of your plants—shrubby, spiky, mounded, and so forth. Make a copy for each bloom season. To see if the colors really work well together, find color photos of all the perennials in your design. Cut out strips of each perennial, and position them on the design according to bloom season, with spring-blooming plants on one copy, summer-blooming on another, and so on.

Refining the Design

Take your finished bubble diagram and plant list, and look at your design. Will the plant combinations you've made for the garden work well together? Have you remembered to include plants like bulbs and ornamental grasses to enrich your plant palette? Will the garden be in bloom when you want color most? If the design works on paper, take it outside and review it where you plan to put the garden. Do the heights, colors and textures still work? Have you inadvertently designed a pink garden to go in front of your orange brick wall?

Don't be afraid to modify your design. If you need inspiration before adding the finish-ing touches, refer to the gallery of garden designs in chapter 3 to see how professionals do it. Borrow any ideas or combinations that appeal or work for your site. Once you have added the finishing touches and smoothed out the rough spots, you can make a last check by "bringing your design to life."

Bringing Your Design to Life

An easy way to see what your dream garden will look like is to design it on paper with catalog cutouts. You'll need the list of perennials you'd like to plant, your bubble diagram on graph paper, tracing paper, and mail-order perennial catalogs.

Through the garden gate. Heart-leaved bergenia (*Bergenia cordifolia*) and Carpathian harebell (*Campanula carpatica*) line the path to this lovely arbor of roses and clematis (*Clematis* spp.). A potted calamondin orange adds an Old World touch. As you can see from this garden, softening an entrance with flowers makes it more inviting.

Now you're ready to arrange the plants in your paper garden. To visualize your garden, refer to your bubble diagram and your list of plants. Using the size and height information for guidance, draw a profile of the garden by placing a sheet of tracing paper over the graph paper.

Use the bubble diagram on your graph paper as an outline, and draw the shapes of the plants you plan to use on the tracing paper. Draw spikes, mounds, lumps, and mats as appropriate, keeping the heights and widths in scale with the other perennials. When you've outlined the clumps of perennials on your tracing paper, make three copies, so you'll have outlines for spring, summer, and fall. Save the original drawing in case you want to change the design later.

Next, take your list of perennials and find photos of them in mail-order catalogs. Cut out the catalog pictures, clipping a 1×2-inch strip of each plant. (This is a good size to get a clear idea of the impact the color will have in that part of the garden. The size of the cutout doesn't need to relate to the scale of your design.) Refer to the encyclopedia section again for bloom season, and arrange the strips of catalog photos for spring-blooming perennials in the appropriate places on one diagram; do the same for summer and fall (and winter, if appropriate). Then you can see for yourself if the colors, shapes, and sizes look right.

If you don't like your combinations, rearrange them, or try perennials or cultivars that have different flower colors. When the design looks like what you had in mind, you can make a more permanent record by pasting or taping the cutouts down on paper. If you can't find photos of some of the plants, fill them in on the appropriate diagram with colored pencils or crayons that match their flower colors.

Remember that your design is really just a starting point. When you're working on a garden design, it's important to bear in mind that your medium is plants, which can be moved easily and are very forgiving. You're not sculpting in stone. As you begin to look more closely at other people's gardens and at garden designs like the ones in chapter 3, you'll find plant combinations and other elements you'd like to include in your design. Don't be afraid to change it. Change is one of the best-kept secrets of successful design. You'll learn more about changing your garden in chapter 4.

A Gallery of Garden Designs

Whether you're thinking about putting in a new perennial garden or redoing an existing one, one of the toughest parts of the job can be coming up with interesting designs and plant combinations. Existing garden designs are a great place to start when you are looking for new ideas. This chapter showcases seven garden designs by well-known garden designers for a range of sites and purposes. Each one contains a plot plan and plant list, along with color realizations of the garden in different seasons or from different views. You'll also find helpful tips on adapting the design to your particular needs, as well as pointers to help you maintain the garden for the best show possible. Below is a brief discussion of each of the gardens, along with the page number on which each design begins.

Gardens for Sun and Shade

A Four-Season Perennial Garden. This island bed is packed with perennials and grasses for all-season interest. Page 84.

A Sunny Perennial Border. Try this classic perennial border to accent a sunny spot along a fence or driveway. Page 94.

A Shady Wildflower Garden. This woodland garden is full of spring wildflowers and other shade-loving plants that can brighten a dark corner. Page 114.

A Bed for a Shaded Terrace. Surround your shaded terrace or patio with this lovely perennial bed for season-long color. Page 122.

Gardens for Special Places and Purposes

A Fragrant Cottage Garden. If you enjoy the informality of a cottage garden and the fragrance of scented flowers, indulge yourself in this delightful garden. Page 104.

A Color Theme Garden. Pick your favorite flower color and use this design to help you create a tasteful, beautiful border. Page 132.

A Simple Rock Wall Garden. Liven up a sunny rock wall with this colorful collection of perennials, grasses, shrubs, and bulbs for all-season interest. Page 140.

A Four-Season Perennial Garden

In cool-climate areas, gardeners often think of the year as two seasons: the growing season and the dreaming season. But as you spend the cold winter months reviewing the previous season's successes and planning for next year's triumphs, consider the benefits of a garden that offers year-round interest—one that pulls you out into the landscape even when everything else is dull and boring. This island bed features a variety of perennials and grasses to add loads of color and excitement to any yard.

White, pinks, yellows, and blues predominate in this garden for most of the year. Spring, for example, brings splashes of color to the garden with the rosy-red flowers of 'Perfecta' heart-leaved bergenia (*Bergenia cordifolia* 'Perfecta') and 'Bountiful' bleeding heart (*Dicentra* 'Bountiful'), combined with yellow lady's-mantle (*Alchemilla mollis*) and white 'Autumn Beauty' candytuft (*Iberis sempervirens* 'Autumn Beauty'). Later on, double pink 'Pillow Talk' peony (*Paeonia lactiflora* 'Pillow Talk') forms a striking combination with the delicate blooms of 'Caesar's Brother' Siberian iris (*Iris sibirica* 'Caesar's Brother').

In summer, a variety of other plants carry on the color themes. Some of them bloom over several months, giving continuity to the design. The spiky flowers of 'Sunny Border Blue' speedwell (*Veronica* × 'Sunny Border Blue') and 'Lochinch' butterfly bush (*Buddleia* × 'Lochinch') complement the daisylike 'Magnus' purple coneflower (*Echinacea purpurea* 'Magnus') and 'Goldsturm' black-eyed Susan (*Rudbeckia fulgida* var. *sullivantii* 'Goldsturm').

When planning a garden, it's not difficult to choose plants for spring and summer color, but designing a garden with year-round interest can be a challenge. One way to extend the bloom season is with plants that flower late in fall or very early in spring. Asters and goldenrods (*Solidago* spp.), for example, put on their best show in the cooler days of fall. And if you add some early-spring-blooming bulbs to the garden, such as 'Jack Snipe' daffodil (*Narcissus* 'Jack Snipe'), you could cut the "down time" of the garden to just three to four months.

A great way to add winter interest is to spare the garden a fall cleanup and let the plants continue their show until spring. Many have leaves, pods, or seeds that remain interesting all winter long. Grasses, for example, can add color and motion to the winter garden. And the coneflowers, including *Echinacea* and *Rudbeckia* species, form striking clumps of brownish black seed heads.

The one drawback to letting seed heads remain is the problem of the plants self-sowing. If you are willing to risk some weeding, you can wait until late winter to cut seed heads down. By removing and composting the winter mulch and applying a fresh mulch in spring, you can keep self-sown seedlings to a minimum.

Otherwise, this sunny garden needs little maintenance to keep looking its best. Regularly removing spent flowers can encourage the yarrows to produce more blooms. Shearing back candytuft after it flowers can also encourage rebloom. And thinning the stems of garden phlox will encourage better air circulation through the plant and reduce the chances of powdery mildew disfiguring the leaves.

In Another Place

Island beds have many uses in the garden. They make attractive, colorful dividers between outdoor living areas, or they can liven up an expanse of lawn, punctuating the sea of green with a pool of bright colors. If you don't have space to plant the whole bed where it could be viewed from all sides, consider splitting the design lengthwise and using either half as a border along a fence or wall. (Remember to include a narrow path between the bed and the fence or wall so that you can get to the back of the bed for maintenance.)

Evergreen Perennials: Myth or Reality?

As you plan your garden with winter interest in mind, you may be tempted to include a lot of perennials with evergreen foliage. After all, why not have some color, even if it's only green, all year long in the perennial garden? Well, depending on where you live, a winter garden based on "evergreen" perennials can be a delight or a disappointment.

A wide variety of perennials are commonly touted as evergreens, including epimediums (*Epimedium* spp.), bergenias (*Bergenia* spp.), ajugas (*Ajuga* spp.), European wild ginger (*Asarum europaeum*), pinks (*Dianthus* spp.), rock cresses (*Arabis* spp.), thrifts (*Armeria* spp.), thymes (*Thymus* spp.), and periwinkles (*Vinca* spp.). Whether or not these plants are worth adding to your winter garden depends a great deal on your climate.

In general, perennials growing in mild-winter areas tend to hold their leaves longer than those in climates with cold, dry winters. Winter winds can dry out the soil and sap water from plant leaves, causing the leaves to discolor and droop. Bergenias and epimediums, for example, often get browned and tattered by midwinter storms and end up looking unattractive until the new leaves emerge.

So If you live in an area where even evergreen trees and shrubs look ratty by winter's end, don't count on evergreen perennials to keep your garden attractive all winter. But if you grow these plants anyway, for their warm-season flowers and foliage, enjoy their green leaves as long as the winter winds hold off, and try some of the other tricks discussed in "Winter Interest" on page 39 to carry the show in mid- to late winter.

Or use the halves to flank a path or driveway where you can enjoy the beauty of the garden all year long.

Four-Season Perennial Garden

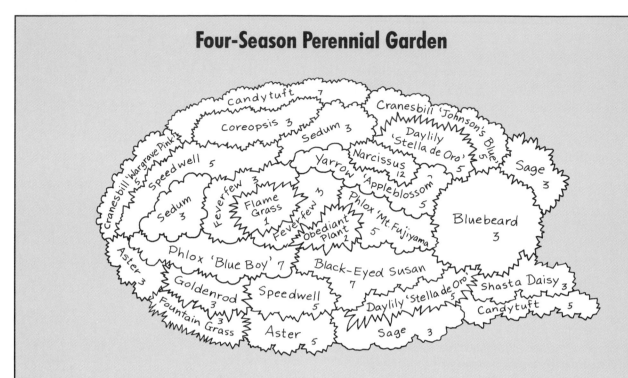

This colorful island bed provides year-round interest for any site, with whites, pinks, yellows, and blues as the predominant colors for most of the year. Below is a list of plants included in this design. For more information on the perennials used, look them up in the table on page 90, or turn to the appropriate entry in the encyclopedia section beginning on page 280. (Note: The numbers in the diagram refer to the quantity of each plant used.)

Plants for the Four-Season Perennial Garden

Anemone (*Anemone × hybrida* 'Margarete')
Aster (*Aster novae-angliae* 'Purple Dome')
Astilbe 'Finale' (*Astilbe × arendsii* 'Finale')
Astilbe 'White Gloria' (*Astilbe × arendsii* 'White Gloria')
Bergenia (*Bergenia cordifolia* 'Perfecta')
Black-eyed Susan (*Rudbeckia fulgida* var. *sullivantii* 'Goldsturm')
Bleeding heart (*Dicentra* 'Bountiful')

Bluebeard (*Caryopteris × clandonensis* 'Blue Mist')
Butterfly bush (*Buddleia × 'Lochinch'*)
Candytuft (*Iberis sempervirens* 'Autumn Beauty')
Coreopsis (*Coreopsis verticillata* 'Moonbeam')
Cranesbill 'Johnson's Blue' (*Geranium × 'Johnson's Blue'*)
Cranesbill 'Wargrave Pink' (*Geranium endressii* 'Wargrave Pink')
Daylily 'Green Flutter' (*Hemerocallis* 'Green Flutter')
Daylily 'Stella de Oro' (*Hemerocallis* 'Stella de Oro')
Feverfew (*Chrysanthemum parthenium*)
Flame grass (*Miscanthus sinensis* 'Purpurascens')
Fountain grass (*Pennisetum alopecuriodes* 'Moudry')
Goldenrod (*Solidago × 'Peter Pan'*)
Harebell 'Blue Clips' (*Campanula carpatica* 'Blue Clips')
Harebell 'White Clips' (*Campanula carpatica* 'White Clips')

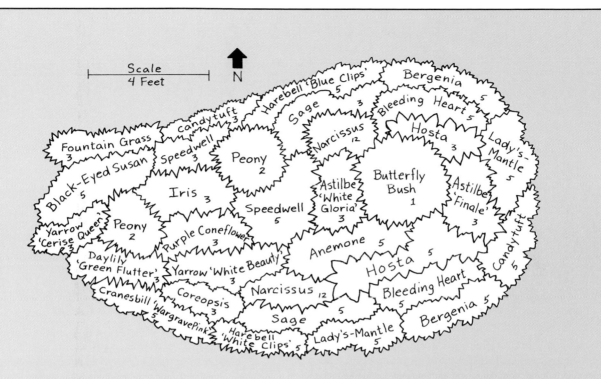

Scale
4 Feet

N

Fountain Grass 3
Black-Eyed Susan 5
Candytuft 3
Harebell 'Blue Clips' 5
Sage 3
Bergenia 5
Speedwell 3
Narcissus 12
Bleeding Heart 5
Hosta 3
Peony 2
Butterfly Bush 1
Lady's-Mantle 5
Iris 3
Astilbe 'White Gloria' 3
Astilbe 'Finale' 3
Yarrow 'Cerise Queen' 3
Peony 2
Speedwell 5
Candytuft 5
Purple Coneflower 3
Daylily 'Green Flutter' 3
Anemone 5
Hosta 5
Yarrow 'White Beauty' 3
Bleeding Heart 5
Cranesbill 'Wargrave Pink' 5
Coreopsis 3
Narcissus 12
Bergenia 5
Sage 5
Harebell 'White Clips' 5
Lady's-Mantle 5

Hosta (*Hosta* 'Francee')
Iris (*Iris sibirica* 'Caesar's Brother')
Lady's-mantle (*Alchemilla mollis*)
Narcissus (*Narcissus* 'Jack Snipe')
Obedient plant (*Physostegia virginiana* 'Pink Bouquet')
Peony (*Paeonia lactiflora* 'Pillow Talk')
Phlox 'Blue Boy' (*Phlox paniculata* 'Blue Boy')
Phlox 'Mt. Fujiyama' (*Phlox* × 'Mt. Fujiyama')
Purple coneflower (*Echinacea purpurea* 'Magnus')
Sage (*Salvia* × *superba* 'May Night')
Sedum (*Sedum* × 'Autumn Joy')
Shasta daisy (*Chrysanthemum* × *superbum* 'Silver Princess')
Speedwell (*Veronica* × 'Sunny Border Blue')
Yarrow 'Apple Blossom' (*Achillea millefolium* 'Apple Blossom')
Yarrow 'Cerise Queen' (*Achillea millefolium* 'Cerise Queen')
Yarrow 'White Beauty' (*Achillea millefolium* 'White Beauty')

Island Beds for Easy-Care Gardens

If you like the look of formal perennial borders but don't enjoy struggling with a lot of plant maintenance, consider trying an island bed. "Island beds are one of the easiest kinds of gardens to maintain," claims Stephanie Cohen, who designed this garden. You can reach into the garden from all sides to tidy up sprawling stems or snip off a few spent flowers, without having to step into the bed or lean precariously over a prized specimen. And when plants are within easy reach, you'll be more likely to spot problems like diseases or insect infestations before they get out of hand.

Cohen points out that, besides being easy to maintain, island beds encourage you to go out and walk around in the garden, "to look at all sides of the beds and enjoy the view that changes constantly as you move around. You become an active participant in the garden, rather than just a spectator."

THE GARDEN IN SUMMER

Enjoy the splendor of summer in your four-season garden with masses of bright flowers and fabulous foliage.

Notice how the feathery flower heads and narrow leaves of flame grass (*Miscanthus sinensis* 'Purpurascens') arch over the lower-growing perennials. Feverfew (*Chrysanthemum parthenium*), planted at the feet of the flame grass, provides masses of delicate white, yellow-centered daisies that form a striking contrast to the bold form of the grass. Nearby, 'Silver Princess' Shasta daisy (*Chrysanthemum × superbum* 'Silver Princess') contributes similar but larger flowers on compact (1-foot tall) plants. And in between, the large flower clusters of 'Mt. Fujiyama' phlox (*Phlox* × 'Mt. Fujiyama') add another splash of white to the summer garden.

The yellow centers of the daisies are highlighted by the many yellow-flowering perennials in bloom at this time. The lemon-yellow flowers of 'Moonbeam' threadleaf coreopsis (*Coreopsis verticillata* 'Moonbeam') are a perfect complement to the white daisies. 'Goldsturm' black-eyed Susan offers masses of golden-yellow daisylike flowers from summer into fall. And daylilies (*Hemerocallis* 'Green Flutter' and 'Stella de Oro') shine in the summer garden with funnelform yellow blooms.

Not to be outdone by the whites and yellows, the pinks and blues put in an appearance in a wide range of flower forms. The spiky flowers of 'May Night' violet sage (*Salvia × superba* 'May Night'), 'Sunny Border Blue' speedwell, and 'Pink Bouquet' obedient plant (*Physostegia virginiana* 'Pink Bouquet') complement the vertical form of the flame grass. Mounds of pink-flowered 'Wargrave Pink' cranesbill (*Geranium endressii* 'Wargrave Pink') and flat-topped 'Cerise Queen' yarrow (*Achillea millefolium* 'Cerise Queen') add rounded forms to complete the scene.

THE GARDEN IN FALL

Vivid blues, pinks, yellows, and whites provide new interest in the fall garden. In a season often predominated by rusts and golds, this colorful bed adds a touch of summer to the waning days of autumn.

The most outstanding feature of this bed is the bright-red column of flame grass topped with airy, white, plumelike seed heads. Next to the flame grass, the bronze-red flower heads of 'Autumn Joy' sedum bring the bright color of the grass down to the level of the lower perennials.

Plenty of pink flowers help to soften and blend the bright color of the flame grass with the softer colors of the perennials. The bold, daisylike, rose-pink blooms of 'Magnus' purple coneflower are complemented by the flat flower heads of light-pink 'Apple Blossom' and rose-pink 'Cerise Queen' yarrow (*Achillea* Galaxy Series 'Apple Blossom' and *A. mille-folium* 'Cerise Queen').

At the base of the flame grass, a vivid combination of white-flowered feverfew and 'Peter Pan' goldenrod (*Solidago* 'Peter Pan') makes a bold contrast to the bright-red grass foliage. 'Sunny Border Blue' speedwell adds a vertical touch with its spiky navy-blue flowers. And the floriferous mounds of 'Purple Dome' aster (*Aster novae-angliae* 'Purple Dome') edge the bed with hundreds of rich purple fall flowers. Toward the middle of the bed, the shrubby form of 'Blue Mist' bluebeard (*Caryopteris* × *clandonensis* 'Blue Mist') offers airy clusters of deep purple-blue flowers over mounds of gray-green leaves.

As the fall progresses, most of these flowers will keep blooming until touched by frost. To help the show continue, remember to deadhead the yarrows regularly. After frost hits, cut down all of the browned perennials to tidy the garden, or allow them to remain for winter interest.

Four-Season Perennial Garden

Plant Name	Description	Bloom Season	Comments
Achillea Galaxy Series 'Apple Blossom' ('Apple Blossom' yarrow)	Grows to 3' tall; flat heads of light-pink flowers over clumps of ferny foliage.	Summer and fall	Deadhead regularly to encourage flowering.
Achillea millefolium 'Cerise Queen' ('Cerise Queen' yarrow)	Grows to 1½' tall; flat heads of rose-pink flowers over clumps of ferny foliage.	Summer and fall	Flowers may vary in color from light- to dark-pink; choose plants in bloom to get the color you want.
Achillea millefolium 'White Beauty' ('White Beauty' yarrow)	Grows to 1½' tall; flat heads of pure-white flowers over clumps of ferny foliage.	Summer and fall	Deadhead regularly to encourage flowering.
Alchemilla mollis (lady's-mantle)	Grows to 1' tall; sprays of starry, yellow-green flowers over rounded, downy leaves.	Spring	If foliage looks tattered, cut it back to the ground and fresh leaves will emerge.
Anemone × hybrida 'Margarete' ('Margarete' Japanese anemone)	Grows to 3' tall; semidouble to double deep-pink flowers over mounds of broad, lobed leaves.	Summer into early fall	Plants produce large quantities of flowers; foliage is attractive all season.
Aster novae-angliae 'Purple Dome' ('Purple Dome' New England aster)	Grows to 2' tall; daisylike, rich purple flowers on clumping stems clothed with narrow leaves.	Fall	Mildew-resistant.
Astilbe × arendsii 'White Gloria' ('White Gloria' astilbe)	Grows to 2' tall; airy plumes of pure-white flowers over mounds of deeply cut leaves.	Early summer	Let the spent flowers remain for winter interest.
Astilbe chinensis 'Finale' ('Finale' Chinese astilbe)	Grows to 1½' tall; airy plumes of pale rose-pink flowers over mounds of deeply cut foliage.	Summer	Let the spent flowers remain for winter interest.
Bergenia cordifolia 'Perfecta' ('Perfecta' heart-leaved bergenia)	Grows to 20" tall; clusters of glossy, rosy-red flowers over clumps of broad, glossy leaves.	Spring	Green leaves take on a purplish tinge in winter.
Buddleia × 'Lochinch' ('Lochinch' butterfly bush)	Grows to 5' tall; narrow wands of blue flowers on arching stems clothed in narrow gray-green leaves.	Summer into fall	Stems may die down in winter; cut back to 6"–12" in early spring.
Campanula carpatica 'Blue Clips' ('Blue Clips' Carpathian harebell)	Grows to 8" tall; cup-shaped medium-blue flowers over clumps of triangular leaves.	Summer	Mulch in summer to keep roots cool.

Plant Name	Description	Bloom Season	Comments
Campanula carpatica 'White Clips' ('White Clips' Carpathian harebell)	Grows to 8″ tall; cup-shaped white flowers over clumps of triangular leaves.	Summer	Mulch in summer to keep roots cool.
Caryopteris × *clandonensis* 'Blue Mist' ('Blue Mist' bluebeard)	Grows to 3′ tall; airy clusters of deep purple-blue flowers on shrubby mounds of gray-green leaves.	Late summer and fall	Cut plants back to the ground in early spring to encourage strong new growth.
Chrysanthemum parthenium (feverfew)	Grows 2′–3′ tall; white daisies with yellow centers over bushy clumps of bright-green lobed leaves.	Summer into fall	Shear plants after flowering to encourage rebloom.
Chrysanthemum × *superbum* 'Silver Princess' ('Silver Princess' Shasta daisy)	Grows to 1′ tall; yellow-centered white daisies on clumping stalks clothed in dark-green leaves.	Summer	Easy to grow from seed; long flowering season.
Coreopsis verticillata 'Moonbeam' ('Moonbeam' threadleaf coreopsis)	Grows 1′–2′ tall; daisylike, pale-yellow flowers over mounds of soft, needle-like leaves.	Summer into fall	Long blooming season (June to October).
Dicentra 'Bountiful' ('Bountiful' bleeding heart)	Grows to 1′ tall; rose-pink heart-shaped flowers over mounds of finely cut blue-gray foliage.	Spring and summer	Long blooming season; foliage is quite attractive.
Echinacea purpurea 'Magnus' ('Magnus' purple coneflower)	Grows to 3′ tall; rose-pink daisy-like flowers on stout stems clothed with coarse lance-shaped leaves.	Summer and fall	Let the spent flower heads remain for winter interest, or remove them to avoid self-sowing.
Geranium endressii 'Wargrave Pink' ('Wargrave Pink' Endres cranesbill)	Grows to 15″ tall; rounded, rich pink flowers over mounds of starry leaves.	Summer	Can flower into the fall in the North.
Geranium × 'Johnson's Blue' ('Johnson's Blue' geranium)	Grows to 1½′ tall; rounded, clear-blue flowers over mounds of sprawling but bushy clumps of deeply cut leaves.	Summer into fall	Foliage is attractive all season.
Hemerocallis 'Green Flutter' ('Green Flutter' daylily)	Grows to 20″ tall; funnelform canary-yellow flowers with green throats on stiff stalks over clumps of straplike leaves.	Late summer	Plants are semi-evergreen in the South.

(continued)

Four-Season Perennial Garden—Continued

Plant Name	Description	Bloom Season	Comments
Hemerocallis 'Stella de Oro' ('Stella de Oro' daylily)	Grows to 1½' tall; yellow funnel-form flowers on stiff stalks over clumps of straplike leaves.	Summer	Long blooming season.
Hosta 'Francee' ('Francee' hosta)	Grows to 2' tall; spikelike stalks carry trumpet-shaped lavender flowers over clumps of white-edged green leaves.	Summer	Leaves are attractive all season.
Iberis sempervirens 'Autumn Beauty' ('Autumn Beauty' perennial candytuft)	Grows to 8" tall; rounded clusters of white flowers over clumps of narrow evergreen leaves.	Spring and fall	Cut back after bloom in spring to promote rebloom.
Iris sibirica 'Caesar's Brother' ('Caesar's Brother' Siberian iris)	Grows to 3' tall; dark violet-blue flowers on thin but strong stems over clumps of narrow upright leaves.	Spring	Plants are generally problem-free.
Miscanthus sinensis 'Purpurascens' (flame grass)	Grows to 4' tall; plumes of white flowers over upright clumps of reddish green leaves that turn red in fall.	Summer and fall	Leave foliage and spent flower heads for winter interest.
Narcissus 'Jack Snipe' ('Jack Snipe' daffodil)	Grows to 8" tall; white flowers with yellow center cups over clumps of grasslike leaves.	Mid-spring	Allow foliage to ripen completely after bloom.
Paeonia lactiflora 'Pillow Talk' ('Pillow Talk' common garden peony or another double pink cultivar)	Grows to 3' tall; double pink flowers over upright clumps of broad, lobed leaves.	Spring	Foliage takes on a bronze tint in fall.
Pennisetum alopecuriodes 'Moudry' ('Moudry' fountain grass)	Grows to 2' tall; soft pinkish brown flower spikes over mounds of narrow leaves.	Summer and fall	Leave foliage and spent flower heads for winter interest, or remove seed heads in late fall to prevent self-sowing.

Plant Name	Description	Bloom Season	Comments
Phlox × 'Mt. Fujiyama' ('Mt. Fujiyama' phlox)	Grows to 3' tall; large clusters of white flowers atop stiff, clump-forming stems clothed in lance-shaped, dull-green leaves.	Summer	Moderately mildew-resistant.
Phlox paniculata 'Blue Boy' ('Blue Boy' garden phlox)	Grows to 3' tall; clusters of lavender-blue flowers atop stiff, clump-forming stems clothed in lance-shaped, dull-green leaves.	Summer	Thin stems in early spring to avoid powdery mildew.
Physostegia virginiana 'Pink Bouquet' ('Pink Bouquet' obedient plant)	Grows to 4' tall; spikes of bright-pink flowers on stiff, clump-forming stems clothed in narrow dark-green leaves.	Late summer into fall	Divide clumps frequently to rejuvenate plants.
Rudbeckia fulgida var. *sullivantii* 'Goldsturm' ('Goldsturm' black-eyed Susan)	Grows to 2' tall; golden yellow, dark-centered daisylike flowers over upright clumps of dark-green leaves.	Summer into fall	Long flowering season; leave spent flower heads for winter interest, or remove them to prevent self-sowing.
Salvia × *superba* 'May Night' ('May Night' violet sage)	Grows to 1½' tall; spikes of deep indigo-blue flowers cover the stiff, clump-forming stems clothed in hairy, bright-green leaves.	Late spring and early summer	Plants may rebloom in the fall.
Sedum × 'Autumn Joy' ('Autumn Joy' sedum)	Grows to 2' tall; flat-topped heads of pink flowers that turn bronze-red with age atop succulent, clump-forming stems.	Summer and fall	Leave spent flower heads for winter interest.
Solidago 'Peter Pan' ('Peter Pan' goldenrod)	Grows 2'–3' tall; arching sprays of canary-yellow flowers on upright clump-forming stems.	Fall	Long blooming season; good as a cut flower.
Veronica × 'Sunny Border Blue' ('Sunny Border Blue' veronica)	Grows to 1½' tall; spikes of deep navy-blue flowers over bushy clumps of glossy green leaves.	Summer into fall	Long flowering season.

A Sunny Perennial Border

This classic perennial border is a perfect choice for a sunny, well-drained site. Packed with traditional favorites like peonies, irises, and daylilies, this design also offers a few surprises with the addition of some underused but worthwhile plants like white gaura (*Gaura lindheimeri*) and rattlesnake master (*Eryngium yuccifolium*). With its wonderful diversity of colors, textures, and plant forms, this perennial border will brighten any yard.

The garden is designed to be set against a wall, fence, or hedge and viewed from the front. If you do place the garden in front of a wall or fence, leave room for a 2-foot path or mowing strip between the back of the garden and the wall or fence. This strip allows you to get behind the bed to maintain it.

The sunny perennial garden is symmetrically designed, with complementary arcs of the same species and a mirror-image border planting divided down the middle. The garden is built around a central clump of Japanese silver grass (*Miscanthus sinensis* 'Variegatus'). The color scheme runs from pale-yellow, cream, soft-pink, and light-blue on the left through soft-purple and yellow to deep purples, stronger yellows, and pure-white on the right side.

Surrounding the Japanese silver grass are two large but airy clumps of rose-pink Joe-Pye weed (*Eupatorium purpureum* 'Atropurpureum'). In front of these are several plants of a lilac cultivar of garden phlox (*Phlox paniculata*). The phlox is repeated on either side of the bed: On the right, it's a pale-pink cultivar, and on the left, a purple cultivar. Together, the phlox cultivars form a broad symmetrical arc.

This arc is repeated with smaller plants on either side of the design: On the right, clumps of yellow daylilies, a blue cultivar of violet sage (*Salvia × superba*), blue catmint (*Nepeta × faassenii* 'Six Hills Giant'), and rose-purple Kansas gayfeather (*Liatris pycnostachya*) arc forward, while on the left, a pink daylily, a purple cultivar of violet sage, and the catmint and Kansas gayfeather arc backward.

Planting masses of perennials in arcs rather than clumps helps to keep your eyes moving over the design, rather than stopping them at each distinct clump. This effect gives a sense of rhythm and continuity to the design.

Like the inside of the garden, the outer edge is symmetrically planted, working out to either side from a central clump of Frikart's aster (*Aster* × *frikartii*). Next to the aster on both sides is 'Vera Jameson' sedum (*Sedum* × 'Vera Jameson'), which has rose-pink flowers and soft blue-purple foliage.

Spreading out on either side of the sedum are pale-yellow 'Moonbeam' threadleaf coreopsis (*Coreopsis verticillata* 'Moonbeam'), pink- and violet-flowered cranesbills (*Geranium sanguineum* var. *striatum* and *G.* × *magnificum*), chartreuse-flowered lady's-mantle (*Alchemilla mollis*), pink Japanese anemone (*Anemone* × *hybrida*), and lavender columbine meadow rue (*Thalictrum aquilegifolium*). At each end of the design, the lovely vertical foliage and showy blue or deep-purple flowers of Siberian iris (*Iris sibirica*) emerge from the clumps of lady's-mantle.

To accent the garden and avoid the monotony of perfect symmetry, the design also features a large clump of blue oat grass (*Helictotrichon sempervirens*) on the right side, highlighted by a bright-pink chrysanthemum (*Chrysanthemum zawadskii* var. *latilobum* 'Clara Curtis') and backed by three clumps of the bold rattlesnake master. To the left, a broken line of primrose-yellow and sulfur-yellow yarrows surrounds the Frikart's aster. These bold combinations give the garden a sense of balance without repeating the exact plants on each side of the design.

This garden is designed for a sunny, south-facing spot on flat or slightly rising ground. The plants included need rich, loamy, moist but well-drained soil. If your soil is heavy clay, add compost and other organic

matter to improve aeration and drainage. You might also consider double digging. (See "Double Digging" on page 183 for more information on this technique.) If you have light, sandy soil, incorporate compost and aged manure to at least a spade's depth.

In Another Place

While this border is designed to stand against a wall, fence, or hedge, you could set the garden out in the yard as an island bed where it can be viewed from the back as well as the front. To do this, double the depth of the garden by repeating the front pattern on the reverse side. If you choose this layout, include a maintenance path down the center of the bed for easy access.

Extending Seasonal Interest

This sunny perennial garden gives the most pleasure from late spring through summer, when flowering is most abundant and varied. But it's designed to offer seasonal interest the rest of the year, too. In fall, the varied perennial foliage comes into prominence, providing a lush backdrop for autumn flowers. Boltonia, Frikart's asters, chrysanthemums, phlox, and 'Vera Jameson' sedum continue to bloom through September; Japanese anemones will flower into October. The majestic clump of variegated Japanese silver grass that anchors the garden comes into bloom in September and continues to bloom through October.

The dried seed heads of the Japanese silver grass extend garden interest into winter. If you leave the dried flower heads of the yarrows, the orange cones of the purple coneflower, and the attractive pods of the Siberian irises and rose mallows on the plants, they, too, will add winter interest to your sunny perennial garden.

Sunny Perennial Border

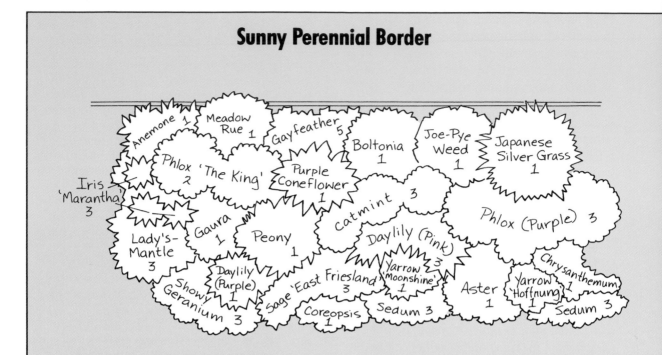

This easy, colorful border is a perfect fit along a fence or wall in full sun. Below is a list of the plants included in this design. For more information on these plants, look them up on the table on page 100, or turn to the appropriate entry in the encyclopedia section beginning on page 280. (Note: The numbers in the diagram refer to the quantity of each plant used.)

Plants for a Sunny Perennial Border

Anemone (*Anemone tomentosa* 'Robustissima' or *A.* × *hybrida*, any pink cultivar)
Aster (*Aster* × *frikartii* 'Monch')
Blue oat grass (*Helictotrichon sempervirens*)
Boltonia (*Boltonia asteroides* 'Pink Beauty')
Catmint (*Nepeta* × *faassenii* 'Six Hills Giant')
Chrysanthemum (*Chrysanthemum zawadskii* var. *latilobum* 'Clara Curtis')
Coreopsis (*Coreopsis verticillata* 'Moonbeam')
Daylily (pink) (*Hemerocallis* hybrid, any pale-pink cultivar)

Daylily (purple) (*Hemerocallis* hybrid, any purple cultivar)
Daylily (yellow) (*Hemerocallis* hybrid, any pale-yellow cultivar)
Gaura (*Gaura lindheimeri*)
Gayfeather (*Liatris pycnostachya* or *L. scariosa*)
Goat's beard (*Aruncus dioicus*)
Iris 'Marantha' (*Iris sibirica* 'Marantha')
Iris 'Summer Sky' (*Iris sibirica* 'Summer Sky')
Japanese silver grass (*Miscanthus sinensis* 'Variegatus')
Joe-Pye weed (*Eupatorium purpureum* 'Atropurpureum' or *E.* × 'Gateway')
Lady's-mantle (*Alchemilla mollis*)
Lancaster cranesbill (*Geranium sanguineum* var. *striatum*)
Meadow rue (*Thalictrum aquilegifolium*)
Peony (*Paeonia lactiflora*, any white single cultivar)
Phlox 'Fairy's Petticoat' (*Phlox paniculata* 'Fairy's Petticoat')
Phlox 'The King' (*Phlox paniculata* 'The King')

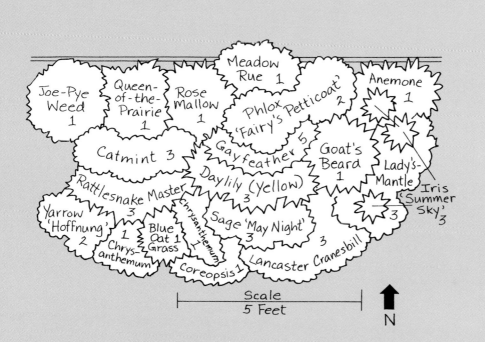

Diagram labels:
Joe-Pye Weed 1
Queen-of-the-Prairie 1
Rose Mallow 1
Meadow Rue 1
Phlox 'Fairy's Petticoat' 2
Anemone 1
Catmint 3
Gayfeather 5
Goat's Beard 1
Lady's-Mantle
Iris 'Summer Sky' 3
Rattlesnake Master 3
Daylily (Yellow) 3
3
Yarrow 'Hoffnung' 2
Chrysanthemum 1
Blue Oat Grass 1
Chrysanthemum 1
Sage 'May Night' 3
Lancaster Cranesbill 3
Coreopsis 1

Scale
5 Feet

N

Phlox (purple) (*Phlox paniculata*, any lilac or pale-purple cultivar)
Purple coneflower (*Echinacea purpurea* 'Bright Star', another cultivar, or the species)
Queen-of-the-prairie (*Filipendula rubra*)
Rattlesnake master (*Eryngium yuccifolium*)
Rose mallow (*Hibiscus moscheutos*, any white cultivar)
Sage 'East Friesland' (*Salvia* × *superba* 'East Friesland')
Sage 'May Night' (*Salvia* × *superba* 'May Night')
Sedum (*Sedum* × 'Vera Jameson')
Showy geranium (*Geranium* × *magnificum*)
Yarrow 'Hoffnung' (*Achillea* × 'Hoffnung')
Yarrow 'Moonshine' (*Achillea* × 'Moonshine')

Return to the Natives

When they hear the term "native plant," many gardeners envision the delicate ephemeral wildflowers that grace shady woodlands in early spring. But don't ignore the unusual native perennials for sunny borders, reminds C. Colston Burrell, who designed this garden. It is definitely worth searching for sources. Many of these plants bloom over a long period of time, or are useful architectural plants or weavers. Many perennial catalogs feature native plants, and you can also find them at good local garden centers.

This sunny perennial border includes two sun-loving native favorites: white gaura (*Gaura lindheimeri*) and rattlesnake master (*Eryngium yuccifolium*). Long-blooming white gaura produces clouds of attractive white flowers from summer into fall. And the striking form of rattlesnake master, with its clumps of spiky leaves topped with round, white flower heads, adds a distinctive touch to any perennial planting.

THE GARDEN IN SPRING

Spring is the best time to enjoy the mixed foliage of this beautiful border, as plants begin their growing season. Spiky leaves of the ornamental grasses, Siberian irises, rattlesnake master, and daylilies combine and contrast with the ferny foliage of the columbine meadow rue, yarrows, and 'Moonbeam' threadleaf coreopsis. The glossy leaves of peonies, the blue-purple foliage of 'Vera Jameson' sedum, and the lobed or fingered leaves of lady's-mantle, chrysanthemums, anemones, and cranesbills (*Geranium* spp.) join in to add a wealth of textural interest.

Spring bloom starts in the sunny perennial garden with the chartreuse flower sprays of lady's-mantle in April. 'Blue Hills Giant' catmint becomes a blue-violet cloud in May, when columbine meadow rue sends up airy light-purple flowers and violet sage sports deep-blue or purple spikes. The pale-pink May

flowers of Lancaster cranesbill (*Geranium sanguineum* var. *striatum*) turn this dapper little plant into a showy groundcover at the front of the garden. May is also the month for Siberian iris, with handsome light-blue or royal-purple flowers. In late May, the starry white plumes of goat's beard offer a promise of summer's delights.

A little extra care in spring will help this garden get off to a good start for its main summer show. In early spring, cut back any seedstalks and foliage you left standing for winter interest. As you do this, keep a close eye on what you are cutting to avoid damaging emerging shoots. You may want to stake the peony to keep the plant upright and the flowers clean. Otherwise, though, most of the plants in this design will thrive with a minimum of fuss as they prepare for the summer bloom season.

THE GARDEN IN SUMMER

From its promising spring beginnings, this garden reaches its peak in summer. Bushy 'Six Hills Giant' blue catmint bridges the seasons, continuing to bloom through June. The butterfly-like blooms of white gaura, pale-yellow 'Moonbeam' threadleaf coreopsis, and pink, yellow, and purple daylilies open throughout the summer. Blue oat grass complements its needle-like blue foliage with tawny flower spikes that persist through summer. Late June starts the summer-long show of purple coneflower, with its orange centers that glow like hot coals.

June is the month for the white, bowl-shaped flowers of peony and the startling violet-blue flowers of showy geranium. Primrose-yellow and sandy-peach yarrows bloom in June and July. Fluffy pink panicles of queen-of-the-prairie and huge, glossy white flowers of common rose mallow carry the summer bloom season into July.

July brings a profusion of lavender-blue daisy flowers on 'Monch' Frikart's aster. The fluffy violet-pink pokers of gayfeathers also add excitement to the garden. Showy phlox sports large clusters of pink, lilac, and purple blooms across the width of the border, continuing to flower through August. And the round flower heads of rattlesnake master add a splash of white in mid- and late summer.

In August, a wealth of rose and pink shades light up the sunny garden. Rose-pink 'Clara Curtis' chrysanthemums, pink 'Vera Jameson' sedum, and pink-flowered 'Robustissima' anemone (*Anemone tomentosa* 'Robustissima') are all late-summer bloomers. Rising tall on either side of the variegated Japanese silver grass, stately Joe-Pye weed opens eye-catching clouds of dusty-rose flowers over wine-red stems. Most of these perennials bloom into fall, often extending the season until the garden is nipped by frost.

Sunny Perennial Border

Plant Name	Description	Bloom Season	Comments
Achillea Galaxy Series 'Hoffnung' ('Hoffnung' yarrow)	Grows to 2' tall; flat heads of pale primrose-yellow flowers over clumps of ferny foliage.	Summer	Remove spent flowers to prolong blooming.
Achillea × 'Moonshine' (moonshine yarrow)	Grows 1'–2' tall; flat heads of pale yellow flowers over dense clumps of ferny blue-gray leaves.	Summer	This compact yarrow seldom needs staking.
Alchemilla mollis (lady's-mantle)	Grows to 1' tall; sprays of starry, soft-yellow flowers over rounded, downy leaves.	Spring	If foliage looks tattered, cut it back to the ground and fresh leaves will emerge.
Anemone tomentosa 'Robustissima' or *A.* × *hybrida* (Japanese anemone, any pink cultivar)	Grows 2'–3' tall; single metallic-pink flowers over clumps of dark-green lobed leaves.	Fall	One of the hardiest anemones.
Aruncus dioicus (goat's beard)	Grows 3'–6' tall; open plumes of white flowers on stout stems over clumps of ferny green leaves.	Late spring	Foliage is attractive all season.
Aster × *frikartii* 'Monch' ('Monch' Frikart's aster)	Grows to 2' tall; daisylike violet-blue flowers on upright stems clothed in lance-shaped green leaves.	Summer to fall	Plants need well-drained soil.
Boltonia asteroides 'Pink Beauty' ('Pink Beauty' boltonia)	Grows 4'–6' tall; pale-pink daisy-like flowers bloom on upright stems clothed in narrow blue-green leaves.	Late summer and fall	Plants growing in rich soil may require staking.
Chrysanthemum zawadskii var. *latilobum* 'Clara Curtis' ('Clara Curtis' chrysanthemum)	Grows 2'–2½' tall; deep-pink daisylike flowers over mounds of deeply lobed green leaves.	Late summer and early fall	Pinch plants in June to encourage compact growth.
Coreopsis verticillata 'Moonbeam' ('Moonbeam' threadleaf coreopsis)	Grows 1'–2' tall; soft-yellow flowers atop airy mounds of needle-like leaves.	Summer	Plants are quite drought-tolerant once established.
Echinacea purpurea 'Bright Star' ('Bright Star' purple coneflower, another cultivar, or the species)	Grows 2'–4' tall; daisylike rose-pink flowers on stiff stalks clothed in lance-shaped green leaves.	Summer	Let the seed heads remain for winter interest, or remove them to prevent self-sowing.

Plant Name	Description	Bloom Season	Comments
Eryngium yuccifolium (rattlesnake master)	Grows 2'–3' tall; open clusters of round, pale-green flower heads over leafy rosettes of lance-shaped gray-green leaves.	Summer	Plants are adaptable to a wide range of growing conditions.
Eupatorium purpureum 'Atropurpureum' or *E.* × 'Gateway' (Joe-Pye weed)	Grows 3'–6' tall; mounded or domed clusters of pale-rose or light-purple, sweetly scented flowers atop strong stems clothed in lance-shaped leaves.	Late summer to fall	The cultivar 'Atropurpureum' has deep wine-red stems.
Filipendula rubra (Queen-of-the-prairie)	Grows 4'–6' tall; large clusters of pink or rose flowers over large clumps of dark-green lobed leaves.	Summer	If foliage appears tattered after blooming, cut it back to the ground and new leaves will appear.
Gaura lindheimeri (white gaura)	Grows 3'–4' tall; spikes of white flowers that blush to pale-rose over dense clumps of narrow deep-green leaves.	Summer	Remove spent flowers to keep plants blooming all summer.
Geranium × *magnificum* (showy geranium)	Grows 1½'–2' tall; clusters of blue-violet flowers over bushy mounds of large, lobed, velvety leaves.	Early summer	Plants spread slowly to form large clumps.
Geranium sanguineum var. *striatum* (Lancaster cranesbill)	Grows 6"–8" tall; flat pale-pink flowers with deep-rose veins over dense spreading mounds of deeply cut leaves.	Early summer	Foliage turns wine-red in fall.
Helictotrichon sempervirens (blue oat grass)	Grows 2'–2½' tall; airy clusters of tawny flowers over spiky tufts of blue leaves.	Summer	The leaves are evergreen, giving the plant year-round interest.
Hemerocallis hybrid, pink (daylily, any pale-pink cultivar)	Grows 2'–3' tall; funnel-shaped pink flowers over clumps of straplike green leaves.	Summer	Daylilies spread quickly to form dense, broad clumps.
Hemerocallis hybrid, purple (daylily, any purple cultivar)	Grows 2'–3' tall; funnel-shaped purple flowers over clumps of straplike green leaves.	Summer	Remove spent flower spikes on all daylilies.
Hemerocallis hybrid, yellow (daylily, any pale-yellow cultivar)	Grows 2'–3' tall; funnel-shaped yellow flowers over clumps of straplike green leaves.	Summer	Divide daylilies every few years for propagation or to control their spread.

(continued)

Sunny Perennial Border—Continued

Plant Name	Description	Bloom Season	Comments
Hibiscus moscheutos (common rose mallow, any white cultivar)	Grows 4′–8′ tall; saucer-shaped white flowers atop thick, upright stalks clothed in broad, bright-green leaves.	Summer	Attractive seedpods provide winter interest.
Iris sibirica 'Marantha' ('Marantha' Siberian iris or another purple cultivar)	Grows to 3′ tall; royal-purple flowers over clumps of narrow, sword-shaped green leaves.	Late spring	Foliage is attractive all season.
Iris sibirica 'Summer Sky' ('Summer Sky' Siberian iris or another light-blue cultivar)	Grows 2½′–3′ tall; pale ice-blue flowers over clumps of narrow, sword-shaped green leaves.	Late spring	Foliage is attractive all season.
Liatris pycnostachya or *L. scariosa* (gayfeather)	Grows 2½′–5′ tall; spikes of densely packed red-violet to mauve flower heads on stiff stems clothed in narrow green leaves.	Summer	*L. pycnostachya* grows taller than *L. scariosa* and blooms a few weeks earlier.
Miscanthus sinensis 'Variegatus' (variegated Japanese silver grass)	Grows 4′–6′ tall; airy, silvery plumes over upright clumps of grassy green leaves striped with white.	Fall	Tender north of Zone 6 without winter protection.
Nepeta × *faassenii* 'Six Hills Giant' ('Six Hills Giant' blue catmint)	Grows to 3′ tall; spiky clusters of deep-violet flowers over mounds of small gray-green leaves.	Early summer	Cut plants back by ½–⅔ after flowering to encourage compact growth and possible rebloom.
Paeonia lactiflora (common garden peony, any single white cultivar)	Grows 1½′–3′ tall; single bowl-shaped flowers over shrubby clumps of lobed green leaves.	Early summer	Attractive foliage adds season-long interest.
Phlox paniculata 'Fairy's Petticoat' ('Fairy's Petticoat' garden phlox or another pale-pink cultivar)	Grows 3′–3½′ tall; clusters of light-pink flowers with darker-pink centers atop stiff upright stems clothed in dull-green, lance-shaped leaves.	Summer to early fall	Deadhead to avoid self-sowing.

Plant Name	Description	Bloom Season	Comments
Phlox paniculata, purple (common garden phlox, any lilac or pale-purple cultivar)	Grows 3'–3½' tall; clusters of lilac or pale-purple flowers atop stiff upright stems clothed in dull-green, lance-shaped leaves.	Summer to early fall	Thin stems on all phlox to provide good air circulation and discourage powdery mildew.
Phlox paniculata 'The King' ('The King' garden phlox or another deep-purple cultivar)	Grows 2'–2½' tall; clusters of deep-purple flowers atop stiff upright stems clothed in dull-green, lance-shaped leaves.	Summer to early fall	Long blooming period.
Salvia × *superba* 'East Friesland' ('East Friesland' violet sage)	Grows 1'–1½' tall; stiff spikes of deep-purple flowers over clumps of triangular bright-green leaves.	Early to mid-summer	Encourage violet sage to rebloom by deadheading regularly or by cutting plants back after the initial flush of bloom.
Salvia × *superba* 'May Night' ('May Night' violet sage)	Grows to 1½' tall; spikes of deep indigo-blue flowers cover the stiff, clump-forming stems clothed in hairy, bright-green leaves.	Late spring and early summer	Plants may rebloom in the fall.
Sedum × 'Vera Jameson' ('Vera Jameson' sedum)	Grows 9"–12" tall; domed clusters of pink flowers on weakly upright succulent stems with waxy bluish or purple leaves.	Late summer to early fall	Foliage is blue-green in warmer areas and blue-purple in cooler areas.
Thalictrum aquilegifolium (columbine meadow rue)	Grows 2'–3' tall; domed clusters of light-purple flowers over clumps of ferny blue-gray leaves.	Early summer	The columbine-like leaves are particularly attractive.

A Fragrant Cottage Garden

While good design principles and attractive plant combinations go a long way to making a perennial garden a success, the added element of fragrance can turn a pleasant garden into a memorable experience. Fragrant flowers and foliage encourage visitors to linger.

This design combines a wide variety of fragrant perennials as well as annuals, bulbs, shrubs, vines, and groundcovers in a delightfully informal cottage garden. It is planned for a south-facing wall along a house and is divided into four quadrants. A gravel path allows visitors easy access between the garden and other parts of the yard. The center of this garden is accented with a circular bed and a sundial.

Herbs, annuals, shrubs, and vines are ideal companions for the perennials in this informal planting. Several kinds of herbs—including thyme, sage, lemon balm, fennel, and lavender—form mounds of foliage in a variety of colors and fragrances. And while some people turn up their nose at the thought of adding annuals to perennial plantings,

smart gardeners know that annuals such as strawflower (*Helichrysum bracteatum*) and sweet alyssum (*Lobularia maritima*) are useful for adding season-long color and filling in gaps among slower-growing plants.

Like annuals and herbs, many shrubs and vines are ideal companions for perennials. They can add height and vertical interest to a planting, as well as provide a sense of structure to the garden when the herbaceous plants have gone dormant for the winter. In this garden, two of the quadrants are graced with the striking evergreen 'Carol Mackie' daphne (*Daphne* × *burkwoodii* 'Carol Mackie'), while another holds a sweetly fragrant 'Petite Plum' butterfly bush (*Buddleia* × 'Petite Plum'). A trellis supports the climbing stems of fragrant goldflame honeysuckle (*Lonicera* × *heckrottii*), which are covered with tubular flowers in early to mid-summer.

Of course, no cottage garden would be complete without its perennials, and this design showcases many traditional plants along with some newer favorites. The showy blooms of daylilies (*Hemerocallis* spp.), Siberian iris (*Iris sibirica*), bee balm (*Monarda didyma*), lilies (*Lilium* spp.), and hollyhocks (*Alcea* spp.) are natural choices for this sunny garden. The domed flower clusters of garden phlox add both color and fragrance to the planting. Sprawling mounds of blue catmint (*Nepeta* × *faassenii*) and patches of sweet violet (*Viola odorata*) add to the informal feel, along with mats of pinks (*Dianthus* spp.) and open clumps of sweet rocket (*Hesperis matronalis*). Other species of perennials contribute masses of flowers or foliage to accent this design.

While summer is a peak time of year for most perennials, the variety of plants in this garden ensures that you'll see something to enjoy virtually year-round. Plants with variegated or colored leaves are attractive even when they're not in bloom. Others produce evergreen leaves that add all-season interest.

This garden was designed for a sunny site with moist but well-drained soil. Most of these plants need little maintenance. Since the charm of a cottage garden is its informal look, you can let plants sprawl a little and lean on each other for support rather than staking them. Thinning the stems of the garden phlox (*Phlox paniculata*) will encourage good air circulation among the stems and lessen the chances of powdery mildew affecting the leaves. In areas north of Zone 7, treat some of the tender perennials (like the *Verbena* species and the flowering tobacco) as annuals, and replant them each year. Some may self-sow if you allow the plants to set seed. You'll find that those self-sown seedlings often pop up in the most delightful places!

In Another Place

This cottage garden is designed to be located close to a house, where visitors can

Scents and Sensibility

Fragrance is one of the most elusive qualities of any plant. Some fragrances, such as those of lavender or roses, are almost universally loved. But in other cases, what smells delightful to one gardener is enough to send others reeling in the opposite direction. Our reactions to certain odors are based not simply on the chemicals involved but also on our memories and associations with those scents. So it's particularly important that the plants you choose for your garden should offer fragrances that you personally find appealing.

If possible, it's wise to smell a fragrant plant before you buy it. You may find that the scent that your friend raves about is undetectable to your nose. Some plants you can smell from hundreds of feet away, while others require you to get right up close before you notice any fragrance. Many herbs, such as thyme, sage, and lemon balm, only release their fragrant oils when you rub or crush the leaves. When you are deciding which fragrant plants to grow, consider a mixture of plants with these different qualities—some strong, some subtle—so you're not overwhelmed by several powerful fragrances competing for attention.

stop for a sniff on their way to and from the house and where open windows allow the wonderful mix of fragrance to waft indoors. If you don't have room to plant the full garden, consider planting just two of the quadrants: one on each side of a door. Or, in another sunny part of your yard, link two quadrants with a comfortable bench where you can sit and enjoy the sweet scents and beautiful flowers. Even a single quadrant, tucked in a sunny corner of a fence or wall, can bring a touch of fragrance to your property.

Fragrant Cottage Garden

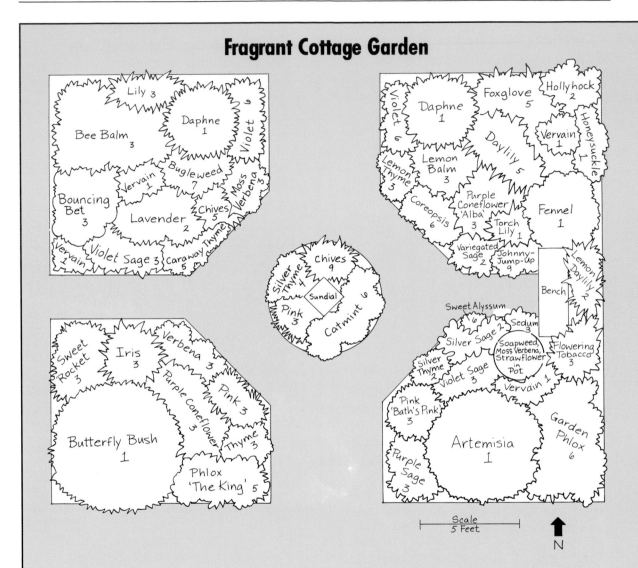

Scale
5 Feet

N

This delightful garden is packed with a variety of plants that provide fragrance as well as beautiful colors and flower forms. Below is a list of the plants that are included in this design. For more information on these plants, look them up on the table on page 110, or turn to the appropriate entry in the encyclopedia section beginning on page 280. (Note: The numbers in the diagram refer to the quantity of each plant used.)

Plants for a Fragrant Cottage Garden

Artemisia (*Artemisia* × 'Powis Castle')
Bee balm (*Monarda didyma* 'Beauty of Cobham' or 'Croftway Pink')
Bouncing bet (*Saponaria officinalis* 'Rosea Plena')
Bugleweed (*Ajuga reptans* 'Burgundy Glow')
Butterfly bush (*Buddleia* × 'Petite Plum', or any silver-leaved, red-flowered cultivar)
Caraway thyme (*Thymus herba-barona*)

Catmint (*Nepeta × faassenii* 'Six Hills Giant'
   or the species)
Chives (*Allium schoenoprasm*)
Coreopsis (*Coreopsis verticillata* 'Moonbeam')
Daphne (*Daphne × burkwoodii* 'Carol Mackie')
Daylily (*Hemerocallis* 'Pardon Me')
Fennel (*Foeniculum vulgare* var. *purpureum*)
Flowering tobacco (*Nicotiana alata*)
Foxglove (*Digitalis purpurea* 'Alba' or *D.
   grandiflora*)
Garden phlox (*Phlox paniculata,* or a tall pink
   cultivar)
Hollyhock (*Alcea rugosa,* or another single
   yellow hollyhock)
Honeysuckle (*Lonicera × heckrottii*)
Iris (*Iris sibirica* 'Sparkling Rosé')
Johnny-jump-up (*Viola tricolor*)
Lavender (*Lavandula × intermedia* 'Grosso')
Lemon balm (*Melissa officinalis* 'All Gold')
Lemon daylily (*Hemerocallis lilioasphodelus*)
Lemon thyme (*Thymus × citriodorus* 'Gold
   Edge')
Lily (*Lilium,* any pink cultivar)
Moss verbena (*Verbena tenuisecta* 'Edith', or
   any pink creeping verbena)
Phlox 'The King' (*Phlox paniculata* 'The King')
Pinks (*Dianthus* spp., any pink species or
   cultivar)
Pinks 'Bath's Pink' (*Dianthus* 'Bath's Pink')
Purple coneflower (*Echinacea purpurea*)
Purple coneflower 'Alba' (*Echinacea purpurea*
   'Alba')
Purple sage (*Salvia officinalis* 'Purpurea')
Sedum (*Sedum ×* 'Vera Jameson')
Silver sage (*Salvia argentea*)
Silver thyme (*Thymus × citriodorus* 'Argenteus')
Soapweed (*Yucca glauca*)
Strawflower (*Helichrysum bracteatum*)
Sweet alyssum (*Lobularia maritima*)
Sweet rocket (*Hesperis matronalis*)
Thyme (*Thymus vulgaris*)
Torch lily (*Kniphofia* 'Primrose Beauty')
Variegated sage (*Salvia officinalis* 'Icterina')
Verbena (*Verbena canadensis* 'Abbeyville')

Vervain (*Verbena bonariensis*)
Violet (*Viola odorata* 'Royal Robe')
Violet sage (*Salvia × superba* 'May Night', or
   another cultivar)

Please Don't Disturb the Bees

One concern some gardeners have about
fragrant plants is the insects they can attract,
including bees. Some people even go so far as
to advise against planting any fragrant plants
near doors or pathways. But if you take this
advice, you could be missing out on some
wonderful plants.

Yes, many fragrant flowers attract bees,
but so do nonscented ones. It's often the
color (blues and yellows, primarily), more
than the scent, of a flower that attracts
pollinators like honeybees. So avoiding all
fragrant plants will not guarantee that your
family and your guests will never get stung.
There are still plenty of other common garden
plants that will attract bees to your yard.

Of course, there are some commonsense
guidelines for using fragrant plants around the
home. If you're really concerned about getting stung, avoid siting plants close to the
paths where you may step on or brush against
them, or next to benches where you might sit
on them. Also, leave room around entrance-
ways so guests can exit and enter without
knocking against the plants. That way, both
your guests and the bees can enjoy the garden
without disturbing each other. The old saying
"Don't hurt them, and they won't hurt you" is
a good thing to keep in mind. "People need to
take personal responsibility," reminds this
garden's designer Edith Eddleman. "You can't
protect everyone from everything. Planting a
fragrant plant by your door is not a sign of
social irresponsibility or malice toward your
fellow human beings." So go ahead and take
time to smell the flowers. Just first make sure
that there aren't any bees in them!

A VIEW OF THE GARDEN IN SUMMER

Yellows and creams predominate in this quadrant of the garden in summer. Accented with touches of red, pink, and blue, this bed offers colorful and scented flowers and foliage that encourage visitors to rest on the bench and enjoy the scene.

Along the one edge, a trellis covered with the fragrant, pink-and-yellow-flowered goldflame honeysuckle is framed by the tall spires of yellow hollyhock (*Alcea rugosa*) and feathery clumps of licorice-scented bronze fennel (*Foeniculum vulgare* var. *purpureum*). This combination is fronted by a drift of white common foxglove (*Digitalis purpurea* 'Alba'), with its tall spikes of creamy-white flowers, and is accented by the airy, violet-flowered Brazilian vervain (*Verbena bonariensis*).

In front of the foxgloves, a bold clump of rusty-red 'Pardon Me' daylily (*Hemerocallis* 'Pardon Me') punctuates the center of the bed. The yellow-green throats of the daylily flowers are highlighted by the golden leaves of 'All Gold' lemon balm (*Melissa officinalis* 'All Gold') and the gold-edged evergreen leaves of 'Carol Mackie' daphne.

This bed is edged with a variety of low-growing plants, including fragrant 'Royal Robe' sweet violet and tiny-flowered Johnny-jump-up (*Viola tricolor*). Scented thymes and sages are represented by their striking green-and-yellow-leaved cultivars: 'Gold Edge' lemon thyme (*Thymus* × *citriodorus* 'Gold Edge') and variegated garden sage (*Salvia officinalis* 'Icterina').

FROM A DIFFERENT PERSPECTIVE

Pinks, white, and silver, with touches of purple and violet, give this quadrant of the fragrant cottage garden a feel of its own. It also complements the adjoining yellow bed. These two beds are linked physically by the bench and visually by clumps of Brazilian vervain.

Anchoring this bed is a massive specimen of 'Powis Castle' artemisia (*Artemisia* × 'Powis Castle'). This plant forms a shrubby mound of lacy, silvery white aromatic leaves. In the North, it may die back to the main stems in winter; consider planting three plants instead of one to fill the space allowed in the plan.

Behind the artemisia, a large clump of pink garden phlox adds a vertical accent to the artemisia's mounding form. Next to the bench, flowering tobacco (*Nicotiana alata*) perfumes the garden when its white flowers open at dusk. A container planting of soapweed (*Yucca glauca*), white and pink strawflowers, and 'Edith' moss verbena (*Verbena tenuisecta* 'Edith') provides season-long color.

In front of the 'Powis Castle' artemisia and the container, a mass of 'May Night' violet sage (*Salvia* × *superba* 'May Night') accents the bed with rigid spikes of deep indigo-blue flowers in late spring and summer. Silver sage (*Salvia argentea*) forms bold rosettes of fuzzy, silvery leaves that provide a good texture contrast for smaller-leaved plants such as sweet alyssum. And a clump of 'Bath's Pink' pinks (*Dianthus* 'Bath's Pink') provides spicy-scented, fringed pink flowers to brighten the early-summer garden.

Summer is a peak time for this garden, but the choice of perennials with long bloom periods and attractive foliage gives the garden season-long interest. The 'Bath's Pink' pinks and the silver thyme (*Thymus argenteus*) provide early-summer interest until the long-blooming perennials are under way. In fall, the pink flowers and bluish or purplish leaves of 'Vera Jameson' sedum (*Sedum* × 'Vera Jameson') add an extra splash of color.

Fragrant Cottage Garden

Plant Name	Description	Bloom Season	Comments
Ajuga reptans 'Burgundy Glow' ('Burgundy Glow' bugleweed)	Grows to 6″ tall; spikes of blue flowers above rosettes of green leaves mottled with white and pink.	Spring	Plants spread quickly to form a groundcover.
Alcea rugosa (yellow hollyhock, or another single yellow hollyhock)	Grows to 6′ tall; spikes of single pale-yellow flowers on stiff stems clothed in large, green, lobed leaves.	Summer	Long blooming period.
Allium schoenoprasum (common chives)	Grows 10″–20″ tall; rounded clusters of pink to mauve flowers over clumps of grassy green leaves.	Summer	Leaves and flowers are edible; remove spent flowers to reduce self-sowing.
Artemisia × 'Powis Castle' ('Powis Castle' artemisia)	Grows 2′–3′ tall; shrubby mounds of deeply cut silvery white leaves.	Spring through fall	Aromatic foliage is attractive all season.
Buddleia × 'Petite Plum' or *B. davidii* 'Nanho Purple' ('Petite Plum' or 'Nanho Purple' butterfly bush)	Grows 4′–5′ tall; spikes of reddish purple flowers over arching stems with narrow silvery leaves.	Summer to early fall	Flowers are fragrant and attract butterflies.
Coreopsis verticillata 'Moonbeam' ('Moonbeam' threadleaf coreopsis)	Grows 1′–2′ tall; daisylike, pale-yellow flowers over mounds of soft, needle-like leaves.	Summer into fall	Long blooming season (June to October).
Daphne × *burkwoodii* 'Carol Mackie' ('Carol Mackie' daphne)	Grows 3′–4′ tall; clusters of pale-pink fragrant flowers over mounds of green leaves edged with creamy-white.	Spring	Foliage is attractive all season.
Dianthus 'Bath's Pink' ('Bath's Pink' pinks)	Grows 8″–12″ tall; fragrant, fringed, pale-pink flowers over mats of narrow gray-green leaves.	Early summer	Lightly shear back after flowering to encourage compact growth.
Dianthus spp. (pinks, any pink species or cultivar)	Grows 1′–2′ tall; showy pink flowers, single or in loose clusters over low carpets or rosettes of green or gray-green leaves.	Early summer	Flowers are delightfully fragrant.
Digitalis purpurea 'Alba' or *D. grandiflora* (white common foxglove or yellow foxglove)	Grows 2′–5′ tall; spikes of creamy-white or yellow tubular flowers over rosettes of broad green leaves.	Summer	*D. purpurea* 'Alba' grows as a biennial or short-lived perennial; *D. grandiflora* is a true perennial.
Echinacea purpurea (purple coneflower)	Grows 2′–4′ tall; rose-pink to red-violet daisylike flowers on stout stems clothed in coarse, lance-shaped green leaves.	Summer	Leave the seed heads for winter interest, or remove them to prevent self-sowing.

Plant Name	Description	Bloom Season	Comments
Echinacea purpurea 'Alba' (white purple coneflower)	Grows 2½'–3' tall; daisylike white flowers with orange-brown centers on stout stems clothed in coarse, lance-shaped green leaves.	Summer	Coneflowers are good for use in fresh arrangements.
Foeniculum vulgare var. *purpureum* (bronze fennel)	Grows 4'–6' tall; flat heads of yellow flowers atop upright stems clothed in feathery purplish green leaves.	Summer	Remove spent flowers to prevent self-sowing.
Helichrysum bracteatum (strawflower)	Grows 1'–4' tall; papery flowers in a wide range of colors on stems clothed in narrow green leaves.	Summer	Flowers dry well and are popular for use in arrangements.
Hemerocallis lilio-asphodelus (lemon daylily)	Grows 2½'–3' tall; funnel-shaped lemon-yellow flowers over clumps of straplike green leaves.	Early summer	Flowers are fragrant.
Hemerocallis 'Pardon Me' ('Pardon Me' daylily)	Grows 2½'–3' tall; funnel-shaped rusty-red flowers over clumps of straplike green leaves.	Midsummer	Remove spent flowerstalks to keep plants looking neat.
Hesperis matronalis (sweet rocket)	Grows 2'–3' tall; open clusters of magenta, pink, or white flowers atop stout stems clothed in lance-shaped green leaves.	Spring	Flowers are fragrant.
Iris sibirica 'Sparkling Rosé' ('Sparkling Rosé' Siberian iris)	Grows 2½'–3' tall; rose-pink flowers on thin stems over grassy clumps of narrow green leaves.	Late spring	Foliage adds all-season interest.
Kniphofia 'Primrose Beauty' ('Primrose Beauty' torch lily)	Grows to 3' tall; dense spikes of tubular light-yellow flowers over tufts of stiff, narrow, evergreen, gray-green leaves.	Early summer	Could be replaced with *Hemerocallis* 'Corky'.
Lavandula × *intermedia* 'Grosso' ('Grosso' lavender)	Grows to 2' tall; long spikes of violet-blue flowers atop thin stems clothed in narrow, evergreen, gray-green leaves.	Summer	The flowers and foliage are both quite fragrant.
Lilium spp., pink (lily, any pink cultivar)	Grows 3'–6' tall; trumpet-shaped pink flowers atop tall stalks clothed in narrow green leaves.	Summer	Tall cultivars may need to be staked.
Lobularia maritima (sweet alyssum)	Grows 4"–6" tall; clusters of tiny white or lavender flowers over sprawling mats of narrow green leaves.	Late spring through fall	Flowers are sweetly fragrant.

(continued)

Fragrant Cottage Garden—Continued

Plant Name	Description	Bloom Season	Comments
Lonicera × heckrottii (goldflame honeysuckle)	Grows 6'–8' tall; fragrant tubular rose-pink flowers with yellow insides on climbing stems clothed in deep-green leaves.	Summer through mid-fall	Honeysuckles are generally problem-free.
Melissa officinalis 'All Gold' ('All Gold' lemon balm)	Grows to 1½' tall; grown for its fragrant, heart-shaped, golden-yellow leaves.	Spring through fall	Pinch plants back lightly in late spring to promote compact growth.
Monarda didyma 'Beauty of Cobham' or 'Croftway Pink' ('Beauty of Cobham' or 'Croftway Pink' bee balm)	Grows 2½'–3' tall; rounded heads of tightly packed tubular pink flowers atop square stems clothed in aromatic green leaves.	Summer	Thin stems to reduce the chances of powdery mildew affecting the foliage.
Nepeta × faassenii 'Six Hills Giant' ('Six Hills Giant' blue catmint or the species)	Grows to 3' tall; spiky clusters of deep-violet flowers over mounds of small gray-green leaves.	Early summer	Cut plants back by ½–⅔ after flowering to encourage compact growth and possible rebloom.
Nicotiana alata (flowering tobacco)	Grows 3'–4½' tall; clusters of fragrant, tubular white flowers atop stems with oval green leaves.	Early summer through fall	Flowers open fully in the evening.
Phlox paniculata (garden phlox or a tall pink cultivar)	Grows 3'–4' tall; clusters of pink flowers atop stiff upright stems clothed in dull-green, lance-shaped leaves.	Summer to early fall	Thin stems on all phlox to provide good air circulation and discourage powdery mildew.
Phlox paniculata 'The King' ('The King' garden phlox)	Grows 2'–2½' tall; clusters of deep-purple flowers atop stiff upright stems clothed in dull-green, lance-shaped leaves.	Summer to early fall	Long blooming period.
Salvia argentea (silver sage)	Grows 2'–4' tall; grown for its crinkled, soft, silver-gray foliage.	Summer	Remove flower spikes when they appear.
Salvia officinalis 'Icterina' (variegated sage)	Grows 12"–15" tall; clumps of oblong leaves variegated with green and gold.	Spring and early summer	The aromatic leaves can be used as a seasoning.
Salvia officinalis 'Purpurea' (purple sage)	Grows 15"–18" tall; clumps of oblong, gray-violet leaves.	Spring and early summer	Sages are generally problem-free.
Salvia × superba 'May Night' ('May Night' violet sage or other cultivar)	Grows to 1½' tall; spikes of deep indigo-blue flowers cover the stiff, clump-forming stems clothed in hairy, bright-green leaves.	Late spring and early summer	Plants may rebloom in the fall.

Plant Name	Description	Bloom Season	Comments
Saponaria officinalis 'Rosea Plena' ('Rosea Plena' bouncing bet)	Grows to 2' tall; loose clusters of fragrant, double rose-pink flowers on sprawling stems clothed in oval green leaves.	Summer	Cut plants back after blooming to encourage new growth.
Sedum × 'Vera Jameson' ('Vera Jameson' sedum)	Grows 9"–12" tall; domed clusters of pink flowers on weakly upright succulent stems with waxy bluish or purplish leaves.	Late summer to early fall	Foliage is blue-green in warmer areas and blue-purple in cooler areas.
Thymus × *citriodorus* 'Argenteus' (silver thyme)	Grows 6"–8" tall; clusters of pink flowers over mounds of tiny green leaves edged with silver.	Early summer	If thyme plants sprawl, shear them back by ½ to encourage compact growth.
Thymus × *citriodorus* 'Gold Edge' ('Gold Edge' lemon thyme)	Grows 6"–8" tall; clusters of soft-pink flowers over mounds of green leaves edged in golden-yellow.	Early summer	Leaves are strongly lemon-scented.
Thymus herba-barona (caraway thyme)	Grows to 2" tall; clusters of soft-lavender flowers over mats of tiny green leaves.	Early summer	Leaves are caraway-scented.
Verbena bonariensis (Brazilian vervain)	Grows 3'–4' tall; rounded clusters of violet flowers on branching stems sparsely clothed in oblong green leaves.	Summer through fall	Grow as an annual north of Zone 7.
Verbena canadensis 'Abbeville' ('Abbeville' verbena)	Grows 8"–18" tall; clusters of fragrant, soft-lavender flowers on trailing stems with oblong green leaves.	Late spring through fall	Verbenas are tough, heat- and drought-tolerant plants.
Verbena tenuisecta 'Edith' ('Edith' moss verbena or any pink creeping verbena)	Grows to 6" tall; clusters of mauve-pink flowers on trailing stems with oblong green leaves.	Late spring through fall	Grow as an annual north of Zone 7.
Viola odorata 'Royal Robe' ('Royal Robe' violet)	Grows 6"–8" tall; deep-purple flowers over clumps of heart-shaped leaves.	Spring	The fragrant flowers are excellent for cutting.
Viola tricolor (Johnny-jump-up)	Grows 6"–8" tall; pansylike purple-and-yellow flowers on stems clothed in small green leaves.	Spring	Flowers are good for cutting.
Yucca glauca (soapweed)	Grows 4'–5' tall; spikes of creamy-white bell-shaped flowers over rosettes of stiff, narrow leaves edged in white.	Summer	Yuccas are generally problem-free.

A Shady Wildflower Garden

In their quest for the "perfect" area for a perennial planting, many gardeners only consider sites with full sun and well-drained soil. Don't overlook the many charms of a moist, shady spot and all the wonderful and diverse plants that can thrive in just such an area. With a little care and planning, a shade garden will provide years of pleasure as a place to enjoy spring wildflowers or just to cool off on a hot summer day.

This wildflower garden is designed for a corner between two walls of a building. A 2-foot-wide path leads to a side door, providing a pleasant transition area between the house and the landscape beyond. The land slopes up toward the house, and the path has two steps and an informal rock ledge to accommodate the slope. The open canopy of mature deciduous trees allows sun to reach the garden in spring but provides cool shade in summer. The design will work facing southwest, as it is now, or any direction where the sun will strike the ground in spring.

The garden is fronted by low groundcover plants with attractive flowers and excellent summer foliage. The groundcover carpets of Allegheny foamflower (*Tiarella cordifolia*), Canada wild ginger (*Asarum canadense*), and creeping phlox (*Phlox stolonifera*) are punctuated with early-blooming plants, such as shooting-star (*Dodecatheon meadia*) and yellow trout lily (*Erythronium americanum*), that go dormant after flowering.

Moving inward from the path and the front of the garden, the taller plants provide a visual link between the lower groundcovers and the trees that shade this garden. Jack-in-the-pulpit (*Arisaema triphyllum*), Solomon's plume (*Smilacina racemosa*), great Solomon's seal (*Polygonatum commutatum*), and black snakeroot (*Cimicifuga racemosa*) provide tall, leafy stems that arch over the bushy mounds of fringed bleeding heart (*Dicentra eximia*) and creeping Jacob's ladder (*Polemonium reptans*) and the lush carpet of Allegheny pachysandra (*Pachysandra procumbens*).

Foliage plants and their various shades of green play an important part in this design.

Besides complementing the colorful spring flowers, the soothing greens make this shady garden a restful place to be on a sultry summer day. Foliage also adds a range of interesting textures that can liven up even a simple design. The various ferns, for example, add a lacy feel to the middle of the garden and form a lush green background at the edges along the building. The arching mounds of southern bush honeysuckle (*Diervilla sessilifolia*) also add to the green backdrop when not in flower.

Ferns and wildflowers are planted along each side of the path to draw visitors along the path to the door. The break in the path at the stairs is accented by clumps of spiky-leaved, blue-flowered crested iris (*Iris cristata*). Delicate maidenhair fern (*Adiantum pedatum*) unifies the two sides of the garden as the path nears the house. The bright-green fronds are lovely in early spring with the ephemeral Virginia bluebell (*Mertensia virginica*) and the emerging purple stalks of black snakeroot.

The plants in this garden require moist, humus-rich soil. A well-prepared bed will ensure success, but you should also avoid doing too much damage to the tree roots when you plant. For tips on planting a garden under trees, see "Wrestling with Roots" on page 117. Annual topdressing with an organic mulch of composted manure and chopped leaves will help to keep the soil loose and fertile.

One important aspect of this garden is the plants' light requirements. Many of the wildflowers bloom in early spring and start their dormant period as the overhanging deciduous trees begin to leaf out. For the rest of the season, the remaining plants prefer light, dappled shade. This garden will not succeed in a dark, dingy corner. If your spot is too shady, consider thinning the lower branches of the trees to let in more light.

Stretching Your Budget

Most of the plants used in this design spread quickly, either by seed or by spreading rhizomes. If you can't afford to buy all of the plants called for in the finished design, start with a few plants of each species and propagate them to build up your stock. Some of the plants, such as wild columbine (*Aquilegia canadensis*), creeping Jacob's ladder (*Polemonium reptans*), and wild cranesbill (*Geranium maculatum*), are easy to start from seed and will often reproduce themselves by self-sowing. Many others, including the ferns, Allegheny foamflower (*Tiarella cordifolia*), and Solomon's plume (*Smilacina racemosa*), are easy to divide. And some, like the wild blue and creeping phlox (*Phlox divaricata* and *P. stolonifera*), are easy to increase by cuttings as well as division. Refer to the individual encyclopedia entries for specific propagation information.

In Another Place

Many elements of this design would work equally well if you modified them to fit your particular site. If you like the secluded feeling of this shady nook but don't have a suitable spot around your house, try planting it along a fence in the corner of your yard. Instead of leading to a side door, the path could just as easily lead to a comfortable bench where you could relax and enjoy the shade. And although the garden is designed for an area with a slight slope, it would look fine in a flat area, too.

If you have a smaller corner, or if you are limited by time or money, consider dividing the garden into smaller sections. If your corner is small, divide the garden at the steps and rock wall, and only plant the section from the rock wall to the house. To fit the design to a straight wall or open area, divide the garden along the full length of the path.

Shady Wildflower Garden

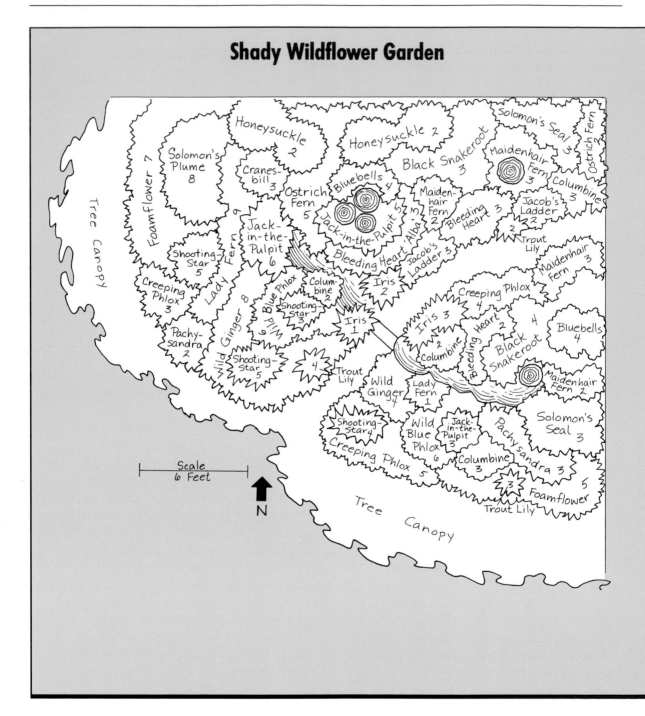

Many gardeners think that a shady spot limits their plant choices, but this lovely garden proves otherwise. Mature trees and moist areas provide new and exciting possibilities. Liven up a shady corner in your yard with this richly diverse planting of wildflowers and ferns. Below is a list of the plants that are included in this design. For more information on these plants, look them up in the table on page 120, or turn to the appropriate entry in the encyclopedia section beginning on page 280. (Note: The numbers in the diagram refer to the quantity of each plant used.)

Plants for a Shady Wildflower Garden

Black snakeroot (*Cimicifuga racemosa*)
Bleeding heart (*Dicentra eximia*)
Bleeding heart 'Alba' (*Dicentra eximia* 'Alba')
Bluebells (*Mertensia virginica*)
Columbine (*Aquilegia canadensis*)
Cranesbill (*Geranium maculatum*)
Creeping phlox (*Phlox stolonifera*)
Foamflower (*Tiarella cordifolia*)
Honeysuckle (*Diervilla sessilifolia*)
Iris (*Iris cristata*)
Jack-in-the-pulpit (*Arisaema triphyllum*)
Jacob's ladder (*Polemonium reptans*)
Lady fern (*Athyrium filix-femina*)
Maidenhair fern (*Adiantum pedatum*)
Ostrich fern (*Matteuccia struthiopteris*)
Pachysandra (*Pachysandra procumbens*)
Shooting-star (*Dodecatheon meadia*)
Solomon's plume (*Smilacina racemosa*)
Solomon's seal (*Polygonatum commutatum*)
Trout lily (*Erythronium americanum*)
Wild blue phlox (*Phlox divaricata*)
Wild ginger (*Asarum canadense*)

Wrestling with Roots

Depending on your site, planting under trees can be stressful for both you and your trees. It can be difficult and frustrating when you just keep digging up roots instead of soil. But don't be tempted to start a garden by dumping a thick layer of fresh topsoil on the area. While it makes planting easier, the soil layer can smother the fragile surface feeder roots and interfere with proper root function, which may stunt the growth of the trees and make them more prone to insect and disease problems.

C. Colston Burrell designed the shady wildflower garden on the opposite page with tree roots in mind. He suggests creating "planting pockets" close to the tree trunk, where there are fewer feeder roots to damage. Loosening up and amending the soil in these pockets will both save you from trying to dig up the whole area and reduce the damage to the tree's roots. You may also want to start with smaller plants, which will need smaller holes than plants with larger root balls.

If you want to plant a garden under shallow-rooted trees, such as Norway maple (*Acer platanoides*) or silver maple (*Acer saccharinum*), keep in mind that their roots will provide stiff competition for your perennials in their search for water. Burrell recommends choosing perennials that are adapted to both shade and drought, such as Solomon's seals (*Polygonatum* spp.), spotted lamium (*Lamium maculatum*), and yellow archangel (*Lamiastrum galeobdolon*). You could also try spring-blooming wildflowers and bulbs like shooting-stars (*Dodecatheon* spp.) and spring crocuses that will go dormant as the season progresses and less moisture is available.

THE GARDEN IN SPRING

Springtime is undoubtedly one of the most exciting times in a shady garden. Many of the woodland wildflowers grow quickly and flower in early spring, so they can take advantage of the spring sunshine before it is blocked by the emerging tree leaves.

On the left side of the path, ferny blue-green mounds of white-flowered bleeding heart (*Dicentra eximia* 'Alba') are nestled under a tree and accented with a variety of blue flowers, including the broad-leaved Virginia bluebells, the leafy clumps of creeping Jacob's ladder, and the spiky clusters of crested iris.

On both sides of the garden, tall clumps of Jack-in-the-pulpit accent the low-growing groundcovers and wildflowers. On the right-hand side, one clump is combined with the soft blue of wild blue phlox (*Phlox divaricata*). This same combination is repeated on the left-hand side and accented by the cheery pink flowers of wild cranesbill (*Geranium maculatum*). Red-and-yellow-flowered wild columbine (*Aquilegia canadensis*) is also scattered throughout the garden to give bright spots of late-spring and early-summer color and to provide motion as the slender stems sway in the breeze.

In this design, groundcovers serve a double purpose: Besides providing leafy green carpets of foliage to unify the design, the groundcovers are ideal companions for spring-blooming wildflowers. Here, masses of Allegheny foamflower, wild blue phlox, and Canada wild ginger are accented with clumps of spring-blooming shooting-stars and yellow trout lilies. After blooming, many of these wildflowers will go completely dormant, leaving gaps that will be filled by the spreading groundcovers.

THE GARDEN IN SUMMER

A woodland garden is always a popular spot on a hot summer day. Its cool shade makes this area a welcome route from the yard to the house. The mixture of colors and textures in the understory provides a lush carpet of greenery with season-long interest.

Once the spring fling of wildflowers has drawn to a close, several species of ferns take over the show and unify the garden with their lacy forms. Ostrich fern (*Matteuccia struthiopteris*) forms bold, upright, vase-shaped clumps of bright-green fronds that add a vertical accent to the garden. Lady ferns (*Athyrium filix-femina*) form more-open clumps of bright-green, dark-stemmed fronds. The ever-popular maidenhair fern produces arching, flat-topped mounds of finely divided light-green fronds that age to a darker green color.

Earlier in the spring, the delicate ferns were lovely in combination with the ephemeral Virginia bluebells and emerging purple stalks of black snakeroot. By summer, the foliage of the ferns and the snakeroot has expanded to fill the space left as the bluebells went dormant. The snakeroot also provides interest to the summer garden with its tall, branching spikes of small white flowers. The southern bush honeysuckle adds to the show with clusters of yellow flowers throughout the summer.

By early fall, the red seeds of Jack-in-the-pulpit and the red-and-white-speckled seeds of Solomon's plume contribute bright splashes of color to the garden. The arrival of winter leaves the canopy trees and the southern bush honeysuckle, along with the evergreen Allegheny foamflower, creeping phlox, and Allegheny pachysandra, to add interest to the garden until the cycle begins again the following spring.

Shady Wildflower Garden

Plant Name	Description	Bloom Season	Comments
Adiantum pedatum (maidenhair fern)	Grows 1'–2½' tall; mounds of fine-textured, light to dark-green foliage on thin black stems.	Spring through fall	Acts as a good "filler" plant.
Aquilegia canadensis (wild columbine)	Grows 1'–3' tall; nodding red-and-yellow flowers over mounds of compound blue-green leaves.	Late spring	Individual plants may be short-lived but self-sow readily.
Arisaema triphyllum (Jack-in-the-pulpit)	Grows 1'–3' tall; hooded purple-and-green flowers under single or paired 3-lobed leaves.	Spring	Red berries appear in late summer.
Asarum canadense (Canada wild ginger)	Grows 6"–12" tall; jug-shaped reddish brown flowers below broadly heart-shaped green leaves.	Spring	Leaves form a good groundcover that is attractive from spring through fall.
Athyrium filix-femina (lady fern)	Grows 1'–3' tall; upright clumps of lacy green leaves.	Spring through fall	If foliage gets tattered in summer, cut it back to get fresh new fronds.
Cimicifuga racemosa (black snakeroot)	Grows 4'–7' tall; tall branching spikes of white flowers over clumps of compound green leaves.	Early summer	Plants grow slowly and take several years to reach their mature size.
Dicentra eximia (fringed bleeding heart)	Grows 10"–18" tall; clusters of pink heart-shaped flowers over mounds of ferny blue-green foliage.	Late spring to early fall	Flowers bloom over a long season.
Dicentra eximia 'Alba' (white fringed bleeding heart)	Grows 10"–18" tall; clusters of greenish white, heart-shaped flowers over mounds of ferny blue-green foliage.	Spring and summer	Flowers bloom over a long season.
Diervilla sessilifolia (southern bush honeysuckle)	Grows 3'–5' tall; yellow flowers on woody stems clothed in dark-green leaves.	Summer	In the North (Zones 4–6), *D. lonicera* can be substituted, if desired.
Dodecatheon meadia (shooting-star)	Grows 1'–2' tall; arching pale-pink or white flowers over rosettes of broadly lance-shaped leaves.	Spring	Plants go dormant after flowering; take care not to dig into the crowns.
Erythronium americanum (yellow trout lily)	Grows 6"–10" tall; nodding yellow flowers over brown-and-green mottled leaves.	Spring	Plants go dormant after flowering.
Geranium maculatum (wild cranesbill)	Grows 1'–2' tall; loose clusters of pink flowers over open clumps of starry rounded leaves.	Late spring	This adaptable wildflower is a perfect addition to a shady woodland garden.

Plant Name	Description	Bloom Season	Comments
Iris cristata (crested iris)	Grows 4″–8″ tall; sky-blue flowers with a yellow-and-white blaze over fans of short, broad leaves.	Spring	A white-flowered variety (*I. cristata* var. *alba*) is also available.
Matteuccia struthiopteris (ostrich fern)	Grows 2′–4′ tall; bold clumps of light-green lacy leaves.	Spring through fall	Plants spread quickly by creeping rhizomes and may require control after 2–3 years.
Mertensia virginica (Virginia bluebells)	Grows 1′–2′ tall; pink buds open to nodding clusters of sky-blue bell-like flowers on thick stems clothed in broad green leaves.	Spring	Plants go dormant after flowering.
Pachysandra procumbens (Allegheny pachysandra)	Grows 4″–6″ tall; short spikes of pinkish white flowers followed by light-green leaves that darken with age.	Spring	An attractive evergreen groundcover.
Phlox divaricata (wild blue phlox)	Grows 10″–15″ tall; open clusters of fragrant sky-blue flowers over clumps of broadly lance-shaped green leaves.	Spring	Plants spread to form dense clumps of evergreen leaves.
Phlox stolonifera (creeping phlox)	Grows 6″–8″ tall; open clusters of lavender to pink flowers over dense clumps of oval evergreen leaves.	Spring	A creeping groundcover with attractive foliage and showy flowers.
Polemonium reptans (creeping Jacob's ladder)	Grows 8″–16″ tall; clusters of deep sky-blue flowers atop succulent stems over mounds of fernlike foliage.	Late spring	Cut plants back after they release their seeds and new foliage will emerge.
Polygonatum commutatum (great Solomon's seal)	Grows 3′–7′ tall; greenish white, bell-shaped clusters hang from arching stems clothed in oval green leaves.	Late spring	Flowers are followed by showy blue-black berries in late summer.
Smilacina racemosa (Solomon's plume)	Grows 2′–4′ tall; plumes of fuzzy white flowers atop arching stems clothed in oval green leaves.	Late spring	Flowers are followed by red-and-white speckled fruit in late summer.
Tiarella cordifolia (Allegheny foamflower)	Grows 6″–10″ tall; spikes of fuzzy white to pale-pink flowers over rosettes of heart-shaped to triangular leaves.	Spring	Plants spread to form an attractive groundcover; leaves are often evergreen.

A Bed for a Shaded Terrace

W hat could be more pleasant than a shady terrace garden on a hot summer day? The cool shade and colorful flowers combine to create a useful and enjoyable outdoor living space. This terrace is a great place to eat, entertain, or just relax and admire the flowers.

The garden has been designed along a 10×12-foot terrace, with a path through one side to allow easy access between the terrace and the yard beyond. Except for one grouping near the house, the plants have been limited to a height of about 2½ feet; this allows for an unobstructed view over the garden as you stand or sit on the terrace.

Besides providing year-round color, this garden takes advantage of some other design tricks that help you get the best effect possible from a small space. A restrained color scheme—here predominantly pink and white with touches of blue and yellow—unifies the garden through the seasons and gives it a stylish, refined look. The light-colored flowers and foliage illuminate the shady garden.

Plants with attractive foliage as well as flowers give you twice the design value for the same amount of space taken up by a single-season plant. 'Royal Standard' hosta (*Hosta* × 'Royal Standard'), for example, produces spikes of tubular white flowers in late summer, but the dense clumps of glossy green leaves are handsome from spring until frost. The short blooming period of 'Sulphureum' Persian epimedium (*Epimedium* × *versicolor* 'Sulphureum') is more than compensated for by the airy mounds of heart-shaped leaves. And astilbes, of course, are beloved by many gardeners as much for their lacy green or reddish leaves as for their plumelike flowers. Selecting plants with variegated leaves, such as those on variegated Japanese kerria, is another way to get double duty from a plant that is not in bloom most of the year.

Interplanting short-season plants like spring bulbs with groundcovers or leafy perennials is a great idea in any garden. After the bulbs bloom, the new foliage of the companion plant hides the dying bulb leaves, so you don't have to look at masses of limp yellow daffodil leaves for weeks at a time. Combinations employed in this design include crocuses or low-growing daffodils with hostas, and full-size daffodils with daylilies. Mixing bulbs with foliage plants is an easy, low-maintenance solution to an unsightly problem.

This lovely garden is designed to look great all season long with very little maintenance. An organic mulch will help keep the soil moist and cool, as well as provide nutrients and add organic matter to the soil as it breaks down. If your site isn't naturally moist, it's a good idea to provide some supplemental water during the warmest months to keep the astilbe and primrose foliage from browning along the edges. And since you'll often be looking at the plants from up close, you may want to remove spent flowers regularly to keep the garden looking its best. (Just remember that the 'Majestic' blue lilyturf and sweet cicely [*Myrrhis odorata*] produce interesting seeds, so let their spent flowers remain if you want to enjoy the bonus display.)

In Another Place

This carefully designed garden is easy to adapt to a variety of sites. Use just two sides of it to flank a smaller patio, or try them as a freestanding border to brighten a dark corner of your yard. Or, since each side of the garden is balanced to stand alone, you could plant just one side and still get a lovely effect in the shady garden. If you are interested in adding a sense of enclosure to your terrace garden, check out "Plants for an Enclosed Area" on page 125 for suggestions of taller plants you can add to the back of the design.

Keep in mind that bulbs, like the crocuses and daffodils included in this design, do need some sun to ripen their foliage properly, so they grow best under the filtered shade of

Dependable Perennials That Deter Deer

While many people associate deer with the beauty and grace of natural woods and fields, gardeners in deer country have a much less benign view of these creatures. Hungry deer can decimate a planting overnight, reducing a carefully planned perennial garden to a shambles of trampled, leafless stems. If you live in an area where deer are a problem, consider trying some deer-resistant plants to discourage deer from feeding in your beds and borders.

Like insect-resistant plants, deer-resistant perennials are a good place to start in a pest-control program. If the deer (or insects) don't like the taste of your plants, they'll search elsewhere for more palatable fare and spare your plantings. If other food is scarce, of course, the deer might overcome their aversions and snack on your sunflowers, but at least the animals are less likely to completely devour these distasteful plants. Some perennials that deer-plagued gardeners have reported success with are listed below.

Astilbes (*Astilbe* spp.)
Bleeding heart (*Dicentra spectabilis*)
Columbines (*Aquilegia* spp.)
Daffodils (*Narcissus* spp.)
Epimediums (*Epimedium* spp.)
Foxgloves (*Digitalis* spp.)
Hellebores (*Helleborus* spp.)
Irises (*Iris* spp.)
Large periwinkle (*Vinca major*)
Lavenders (*Lavandula* spp.)
Lungworts (*Pulmonaria* spp.)
Sunflowers (*Helianthus* spp.)
Yuccas (*Yucca* spp.)

deciduous trees. If the shade of your terrace comes from evergreens, you may want to leave the bulbs out of the design, or else plant new ones each fall to get a good spring show.

Bed for a Shaded Terrace

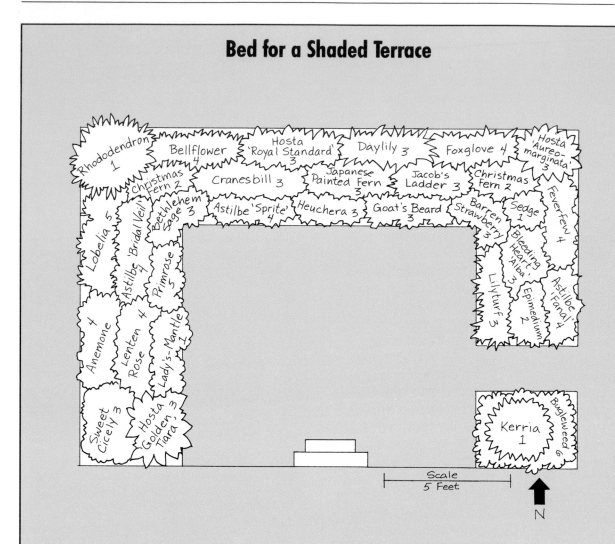

Rhododendron 1

Bellflower 4

Hosta 'Royal Standard' 3

Daylily 3

Foxglove 4

Hosta 'Aureo-marginata' 3

Christmas Fern 2

Cranesbill 3

Japanese Painted Fern 3

Jacob's Ladder 3

Christmas Fern 2

Feverfew 4

Lobelia 5

Astilbe 'Bridal Veil' 4

Bethlehem Sage 3

Astilbe 'Sprite' 4

Heuchera 3

Goat's Beard 3

Barren Strawberry 3

Sedge 1

Primrose 5

Bleeding Heart 'Alba' 3

Astilbe 'Fanal' 4

Anemone 4

Lenten Rose 4

Lady's-Mantle 1

Lilyturf 3

Epimedium 2

Sweet Cicely 3

Hosta Golden Tiara 3

Kerria 1

Bugleweed 6

Scale 5 Feet

N

Plants for a Shaded Terrace

If you have a shaded patio or terrace, highlight it with this planting of perennials, grasses, ferns, and shrubs for season-long interest. Below is a list of the plants that are included in this design. For more information on these plants, look them up on the table on page 128, or turn to the appropriate entry in the encyclopedia section beginning on page 280. (Note: The numbers in the diagram refer to the quantity of each plant used.)

Anemone (*Anemone tomentosa* 'Robustissima')
Astilbe 'Bridal Veil' (*Astilbe* × *arendsii* 'Bridal Veil')
Astilbe 'Fanal' (*Astilbe* × *arendsii* 'Fanal')
Astilbe 'Sprite' (*Astilbe* 'Sprite')
Barren strawberry (*Waldsteinia ternata*)
Bellflower (*Campanula persicifolia*)
Bethlehem sage (*Pulmonaria saccharata* 'Mrs. Moon')

Bleeding heart 'Alba' (*Dicentra eximia* 'Alba')
Bugleweed (*Ajuga pyramidalis*)
Christmas fern (*Polystichum acrostichoides*)
Cranesbill (*Geranium endressii* 'Wargrave Pink')
Crocus 'Jeanne d'Arc' (*Crocus* 'Jeanne d'Arc')
Crocus 'Pickwick' (*Crocus* 'Pickwick')
Daffodil 'February Gold' (*Narcissus* 'February Gold')
Daffodil 'Thalia' (*Narcissus* 'Thalia')
Daylily (*Hemerocallis* 'Stella de Oro')
Epimedium (*Epimedium* × *versicolor* 'Sulphureum')
Feverfew (*Chrysanthemum parthenium*)
Foxglove (*Digitalis grandiflora*)
Heuchera (*Heuchera micrantha* var. *diversifolia* 'Palace Purple')
Hosta 'Aureo-marginata' (*Hosta fortunei* 'Aureo-marginata')
Hosta 'Golden Tiara' (*Hosta* 'Golden Tiara')
Hosta 'Royal Standard' (*Hosta plantaginea* 'Royal Standard')
Goat's beard (*Aruncus aethusifolius*)
Jacob's ladder (*Polemonium* 'Blue Pearl')
Japanese painted fern (*Athyrium goeringianum* 'Pictum')
Kerria (*Kerria japonica* 'Variegata')
Lady's-mantle (*Alchemilla mollis*)
Lenten rose (*Helleborus orientalis*)
Lilyturf (*Liriope muscari* 'Majestic')
Lobelia (*Lobelia siphilitica*)
Primrose (*Primula* × *polyantha* 'Pacific Giant Blue')
Rhododendron (*Rhododendron* 'Yaku Prince')
Sedge (*Carex elata* 'Bowles Golden')
Sweet cicely (*Myrrhis odorata*)

Plants for an Enclosed Area

Although garden designer Mary Ann McGourty planned for an open view beyond the terrace, this design could work equally well on a small lot or in an enclosed city garden. By adding shrubs or taller perennials along the back of the design, you can create a colorful, ever-changing "wall" around your terrace. Below are some tall-growing perennials that McGourty suggests for seasonal interest.

For early flowering, try common bleeding heart (*Dicentra spectabilis*), with its pink or white, heart-shaped blooms, or variegated Solomon's seal (*Polygonatum odoratum* var. *thunbergii* 'Variegatum'), with bell-shaped white flowers and creamy-white-striped leaves.

For mid-season interest, consider the spiky yellow blooms of rocket ligularia (*Ligularia stenocephala* 'The Rocket'), the white spikes of black snakeroot (*Cimicifuga racemosa*), or the fuzzy lilac-purple flowers of lavender mist (*Thalictrum rochebrunianum*). Rodgersias (*Rodgersia* spp.), with their summer clusters of creamy-white flowers, also provide interest in other seasons with their large, lobed leaves.

For late-flowering perennials, choose the sweetly scented white spikes of 'White Pearl' Kamchatka bugbane (*Cimicifuga simplex* 'White Pearl'), the feathery pink plumes of 'Superba' fall astilbe (*Astilbe taquetii* 'Superba'), which become attractive seed heads, or the bright rose-pink flowers and lush foliage of pink turtlehead (*Chelone lyonii*).

THE GARDEN IN SPRING

After surviving the dull days of winter, you'll welcome a reason to sit outdoors and enjoy the flowers in the warm spring sunshine. Spring finds this corner of the garden awash in pinks and blues accented with white.

Dominating the garden is the shrubby form of 'Yaku Prince' rhododendron, with its clusters of funnel-shaped pink flowers. This compact shrub is clothed in leathery dark-green leaves, whose undersides are coated with a light-brown downy material. Along the front of the garden, a leafy mound of 'Mrs. Moon' Bethlehem sage (*Pulmonaria saccharata* 'Mrs. Moon') is also in bloom. It complements the pink of the rhododendron with clusters of pink buds that open pink and turn to blue as they age. Next to the Bethlehem sage, clumps of 'Pacific Giant Blue' primrose (*Primula* × *polyantha* 'Pacific Giant Blue') add their

dainty deep-blue flowers to the show. And to the left, a patch of white 'Jeanne d'Arc' crocus (*Crocus* 'Jeanne d'Arc') is just about over for the season. In the center, the quiet green of Christmas fern (*Polystichum acrostichoides*) forms a restful counterpoint to all the vigorous activity going on around it.

Highlights in other parts of the spring garden are clumps of 'Pickwick' crocus (*Crocus* 'Pickwick') and 'Thalia' and 'February Gold' daffodils (*Narcissus* 'Thalia' and 'February Gold'). Next to the house, a variegated Japanese kerria is underplanted with upright bugleweed (*Ajuga pyramidalis*) to create a smashing yellow-and-blue combination. 'Sulphureum' Persian epimedium and barren strawberry (*Waldsteinia ternata*) are also blooming now, contributing their yellow flowers to complete the spring scene.

THE GARDEN IN SUMMER

In the heat of the summer, blue, white, and soft-pink flowers add a cool touch to this corner of the shady garden. Can you imagine anything more civilized than sipping a cold glass of lemonade as you rest on the terrace and enjoy this combination of colorful perennials?

In this corner, you'll find the feathery white plumes of 'Bridal Veil' astilbe (*Astilbe × arendsii* 'Bridal Veil') make a tasteful companion to the single pink flowers of 'Wargrave Pink' cranesbill (*Geranium endressii* 'Wargrave Pink'). Along with the silver-spotted green leaves of 'Mrs. Moon' Bethlehem sage, the dark-green leaves of 'Yaku Prince' rhododendron and Christmas fern complement the colorful flowers.

In other parts of the bed, other cheerful combinations prevail. The golden-yellow trumpets of 'Stella de Oro' daylily (*Hemerocallis* 'Stella de Oro') and soft-yellow spikes of yellow foxglove (*Digitalis grandiflora*) are complemented by swirling mounds of golden-leaved 'Bowles Golden' sedge (*Carex elata* 'Bowles Golden'). The blue flowers of 'Blue Pearl' Jacob's ladder (*Polemonium* 'Blue Pearl') and tiny white plumes of dwarf goat's beard (*Aruncus aethusifolius*) form bright accents to round out this colorful combination.

Next to this grouping, the bright-red plumes of 'Fanal' astilbe (*Astilbe × arendsii* 'Fanal') form a vivid contrast to the white flowers and bright-green leaves of feverfew (*Chrysanthemum parthenium*). Not to be outdone, the opposite side of the garden showcases a delightful association of flowers, including white sweet cicely, yellow-green lady's-mantle (*Alchemilla mollis*), and lilac-purple 'Golden Tiara' hosta (*Hosta* 'Golden Tiara').

Bed for a Shaded Terrace

Plant Name	Description	Bloom Season	Comments
Ajuga pyramidalis (upright bugleweed)	Grows 6″–9″ tall; spikes of bright-blue flowers over basal clumps of glossy green leaves.	Late spring	This species forms slow-spreading clumps; it is not invasive.
Alchemilla mollis (lady's-mantle)	Grows to 1′ tall; sprays of yellow-green flowers over mounds of rounded, hairy, pale-green leaves.	Early to mid-summer	If foliage appears tattered, cut it to the ground, and the plant will produce a new set of leaves.
Anemone tomentosa 'Robustissima' (Japanese anemone)	Grows 2′–3′ tall; single metallic-pink flowers over clumps of dark-green lobed leaves.	Fall	One of the hardiest anemones.
Aruncus aethusifolius (dwarf goat's beard)	Grows 8″–12″ tall; upright clusters of creamy-white flowers over mounds of shiny, deep-green, compound leaves.	Early to mid-summer	This compact plant is ideal as an edging for beds, borders, and paths.
Astilbe × arendsii 'Bridal Veil' ('Bridal Veil' astilbe)	Grows to 2′ tall; nodding clusters of white flowers over mounds of green foliage.	Summer	Plants are deer-resistant.
Astilbe × arendsii 'Fanal' ('Fanal' astilbe)	Grows to 2′ tall; narrow spikes of deep cherry-red flowers over mounds of red foliage.	Early to mid-summer	Plants are deer-resistant.
Astilbe simplicifolia 'Sprite' ('Sprite' star astilbe)	Grows to 1′ tall; arching clusters of pale creamy-pink flowers over mounds of glossy green lobed leaves.	Late summer	One of the latest-blooming astilbes.
Athyrium goeringianum 'Pictum' (Japanese painted fern)	Grows to 1½′ tall; mounds of lacy silver-and-green foliage with maroon stems.	Spring through fall	The foliage is attractive throughout the growing season.
Campanula persicifolia (peach-leaved bellflower)	Grows 1′–3′ tall; open clusters of bell-shaped blue-violet flowers on wiry stems clothed in narrow leaves.	Summer	Remove spent flowers to encourage rebloom.
Carex elata 'Bowles' Golden' ('Bowles' Golden' sedge)	Grows 2′–2½′ tall; mounds of narrow golden-yellow leaves with thin green margins.	Spring through fall	The mounds of golden foliage are attractive all season.
Chrysanthemum parthenium (feverfew)	Grows 2′–3′ tall; clusters of white daisies over bushy clumps of bright-green lobed leaves.	Summer to fall	Long-lasting as cut flowers.

Plant Name	Description	Bloom Season	Comments
Crocus 'Jeanne d'Arc' ('Jeanne d'Arc' crocus)	Grows 6″–8″ tall; pure-white flowers with purple bases over clumps of grasslike green leaves.	Early spring	Interplant with hostas or other spreading plants whose leaves will cover the withering crocus foliage.
Crocus 'Pickwick' ('Pickwick' crocus)	Grows 6″–8″ tall; purple-and-white striped flowers over clumps of grasslike green leaves.	Early spring	Interplant with hostas or other spreading plants whose leaves will cover the withering crocus foliage.
Dicentra eximia 'Alba' (white fringed bleeding heart)	Grows 10″–18″ tall; clusters of greenish white, heart-shaped flowers over mounds of ferny blue-green foliage.	Spring and summer	Flowers bloom over a long season.
Dicentra 'Luxuriant' ('Luxuriant' bleeding heart)	Grows to 1′ tall; clusters of heart-shaped cherry-red flowers over mounds of ferny blue-gray leaves.	Spring and summer	The delicate foliage is attractive throughout the season.
Digitalis grandiflora (yellow foxglove)	Grows 2′–3′ tall; spikes of soft-yellow tubular flowers over dense rosettes of broad green leaves.	Summer	Plants are deer-resistant.
Epimedium × *versicolor* 'Sulphureum' ('Sulphureum' Persian epimedium)	Grows 10″–12″ tall; airy sprays of yellow flowers followed by mounds of heart-shaped leaves.	Spring	Plants are deer-resistant.
Geranium endressii 'Wargrave Pink' ('Wargrave Pink' Endres cranesbill)	Grows 15″–18″ tall; pink flowers bloom on loose mounds of starry green leaves.	Summer	Plants bloom over a long period in cooler areas.
Helleborus orientalis (lenten rose)	Grows 1′–1½′ tall; clusters of nodding white, pink, rose, or purple blooms on succulent stems clothed in deeply divided, evergreen leaves.	Spring	Foliage is attractive all season.
Hemerocallis 'Stella de Oro' ('Stella de Oro' daylily)	Grows to 2′ tall; trumpet-shaped golden-yellow flowers over clumps of straplike deep-green leaves.	Early summer through fall	Blooms prolifically over a long period.
Heuchera micrantha var. *diversifolia* 'Palace Purple' ('Palace Purple' heuchera)	Grows 1′–2′ tall; airy spikes of tiny white flowers over mounds of shiny, maplelike purple-brown leaves.	Summer	Foliage is attractive all season.

(continued)

Bed for a Shaded Terrace—Continued

Plant Name	Description	Bloom Season	Comments
Hosta fortunei 'Aureo-marginata' ('Aureo-marginata' Fortune's hosta)	Grows 1'–2' tall; spikes of tubular lilac flowers over mounds of dark-green, yellow-edged leaves.	Late summer	Foliage is attractive all season.
Hosta 'Golden Tiara' ('Golden Tiara' hosta)	Grows to 14" tall; spikes of tubular purple flowers over mounds of light-green leaves with yellow margins.	Summer	Plants form compact, small to medium-size mounds.
Hosta × 'Royal Standard' ('Royal Standard' hosta)	Grows 1½'–2' tall; spikes of tubular white flowers over tight mounds of glossy green leaves.	Midsummer to early fall	Flowers are quite fragrant.
Kerria japonica 'Variegata' (variegated Japanese kerria)	Grows 4'–6' tall; single yellow flowers on arching green stems bearing white-edged green leaves.	Spring	Green stems are attractive year-round; foliage is attractive all season.
Liriope muscari 'Majestic' ('Majestic' blue lilyturf)	Grows 1'–1½' tall; spikes of deep lilac-purple flowers over grassy mounds of straplike evergreen leaves.	Late summer	The flowers are followed by glossy black berries that persist into the winter.
Lobelia siphilitica (great blue lobelia)	Grows 2'–3' tall; dense spikes of blue flowers on leafy stems over clumps of medium-green oblong leaves.	Mid- to late summer into fall	Flowers range in color from deep- to light-blue or violet-blue.
Myrrhis odorata (sweet cicely)	Grows to 3' tall; flat clusters of white flowers over clumps of lacy aromatic green leaves.	Spring	Flowers are followed by clusters of large black seeds; both the seeds and foliage can be used as seasonings.
Narcissus 'February Gold' ('February Gold' daffodil)	Grows to 1' tall; golden-yellow blooms among clumps of strap-like green leaves.	Early spring	One of earliest-blooming daffodils.

Plant Name	Description	Bloom Season	Comments
Narcissus 'Thalia' ('Thalia' daffodil)	Grows to 15″ tall; clusters of starry, white, nodding flowers among clumps of straplike green leaves.	Spring	The flowers are quite fragrant.
Polemonium 'Blue Pearl' ('Blue Pearl' Jacob's ladder)	Grows 1′–1½′ tall; clusters of medium-blue bell-shaped flowers over mounds of fernlike foliage.	Late spring through midsummer	Grows best in evenly moist soil in light shade.
Polystichum acrostichoides (Christmas fern)	Grows to 2′ tall; open clumps of shiny medium-green fronds that darken with age.	All year	Evergreen leaves provide year-round interest.
Primula × *polyantha* 'Pacific Giant Blue' ('Pacific Giant Blue' primrose)	Grows 8″–12″ tall; sparse clusters of flat, deep-blue flowers over rosettes of broad, crinkled, green leaves.	Spring	Divide overgrown clumps after flowering.
Pulmonaria saccharata 'Mrs. Moon' ('Mrs. Moon' Bethlehem sage)	Grows 9″–18″ tall; clusters of pink buds and blue flowers over mounds of heart-shaped green leaves spotted with silver.	Spring	Cut back spent bloom stalks after flowering.
Rhododendron 'Yaku Prince' ('Yaku Prince' rhododendron)	Grows to 3′ tall; clusters of funnel-shaped pink flowers on a compact shrub with leathery dark-green leaves.	Late spring	Evergreen leaves give the plant year-round interest.
Waldsteinia ternata (barren strawberry)	Grows 6″–12″ tall; single yellow flowers over mats of glossy lobed green leaves.	Spring	An attractive evergreen groundcover.

A Color Theme Garden

Ask a gardener to describe a plant, and the first thing he or she is likely to tell you is the flower color. Color is one of the most obvious features gardeners consider when deciding which plants to grow. Part of the challenge of garden design is to include all the colors you like without creating a carnival-like atmosphere where reds, blues, yellows, and whites all clamor for attention. One effective way to use color in the garden is to group similar plants together, creating what is known as a color theme garden.

Color theme gardens are often referred to as monochromatic gardens, although that term is not really accurate. To be truly monochromatic, a design would have to use flowers that are all exactly the same color. But even a garden of nothing but pure-white flowers would contain at least two colors—the white of the blooms and the greens of the leaves and flowerstalks—so any attempt at a perfectly monochromatic garden is doomed

from the start. Fortunately, the concept of a color theme garden is much more forgiving. You can mix the dusty-blue leaves of rue with the deep navy-blue spikes of 'Sunny Border Blue' speedwell and the lilac-blue blooms of 'Butterfly Blue' pincushion flower and still brag to your friends about your stunning blue border.

If you'd like to try a color theme border in your garden, you'll find the design in this section to be a good starting point. It has been carefully planned to offer a selection of compatible plants in several color ranges, including blue, yellow, red, pink, and white. Whether you pick one color border or try one of each, you'll be delighted with the results. If you're not sure you'd like a garden based on just one color, you can mix and match from the different plant lists to get the color effect that you find most pleasing.

Besides offering loads of flowers, these gardens also take advantage of the often-overlooked colors of leaves and stems. Many plants bear colorful leaves that make them interesting even when they're not in bloom. Baptisia, for example, produces soft blue-green leaves, while 'Morning Light' Japanese silver grass bears white-striped foliage and 'Vera Jameson' sedum offers succulent bluish or purplish leaves. Other plants are included just for their foliage interest, such as 'Valerie Finnis' artemisia with its silvery white leaves, golden Japanese barberry with bright-yellow foliage, and 'Vulcan' swiss chard with bright-red leafstalks.

These color theme borders include a wide variety of plants—including annuals, perennials, bulbs, grasses, and shrubs—for year-round interest. Flowering annuals and long-blooming perennials help to provide lots of interest throughout the growing season, while bulbs and flowering shrubs contribute bright splashes of color. Grasses and foliage perennials supply season-long color and texture to round out the design. The diversity of plants in each design means you'll always find something to admire when you look at the garden.

All of the plants in these color theme borders grow best in full sun and moist but well-drained soil. The specific maintenance needs of the garden will vary, depending on which plants you include, but it should require little fussing in the way of staking or deadheading. You will need to plant new annuals every year, or else you can let them reseed and then move any errant seedlings to their appropriate place in the design. In the North, treat the tender perennials (like verbenas and cannas) as annuals and replant them every year, or dig them up and bring them indoors for the winter. Verbenas are easy to start from cuttings, too, so root a few stems in fall and use those as a source for fresh cuttings in late winter.

Combining Color Choices

If you find the idea of a monochromatic border to be a bit overwhelming, why not try a combination of two or more colors for a bright, festive look? Use the basic plot plan shown on page 134, and choose a few plants from each of the color-theme plant lists to create a garden design that fits your needs. You can make hundreds of different combinations from these simple ingredients.

Let's say, for example, that you are equally fond of blue and white flowers, and you can't decide which border to use. To solve your dilemma, you could choose numbers 3, 6, 7, 10, 12, 14, and 15 from the list for the white border and fill in with plants from the blue plan to create a quaint blue-and-white border. (To avoid a blocky look, try to choose some shorter and some taller plants of each color, and spread them out through the garden.) If you are more daring, perhaps a garden in pink and yellow, or even in red, white, and blue, might be more to your liking. This tight, adaptable design will show off almost any combination of plants to its best advantage. The color choices are limited only by your imagination.

In Another Place

The basic plot plan for all of the color theme borders is easy to adapt to almost any garden situation. If you want to view the garden from both sides, repeat the plan back-to-back to create an island bed. To create a longer border, link the units side by side until you fill up the space. You can overlap two units to fit the design around a corner, or join three units to create a unique U-shaped garden. This border design would also look stunning along both sides of a path or driveway. With all the different layouts you can create, the possibilities are endless.

Plot Plan for the Color Theme Garden

Scale
4 Feet

N

This color theme border, created by garden designer Edith Eddleman, is based on a single plot plan with accompanying plant lists, so you you can get a variety of effects from a single design. No matter which color you choose, you can use this easy-to-follow plan to lay out your garden.

Using the Plot Plan

You can use the basic plan shown here to create a red, pink, white, yellow, or blue garden. Below you'll find plant lists for the red, white, and yellow borders. The number preceding each plant name on the list corresponds to a number on the basic plan. This gives you the location for that plant. The number following the plant name indicates the quantity needed for planting. For example, the "Red Border Plant List" below starts with "1. 'Ambassador' canna (Canna × generalis 'Ambassador', or another red-flowered, bronze-leaved cultivar), 3." The number 1 means the 'Ambassador' canna should be planted in the area marked with a 1 on the basic plan. The number 3, which follows the plant name, represents the number of cannas needed to

plant that area. If you would like to try a blue border, turn to page 138 for its labeled plan and plant list, followed by a color realization of the garden in the fall. You'll find the labeled plan and plant list for the pink border on page 136, along with a color realization of the garden in summer.

If you plan to install a red, yellow, or white border, you'll probably find that it's handy to photocopy the general plot plan on this page and write the corresponding plant names next to the numbers on the diagram. This will give you an easy reference to use when you are actually planting the garden. If you decide to use the pink or blue border, of course, this step has already been done for you.

Red Border Plant List

1. 'Ambassador' canna (*Canna × generalis* 'Ambassador', or another red-flowered, bronze-leaved cultivar), 3

2. Wild columbine (*Aquilegia canadensis*), 1

3. 'Burgundy' blanket flower (*Gaillardia × grandiflora* 'Burgundy'), 2

4. 'Pardon Me' daylily (*Hemerocallis* 'Pardon Me'), 3

5. Verbena (*Verbena peruviana* or *V. canadensis* 'Bright Red'), 3

6. 'Red Baron' blood grass (*Imperata cylindrica* 'Red Baron'), 7

7. Purple-leaved barberry (*Berberis thunbergii* var. *atropurpurea*), 1

8. 'Haense Herms' switchgrass (*Panicum virgatum* 'Haense Herms'), 2

9. 'Vesuvius' Arkwright's campion (*Lychnis* × *arkwrightii* 'Vesuvius'), 6

10. 'Flame' rose verbena (*Verbena canadensis* 'Flame'), 3

11. 'Vulcan' Swiss chard (*Beta vulgaris*, Cicla Group 'Vulcan'), 1

12. Bronze fennel (*Foeniculum vulgare* var. *purpureum*), 1

13. Sage (*Salvia greggii* or *S. coccinea*), 3 or 5

14. 'Red Velvet' pinks (*Dianthus* 'Red Velvet'), 3

15. 'Venture' lily (*Lilium* 'Venture' or another red-flowered cultivar), 1

White Border Plant List

1. 'Helen Campbell' spider flower (*Cleome hasslerana* 'Helen Campbell'), 3

2. White rose campion (*Lychnis coronaria* 'Alba'), 1

3. White bloody cranesbill (*Geranium sanguineum* 'Album'), 2

4. Flowering tobacco (*Nicotiana alata*), 1

5. White mother-of-thyme (*Thymus praecox* subsp. *arcticus* 'Albus'), 6

6. 'May Queen' oxeye daisy (*Chrysanthemum leucanthemum* 'May Queen'), 3

7. 'Morning Light' Japanese silver grass (*Miscanthus sinensis* 'Morning Light'), 1

8. 'Miss Lingard' wild sweet William (*Phlox maculata* 'Miss Lingard'), 3

9. 'Valerie Finnis' artemisia (*Artemisia* 'Valerie Finnis'), 1

10. White moss verbena (*Verbena tenuisecta* 'Alba' or another white-flowered cultivar), 3

11. 'White Swirl' Siberian iris (*Iris sibirica* 'White Swirl' or another tall white cultivar), 1

12. 'Honorine Jobert' Japanese anemone (*Anemone* × *hybrida* 'Honorine Jobert'), 3

13. Flowering spurge (*Euphorbia corollata*), 3

14. Garlic chives (*Allium tuberosum*), 3

15. 'Casa Blanca' lily (*Lilium* 'Casa Blanca'), 1

Yellow Border Plant List

1. Golden Japanese barberry (*Berberis thunbergii* 'Aurea'), 1

2. 'Happy Returns' daylily (*Hemerocallis* 'Happy Returns'), 1

3. 'Moonbeam' threadleaf coreopsis (*Coreopsis verticillata* 'Moonbeam'), 6

4. 'Butter and Sugar' Siberian iris (*Iris siberica* 'Butter and Sugar'), 1

5. Gold-and-silver chrysanthemum (*Chrysanthemum pacificum*), 1

6. Golden oregano (*Origanum vulgare* 'Aureum'), 6

7. Porcupine grass (*Miscanthus sinensis* var. *strictus*), 1

8. Patrinia (*Patrinia scabiosifolia*), 3

9. 'Yellow Sun' blanket flower (*Gaillardia pulchella* 'Yellow Sun'), 3

10. 'Golden Fleece' goldenrod (*Solidago sphacelata* 'Golden Fleece'), 3

11. Golden columbine (*Aquilegia chrysantha*), 1

12. 'Golden Sword' Adam's-needle (*Yucca filamentosa* 'Golden Sword'), 3

13. 'Limemound' Bumald spirea (*Spiraea* × *bumalda* 'Limemound'), 3

14. Yellow foxglove (*Digitalis grandiflora*), 2

15. 'Citronella' lily (*Lilium* 'Citronella'), 1

The Pink Border Plot Plan

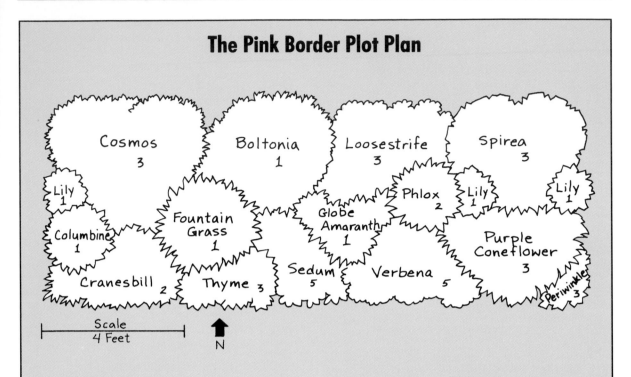

A mixture of soft- and bright-pink flowers makes this border a cheery addition to your landscape. Below is a list of the plants that are included in this design. For more information on the perennials, turn to the appropriate entry in the encyclopedia section beginning on page 280. (Note: The numbers in the diagram refer to the quantity of each plant used.)

Boltonia (*Boltonia asteriodes* 'Pink Beauty')
Columbine (*Aquilegia* × *hybrida* 'Nora Barlow')
Cosmos (*Cosmos bipinnatus*)
Cranesbill (*Geranium sanguineum* var. *striatum*)
Fountain Grass (*Pennisetum orientale*)

Globe Amaranth (*Gomphrena* 'Lavender Lady')
Lily (*Lilium speciosum*)
Loosestrife (*Lythrum virgatum* 'Morden Pink')
Periwinkle (*Catharanthus roseus,* any pink cultivar)
Phlox (*Phlox maculata* 'Omega', or any pink-eyed, white-flowered cultivar)
Purple Coneflower (*Echinacea purpurea*)
Sedum (*Sedum* × 'Vera Jameson')
Spirea (*Spiraea japonica* 'Little Princess')
Thyme (*Thymus* 'Bressingham Pink', or another pink-flowered cultivar)
Verbena (*Verbena tenuisecta* 'Edith', or another pink-flowered cultivar)

THE PINK BORDER IN SUMMER

Nothing beats this pink border for adding loads of color to the early-summer garden. You'll have plenty of flowers to enjoy in the garden and can even cut a few to use indoors. The carefully chosen selection of plants ensures that the stunning display continues throughout the growing season.

Early summer is a particularly lively time in this garden, as the end of the spring bloomers overlaps with the start of the annuals and summer-blooming perennials. The colorful double flowers of 'Nora Barlow' columbine (*Aquilegia* × *hybrida* 'Nora Barlow') are finishing up their season as the Lancaster cranesbill (*Geranium sanguineum* var. *striatum*) and 'Bressingham Pink' thyme (*Thymus* 'Bressingham Pink') are in their full flush of summer bloom.

Other perennials on the scene include 'Omega' phlox (*Phlox maculata* 'Omega'), with its domed clusters of white, pink-centered blooms, and 'Morden Pink' loosestrife (*Lythrum virgatum* 'Morden Pink'), with narrow spikes of bright-pink flowers. Next to the loosestrife,

the shrubby form of 'Little Princess' spirea (*Spiraea japonica* 'Little Princess') contributes to the show with flat clusters of reddish pink flowers on slender, mounding stems. And the magnificent Japanese lily (*Lilium speciosum*) is a lovely addition for its distinctive pink-and-white coloration and powerfully fragrant blooms.

Early summer also marks the start of the blooming season for the annuals and long-flowering perennials. Cosmos (*Cosmos bipinnatus*), 'Lavender Lady' globe amaranth (*Gomphrena* 'Lavender Lady'), and Madagascar periwinkle (*Catharanthus roseus*) add color to the border all season, along with 'Edith' moss verbena (*Verbena tenuisecta* 'Edith'), oriental fountain grass (*Pennisetum orientale*), and purple coneflower (*Echinacea purpurea*). And to accent all of these and extend the season, the daisylike flowers of 'Pink Beauty' boltonia (*Boltonia asteriodes* 'Pink Beauty') and clustered blooms of 'Vera Jameson' sedum (*Sedum* × 'Vera Jameson') flower in fall, continuing the show well into autumn.

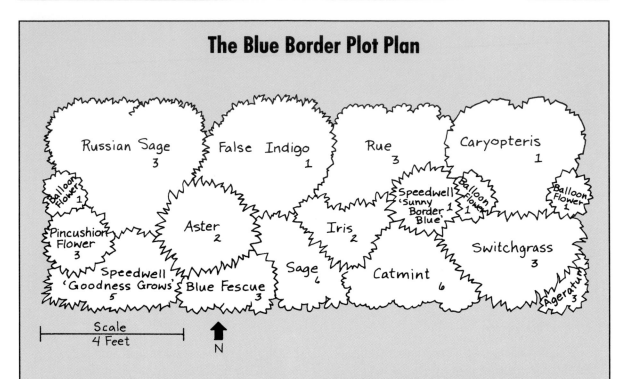

The Blue Border Plot Plan

Russian Sage 3

False Indigo 1

Rue 3

Caryopteris 1

Balloon Flower 1

Pincushion Flower 3

Aster 2

Speedwell 'Sunny Border Blue' 1

Balloon Flower 1

Balloon Flower 1

Iris 2

Switchgrass 3

Speedwell 'Goodness Grows' 5

Blue Fescue 3

Sage 6

Catmint 6

Ageratum 3

Scale 4 Feet

N

A blue border can add a cool, sophisticated touch to any garden. Below is a list of the plants that are included in this design. For more information on the perennials, turn to the appropriate entry in the encyclopedia section beginning on page 280. (Note: The numbers in the diagram refer to the quantity of each plant used.)

Ageratum (*Ageratum* 'Capri')
Aster (*Aster* × *frikartii* 'Monch')
Balloon flower (*Platycodon grandiflorus*)
Blue fescue (*Festuca caesia*)

Caryopteris (*Caryopteris* × 'Dark Knight')
Catmint (*Nepeta* × *faassenii* 'Six Hills Giant')
False indigo (*Baptisia australis*)
Iris (*Iris siberica* 'Sky Wings' or 'Ego')
Pincushion flower (*Scabiosa* 'Butterfly Blue')
Rue (*Ruta graveolens*)
Russian sage (*Perovskia atriplicifolia*)
Sage (*Salvia farinacea*)
Speedwell 'Goodness Grows' (*Veronica* 'Goodness Grows')
Speedwell 'Sunny Border Blue' (*Veronica* × 'Sunny Border Blue')
Switchgrass (*Panicum virgatum* 'Heavy Metal')

THE BLUE BORDER IN FALL

Color in the fall garden isn't limited to yellow goldenrods and bronze-red chrysanthemums. Add a touch of class to the season with this elegant blue border.

Highlights of the fall garden include the powder-blue flowers of Russian sage (*Perovskia atriplicifolia*) and the deeper blue of 'Monch' Frikart's aster (*Aster × frikartii* 'Monch'). Many perennials that started blooming earlier in the summer are still around to add to the fall show. 'Sunny Border Blue' speedwell (*Veronica × 'Sunny Border Blue'*) and 'Butterfly Blue' pincushion flower (*Scabiosa* 'Butterfly Blue') are two dependable, long-blooming perennials that are a great addition to any garden. 'Goodness Grows' speedwell (*Veronica × 'Goodness Grows'*) puts on its main flush of bloom in summer but continues to bloom sporadically until frost. 'Six Hills Giant' catmint (*Nepeta × faassenii* 'Six Hills Giant') can be encouraged to rebloom in fall if it is cut back by half and fertilized lightly after its early-summer bloom.

Annuals, grasses, and foliage perennials also contribute to the autumn spectacle. The spiky blue flowers of mealycup sage (*Salvia farinacea*) and fuzzy, white-centered blooms of 'Capri' ageratum bloom from late spring up to frost. The dramatic upright form of 'Heavy Metal' switchgrass (*Panicum virgatum* 'Heavy Metal') and spiky tufts of blue fescue (*Festuca caesia*) accent the garden from spring through late winter. Aromatic rue (*Ruta graveolens*) forms a leafy mound of blue-gray leaves that continues to add interest long after its early-summer blooms have passed.

To accent the backbone of long-blooming and foliage plants, this design also includes a few favorite perennials for early- to mid-summer color. The unique inflated buds and starry open blooms of balloon flower (*Platycodon grandiflorus*) are a must for a blue border, as are the distinctive flowers of Siberian iris (*Iris sibirica*). And no blue garden would be complete without the summer spikes of blue false indigo (*Baptisia australis*), whose blue-green foliage remains as shrubby mounds in the fall border.

A Simple Rock Wall Garden

If you're lucky enough to have a sloping rock wall on your property, or are considering building one, this garden offers season-long interest and color from a few easy-to-grow plants. It adapts easily to a traditional rock garden, too, since the wall plants all grow best with full sun and good drainage: typical rock-garden conditions. Remember that the beauty of a rock wall garden or rock garden is the contrast of the plants against the rock—don't overplant.

Perennials on the wall include low-growing, cheerful dwarf bearded iris (*Iris pumila*), red-and-yellow wild columbine (*Aquilegia canadensis*), blue or white Carpathian harebell (*Campanula carpatica*), yellow basket-of-gold (*Aurinia saxatilis*), and blue, pink, or white moss pink (*Phlox subulata*). Succulent 'Ruby Glow' sedum (*Sedum* × 'Ruby Glow') provides contrast with its thick, waxy leaves and starry red flowers, as do the hens-and-chickens (*Sempervivum tectorum*) with their fleshy green and burgundy rosettes.

The perennials at the bottom of the wall

enjoy the same conditions as most popular border perennials—full sun, good drainage, and average to rich soil—so if you don't have a rock wall, you could grow these plants as a border or in front of an upright stone wall, brick wall, or fence. They include such reliable landscape standards as 'Hyperion' daylily (*Hemerocallis* 'Hyperion'), 'Caesar's Brother' and 'White Swirl' Siberian irises (*Iris sibirica* 'Caesar's Brother' and 'White Swirl'), 'Hoffnung' yarrow (*Achillea* 'Hoffnung'), Russian sage (*Perovskia atriplicifolia*), and perennial candytuft (*Iberis sempervirens*).

The mixed border on top of the wall could also stand alone. In addition to the moss pinks, candytuft, basket-of-gold, and dwarf bearded iris that also accent the wall, dwarf fountain grass (*Pennisetum alopecuroides* 'Hameln') and cranberry cotoneasters (*Cotoneaster apiculatus*) add height and structure. Both the cotoneasters and fountain grass arch over, their fountaining form emphasizing the slope of the wall and the flowing shape of most of the wall plants. The borders on the top and bottom of the wall are tied together by the lovely white-variegated 'Silver Beauty' ajuga (*Ajuga reptans* 'Silver Beauty'), which provides a cool contrast to the bright blue, pink, yellow, and white of the perennials.

In Another Place

This garden was designed for a sunny site, but if your rock wall or rock garden area is shaded, you can create a design that's just as beautiful. Intead of the dwarf bearded iris, plant crested iris (*Iris cristata*), with pale-blue flowers and fans of 4-inch leaves. Replace the candytuft with lady's-mantle (*Alchemilla mollis*), with lovely scalloped leaves and sprays of chartreuse flowers in spring. Grow creeping phlox (*Phlox stolonifera*) instead of the moss pinks; you can buy cultivars in the same color range—white, lilac-blue, mauve-pink, and purple-blue.

Try maidenhair fern (*Adiantum pedatum*), corydalis (*Corydalis lutea*), fringed bleeding heart (*Dicentra eximia*), and coral bells (*Heuchera sanguinea*) instead of the hens-and-chickens, sedum, harebells, and basket-of-gold. Both the yellow-flowered corydalis and the rose-pink bleeding heart have ferny blue-green foliage and sprays of heart-shaped flowers. Coral bells bear a rosette of attractive scalloped leaves and tall sprays of delicate white, red, salmon, or pink bell-shaped flowers.

If you live in Zone 6 or south, you can grow Kenilworth ivy (*Cymbalaria muralis*), with tiny scalloped leaves and cheerful lavender flowers, to add a delicate touch to a shaded rock wall. Wild columbine will grow well in shade, but might look better with this color scheme if you plant its pale-yellow-flowered cultivar 'Corbett' instead of the red-and-yellow species.

At the top and bottom of the wall, use shade-tolerant periwinkle (*Vinca minor*) to

Adding Annuals and Biennials

One way to add more summer punch to your rock wall garden is with colorful, easy-care annuals and biennials. Great annuals for the rock wall are the shorter cultivars of snapdragon, with their distinctive spikes of dragon-head flowers in a rich range of colors from white, pink, and yellow through velvet-red. You can plant taller cultivars at the base of the wall. Other excellent choices that self-sow are sweet alyssum (*Lobularia* spp.), with its clouds of flowers, and annual candytuft (*Iberis umbellata*), with flowers that look like the perennial candytuft's but are borne all summer; both are available in shades of white, pink, rose, and lavender.

If you'd like to add splashes of brilliant color that will spill down the rock wall, grow lobelias (*Lobelia erinus*) and baby-blue-eyes (*Nemophila menziesii*). Lobelias form trailing mats of fine foliage that are covered with tiny flowers in jewel tones—sapphire, amethyst, and garnet—often with a white eye. Make sure you choose a trailing or hanging-basket cultivar. Baby-blue-eyes bears clouds of open cup-shaped flowers over mossy foliage. The bright blue-and-white flowers are 1½ inches wide, so they're quite showy even from a distance. An unusual annual that will add sparkle to your wall garden is Moroccan toad-flax (*Linaria maroccana*), with feathery foliage and tiny snapdragon-like flowers in a bright range of colors, including yellow, pink, mauve, and scarlet. It will grow 8 to 15 inches tall.

For bright biennial color, try sweet William (*Dianthus barbatus*), which produces clusters of glowing red, dark-red, pink, scarlet, salmon, rose, and white flowers; the petals often look like rich velvet. And for the foot of the wall, plant foxgloves (*Digitalis* spp.), which add a vertical element with their stately spikes of purple, lavender, white, yellow, pink, and salmon flowers; 'Foxy' is shorter than the species, reaching only 2½ feet, and often blooms the first year.

Simple Rock Wall Garden

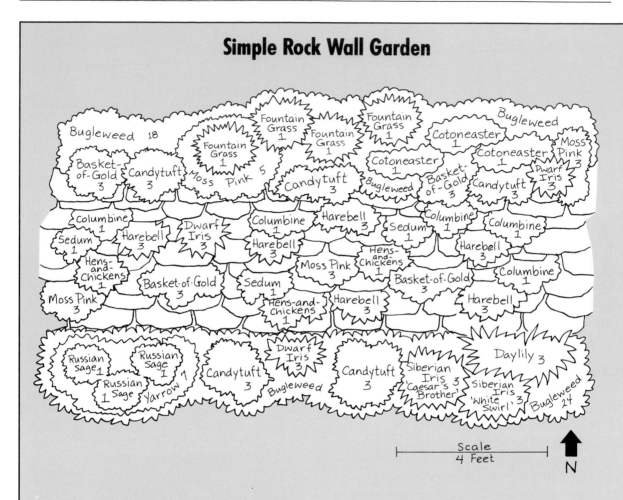

Scale
4 Feet

N

Spruce up a plain stone wall with this colorful combination of perennials, bulbs, grasses, and shrubs. Spring crocuses are included in the design, although they are not shown in the plot plan. Simply scatter them throughout the garden. Below is a list of the plants that are included in this design. For more information on these plants, look them up on the table on page 146, or turn to the appropriate entry in the encyclopedia section beginning on page 280. (Note: The numbers in the diagram refer to the quantity of each plant used.)

Plants for a Simple Rock Wall Garden

Basket-of-gold (*Aurinia saxatilis*)
Bugleweed (*Ajuga reptans* 'Silver Beauty')
Candytuft (*Iberis sempervirens*)
Columbine (*Aquilegia canadensis*)
Cotoneaster (*Cotoneaster apiculatus*)
Daylily (*Hemerocallis* 'Hyperion')
Dwarf iris (*Iris pumila*)
Fountain grass (*Pennisetum alopecurioides* 'Hameln')
Harebell (*Campanula carpatica*)
Hens-and-chickens (*Sempervivum tectorum*)

Moss pink (*Phlox subulata*)
Russian sage (*Perovskia atriplicifolia*)
Sedum (*Sedum* × 'Ruby Glow')
Showy crocus (*Crocus speciosus*)
Siberian iris 'Caesar's Brother' (*Iris sibirica* 'Caesar's Brother')
Siberian iris 'White Swirl' (*Iris sibirica* 'White Swirl')
Spring crocus (*Crocus* spp., any species or cultivar)
Yarrow (*Achillea* Galaxy Hybrid 'Hoffnung', or another cultivar)

For Southern Gardens

If you live in the South, where Ellen Phillips (designer of the simple rock garden on the opposite page) grew up, you may have never seen a bellflower (*Campanula* spp.). That's because they don't tolerate the steamy summers so characteristic of southern states. Instead of trying to grow Carpathian harebell (*C. carpatica*) in your garden, substitute sun-loving, heat-tolerant pinks (*Dianthus* spp.).

Pinks form neat, matlike tussocks of grassy green, blue-green, or gray-green foliage and bear cheerful carnation-like flowers in spring or summer. Some of the best for rock walls or rock gardens are Allwood pinks (*D.* × *allwoodii*), maiden pinks (*D. deltoides*), and cheddar pinks (*D. gratianopolitanus*), which stay low, bloom for two to three months, and have cultivars in white, pink, rose, red, maroon, purple, salmon, and bicolors.

replace the ajuga. It's an excellent groundcover, and you'll appreciate its pinwheel flowers twinkling against the dark foliage, especially if you plant a white-flowered cultivar.

At the bottom of the wall, you can replace the daylily and Siberian irises with a large blue-leaved hosta (such as 'Krossa Regal') and Japanese anemones like 'September Charm' (*Anemone* × *hybrida* 'September Charm') or 'Robustissima' (*A. tomentosa* 'Robustissima'), both with pink flowers. Plant lavender mist (*Thalictrum rochebrunianum*), with airy, blue-green foliage and clouds of pale-purple flowers, instead of the Russian sage, and replace the yarrows with chartreuse or white-variegated hostas and the dramatic red-purple foliage of 'Palace Purple' heuchera (*Heuchera micrantha* var. *diversifolia* 'Palace Purple').

On top, replace the fountain grass with a fountaining fern like ostrich fern (*Matteuccia struthiopteris*), and use a sweetspire like 'Henry's Garnet' (*Itea virginica* 'Henry's Garnet') instead of the cotoneasters. This lovely shrub bears 6-inch spires of white flowers in summer and has intense maroon fall foliage. It's larger than the cotoneasters, so just plant one as a specimen.

For a fun *trompe l'oeil* effect, you can create the illusion that your rock wall was built behind a water garden. Just sow biennial forget-me-nots (*Myosotis sylvatica*) as a groundcover at the base of the wall. These shade-loving 6- to 18-inch plants will create a sea of cornflower-blue flowers over grass-green leaves. They self-sow profusely and will soon "lap" in blue waves against your wall, blooming from spring into early summer. When blooming ends, pull the plants; they'll have produced plenty of seed to create the same effect next year.

THE GARDEN IN SPRING

Masses of color make this rock wall garden the place to be on a sunny spring day. The delightful mixture of yellows, blues, and white, accented with touches of red, is sure to brighten up any area.

At the base of the wall, a range of plant heights and textures add extra interest to the colorful flowers. The flat, spiky leaves and dainty blue or yellow blooms of low-growing dwarf bearded iris are particularly striking against the mounds of perennial candytuft, with their narrow leaves and round clusters of white flowers. Alongside, 'Caesar's Brother' and 'White Swirl' Siberian irises form tall, narrow-leaved clumps of violet-blue or white flowers that draw your eye up from the ground and help link their low-growing companions to the rest of the garden.

Many of the plants growing in and above the wall also contribute their bright colors to the spring show. Bold clumps of yellow basket-of-gold and pale-blue moss pink complement the yellow and blue dwarf irises scattered throughout the garden. Masses of white perennial candytuft also help to unify the design. And delicate clumps of wild columbine accent the softer colors with their nodding red-and-yellow blooms that sway gently in each passing breeze.

Even plants that aren't blooming now have something to offer. The spiky mounds of 'Hameln' fountain grass on top of the wall are complemented by the grassy clumps of 'Hyperion' daylily growing at the base. And in the wall itself, hens-and-chickens form striking rosettes of fleshy, pointed leaves.

THE GARDEN IN SUMMER

Summer finds the rock wall garden glowing with yellows and golds, along with touches of blue and pink. Masses of foliage in varying shades of green add a restful touch to the otherwise vibrant combinations.

At the base of the wall, grassy mounds of 'Hyperion' daylily display their sweetly fragrant soft-yellow blooms against the dark background of the stone. Nearby, the shorter 'Hoffnung' yarrow offers flat-topped clusters of complementary soft sandstone-yellow blooms over clumps of ferny foliage. Later in summer, the gray-green mounds of Russian sage will be topped with powder-blue flowers that accent the yarrow and the daylily.

The wall itself is adorned with the cool-blue, bell-shaped flowers of Carpathian harebell. If you allow them to set seed, these delightful flowers often self-sow into other cracks in the wall, adding to the summer display in following years. Other plants of particular interest include the straplike leaves of spring-blooming dwarf bearded iris and the fleshy rosettes of hens-and-chickens. The leafy stems of 'Ruby Glow' sedum (*Sedum* 'Ruby Glow') are topped with broccoli-like flower heads that will soon open to display cheery pink flowers.

The top of the wall is graced with a mass of 'Hameln' fountain grass. Its clumps of arching green leaves and fuzzy, silvery pink flower heads add interest all summer and remain attractive well into winter. Alongside, cranberry cotoneaster complements the mounding form of the fountain grass with arching woody stems clothed in glossy, dark-green leaves and, later in the fall, bright-red berries.

Simple Rock Wall Garden

Plant Name	Description	Bloom Season	Comments
Achillea Galaxy Series 'Hoffnung' ('Hoffnung' yarrow, or another Galaxy Series hybrid)	Grows to 2' tall; flat heads of pale primrose-yellow flowers over clumps of ferny foliage.	Summer	Remove spent flowers to prolong blooming.
Ajuga reptans 'Silver Beauty' ('Silver Beauty' bugleweed)	Grows 4″–6″ tall; spikes of blue flowers over rosettes of gray-green leaves edged in white.	Late spring	Plants spread to form an attractive groundcover.
Aquilegia canadensis (wild columbine)	Grows 1'–3' tall; nodding red-and-yellow flowers over mounds of compound blue-green leaves.	Late spring	Individual plants may be short-lived but self-sow readily.
Aurinia saxatilis (Basket-of-gold)	Grows 10″–12″ tall; dense clusters of yellow flowers above rosettes of fuzzy, oblong, gray-green leaves.	Spring	Cut plants back by ⅓ after flowering to encourage compact growth.
Campanula carpatica (Carpathian harebell)	Grows 8″–18″ tall; cup-shaped blue or white flowers over clumps of triangular leaves.	Spring through summer	Mulch in summer to keep roots cool.
Cotoneaster apiculatus (cranberry cotoneaster)	Grows to 3' tall; single pink flowers on arching stems clothed in glossy, dark-green, small semi-evergreen leaves.	Late spring	Flowers are followed by red fruit in fall.
Crocus speciosus (showy crocus)	Grows 4″–6″ tall; lavender-blue flowers.	Early fall	Flowers bloom in fall without the grasslike leaves, which are produced in spring.
Crocus spp. (spring crocus, any species or cultivar)	Grows 4″–6″ tall; white, cream, yellow, lilac, or purple flowers over clumps of grasslike green leaves.	Spring	Plants go dormant after flowering.
Hemerocallis 'Hyperion' ('Hyperion' daylily)	Grows to 3½' tall; yellow funnel-shaped flowers on stiff stalks over clumps of straplike green leaves.	Summer	The large flowers are quite fragrant.

Plant Name	Description	Bloom Season	Comments
Iberis sempervirens (perennial candytuft)	Grows 6"–12" tall; round clusters of white flowers over mounded clumps of narrow green leaves.	Spring	Foliage is evergreen.
Iris pumila cultivars (dwarf bearded iris)	Grows 4"–8" tall; flowers in a range of colors over fans of broad straplike leaves.	Spring	Dwarf bearded irises look just like full-size bearded irises and are available in a wide color range.
Iris sibirica 'Caesar's Brother' ('Caesar's Brother' Siberian iris)	Grows to 3' tall; dark violet-blue flowers on thin but strong stems over clumps of narrow upright leaves.	Spring	Plants are generally problem-free.
Iris sibirica 'White Swirl' ('White Swirl' Siberian iris)	Grows to 3' tall; pure-white flowers on thin stems over clumps of narrow leaves.	Summer	The petals are slightly twisted, giving the flower a striking appearance.
Pennisetum alopecuriodes 'Hameln' ('Hameln' fountain grass)	Grows 2'–3' tall; silvery pink flower spikes over clumps of arching, narrow green leaves.	Midsummer to fall	The cultivar 'Moudry', with dark-brown flower spikes, can also be used.
Perovskia atriplicifolia (Russian sage)	Grows 3'–5' tall; airy sprays of powder-blue flowers on stems clothed in deeply toothed, gray-green leaves.	Summer	Plants often die back to the roots in winter but resprout from the roots in spring.
Phlox subulata (moss pink)	Grows 4"–8" tall; single pink, magenta, or white flowers over mounds of needle-like green leaves.	Spring	Shear plants back by ⅓ after flowering to keep plants looking tidy.
Sedum × 'Vera Jameson' ('Vera Jameson' sedum)	Grows 9"–12" tall; domed clusters of pink flowers on weakly upright succulent stems with waxy bluish or purplish leaves.	Late summer to early fall	Foliage is blue-green in warmer areas and blue-purple in cooler areas.
Sempervivum tectorum (hens-and-chickens)	Grows to 1' tall; pink or purplish flowers over wide rosettes of succulent pointed leaves.	Summer	Many hybrids are available.

CHAPTER FOUR

Growing with the Design

Like a good marriage, a good garden is an ongoing process. There's never a point where you can sit back and say, "Well! I've done it now. Everything's going so well, I'll just take it easy and let the garden fend for itself." A garden left to itself will follow the laws of natural succession and revert to the wild. To remain a perennial garden, your beds or borders need *you,* and your care and input, on an ongoing basis.

A garden develops in three stages: design, installation, and ongoing care or maintenance. The first three chapters of this book show you how to create a garden on paper, this chapter tells you how to get the garden in the ground, and Part 2 covers ongoing care. Though each of the stages is enjoyable, this one, making your dream garden a reality, is the most exciting. Let's get started!

PREPARING THE BED

The first step toward in-ground gardening is making your bed (or island, or border). If you're digging a garden in what is now lawn,

first outline the bed with garden hose, ground limestone, or flour. With an edging tool or a sharp spade, cut around the outline of the bed. Then use the spade to cut strips of sod and roll them up for reuse or composting. When you've removed the sod from the bed area, you're ready to work the soil.

Good soil is humus-rich and well-drained but moisture-retentive. If your grass is growing well without fertilizer and the ground drains quickly, your soil is probably average to good. Work the soil from one edge of the bed to the other with a garden fork or a shovel, breaking up clods and removing rocks, large roots, and other debris. Add soil amendments like compost and aged manure, and work it again to a fork's (or shovel's) depth. Rake the surface smooth. Then cover the bed with a light mulch like shredded leaves to prevent erosion until your plants arrive.

If your soil is heavy clay, it needs more intensive care. Making a raised bed or double digging are two ways to improve the structure and drainage of clay soils. Adding ample organic matter will increase the humus content.

If your soil is extremely sandy, treat it like average soil, but add lots of organic matter and mulch it heavily.

The time you spend improving your soil is the most important time you'll ever spend in the garden. And it will repay you over and over as your garden grows. You'll find out all about digging, double digging, soil types, organic matter, and soil amendments in chapter 6.

BUYING PERENNIALS

After you've dug your garden and prepared the soil, the next step is getting your plants. The most common way to acquire perennials is to buy them, though we discuss money-saving alternatives like seed starting and plant swaps in "Seeds and Seedlings" and "Plant Exchanges and Societies" on page 158.

You can buy perennials at a local nursery or garden center, where you pick out each plant yourself, load them in the car, and take them home for same-day planting. Or you can order perennials through the mail from nursery catalogs. Both ways have advantages, so most gardeners end up buying some of their plants locally and some by mail order.

Plants by Mail

There are two big advantages to mail-order shopping: convenience and selection. With mail-ordering, you can have perennials delivered right to your door. And mail-order nurseries offer a much larger selection than most garden centers are able to because the mail-order companies usually have large growing fields.

If you're looking for an unusual species or a particular cultivar, you'll often have the best luck by turning to a catalog. It's fun to compare catalogs, too. Many provide valuable

How to Be a Smart Mail-Order Shopper

Mail-order shopping is a convenient way to order a large selection of perennials. But it pays to be cautious; some mail-order nurseries are better than others. Here's how to get the most from mail-order shopping:

▶ Order early for the best selection.

▶ Specify a desired shipping time, so plants will arrive when you want them.

▶ When plants arrive, get out your plant journal and write down when you received them, from where, and what condition they arrived in. This information will come in handy when you choose nurseries to order from next time.

▶ Evaluate containerized mail-order plants just as if you were looking them over at the garden center. Don't expect perfect foliage, though—shipping often leads to broken or bruised leaves. If the plants are healthy, they'll recover quickly. Diseased foliage or insects are more serious matters; return plants that show signs of infection or infestation.

▶ Examine bareroot plants for pests and diseases, too. Check the roots, crowns, and stems for pests or signs of pest damage.

▶ If the roots of your bareroot plants are sparse or in poor condition, return the plants.

▶ Rewrap bareroot plants after you've inspected them, and store in a cool place until you are ready to plant them.

▶ Before planting, soak the roots of bareroot plants in water for at least 1 hour.

▶ If you receive substandard or damaged plants and want a refund or replacement plant, contact the nursery immediately.

▶ Avoid hype and exaggerated claims. If it sounds too good to be true, it usually is. However, reputable nurseries sometimes offer collections of perennials that are excellent buys (but not *unbelievable* buys).

growing tips, information on good plant combinations, entertaining plant anecdotes, and design suggestions, as well as clear descriptions and color photos of the perennials.

The drawback of mail-ordering is that you can't see the plants you're buying until they arrive. The best way to avoid disappointment is to start with a small order from each nursery you want to try. Some nurseries ship plants in containers; others ship bareroot; and others use both techniques. Specify shipping times when ordering by mail to make sure your plants arrive when you can actually plant them. A nursery in another part of the country may not know when planting conditions will be right in your area.

At the Nursery or Garden Center

The advantages of buying perennials from a local nursery or garden center are that

At the garden center. After good soil, a good nursery or garden center can be a gardener's most valuable asset. Look for one that labels plants clearly, including cultivar name where appropriate, gives specific cultural information, and offers healthy plants.

you can get your plants the minute you need them and you can choose the healthiest, most attractive plants. Many garden centers also have display gardens where you can see the mature sizes and forms of the plants. The plants will be larger than those available by mail, so you'll get more "instant gratification" when you put them in the ground (the mail-order plants usually catch up by the end of the season).

There's a hidden drawback to garden-center shopping, though—the candy-store syndrome. When you see all those wonderful plants, it's tempting to buy one of each. The best way to avoid temptation is to make a list of the plants you plan to buy, then stick to it. Otherwise, you might set out to buy five irises and return home with a carload of mixed plants that looked great in the store but not in your garden design. Another drawback is that your selection may be limited. Here are some tips for getting the most from buying plants at a garden center:

▶ The best selection is available in spring.

▶ If you want a specific color, buy a cultivar.

▶ Avoid plants that are visibly rootbound. Check the root systems of plants that are leggy or too large in relation to the size of the pot by gently tipping the plants out of their pots.

▶ Choose plants with lush foliage and multiple stems. Avoid plants with dry, pale, or shriveled leaves.

▶ Check for insects on the leaves (examine both the tops and undersides) and along the stems.

▶ Plants bought in fall will look weather-beaten, since they may have been sitting on a bench all summer. So don't go by appearances—check the root system. If it's in good shape, the plant is probably healthy.

▶ If you can't plant immediately, keep containers well-watered. Check them daily.

WHEN YOUR PLANTS ARRIVE

Let's back up a minute here to stress a vital point: Dig your beds *before* your plants arrive. Don't order plants or buy them locally unless you've prepared a place to put them. You'll be rushed enough at planting time without having to start from scratch, and your plants deserve a better start than you could give them with last-minute bed making.

Even if you've already prepared your garden bed, you still may not be able to put your plants in the ground as soon as they arrive, especially if they're mail-order. More likely, you'll come home after a long day's work, with hours of chores still before you, and find them on the doorstep. You may have to wait until the next day—or even the weekend—before you can plant. Here's what to do with your plants in the meantime:

▶ Take mail-order plants out of the box as soon as you get them.

▶ Water container-grown plants whenever the soil dries. The smaller the pot, the more often you'll have to water.

▶ Set container-grown plants outside in a shaded area until you can plant them.

▶ If bareroot plants are wrapped in a protective material like peat or shredded wood, keep the material damp. If the plants aren't wrapped in protective material, soak the roots in lukewarm water, then cover them with moist soil or compost.

▶ Keep bareroot perennials in a protected place until you can plant them.

▶ Plant your perennials as soon as you are able to.

Beginning a border. The owners of this yard have their site ready and waiting to plant: They have stripped off the sod, worked the soil, set in an edging, and placed stepping stones.

A year later. Only a year later, the border (shown at a slightly different angle) looks lush and established. Evening primroses (*Oenothera* spp.) make a bold splash of yellow in the back, echoed by the 'Stella de Oro' daylily in front. Bellflowers (*Campanula* spp.) and lavender add blue accents, while lamb's-ears (*Stachys byzantina*), silvermound artemisia (*Artemisia schmidtiana*), and a variegated iris add silver foliage to the garden. Mixed shrubs provide a framework for the border, and a 'Dynasty' rose blooms at one end.

You'll find detailed instructions on caring for your new perennials in "What to Do Once the Plants Come Home" on page 184.

PLANTING TIME

When you're ready to plant, remove the mulch from your prepared bed. Choose an overcast day if possible, and don't plant during the heat of the day. Place container-grown plants, pots and all, on the bed where you plan to plant them. (Consult your design to make sure you're putting them in the right spots.)

You can dig the holes for as many perennials as you think you're going to plant that day, but plant only one perennial at a time. Remove it from its pot by turning the pot upside down, with one hand spread over the soil around the stem, and tapping the bottom of the pot with your trowel to loosen the roots. The roots may have grown into a tangled mass. Separate them by gently pulling them apart or quartering the root ball with a knife—this will make it easier for the roots to spread through the soil, and the plant will establish more quickly. Remove any broken or diseased roots.

Place each container-grown perennial in the ground so its crown is at the same depth at which it grew in the pot, or slightly higher; the soil will settle a bit over the next few weeks. Make sure you spread the roots out in the hole as you plant.

If you're planting bareroot perennials, remove protective material from the roots, then soak the roots in a bucket of lukewarm water for 1 or 2 hours to hydrate them before planting. Again, plant one perennial at a time. Dig a large enough hole so you'll have room to spread out the roots. Prune off diseased or damaged roots. Mound up soil in the center of the hole and set the plant on top of the mound, spreading its roots out over the sides.

Make sure the mound is the right size to position the plant's crown at the soil surface. Fill in the hole with soil, then firm it down.

One last point that's important but easy to forget: Keep the plant labels with your perennials, and stick them firmly in the ground next to each plant as you plant it. You'll find step-by-step directions for planting container-grown and bareroot perennials in "Putting in the Plants" on page 185.

AFTERCARE: A TIMETABLE

How well your plants will thrive depends on the care you give them after planting. You can't just plop them in the ground and walk away. Newly planted perennials need more attention than established plants. You'll find detailed how-to information on every aspect of growing perennials in chapter 6. Use this care calendar to make sure you're giving your new plants what they need.

Right Away

Water. Water both bareroot and container-grown perennials as soon as you've planted them.

Cut back foliage. If the nursery hasn't already done this, cut off one- to two-thirds of the foliage on bareroot plants; otherwise plants will lose water through their leaves faster than their damaged roots can take it up, causing wilting. If they wilt even after you've cut them back, you probably were too tender-hearted; cut back to a few inches to give plants a chance to recover.

Mulch. Mulch your plants after watering them to maintain soil moisture and guard against wilting. Mulch will keep weeds from competing with your new plants, too.

Provide shade. Shade your newly planted perennials from direct sunlight until they've had a chance to recover from the shock of transplanting. Cover them with a spunbonded row cover like Reemay or with shade cloth, screening, or a lath cover for the first two or three days after planting.

The First Week

Water. Your plants' primary need will continue to be water. Check at least once a day—before and after work is even better.

Check for bugs. Check your perennials daily for signs of pests and pest damage. New plants are smaller, so they're particularly vulnerable to pest damage. If you find insects or damage, check in chapter 7 for the culprit and what to do about it. Remember that animals and birds can decimate a planting, too—if you see signs of their damage, protect your plants with screens.

Remove shade. Gradually remove your shade cover after the first few days—ideally, leave it on only during the heat of the day, and remove it in the morning and late afternoon. If you work and can't get home to move the cover, take it off completely after the third day; make doubly sure that plants are well-watered and mulched.

The First Season

Water. Watering will remain critical during the first growing season. Make sure your perennials get 1 inch of water a week, either from rain or the hose.

Weed. Weeding is most important the first two years after planting; after that, plants will be established and large enough to shade out most weed seedlings. Mulch will help control weeds, but check for them every time you're in the garden.

Feed. If you've prepared the soil well, your perennials won't need more than an application of compost in the middle of the season, or compost (or manure or seaweed)

tea once a month, to grow vigorously.

Monitor for insects and diseases. Continue to keep an eye out for pests and diseases and apply appropriate controls.

Stake. In the first year after planting, stake perennials like peonies and delphiniums that might have weak stems.

Disbud. If you buy perennials bareroot in May or June that are late-blooming (like asters and mums), remove all their flower buds. They need to establish themselves the first growing season, not put their energy into flowering.

Deadhead. Cut off spent flower heads to keep your perennials from wasting energy by setting seed.

Move things around. If plants don't look right where you've placed them, don't be afraid to move them around. Don't move perennials in bloom. Wait until they've stopped blooming, then move them with a large soil ball around their roots; or mark them and their new location on a copy of your design and move them at the end of the season.

Add new plants. If you find you've left a gap in your bed that won't be filled in by the following season, add more plants to cover the bare spot.

Enjoy. Take time to appreciate the beautiful garden you've made.

PUTTING IN YOUR GARDEN OVER TIME

It's great if you can design a garden, then buy all the perennials you've included and plant them. Your garden will mature at the same rate, so it has an even, finished look. And you'll see the complete design—outdoors, growing, in full color—within one season.

But for many of us, a one-shot garden is just an ideal. For one reason or another—time, money, an unexpected trip or other interruption to our plans—we have to implement our garden in stages. Instead of the three to four years it usually takes a perennial garden to mature, it may take ours five or six. In the end, though, a multi-step garden will look just like the one-shot. And you can use time-tested techniques to make sure it looks lovely every step of the way.

If you're planting your garden in stages, one of the most sensible steps is to put in the slower-growing perennials first. Perennials like peonies, oriental poppies, daylilies, blue false indigo (*Baptisia australis*), gas plant (*Dictamnus albus*), balloon flower (*Platycodon grandiflorus*), Siberian iris (*Iris sibirica*), large-leaved hostas (*Hosta* spp.), and baby's-breath (*Gypsophila paniculata*) are slow to establish. If your design includes any of these plants, start with them.

Ways to Approach a Design

Every gardener faces the problem of putting a good face on a new garden. Perennials take a long time to mature—often three or four growing seasons—and the garden can look bare or haphazard in the meantime. One way to give your new garden a fuller, more mature look is to fill in the gaps with colorful annuals while the perennials mature.

You'll be more successful if you choose annuals with the same color, form, and texture as the perennials that will grow to replace them. This designer trick will give your garden a unified look, and let you try out your color scheme the first season. Snapdragon (*Antirrhinum majus*) and sweet alyssum (*Lobularia*

Filling in with annuals. One of the best ways to make a garden look established is to interplant with annuals while waiting for the perennials to fill in. You'll get lots of season-long color from the annuals if you keep them watered and deadheaded. (Many perennials take at least two seasons to reach flowering size.) Here, geraniums, sweet alyssum (*Lobularia* spp.), petunias, lobelias (*Lobelia* spp.), celosias (*Celosia* spp.), and verbenas (*Verbena* spp.) put on a showstopping display in this two-year-old daylily border.

maritima) mix especially well with perennials; use them in the front and middle of the bed or border. For height, try annuals like spider flower (*Cleome hasslerana*) and cosmos (*Cosmos bipinnatus*).

A drawback is the cost of annuals—if you buy bedding plants rather than starting them from seed, annuals cost almost as much as the least expensive perennials. A different alternative—especially if you're planning to add another bed or border in a few years—is to overplant rather than use a lot of annuals. Plant three perennials where your design calls for one, then move the two extras out as plants mature. This technique gives your garden a fuller look, and you'll have good-size plants on hand when you're ready to start the new garden.

A final trick that's really effective is to plants lots of bulbs for a bright first-season show. Daffodils, species tulips, crocuses, and other "little bulbs" will make your garden sparkle in spring, while lilies will pick up the show in summer. Plant bulbs thickly—in groups, rather than singly—for a dazzling display.

When You Don't Have Time

One obvious solution to a time crunch is to plant a piece of the garden rather than trying to do it all at once. You can put in part of the bed or border each year until it's all planted. An advantage of this technique is that if you don't like part of the design, you won't have to redo the entire garden—you may only have to move or replace 3 plants rather than 30. A drawback is that each section will mature in the order you planted, so one end of the border may just be filling in when the other is peaking.

Another way to tackle the time problem is to start with the parts of your yard that will make the most impact. Put in the colorful sunny border this year, and worry about more intricate and less showy plantings like the shade and bog gardens later. If your terrace is the central feature of your yard, put in a bed around it now; save the property-line border for another year.

Don't forget ongoing time concerns, too—the larger the garden, the more time it will take to weed, water, deadhead, and do other routine chores. When you're planning your bed or border, don't bite off more than you can chew.

When You Don't Have Cash

If ready money is the problem rather than time—and with plant prices what they are today, planting an entire garden isn't an inexpensive undertaking—there are plenty of ways to get garden color for a minimum of cash. Here are some ideas to get you started:

▶ Trade plants with neighbors. Almost everybody has a little too much of something, and these "extra" plants are often fast-growing—just what you need for quick color.

▶ Start perennials from seed. (See "Seeds and Seedlings" on page 158.)

▶ Start with commonly available plants and replace them with more choice perennials when you can afford them. For example, plant a "ditch daylily" this year, and replace it with a favorite cultivar in a couple of years. While you wait, you'll still be able to enjoy daylily form and flowers.

▶ Use fast-growing plants—spotted lamium (*Lamium maculatum*) in shade, coneflowers (*Rudbeckia* spp.) and bee balm (*Monarda didyma*) in sunny areas—until you can afford to replace them with a more diverse selection. Other fast-growing perennials include mums, catmints (*Nepeta* spp.), fringed bleeding heart (*Dicentra eximia*), and gayfeathers (*Liatris* spp.). In a shady site, fill in with running ferns like lady fern (*Athyrium filix-femina*), New York fern (*Thelypteris noveboracensis*), and sensitive fern (*Onoclea sensibilis*).

Help for a Large Garden

If you have a large yard—or just want a sizable garden—and you're starting from scratch, you need an excellent strategic plan or you'll quickly exceed your gardening time and budget. Another danger is that impulse planting will result in a haphazard look. Here are some tips to get your garden up and running without breaking either your back or the bank.

Plan Ahead

Before you begin to dig or plant, be sure you take time to consider the following points.

▶ Think about where you'll enjoy the garden as you plan beds and borders. What will you see from your windows? What will your neighbors see? (Remember, good gardens make good neighbors.)

▶ Plan a maintenance program. Site fussier plants in beds closer to the house, where it's easier to care for them, and tough, self-sufficient perennials at a distance.

▶ Don't site a bed or border in a high-traffic area—where family and friends will be tempted to tramp through it. If some "through traffic" is unavoidable, add large, flat stepping stones to make a convenient path.

▶ To eliminate hard-to-maintain areas, plant perennials and groundcovers around trees to eliminate trimming, and on slopes that are difficult to mow.

▶ Put in permanent elements first, like a hedge or an evergreen border. They'll frame the garden or hide unattractive views. Once the trees or shrubs are growing, plant your perennials.

▶ Make both shady and sunny nursery beds. Don't make the beds too small—you'll be propagating your plants and growing them on, so you'll need more space than seems likely at first.

Choosing Plants

When you're ready to pick out plants, use these tips to decide what to buy and where to plant it.

▶ Buy essential plants first—groundcovers, hostas, daylilies, and other basic,

---

▶ Start with a small garden and a limited color scheme, then expand to a larger garden with a broader color scheme when you're able.

The Nursery Bed

Creating a private nursery of their own is a fantasy for many gardeners. Make it a reality of sorts in your garden with a nursery bed, a great way to save money and protect small, vulnerable plants.

If your design calls for lots of groundcovers or other perennials that are easy to propagate, like mums, start with a plant or two of each.

Then make lots of divisions or take lots of cuttings from the parent plants—many more than you would from a plant in your garden. (For example, if you were dividing a daylily to replant in your garden, you might cut it into two to four divisions; for the nursery bed, you might separate and plant out every fan of leaves. After all, this isn't a display garden; a nursery bed, like a compost pile, is one of the working areas of the garden.)

A nursery bed is ideal for perennial seedlings, too, since they often take two to three years to grow large enough to hold their own in the garden. Meanwhile, keeping the

easy-to-move plants. Divide them regularly, and put the divisions in a nursery bed. Move divisions to the garden as you create it.

▶ Don't be afraid to invest in top-quality cultivars if you can divide or propagate them.

▶ For plants that resent transplanting, like peonies, baptisias (*Baptisia* spp.), and gas plant (*Dictamnus albus*), dig small sections of the future border and put these plants in where you'll eventually want them. Mow around the sections until you can dig the spaces in between and connect them.

▶ In a big garden, you can tolerate more invasive plants than in a small garden. Site aggressive thugs where you can mow around them—under trees or up against hedges, for example—to keep them from getting out of hand.

Getting Good Buys

To get the most greenery for your green-backs, follow these tips.

▶ Save money by buying from nurseries that sell seedling-size plants. Then grow them on in your nursery beds.

▶ Look for special packages from nurseries—group offers of daffodils, hostas, and other popular perennials. You can save money with these packages, but be aware of the trade-offs: If you buy a group of unnamed plants, don't expect cultivar quality—put them on a slope or distant area that needs color rather than in a nearby bed or border. If you buy a "named, our choice" special, you won't sacrifice quality—you just won't know exactly what you're getting.

▶ You can also take advantage of summer sales, when many nurseries try to sell stock quickly so that they don't have to maintain it into fall. Don't plant your bargains right away, though—it's too hard on the plants. Instead, keep the pots in a shady area near the house, where you can water them often, then plant them in fall.

▶ With big gardens it is time- and cost-effective to start plants from seed. Many perennials, including species hostas and daylilies, are easy to grow if you use fresh seed.

young plants together makes it easier to give them the care they need.

The best nursery bed is a large, open-topped cold frame, since you can set screening in the bottom to keep voles out and put shading like lath or screen over the top without fear of crushing the plants. If you don't want to make a cold frame or don't think it would look right in your garden, make a raised bed for your nursery. An east-facing site in partial shade is best, since it gets indirect light.

Prepare the soil for your nursery bed the same way you would for a perennial bed, but screen it to remove clods, twigs, and rocks; the soil texture should be fairly fine. Add plenty of compost or other organic matter. Use the same kind of soil in your nursery bed that the plants will eventually grow in. Don't overfeed your nursery plants, or they'll grow spindly and susceptible to pest and disease attack.

The plants in your nursery bed are small and vulnerable—you'll need to protect them from sun, driving rain, and pests. Fine window screen will serve all three purposes; it provides shade, breaks the force of raindrops that could flatten seedlings, and keeps pests from reaching plants. You can also put slats or shade cloth over the bed, or protect it with wood lath. When you're siting your nursery bed, make sure it's within reach of your hose; you'll be watering often. For more on nursery beds, see "Make Your Own Nursery Bed" on page 250.

Seeds and Seedlings

If you have more time and patience than money to spend on your perennials, starting plants from seed is an excellent choice. A packet of seed is much cheaper than the equivalent number of plants (or even one plant!). In exchange for a good buy, though, you must be willing to wait. And you must limit your selection to perennials that come true from seed—mostly species, though some cultivars can be seed-grown.

In addition to simply germinating your seeds, you'll need to set up a cold frame or nursery bed to protect the seedling perennials while they grow. Seedlings require considerable care for the first season, and continuing care for the following year or two until they reach blooming size. For more on growing perennials from seed, see chapter 9.

Plant Exchanges and Societies

Plant societies like the American Rock Garden Society and the Hardy Plant Society are great sources of inexpensive seeds and plants, since many have seed and plant swaps and sales. You'll find rare and unusual plants in addition to popular perennials. Societies are also excellent sources of information, and joining one is a good way to meet fellow enthusiasts. Some of the plant societies of interest to perennial gardeners are listed in "Resources" on page 500.

Botanical gardens, public gardens, and arboreta also often have plant and seed sales.

Sometimes universities with horticulture programs sponsor plant sales, too. You must join the plant societies to participate in their programs, but the garden, arboretum, and university sales are often open to the general public. Contact your local university's horticulture department and the nearest botanical garden to see if they have plant sales; you'll enjoy the gardens, too.

WAYS A DESIGN CAN CHANGE AS PLANTS MATURE

Plants grow and change as long as they live, so it's a mistake to think that once your garden has matured, it will continue to look exactly the same forever after. In reality, no two years in the garden ever look the same—it's one of the pleasures of gardening.

Slow-growing perennials like peonies, oriental poppies, and blue false indigo (*Baptisia australis*) will change predictably: As long as they're healthy, they'll just get bigger every year. Other perennials may peak and decline, disappear from where you planted them and pop up in another part of the garden, or return from seedlings that bloom in a completely different color than the original plants.

Change for the Better

Often, changes in the garden are for the better. Forty blooms on a mature peony are a far more spectacular sight than four on a third-year plant. Creeping perennials will spread to fill in gaps, making the plants seem to flow together in a beautiful blend of color and texture. Bulbs will multiply, forming sizable clumps.

Other changes are less predictable but equally delightful. The stems of perennials

Perennials from seed. If you don't have a lot of spare cash, one way to have an affordable garden is to grow most of your perennials from seed. It takes a little more time, but the results are just as spectacular. Buy plants of the cultivars you really want immediately, then sow easy-from-seed perennials like the yarrow, gloriosa daisy (*Rudbeckia hirta* 'Gloriosa Daisy'), and rose campion (*Lychnis coronaria*) in this exuberant garden.

may weave among those of neighboring plants, so those plants may suddenly "bloom" out of season. A perennial may not be the color you expected—but the new color may work even better than the one you wanted. You may find you've accidentally created a haven for butterflies or hummingbirds.

Change for the Worse

Unfortunately, not all changes are for the better. A perennial may grow too large for its space, crowding out less vigorous neighbors. A tall plant may flop over on adjacent plants or may shade them too much when they need full sun. Plants like yarrows and artemisias (*Artemisia* spp.) that prefer poor, dry soil may lodge (fall open from the center, leaving a hole) if they're grown in the rich, moist soil preferred by most perennials.

Other problems may show up as your garden matures. One of the most frequent is decreased vigor—perennials that aren't growing as strongly or flowering as well as they were a season or two ago. Another is self-sowing, where seedlings from plants like garlic chives (*Allium tuberosum*), columbines (*Aquilegia* spp.), or coneflowers (*Rudbeckia* spp.)

Keep up the good work. This well-designed garden presents a delightful combination of color, texture, and form — the upright yucca (*Yucca smalliana*) in a sea of silvery 'Powis Castle' artemisia in back and 'Marie's Rose' verbena (*Verbena* × 'Marie's Rose') in front. The perennials look great this year, but the owners of this garden can't rest on their laurels. If they don't want the artemisia to be sprawling and overgrown next year, they'll need to cut it back at the end of this season; to make sure they have verbena next year, they should take cuttings.

may crop up all over the bed, crowding out other plants and sometimes creating jarring color combinations.

What to Do: Alternatives

If the perennials in your garden don't look right or aren't growing compatibly with their neighbors, remember the gardener's most valuable design tools—a trowel and shovel. Don't be afraid to move plants around, even if it's only a foot to the right or left. Unless they have a taproot, most perennials are very forgiving. Move them in the cooler part of the day with a large soil ball around their roots and water them carefully until they're re-established. Often, moving plants will solve design problems simply and effectively.

If your plants are losing vigor, they probably need to be divided. As its name implies, this technique involves taking the plant out of the ground and splitting it into smaller pieces. Replant one of these pieces in improved soil in the original hole, and plant the rest elsewhere or give them to friends. The smaller pieces usually take a season to get established, then display all the vigor of new plants. (For more on how to divide perennials, see "Divide and Multiply" on page 241; check the encyclopedia entries beginning on page 280 to see if individual plants divide best in spring or fall.)

If volunteer seedlings are a problem, deadhead the offending parent plants before they can set seed. In fact, deadheading and other routine chores—watering, feeding with compost, weeding, mulching, and keeping a

On the cutting edge. An edging is the best way to keep lawn grass where it belongs—in the lawn, not in your beds. This colorful garden of annuals, perennials, and bulbs is edged with a flexible plastic edging strip that conforms easily to curves. Metal edging strips are also available. For formal gardens, brick and stone make elegant edgings.

sharp eye out for pests and diseases—are the best ways to prevent problems. In Part 2, you'll learn how to give your plants the care they need to grow and perform at their best—wherever you live and however large or small your garden is.

Growing plants well and keeping them happy is a delightful pastime with ample rewards, as this colorful cottage garden shows. If you work a little every day, you can keep up with your plants' needs. In this section, you'll find step-by-step information on every aspect of perennial culture.

PART TWO

GROWING PERENNIALS

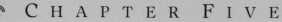
Climate Considerations

The single most critical factor in perennial gardening is climate. It's the primary reason new gardeners fail, and even seasoned gardeners can lose plants when they forget to take climate into account. In this chapter, you'll learn what climate is and why it matters, what catalogs mean when they refer to hardiness zones, how to determine what your garden's climate is, and how to choose plants that are adapted to your conditions. You'll also find lists of the best perennials for hard-to-please climates (like those of New England and the Southwest).

WHAT IS CLIMATE?

Most people think of climate in terms of heat and cold. If your summers are hot enough to melt plastic and your winters are frost-free, you'd probably say you live in a warm climate. Alternatively, if you live in northern Vermont where, as the natives say, you have 11 months of winter and 1 month of mighty cold weather, you could say your climate was cold. Temperature extremes do play an important part in determining what you can—and, more important to some gardeners, can't—grow. But temperatures are only a part of the climate picture.

Humidity is as important to climate as temperature. Summers may be equally hot in Arizona and Alabama, but the plants that do well in each state are radically different. Arizona plants are adapted to hot, dry summers and would rot in the foglike dampness of an Alabama August. When you're choosing plants for your perennial border, find out if they're adapted to dry areas (these are often listed as plants for *xeriscapes*, or dryland conditions), or if they thrive in a more humid environment. Then buy the ones that match your conditions.

Snow cover is another important consideration. If you live in an area that is usually blanketed with snow all winter long, you can grow plants that would die farther south if grown in a site with sporadic snow cover. That's because snow acts as a natural insulator, keeping the soil evenly frozen. Perennials are most likely to die over winter if the soil repeatedly freezes and thaws, since the freezing and thawing action tends to heave the plants out of the ground, exposing their roots to freezing and drying out. (The other cause of perennials dying in winter is cold, wet soil, which isn't a problem if the soil stays frozen.)

Other aspects of climate that may determine what grows well for you are wind, rain, and the types of "natural disaster" conditions that make the paper. If your garden is in an exposed site and you live in an area with high winds, your plants will face a triple threat. First, the wind beating against the unprotected plants will batter them and knock them over unless they're sturdily staked. Second, winds dry out plants and soil, so your plants will need a deep mulch and frequent watering or they may scorch. And third, winds create colder temperatures (the dreaded windchill factor), so your plants may in fact be growing in a colder climate than simple geography might lead you to believe.

Rains that sheet down in torrents can also flatten your plants; if you live in an area where downpours are the norm, consider siting your garden where it gets some shelter from overhanging branches, walls, or other structures. Hailstorms can turn flowers and foliage into streamers or punch holes in leaves like a hungry caterpillar. If you live in a hail zone, minimize the damage by growing plants with small or fine leaves, rather than plants with large, showy leaves.

You can see that what we call "climate" is actually a complex interaction of geography and weather patterns. The way your climate is pieced together determines what you can grow, or at least imposes significant limits. But by finding out what these limits are, you'll be that much closer to a garden that grows well and looks great with only routine care.

Know Your Limitations

No gardener can grow every perennial, because every property has its climatic limitations. Even gardeners in England envy our warm, dry summers and stunning autumns, just as we envy their mild winters and moderate summers. A Denver gardener might have a showstopping rock garden that's the envy of his Nashville friends, while he covets the beautiful border of peonies and irises that they take for granted.

What about all those "perfect" perennial gardens that are photographed for magazines and books? No matter how large or complicated they are, even the best gardens have only a selection of the many available perennials. Whenever you look at a photo of a lush, gorgeous garden, you don't see the plants the gardener tried—and failed—to grow. What you *do* see is the eventual success that the gardener achieved from finding out what plants grow well together in his or her garden's conditions.

The secrets of this success are learning about your particular climate—and it can be quite a bit different from the climate two blocks over—and learning about the climatic needs of the perennials you'd like to plant. In addition to the plant lists in this chapter, the encyclopedia entries provide growing specifics for every plant, so you can refer to the encyclopedia section when considering whether a given perennial would be suitable.

Climate Checklist

To focus in on your own climate, run through the following climate checklist. (If you don't know an answer, you can often get it by calling your local weather station or Coopera-

Weather Lore

One part of climate that's hard to overlook is the weather. We check the forecast in the paper and on the news at night and in the morning, and perk up for the weather announcements on the radio. We may even buy a weather radio if we commute in cold-weather areas or are concerned for our crops. We scan the skies and stick our arms or heads out the door to see if we'll need a jacket or an umbrella. Each of us is a sort of weather prophet, making our best guess and proceeding accordingly.

Fortunately, our ancestors have left us a rich mine of lore about the weather to help us make our guesses. For them, weather was often a matter of life and death, since many made their living from agriculture or the sea. Even for those who didn't, transportation was neither as safe nor as weatherproof as it is today, so they needed a forecast they could rely on before setting out on a journey. As a result, they studied the weather closely and passed on their observations from generation to generation.

Here are some sayings that still stand the test of time. Keep them in mind the next time you're trying to decide if it will rain or if you need to water.

▶ "When ye see a cloud rise out of the west, straightway cometh the rain" (Luke 12:54). This refers to the fact that weather fronts usually move from west to east.

▶ "Rainbow in the morning, shepherd take warning. Rainbow toward night, shepherd's delight." A morning rainbow, caused by the rising sun from the east shining on rainclouds in the west, indicates rain heading your way from the west. A rainbow seen in the evening is caused by the setting sun shining from the west on rainclouds in the east, indicating fair weather approaching from the west.

▶ "If the sun goes pale to bed, 'twill rain tomorrow, it is said." High cirrus clouds in the west give the setting sun a veiled look. When appearing as bands or mare's tails, they signal an approaching storm.

▶ "Clear moon, frost soon." Cloud cover acts like a blanket over the earth, keeping temperatures from dipping as low as they would on a clear night.

Animal and Plant Predictors

Another body of weather lore involves the appearance or behavior of plants and animals. Even today, we grow up with sayings about unusually large woolly bear caterpillars and extra-plump squirrels or other hibernators being signs of a cold winter to come. Some of this lore has a basis in science. Here are some reliable weather indicators to watch for:

▶ "The darker the color of a caterpillar in fall, the harder the winter." This indicator has proven reliable, but we don't yet know why.

▶ "When the sheep collect and huddle, tomorrow will become a puddle." Sheep respond in this way to a change from a high- to a low-pressure system, which often brings rain.

▶ "The higher the geese, the fairer the weather." High flying is a response to a high-pressure system; if geese fly low, a low-pressure system is coming, and rain with it. This saying applies to all migratory birds.

▶ "When the wild azalea shuts its doors, that's when winter tempest roars." Azaleas and rhododendrons draw their leaves in when the temperature drops.

tive Extension Service.) Review the results and you'll have a good idea of your yard's general climate as well as the specific conditions prevailing in different parts of the yard. Both your yard's overall climate and the climates of smaller areas in the yard are called *microclimates,* since they reflect the specific conditions of small sites.

▶ What is the average date of your first fall frost?

▶ What is the average date of your last spring frost?

▶ Do you have winter snow cover? If so, is it constant or sporadic?

▶ Do you have fairly consistent rains in summer? Or are some months usually dry? Which ones?

▶ Is your area humid all year? Very humid in summer? Or is the air usually dry?

▶ What is each month's average high temperature in your area?

▶ What is each month's average low temperature in your area?

▶ What is each month's average precipitation in your area?

▶ Does your area have frequent high winds, torrential rains, dust storms, or hailstorms?

▶ Think about what your yard looks like. Are there exposed, open places that seem more windy than other areas? Are there low areas that get frost earlier and that seem to stay cold longer than the rest of the yard? What about hills or other high places that might suffer from windchill more than the rest of the yard, or that warm up too early and might be hit hard by late frosts?

▶ Do trees, hedges, walls, or fences create shady areas that tend to be cooler than the surrounding yard? Are there bright areas that heat up faster?

Record the climate information from the checklist in your garden journal. When you're tempted by a perennial you are reading about or looking at in a catalog, refer to the journal. You'll have a good idea whether or not the plant will grow well in your conditions.

Fooling Mother Nature

Plants usually grow best and are healthiest when given the conditions they prefer. But sometimes you can still grow "impossible" plants—the ones that "just don't grow here"—if you are able to compensate for growing them outside their natural range.

For example, tulips need a certain amount of chilling to bloom. If you live in the Deep South, where the winters don't stay cold for the required number of weeks, your tulips will come up, but they won't bloom. You can still have blooming tulips—if you prechill the bulbs in the refrigerator every year. But you can also have beautiful bulbs like African lilies (*Agapanthus* spp.) and crinums (*Crinum* spp.) that would freeze and die with the first frost farther north.

Peonies also bloom better in cold-winter areas. If you're a Deep South gardener whose heart is set on peonies, the trick here is to look for cultivars that have been specially bred to do well in hotter areas. Researchers at colleges like the University of Georgia are always testing and evaluating perennials to find those that are adapted to southern conditions.

Gardeners in the North often envy the beautiful rosemary bushes that grow in southern colonial and cottage gardens. In areas where rosemary won't overwinter outdoors, you can still have stately rosemary bushes if you grow them in pots and bring them in each fall. You can choose ornamental pots for a formal touch, or sink the pots into the ground to make it look like the plants are growing in your garden bed. Northerners can grow many tender perennials if they are willing to over-winter them indoors.

Remember that where you put a plant can help it survive, too. Chancy perennials sited in front of a south-facing wall are more likely to live through the winter than similar plants in colder, exposed sites. Sometimes a well-drained site can make the difference between death and survival. For more about these and other ways to protect your plants in winter, see "Winter Protection" on page 205. But although these tactics can make a real difference, your plant selection will ultimately depend on the plants' hardiness.

PLANT HARDINESS AND HARDINESS ZONES

Hardiness can mean a lot of things, from a plant's ability to withstand drought and neglect to its pest-resistance and durability. But most often, it is used to refer to cold-hardiness—the coldest temperature a plant can live through. If a plant can survive low temperatures of $-10°F$ but will die at $-11°F$ or below, it is considered hardy to $-10°F$.

Information about plant hardiness has been collected for most perennials and is readily available. But for this information to be useful, you need to be able to connect it to your climate. It doesn't help to know that a perennial is hardy to $-10°F$ if you don't know whether the temperature gets below $-10°F$ in your area. Fortunately, plant scientists and meteorologists have gotten together and mapped North America in terms of plant hardiness, dividing it into hardiness zones. By finding your area on a plant hardiness zone map, you can also see which hardiness zone you live in.

Hardiness Zone Maps

Plant hardiness zone maps give the range of the average annual minimum temperatures for areas across North America. These areas are assigned zone numbers from 1 to 10 or 11 (depending on the map), with the zones stretching in rough bands across the continent. The zones start with the coldest, Zone 1, and move south to the warmest, Zone 10 or 11. Each zone represents a minimum tempera-ture range, such as 10° to 20°F. This is the coldest it is likely to get in that area.

Of course, plant zones are created from temperature averages, so some winters will be colder. If there's solid snow cover or your plants are buried under a heavy winter mulch, most likely no harm will be done; if they're exposed, a freak cold spell may kill the less hardy perennials. Gardening is a gamble, and few seasons see every plant through alive. You're just as likely to lose plants in a cool, wet winter where the soil stays damp as you are in cold snaps (many perennials don't tolerate wet feet for prolonged periods).

The USDA Plant Hardiness Zone Map

The hardiness map that's now consid-ered the standard is the new USDA Plant Hardiness Zone Map. This map, revised in 1990 from the 1965 version, incorporates data from weather stations across North America. It accurately reflects current minimum tempera-tures for the United States, Canada, and Mexico.

The USDA map divides the country into 11 plant hardiness zones. Each zone except the coldest (Zone 1) and warmest (Zone 11) is subdivided into two sections, A and B, each representing a 5°F range. This means, for example, that Emmaus, Pennsylvania, where Rodale Press is located, is in Zone 6B, with average winter minimum temperatures of 0° to

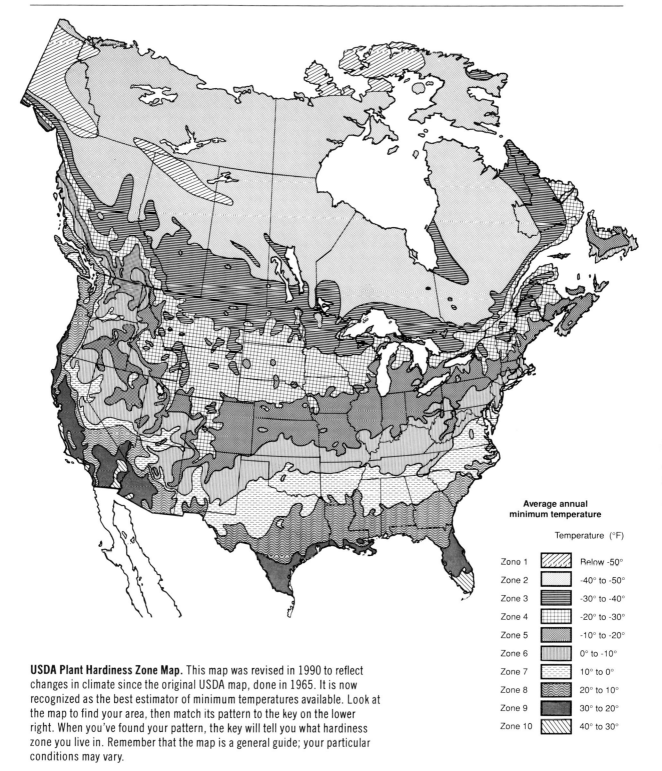

USDA Plant Hardiness Zone Map. This map was revised in 1990 to reflect changes in climate since the original USDA map, done in 1965. It is now recognized as the best estimator of minimum temperatures available. Look at the map to find your area, then match its pattern to the key on the lower right. When you've found your pattern, the key will tell you what hardiness zone you live in. Remember that the map is a general guide; your particular conditions may vary.

Average annual minimum temperature

Temperature (°F)

Zone		Temperature
Zone 1		Below -50°
Zone 2		-40° to -50°
Zone 3		-30° to -40°
Zone 4		-20° to -30°
Zone 5		-10° to -20°
Zone 6		0° to -10°
Zone 7		10° to 0°
Zone 8		20° to 10°
Zone 9		30° to 20°
Zone 10		40° to 30°

−5°F. Gardeners in Emmaus can feel confident about planting perennials that are hardy to −5°F or below. They're on fairly safe ground planting perennials that are hardy to 0° to −5°F. But they risk losing plants to the cold if they choose plants that are not hardy to 0°F.

Unless you see a detailed copy of the USDA map, however, you'll probably see only Zones 1 to 10. Zone 11 can't be seen on most zone maps; it includes only the very warmest parts of the country where temperatures remain above 40°F year-round. Most zone maps also don't include the A and B divisions. Though the A and B divisions are more precise, the broader zones are still a useful guide and are the zones referred to in most gardening books, magazines, and catalogs. When you look up an entry in this encyclopedia, you'll see hardiness listed in whole zones rather than half zones.

Arnold Arboretum Zone Map

Occasionally, you'll find references to the Arnold Arboretum zone map in a gardening book. This map was compiled by the Arnold Arboretum in Jamaica Plain, Massachusetts, and last revised in 1967. It has slightly different hardiness zones and is considered by some horticulturists to be more accurate than the old USDA map.

The Arnold Arboretum map divides the United States and Canada into 10 zones, which represent 5°, 10°, or 15°F ranges rather than the standard 10°F zones of the USDA map. However, the painstaking data collection that went into the new USDA Plant Hardiness Zone Map convinced the Arnold Arboretum to switch to the USDA map. Newer references should all feature the USDA zones.

Using Hardiness Zones

Here's how to use plant hardiness zones. You're looking at a perennial you'd like to grow in your garden—say, garden phlox (*Phlox paniculata*). The catalog or plant tag says the phlox is hardy to Zone 4. That means that if you live in Zone 4 or in a warmer zone (such as Zone 7), garden phlox will be cold-hardy in your area. If you live in a colder zone, garden phlox will not be reliably hardy in your area. Gardeners in colder zones should choose another phlox or a similar but hardier perennial. Moss pink (*Phlox subulata*) and creeping phlox (*P. stolonifera*) are hardy to Zone 2, while woodland phlox (*P. divaricata*) and wild sweet William (*P. maculata*) are hardy to Zone 3. If you live in the southern part of Zone 3, you could take a chance on garden phlox, giving it a protected site and a heavy winter mulch. But there are no guarantees—try a plant or two, not a large group.

Deep South gardeners are often confronted with the opposite problem—plants that grow well in colder areas can't take the heat. Fortunately, some catalogs and books, including this encyclopedia, give a hardiness range rather than simply listing the coldest zone a plant will grow in. If you're a southern gardener and want to grow the bold, colorful hybrid lupines (*Lupinus* spp.), a cold-hardiness limit (Zone 3) would imply that you're on solid ground. However, a hardiness range (Zones 3 to 5) shows you that lupines won't survive the humid heat of a southern summer.

GEOGRAPHICAL REGIONS

For most gardeners, their hardiness zone is a good guide to what they can grow. But in some parts of the country, special conditions like highly alkaline soil, drought, high rainfall, or high humidity are limiting factors. This is especially true of the Southwest, the Far North, the Deep South, and the Rockies.

Making the Desert Bloom

In the Southwest, humidity and rainfall are low and watering is often restricted. It makes sense to grow perennials that don't need a lot of water, especially since what rain does fall often comes in winter rather than during the growing season. Perennials for the Southwest also have to be both heat- and cold-tolerant, since days are often scorching, while nights can drop near or below freezing.

These daunting requirements have led to the development of xeriscaping, a style of dryland gardening that uses only tough, drought-tolerant plants. For a list of perennials that grow well in Southwest conditions, see "Best Perennials: A Regional Guide" on page 172. You can also check with your local extension agent or arboretum for a broader selection. But successful xeriscaping depends on more than plant selection. To get the most from dryland perennial gardening, give your plants a protected site: Use windscreens—either fencing or hedges—and trees, shrubs, or structures to shade your garden. Use drip irrigation, and mulch your beds.

The drier the climate, the more alkaline the soil is likely to be. If you live in near-desert conditions, your selection of plants will be fairly restricted unless you garden in raised beds with imported topsoil or lower your soil's pH. You'll find more information in "Changing Your pH" on page 178.

Perennials Southern Style

The high humidity and relentless summer heat combine to make Deep South gardening a challenge. While gardeners swelter in an atmosphere as inviting as a wet sleeping bag, pests and diseases thrive. In addition, southern gardeners may face heavy-clay soil or thirsty sand. For perennials to grow well in the South they must be heat-tolerant and disease-resistant. For a list of top perennials for Deep South gardens, see "Best Perennials: A Regional Guide" on page 172. Or, consult your local extension agent for more perennials that do well in your area.

Dr. Allan Armitage of the University of Georgia has done extensive trials to see which perennials stand up to southern conditions. He has developed the following recommendations that will help you have a better garden.

▶ Avoid taller cultivars. The abundant heat and moisture and longer growing season cause plants to grow bigger in the South, so starting with tall plants invites lots of staking. Look for short or dwarf cultivars of your favorite perennials.

▶ Hold off on fertilizer. High-nitrogen fertilizers will cause loose, lanky growth at the expense of flowers.

▶ Improve your soil by adding organic matter like compost and shredded leaves. Organic matter increases drainage and aeration in clayey soil, while it increases water- and nutrient-retention in sandy soil. For more on organic matter, see "Soil Amendments" on page 178.

Dr. Armitage has also found that southern gardeners can grow some perennials that traditionally do poorly in the South. The trick is to plant beautiful but heat-intolerant plants like delphiniums, lupines, and primroses in the fall, enjoy their bloom the following spring and summer, then dig them up and consign them to the compost heap. If you're willing to treat them as annuals, you'll get a fine show from these finicky beauties, and you can use heat-tolerant bedding plants to fill in the gaps left when you pull them. This works for bulbs like tulips that need chilling, too. Simply treat them as annuals, and replant each fall.

Best Perennials: A Regional Guide

These perennials are proven performers in their areas. Use them as the basis for a bed or border if you live in one of these challenging regions. To expand your selection, see what sells well in a good local garden center, visit a botanical garden if one is nearby and see what they're growing, and try to find mail-order nurseries that specialize in regional plants. Experiment with other perennials and add the ones that are successful for you. In a few years, you'll have your own customized list.

Note that if only a genus name is listed (indicated by "spp." after the name), more than one species in that genus can be grown in your region, but not every species will be suitable. Similarly, hardiness zones given after the genus name will reflect the range for the genus and won't apply to every species. Look up the genus in the encyclopedia section to find which species you can grow.

Ten for the Southwest

Artemisia spp. (artemisias): Zones 3–9
Chrysanthemum leucanthemum (oxeye daisy): Zones 2 to 10
Gaillardia spp. (blanket flowers): Zones 2–10
Gaura lindheimeri (white gaura): Zones 5–9
Oenothera spp. (evening primroses): Zones 3–8
Penstemon spp. (penstemons): Zones 2–9
Salvia spp. (sages): Zones 3–10
Verbascum spp. (mulleins): Zones 4–8
Verbena spp. (verbenas): Zones 3–10
Yucca spp. (yuccas): Zones 3–10

Ten for the Deep South

Achillea spp. (yarrows): Zones 3–9
Asclepias tuberosa (butterfly weed): Zones 4–9
Chrysanthemum × *superbum* (Shasta daisy): Zones 4–9
Crocosmia spp. (montbretias): Zones 5–9
Eupatorium coelestinum (hardy ageratum): Zones 6–10
Gaillardia × *grandiflora* (blanket flower): Zones 2–10
Hemerocallis spp. and hybrids (daylilies): Zones 2–9
Hibiscus spp. (hibiscus): Zones 4–10
Salvia spp. (sages): Zones 3–10
Verbena spp. (verbenas): Zones 3–10

Ten for the Far North

Anemone spp. (anemones): Zones 2–9
Campanula spp. (bellflowers): Zones 2–8
Delphinium hybrids (delphiniums): Zones 2–7
Dicentra spp. (bleeding hearts): Zones 2–9
Eryngium spp. (sea hollies): Zones 2–9
Hemerocallis spp. and cultivars (daylilies): Zones 2–9
Lupinus hybrids (hybrid lupines): Zones 2–5
Paeonia lactiflora cultivars (peonies): Zones 2–8
Papaver orientale (oriental poppy): Zones 2–10
Phlox spp. (phlox): Zones 2–9

Ten for the Rockies

Artemisia spp. (artemisias): Zones 3–9
Aurinia saxatilis (basket-of-gold): Zones 3–7
Campanula spp. (bellflowers): Zones 2–8
Centaurea spp. (centaureas): Zones 3–8
Dictamnus albus (gas plant): Zones 3–8
Iberis sempervirens (perennial candytuft): Zones 3–9
Lupinus spp. (lupines): Zones 2–6
Salvia spp. (sages): Zones 3–10
Santolina spp. (lavender cottons): Zones 6–8
Veronica spp. (speedwells): Zones 2–8

The Big Chill

Perennial gardening in the Far North presents a different challenge—winter. Temperatures far into the minuses may be the norm at night for months, often accompanied by high winds. Ice storms may coat the garden with "glass." Arctic winds may whip your fragile plants, causing breakage and dehydration. And frosts may continue to strike into June, take a month off, and start up again in August.

Fortunately, gardeners from Maine to Minnesota have a broad selection of perennials that withstand cold. For a list of some of the best, see "Best Perennials: A Regional Guide" on the opposite page. And there are a number of ways to reduce the risks and guarantee a beautiful garden display. One way is to choose perennials that bloom when frost is unlikely. If you want to plant fall-flowering perennials like chrysanthemums and asters, buy cultivars that bloom in September rather than October. On the other hand, if your heart is set on spring-flowering perennials, buy late-blooming cultivars that are likely to escape late-spring frosts.

Another way to ward off winter fatalities is to protect your plants' roots. Make sure your beds are well-drained to avoid root rot. When the ground freezes, mulch your perennials deeply to guard against frost heaving. A deep snow is an excellent insulator. Pile it on your beds to keep the soil frozen and plants protected. And site beds in areas where they're protected from chilling, drying winds.

Rocky Mountain High

Rocky Mountain gardeners have their own distinct set of climatic conditions. They face severe winter cold and intense summer heat. Like the Southwest, humidity and rainfall are extremely low, and like the North, wind exposure creates both windchill and serious drying. On the plus side, the benefits of high-altitude gardening are bright sunlight and well-drained, gravelly soils—perfect conditions for rock gardening. Rocky Mountain gardeners can easily grow the gorgeous alpine plants that avid rock gardeners in other parts of the country can only dream about.

If a beautiful rock garden isn't your ideal, you can create a standard perennial bed or border if you can irrigate your plants, or a lovely xeriscape with little or no additional water. Make sure you choose plants adapted to Rocky Mountain conditions. See "Best Perennials: A Regional Guide" on the opposite page for a list of some of the best, and check with the Denver Botanic Garden or your local extension agent for others. Site your garden in a sheltered location where plants will be protected from wind, use drip irrigation, and mulch your perennials. Then you can enjoy the plants and their beautiful mountain backdrop.

OTHER CONSIDERATIONS

When you've matched your perennials to your climate, you've come a long way toward a great garden. But there are other conditions that must be met.

First, site plants where they'll get the exposure they need. Plants that prefer to grow in full sun will languish in deep shade; shade-loving plants will fry in the sun. Matching a plant's soil preferences is another way to ensure success. You'll find out what exposure specific perennials prefer, how to prepare the soil for perennials, and other cultural tactics in chapter 6. You can look up specific perennials' needs in chapter 10 or in the individual entries in the encyclopedia section.

CHAPTER SIX

Perennial Gardening Basics

Sound gardening principles are the same, whether you're growing squash, shrubs, or Siberian irises. In this chapter, you'll learn how to prepare your garden, how to put in your plants, and how to take care of them once they're planted. Once you've mastered the basics, you can grow any perennial in this encyclopedia. But, as with any skill, you have to start from the ground up.

Remember the name "perennial" when you're preparing a garden bed or border for these beautiful and durable plants. A clump of peonies or poppies can live for 75 years, and all perennials live for at least 3 to 5 years. So give your garden the attention it needs *before* you put in your plants.

SIZING UP YOUR SOIL

Good soil is the backbone of a good garden. Well-prepared soil is fluffy and loose, so water, air, and nutrients can filter down easily, and roots have room to stretch. You can grow a lovely garden without knowing anything about soil if you have good soil to begin with and use sound gardening techniques like mulching, composting, and adding organic matter to your garden beds. But if your soil is hard to work, if it drains too quickly or too slowly, or if your plants aren't as lush and healthy as they should be, you'll have a better garden if you learn a few things about soil.

Soil 101

Most people think of soil as a layer of decayed leaves, twigs, and so on, but this organic matter and the organisms that live in it really make up only 5 percent of the soil. Soil is 45 percent mineral particles—the bedrock of the earth broken down over time—and 50 percent space between particles, space that's filled with air and water. Your soil will be made of particles of whatever rocks are prevalent in your area. The reason you don't recognize soil as crushed limestone, granite, sandstone, or whatever is because soil particles are so small that they've lost these distinguishing characteristics.

Sand, Silt, and Clay

Soil particles are classified by size. The three particle sizes are sand, silt, and clay.

Sand. The largest particle is sand, which can be seen by the naked eye and is pinhead-size or larger. Sand particles fit together loosely, leaving space for oxygen to reach plant roots for good growth. This space between particles also means that sandy soils drain quickly and don't hold many nutrients.

Silt. The next soil component is silt, which is barely visible as individual particles. Silt particles fit together more tightly, so they hold more water and nutrients while still allowing room for oxygen to get to the roots.

Clay. Clay, the smallest particle, can only be seen individually under a microscope. Clays can hold large amounts of water and nutrients, but they pack together so tightly that little air is available to plant roots.

Most soils in residential areas are loams—combinations of sand, silt, and clay. If the soil has a high percentage of sand, it will be a sandy loam, whereas a high percentage of clay results in a clay loam, and so on. Unless you live on the beach, in a swamp, or on a mud slick, you won't have to garden in pure sand, silt, or clay.

Soil scientists consider the ideal garden soil to be 20 percent clay, 40 percent silt, and 40 percent sand. The sand encourages good drainage, while the clay and silt help to hold nutrients and some moisture for good root growth. But remember that this is just an ideal—there's a lot of leeway for good garden performance, since different plants have different soil requirements. And adding lots of organic matter like shredded leaves or strawy

manure will bring your soil into better balance no matter what its composition is, since organic matter both aerates the soil and retains water and nutrients. (For more on organic matter, see "Soil Amendments" on page 178.)

Simple Soil Tests

How do you know if you have good loam soil, or if you have too much clay or sand? There are simple tests you can do at home to find out what kind of soil you have. These tests are easy, and they just take a few minutes.

The Watering Test

This simple test looks at how your soil handles water. When you're watering the lawn or garden, does the water disappear so fast it looks like only the leaves have gotten wet, rather than the soil surface? And do you find that you have to water frequently to keep plants from wilting? If so, you have a lot of sand in your soil. On the other hand, if water puddles up and seems to take forever to sink into the soil, you have a high percentage of clay. Soil with very high clay content may dry and crack apart in clods or plates between rains, and becomes sticky or very slippery when it's wet.

The Soil Ball Test

Try the soil ball test after a rain or after you water, when the soil is moist but not soggy. Take a handful of soil from the site where you want to grow perennials and squeeze it. When you open your hand, see what happens to the soil. If it crumbles apart, it's a loam. If it stays in a ball, it's basically clay. If it disintegrates easily and you can see and feel gritty little crystals in it, it's a sandy soil. And if it crumbles but feels greasy, it's silt.

The Water Jar Test

For a slightly more scientific evaluation, try the water jar test. Collect several soil samples where you want to site your flower bed and mix them. Sieve or pick out any pebbles, roots, and other large debris. Put a cup of the mixed soil in a clear quart jar, fill the jar with water, and seal it. Then shake the jar vigorously and watch the particles settle out.

Let the jar stand for 24 hours to settle the contents, then examine the soil layers that have formed in the bottom of the jar. Don't move the jar, or all the clay will float up again. (Remember that the organic particles in the soil—bits of leaves, twigs, and so on—will be lighter than the soil particles and will be floating or lying on top of the soil layers; for the purposes of this test, just ignore them.)

The largest and heaviest particles—sand—will have settled on the bottom, the medium-size and medium-weight particles—silt—will be in the middle, and the smallest and lightest—clay—will be on top. Estimate the percentage of each layer, and you can make an educated guess at your soil's texture. If you have a grease pencil, crayon, or indelible marker, you can mark off the level of each layer for easy reference.

For example, if you have a ¼-inch layer of sand, a ½-inch layer of silt, and a ¼-inch layer of clay (totaling 1 inch), your soil would be 25 percent sand, 50 percent silt, and 25 percent clay.

Once you've estimated the percentages of each particle type, you can see if you have a sandy loam, a silt loam, or a clay loam. Here's how to interpret the percentages.

Clay soils. Clay loams are common. If your soil has 20 to 35 percent clay and at least 45 percent sand, it's a sandy clay loam. If it's 25 to 40 percent clay and up to 20 percent sand, it's a silty clay loam. And if it's over 45 percent clay, it is classed as clay.

Sandy soils. Sandy loams are also common, with 50 to 70 percent sand. Loamy sand soils have 70 to 85 percent sand. The soil must be 85 to 100 percent sand before it can be classed as sand.

Silt soils. Silt loams, with 45 to 80 percent silt, are common in the Midwest. But high-silt soils are rare, mainly occurring on river deltas. You'd have to have 80 to 100 percent silt before the soil could be classed as silt rather than silt loam.

Professional Soil Tests

Once you've determined what type of soil you have, you may want to know what's *in* the soil. Is it phosphorus-rich? Does it have too much calcium? The best way to find out is to have your soil tested. Private soil labs and Cooperative Extension Services across the country will analyze soil samples for pH and nutrient content.

Each soil testing service has its own procedures, so don't just send off soil; write or call for instructions first. You'll receive a variation of the following general directions. Remove the surface debris from the area you plan to sample, then dig a small hole 6 inches deep. With a clean stainless-steel trowel or large stainless-steel spoon, cut a slice of soil from the side of the hole and put it in a clean plastic bucket. Take 10 to 15 samples around the garden area, then mix them in the bucket. Put the required amount of mixed soil in a plastic bag, then mail it and any required information in the package provided by the soil testing service. Be sure to ask for organic recommendations.

It usually takes four to six weeks to get the results of your soil test, so give yourself plenty of time. If you're planning to put in a new flower bed in fall, take your soil test in spring; if you want to upgrade your garden in spring, take it the previous fall. You can test for pH any time the soil isn't frozen. When the results come back, you can start collecting soil amendments to correct deficiencies and balance pH. Then you'll be ready when it's time to dig your beds.

Understanding pH

Soil pH is one of the simple mysteries of gardening: It sounds like a concept straight out of higher physics, but it's actually easy to determine, and except in extreme cases, it's easy to correct. Soil pH is a measure of the acidity or alkalinity of your soil. It's measured on a scale from 0 (highly acidic) to 14.0 (highly alkaline) with 7.0, the pH of water, considered neutral. Most garden perennials grow best in soil with a pH of 6.0 to 7.0—slightly acidic to neutral. Many woodland perennials prefer a more acidic soil—pH 5.5 to 6.5.

Most perennials are flexible in their pH requirements; the problems start when soils are very acid or alkaline. Strongly acid and alkaline soils bind essential nutrients, making them unavailable to plants. The plants then exhibit deficiency symptoms, such as stunted growth or yellowed leaves. Acid soils can release heavy metals like aluminum, lead, and cadmium in harmful concentrations and create an unfavorable environment for beneficial soil organisms. Alkaline soils are also often highly saline, a condition toxic to plants.

Once you've determined your soil's pH, you can bring acid soils closer to neutral by adding lime, while alkaline soils may need sulfur to neutralize them. (See "Changing Your pH" on page 178 to find out how much lime or sulfur to add.) Adding organic matter like leaves, grass clippings, or compost to your soil will level out the pH reading from either end: It raises the pH of acid soils and lowers the pH of alkaline soils. If your soil pH is mildly acidic

---

Get Your Soil Test Here!

Your local Cooperative Extension Service is the first place to call about a soil test. Look them up in the phone book under the city or county government listings, then call to see what you need to do. Don't forget to request organic recommendations. There are also a number of private labs that will do soil tests and provide organic recommendations, including:

A & L Agricultural Labs, 7621 White Pine Road, Richmond, VA 23237

Brookside Labs, 308 South Main Street, New Knoxville, OH 45871

Biosystem Consultants, P.O. Box 43, Lorane, OR 97451

Cook's Consulting, R.D. 2, Box 13, Lowville, NY 13367

Erth-Rite, R.D. 1, Box 243, Gap, PA 17527

Peaceful Valley Farm Supply, P.O. Box 2209, Grass Valley, CA 95945

As with the Cooperative Extension Service, write for instructions and testing fees before sending off your soil.

(pH 5.5 to 6.9) to mildly alkaline (pH 7.1 to 7.8), you should be able to balance it with organic matter alone. You'll learn more about organic matter in "Soil Amendments" on page 178.

Checking Your Soil's pH

You can test soil pH yourself with a home soil test kit or a pH meter (both are available from garden centers and catalogs). But instead of testing, you might be able to guess your soil's pH by learning a little about the geology and native plants of your area. Nature preserves, parks, botanical gardens, and other public gardens often offer books on the natural history of their area for sale; you can also try local colleges, libraries, and the nature and geography sections of bookstores.

If the predominant rock in your area is limestone, your soil is probably neutral to slightly alkaline, but if it's sandstone or granite, you may have acid soil. If you live in an eastern woodland area, where azaleas, rhododendrons, mountain laurel, blueberries, bayberries, ferns, and hemlocks are common,

your soil is probably acidic; if you live in the arid Southwest, it's likely your soil is alkaline.

Matching Plants to pH

If your soil is acidic and you'd like to keep it that way for your rhododendrons, ferns, hemlocks, and oaks, grow perennial woodland wildflowers and lilies, which prefer more acidic soil, rather than garden perennials that grow best in near-neutral soil.

If your soil is alkaline and you're having a hard time lowering the pH, there are a number of lovely and popular perennials that appreciate mildly alkaline conditions, including baby's-breath, bearded iris, delphiniums, lavender, clematis (*Clematis* spp.), and pinks (*Dianthus* spp.).

One way to grow favorite plants that aren't adapted to your soil's pH is to grow them in containers. You can buy or mix your own potting soil to match the plants' pH requirements. If, on the other hand, you'd like to bring your pH closer to neutral, the best time to amend the soil is when you dig your beds.

SOIL AMENDMENTS

Soil amendments benefit your garden—and your perennials—by supplying the humus that's the basis for good plant growth. Adding amendments loosens the soil so there are more spaces for air and nutrient-bearing water, increases water retention so you don't have to irrigate as often, improves drainage, and creates a favorable microclimate for beneficial soil organisms, including earthworms.

Unlike fertilizers, which provide plant nutrients without adding organic matter to the soil, the primary function of soil amendments is to improve soil structure. The phrase "soil structure" refers to the way soil particles fit together. Particles in a soil with good structure are close enough together to retain water and

Changing Your pH

If your soil is too acidic—a frequent problem in high-rainfall areas, where calcium leaches from the soil—you can add ground limestone, wood ashes, or bonemeal to correct the problem. Choose calcitic limestone if your soil has enough magnesium, and dolomite if your soil needs magnesium as well as calcium. To raise pH 1 point, add 5 pounds of calcitic limestone or 7 pounds of dolomite per 100 square feet. Add 6 pounds of wood ashes (instead of the limestone) per 100 square feet if you want faster results. Broadcast these materials by hand and rake them into the surface of your beds, or, for larger areas, apply them with a small garden spreader. If you broadcast by hand, wear gloves.

Don't get carried away when adding dolomite or wood ashes. Repeated applications of dolomite can cause an excess of magnesium, which can harm your plants, while an overdose of wood ashes will create a potassium overload. Use these materials cautiously.

If your soil is too alkaline—a particular problem in dryland areas—you can add powdered elemental sulfur to lower pH. To lower pH 1 point, add 1 pound of sulfur per 100 square feet. You can also add evergreen needles to the soil or use them as mulch, or work peat moss into the soil to help lower soil pH.

Perennial Gardener's Guide to Organic Soil Amendments

Organic soil amendments are the core of the perennial gardener's soil-improvement program. Choose the amendments that are most readily available to you, and turn them into the soil when you prepare your beds. Chop and compost hay, straw, and leaves first for quicker decomposition. You'll be adding humus, improving soil structure and water-retention, and neutralizing pH every time you add soil amendments. Your perennials will thank you!

Organic Amendment	Average NPK Analysis	Average Application Rate per 100 sq. ft.	Comments
Compost, dry commercial	1-1-1	10 lb.	Balanced amendment; good when homemade compost is in short supply.
Compost, homemade	0.5-0.5-0.5 to 4-4-4	100 lb.	Ideal, balanced amendment; add at any time.
Grass clippings, green	0.5-0.2-0.5	30 lb.	Decompose quickly, adding little bulk to soil.
Hay, weed-free	2.2-0.6-2.2	15 lb.	Add nitrogen source, such as blood meal, to speed breakdown.
Manure (dry)			Manures add balanced nutrients to soil; dry manure won't burn plants.
cow	2-2.3-2.4	15 lb.	
horse	1.7-0.7-1.8	15 lb.	
sheep	4-1.4-3.5	5 lb.	
swine	2-1.8-1.8	15 lb.	
Oak leaves	0.8-9.4-0.1	15 lb.	Add nitrogen source, such as blood meal, to speed breakdown.
Peat moss	Negligible	3–6 cu. ft.	Lowers pH; do not use on acid soils.
Sawdust	Negligible	15 lb.	Add nitrogen source, such as blood meal, to speed breakdown.
Wheat straw	0.7-0.2-1.2	15 lb.	Add nitrogen source, such as blood meal, to speed breakdown.
Worm castings	0.5-0.5-0.3	10 lb.	Good soil conditioner.

nutrients, but far enough apart to allow air and water to reach plant roots. When soil particles are too closely packed together, as in heavy clays, air and water can't get in; when they're too far apart, as in sands, they won't hold necessary water and nutrients long enough for plants to take them up. Adding soil amendments balances these extremes by loosening up clay soils and adding moisture-retentive organic matter to sandy soils. Many amendments add nutrients as well, but when you're turning in shredded leaves, compost, or even manure, you're first and foremost adding organic matter to the soil. (For more on fertilizers, see "Fertilizing" on page 187.)

All garden soils, even good garden loams, benefit from regular additions of organic matter. You need to apply more every season because organic matter isn't stable in the soil. This essential material is constantly being broken down into humus by soil organisms. Humus binds nutrients and holds them in the soil of the root zone. To continue to give your perennials the benefits of organic matter, you must give your soil a steady supply. Fortunately, that's easy to do—just incorporate organic matter into new beds, and add compost and mulch to established beds. (Remember that many of the same materials are used as both soil amendments and mulches, including compost and shredded leaves.)

The most commonly available soil amendments are compost, shredded leaves, grass clippings, hay and straw, aged manure, aged sawdust, and peat moss. You may be able to get other amendments locally, like alfalfa meal, seaweed, mushroom compost, ground corncobs, and apple pomace.

Compost and aged manure are balanced amendments and can be turned into the soil as is, at any time. Grass clippings are a good source of fast-release nitrogen, but they decompose quickly, adding little bulk to the soil. Peat, on the other hand, decomposes extremely slowly, so it will stay in the soil a long time. However, peat has a serious drawback if you live in an area where the soil is neutral to acidic—it is a low-pH material and will acidify the soil if you add enough of it to have an impact on soil structure.

Shredded leaves, aged sawdust, hay, and straw need time to break down. Soil organisms use nitrogen in the decomposition process and may compete with your perennials for the nitrogen if you add amendments the same season you plant. Ideally, you should prepare your beds in fall for spring planting or in spring for fall planting, giving these amendments plenty of time to break down before you put in plants. If that's not possible, prepare the beds at least six weeks before you plant, and add a high-nitrogen fertilizer like blood meal or chicken manure with your soil amendments to speed decomposition. If you use sawdust, which is woody and needs a lot of nitrogen to break down, make sure it's well-aged—the best sawdust will be so old it's black. Pile fresh sawdust outside to weather until it has aged for a few seasons.

HOW TO MAKE COMPOST

Compost is the gardener's black gold—the perfect soil amendment and fertilizer. Its low nitrogen content provides the right amount of fertility for perennials. Too much nitrogen can cause weak, leggy growth that looks unattractive, flops over, and invites disease and insect invasions. If you've prepared your bed well before planting, compost is often the only fertilizer your perennials will need. Making your own compost is easy and fun, and it only takes 3 square feet of garden space.

Composting is controlled decomposition, with finished compost about halfway between fresh organic matter and humus. It works the same way as decomposition in the ground—beneficial decomposer microorganisms feed on nitrogen and carbon in the plant material, breaking it down. But because you're controlling the process, you can monitor the composting and speed it up, and because it's occurring above ground, it doesn't compete with your plants for nitrogen.

Materials for Your Pile

To make compost, just mix high-carbon and high-nitrogen materials and add air.

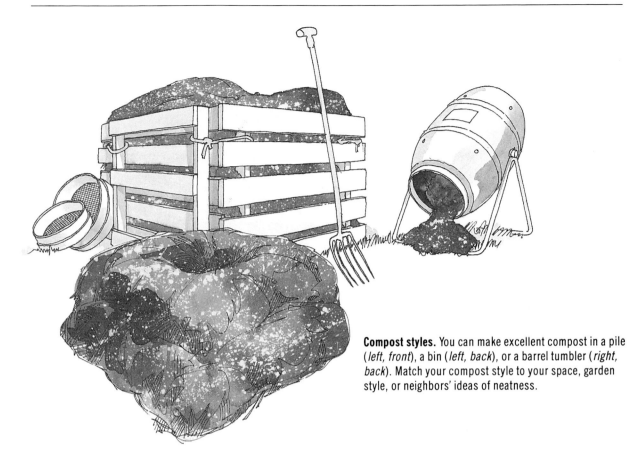

Compost styles. You can make excellent compost in a pile (*left, front*), a bin (*left, back*), or a barrel tumbler (*right, back*). Match your compost style to your space, garden style, or neighbors' ideas of neatness.

High-carbon materials are easy to recognize: They're the fibrous ones that take a while to break down. Straw, hay, leaves, sawdust, shredded newspaper, pine needles, hedge trimmings, and the woodier parts of perennials (like old daylily flowerstalks) are all high-carbon.

High-nitrogen materials are the succulent plant materials that break down quickly, like grass clippings, fresh weeds or perennial prunings, fruits, and vegetables. Other nitrogen sources you can add to balance the compost pile are farmyard manure, blood meal, chicken manure, cottonseed meal, and guano.

You can also add kitchen scraps like eggshells, vegetable and fruit peelings, coffee grounds, and tea leaves. Don't add dog droppings or the contents of the cat's litter box, both of which may carry disease, or meat

scraps, bones, or grease, which attract rodents and other scavengers. And don't add diseased plants to your pile—throw them out. Otherwise, you might be spreading disease along with your compost.

Siting and Building the Pile

Site your compost pile in a spot close to the garden—you want the compost within easy reach. You can make a simple pile, or build a wire or wooden bin for your compost. While the bin is more attractive, the pile blends in better with the landscape and is easier to work since you aren't restricted by the walls of the bin. If your garden features formal elements such as a picket fence, you might want to make compost bins to match.

Build your pile as materials become available. Add kitchen scraps after dinner, grass clippings after you mow the lawn, and the trimmings from shrubs after you finish pruning. Sprinkle thin layers of topsoil or finished compost throughout the pile to introduce the organisms that create compost. If you have a lot of grass clippings, mix fibrous materials, like shredded newspaper or straw, with them or add small amounts to the pile at a time. Large amounts of grass clippings can pack down and exclude air. Don't make the pile too tall, either. It needs air to "cook," or heat up, and a tall pile can pack down under its own weight. When that happens, anaerobic bacteria take over and turn your would-be compost into a smelly, slimy mess. Three feet tall and wide is the ideal size for a compost pile; when you've reached that size, just start another pile.

If you're not in a rush for compost, you can build a pile (or several) and let it compost on its own for a season. By the following year, you'll have beautiful, dark, crumbly compost with no further effort on your part.

Tricks for Quick Compost

If you need compost soon, there are tricks for speeding up the process. You can add more nitrogen, water the high-carbon layers to dampen (but not drown) them, and turn the pile every third day with a pitchfork to add more air. You can also shred or chop the high-carbon materials before adding them to the pile—the smaller the pieces, the quicker the process. All these techniques will make your pile cook faster, resulting in finished compost in as little as three weeks. (Remember that composting slows down in cold weather and speeds up when it's hot, so you'll get finished compost faster in hot weather.)

DIGGING AND DOUBLE DIGGING

Gardening is digging—digging out weeds, digging up plants to move or divide, digging in soil amendments. But the biggest digging job a perennial gardener faces is making a new flower bed or border. Unless you have heavy clay, digging a bed shouldn't be daunting—just remove the sod, turn over the soil, add organic matter, settle the bed, and you're ready to plant. If you do have heavy clay soil, you can use a special technique called double digging to improve drainage and aeration so you can have a beautiful perennial bed (see "Double Digging" on the opposite page).

Digging a New Bed

Before you make a new perennial bed or enlarge a bed or border, test the moisture content of the soil. Don't dig a bed when the soil is wet—you'll destroy the soil's structure, creating clods and compaction. Don't dig when the soil is powder-dry, either; this also destroys the soil's structure and can cause erosion. The best time to work the soil is when it's slightly moist.

When you're ready to dig, mark off the area with lime, flour, stakes and string, or even a garden hose. Then slice off the sod in the marked area by sliding a spade under the roots. (Sod makes great compost, or you can use it to patch sparse lawn areas.) Turn the soil to a spade or fork's depth. Add compost or other organic matter and any soil amendments, then work over the area again with your fork or spade to incorporate these materials and to break up clods. To settle the soil, water it several times.

The soil will settle on its own if you prepare the bed in fall for spring planting or in spring for fall planting, mulch it to keep out weeds, and let it sit until planting time. This waiting period is especially important if you're turning in fresh manure because it can burn plants; let it age in the soil for three or four weeks before planting, or better yet, compost it before using.

Perennial Beds and Problem Soils

If you have a loose, friable loam soil that's easy to turn over with a garden fork or spade, digging a perennial bed is a simple job. If you don't have good soil to begin with, analyze the problem before you jump in.

Help for Sandy Soils

If you have a high-sand soil that drains too fast, water carries nutrients out of the root zone before plants can take them up. Add large amounts of organic matter (shredded leaves, strawy manure, grass clippings, compost, and so on) to improve water- and nutrient-retention. The soil will be easy to work because sandy soils are generally loose.

If, on the other hand, your soil is so extremely sandy that you can't grow many of the perennials you'd like to have, you might want to consider raised beds. By creating raised beds of good topsoil and working in plenty of organic matter, you'll make a kind of giant planter for your perennials. Keep the plants watered, fed, and mulched, and your perennials will thrive.

Coping with Clay Soils

Your problem is more likely to be subsoil or heavy clay soil rather than sandy soil, though. If yours is the kind of soil that water just sits on rather than soaks into, and you can bend a spade trying to dig it, make raised beds as you would for super-sandy soil. (This works well with boggy soils, too, when it would cost too much to drain them.) If the soil is heavy and difficult but not impossible to work, and if water does eventually soak in rather than puddling up until it evaporates, try double digging.

Double Digging

Double digging is working the soil to twice the ordinary depth—two spades' depth rather than one. Double digging is hard work, but the results are worth it—you'll turn second-class soil into first-rate beds—and you only have to do it once for each bed. As with any digging, don't double dig when the soil is wet or bone-dry. Here's how to double dig.

1. Mark off the area to be worked, and remove the sod as you would for normal digging (see "Digging a New Bed" on the opposite page).

2. Starting at one end of the bed, dig a trench across the bed that's 1 foot wide and the depth of your spade (not including the handle). Pile the soil into a wheelbarrow or garden cart.

3. When you've removed the soil from the trench, work back across it with a garden fork, loosening (but not removing) the soil to the depth of the tines.

4. Repeat the procedure, creating a second trench next to the first. Move the soil from the second trench into the first trench.

5. Continue trenching and replacing soil in the trenches until you reach the end of the bed.

6. Use the soil in the wheelbarrow to fill the last trench.

7. Spread organic matter and any additional soil amendments over the bed, then work them into the top 4 to 6 inches of soil.

The loosened soil and added amendments will raise the level of your bed a few inches. Note that added organic matter is critical to the success of double digging; without it, you'll just have loosened heavy soil that will soon become compacted again.

WHAT TO DO ONCE THE PLANTS COME HOME

When you've made your beds and amended your soil, you're ready for plants. But often, you're not ready to plant when your perennials arrive in the mail or the minute you get home from the nursery. You don't have to plant right away, but there are things you can do to get your perennials off to a good start even before you put them in the ground. If you've bought container-grown plants at a garden center or nursery, care is simple: Don't let them dry out (this may mean watering every day—in summer, maybe twice a day), and set them out under trees or in another place where they'll be protected from full sun until you can plant them. Try to plant them as soon as possible.

Mail-order plants may arrive in containers or bareroot. The first thing to do when you get the box is open it; get those plants into the light and out of the cramped conditions of the box. When you take out your plants, they may look the worse for wear. Some may be shipped dormant and look mummified. But even the most wilted or battered specimen will revive quickly with a little coddling.

Care for Container-Grown Plants

If you've ordered container-grown plants, don't be surprised if the containers are smaller than you expect; even plants that are large when they mature are often shipped small. (This is *not* a bad thing; healthy, well-grown small plants will suffer less transplant shock and establish themselves faster than large plants.) The smaller the container, the more often you'll have to water. Don't put plants in small containers out in full sun, or you'll stress them and bring on wilting and dehydration. Keep them in partial shade until you can plant them, and try to get them in the ground as soon as you can.

Care for Bareroot Plants

Bareroot perennials need more initial care than container-grown plants, but otherwise they'll get established and grow just as vigorously. When you order bareroot plants, they usually come with the roots in peat, shredded wood, or some other protective substance. If you can plant right away, remove the protective material and soak the roots in a bucket of lukewarm water for 1 to 2 hours to rehydrate them before planting. If you must delay planting, keep the material damp (but not soggy) and keep the plants out of the sun until you can plant them. If your plants arrive without a protective covering on their roots, soak the roots to rehydrate them, and then cover them with moist potting soil or compost until you can plant.

Before planting, remove all protective material from your bareroot perennials and compost it; it would wick water away from the roots, causing them to dry out, if you put it in the planting hole. Remember that bareroot perennials have less holding capacity than container-grown plants; try to get them in the ground within three days of their arrival. If you have to wait longer than that, pot them up until you can plant them. And don't forget to keep the labels with the plants!

PUTTING IN
THE PLANTS

When you have a plan, a prepared bed, and your perennials, you're ready to plant. If you can, choose an overcast day for planting—hot sun stresses transplants. If you're planting container-grown perennials during the growing season, remember to set them out (pots and all) on the bed before you plant. Then you can make any last-minute design changes without having to dig up your plants.

Planting Container-Grown Perennials

Plant container-grown perennials a little higher than they sit in the pots if you're planting in newly prepared soil, since it will settle. In established beds, plant these perennials at the level at which they sit in the pots. Don't plant perennials deep, or the crowns will be buried and the plants will struggle or even die.

Start small. Plant one perennial at a time, rather than taking them all out of their pots and leaving them to dehydrate. And don't just grab a plant by the stem and pull it out of its pot. Instead, cover the surface of the pot with one hand, spreading your fingers over the soil on either side of the stem. Invert the pot so it's resting upside down on your hand, then pull off the pot. (If it doesn't pull off easily, tap or squeeze it a few times and try again. Really stubborn pots may have to be cut off.)

If the roots have filled the pot so tightly that they hold its shape once you've removed the pot, or if they circle the container, gently pull them loose or quarter the root ball before planting. To quarter the root ball, take a sharp knife or trowel, turn the plant upside down, and slice the root ball into four equal sections, stopping about an inch from the top of the soil ball. Spread the quarters out in the planting hole. This will make sure the roots grow out into the soil instead of remaining in a ball.

Planting Bareroot Perennials

Again, bareroot perennials are a bit trickier. Before you plant a bareroot perennial, cut off any dead, damaged, or diseased roots with sharp, clean scissors-style pruners or a sharp knife—dull blades will damage roots.

Mound soil in the bottom of the planting hole and spread the roots out so the crown rests on top of the mound. You'll have to tell from looking at the plant where the roots end and the crown begins. If you can see a soil line on the perennial, where stems or leaf bases change from green to yellow or white, plant it at the same depth as it grew in the nursery. If not, plant it so the soil comes up to, but not over, the crown. When you've filled in around the plant, pat the soil down firmly to create good contact between roots and soil. As with container-grown perennials, try to plant one at a time.

If you're adding plants to an established bed, dig a hole as wide as the roots are long. Try not to disturb the roots of adjacent perennials— make sure there's room for the new plant before you start digging.

Fibrous-Rooted Plants

If you're planting a fibrous-rooted perennial—one with lots of roots coming down from the crown—form a cone of soil in the center of the hole, making the cone high enough to position the crown at the surface of the soil. Snip off any damaged roots, then take the plant, turn it upside down, and shake it so the roots fall evenly on every side of the crown. Turn the plant over on top of the soil cone so that the roots spread out evenly rather than clumping. Add the remaining soil to the hole, tamp it down, and check to make sure the crown of the plant is at the right level.

Taprooted Plants

For taprooted perennials, which have one long root, you need a deep, narrow hole without a soil cone. Make this hole by inserting a trowel in the place you want your plant and pulling the trowel toward you to make a V-shaped incision. Slide the taproot into the hole, make sure the crown is at the correct level, and step on the soil beside the newly planted perennial to close the hole and tamp down the soil.

After You Plant

Whether you're planting bareroot or container-grown perennials, and no matter how many you're planting, keep the identification labels with the plants. Insert them firmly in the ground at the base of the plant, where you can find them but they'll be discreetly hidden as the plant grows. Don't lose them! Even the most detailed garden plan can't beat on-the-spot identification.

Once your plants are in the ground, water them in thoroughly. Keep an eye on them over the next few weeks and make sure they

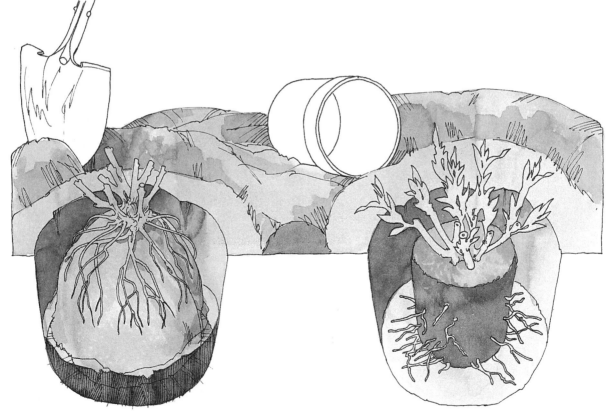

How to plant perennials. To plant a bareroot perennial (*left*), mound soil in the bottom of the planting hole and set the plant on top of the mound, spreading its roots down the sides. Fill in around the plant with soil. Plant these perennials at the same depth they grew in the nursery—don't

cover the crowns. Container-grown perennials (*right*) are a snap to plant. Plant them at the same depth they sit in the pot. If the surrounding soil is loose, plant them a little high. The plant will sink when the soil settles. If the plant is rootbound, loosen the root ball before planting.

stay watered and don't dehydrate. Otherwise, leave them alone until they start growing—don't fertilize them. They won't need additional nutrients until they're growing well. And never put fertilizer in the planting hole—it could burn the roots, and a nutrient boost is the last thing a stressed plant needs as it tries to recover from planting.

FERTILIZING

Once your perennials are in the ground and growing, you can consider fertilizing them. If you've faithfully improved the soil, they may not need more than a dose of compost and a spray of liquid seaweed or compost tea to perform well all season. However, if your beds have been in place for a few years or you're growing heavy feeders like peonies, delphiniums, and phlox, fertilizers can give your perennials a needed boost. But remember that it's easy to overfertilize perennials, especially with nitrogen, causing tender, lanky growth and fewer flowers. Moderation is the key here: See what your plants need, then give it to them.

Fertilizer Basics

To get the most from fertilizing, it helps to know a bit about plant nutrition. Fertilizers supply three major nutrients to plants—nitrogen (N), phosphorus (P), and potassium (K). If you buy a commercial fertilizer, the percentage of each of these key nutrients will be expressed as a ratio, called the NPK ratio. For example, if your bag says 1-2-2, the fertilizer contains 1 percent nitrogen, 2 percent phosphate (the form of phosphorus used by plants), and 2 percent potash (the form of potassium used by plants).

Different fertilizers have different NPK ratios, which is important because each of these major nutrients does something different for your plants. Nitrogen boosts vegetative growth—the leaves and stems. Phosphorus stimulates flower and fruit production. And potassium enhances root growth. Plants need all three of these nutrients to grow, but they may need different levels at different times—more nitrogen in springtime when growth starts, more phosphorus when they're flowering, and more potassium in fall when major root growth occurs. You can also match the NPK ratio to your soil's supply of these nutrients—for example, your soil may have enough potassium but need more nitrogen and phosphorus, so you'd want to choose a low-potassium fertilizer.

Choosing the Right Fertilizer

By knowing a fertilizer's NPK ratio, you can choose the best combination for your plants. For example, if you need to add a high-nitrogen fertilizer, you could choose blood meal, with a 10-0-0 NPK ratio; bat guano, at 10-3-1; or cottonseed meal, at 6-2-1. Good sources of phosphorus include bonemeal, with a 1-11-0 NPK ratio; colloidal phosphate, at 0-2-2; and rock phosphate, at 0-3-0. For potassium, you could add greensand, with a 0-0-7 NPK ratio; Sul-Po-Mag, at 0-0-22; or wood ashes, at 0-1.5-8. These and other good nutrient sources are listed in the "Perennial Gardener's Guide to Organic Fertilizers" on page 190, along with their suggested application rates. Balanced, pre-mixed organic fertilizers are also readily available from garden centers and mail-order catalogs.

Secondary and Trace Elements

In addition to the primary nutrients, perennials need secondary nutrients—calcium, magnesium, and sulfur—as well as trace quantities of micronutrients—boron, chlorine,

Are Your Perennials Missing Something?

If your plants have a nutrient deficiency, they may look stunted, or they may look as if they have a disease. Deficiency "diseases" are called disorders. Unless you see mold, rot, or another definite disease symptom on your plants, check this list for deficiency symptoms before concluding that your perennials are diseased.

If your plants' symptoms match one of the deficiencies in this table, turn to the "Perennial Gardener's Guide to Organic Fer-tilizers" on page 190 to find a source of the missing nutrient. But bear in mind that pH may be the real culprit: If your soil is alkaline, your plants may exhibit symptoms of iron, zinc, or phosphorus deficiency, while an acidic soil can cause magnesium, potassium, and boron deficiencies. Even though these nutrients are present in adequate quantities in the soil, they're "locked up," unavailable to your perennials. So bringing your pH closer to neutral may solve your deficiency problems.

Symptom	Deficiency
Leaves small; lower leaves turn pale-green; chlorosis (yellowing) follows; older leaves drop. Eventually, all leaves may turn yellow. Undersides of leaves may turn bluish purple.	Nitrogen
Plant grows slowly and becomes spindly and stunted; individual branches may die.	Nitrogen
Leaves small, but not chlorotic (yellowed). Undersides of leaves turn reddish purple in spots in the web of the leaf; color then spreads to entire leaf.	Phosphorus
Stems slender, fibrous, and hard; plants and roots may be stunted.	Phosphorus
Leaves small, turning dark-purple to black while young. Leaf petioles and midribs become thickened, curled, and brittle. Terminal shoots curl inward, turn dark, and die.	Boron
Lateral buds grow, then die, creating a bushy witches'-broom effect.	Boron

copper, iron, manganese, molybdenum, and zinc—to grow well. If your plants aren't getting enough of any of these essential elements, they'll let you know by showing deficiency symptoms—the plant may be stunted, or the leaves may turn yellow along the veins or even display purple blotches. (For a rundown of deficiency symptoms, see "Are Your Perennials Missing Something?" above.) Fortunately, many fertilizers also supply these elements, and some, such as seaweed and compost, supply all of the micronutrients.

If you've taken a soil test, the results will tell you how much nitrogen and so on to apply. If you don't have soil test recommendations to guide you, there are also general application guidelines for each fertilizer. (See the "Perennial Gardener's Guide to Organic Fertilizers" on page 190 for descriptions and application rates.) Calcium, magnesium, and sulfur are often supplied by materials you'd use to balance soil pH, like dolomitic lime-

Symptom	Deficiency
Leaves normal size, but new leaves and terminal branches deformed. Upper leaves may be dark-green, but they curl upward and leaf edges turn yellow, then leaves dry up and fall. Lower leaves normal.	Calcium
Stems fibrous and hard; roots short and brown.	Calcium
Plant wilts, becoming weak and flabby, even though it's adequately watered.	Calcium
Leaves small and/or mottled with yellow or necrotic (dead) areas.	Zinc
Internodes are shortened. Plant may form a rosette of leaves.	Zinc
Leaves normal size, but leaf margins of older leaves are tanned, scorched, or have black or brown necrotic (dead) spots. Leaf margins become brown and cup downward. Leaves are mottled with yellow and may turn ashen gray-green, bronze, or yellowish brown. Symptoms begin at the bottom of the plant and work up. Young leaves crinkle and curl.	Potassium
Roots are poorly developed and brown. Stems are slender, hard, and woody. Plants may be stunted.	Potassium
Leaves normal size, but veins of lower leaves remain dark-green while the area between veins turns yellow and then dark-brown. Leaves are brittle and curl upward. Tissue breaks down; leaves fall prematurely.	Magnesium
Leaves normal size. New leaves turn yellow, but chlorotic (yellowed) spots not usually followed by necrosis (dead tissue). Distinct yellow or white areas appear between veins; veins eventually become chlorotic. Symptoms are rare on mature leaves.	Iron

stone (usually sold as dolomite) and elemental sulfur.

Applying Fertilizers

Commercial organic fertilizers are usually packaged as a dry powder, though some may be pelleted. Spread these fertilizers around your plants before you mulch, then mulch over the fertilizers. If your beds are already mulched, pull the mulch back, fertilize, then replace the mulch. Don't dump fertilizer right on your plants—it's concentrated and could burn them. Some organic fertilizers, like fish emulsion and liquid seaweed, are sold in liquid form. Dilute them according to package directions and water them in, or use them as the base ingredient for foliar feeding.

Foliar Feeding

Foliar feeding is the best way to supply nutrients to your perennials quickly. Instead of

(continued on page 192)

Perennial Gardener's Guide to Organic Fertilizers

Organic fertilizers are gentle on the soil and good for your plants. Use blood meal, cottonseed meal, fish meal, guano, hoof and horn meal, leatherdust, or chicken manure if your perennials need nitrogen. Bonemeal, fish meal, guano, colloidal phosphate, rock phosphate, and wood ashes are good sources of phosphorus. If your perennials need more potassium, choose granite dust, greensand, langbeinite, seaweed, or wood ashes. Bonemeal, dolomite, gypsum, and wood ashes provide calcium; gypsum, langbeinite, and elemental sulfur are good sulfur sources. For trace minerals, choose materials like granite dust, greensand, guano, colloidal or rock phosphate, seaweed, or wood ashes. Don't apply more than the recommended amount of any of these additives; more is definitely *not* better where fertilizers are concerned.

Organic Fertilizer	Nutrients Supplied	Application Rate	Comments
Blood meal, dried blood	Blood meal: 15% nitrogen, 1.3% phosphorus, 0.7% potassium. Dried blood: 12% nitrogen, 3% phosphorus, 0% potassium.	Up to 3 lb. per 100 sq. ft. (more will burn plants).	Source of readily available nitrogen. Add to compost pile to speed decomposition. Repels deer and rabbits. Lasts 3–4 months.
Bonemeal	3% nitrogen, 20% phosphorus, 0% potassium, 24–30% calcium.	Up to 5 lb. per 100 sq. ft.	Excellent source of phosphorus. Raises pH. Lasts 6–12 months.
Cottonseed meal	6% nitrogen, 2–3% phosphorus, 2% potassium.	2–5 lb. per 100 sq. ft.	Acidifies soil, so it's best for plants that prefer low pH, or use it with bonemeal or wood ashes. Lasts 4–6 months.
Dolomite	90–100% MgCa $(CO_3)_2$ (51% calcium carbonate, 40% magnesium carbonate).	To raise pH one point, use 7 lb. per 100 sq. ft. on clay or sandy loam, 5½ lb. on sand, and 10 lb. on loam soil.	Raises pH and adds magnesium, which is needed for chlorophyll production and photosynthesis. Repeated use may cause magnesium excess. Also sold as Hi-Mag or dolomitic limestone.
Fish meal, fish emulsion	Fish meal: 10% nitrogen, 4–6% phosphorus, 0% potassium. Fish emulsion: 4% nitrogen, 4% phosphorus, 1% potassium.	Fish meal: up to 5 lb. per 100 sq. ft. Fish emulsion: dilute 20:1 water to emulsion.	Fish meal: Use in early spring, at transplanting, and anytime plants need a boost. Lasts 6–8 months. Fish emulsion: Apply as a foliar spray in early morning or evening. Distinctive smell. Also sold as fish solubles.
Granite dust	0% nitrogen, 0% phosphorus, 3–5% potassium, 67% silica; 19 trace minerals.	Up to 10 lb. per 100 sq. ft.	Very slowly available. Releases potash more slowly than greensand but lasts up to 10 years. Improves soil structure. Use mica-rich type only. Also sold as granite meal or crushed granite.

Organic Fertilizer	Nutrients Supplied	Application Rate	Comments
Greensand	0% nitrogen, 1% phosphorus, 5–7% potassium, 50% silica, 18–23% iron oxide; 22 trace minerals.	Up to 10 lb. per 100 sq. ft.	Slowly available. Lasts up to 10 years. Loosens clay soils. Apply in fall for benefits next season. Also sold as glauconite or Jersey greensand.
Guano, bat	8% nitrogen, 4% phosphorus, 2% potassium average, but varies widely; 24 trace minerals.	Up to 5 lb. per 100 sq. ft; 2 T. per pint of potting soil; 1 lb. per 5 gal. water for manure tea.	Caves protect guano from leaching, so nutrients are conserved.
Guano, bird	13% nitrogen, 8% phosphorus, 2% potassium; 11 trace minerals.	3 lb. per 100 sq. ft.	Also sold as Plantjoy.
Gypsum (calcium sulfate)	23–57% calcium, 17.7% sulfur.	Up to 4 lb. per 100 sq. ft.	Use when both calcium and sulfur are needed and soil pH is already high. Sulfur will tie up excess magnesium. Helps loosen clay soils.
Hoof and horn meal	14% nitrogen, 2% phosphorus, 0% potassium.	Up to 4 lb. per 100 sq. ft.	High nitrogen source but more slowly available than blood meal. Unpleasant smell. Takes 4–6 weeks to start releasing nitrogen; lasts 12 months.
Langbeinite	0% nitrogen, 0% phosphorus, 22% potassium, 22% sulfur, 11% magnesium.	Up to 1 lb. per 100 sq. ft.	Will not alter pH. Use when there is abundant calcium but sulfur, magnesium, and potassium are needed. Also sold as Sul-Po-Mag or K-Mag.
Leatherdust	5.5–12% nitrogen, 0% phosphorus, 0% potassium.	½ lb. per 100 sq. ft.	2% nitrogen is immediately available; rest releases slowly over growing season. Does not burn or leach.
Manure, chicken	1.3% nitrogen, 2.7% phosphorus, 1.4% potassium.	10 lb. per 100 sq. ft.	Good source of fast-release nitrogen. Use dry or compost; fresh chicken manure can burn plants.
Phosphate, colloidal	0% nitrogen, 18–22% phosphorus, 0% potassium, 27% calcium, 1.7% iron; silicas and 14 other trace minerals.	Up to 10 lb. per 100 sq. ft.	More effective than rock phosphate on neutral soils. Phosphorus availability higher (2% available immediately) than rock phosphate because of small particle size of colloidal clay base. Half the pH-raising value of ground limestone. Lasts 2–3 years.

(continued)

Perennial Gardener's Guide to Organic Fertilizers—Continued

Organic Fertilizer	Nutrients Supplied	Application Rate	Comments
Phosphate, rock	0% nitrogen, 33% phosphorus, 0% potassium, 30% calcium, 2.8% iron, 10% silica; 10 other trace minerals.	Up to 10 lb. per 100 sq. ft.	Releases phosphorus best in acid soils below pH 6.2. Slower release than colloidal phosphate. Will slowly raise pH 1 point or more. Also sold as phosphate rock.
Seaweed (kelp meal, liquid seaweed)	1% nitrogen, 0% phosphorus, 12% potassium; 33% trace minerals, including more than 1% of calcium, sodium, chlorine, and sulfur, and about 50 other minerals in trace amounts.	Meal: up to 1 lb. per 100 sq. ft. Liquid: dilute 25:1 water to seaweed for transplanting and rooting cuttings; 40:1 as booster.	Contains natural growth hormones. Best source of trace minerals. Lasts 6–12 months. Also sold as Thorvin Kelp, FoliaGro, Sea Life, Maxicrop, Norwegian SeaWeed, liquid kelp.
Sulfur	100% sulfur.	1 lb. per 100 sq. ft. will lower pH one point.	Lowers pH in alkaline soil. Ties up excess magnesium. Also sold as Dispersul.
Wood ashes	0% nitrogen, 0–7% phosphorus, 6–20% potassium, 20–53% calcium carbonate; trace minerals such as copper, zinc, manganese, iron, sodium, sulfur, and boron.	1–2 lb. per 100 sq. ft.	Nutrient amounts highly variable. Minerals highest in young hardwoods. Will raise soil pH. Put on soil in spring, and dig under. Do not use near young stems or roots. Protect ashes from leaching in winter. Lasts 12 or more months.

becoming available in solution in the soil—a process that can take years for some rock fertilizers—then being taken up by plant roots, the nutrients are absorbed directly through the leaves and can be used by the plant at once.

If your perennials are showing deficiency symptoms, use foliar feeding to provide a fast but temporary cure. First, identify the deficiency, then apply compost tea, manure tea, or fish emulsion directly to the leaves to correct major nutrient deficiencies, or apply liquid seaweed for micronutrient deficiencies. You can also buy fish-emulsion/seaweed combinations. For a long-term solution, amend the soil; meanwhile, foliar-feed as often as necessary to keep your plants growing and healthy.

When and How to Foliar-Feed

Even if your perennials don't have obvious deficiencies, they may start looking a bit peaked as the season wears on. And they'll flower better with a gentle boost when they're setting buds. If they have a long bloom season, they'll appreciate additional nutrients every two weeks during flowering. Foliar feeding is perfect for these uses.

To foliar-feed, choose a cloudy day, if possible, and fertilize in the morning or evening, when absorption is highest. If you're using a commercial organic fertilizer, dilute it according to package directions. If you want to make your own compost or manure tea, see the directions in "Tea Time for Your Plants" below. Use a clean plant sprayer turned to its finest setting, or a plant mister, and spray your perennials' leaves thoroughly, including the undersides of the leaves.

WATERING

There are two rules to keep in mind when it comes to watering perennials: When you need to water, water deeply, and put the water on the ground, not in the air or on the plants. If you break the rules, you'll end up with shallow-rooted, wilt-prone plants and mildewed foliage.

With a few exceptions, perennials like consistently (and preferably evenly) moist soil. In general, you need to water when the top inch or two of soil dries out and no rain is predicted. When you water, be sure to moisten the top 5 to 6 inches of soil to encourage deep root growth. Also, use a hose instead of a sprinkler, so you can direct the water to the base of the plants without wetting the foliage. (An even better alternative is drip or trickle irrigation; for more on this method, see "Drip Irrigation" on page 194.) Don't water in the evening, when the water will stay on your

---

Tea Time for Your Plants

Your perennials will find a bucket of manure or compost tea as refreshing as you find your morning cup, and it's just as easy to make. Put a shovelful of fresh or dried manure (or finished compost) in a burlap or cheesecloth bag. Tie the top closed and sink the sack in a large bucket or barrel of water. Cover the container, and steep the "tea" for one to seven days. (As with real tea, the longer it steeps, the stronger it is.)

Use compost tea full strength as a liquid fertilizer around your plants. Or dilute either tea and use it to give plants a boost when you water. (Don't use manure tea full strength or it may burn your plants.) You can also use manure or compost tea with drip irrigation systems if you filter it through cheesecloth or old pantyhose first so it doesn't clog the tubes. Manure and compost tea are both great for foliar feeding; for more on this technique, see "Foliar Feeding" on page 189.

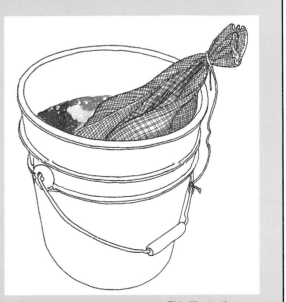

Making manure or compost tea. This illustration shows how easy it is to make "tea" for your plants—just like steeping a tea bag.

plants all night, encouraging fungal infections like powdery mildew. There is a third rule of perennial irrigation, where conditions permit: mulch. A mulch will slow down soil water evaporation, but it won't stop it completely. (For more on mulch, see "Much Ado about Mulch" on the opposite page.)

Drip Irrigation

Drip irrigation systems are ideal for perennial beds because you don't have to disturb the plants or beds to use them. Just lay one down after you plant your bed, or snake it between plants in an established bed. Mulch over the hoses and you have an invisible, but very effective, watering system. You won't waste water since very little will be lost to evaporation, and the water will go where it does the most good—in the soil of the root zone. Another benefit is that, because the water oozes out slowly but evenly, it saturates the soil rather than puddling or running off. You can also use drip systems in the evening or at night, since they don't wet the foliage.

Drip irrigation benefits the gardener as well as the garden. You won't have to haul out a hose every time you need to water, then run back and forth moving it every 10 minutes, battering plants as you drag the hose over them. Instead, you just turn on the faucet and relax.

The first time you use drip irrigation, you'll need to fine-tune your watering time. Start when the soil is dry. Check the soil every hour—just stick a finger into it. When the soil is moist 5 to 6 inches deep at the far edge of the hose's range, turn off the faucet and record the amount of time it was on. This will be a good guideline for future watering. Since you'll only be watering for a few hours at a time, you can disconnect the system from the faucet when it's not in use, or disconnect the hose at

the end of the bed so the connector hose isn't trailing across the lawn.

Soaker Hoses

The simplest and least expensive drip system is a soaker hose, a black rubber hose (usually made from recycled tires) with pinpoint holes all over it. The hose attaches to a regular garden hose and water oozes out of all the holes as long as the water is on, irrigating an area about 2 to 3 feet wide along the hose's length. A plug keeps the water from running out the end of the hose. You can buy soaker hoses through garden centers and mail-order garden supply catalogs in 25- to 250-foot lengths. (For longer hoses, simply screw several together.) Suppliers also sell flow and pressure regulators for the longer hoses.

To use a soaker hose, attach it to a length of garden hose that runs between your faucet and your perennial bed. If your bed is 5 × 25 feet, you'll need at least 50 feet of soaker hose. Run the soaker hose up one side of the bed about 1½ feet from the edge, turn it about a foot from the end of the bed, and run it back down the other side, again about 1½ feet from the edge. When you've got the hose down the way you want it, cover it with mulch so it will "disappear" into the bed. You can leave the hose in place all season, then drain and store it over the winter.

A Drip System

A drip irrigation system is more complex, but more precise, than a soaker hose. Instead of soaking the ground around the hose, these plastic hoses deliver water directly to the base of each plant through a thin plastic pipe called a spaghetti tube. An emitter at the end of the tube delivers water or liquid fertilizer solution slowly and evenly.

Drip systems can have timers, pressure regulators, filters, and feeder tubes for fish

Soaker hose

Drip irrigation system

Soaker hoses and drip irrigation. For small beds, soaker hoses (*left*) are great, releasing water slowly and evenly to the whole bed. Cover the hoses with mulch to conserve moisture. For large beds, use a drip system (*right*), which delivers water through spaghetti tubes directly to the base of each plant.

emulsion or other liquid fertilizers. Better systems allow you to attach the spaghetti tubes precisely where they'll reach your plants. And unlike soaker hoses, drip systems can branch, eliminating multiple hose lines down the beds. A drawback of drip irrigation, besides the cost, is the tendency of emitters to clog from hard water or fertilizer buildup, but you can soak them in vinegar to clear them.

If you decide to invest in a drip system, explore the market carefully. There are many systems available through garden centers and specialty catalogs. Familiarize yourself with the types offered, and choose the system that suits your budget and garden best. Most drip systems can be installed under mulch like soaker hoses, so they're less visible. And like soaker hoses and garden hoses, drip systems are durable.

MUCH ADO ABOUT MULCH

Mulch has come into its own as a prime garden problem-solver. After good soil, mulch does more for plants than any other additive or technique. Here are the major benefits of mulch:

▶ Mulch conserves water, so mulched soil stays more evenly moist, stays moist longer, and requires less frequent watering.

▶ Mulch keeps down weeds, since many weed seeds need light to germinate, so you save weeding time.

▶ Organic mulches add humus and some nutrients to the soil as they break down.

▶ Mulch keeps soil and nutrients from washing away during hard rains.

▶ Mulch keeps soil temperatures more even, protecting plant roots and beneficial soil organisms against violent swings in soil temperature. This is especially critical in winter, when unmulched soil is prone to freezing and thawing, causing frost heaving and exposing sensitive roots to freezing air and drying out.

In addition, mulch protects plants from some soilborne diseases and nematodes that could splash up onto the foliage when it rains or you water your plants. It keeps dirt off your plants, so they stay clean and attractive. Pale mulches like straw can reflect light back onto foliage. But the main benefit of mulch to many gardeners is aesthetic—it just looks good. To make sure it looks attractive but also provides the other benefits that have made it famous, use mulch with moderation. Don't bury your perennials in a mound of mulch. Two to 3 inches is plenty. When the mulch begins to break down, turn it into the soil, or remove and compost it. Replace it with fresh mulch.

Types of Mulch

Actually, one of the best mulches you can use is simply a thick covering of plants over the soil. A thickly planted garden, where foliage shades the ground and there are no bare patches of soil, provides all the advantages of other types of mulch. The plant cover helps retain water, protects the soil, and keeps down weeds. When the garden dies down in fall, you need to apply a winter mulch to protect the plants. By the time the winter mulch decomposes in late spring, the foliage will once again have taken over as a living mulch.

There are two categories of applied mulch: organic and inorganic. Organic mulches are made from plants: shredded leaves, bark or wood chips, straw and hay, newspapers,

compost, and so on. Inorganic mulches include plastics, pebbles, and landscape fabrics (also called geotextiles).

Inorganic mulches are most useful in the landscape and the vegetable garden: Black plastic heats up the soil and suppresses weeds, clear plastic can be used to solarize the soil, while landscape fabrics prevent erosion on slopes and are used to keep weeds down around shrubs. Water can't soak through a plastic mulch (many gardeners lay irrigation systems under the plastic), but landscape fabrics are water-permeable. Landscape fabric works best when it's set in place and not removed (as it would be when you're transplanting or dividing plants). Moving the fabric can cause it to tear and may also injure established roots. Pebbles, bark, or wood chips can be used to disguise plastics and landscape fabrics, making them look more natural.

For the perennial garden, organic mulches are best. They hold in soil moisture, keep down weeds, and add organic matter to the soil as they decompose. Don't overlook local materials when you're choosing a mulch. Nearly everyone has leaves they can shred, and they make an ideal mulch. In areas where they are readily available, cocoa hulls or peanut shells make an excellent, affordable, and attractive mulch. If you decide to use shredded wood chips or bark, such as those available free from tree trimmers, it's best to compost them for a year by just letting them sit in an out-of-the-way spot before using them. That way, they can begin to decompose and aren't so sharp and hard to work with when you apply them. For an overview of the use and advantages of other organic mulches, see "More on Mulch" on the opposite page.

Consider attractiveness when you're choosing a mulch: The perennial garden is, first and foremost, ornamental. Newspaper is a good mulch material, since it's readily available,

More on Mulch

These are the best mulches for perennial gardens. All of them will biodegrade over time, adding humus to the soil. They provide mulch's other benefits as well—retaining moisture and suppressing weeds. Shredded leaves, compost, and pine needles are the most attractive, while newspaper and straw are most readily available (of course, leaves are abundant in fall). Grass clippings will give your perennials a nitrogen boost. But they break down fast and are best used to supplement more stable mulches in areas where appearance is not so important.

Material	Primary Benefits	When to Apply	How to Apply
Compost	Adds humus. Suppresses weeds. Fertilizes. Warms soil.	At planting time and as needed throughout the season.	Spread 1″ or more as a top-dressing around plants.
Grass clippings	Add nitrogen and humus.	At planting time and as needed throughout the season.	Apply a 1″–4″ layer around plants. May burn plants if placed too close to stems.
Leaves, shredded	Add humus. Suppress weeds well. Modulate soil temperature.	At planting time and as winter cover.	Apply in 3″ layers; best if chopped and composted.
Newspaper	Suppresses weeds well. Retains moisture.	At planting time.	Lay down whole sections of the paper and anchor with soil or stones, or shred paper and apply 4″–6″ layers. Use under more attractive mulches.
Pine needles	Attractive. Suppress weeds well. Some control of fungal diseases.	At planting time and as winter cover.	Apply in 2″–4″ layers. Needles tend to acidify soil; don't use around non-acid-loving plants.
Straw	Adds humus. Suppresses weeds well. Cools soil.	At planting time and as winter cover.	Lay down 8″ layers around but not touching plants. May tie up nitrogen in soil; oat straw best.
Wood or bark chips, shredded	Attractive. Suppress weeds well. Cool soil and retain water.	At planting time and as needed throughout the season.	Best to compost before using. Apply in 1″–2″ layer.

holds water, and biodegrades, but if you use it, cover it with something more appealing, like a thick layer of shredded leaves or shredded wood or bark chips.

There are also some organic mulches to avoid, like sawdust and peat moss. Sawdust has several drawbacks: It's unattractive, it's often splintery and hard to work through, and it steals soil nitrogen from your perennials as it breaks down, causing poor plant growth. Peat forms a hard, dry crust on the soil, making it hard for water and nutrients to get through. It's also acidic, lowering soil pH as it leaches. If you'd like a lower pH in your perennial bed, incorporate the peat into the soil—don't use it on top.

Applying Mulch

The best time to put a winter mulch on your beds or to mulch fall transplants is when the soil cools and the plants have been killed back by a hard frost. Good materials for winter mulch are pine needles, shredded leaves, and straw that's free of weed seeds. (Don't use unshredded leaves, which can pack down and encourage disease.) But the best material for winter mulch is snow, a natural insulator. Don't be afraid to pile it up on your beds for a uniform winter cover. Follow nature's example: Put down your leaves or other mulch, then add a snow blanket.

In spring, pull back a winter mulch until the soil has warmed, then pull it back up to—but not over—the plants. This is important when setting out transplants as well. If you cover the crowns of the plants with mulch, you'll encourage crown rot, and mulching up to the stems of tender transplants creates an ideal environment for cutworms. So leave a mulch-free ring about 1 inch out from the crown.

As summer wears on, mulches may begin to break down, since they'll compost under the surface layer. Watch organic mulches through the summer and renew them when they start to look thin. This is especially important in the Deep South, where high heat and humidity combine to create rapid decomposition.

WEEDING WISELY

Weeding is a fact of life in the perennial garden. It will be easier and more effective if you start weeding as soon as you see a problem and then continue to monitor for any new weeds. Control is much more difficult if you let the weeds take over the garden and then try to bring the situation under control in one marathon weeding session.

Here are some surefire ways to minimize your weeding chores:

▶ Mulch your garden. Mulch not only suppresses weed germination and growth, it also makes those weeds that do turn up easier to pull, since the soil stays soft and moist beneath the mulch.

▶ Get out the whole weed the first time. A lot of weeds can spread from a tiny piece of root or stem left in the ground, and taprooted weeds like dandelions grow back if you don't take out the whole taproot.

▶ Don't let weeds set seed. Some perennials like coneflowers, alliums, and ornamental grasses self-sow so enthusiastically that they fall into the weed category here, too. If you don't plan to start your own nursery, cut their flower heads before the seed ripens and drops.

▶ Don't bring potential weed problems (like uncomposted manure, which may carry weed seeds, and seed-rich hay) into the garden with you. Always specify weed-free straw or hay if you use them in your garden.

▶ Don't compost mature weed seed heads. A really hot compost pile will kill weed seeds, but you can't guarantee that the seeds will be in the hottest part of the pile or that your pile will get hot enough. It's better to throw them out than to spread weeds along with your compost.

Even if you use these preventive tactics, you'll have weeds. There are weed seeds, roots, and crowns already in your soil. Birds, wind, and even pets can bring in weed seeds from outside. But only 5 to 10 minutes a day can keep weeds in a mulched perennial garden under control, even if the garden is fairly large. The key to effective weeding is persistence. A year-round weeding program saves time and labor in the long run. Weed in winter, when

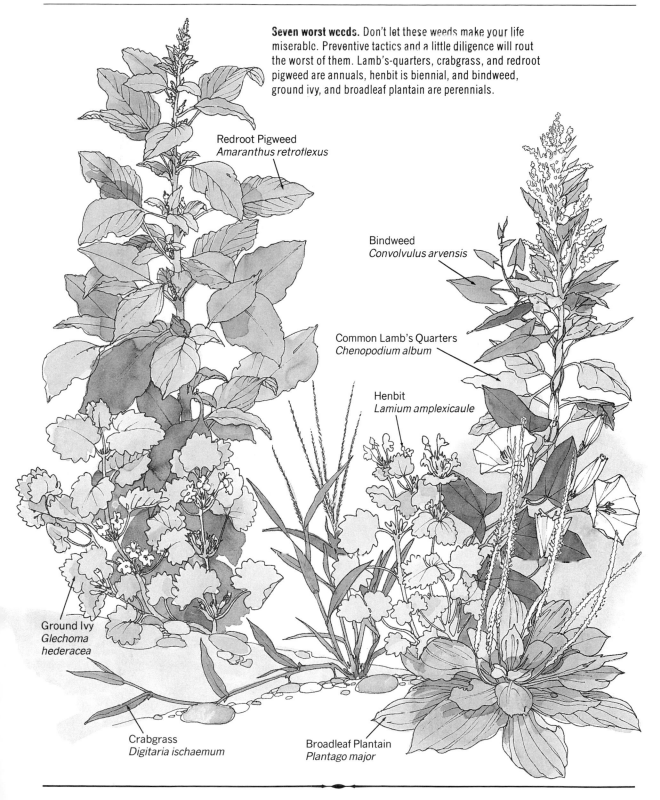

Seven worst weeds. Don't let these weeds make your life miserable. Preventive tactics and a little diligence will rout the worst of them. Lamb's-quarters, crabgrass, and redroot pigweed are annuals, henbit is biennial, and bindweed, ground ivy, and broadleaf plantain are perennials.

Redroot Pigweed
Amaranthus retroflexus

Bindweed
Convolvulus arvensis

Common Lamb's Quarters
Chenopodium album

Henbit
Lamium amplexicaule

Ground Ivy
Glechoma hederacea

Crabgrass
Digitaria ischaemum

Broadleaf Plantain
Plantago major

the soil tends to be damp and weed seedlings are vulnerable, as well as throughout the growing season.

Types of Weeds

Like flowers, there are annual, biennial, and perennial weeds. Each group poses its own control problems, so you can control weeds more effectively if you know which group they fall into.

Annual Weeds

Annual weeds, like lamb's-quarters, wild mustard, pigweed, purslane, crabgrass, and ragweed, live only a season. But they produce thousands of seeds, guaranteeing success through strength of numbers. Most garden weeds will be annuals. Control them by pulling them before they flower and set seed.

Biennial Weeds

Biennial weeds, like mullein and Queen-Anne's-lace, form a rosette of leaves their first season. The following year, they flower, set seed, and die. Control them by looking for their rosettes and removing them the first season. If you miss some, pull them the second season before they set seed.

Perennial Weeds

Perennial weeds include dandelion, bindweed, dock, wild garlic, ground ivy, plantain, pokeweed, and wood sorrel. Some of the worst perennial weeds are grasses, including Johnson-grass and quack grass. They live for years, set seed, have deep, persistent root systems, and often have creeping stems as well, so a single plant can send up offspring all over the perennial bed. The same is true for woody weeds like poison ivy and multiflora roses. To control these difficult weeds, dig carefully to try to remove as much of the root

system as possible. Then pull up the plants that grow from the pieces you've missed. Don't give up; persistence will pay off.

Rooting Out Weeds

Hand weeders will help you get the better of really stubborn weeds. A dandelion weeder (also called an asparagus fork), with a blade like a snake's forked tongue, is great for rooting out deep taproots without disturbing nearby perennials. You can use a three-tined hand cultivator to shallowly disturb soil between perennials, uprooting weed seedlings. And bent-bladed pavement weeders will remove weeds in cracks between bricks or flagstones, which are notoriously hard to hand-pull. There's even a soap-based organic herbicide, SharpShooter. It's a last resort, though, since it will kill your perennials if it gets on them. It's also most effective on seedling weeds; for mature weeds, you're better off digging.

STAKING

Gardening with perennials means gardening for beauty. Many plants are beautiful whether their stems are straight, curved, or trailing. But there's nothing attractive about delphiniums or glads pitched flat on their faces after a high wind, or the peonies you'd been waiting for bent facedown in the mud after a hard rain. An entire season can be ruined by a single violent storm. Some perennials—usually the ones with tall flower spikes or full, heavy flowers—are especially prone to toppling.

The solution to flopped flowers is staking. If this brings to mind giant tomato stakes or cages, remember that you want to see the flowers, not the stakes. If you've chosen the right kind of staking for each plant and done a good job, the stakes should disappear in the bed's foliage. The only sign of good staking is that the plants remain upright.

Staking Tall Flowers

Match the kind of staking you use to the plant's growth habit. For perennials with tall, slender bloom stalks like foxgloves (*Digitalis* spp.) and delphiniums, use a tall, slender branch, a slender bamboo cane, or a dark-green plastic "cane" for each stalk. Insert the stakes as soon as you see the bloom stalks emerging. Place the stake as close to the stalk as you can without damaging the plant's crown, and push it deep enough into the ground so a storm won't knock it over. (The final height of the stake should be about 6 inches shorter than the mature bloom stalk.)

The best way to tie the bloom stalk to the stake is with a loop, so you don't put pressure on the stem or even cut or snap it off as it grows. Put soft string, yarn, or a fabric strip around the stem, turn it to form a loop or circle, then tie it to the stake. As the stem grows taller, add more ties as needed.

Plant Frames for Bushy Flowers

For perennials like peonies, chrysanthe-mums, and bleeding hearts that have a bushy habit, circular plant frames are ideal. These are circles of wire with three or four wire legs that hold the entire plant upright. Again, set them out over the plant when growth begins, pushing them deeply into the ground and avoiding the crown. As the plant grows, gently pull stray stems back into the circle. An alternative is putting four stakes around the plant and connecting them with string to make a frame.

Supporting Airy Flowers

Some perennials, like baby's-breaths, artemisias, and yarrows, have an airy habit but still tend to fall over. Support them with

---

Perennials at Stake

The perennials listed below are especially prone to flopping and are therefore good candidates for staking. Stake each flower spike of hollyhocks, delphiniums, foxgloves, glads, lilies, and lupines. Grow yarrows, asters, baptisias, hardy mums, blanket flowers, heleniums, peonies, and sages in a wire ring or cage. And use twiggy brush or a branch-and-string "web" to hold up coreopsis and baby's-breath.

Achillea spp. (yarrows)
Alcea spp. (hollyhocks)
Aster spp. (asters)
Baptisia australis (blue false indigo)
Chrysanthemum × *morifolium* (garden mum)
Coreopsis spp. (coreopsis)
Delphinium spp. and hybrids (delphiniums)
Digitalis spp. (foxgloves)
Gaillardia × *grandiflora* (blanket flower)
Gladiolus spp. (glads)
Gypsophila paniculata (baby's-breath)
Helenium spp. (sneezeweeds)
Lathyrus latifolius (perennial sweet pea)
Lilium spp. (lilies)
Lupinus hybrids (lupines)
Paeonia lactiflora hybrids (common garden peonies)
Salvia spp. (sages)

---

slender, twiggy branches set into the ground around the plant's perimeter. Another effective staking system for these ferny or feathery plants is a network of slender branches or stakes with a netting of string woven between them. Again, place these supports when growth begins. Dark string will be less obtrusive than white.

A More Relaxed Look

If you don't want stakes in your garden, you can avoid them by using one of several

Three standard methods of staking. Match your staking method to each plant's growth habit: Use a single stake per bloom stalk for perennials with heavy flower spikes, like this delphinium (*left*). Plants with airy habits, like coreopsis (*center*), do best staked with twiggy brush. Hold up bushy plants with heavy flowers, like peonies (*right*), by growing them in a wire ring. The foliage will hide the stakes as the plants grow.

strategies. The keys to their success are planning ahead and knowing your plants' habits. One way to avoid staking is by selecting lower-growing plants that don't fall over. You can also design your border with an English or cottage-garden feel, allowing plants like asters to sprawl and encouraging perennials like boltonia (*Boltonia asteroides*) and coreopsis (*Coreopsis* spp.) to weave their feathery branches over and through surrounding plants. Results can be surprising and delightful.

Planting perennials closer together can also provide natural staking—a peony is less likely to be bent to the ground by a storm if it has Siberian iris (*Iris sibirica*) on either side. Giving plants the right cultural conditions can also make them sturdier, requiring less staking.

Yarrows will grow leggy and fall over in a shady site with rich soil, but will stay compact and upright in full sun and average to poor soil. Baptisias (*Baptisia* spp.) will become spindly and need staking in shade, but grow bushy in full sun and rich soil. Check your plants' cultural requirements in the encyclopedia section, and give them what they need.

GROOMING

Some gardens look better than others, even when their gardeners are growing the same plants. If plant selection and cultural conditions are similar, plant grooming is usually the reason a garden looks better. Grooming is the finishing touch for perennials.

And fortunately, grooming techniques—thinning, pinching, disbudding, and deadheading—are easy and fast. But grooming provides more than a tidy garden. It can change the shape of your plants, double your bloom, or produce huge, showy flowers.

Thinning

Thinning is removing some of the stems of dense, bushy plants to let in light and air circulation. This technique helps prevent mildew on susceptible plants like garden phlox (*Phlox paniculata*), bee balm (*Monarda didyma*), and delphiniums. Thin in spring by cutting or pinching out stems at soil level. Thin each plant to the four or five strongest shoots, leaving 2 to 4 inches between each stem.

Pinching

Pinching creates more compact, bushier plants, prevents flopping, and ensures more bloom. To pinch a plant, start in late spring or early summer. With forefinger and thumb, pinch out the tips of the stems. From each pinched stem, two branches will grow. You can pinch again a few weeks later for even bushier plants with still more flowers, but don't pinch after flower buds are set or you'll cut off flowers rather than encouraging them.

If you aren't sure when to pinch your perennials, keep these basic guidelines in mind. For fall-blooming plants like mums, you'll need to stop pinching around the first of July so that the plants can set flower buds for fall bloom. Pinch plants that bloom in late spring or summer once or twice in early spring, so you don't risk removing the flower buds by pinching later. Experiment by pinching one or two stems on different plants, and note the results in your garden journal so that you'll know what to do the following year. But don't pinch an entire plant if you're not sure

---

Pinch These Perennials!

Curb the often-leggy habit of these perennials by pinching back the stems when growth takes off in spring. You'll be rewarded with compact growth and heavier flowering.

Artemisia spp. (artemisias)
Aster spp. (asters)
Boltonia asteroides (boltonia)
Chelone lyonii (pink turtlehead)
Chrysanthemum spp. (chrysanthemums)
Helianthus spp. (sunflowers)
Lobelia spp. (lobelias)
Lychnis spp. (campions)
Monarda didyma (bee balm)
Phlox paniculata (garden phlox)
Physostegia virginiana (obedient plant)
Salvia spp. (sages)
Sedum spp. (sedums)

---

it's the right time; it's better to have a leggy plant that blooms than a compact one that doesn't.

Pinching produces more flowers, but the individual flowers will be slightly smaller than those from an unpinched plant. If you want extra-large, fair-prize-size flowers, the technique for you is disbudding.

Disbudding

Like pinching, disbudding is a simple technique: Where one bud is larger than the others in a cluster, pinch out the smaller buds and just leave the largest. Disbudding will give you showy results on plants like peonies and roses. Don't use this technique on spike-blooming perennials like delphiniums and lobelias (*Lobelia* spp.), since a single large flower on the top of a denuded flower spike wouldn't be ornamental. However, you can

Pinching, disbudding, and deadheading. Pinch out the growing tips of each stem of perennials like this chrysanthemum (*left*) for bushier plants with more flowers. To disbud perennials like this dahlia (*center*) for fewer but larger blooms, pinch out side buds, leaving only the central or highest bud in each cluster. Deadhead flowers like this daylily (*right*) by pinching or cutting off spent flowers.

pinch out smaller side spikes of perennials like delphiniums and monkshoods (*Aconitum* spp.) for a larger central spike.

Deadheading

Deadheading is a gruesome name for a very useful technique—removing spent flowers. Some perennials deadhead themselves, dropping old flowers unobtrusively to the ground. But the brown, papery ruins of other flowers will spoil your pleasure in a perennial border unless you take them off regularly. (Daylilies and bearded irises are prime offenders.)

Deadheading provides your perennials with more than good looks, though. It's an important maintenance technique for several reasons.

▶ Flowers usually fade after pollination, so if you leave them on the plant, you're encouraging seed formation. This robs the plant of vigor, since it takes a great deal of the plant's energy to mature seed. By deadheading, you'll allow the plant to channel that energy back into flower, leaf, and root production.

▶ Removing spent flowers (and potential seeds) keeps invasive perennials from self-sowing all over your garden—always an unwelcome surprise the following season.

▶ Deadheading often extends the bloom season, since the plants will keep flowering rather than stopping after the first flush, as they would if they had set seed. In fact, if you shear back some plants after blooming, you'll often get a second flush of bloom later in the season.

You can deadhead as you're weeding, throwing the spent flowers into a bucket with the weeds, then taking it all off to the compost pile. As with weeding, it pays to keep up with deadheading. Don't let it get away from you.

If there's more than one flower on a single stalk and the flowers open at different times, like daylilies, carefully snap off the faded blooms with your fingers or trim them off with garden shears. With plants like yarrows that bear one flower head on the end of each stalk, cut the stalks at or near the ground when the flowers fade.

Some spring-blooming plants get leggy by midsummer and benefit from harsher treatment. This is especially true of mat-forming plants such as wall rock cress (*Arabis caucasica*), perennial candytuft (*Iberis semper-virens*), and moss pinks (*Phlox subulata*). After bloom, shear these perennials back to half their former height. Besides keeping them from sprawling, cutting back hard sometimes results in a second flush of bloom later in the season.

Some plants like ornamental grasses and coneflowers (*Rudbeckia* and *Echinacea* spp.) have attractive seed heads that you may want to leave on the plants for winter interest. Deadhead these plants in early spring before growth resumes.

WINTER PROTECTION

In areas where the temperature drops below freezing, your plants need winterizing as much as your car. Begin in fall with a thorough cleanup. After frosts have killed back your plants, cut them back to the ground and compost the trimmings. (Throw out diseased trimmings rather than composting them.) When the ground is cold, give your plants a winter mulch. (For more on winter mulching, see "Applying Mulch" on page 198.) Water the garden thoroughly whenever the soil is dry but not frozen—drought is actually a bigger threat to most perennials than cold.

Plan for Protection

There are commonsense measures you can take all year to help your perennials face winter. First, site your garden in a protected place where winds won't roar over it, dropping temperatures and drying out the ground. (This is even more critical if you leave four-season perennials like ornamental grasses and cone-flowers standing in winter to add landscape interest.) If the only place you can grow peren-nials is exposed, add extra protection like pine branches over your mulch, and consider investing in a fence or shrub border to block the wind and provide permanent protection.

Check Plant Hardiness

Next, make sure the perennials you grow are hardy in your area. Check the USDA Plant Hardiness Zone Map on page 169 to find your zone. (Since climate varies so much regionally, it's wise to discuss your immediate area with gardening neighbors or your local garden club. They can tell you if your garden might be a zone warmer or colder than the base zone shown on the map.) Then look up the perennials you want to plant in the encyclo-pedia section or in mail-order plant catalogs to make sure they're hardy in your zone.

If you'd like to try growing perennials that are hardy in the next zone down but question-able in yours, site them in your warmest, most protected place (like in front of a south-facing wall), mulch heavily over winter, and hope for

the best. In areas with consistent snow cover, plants can often survive farther north than in warmer zones with uneven winter conditions. If you want to grow tender perennials (those that definitely won't overwinter outdoors in your area), either treat them like annuals or pot them up and bring them in for the winter.

Avoid These Mistakes

Finally, avoiding two common mistakes can give your perennials a better chance of survival. First, don't fertilize your plants after they stop active growth in late summer. Give them time to prepare for dormancy, rather than pushing them to grow tender, leafy shoots into the fall. Overfertilizing is one of the main reasons plants don't survive the winter. Second, don't ignore drainage problems. Waterlogged soil causes rotten roots and crowns and is another reason plants often don't survive the winter. Your goal, summer and winter, is moist but well-drained soil. Prepare your garden soil with lots of organic matter before you put in plants, and keep mulch pulled back from

Plan for protection. If you live in a cold-winter area or on a flat, exposed site that's windy, plan to place your borders in a protected spot. Plant them on the south side of a wall, hedge, or fence, or where a dip in the landscape will offer some shelter. (Remember, snow is good insulation.) If you grow perennials in sheltered sites like the one shown at left, you can often gamble successfully on plants that are normally hardy a zone warmer than your garden. If you leave your plants exposed like the garden on the right, you'll be lucky if perennials that are normally hardy in the next-coldest zone come through the winter.

plant crowns. If you think you have a drainage problem, site your garden elsewhere or consider raised beds.

Welcoming Spring

Don't succumb to the need to see green and pull back your winter mulch on the first warm day. When days are reliably warm, carefully remove the mulch, watching for tender shoots that are easy to damage or snap off. Leave the mulch alongside the bed so you can pull the "blanket" back over it if freezing temperatures threaten. You may have to remove and replace the mulch several times before the weather evens out. Once the weather has moderated and growth has begun, take your winter mulch to the compost pile.

THE PERENNIAL GARDENER'S TOOLSHED

You can have a wonderful perennial garden with only three tools: a trowel, a garden fork, and a bucket. The trowel will take care of planting, transplanting, weeding, and other close work. The garden fork is for digging and double-digging beds, compost turning, lifting and dividing perennials, mulching, and other heavy chores. And the bucket does everything else: It carries water or soil amendments; holds cut flowers, trimmings, or weeds; and even provides a crude seat for the worn-out gardener.

Of course, a few more tools are helpful. A shovel is good for digging and soil lifting. You can carry a lot more in a wheelbarrow or garden cart than you can in a bucket. And a hose or irrigation system beats a bucket for watering any day. Hedge shears, scissors, and hand pruners are helpful for cutting flowers, shearing back plants, and pruning off dead or diseased stems. And stakes and string are great for propping and tying up floppy perennials.

Buy Well-Made Tools

Tools are like clothes: Cheap ones wear out fast, but good ones last. Whether your tool collection has outgrown your garage or you have only a trowel and spade by the back door, make sure your essential tools are well-made and well-maintained. Good tools make work easier and faster. Having a spade break off in the middle of planting is a high price to pay for choosing a shoddy tool. (For more on choosing good tools, see "How to Choose a Quality Tool" on the opposite page.)

Earth-Working Tools

When you're getting ready to dig or enlarge a perennial bed, carve out a path, or

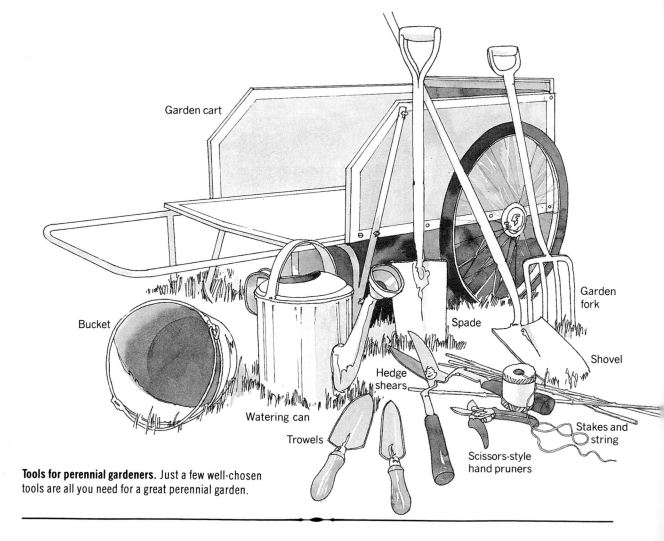

Tools for perennial gardeners. Just a few well-chosen tools are all you need for a great perennial garden.

How to Choose a Quality Tool

Even in this age of instant breakdown, a tool can still last a lifetime—if it's a good tool, and if you use it for its intended purpose. (Levering out boulders can break even the best garden fork.) The best tool isn't necessarily the most expensive, but it certainly isn't the cheapest. Here are some things to look for—and things to avoid—when you're tool shopping.

Handles. The best wood for a tool handle is white ash, which is strong and light. Check the grain of the wood when you're looking at a handle. The lines should run up and down the length of the handle, not from side to side or in irregular patterns, which can cause breakage. Don't buy handles that have knots in the wood—they also weaken the handle. And pass up tools with painted handles, which can hide cheap wood or bad grain lines. If the tool has a short handle with a grip on top, make sure the grip is sturdy and you can see that it's securely fastened to the handle, not stuck on.

Sockets. The socket is the metal "collar" that attaches the blade to the handle. Avoid tools that have jagged rivets or sharp edges on the socket. Choose solid-socket rather than open-socket construction. In solid-socket tools, the base of the handle is completely enclosed by a seamless, single-forged piece of steel. An open-socket tool, where the metal wraps around the handle, leaves an open strip of wood where the base of the handle is exposed to mud and water. This can cause rot and warping, as well as rusting the inside of the socket. Open-socket construction is also weaker than solid-socket construction, making the blade more likely to snap off during use.

Blades. Make sure a tool's blade is smooth and strong. Don't buy tools with warped, jagged, or cracked blades. Most good carbon steel blades are half-painted, so you can see the steel on the business end of the tool. Avoid tools with com-pletely painted blades; they're usually cheaply made. Stainless blades are unpainted, so you can enjoy their sleek look. Also, spades that have a flattened tread on either side of the handle to hold your foot are a lot more comfortable to use than those without.

Metal. The most expensive tools have stainless steel blades, which don't rust, so they require minimal maintenance. However, they cost as much as three times the price of a good carbon steel blade, and they don't hold a sharp edge as well as carbon steel. If you want to go all out, stainless steel is great for spades, forks, and trowels, but well-maintained carbon steel tools will give you more than your money's worth. (For more on tool maintenance, see "Ten Commandments of Tool Maintenance" on page 211.)

Size. Bigger isn't always better when it comes to tools—a large, heavy tool may be harder and more exhausting to use than a lighter model. And when doing garden chores, you want your tools to work with you, not against you. Pick up the tools in the store and pretend you're hoeing, spading, or doing whatever you'd do with that tool in the garden. Make sure the handle length and the weight of the tool are comfortable for you. If the tool has a grip on the handle end, make sure your hand fits in it comfortably. If you garden in gloves, take the extra size into account.

Shape. If you have arthritis or are handicapped, or if gardening's not as easy as it used to be, there are specially shaped tools to help you. Trowels and hand forks have special grips that take the pain out of gardening for arthritis sufferers. Others have longer handles for wheelchair gardening. And ergonomically shaped tools have handles that seem bent at odd angles, but that really work with your body to make gardening chores much easier. Buy the tool that's shaped for your needs.

do some transplanting, you need earth-moving tools: forks, shovels, spades, and trowels.

Forks

Garden forks are wonderful for loosening soil, removing stones and other debris, and lifting and dividing perennials. They have thick, square, fairly blunt-tipped tines. Manure forks, which have a scooped head with slender, rounded, sharp-tipped tines, are better for lifting compost, mulch, and manure, though a garden fork will do if you only want to buy one fork.

Spades and Shovels

Beginning gardeners may not know the difference between a spade and a shovel. A spade has a slender, straight, rectangular blade. It's ideal for creating straight sides in perennial beds, edging lawns and paths, and slicing under and removing sod from new beds. A shovel has a scooped blade with a rounded edge that comes to a point. As its shape suggests, a shovel is designed for scooping and lifting soil and soil amendments, for digging large holes, and for removing large perennials from their holes. Different blade widths are available for different purposes; for example, you might buy a small-bladed "poacher's spade" for working between perennials.

Trowels

For close work, the best earth-moving tool is a trowel. A wide, sturdy trowel with a comfortable grip is indispensable for digging around established plants, digging up weeds and small plants, and transplanting small perennials. Hold a trowel handle as if you were shaking hands with it. Try a number of different trowels in your garden center, making digging motions with your wrist and hand. Buy the most comfortable trowel—it's the tool you'll use most often. You can also buy a narrow-bladed trowel for transplanting bulbs, volunteer seedlings, and other very small plants. It's the best trowel for digging in extremely tight quarters, and its slim, sharp sides are also excellent for hacking off divisions.

Weeding Tools

As with earth-moving tools, there are weeding tools for close work—hand weeders—and weeding tools for larger areas—hoes. For more on hand weeders, see "Rooting Out Weeds" on page 200.

Hoes

A straightforward garden hoe, with a squared-off blade, is all you really need for weeding the perennial garden. Use the hoe to skim off weeds just below the surface of the soil, pulling the blade lightly toward you with the blade's edge horizontal to the soil. Since you're planting perennials in mulched beds rather than as row crops, you shouldn't have to hoe among the perennials very often.

Pruners and Other Maintenance Tools

A sharp pair of scissors can cut many flowers in the perennial garden, but for plants with thick-stemmed blooms like peonies or woody stems like Russian sage (*Perovskia atriplicifolia*), hand pruners are indispensable. You also need them for surgically precise removal of damaged and diseased branches, and for cutting perennials back after bloom. They're handy for taking cuttings and trimming stakes to size. Use scissors-style pruners rather than anvil pruners. Scissors-style pruners cut the stems neatly, while anvil pruners mash the stems against their flat anvil blade.

Ten Commandments of Tool Maintenance

Tool maintenance makes sense. You wouldn't leave shop tools or sewing supplies lying around the yard, or leave pots and pans unwashed for months after you used them. You've invested in good garden tools; you might as well spend a few minutes taking care of them. And a few minutes per use is all it takes! Here are the "Ten Commandments of Tool Maintenance."

1. Buy the best tools you can afford. You'll be surprised by how much less maintenance good tools need.

2. Know where your tools are. The most expensive tool is useless if you can't find it. If you have lots of tools, it might be worthwhile to rig up a hanging wall system to store them in the basement, garage, or toolshed. But however many you have, keep them all in the same place.

3. Keep your tools indoors. They'll last longer and stay in better shape if they're protected from the elements.

4. Get the dirt off. When you're through in the garden, clean and dry your tools. Knock off soil with a wooden scraper. A bucket of sand will remove stubborn particles if you plunge the blade in a few times.

5. Get rid of rust. Use a wire brush to remove rust regularly. If you disinfect your tools with alcohol or bleach solution, dry and oil them afterward to prevent rust.

6. Heal your handles. Smooth handles are essential—you're not going to use a tool that hurts your hands. Keep wooden handles oiled. If they start splintering, sand them smooth, then oil them with linseed oil.

7. Keep sharp tools sharp. If you've ever tried to use dulled pruners, you'll know why this is necessary—dull tools need more strength behind them, take longer to do the job, and do a poor job. Keep an eye (or a cautious finger) on your tools' edges: Sharpen them yourself if you know how, or take them to a tinker shop for sharpening.

8. Keep smooth edges smooth. Nicks and burrs on a spade or shovel blade cause soil to stick and make more work for you. Use a ball-peen hammer to flatten burrs, and smooth out nicks with a fine-gauge metal-cutting file.

9. Make your tools hard to lose. It's amazing how easy it is to lose tools in the yard—sometimes they just seem to disappear, turning up warped and rusted months later. You'll be able to spot them before they get away if you paint a bright stripe or circle on each handle—preferably in fluorescent-orange.

10. Give your tools a rest. At the end of the season, polish tool blades with steel wool, oil them to prevent rust, and store them in a dry place.

Shears

Hedge shears are excellent for shearing plants back. They're also useful for cutting the flowering tops off self-sowing ornamental grasses before they can set seed, or shearing the grasses near the ground in early spring before new growth begins.

That's all there is to basic perennial care—prepare the soil, put in the plants, and maintain them sensibly. Two other aspects of growing perennials are dealt with in later chapters: In chapter 7, we'll discuss the best ways to cope with the garden pests and diseases that plague your plants. Chapter 9 gives you simple techniques for adding more plants to your garden.

Perennial Pest and Disease Control

Effective pest and disease control is a three-step process for the perennial gardener: observe, refer, react. You'll apply the right preventives and controls at the right time if you watch your plants for signs of pests or diseases, check your references to identify pests or symptoms, and then use the recommended control for that particular problem.

In this chapter, you'll find out which pests and diseases attack perennials, what they look like, and what to do about them. But first, you'll learn how to prevent pests and diseases from becoming a major problem through wise plant selection and good cultural practices.

RESISTANT PLANTS

Some species and cultivars of perennials are resistant to certain pests and diseases that plague similar plants. Some of these plants are naturally resistant; others were bred for resistance. Using these plants is one of the easiest ways to solve pest and disease problems. You can either look for and choose resistant plants when you're starting a new garden, or replace susceptible plants with resistant species or cultivars when problems arise.

You can use resistant plants to solve potential garden problems like powdery mildew. Garden phlox (*Phlox paniculata*) is notoriously susceptible to powdery mildew, which disfigures the foliage with a powdery white coating and reduces plant vigor. But phlox is a staple of many summer gardens, with its tall, showy panicles of red, white, pink, or salmon flowers.

If you feel that you must have phlox in your perennial bed or border, you have two choices: You can battle mildew with good cultural practices and preventive spraying, or you can plant mildew-resistant cultivars like 'Bright Eyes', a pink-flowered phlox with crimson centers, or 'David', a sparkling white-flowered form. Wild sweet William (*P. maculata*), which looks like garden phlox, is also mildew-resistant and an excellent substitute; there are pink, white, and rose-colored cultivars.

GROWING PLANTS RIGHT

Good gardening practices result in vigorous, healthy perennials. Careful site selection and soil preparation, adequate irrigation, and mulching are some of the ways you can make sure your plants are ready to resist pest and disease attacks. Just as we are less able to resist a cold when our bodies are already run-down, stressed plants succumb more quickly to infection. Research has shown that weakened plants are the first attacked by pests.

Make sure your plants aren't water-stressed or waterlogged. Keep weeds, which are often alternate hosts for both pests and diseases, away from your garden. Add plenty of organic matter—especially compost—to your beds to enhance water- and nutrient-retention and fight nematodes. Space plants far enough apart for good air circulation. And grow a variety of species; many pests and diseases are species-specific, or are confined to a few related species. Get your perennials off to a good start and keep them growing strongly by using these and other sound gardening practices outlined in chapter 6.

PESTS IN THE PERENNIALS

Pests build up most quickly when just one or two kinds of plants are grown, so a bed of mixed perennials is less likely to be decimated than a bed of roses or petunias. That's because the pests that prefer specific plants will have a harder time finding them when they're "hidden" among all those other perennials. That doesn't mean perennials are pest-free, though, as gardeners who've encountered borers in their bearded irises, Japanese beetles on their hollyhocks, or slugs on their hostas can attest.

One cause of pests in perennial beds is the nature of perennials themselves: The plants are in place a long time, giving pest populations a chance to establish themselves over many growing seasons. Fortunately, there are five ways to keep pests at an acceptable level in your garden.

1. Grow resistant species and cultivars when available.

2. Use good cultural practices.

3. Apply biological controls, which are alive and often self-perpetuating.

4. Use manual controls, including barriers and traps.

5. Use insecticidal sprays and dusts when required.

These five tactics should keep perennial pests at the "few and far between" state, so your plants can bloom and thrive unmolested.

We've discussed resistant plants and cultural controls earlier in the chapter; here's an overview of biological controls, manual controls, and sprays and dusts. But first, there are two techniques that are more important than any control: monitoring and using common sense.

Monitoring

The best and easiest way to keep pests under control is to find them when they've just arrived and there aren't many of them. If you can start control early, your perennials will suffer minimal damage, and you can usually use a simple control. Handpicking a few Japanese beetles is far better than coping with bug sprays and stripped plants. Become a garden detective: When you're weeding, watering, or just out strolling in your garden, check your plants for pests and signs of feeding injury. Make sure you're in the garden every day—pest populations can build up fast. Try to

(continued on page 216)

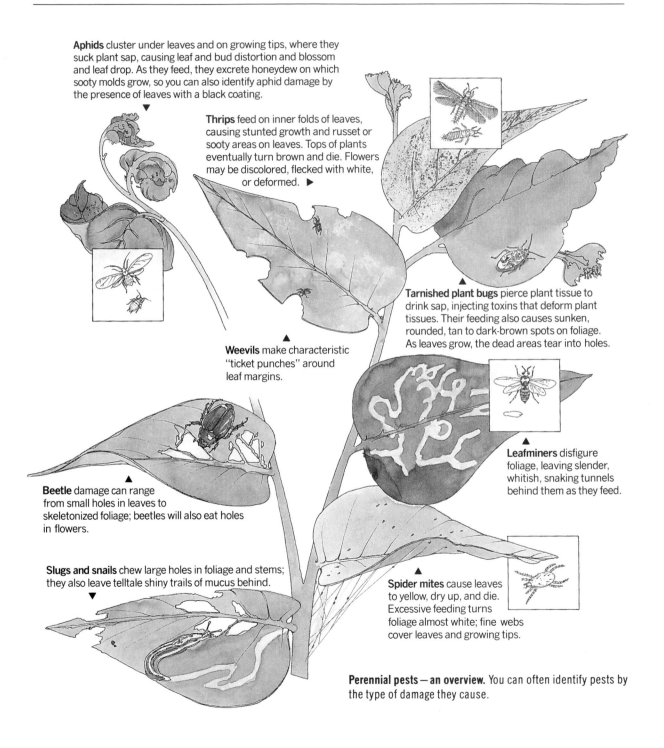

Aphids cluster under leaves and on growing tips, where they suck plant sap, causing leaf and bud distortion and blossom and leaf drop. As they feed, they excrete honeydew on which sooty molds grow, so you can also identify aphid damage by the presence of leaves with a black coating.

Thrips feed on inner folds of leaves, causing stunted growth and russet or sooty areas on leaves. Tops of plants eventually turn brown and die. Flowers may be discolored, flecked with white, or deformed. ▶

Tarnished plant bugs pierce plant tissue to drink sap, injecting toxins that deform plant tissues. Their feeding also causes sunken, rounded, tan to dark-brown spots on foliage. As leaves grow, the dead areas tear into holes.

Weevils make characteristic "ticket punches" around leaf margins.

Leafminers disfigure foliage, leaving slender, whitish, snaking tunnels behind them as they feed.

Beetle damage can range from small holes in leaves to skeletonized foliage; beetles will also eat holes in flowers.

Slugs and snails chew large holes in foliage and stems; they also leave telltale shiny trails of mucus behind. ▼

Spider mites cause leaves to yellow, dry up, and die. Excessive feeding turns foliage almost white; fine webs cover leaves and growing tips.

Perennial pests — an overview. You can often identify pests by the type of damage they cause.

Perennial Pests at a Glance

This table lists the 13 top perennial pests. If pests are plaguing your plants and you can see them, check the description column and match your pest; if you can't find a pest, check the damage column for a match. Once you've found the culprit, a glance across the page will show you the most effective controls and which other perennials are likely to be attacked.

Pest Name and Description	Damage	Controls	Plants Attacked
Aphids. *Adults:* 1/12″–1/5″ long; green, reddish, or blue-black; pear-shaped, with 2 tubes projecting back from abdomen; some are winged, some wingless. *Larvae:* smaller version of adults.	Leaves, stems, and buds distorted, sticky; look for clusters of small insects.	Wash pests from plants with a strong spray of water; use insecticidal soap sprays for serious infestations.	Many
Beetle, Asiatic Garden. *Adults:* 1/3″-long, brown, velvety beetles. *Larvae:* 3/4″-long, white grubs with light-brown heads.	Leaves with irregular holes in edges.	Handpick adults at night into can of soapy water; spray heavily infested plantings with pyrethrins or rotenone.	Many
Beetle, Fuller Rose. *Adults:* 1/3″-long, gray, long-nosed weevils. *Larvae:* white or yellowish grubs with brown heads.	"Ticket-punch" holes around leaf margins.	Handpick adults at night into can of soapy water; shake plants over dropcloth or sheet in early morning and collect weevils.	*Chrysanthemum, Hibiscus, Penstemon, Plumbago, Primula, Rubdeckia, Scabiosa*
Beetle, Japanese. *Adults:* 1/2″-long, metallic-blue or green beetles with coppery wing covers. *Larvae:* 3/4″-long, plump, grayish white grubs.	Leaves and flowers with holes; may be skeletonized.	Handpick adults into can of soapy water; apply milky disease spores to lawn to control grubs; set up traps away from beds; spray heavily infested plants with pyrethrins or rotenone.	*Alcea, Aster, Astilbe, Digitalis, Gaillardia, Hemerocallis, Hibiscus, Paeonia*
Borers. *Adults:* moths or beetles. *Larvae:* caterpillars or grubs.	Stems exude sawdustlike material and break; leaves wilt; iris borers cause irregular tunnels in leaves, damaged or rotted rhizomes.	Apply *Bacillus thuringiensis* (BT) at first sign of borers. Destroy weeds where borers overwinter. Crush borers in iris leaves; dust the base of iris plants with pyrethrins in spring.	Many

(continued)

Perennial Pests at a Glance—Continued

Pest Name and Description	Damage	Controls	Plants Attacked
Bugs, True. *Adults:* ¹⁄₁₆″–½″ long, usually shield-shaped; may be brown, black, green, or brilliantly colored and patterned. *Larvae:* oval to rounded nymphs with long snouts; may be yellow, red, bluish gray, or yellow-green; often patterned.	Buds and leaves deformed or dwarfed.	Handpick into can of soapy water. Spray with insecticidal soap; treat severe infestations with rotenone. Destroy weeds where bugs overwinter.	Many
Cutworms. *Adults:* gray or brownish moths. *Larvae:* 1″–2″-long, grayish or brown caterpillars that curl up when disturbed.	Seedlings or young plants cut off at soil level.	Place plant collars in soil around seedlings or transplants.	Many
Leafminers. *Adults:* ¹⁄₁₀″ long; wasplike, with yellow-striped black bodies and clear wings. *Larvae:* yellowish, stout, wormlike maggots.	Leaves with tan or brown blotches or serpentine tunnels.	Prune off and destroy infested leaves. Spray leaves weekly with insecticidal soap at the first sign of leafminers. Remove garden debris in fall.	*Aconitum, Aquilegia, Chrysanthemum, Delphinium, Dianthus, Eupatorium, Gypsophila, Heuchera, Lobelia, Primula, Salvia, Verbena*
Scales. *Adults:* ¹⁄₁₂″–⅕″ long, with grayish, brownish orange, reddish brown, or cottony white shells; males are winged, females wingless. *Larvae:* tiny yellow, brown, or red nymphs.	Leaves turn yellow, drop; plants may die.	Prune off infested stems and leaves. Remove scales with a cotton swab dipped in rubbing alcohol; spray severe infestations with pyrethrins or rotenone.	*Helianthus, Iberis, Monarda, Opuntia, Paeonia, Phlox, Verbena*

familiarize yourself with the major perennial pests so you'll know what you're looking at, then apply appropriate controls.

Using Common Sense

Don't panic at the first sight of a slug or a ragged leaf. Unless you're growing perennials for the florist industry or a flower show, a little damage is as acceptable as it is inevitable. The techniques we recommend will ensure you have lush, healthy plants and plenty of perfect flowers. Your garden is a natural system, so be prepared for the occasional flaw. Use good sense; don't overreact.

Pest Name and Description	Damage	Controls	Plants Attacked
Slugs and Snails. *Adults:* ⅛″-8″ long; gray, tan, green, black, yellow, or spotted, with eyes at the tips of small tentacles; snails have a single spiral shell; slugs are shell-less. *Young:* smaller, paler versions of adults.	Leaves with large, ragged holes.	Place copper strips around beds; sprinkle sawdust, ashes, or diatomaceous earth around plants. Set beer traps in garden. Hand-pick at night into can of soapy water.	*Alcea, Asarum, Begonia, Bergenia, Campanula, Delphinium, Hemerocallis, Hosta, Iris, Ligularia, Primula, Sedum, Viola*
Spider Mites. *Adults:* 1/50″-long, reddish brown or pale spider-like mites with 8 legs; wingless. *Larvae:* smaller version of adults.	Leaves stippled, reddish to yellow, with fine webbing.	Spray plants daily with a strong stream of water. Keep soil moist. Use insecticidal soap sprays for serious infestations.	Many
Thrips. *Adults:* 1/50″-1/25″ long, with yellow, brown, or blackish bodies and two pairs of fringed wings. *Larvae:* white or yellow with red eyes; wingless.	Flower buds die; petals distorted; growth stunted.	Remove and destroy infested plant parts. Destroy weeds where thrips overwinter. Use insecticidal soap for serious infestations.	Many
Whiteflies. *Adults:* 1/12″-long, white, mothlike insects. *Larvae:* green, translucent, flat nymphs.	Leaves yellow; plant weakened.	Spray leaves with insecticidal soap. Destroy weeds to reduce whitefly populations.	*Chrysanthemum, Hibiscus, Lupinus, Primula, Rudbeckia, Salvia, Verbena*

The second time to let common sense come to your rescue is at the other end of the control spectrum. If, in spite of your best efforts, certain perennials are decimated every year, give up the fight. No matter how much you love columbines, if leafminers make them unsightly every season, it's time to throw in the trowel. There are plenty of other lovely perennials to choose from. Give it your best shot, but then let common sense be your guide. Don't let pest-pocked perennials ruin the looks of your perennial garden. Remember that you can always hide favorite but pest-plagued perennials in the cutting garden, where the colorful chaos will make pest damage less noticeable.

For a rogues' gallery of the worst perennial pests with descriptions, damage, and

Grub

Adult

Japanese beetles. These ½-inch-long, metallic blue-green beetles consume the leaves, stalks, and flowers of many perennials. The ¾-inch-long, C-shaped grub larvae feed on the roots of lawn grasses. Handpick adults into a can of soapy water. Traps will attract these pests to your yard unless you get your neighbors to set them up, too. Use milky disease on lawn areas to control beetle larvae.

controls listed for each pest, see "Perennial Pests at a Glance" on page 215.

Using Biological Controls

Biological controls are microscopic living organisms that infest or attack pests. They are usually pest-specific, attacking only one kind of insect, and are thought to be harmless to the environment and nontargeted species. To be effective, they must be applied early, since the infection takes several days to kill the pest. All are available from garden suppliers; apply according to directions.

BT. *Bacillus thuringiensis,* known as BT, is a bacterial disease that infects insect larvae. Different strains of BT have been isolated for different pests: One infects caterpillars, a second attacks the grubs of Colorado potato beetles, and a third infects mosquito and black fly larvae. Make sure you buy the strain of BT that targets your pest problem.

Milky disease. *Bacillus popilliae,* milky disease, attacks Japanese beetle grubs. Apply this bacterial disease, often sold as milky spore, to the lawn where these grubs live. Milky disease is most effective in providing grub control if everyone in your neighborhood applies it to their lawns; one application will be effective for years.

Parasitic nematodes. These microscopic roundworms parasitize and kill insect larvae, including ground-dwelling caterpillars (like cutworms) and grubs. The nematodes feed on the dead insect, and about 10 to 20 days after first infection, huge numbers of nematodes leave the dead insect in search of new victims. Because nematodes perish in sunlight or dry places, they are most useful against pests in soil or hidden locations. Although the larval stage can survive for long periods in the soil, for the greatest effect you need to release more nematodes each year.

Using Manual Controls

Manual controls are simple, low-tech methods like handpicking pests or putting barriers around plants. Some manual controls are preventive, like cutworm collars; their aim is to keep pests from reaching your plants. Others, like handpicking, come into play once pests attack. When you notice a pest problem, try these controls first; they're often all you'll need. If pest populations are too great for effective manual control, move on to dusts and sprays.

Handpicking. This is a simple technique that merely involves plucking a pest off a plant and squashing it or drowning it in a can of soapy water. (Soap breaks the surface tension of the water, so the pests can't climb out.) It's not for the squeamish but is highly effective when used early when populations arc light.

Copper barriers. Slugs and snails get an electric shock when their slimy bodies touch copper, so these copper strips keep them out of your beds. They're easiest to use if you have wood-sided raised beds and can nail the strip around the outside of the bed. This works on a barrel garden, too. Copper strips are available from garden supply companies and are sold as Snail-Barr.

Cutworm collars. Make your own "collars" to keep cutworms from attacking your seedlings and transplants. Use cardboard cylinders like toilet paper or paper towel rolls, or roll your own. Make each collar 2 or 3 inches tall and 1½ to 2 inches wide; push them into the soil so that about half the collar is below the soil surface. Remove the collars once plants are past the seedling stage.

Diatomaceous earth. This mineral dust is composed of fossilized diatom shells. The microscopic fossil shells have razor-sharp edges that pierce the skin of soft-bodied pests

Iris borers. In spring, borer larvae enter a fan of iris leaves at the top and burrow down to the rhizome. Pale, irregular tunnels in the leaves mark their travels. Borers also spread soft rot bacteria as they feed. To control borers, pinch and crush them in the leaves. Also, remove dead leaves in fall and destroy infested fans in spring. If you've had serious borer problems, grow Siberian iris (*Iris sibirica*), which is usually borer-free, rather than bearded iris.

Slug eggs
in soil

Snail

Slug

Slugs and snails. These pests prefer the cool, moist soil preferred by many perennials like hostas. Mulches and plants with low-growing leaves provide shady hiding places from which they emerge to feed at night. They rasp large holes in leaves and stems and leave a characteristic shiny slime trail. To control these pests, drown them in beer traps or sprinkle bands of coarse, dry, scratchy materials such as wood ashes or diatomaceous earth around plants or beds.

like caterpillars, slugs, and snails. The pests dehydrate and die. Diatomaceous earth also works as a repellent: Use it as a barrier on the soil around plants or around the outside of beds.

Traps. Shallow pans of beer will lure slugs and snails to a watery death. (Alcohol-free beer is effective, too.) Set the pans into the soil, placing the lip flush with the soil surface, and fill with stale beer; empty the traps daily. Snail traps are also commercially available. Other traps, like Japanese beetle traps, are available commercially but are less relevant to perennial gardeners; in fact, studies have shown that Japanese beetle traps often act as a lure, drawing pests into your garden.

Using Sprays and Dusts

The best control for a severe pest out-break is sometimes a spray or dust. Some sprays and dusts are harmless (like water); others are relatively harmless (like insecticidal soap); and others may be highly toxic for a short time (pyrethrins are toxic for about a day, rotenone for about a week). Don't underestimate the potential toxicity of organically acceptable insecticides like rotenone or pyrethrins. If you choose to use them, wear protective clothing, a face mask, and gloves when handling or applying them. Whichever spray or dust you use, make sure you coat the undersides of the leaves; many pests congregate there, out of sight of potential predators.

Water. A forceful spray of water is often enough to control aphids and spider mites; it knocks them off the plants, and these slow-moving pests can't find their way back.

Insecticidal soap. Soap sprays are contact poisons that are effective against outbreaks of soft-bodied pests like aphids and whiteflies. You can buy insecticidal soap commercially (Safer is a commonly available brand) and dilute it according to directions, or make your own by mixing 1 to 3 teaspoons of liquid dish soap (not laundry or dishwasher detergent) in 1 gallon of water. For best control, spray plants every two or three days for two weeks.

Pyrethrins. Pyrethrin insecticides are made from the pulverized dried flowers of pyrethrum daisies (*Chrysanthemum cinerariifolium* and *C. coccineum*). Pyrethrins can be applied as a dust or used as a spray and are effective against a wide range of insects. For best control, apply pyrethrins in the early evening; two applications 2 hours apart may be most effective. Because pyrethrins are not pest-specific, don't use them near water (they are extremely toxic to fish) or pets. Make sure you buy plant-derived pyrethrins, not synthetic pyrethroids.

Rotenone. Rotenone is made from the dried powdered roots of *Lonchocarpus,* a genus of South American legumes. It is effective against a wide range of insects and is more toxic to pests than pyrethrins, usually

requiring only one application. Rotenone is available as a dust or spray. It is not pest-specific and is highly toxic to fish and birds; don't use it near water or pets.

PERENNIAL DISEASES

Perennials are more likely to be disease-free than annuals or vegetables because perennial beds usually contain a mixture of plants, rather than a single species or cultivar

---

Sources of Organic Pest and Disease Controls

Many garden centers, nurseries, and hardware stores now carry a wide range of organic pest and disease controls. If you can't find a source near you, these mail-order suppliers offer an excellent selection.

Gardener's Supply Company, 128 Intervale Road, Burlington, VT 05401

Gardens Alive!, 5100 Schenley Place NE, Lawrenceburg, IN 47035

Growing Naturally, P.O. Box 54, 149 Pine Lane, Pineville, PA 18946

Harmony Farm Supply, P.O. Box 460, Graton, CA 95444

The Natural Gardening Company, 217 San Anselmo Avenue, San Anselmo, CA 94960

Necessary Trading Company, 703 Salem Avenue, New Castle, VA 24127

North Country Organics, R.R. 1 Box 2232, Bradford, VT 05033

Peaceful Valley Farm Supply Company, P.O. Box 2209, Grass Valley, CA 95945

Ringer Corporation, 9959 Valley View Road, Eden Prairie, MN 55344

Smith & Hawken, 25 Corte Madera, Mill Valley, CA 94941

(a monoculture). Monocultures draw diseases—and the pests that often spread them—like a magnet. Good cultural practices, like adding plenty of compost and other organic matter to the soil, mulching, and cleaning up plant debris in fall, also reduce the likelihood of diseases getting a foothold in your garden.

No matter how careful you are, though, you'll probably encounter diseases in your perennials from time to time. An especially hot, wet summer might provoke an outbreak of powdery mildew, a friend might inadvertently give you a peony division with botrytis blight, or an unusually high leafhopper population might spread aster yellows to your chrysanthemums. Familiarize yourself with disease symptoms, so when your plants show signs of infection, you can take prompt action to save them.

There are three types of diseases that infect perennials—bacteria, fungi, and viruses—as well as a related category of pests and problems that cause diseaselike symptoms in plants. These include microscopic nematodes, nutrient deficiencies, and other disorders like herbicide drift. Check the table "Are Your Perennials Missing Something?" on page 188 to make sure your plants don't have a simple deficiency before treating them for disease. For descriptions of perennial disease symptoms and controls, see "Perennial Pests at a Glance" on page 215.

Preventing Diseases

Prevention is the best—and often the only—cure for plant diseases. There is no cure for viral diseases, and once your garden soil becomes infested with nematodes, you may have to remove all the plants in your perennial bed and solarize the soil before trying again

with new plants. Even fungi like *Verticillium* can survive for 20 years in the soil. So good gardening practices and commonsense precautions can be critical in keeping diseases out or minimizing their damage.

You might start with resistant species and cultivars, especially if a disease has been a problem in the past. For example, if powdery mildew has been a plague on your bee balm, try 'Marshall's Delight', which is mildew-resistant. You might have to search for disease-resistant cultivars; breeding for resistance in perennials is a fairly new phenomenon. Resistant species and cultivars are mentioned in encyclopedia entries when a disease is a particular problem for a perennial.

Site selection is also important. If you're planning a new perennial bed, site it in well-drained soil in full sun and where it will get good air circulation. Don't overcrowd plants; space them far enough apart so air can circulate between them. If you have an established bed that has become overcrowded, thin plants to improve circulation. (You'll find more on this technique in "Thinning" on page 203.)

Fungal and bacterial diseases and nematodes can all spread by water. You can avoid encouraging infections by careful watering. Water your perennials in the morning, so they'll dry before night. Water the ground around the plants, not the foliage. And don't work in your perennial beds when the foliage is still wet from a rain.

Another time-honored preventive tactic is to practice good garden hygiene: Wash your hands and tools after working with diseased plants. Keep the garden clean of potentially diseased plant debris, and weed religiously to remove alternate hosts of diseases and their carriers. Cut plants to the ground at the end of the growing season; compost healthy trimmings, but destroy any that look diseased.

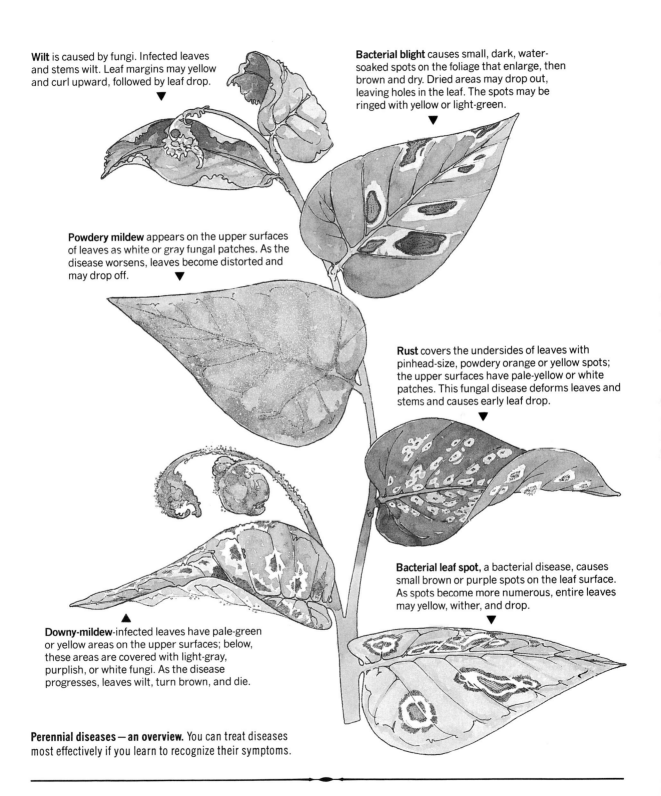

Wilt is caused by fungi. Infected leaves and stems wilt. Leaf margins may yellow and curl upward, followed by leaf drop. ▼

Bacterial blight causes small, dark, water-soaked spots on the foliage that enlarge, then brown and dry. Dried areas may drop out, leaving holes in the leaf. The spots may be ringed with yellow or light-green. ▼

Powdery mildew appears on the upper surfaces of leaves as white or gray fungal patches. As the disease worsens, leaves become distorted and may drop off. ▼

Rust covers the undersides of leaves with pinhead-size, powdery orange or yellow spots; the upper surfaces have pale-yellow or white patches. This fungal disease deforms leaves and stems and causes early leaf drop. ▼

Bacterial leaf spot, a bacterial disease, causes small brown or purple spots on the leaf surface. As spots become more numerous, entire leaves may yellow, wither, and drop. ▼

▲ **Downy-mildew**-infected leaves have pale-green or yellow areas on the upper surfaces; below, these areas are covered with light-gray, purplish, or white fungi. As the disease progresses, leaves wilt, turn brown, and die.

Perennial diseases — an overview. You can treat diseases most effectively if you learn to recognize their symptoms.

Perennial Diseases at a Glance

This chart gives you an overview of the major diseases that infect perennials. If your plants have contracted a disease, they may display classic symptoms like spotted leaves, wilting, mold, or stunting. Look at the symptoms column of this table and match the symptoms described with those on your plant. Then you can look in the other columns to find out the name of the disease, how to control it, and what other perennials it's most likely to strike.

Disease Name	Symptoms	Controls	Plants Affected
Anthracnose	Stems with sunken lesions and pink blisters; plants may die.	Thin stems to improve air circulation; clean up garden in fall, destroying infected plant material. Treat severe infections with copper fungicide sprays.	*Alcea, Hemerocallis, Hosta, Paeonia, Tulipa, Viola*
Aster Yellows	Leaves yellow, flowers small and green; witches'-brooms at base of plant.	Remove and destroy infected plants. Control leafhoppers, which spread the disease; remove weeds, which may carry the disease.	*Campanula, Chrysanthemum, Coreopsis, Delphinium, Gaillardia, Rudbeckia, Salvia*
Botrytis Blight	Shoots wilt suddenly and fall over; stem bases blacken and rot; gray mold may appear on crowns; buds wither and blacken; flowers and leaves turn brown.	Remove and destroy infected plant parts. Clear mulch from crowns in spring to let soil dry; site plants in well-drained soil. Spray shoots with bordeaux mix in spring.	*Gladiolus, Lilium, Paeonia, Tulipa*
Leaf Spot, Bacterial	Leaves with many small brown or purple spots; heavily spotted leaves may yellow and drop.	Remove and destroy infected plants. Wash hands and tools after handling diseased plants. Avoid injuring healthy plants and splashing water on plant foliage. Clean up garden debris.	*Aconitum, Delphinium, Geranium, Iris, Papaver*
Leaf Spot, Fungal	Leaves with yellow, brown, or black spots; leaves may wither.	Remove and destroy infected foliage; thin stems or space plants to encourage air circulation; avoid wetting foliage when watering. Apply preventive sulfur sprays if leaf spot was severe last season. Clean up garden debris in fall.	Many
Mildew, Downy	Cottony gray or white spots on undersides of leaves; angular yellow spots form on upper leaf surfaces.	Grow resistant species and cultivars. Space plants and thin stems to encourage air circulation. Remove and destroy infected leaves. Spray severe infections with bordeaux mix.	*Artemisia, Aster, Centaurea, Geranium, Geum, Lupinus, Rudbeckia, Veronica*
Mildew, Powdery	Leaves covered with white powder.	Grow resistant species and cultivars. Spray with sulfur fungicide every 10 days during warm, wet weather. Water in the morning, and avoid wetting the foliage. Destroy infected leaves.	*Achillea, Aster, Coreopsis, Delphinium, Monarda, Phlox, Rudbeckia*

Disease Name	Symptoms	Controls	Plants Affected
Nematodes, Foliar	Leaves with yellow-brown spots or blotches; leaves die and turn brittle; symptoms move up the plant.	Remove and destroy infested plants and the soil surrounding them. Clean up garden debris in fall. Mulch in spring to keep nematodes from leaves. Avoid wetting foliage when watering.	*Bergenia, Chrysanthemum, Heuchera, Phlox*
Nematodes, Root Knot	Plants stunted; leaves yellow, spotted; roots have tiny galls.	Increase soil organic matter; apply chitin or parasitic nematodes to soil.	*Clematis, Geranium, Gladiolus, Hemerocallis, Iris, Paeonia, Viola*
Rot, Bacterial Soft	Leaves with water-soaked spots; rhizomes rotted and soft.	Control iris borers; remove and destroy rotting rhizomes. Wash tools between plants. Plant iris in well-drained soil in full sun.	*Iris*
Rot, Crown	Stems blacken and rot at base; foliage turns yellow and wilts; crowns may mold.	Plant perennials in well-drained soil; avoid damaging crowns when digging around plants. Keep winter mulch away from crowns. Wash tools between plants. Remove and destroy infected plants.	*Ajuga, Delphinium, Eremurus, Iris, Kniphofia, Platycodon*
Rot, Root	Leaves yellow; plant growth slows; roots rot off.	Plant perennials in well-drained soil; avoid damaging roots when digging around plants. Keep mulch away from base of plants. Wash tools between plants. Remove and destroy infected plants.	Many
Rust	Leaf surfaces pale, with powdery orange spots beneath.	Grow resistant cultivars; keep leaves dry; thin stems to encourage air circulation. Remove and destroy infected plant parts. Apply wettable sulfur.	*Achillea, Aconitum, Alcea, Anemone, Aquilegia, Campanula, Clematis, Delphinium, Dianthus, Iris, Liatris, Monarda*
Viruses	Leaves and flowers greenish yellow, distorted; leaves mottled or streaked; new growth spindly; plants stunted.	There is no cure for viral plant diseases; remove and destroy plants showing viral symptoms. Viruses are spread by sucking insects like aphids and leafhoppers; control them to limit the spread of viruses.	*Aquilegia, Aster, Chrysanthemum, Delphinium, Gaillardia, Iris, Lilium, Paeonia*
Wilt, Fusarium	Leaves wilt, yellow, and die; stems droop; symptoms may first appear on a single branch.	Dig and destroy infected plants. Clean up garden debris thoroughly in fall. Plant resistant species and cultivars.	*Chrysanthemum, Dianthus*
Wilt, Verticillium	Leaves and stems wilt; leaf margins may curl upward; leaves yellow and drop off; plants may die.	Dig and destroy infected plants. Clean up garden debris thoroughly in fall. Plant resistant species and cultivars.	*Aconitum, Aster, Chrysanthemum, Coreopsis, Delphinium, Paeonia, Papaver, Phlox*

Curing or Controlling Disease

If disease strikes in spite of your attempts to prevent it, take prompt action to curtail its development and spread. In the following sections, specific controls are discussed with each disease category; for example, you'll find organic fungicides under "Fungal Diseases" on the opposite page. However, there are two control techniques that are effective for a range of diseases.

The simplest but most painful control is to promptly remove and destroy infected foliage, flowers, or entire plants, if necessary. It's heartrending to pull out prized perennials, but sometimes that's the only alternative, especially if they have viral diseases or foliar nematodes. Better to lose a plant or two than an entire bed. This technique will help control fungal and bacterial diseases as well. A more specialized technique that can be quite effective is called soil solarization.

Soil Solarization

If soilborne problems like wilts and nematodes have plagued your perennials in the past few seasons, try soil solarization. This is an easy technique, but it does require planning, since it takes several months to be effective. If you're starting a new bed, prepare the bed a season before you plan to use it if you live in the North; in the South and Southwest, you can dig the bed, solarize it, and be ready to plant the same growing season.

In spring in the South and midsummer in the North, rake the new bed smooth and water it well. Dig a trench several inches deep around the outside of the bed. Spread a thin (1 to 4 mils), clear plastic sheet over the bed and press it down against the soil surface. Press the edges of the sheet into the trench, and seal the plastic by filling the trench with soil. Leave the sheet in place for one to two months.

The technique works because heat builds up under the plastic sheet, essentially cooking the top 6 to 12 inches of soil in the bed. In addition to killing nematodes and diseases, solarization will also kill weeds, weed seeds, and insect pests. The drawback is that you need bare soil; if you have a serious nematode infestation in an existing bed, you may have to dig out and discard all the perennials, solarize the soil, and replant in the fall.

Bacterial Diseases

Bacteria are microscopic organisms. Most are beneficial decomposers—vital to the decay cycle and to composting—and some are major pest controls, like *Bacillus thuringiensis*. A few bacteria cause diseases in perennials. Bacterial infections can be spread by wind, water, and contact with contaminated tools or carrier pests. Once contracted, these diseases are difficult to control; use preventive tactics and treat signs of disease promptly.

Controlling Bacterial Diseases

To control bacterial diseases, remove and discard infected plant parts. Thin plants and avoid crowding future plantings. Wash your tools and hands after handling infected plants. Avoid overhead watering. Clean up plant debris to remove overwintering sites. The most common bacterial diseases of perennials are bacterial soft rot of iris and leaf spot, which infects a number of plants. If you live in the South, your perennials may also be infected by pseudomonas wilt, which causes leaves and stems to wilt and may kill infected plants. Keep pseudomonas wilt from spreading by digging and destroying infected plants.

Fungal Diseases

Most perennial diseases are fungal. Fungi are organisms like mushrooms that reproduce by spores, lack cholorphyll, and live on organic matter. Most fungi are beneficial, but parasitic fungi cause diseases, sapping the strength of host plants by growing and feeding on them. These fungi are microscopic but produce visible spores that are often easy to identify, like the white, cottony spores of powdery mildew or the orange spores of rust.

Controlling Fungal Diseases

Fortunately, since they're the diseases you're most likely to encounter in your garden, fungal diseases are the easiest to control. Besides growing resistant species and cultivars and using cultural practices to reduce the likelihood of infection, you can choose from a number of organic fungicides to treat stricken plants. These fungicides won't cure disease on infected plant parts, but will keep the disease from spreading to healthy parts of the plant once you've removed the infected portions. Always follow label directions. Remember that some of these sprays may leave an unattractive coating on foliage, but this is a temporary effect, and it certainly looks no worse than fungus-covered leaves.

The most effective fungicide sprays include:

▶ **Antitranspirants.** Sprays like Wilt-Pruf that are intended to keep leaves from dehydrating have also been proven effective in preventing powdery mildew. Use ⅓ of the recommended summer rate and reapply to cover new growth and after rain.

▶ **Baking soda.** One homemade spray that tests have shown to be effective in controlling a wide range of fungal diseases, including leaf spot, anthracnose, and powdery mildew, is a 0.5 percent solution of baking

Botrytis blight. Peony shoots afflicted with this fungal disease wilt and fall over. Stem bases blacken and rot, and buds may wither and blacken. Flowers and leaves may turn brown and moldy. Remove and destroy infected plant parts. Avoid overwatering and wet, poorly drained soil. Clear mulch from crowns in spring to let the soil dry, and spray shoots with bordeaux mix if botrytis was a problem the previous season.

soda and water. Mix 1 teaspoon of baking soda in 1 quart of water, add a few drops of liquid dish soap or cooking oil to help the mixture adhere to the leaves, and spray on infected plants.

Crown rot. Overcrowded plants and wet, poorly drained soil are the main causes of crown rot. The leaves and stems of afflicted plants turn brown or black at the base and black spores may appear on stems. Plants may wilt suddenly or yellow and wilt slowly. Prevention is the best control: Avoid sites with poorly drained, wet soil; divide plants regularly; don't damage crowns when digging near plants; and keep winter mulch away from the base of the plant. Remove and destroy infected plants.

▶ **Bordeaux mix.** This powerful fungicide is a combination of hydrated lime and copper sulfate. It will control a wide range of fungal diseases. You can apply it as a dust or spray. If you spray, choose a dry day when the spray will evaporate quickly; otherwise, you might get leaf damage.

▶ **Copper.** Copper is also a powerful broad-spectrum fungicide. Use copper fungicides sparingly, since repeated applications may stunt or damage plants.

▶ **Fungicidal soap.** Safer Garden Fungicide, which contains sulfur in a soap emulsion, controls fungi including powdery mildew, leaf spot, and rust on perennials. You can buy it in ready-to-spray or concentrate form.

▶ **Sulfur.** Milder than copper or bordeaux mix, sulfur still prevents fungi from growing on perennials. You can apply elemental sulfur as a dust, or spray wettable or liquid sulfur onto your plants. Apply sulfur only when temperatures will stay below 85°F; higher temperatures make sulfur toxic to plants.

Viruses and Viruslike Diseases

Viral diseases aren't as common in perennials as fungal and bacterial infections and nematodes. But it's important to recognize the symptoms of viral infection and eliminate infected plants before they can spread disease because there is no cure. Symptoms can vary from plant to plant, but infected plants tend to show certain characteristic traits like greenish flowers, ring spotting, and rosetting. Mosaic virus and aster yellows are common.

Viruses are spread from plant to plant by direct contact rather than by wind or water. The virus must be either rubbed against or injected by pests into a susceptible plant for it to contract the disease. You can spread viral diseases to your perennials by brushing against first infected plants and then healthy plants, especially when plants are wet. Smokers can transmit tobacco mosaic virus from touching cigarettes or other tobacco products and not washing up before heading out to the garden. If you inadvertently propagate infected plants, you may also be spreading viral diseases.

Viral diseases. Perennials may be attacked by several viral diseases that cause symptoms such as spindly new growth and distorted, greenish yellow flowers and leaves. Viruses are spread by sucking insects such as aphids and leafhoppers; control these pests to limit virus problems. There's no cure for infected plants: Remove and destroy them; do not compost them. Viruses overwinter in perennials and perennial weeds; clean up the garden thoroughly in fall if you've had problems with them. Wash any tools that come in contact with infected plants.

Controlling Viruses

Since there is no cure for plants that are infected by viruses, try to keep your garden virus-free. Plant resistant species when possible. Viruses are carried by sucking insects such as aphids, whiteflies, and leafhoppers, which spread the diseases as they feed. Control these pests by spraying plants with a mixture of insecticidal soap and 70 percent isopropyl alcohol (1 tablespoon alcohol to 1 pint soap solution) to reduce the risk of infection. Wash tools used around infected plants. Viruses overwinter in perennials and weeds such as daisies and plantains; a good fall cleanup will reduce the chances of reinfection.

Viruses infect entire plants, so you can't control their spread by removing infected leaves or stems. Once perennials show viral symptoms, remove and destroy them. Do not compost infected plants.

Nematodes

Nematodes are microscopic roundworms, but when they attack plants, they produce disease-like symptoms rather than the damage typical of other insects. Three types of nematodes—root knot, foliar, and stem-and-bulb—attack a wide range of perennials. Nematodes are more likely to be a problem in the South, or in perennial beds that were previously used for growing susceptible vegetables.

Controlling Nematodes

Nematodes travel over wet plants on a film of water, or on garden tools and gardeners moving among plants. Promote natural nematode controls by increasing soil organic matter. You can control root knot nematodes by applying chitin (ground seafood shell wastes) or parasitic nematodes to the soil; both are available from garden supply companies. In severe cases, remove plants, solarize the soil, and replant with nematode-free stock.

There is no cure for either stem-and-bulb or foliar nematodes. Remove and destroy infested plants and the surrounding soil; do not compost the debris. Clean up debris in fall to destroy overwintering nematodes. Mulch in spring to keep nematodes from climbing up plants; avoid wetting leaves when watering.

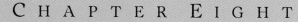
Perennial Care Calendar

T he perennial gardener's year doesn't start in January and end in December. Instead, it starts in fall, when plants are ordered, beds are prepared and planted, and the garden is protected for winter. In this chapter, we'll give a brief overview of each season's garden activities, then go through the garden month by month. For much of the country, these activities will be the same; however, the calendar is different for the South and West Coast, where the climate is much milder. These regions have a separate listing each month. Wherever you live, treat these timelines as guidelines, not gospel; experience (and accurate records in your own garden journal) makes the most accurate calendar. If you're unsure, check with your local extension office, a garden club, or seasoned gardeners in your area about the best timing for any garden chore.

THE GARDEN IN FALL

Fall brings relief to sun-scorched gardens and gardeners. It's finally cool enough to water, weed, deadhead, and perform all those other chores in comparative comfort. Fall is also the time of harvest shows. Visit one in your area for a refreshing display of flower color before winter white takes over.

September

This month, plant spring-flowering bulbs. Buy fall mums. Divide daylilies. Buy a soil test kit and take samples, so you'll be able to amend the soil for next month's planting. Cut and dry perennial flowers. Keep after weeds, and continue to water perennials when the soil dries. Watch for powdery mildew. In New England and the Upper Midwest, killing frosts may end the garden display this month. When perennial foliage dies back, clean up the garden and compost the debris, but don't put down winter mulch until the soil has frozen.

South and West Coast

In the South, prepare beds for fall planting. Divide perennials. Watch for spider mites. Sow perennial seeds in garden or nursery beds. Set out fall-flowering bulbs. Order spring bulbs now for later planting; store all at room temperature except tulips and hyacinths. Store tulips and hyacinths in the refrigerator for six to eight weeks before planting. On the West Coast, prepare garden beds for planting. Plant nursery-grown perennials and sow perennial seeds in garden or nursery beds.

October

This month is planting and maintenance time in the garden. Plant bareroot and container-grown perennials in well-prepared beds as they arrive. Keep the labels with the plants, and make a garden diagram for your records so that you'll know where plants are if a label gets lost. Continue to water perennials until they're dormant, then give the garden a thorough cleaning, cutting back the plants and composting debris. Take a pH test and add lime, if needed. Add compost or composted manure to your beds. Continue weeding. Dig and store glads. Plant spring-blooming bulbs. When the ground freezes, mulch beds deeply. Once garden chores are over, clean and store your tools.

South and West Coast

In the South, divide perennials. Mulch perennial beds and water deeply. Sow perennial seeds in garden or nursery beds. Prepare new beds for planting. In the Upper South, plant spring-flowering bulbs. Dig and store tender bulbs if they won't overwinter in your area. On the West Coast, plant container-grown perennials, spring bulbs, and lilies. Sow perennial seeds in garden or nursery beds.

November

Put the garden to bed this month. Complete garden cleanup. Make sure plant labels are still in place and easy to read. Mulch deeply when the soil has frozen. Drain and store hoses. Store stakes and other supports. Review the garden year—go through your records, noting what looked and did well as well as any problems. Send for seed and plant catalogs to get an early start.

South and West Coast

In the South, plant spring bulbs, peonies, and irises this month. Clean up established beds, composting debris, and prepare new beds for planting. Keep the compost pile moist during dry spells. On the West Coast, divide perennials and plant newly purchased plants. Plant prechilled tulips and hyacinths. Mulch your garden this month; give summer bulbs extra protection.

THE GARDEN IN WINTER

In most of the country, the garden rests in winter, blanketed by mulch and often by snow. It's also a restful time for the gardener—a time to learn and plan. Now is the time to join garden clubs and plant societies, subscribe to gardening magazines, read a good gardening book, even watch a gardening video. In winter, you have a chance to tally the year's successes and failures. It's also the time to compile plant and seed orders from those tempting catalogs, and to ruthlessly cut down those orders to fit your garden space.

December

Send for seed and plant catalogs this month. Make sure Santa has your garden wish list. Remember to buy catalog and gardening magazine gift certificates for your gardening friends. Don't throw away your tree after Christmas—use its branches to mulch the perennial bed. Check stored bulbs and tubers and discard any that show signs of rot.

South and West Coast

In the South, order seeds this month so you'll have enough time to start transplants. On the West Coast, inventory your stored seed this month and test its viability. Order seeds and plants. Divide established perennials and plant new ones. Plant summer bulbs.

January

This is the month to plan your planting program. Look over last year's leftover seeds and test them for viability before ordering new seed. Start a new garden journal. Mail catalog seed orders. Look over your garden now that you can see its structure, and think about any changes you'd like to make. Try your hand at garden design—maybe you'd like a shade garden or color theme garden. Don't forget to inspect stored bulbs and tubers.

South and West Coast

In the South, it's time to place catalog orders. Condition and repair garden tools. Cut back ornamental grasses. Buy summer-blooming bulbs now for best selection; store at room temperature until planting time. Keep the compost pile moist so it will continue composting. On the West Coast, plant container-grown and bareroot perennials this month. Plant summer bulbs. Sow perennial seeds.

February

Inventory and repair your garden tools this month. Order perennial plants from catalogs. Sow the earliest seeds under lights. Try an indoor composting system. Continue to check stored bulbs. Weed garden beds as weather permits. Start an exercise program so you'll be ready for garden chores.

South and West Coast

In the South, clean up the garden—cut back dead and winter-damaged perennial foliage. Start seeds under lights or in a cold frame. Watch for aphids on new bulb and perennial growth. Weed now while weeds are small. On the West Coast, plant perennials this month. Make sure seedlings and newly planted perennials are well-watered. Protect seedlings from snails and slugs. Watch for aphids on new growth. Weed now while weeds are small.

THE GARDEN IN SPRING

For many gardeners, spring is the favorite season, when color and bloom return to the garden after winter's absence. It's also a busy season, with soil building, transplanting, dividing, and weeding vying for attention with the arrival of new plants and the emergence of perennials from their winter hiding places.

March

March is garden-show month—try to attend one for inspiration and ideas. It's also soil test time if you didn't test your soil in fall. Buy a home test kit or request testing information from your local extension office. This is the last chance to clean and oil your garden tools before the new season; buy new tools now. Continue starting seeds under lights or in a bright window. Visit garden centers for seeds and supplies. Order summer bulbs. Keep garden records. Don't let sunny days and warm weather trick you into pulling off winter mulch, no matter how tempting it is. Don't work the soil until it's dry enough to crumble when you squeeze a handful, and don't walk on your wet garden soil and compact it.

South and West Coast

In the South, prepare new beds for planting, adding organic matter and soil amendments. Make raised beds for wet sites. Renew mulch in existing beds. Buy summer bulbs now for best selection. Divide coreopsis, mums, and garden phlox as soon as they show new growth. Continue weeding. Start compost piles. On the West Coast, prepare new beds for planting when the soil is dry enough to work. Divide summer- and fall-blooming perennials; replant in amended soil. Plant perennials and summer-blooming bulbs.

April

Clean up the perennial garden this month, and prepare the beds for planting when the soil is dry enough to work. Cut back dead foliage before new growth starts. Use the trimmings to start a compost pile. Make a garden map so that you'll know at a glance where plants are and where you have holes to fill. Continue starting seeds indoors. Harden off transplants. Divide mums. Consider planting ornamental grasses with your perennials. Keep planting records. Save your Easter lily to plant out later. Pest season starts as plants begin to grow, so watch plants closely. In New England and the Upper Midwest, leave winter mulch in place until early May.

South and West Coast

In the South, set out transplants and newly purchased perennials this month. Divide summer- and fall-blooming perennials. Plant summer-blooming bulbs. Plant Easter lilies outdoors when they've finished blooming. On the West Coast, plant glads. Take cuttings of mums. Feed your perennials. Watch for pests.

May

Divide summer- and fall-blooming perennials this month. Harden off transplants and plant them in your beds. Protect transplants from cutworms. Plant bareroot and container-grown perennials. Don't forget to label your plants! Plant glads and other summer bulbs two weeks before your last frost date. Side-dress spring-flowering bulbs. Give your beds 1 inch of water a week if it doesn't rain; don't let transplants and newly planted perennials dry out. Pinch mums, asters, Shasta daisies, and other perennials that tend to grow leggy. Try a wildflower garden or container garden. Mulch your garden. Continue to weed and monitor pests and diseases—the earlier you catch all three, the easier it is to control them. In New England and the Upper Midwest, gradually remove winter mulch early this month; continue to watch for late frosts.

South and West Coast

In the South, stake tall-growing perennials this month. Mulch your perennial beds. Take cuttings from tip growth. Don't let transplants dry out. Cut back dying daffodil and Dutch iris foliage. Watch for and control pests, especially aphids, slugs, snails, thrips, and sow bugs. Plant new mums and divide established ones. Store unused seed in airtight jars in the refrigerator. Side-dress perennials. Keep up with weeds. On the West Coast, deadhead perennials. Pinch mums. Divide coral bells, daylilies, irises, lilies-of-the-valley, and oriental poppies after bloom. Stake tall perennials. Start perennial seeds for fall transplanting.

THE GARDEN IN SUMMER

Summer is maintenance time in the perennial garden—time for watering, weeding, deadheading, feeding, and relentless pest and disease control. Remember to water in the morning, to water deeply, and to put the water on the ground, not on the plants. Think of your own safety as summer progresses. Watch for poison ivy when you're weeding. In hot weather, work in the morning and evening, when it's cooler; wear a large-brimmed hat and sunblock; and drink plenty of fluids to avoid heatstroke. Summer is also vacation time. Think of your garden before you go—leave it in good shape, water well, and see if you can find a neighbor to "garden-sit."

June

Fertilize perennials now to encourage flowering and strong growth. Prune back spring-flowering perennials, if needed. Store unused seed in airtight jars in the refrigerator. Leave foliage on spring bulbs until it dies back. Order next year's spring bulbs now—they'll arrive in time for fall planting. Stake vining perennials or train them on strings. Mulch your beds to conserve moisture and cut down on weeding, but continue watering deeply as needed, and pull or hoe out weeds as they appear. Keep on the pest and disease patrol and control problems promptly—spider mites are especially bothersome when the weather is hot and dry. Compost!

South and West Coast

In the South, deadhead spent flowers. Stake glads and other perennials that need it. Pinch mums and other tall fall bloomers for bushier plants with more flowers. Order spring bulbs now for fall planting. Mulch beds or renew existing mulch. Continue to weed, water, and monitor pests and diseases. Feed your perennials lightly this month. On the West Coast, plant fall-blooming perennials now. Order spring bulbs. Cut flowers for drying.

July

This month, your perennials are full-grown, so it's a good time to take stock of the garden. How do the combinations look? Are some plants crowding out others? Take notes of plants you should move in the fall. Mulch the garden or renew existing mulch. Stake tall perennials. Side-dress perennials. Look for nutrient deficiency symptoms, and correct deficiencies. Turn your compost pile. Deadhead perennials. Thin crowded perennials to improve air circulation. Continue to water deeply, weed, and monitor for pests and diseases. Japanese beetles, slugs, and powdery mildew are especially bothersome this month.

South and West Coast

In the South, divide bearded irises and daylilies. Deadhead perennials. Start perennial seeds for fall transplanting. Set out mums for fall bloom. On the West Coast, plant fall bulbs. Start perennial seeds for fall transplanting.

August

Order perennials for fall planting from nursery catalogs early this month. Divide bearded irises, oriental poppies, daylilies, and peonies. Deadhead and thin crowded perennials. Cut flowers for drying. Take cuttings from perennials at month's end. Keep the garden mulched and watered. Watch out for slugs, beetles, leaf spots, blights, and mildews. In New England and the Upper Midwest, be prepared to protect tender plants from frost.

South and West Coast

In the South, stake late-blooming perennials. Deadhead, water, and watch for pests and diseases. Start perennial seeds for fall transplanting. Cut flowers for drying. Set out mums. On the West Coast, plant perennials.

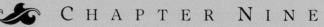
Propagating Perennials

*P*erennials aren't cheap. In fact, if you've ever tried to order a row of peonies or a bed's worth of mixed perennials from catalogs, or filled a shopping cart on impulse one fine spring day at the garden center, you were probably shocked by the total cost. If you need more than a few plants, or if you'd like a large number of a choice cultivar, it pays to propagate your own perennials.

There are two basic ways to propagate perennials—sexually and vegetatively (or asexually). To propagate perennials sexually, you just grow them from seed. On the other hand, there are four methods of vegetative propagation used for perennials—division, stem cuttings, root cuttings, and tissue culture. Tissue culture is a specialized technique used by professional propagators who have access to a lab, but the other three methods require nothing but a little straightforward know-how.

In this chapter, we'll discuss each type of propagation (except tissue culture), how to do it, its advantages and drawbacks, and which perennials respond best to each technique.

Then you can choose the method or combination that suits your needs. Whichever you choose, the end result is the same—more perennials!

There are two places in this book that you can turn to for specifics on how to propagate each type of perennial. The "Perennial Culture Table" on page 251 features a column on propagation that lists the easiest and most common ways to propagate each type of perennial. So, if seed sowing or stem cuttings are recommended for a particular perennial, you can be sure that is an easy, effective method to use. For more details on propagation, see the individual plant entries in the encyclopedia section on page 280. There, you'll find special seed treatments required and any other details you need to propagate perennials successfully.

STARTING FROM SEED

Growing perennials from seed has definite advantages: It's the cheapest and easiest way to produce a large number of plants.

However, it's usually also the slowest way, since a plant that takes a season or less to reach blooming size from a division or cutting may take three years from a seedling. The other drawback to starting from seed is that many cultivars won't come true—you'll get seedlings of the same species, but most likely they won't carry the traits that made their parents outstanding. (For a list of cultivars that *do* come true from seed, see "Cultivars from Seed" on page 239.) However, if you're not in a hurry for plants, if money is a factor, or if you're trying to propagate species rather than cultivars, growing your plants from seed is the way to go.

When you order perennial seed, check the catalogs for planting depth, germination time, and other useful information. Seed packets feature this information, too. Keep germination data handy where you plan to sow the seed, so you can refer to it easily during planting. Once you've decided which seeds to order, it makes sense to copy the germination information for your seeds onto a sheet of paper, which you can post near your propagating area.

While you wait for the seed to arrive, prepare your propagating area. This can be anything from a greenhouse bench, cold frame, or plant stand with lights to a card table in front of a bright window. Just make sure it's clean, sturdy, and in bright but indirect light.

You have several options for seed-starting containers. If you're not starting a lot of perennials, one of the best containers is the kind that comes in a tomato-growing kit (available at garden centers and from catalogs). These come with bottom-watering trays, and bottom watering is ideal for seedlings: It provides even moisture without getting the plants wet, which is an invitation to fungi.

If you're growing lots of perennials or don't want to invest in tomato kits, you'll want nursery flats—plastic trays shaped like oblong cake pans—to sow the seed in. Flats are available from seed and garden supply catalogs, garden centers, and nurseries. Make sure your flats have drainage holes. (Set them on cookie sheets with sides or other shallow trays if draining water would be a problem.) The long, shallow flat is ideal for seedlings, since it's easy to keep the soil moist but not soggy, and no space is wasted between pots. Of course, if you only want to grow a few seedlings, 4-inch plastic pots on the windowsill or recycled cell packs (like the ones annuals are sold in) are fine.

Sterile conditions are vital to seed-starting success, since fungal diseases (especially damping off) are the bane of seedlings. So start with new flats or pots, or sterilize them in a 5 percent bleach solution (1 part bleach to 20 parts water). This also discourages algae, which can take over an uncleaned flat. Use a sterile soil mix—some are sold specially for seedlings. You can also make your own soil mix from equal portions of peat and perlite. Moisten the soil mix thoroughly before planting.

Remember that timing is important when you're sowing seed—you'll have to transplant all those seedlings. To avoid a monster transplant job, stagger sowing of perennials that germinate in the same amount of time, so your transplanting job will be manageable.

Special Seed Treatments

Many perennial seeds are ready for sowing straight from the packet. But others need special treatments that mimic the conditions they'd get outdoors before they'll come up. They may need to have their thick seed coats scratched—a process called scarification—or soaked so the seedling can break through. Or they may need a period of moist chilling—called stratification—to mimic winter conditions in order to germinate.

Scarifying Seed

Perennials with hard seed coats like baptisias (*Baptisia* spp.) and lupines (*Lupinus* spp.) often need more help germinating than a moist soil medium provides. Fortunately, scarification is an easy technique. If you have only a few seeds to treat, you can scrape the seed coats with a nail file. Or, you can scarify seeds by putting a sheet of medium-grade sandpaper inside a cookie sheet or rectangular metal cake pan (one you don't mind getting scraped up), putting a layer of seeds on top of the sandpaper, and rubbing over them with a sander block to wear down the seed coats.

An equally effective and even easier method is soaking the seeds, as you do before cooking dried beans. Just boil water, take it off the burner, wait until the water stops boiling, and put in the seeds. Then leave them in the water overnight. The seeds will swell and germinate faster.

Stratifying Seed

Perennial seeds that need moist chilling, or stratifying, have inhibitors that prevent them from sprouting until they've been through six to eight weeks of winterlike conditions. This is especially true for perennial woodland wildflowers like trout lilies (*Erythronium* spp.) that bloom in spring and ripen seed in summer, and for fall-bloomers like asters (*Aster* spp.). If the seeds germinated in fall, they'd be killed by the harsh winter that followed. Instead, they lie dormant through the winter and sprout the following spring. They'll have a whole season to grow before winter comes again.

If you've purchased or collected seeds that need stratifying, it's important to sow them outdoors while they are fresh. (Check the encyclopedia entries for seeds that should be stratified.) If you do not sow them soon after you collect or receive them, germination rates can drop drastically. Seeds sown out-doors will receive moist chilling naturally during winter. If you must start the seeds indoors, provide winter conditions by stratifying them. To stratify seeds, sow them in moist sand and store for six to eight weeks in the refrigerator. Or sow the seeds in flats or pots and set them outdoors in a cold frame for the same time period. The seeds will actually respond better to the natural cycle of winter freezing and thawing.

Sowing Seed

Sow your perennial seed in rows rather than randomly over the soil surface. Rows of plants are easier to transplant, and you can water the soil between rows, cutting the risk of fungal attack. To get neat rows, pour some seed from your pack onto a 3 × 5-inch card with a fold in the middle. The card lets you see what you're sowing and sow evenly. Shake the seed from the card onto the soil. Sow one cultivar or species in each row to avoid confusion, rather than mixing them up in the rows. If you're sowing in pots, stick to one cultivar or species per pot.

Small seeds are hard to handle, even with the card trick. Mix them first with a small quantity of sterilized play sand (the pure-white sand sold for sandboxes, not coarse builder's sand), so you'll be able to see what you're sowing and won't scatter the fine, dustlike seed all in one spot. Press the row of sand and seed into the soil surface, but don't cover it with soil.

Tamp down larger seeds after sowing to achieve good contact between the soil and the seeds. Cover seeds that don't need light to germinate to the depth recommended on the packet—a safe general rule is to cover them with a layer of soil one to three times their width. Then tamp the soil down. For a light, even cover, you can use a flour sieve or

Cultivars from Seed

If you want named cultivars without paying for individual plants, look for seed packets of the perennials in this list. Unlike many perennials—like hosta, peony, or iris cultivars, which must be propagated vegetatively by division to preserve their special characteristics—these come true from seed.

Achillea ptarmica 'The Pearl'
Achillea taygetea 'Debutante'
Aquilegia × *hybrida* 'McKana' hybrids, 'Biedermeier', and 'Nora Barlow'
Armeria hybrida 'Ornament'
Asclepias × 'Gay Butterflies'
Aurinia saxatilis 'Gold Dust'
Bergenia cordifolia 'Redstart'
Campanula carpatica 'Blue Clips' and 'White Clips'
Chrysanthemum × 'Autumn Glory'
Chrysanthemum coccineum 'James Kelway' and 'Robinson's Mix'
Chrysanthemum × *superbum* 'Alaska' and 'Snow Lady'
Coreopsis grandiflora 'Early Sunrise' and 'Sunburst'
Delphinium × *elatum* 'Pacific Giant' (or 'Round Table') series
Dianthus deltoides 'Zing Rose'
Digitalis purpurea 'Excelsior Hybrids' and 'Foxy'

Echinacea purpurea 'Bravado' and 'White Swan'
Erigeron karvinskianus 'Profusion'
Gaillardia × *grandiflora* 'Torch Light'
Geum 'Mrs. Bradshaw'
Heuchera micrantha var. *diversifolia* 'Palace Purple'
Heuchera sanguinea 'Bressingham Mix'
Liatris spicata 'Floristan Violet', 'Floristan White', 'Kobold'
Linum perenne 'Saphyr'
Lobelia cardinalis 'Queen Victoria'
Lobelia speciosa 'Compliment Scarlet'
Lupinus Russell hybrids and 'Minarette'
Lychnis × *arkwrightii* 'Vesuvius'
Lychnis coronaria 'Angel Blush'
Monarda didyma 'Panorama Mix'
Papaver orientale 'Brilliant' and 'Dwarf Allegro'
Physostegia virginiana 'Crown of Snow'
Platycodon grandiflorus 'Fugi' series and 'Shell Pink'
Potentilla nepalensis 'Miss Wilmott'
Rudbeckia fulgida var. *sullivantii* 'Goldsturm'
Scabiosa caucasica 'Fama'
Solidago canadensis 'Golden Baby'
Veronica spicata 'Sightseeing'

---

collander to scatter soil over the seeds. Once you've covered the seeds, moisten the soil gently and evenly.

There aren't many perennials that need light to germinate, but if you're starting seed of one that does, treat it as you would fine seed—just press it into the soil surface. (The encyclopedia entries and the seed packets will tell you if your perennials need light to germinate.)

As you sow the seed, label each row in the flat or each pot clearly, so you'll know what you have and can monitor each perennial's progress. Write the name of the perennial and the date you sowed the seed clearly on the label. Then cover the flat or pots with plastic wrap, a sheet of plastic, a pane of glass, or a rigid plastic cover (available from catalogs). One way to maintain humidity with pots is to set them in an empty aquarium and cover it with glass or a sheet of plastic. Or, you can sit each pot in a plastic bag and close the top with a twist tie.

Set the flats or pots in a bright place out of direct sunlight. Make sure the top ⅛ to ½ inch of soil stays evenly moist (not soaked) until the seeds germinate. With covered flats or pots, you shouldn't have to water again until the seeds germinate, but it won't hurt to check soil moisture every day or two.

Dos and Don'ts When the Seeds Come Up

Once the seeds have germinated and become seedlings, they need different conditions. Here's what to do—and what not to do—to get healthy seedlings:

▶ **Do** remove plastic or glass covers to bring the humidity down and give the seedlings as much light as possible.

▶ **Do** cut down on water—let the top ¼ inch of soil dry between waterings—and resist the urge to feed the emerging plants. Both overwatering and fertilizing result in soft, tangled growth and rot.

▶ **Do** water carefully—remember that damping off threatens seedlings. If you are watering from above, water next to the row of seedlings rather than on top of them. Water as gently as possible—you can use a nozzle to break the force of the water. If possible, water seedlings from below by pouring water into the tray or saucer in which the flats or pots are sitting and letting it soak up into the soil. And water in the morning, not in the evening.

▶ **Do** transplant before the roots of adjacent seedlings get tangled together. The best time is when the seedlings have developed their first set of true leaves. When seedlings sprout, they first send up seed leaves, called cotyledons, which are shaped

like the seed coat. The next set of leaves, the true leaves, often look very different from the seed leaves. All the rest of the leaves will be true leaves.

▶ **Don't** handle seedling stems—they're very fragile and easy to crush. Instead, dig up the seedling with a houseplant trowel or Popsicle stick, then hold it by the leaves to move it.

▶ **Do** plant each seedling in a clean cell pack, Styrofoam cup (with drainage holes added), or plastic pot of its own. Replant the seedling at the depth at which it grew in the flat, and firm the soil to make sure there's good root-to-soil contact.

▶ **Do** handle seedlings as little and as quickly as possible, and **don't** leave them lying out. Have your pots set up and ready before you start to transplant, and transplant one seedling at a time. The roots can dry out in a matter of minutes.

▶ **Do** protect newly transplanted seedlings until they've re-established themselves. Keep them in bright but indirect light.

▶ **Don't** fertilize the plants until they're established or you'll shock them. Once they're growing again, you can give them a boost with one-third- to one-half-strength liquid seaweed.

▶ **Don't** let your seedlings overheat. Seedlings prefer cooler temperatures than you might think—around 60°F is fine for most species. When in doubt, keep them cool.

▶ **Do** start hardening off the plants when frost danger is over and the soil has warmed by setting them outside during the day and bringing them in again at night. Select a protected location, such as a spot against a north-facing wall. If possible, mist them in the heat of the day, and put them in the shade or cover them with moist newspaper or a spunbonded row cover like Reemay. After a week of this, you can put them in a cold frame or nursery bed until they're big enough to hold their own in the perennial bed. (To learn more about setting up a nursery bed for your perennials, see "Make Your Own Nursery Bed" on page 250.)

Storing Seed

Whether you collect seed from your perennials, have some left over from the packets you ordered, or aren't ready to plant your seeds when they arrive, how you store them can make a big difference as to how well they'll come up when you plant them. The best place to store them is in the refrigerator, where the seed ages more slowly and stays fresher. Make sure you put the seed on the bottom shelf of the refrigerator, far from the freezer.

If you have a lot of one kind of seed, put it in a small jar with a label in the jar. If you have packets of several types of seed, store them all in a mayonnaise jar, pint canning jar, or other medium-size jar.

Seeds will live longer and germinate better if they're kept dry. To keep moisture away from your seeds, wrap 2 heaping tablespoonfuls of powdered milk in four layers of facial tissue, and secure the packet with a rubber band. Put the packet in the bottom of the jar to absorb moisture, and be sure to replace it every six months. You can also use 1 tablespoon of silica gel—available at drugstores, camera shops, hardware stores, or craft suppliers—instead of the powdered milk.

When you're ready to plant, take the seeds out of the refrigerator. Keep them in the closed jars and let them warm up to room temperature before planting. Otherwise, moisture will condense on the seeds and they'll clump together.

Don't get carried away and store seeds in the freezer or they'll die from shock. It's true that seeds overwinter in the freezing ground,

> ## Tips for
> ## Seed-Starting Success
>
> Perennial gardeners have developed many secrets for successful seed starting. Here are some favorites:
>
> ▶ Mix clean clay cat-box litter in your potting mix to loosen up a heavy mix; it also retains moisture and nutrients.
>
> ▶ Try soaking seeds in black tea to scarify tough seed coats—the tannin in the tea does the trick.
>
> ▶ If your seed flats are in a greenhouse or cold frame, watch out for mice—they love freshly sown seed.
>
> ▶ When sowing fine seed, mix it with unflavored Knox powdered gelatin, which is orange and easy to see, and will actually nourish the seedlings by releasing a little nitrogen as it breaks down.
>
> ▶ Use those discarded cell packs (the kind bedding plants are sold in) to save steps in seed starting. Sow one seed in each cell, then just pop the seedlings out when it's time to transplant. If you're not sowing a lot of seeds and have room, this will really reduce transplant shock.
>
> ▶ Store seeds in plastic Ziploc Storage Bags in the refrigerator—they take up less space than jars.

but in the ground, they freeze gradually in a high-humidity environment, not instantly in a low-humidity freezer.

DIVIDE AND MULTIPLY

Division is the method of choice for the backyard gardener—it's low-tech, reliable, and easy. Basically, you're just digging up established plants and cutting or pulling them

Division Step-by-Step

Division is a great way to propagate your perennials. Here are the basic steps to follow.

1. To start dividing a clump, cut around the mother plant with a trowel or spade (depending on the size of the plant), or loosen the soil with a garden fork. Then lift the plant from the ground, shaking enough soil from the roots so you can see what you're doing when you divide the plant. If there's still too much soil clinging to the roots, you can hose it off.

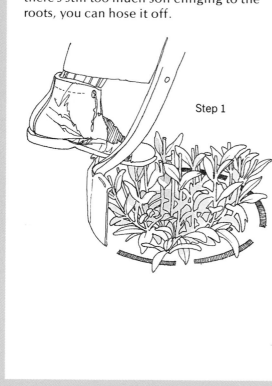

Step 1

2. Plunge two garden forks back-to-back into the clump, then press the handles together until the clump separates into two parts. Divide each part into halves to quarter the perennial, or pull off sections for smaller divisions.

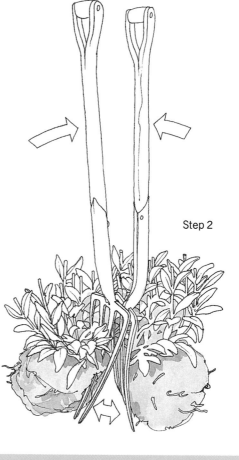

Step 2

apart. In addition to making more plants, division is an excellent way to rejuvenate an old, overgrown perennial that's no longer flowering well and is crowding its neighbors.

The time to divide your perennials is when they're growing vegetatively, not when they're blooming. As a general rule, divide midsummer- to fall-blooming perennials like

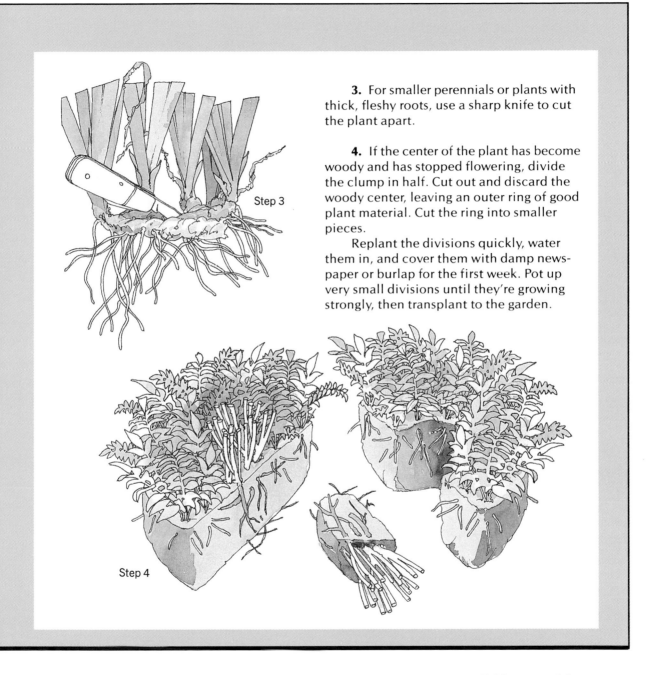

Step 3

3. For smaller perennials or plants with thick, fleshy roots, use a sharp knife to cut the plant apart.

4. If the center of the plant has become woody and has stopped flowering, divide the clump in half. Cut out and discard the woody center, leaving an outer ring of good plant material. Cut the ring into smaller pieces.

Replant the divisions quickly, water them in, and cover them with damp newspaper or burlap for the first week. Pot up very small divisions until they're growing strongly, then transplant to the garden.

Step 4

coneflowers (*Rudbeckia* spp.) in early spring, and spring and early-summer bloomers like astilbes and daylilies in late summer or early fall.

There are two ways to divide perennials once you've dug them up. You can divide them into either a few large pieces or many smaller pieces, depending on your needs.

Division for a Few Big Plants

If you want each parent plant to yield a few large plants that will get established and bloom in a short time, just quarter the original plant. Use a tool that's the right size for the job: A trowel is fine for a loose-knit plant like a coneflower, while a sharp knife is better for perennials like astilbes and peonies that have a more solid crown. A heavy-crowned plant like a daylily may need a very sharp spade or two garden forks set back to back. (Remember that big, old clumps of perennials are heavy. Try to get someone to help you lever them out of the ground.) Leave the daughter plants' healthy roots as intact as possible.

Division for Many Small Plants

If, instead of a few large divisions that will re-establish themselves quickly and bloom the following season, you want the largest possible number of divisions: Dig up the parent plant and cut off the lower roots—up to two-thirds of their total length. Then, with a propagating knife or other sharp knife, cut the parent plant into 1- or 2-inch plugs (in the case of plants with multiple crowns like asters, boltonias, and coneflowers) or individual fans (in the case of plants like daylilies and irises).

You'll get lots of new plants, but they'll take longer to reach blooming size than larger divisions, and the smaller plants will require more care. In fact, you'll have the best luck with this technique if you pot up the divisions and grow them under a watchful eye until they're well-established.

Division Dos and Don'ts

No matter which method of division you use, there are some basics that apply. Remember that division shocks your plants—treat them like the postoperative patients they are.

▶ **Do** prepare the site for your new divisions before you divide your perennials.

▶ **Do** take plants out of the ground before you divide them.

▶ **Do** make sure your tools are sharp. Sharp knives, trowels, or other tools cause fewer open wounds. Since they damage the roots less, plants are less susceptible to disease.

▶ **Do** discard or compost the dead, woody centers of old plants. Cut the remaining section of healthy plant into smaller pieces and replant.

▶ **Do** remove one-half to two-thirds of the foliage on your divisions so it won't wick water away from the plant, but **don't** cut off more than that or you'll slow growth and invite rot.

▶ **Do** replant divisions as soon as possible. Divisions are vulnerable—**don't** leave them lying in the sun.

▶ **Do** plant divisions ½-inch higher than they were planted originally; they'll sink a little as the soil settles. The goal is for them to end up at the same level as the original plants were growing.

▶ **Do** water your divisions well. Give them a good soaking as soon as you plant them, and continue to water them regularly until they're established.

▶ **Do** shade newly planted divisions to protect them. Cover the plants with moist newspaper or burlap held down with rocks or soil for the first week after planting.

▶ **Do** give divided perennials and ornamental grasses a foliar feed of liquid seaweed or fish emulsion to provide trace elements and speed establishment.

▶ **Do** heavily mulch plants divided in fall when the soil cools, to prevent shallow freezing and frost heaving.

▶ **Don't** divide perennials after early October, since the roots need time to establish themselves while the soil is warm.

▶ **Don't** divide taprooted perennials—start them from stem cuttings or seed. These include plants such as butterfly weed (*Asclepias tuberosa*), gas plants (*Dictamnus* spp.), and rues (*Ruta* spp.).

A CLEAR VIEW OF CUTTINGS

Cuttings are a mixed blessing for the perennial gardener. They're easy to make, but it's hard to get them to take. There are two big advantages to cuttings. First, they come true to type: No matter how many cuttings you take of *Veronica* × 'Sunny Border Blue', they'll all be the same, not variations of 'Sunny Border Blue', as they would be from seed. But this is also true of divisions, which are a lot less trouble than cuttings. This brings us to another advantage of cuttings: You can take a lot of them, usually many more pieces than you'd get from dividing. In addition, cuttings are the way to go if you want to propagate a plant that is not yet large enough to divide or is one of the species that resents the disturbance associated with dividing.

That means that, on the plus side, cuttings provide some of the advantages of seed *and* division. The down side is that cuttings are tricky—you have to take them from growth in the right stage, then grow them in warm, humid conditions in a sterile medium. And you have to protect them from rot and other fungal problems, which are encouraged by the heat and high humidity. The upshot is that if you're prepared to coddle your cuttings, and you want a lot of plants that are true to type, this is a good technique for you. Otherwise, stick with division and seed starting.

There are two kinds of cuttings you can make with perennials—stem and root cuttings. Stem cuttings are pieces of a stem, usually with leaves attached (stem cuttings taken from the growing tip of a stem are called tip cuttings), while root cuttings are, as their name implies, pieces of roots. Stem cuttings are easier, so let's start with them.

STEM CUTTINGS

The best time to take stem cuttings is when plants are putting out shoots and leaves, not when they're blooming or getting ready to bloom. So make your cuttings from the first flush of growth, in April through June or July in most of the country. If you want to take cuttings from an early-spring bloomer like woodland phlox (*Phlox divaricata*), wait for the first flush of foliage after bloom. You can also take perennial cuttings when vegetative growth resumes in fall.

When you're ready to take cuttings, choose the parent plant carefully. Don't take cuttings from wilted plants or from plants that are undernourished and stunted. On the other hand, don't take cuttings from an overfed plant with elongated, straggly stems, either. The ideal is soft but vigorous growth: soft enough so you can bend it, but strong enough to stand upright on its own.

Knowing about nodes is an essential part of taking cuttings. Nodes are the little bumps on the stem where leaves will or have come out, and where the roots will emerge from the buried part of the cutting. When taking cuttings, make each cut slightly below a node, as shown in the illustration on page 246.

Success with Stem Cuttings

Smaller cuttings tend to root better and faster—you'll root close to 100 percent of 1½-inch-long rosemary cuttings, while only

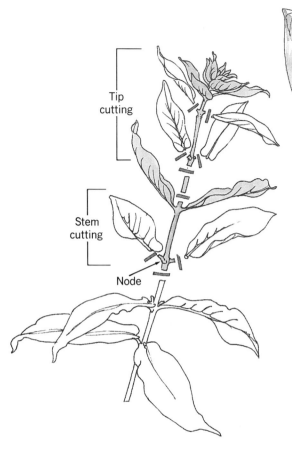

Tip cutting

Stem cutting

Node

Taking stem cuttings. Make stem cuttings from first-flush growth that's firm but not hard. Cut 1½- to 2-inch-long pieces with a sharp, sterile knife. Remove the lower leaves and stick the cuttings in a pot or flat in moist, sterile potting medium so the bottom inch of the stem is in the medium and at least one node is at or below the soil surface. When all the cuttings are in the flat or pot, cover it with clear plastic draped over wire hoops so the plastic doesn't touch the plants.

about 10 percent of 4-inch cuttings will root. The only drawback is that smaller cuttings are also more prone to wilt, so they need more immediate attention. Take only as many cuttings at one time as you can stick into the soil in a half hour. Keep the cuttings out of the sun. Even though you're going to plant them up almost immediately, be sure to wrap them in a damp paper towel to keep them moist.

For rooting cuttings, you'll want a pot or flat filled with sterile, fluffy potting soil. (A 50/50 mix of peat and perlite works well.) Premoisten the mix before you start so that you aren't sticking cuttings into dry soil. Unless your cuttings are taken from the tip of a stem, make a straight cut at the top of the cutting and a slanted cut at the bottom or root end. When you are ready to plant the cuttings, this will help you remember which end goes up and which end should be stuck in the potting soil.

Remove the bottom leaves from your

cuttings so that you're sticking bare stem into the soil. If it's summertime and the plant is big and leafy, take off an extra set or two of the bottom leaves on each cutting before you stick it into the potting mix. Don't remove more than half of the leaves from a cutting, though—the goal is to take off enough foliage to cut down on water loss, while leaving enough greenery for photosynthesis to feed the plant. If the remaining leaves are extremely large, you may need to cut them in half to keep them from wilting unless you have a mist bed.

Stick the cuttings so about 1 inch of stem, with at least one node, is below the soil surface. Be sure to put only cuttings from the same species or cultivar in each pot, and label them clearly with the plant name and the date you took the cuttings. You can root different cuttings in rows in a flat—just label each row.

If you have to transport the cuttings any distance and can't plant them immediately, take slightly bigger cuttings than you plan to use. Label them, wrap them in moist newspaper, and put the moist paper in a plastic bag. Don't seal the bag, or the cuttings will rot. Keep the cuttings cool—Styrofoam coolers are ideal for cool transport. When you get the cuttings home, cut them to the right size and stick them in the flat or pot.

Giving Your Cuttings a Good Home

Once you've potted up the cuttings, your goal is to give them an environment with close to 100 percent humidity and good air movement. The first step is to water the cuttings in thoroughly, so the soil is moist to the bottom of the pot or flat. Then put clear plastic over wire hoops on top of the flat or pot, put a rigid plastic hood over them, or put them in an empty aquarium with a sheet of glass or plastic over the top. You can also sit each pot in a plastic bag and tie the top with a twist tie. Whichever method you choose, make sure the

plastic or glass doesn't touch the cuttings, or leaf diseases may develop.

The cuttings also need warm soil to root and not rot. If you're not propagating in summer, give them bottom heat by putting a rubber mat with heating cables (available from garden centers and garden supply catalogs) under your flat or pot. The soil should be at least 60°F—the higher, the better, up to about 75°F.

If you are taking cuttings in summer, make sure they're kept moist and cool and out of the sun, or they'll cook inside the plastic like a microwave dinner. Provide shading like burlap or a newspaper tent over the plastic for extra protection.

Many cuttings will root in seven to ten days. Check rooting after the first week by gently tugging on the plants—if you feel resistance, give them more ventilation and start to remove the shading if you're using it.

Keep the soil in your flats or pots moist. Don't feed cuttings until they're rooted and growing. Then give them a foliar feed with liquid seaweed or fish emulsion for a gentle boost.

Because of the high-humidity environment needed to root stem cuttings, you can't use this technique with every perennial. Succulents like sedums will rot in such high humidity. Root them in moist sand or a mix of half sand and half perlite, and don't cover the pots or flats with plastic so that the humidity stays low. Silver-leaved plants like artemisias and lavender also tend to rot. You may find it easier to divide these plants or grow them from seed rather than from cuttings.

Dos and Don'ts for Stem Cuttings

Fungal problems are the major threat to cuttings. Here are some dos and don'ts for avoiding rots and other fungal disasters:

▶ **Do** sterilize your knife with alcohol between cuts.

▶ **Do** treat each cutting with a 5 percent bleach solution (1 part bleach to 20 parts water) if you want an extra guard against fungi. If you plan to put the cuttings in a plastic propagating tent or enclosure, use chamomile tea instead of bleach solution. Dip the entire cutting for a few seconds to a minute.

▶ **Don't** stick cuttings deeper than 1 inch or they may rot, and **don't** let leaves come in contact with the soil surface.

▶ **Do** stick cuttings far enough apart so the leaves of adjacent plants don't touch.

▶ **Don't** let the plastic you use to enclose the flat or pot touch the cuttings.

▶ **Do** open the plastic on your propagating containers at least once a day—good circulation prevents fungal problems, while stagnant air encourages them.

▶ **Do** check your cuttings daily for mildewed or dropped leaves. Remove dropped leaves and diseased cuttings as soon as you see them to keep fungi from spreading to healthy cuttings.

Tips for Top Cuttings

Perennial gardeners have developed their own tricks for getting good cuttings. Here are some of the best:

▶ Plastic soda bottles make great propagating tents for rooting cuttings. Cut off the bottoms, fill them with potting mix, stick in the cuttings, water, and replace the top part, sealing the sides with tape. Leave the bottle top off for ventilation.

▶ The clear plastic "clamshell" packs you get at salad bars are also great for rooting cuttings. Punch a few holes in the top for ventilation.

▶ If you're taking cuttings of virus-prone perennials, sterilize your knife between plants by dipping it in skim milk. Research has shown that the milk prevents the spread of viruses.

▶ Use willow water to encourage your cuttings to root. Put willow branches in a 5-gallon pail of water to soak for three days, then soak the ends of the cuttings in this water for up to 24 hours before sticking them in the potting mix. The willow extract seems to make rooting hormones more effective. This is especially helpful with woodier perennials like rosemary, baptisia, and thermopsis.

▶ If you need cuttings but have missed your plants' first flush of growth, you can trick plants like yarrows into creating a second flush by cutting the plants back almost to the ground. Take cuttings from the new growth.

▶ Home water softeners use salts that are harmful to plants. Make sure you're using unsoftened water or rainwater.

▶ One way to keep cuttings fresh if you're bringing them back from a friend's garden is to stick them in a raw potato. Slice the potato in half lengthwise, lay the cuttings along one half with the cut ends inside the potato, put the other half over them like a sandwich, and hold the halves together with rubber bands.

ROOT CUTTINGS DONE RIGHT

If you have a cold frame, unheated room, or greenhouse, you can also propagate perennials from root cuttings. The best perennials for root cuttings have fleshy roots, like Japanese anemone (*Anemone* × *hybrida*), grape leaf anemone (*A. vitifolia*), snowdrop anemone (*A. sylvestris*), great coneflower (*Rudbeckia maxima*), Siberian bugloss (*Brunnera macrophylla*), poppies (*Papaver* spp.), ligularias (*Ligularia* spp.), bleeding hearts (*Dicentra spp.*), cranesbills (*Geranium* spp.), and garden phlox (*Phlox paniculata*). Take root cuttings in the fall or winter when plants are dormant, grow them on in the greenhouse or cold frame, and plant them out in a nursery bed when they are growing strongly (see "Make Your Own Nursery Bed" on page 250).

Making Root Cuttings

Taking root cuttings isn't hard if you pay attention to what you're doing. Here's how to do it: First, hose off the roots of your freshly dug perennial so you can find fleshy, mature roots. They're usually tan rather than the white

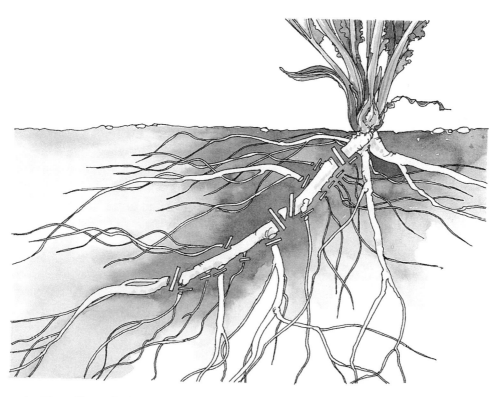

Making root cuttings. Choose fleshy, mature tan roots for root cuttings. Use a sterile propagating knife to cut 1½-inch-long segments of root. Start at the bottom of the root and cut up.

Make a slanted cut at the bottom of the root cutting and a straight cut across the top so that you'll be able to plant it right-side up.

color of immature roots. Use a sterile propagating knife or other sharp knife to make the cuttings. Never use scissors, which will mash the cut surface. Sterilize your knife with alcohol between cuts—root cuttings are very vulnerable to fungal problems.

Bear in mind that perennial roots that grow down in the soil (as opposed to spreading sideways) won't grow if you plant them upside down. For this reason, it's important to plant them in the same direction they were growing in the ground. To remember which end is up, make a slanting cut on the bottom of the root section and a straight cut across the top. (If you forget, plant the root on its side.)

Make your root cuttings about 1½ inches long; you can make many cuttings from each root. Dip cut roots in a 5 percent bleach solution (1 part bleach to 20 parts water) for about a minute to sterilize them.

Pot up your root cuttings in pots or flats filled with a fluffy, sterile potting medium. A seedling mix is a good choice, mixed half-and-half with perlite to make a very porous medium to prevent rotting. When you plant your cuttings, leave about ⅛ inch of the top of each cutting exposed to the light to encourage it to green up and produce top growth.

Perennials with thin, wiry, mat-forming roots aren't as picky when it comes to directional planting. You can scatter root segments of plants like phlox, mulleins (*Verbascum* spp.), Himalayan primrose (*Primula denticulata*), bugloss (*Anchusa* spp.), or hardy ageratum (*Eupatorium coelestinum*) horizontally on the soil surface of your pot or flat, then cover them lightly with one or two times their thickness of soil.

Some perennials produce their own root cuttings when you divide them: The roots that are cut, exposed, and left in the ground when you lift out the mother plant will produce plantlets in the old planting hole, which you can then dig, separate, and replant. Stokes' aster (*Stokesia laevis*), poppies (*Papaver* spp.), blanket flower (*Gaillardia* × *grandiflora*), sea hollies (*Eryngium* spp.), and coneflowers (*Rudbeckia* spp.) are especially prone to this.

Dos and Don'ts for Root Cuttings

Here are the critical dos and don'ts for successful root cuttings:

▶ **Do** keep root cuttings barely moist; they'll rot in wet soil.

▶ **Don't** add fertilizer until the plant is sending up leaves, or you'll promote rot.

▶ **Do** give root cuttings bottom heat: Use a heating pad or heating cable (available from garden supply catalogs) in a cold frame or unheated room. Or set them on a greenhouse bench that has heat running underneath it.

MAKE YOUR OWN NURSERY BED

Once you have seedlings, divisions, and cuttings, where do you put them while they grow big enough for the perennial border? Some perennials may take several years to size up from cuttings or seedlings, and many take a growing season. The ideal is to make a special nursery bed just for growing plants on.

Prepare this bed as you would a standard perennial bed, making sure the soil is rich and smooth and drainage is good. (For more on bed making, see chapter 6.) Site it in partial shade, where the vulnerable plants are protected from heatstroke, where you have easy access to water, and where you'll pass it often so you can keep an eye on it. Mulch the bed, make sure your nursery plants are well-watered, and watch out for rabbits, slugs, and other invaders. One more critical thing: Label plants clearly.

CHAPTER TEN

Perennial Culture Table

This table provides a quick reference to the 161 genera of perennials included in the encyclopedia section. To use the table, find the genus name of the plant you're interested in. The "Name and Page" column tells you the common name most often applied to that genus and the page on which you can find the plant entry in the encyclopedia section. The "Culture" column gives you the cultural requirements of the major species in each genus, including soil, moisture, and light. If a species has different requirements, these will be listed after the general culture notes. You'll find more details on growing these plants in the individual encyclopedia entries, and general culture information in chapter 6.

The "Propagation" column suggests several ways to propagate your perennials. Many perennials are quite easy to divide; if you want to create a number of smaller plants from a large parent, division is the technique of choice. If you don't want to split up the parent plant, other options are also listed here.

Several entries mention seed stratification. This is a simple technique for prechilling seeds that need a cold period before they'll sprout. To stratify, sow the seeds, moisten the soil, and place the pots or flats in the refrigerator for the recommended time period. When their time is up, take them out of the refrigerator and move them to a warm, bright place. For more specifics and other methods, refer to the plant's encyclopedia entry and to chapter 9.

The "Problems" column is for trouble-shooting. We've included potential pest and disease problems, as well as cultural problems that might arise in a typical garden. For more specific problems, see the individual encyclopedia entries; for information on dealing with problems in general, see chapter 7. We've also noted plants that may become invasive through self-sowing or creeping stems; if you don't have room for these plants to spread and don't want to invest extra time keeping them in check, you might choose other perennials that are better-behaved.

251

Name and Page	Culture	Propagation	Problems
Acanthus spp. (bear's-breeches) Page 282	Moist, well-drained soil; full sun or partial shade.	Divide in spring; take root cuttings in spring or late fall.	Spreads rapidly; may be invasive.
Achillea spp. (yarrows) Page 283	Average, well-drained soil; full sun. May need staking.	Sow seeds in late winter; divide in spring or fall; take tip cuttings in spring or early summer.	Powdery mildew or rust may damage leaves; rot is a problem in poorly drained soil.
Aconitum spp. (monkshoods) Page 285	Rich, moist soil; full sun in cooler areas, afternoon shade in Zones 7–8.	Divide in fall or early spring.	Grows less vigorously in areas with high night temperatures (above 70°F).
Aegopodium spp. (bishop's weeds) Page 286	Average soil; partial to full shade.	Divide in fall or spring.	Spreads rapidly; may be invasive. 'Variegatum' is less invasive.
Ajuga spp. (ajugas) Page 287	Average to rich, well-drained soil; sun or shade.	Take cuttings in spring or summer; divide anytime in the growing season.	Common bugleweed (*A. reptans*) may be invasive (other species spread less); crown rot may cause entire clumps to wither and die.
Alcea spp. (hollyhocks) Page 288	Average to rich, well-drained soil; full sun or light shade.	Sow seeds indoors in winter for summer bloom or outdoors in spring for bloom the second year.	Rust, anthracnose, and spider mites can be serious problems on the foliage.
Alchemilla spp. (lady's-mantles) Page 289	Moist, humus-rich soil; full sun to partial shade; likes even moisture but not water-logged soil.	Divide in early spring; sow fresh seeds outdoors in summer; plants often self-sow.	Dry soil will cause the foliage to turn brown.
Allium spp. (alliums) Page 290	Average to rich, well-drained soil; full sun. *A. moly* needs a dry period after flowering.	Divide as leaves yellow and clumps go dormant; sow fresh seeds outdoors; most will self-sow.	Spring-blooming species go dormant after flowering; plant them with bushy summer-blooming plants to hide the tattered, yellowing foliage.
Amsonia spp. (blue stars) Page 292	Average to rich, moist soil; full sun or partial shade.	Divide in fall; sow fresh seeds outdoors in summer; take tip cuttings in early summer.	Clumps are very bushy and may flop; prune stems to 10″–12″ after flowering.
Anaphalis spp. (pearly everlasting) Page 292	Average to rich, moist soil; full sun or light shade. Tolerates damp soil.	Divide in early spring or late fall; take tip cuttings in early summer; sow seeds outdoors in late summer or indoors in late winter.	In dry soils, plants may drop their lower leaves.

Name and Page	Culture	Propagation	Problems
Anchusa spp. (bugloss) Page 293	Rich, well-drained soil; full sun or light shade. Cut plants back after flowering to encourage reblooming.	Divide in spring or fall; take root cuttings in early spring; move self-sown plants into desired locations.	Plants may be short-lived; may self-sow too freely and become weedy.
Anemone spp. (anemones) Page 294	All species prefer moist, humus-rich soil. Spring-blooming species need partial shade; summer- and fall-blooming species thrive in sun or light shade.	Spring-blooming species: divide after flowering or when dormant, or sow fresh seeds outdoors in summer. Summer- and fall-blooming species: divide in spring or after flowering, or take root cuttings when plants are dormant.	All of the spring-blooming species (except for *A. sylvestris*) go completely dormant after flowering. Meadow anemone (*A. canadensis*) may become invasive.
Anthemis spp. (marguerite) Page 296	Average, well-drained soil; full sun. Cut plants back as flower production wanes to encourage new growth.	Divide plants every 2–3 years in spring or fall; take stem cuttings in spring or early summer.	Plants tend to sprawl when grown in light shade. Dead-head regularly to promote bloom.
Aquilegia spp. (columbines) Page 297	Light, average to rich, moist but well-drained soil; full sun or partial shade.	Divide in spring; sow seeds outdoors in fall, or sow indoors in winter. (Store dry seeds in the refrigerator for 4 weeks before sowing.)	Often short-lived; soggy soils hasten their demise. Foliage may be plagued with leaf-miners; borers can also be a problem.
Arabis spp. (rock cresses) Page 299	Average to good, well-drained soil; full sun or light shade. Requires cool temperatures and low humidity for best growth. Cut plants back after flowering to keep them neat.	Divide clumps after flowering; take cuttings in spring.	Highly fertile soil or high heat and humidity can encourage loose, sprawling growth.
Arenaria spp. (sandworts) Page 300	Average, sandy or loamy, well-drained soil; full sun.	Divide in spring or fall.	Plants are shallow-rooted and must be watered regularly during dry spells.
Arisaema spp. (Jack-in-the-pulpits) Page 300	Humus-rich, moist soil. *A. dracontium* prefers full sun to partial shade; *A. triphyllum* tolerates deep shade and poorly drained soils.	Sow cleaned fresh seeds outdoors in fall.	It takes several years for seedlings to grow to flowering size.
Armeria spp. (thrifts) Page 301	Average, well-drained, loamy or sandy soil; full sun. Tolerant of seaside conditions.	Divide in spring or fall; sow seeds indoors in winter in a warm (70°F) growing medium.	–
Artemisia spp. (artemisias) Page 302	Average, well-drained soil; full sun. Generally quite drought-tolerant, but *A. lactiflora* needs moist soil for best growth.	Divide in spring or fall or take cuttings in summer.	In warm, humid regions, the mounding species (especially *A. schmidtiana*) tend to sprawl. Wet soil for extended periods encourages root rot.

(continued)

Name and Page	Culture	Propagation	Problems
Arum spp. (aroids) Page 304	Humus-rich soil; light shade. Needs moist soil when actively growing, but tolerates drier conditions when leafless.	Divide clumps in summer as the leaves wither; sow cleaned fresh seeds outside in fall.	Severe winter weather may cause leaves to turn brown.
Aruncus spp. (goat's beards) Page 305	Moist, humus-rich soil; light to partial shade.	Divide in spring; sow fresh seeds indoors or outdoors in summer in a warm (70°F) growing medium.	Plants will bloom sparsely if shade is too dense.
Asarum spp. (wild ginger) Page 306	Continually moist, humus-rich soil; partial to full shade. *A. canadense* tolerates lime; other species prefer acid soils.	Divide plants in fall; sow fresh seeds indoors or outdoors in summer.	Slugs may devour leaves.
Asclepias spp. (milkweeds) Page 307	Average, well-drained, loamy or sandy soil; full sun. *A. incarnata* prefers moist to wet soil.	Take tip cuttings in late spring or early summer; sow fresh seeds outdoors in fall.	Most species spread by rhizomes and may be invasive.
Aster spp. (asters) Page 308	Cultural needs vary among species. Mountain and seaside species: average to rich soil with excellent drainage; full sun. Meadow, marsh, prairie, and roadside species: average to rich, evenly moist soil; full sun. Woodland species: moist, humus-rich soil; light to partial shade.	Divide clumps in spring; take stem cuttings in late spring or early summer; sow fresh seeds outdoors in fall, or sow indoors in winter (stratify for 4–6 weeks).	Excess moisture or wet soil is sure death to mountain- and seaside-adapted species; they may be short-lived in cultivation. Some asters spread rapidly and need frequent division to keep them attractive. Powdery mildew may be a problem.
Astilbe spp. (astilbes) Page 312	Consistently moist, slightly acid, humus-rich soil; light shade to filtered sun.	Divide in spring or fall.	Wet, poorly drained soil promotes root rot. Dry soil, especially in sunny situations, can also be fatal.
Aubrieta spp. (rock cress) Page 315	Average, well-drained soil; full sun or light shade. Add lime to bring the pH close to neutral. Shear plants after flowering; cut back again in midsummer to promote compact growth.	Divide plants in fall; take cuttings after flowering.	Plants may sprawl by midsummer if not cut back.
Aurinia spp. (basket-of-gold) Page 316	Average, well-drained soil; full sun.	Divide clumps in fall; take cuttings in spring or fall.	In rich and overly moist soils, clumps flop and may rot; treat plants as annuals or biennials in hot areas.

Name and Page	Culture	Propagation	Problems
Baptisia spp. (baptisias) Page 317	Average to rich, moist but well-drained soil; full sun or light shade. Drought-tolerant once established.	Divide in fall; sow fresh seeds outdoors or indoors in summer. (Soak seeds overnight in hot water before planting to speed germination.)	Plants bloom well in light shade but may need staking.
Begonia spp. (begonias) Page 319	Evenly moist, humus-rich soil; partial to full shade.	Plant bulbils (found in the leaf axils) directly out in the garden.	Slugs may eat leaves.
Belamcanda spp. (blackberry lilies) Page 320	Average to rich, well-drained soil; full sun.	Divide clumps in late summer or spring; sow fresh seeds outdoors in fall.	In hot regions, shade from afternoon sun prolongs bloom.
Bergenia spp. (bergenias) Page 320	Moist, humus-rich soil; sun or light shade. Tolerates alkaline soil and drought.	Divide plants in spring; sow fresh seeds indoors or outdoors in summer.	North of Zone 6, the leaves may brown and the growing point may be damaged in winter; slugs may attack leaves.
Boltonia spp. (boltonias) Page 322	Moist, humus-rich soil; full sun or light shade. Drought-tolerant.	Divide in spring or take tip cuttings in May or June.	Plants growing in dry soil may be smaller than normal.
Brunnera spp. (brunneras) Page 323	Moist, humus-rich soil; light to full shade.	Divide in early spring or fall; plants often self-sow. Take root cuttings in fall or winter.	Plants go dormant during long dry spells if not watered.
Caltha spp. (marsh marigolds) Page 324	Constantly moist or wet, humus-rich or loamy soil; full sun to light shade. Can tolerate standing water.	Divide in summer; sow fresh seeds outdoors in late spring in moist soil.	Plants go dormant after flowering.
Campanula spp. (bellflowers) Page 325	Average to rich, well-drained soil; full sun or light shade. Taller-growing species appreciate moist but well-drained soil.	Divide plants in early spring or fall; sow fresh seeds indoors and leave uncovered (light may encourage germination); take tip cuttings in early summer.	Most species grow poorly in areas with high temperatures. Slugs are the only serious pest.
Catananche spp. (Cupid's darts) Page 328	Humus-rich, sandy, well-drained soil; full sun or light shade. Tolerates alkaline soils.	Take root cuttings in fall or winter; sow seeds indoors in late winter.	Plants may be short-lived—especially in heavy clay soils.
Centaurea spp. (centaureas) Page 329	Average to rich, moist but well-drained soil; full sun or light shade.	Divide in spring or fall; sow fresh seeds outdoors in fall or indoors in late winter.	Plants may need to be staked to keep them from flopping.
Centranthus spp. (valerians) Page 330	Average to sandy, neutral or alkaline soil; full sun. Thrives in rockeries and stone walls. Shear plants after flowering if they become floppy.	Easy to grow from seeds sown indoors or outdoors in late winter; plants may self-sow freely under favorable conditions.	—

(continued)

Name and Page	Culture	Propagation	Problems
Cerastium spp. (mouse-ear chickweed) Page 330	Average, well-drained soil; full sun.	Divide plants in spring or fall; take tip cuttings in summer.	Plants may rot unless they have good drainage.
Ceratostigma spp. (plumbago) Page 331	Average to rich, moist but well-drained soil; sun or partial shade. Prune out winter-killed stems before new growth expands in late spring.	Divide clumps in spring; take tip cuttings in summer.	—
Chelone spp. (turtleheads) Page 332	Rich, evenly moist soil; full sun or partial shade. In warmer zones, plants in full sun must have constant moisture.	Divide in spring or late fall; take stem cuttings in early summer.	Plants grow poorly in dry soil, especially if they are in full sun.
Chrysanthemum spp. (chrysanthemums) Page 333	Average to rich, moist but well-drained soil; full sun. *C.* × *morifolium* thrives in neutral or alkaline soils; *C. nipponicum* and *C.* × *superbum* tolerate dry, sandy soils and seaside conditions.	Divide clumps in spring; take tip cuttings in late spring or early summer.	Waterlogged soil is fatal to most species, especially in winter. Aphids and spider mites can be problems.
Chrysopsis spp. (golden asters) Page 337	Average or sandy, well-drained soil; full sun.	Divide in spring; take tip cuttings in early summer; sow fresh seeds outdoors in fall or indoors in winter (stratify for 4–6 weeks).	Plants grow poorly in rich or very moist soils.
Cimicifuga spp. (bugbanes) Page 337	Moist, humus-rich soil; sun or shade. Fairly drought-tolerant once established.	Divide the tough roots in the fall; sow fresh seeds outdoors in fall.	Full sun and dry soil may cause browned leaf edges.
Clematis spp. (clematis) Page 338	Moist, humus-rich soil; full sun. A cool, evenly moist and fertile root zone is as important as sun for good growth.	Take stem cuttings before flowering in spring or early summer.	—
Convallaria spp. (lilies-of-the-valley) Page 339	Moist, rich soil; partial or filtered shade.	Divide in summer or fall.	Spreads rapidly; may be invasive.
Coreopsis spp. (coreopsis) Page 340	Average to rich, moist soil; full sun. Drought-tolerant.	Divide in spring or fall; sow fresh seeds indoors in summer or fall in a warm (70°F) growing medium.	Overly rich soils promote flopping.
Crocosmia spp. (montbretias) Page 342	Moist, humus-rich soil; full sun. In Zones 5 and north, lift bulbs in fall and store indoors.	Divide clumps in fall.	Leaves may be attacked by thrips or spider mites.

Name and Page	Culture	Propagation	Problems
Crocus spp. (crocuses) Page 343	Average to rich, well-drained soil; full sun or light shade. Plant in fall.	Divide after flowering.	Rodents often eat corms.
Delphinium spp. (delphiniums) Page 345	Deep, moist, alkaline to slightly acidic, humus-rich soil; full sun.	Divide in spring; sow fresh seeds outdoors in summer or fall; take stem cuttings in early spring.	Slugs and powdery mildew may damage the leaves. Delphiniums grow best in areas with cool summers.
Dianthus spp. (pinks) Page 347	Moist to dry, well-drained, alkaline to slightly acid soil; full sun. Divide every 2–3 years to keep plants vigorous.	Divide in spring or fall or take stem cuttings in summer; sow seeds outdoors in spring or indoors in winter.	Rust may be a problem on the leaves.
Dicentra spp. (bleeding hearts) Page 350	Evenly moist, humus-rich soil; light to full shade.	Divide in fall or as they go dormant; sow fresh seeds outdoors in summer; take root cuttings in fall.	*D. cucullaria* and *D. canadensis* go dormant in early summer. Leaves are prone to browning if exposed to too much sun.
Dictamnus spp. (gas plants) Page 352	Well-drained, average to rich soil; full sun or light shade.	Sow fresh seeds outdoors in late summer.	Root rot may be a problem in soggy soil and hot weather. Established plants are difficult to divide or transplant successfully.
Digitalis spp. (foxgloves) Page 353	Moist, humus-rich soil; full sun or partial shade. Remove spent flowerstalks from biennials and hybrids to keep plants vigorous.	Sow seeds indoors in late winter or outdoors in summer; plants bloom the second year.	Biennial and hybrids types need frequent division to grow well.
Disporum spp. (fairy-bells) Page 354	Moist, humus-rich soil; partial to full shade.	Divide in fall; sow fresh seeds outdoors in summer.	—
Dodecatheon spp. (common shooting-stars) Page 354	Moist, humus-rich soil; sun or shade; prefer a neutral or slightly acidic soil.	Divide in summer or fall; take root cuttings in summer or fall; sow fresh seeds outdoors in summer.	Plants usually go dormant after flowering.
Doronicum spp. (leopard's bane) Page 355	Consistently moist, humus-rich soil; full sun or partial shade. Mulch to keep the soil cool.	Divide after flowering.	Plants go dormant in summer.
Echinacea spp. (purple coneflowers) Page 356	Average, well-drained, loamy soil; full sun. Drought-tolerant.	Take root cuttings in fall; sow seeds outdoors in fall or indoors in winter (stratify for 4–6 weeks).	Division is not recommended; divided plants become bushy and produce fewer flowers.

(continued)

Name and Page	Culture	Propagation	Problems
Echinops spp. (globe thistles) Page 357	Average to rich, sandy or loamy soil; full sun. Drought-tolerant. Good drainage is essential, especially in winter.	Divide in fall or take root cuttings in spring or fall; sow seeds indoors in late winter.	Plants cannot tolerate water-logged soil.
Epimedium spp. (epimediums) Page 358	Moist, average to humus-rich soil; partial to full shade. Thrives for years with little attention.	Divide plants after flowering or in late summer.	—
Eremurus spp. (foxtail lilies) Page 360	Moist but well-drained, humus-rich soil; full sun or light shade.	Divide clumps in fall; sow fresh seeds indoors or outdoors in fall.	Plants cannot tolerate water-logged soil, especially during the winter months.
Erigeron spp. (fleabanes) Page 360	Moist but well-drained, rich soil; full sun or light shade. Long-lived, but benefits from division every 2–3 years.	Divide in fall; take tip cuttings in early summer; sow seeds indoors in winter.	—
Eryngium spp. (sea hollies) Page 361	Average, well-drained soil; full sun. Move plants when they are young; older plants are difficult to re-establish after transplanting.	Sow fresh seeds outdoors in fall or indoors in winter (stratify for 4–6 weeks).	—
Erythronium spp. (trout lilies) Page 363	Moist, humus-rich soil. Sun is essential when plants are growing in spring, but shade is acceptable when plants are dormant.	Divide in early summer as the leaves are yellowing; sow fresh seeds outdoors in summer.	Plants go dormant after flowering.
Eupatorium spp. (bonesets) Page 364	Moist, average to rich soil; full sun or light shade.	Divide in spring or fall; take tip cuttings in early summer.	Plants may self-sow freely in the garden.
Euphorbia spp. (spurge) Page 365	Well-drained, average to rich soil; full sun or partial shade. Most species are drought-tolerant (except for *E. griffithii*).	Divide in fall; take tip cuttings in summer.	Plants need winter protection in areas with cold temperatures and no snow cover.
Filipendula spp. (meadowsweets) Page 367	Evenly moist, humus-rich soil; full sun or light shade.	Divide clumps in fall.	Leaves become tattered or browned in dry soil.
Fritillaria spp. (fritillaries) Page 369	Light but rich, well-drained soil; full sun or partial shade. Plant in autumn.	Divide after flowering.	*F. imperialis* is usually short-lived but can be grown as an annual.
Gaillardia spp. (blanket flowers) Page 370	Average, well-drained soil; full sun. Thrives on hot sites with little maintenance; perfect for seaside gardens.	Divide in early spring; sow seeds outdoors in fall or indoors in winter (stratify for 4 weeks).	Plants may sprawl and be short-lived when grown in rich, moist soil.

Name and Page	Culture	Propagation	Problems
Galium spp. (bedstraws) Page 371	Moist, rich soil; sun or shade.	Divide in spring or fall; take stem cuttings in early summer.	Spreads rapidly; may be invasive.
Gaura spp. (gauras) Page 372	Moist, well-drained soil; full sun. Drought-tolerant.	Sow seeds outdoors in fall or divide in spring or fall.	—
Gentiana spp. (gentians) Page 372	Evenly moist, humus-rich soil; full sun or partial shade.	Sow fresh seeds outdoors in late fall or indoors in late winter (stratify for 4–6 weeks).	Foliage may turn brown if not shaded from afternoon sun.
Geranium spp. (cranesbills) Page 373	Moist but well-drained, humus-rich soil; sun or partial shade.	Divide in early spring or fall; sow seeds outdoors or indoors in a warm (70°F) growing medium in summer.	Foliage may turn brown if not shaded from hot afternoon sun in warmer zones.
Geum spp. (avens) Page 376	Evenly moist but well-drained, humus-rich soil; full sun or light shade. *G. rivale* will grow in wet soil; *G. triflorum* tolerates drier soils.	Divide in spring or fall; sow fresh seeds outdoors in summer or fall.	Plants growing in hot, dry conditions are susceptible to leaf browning and spider mites.
Gillenia spp. (bowman's-roots) Page 377	Moist, rich soil; sun or partial shade. Drought-tolerant.	Take stem cuttings in spring; sow fresh seeds outdoors in summer.	—
Gladiolus spp. (glads) Page 378	Moist, well-drained, humus-rich soil; full sun. Plant in spring. North of Zone 7, lift corms in fall and store indoors, or treat as annuals.	Divide corms before replanting in spring.	Thrips are a serious problem; aphids may also attack plants.
Gypsophila spp. (baby's-breaths) Page 379	Rich, moist, neutral to slightly alkaline soil; full sun or light shade. Good drainage is essential.	Take cuttings in spring; sow seeds outdoors in spring or fall or indoors in late winter.	Established clumps can be difficult to divide or transplant successfully.
Helenium spp. (sneezeweeds) Page 380	Evenly moist, humus-rich soil; full sun. Pinch stem tips in the spring to promote sturdy, compact growth.	Divide in spring or late fall; take stem cuttings in early summer.	—
Helianthus spp. (sunflowers) Page 381	Moist, average to rich soil; full sun. Drought-tolerant.	Divide in fall; take stem cuttings in early summer; sow fresh seeds outdoors in late summer or fall.	Most species are too large for small gardens.
Heliopsis spp. (heliopsis) Page 383	Moist or dry, average to rich soil; full sun or partial shade.	Divide after flowering; take stem cuttings in late spring.	Plants may need staking.

(continued)

Name and Page	Culture	Propagation	Problems
Helleborus spp. (hellebores) Page 383	Evenly moist but well-drained, sandy, humus-rich soil; light to partial shade. Plants thrive in alkaline to slightly acidic soils.	Sow fresh seeds outdoors in spring or summer.	Plants take 2 years to become established and dislike disturbance.
Hemerocallis spp. (daylilies) Page 385	Average to rich, well-drained soil; full sun or light shade. Hybrids need sun for optimum flowering.	Divide in late summer.	Newer cultivars need daily deadheading to keep them looking their best; aphids and thrips may be a problem on bloom stalks and buds.
Hesperis spp. (dame's rockets) Page 389	Moist, average to rich soil; sun or partial shade.	Sow seeds indoors in late winter or outdoors in summer or fall; plants self-sow prolifically.	Plants go dormant or die soon after flowering.
Heuchera spp. (alumroots) Page 389	Moist but well-drained, humus-rich soil; full sun or partial shade.	Divide in early spring or fall.	In warm regions, plants need shade from hot afternoon sun to prevent leaves from turning brown or pale.
× *Heucherella* spp. (foamy bells) Page 391	Moist, humus-rich soil; light to partial shade.	Divide in early spring or fall.	Leaves may turn brown if they get too much sun, but deep shade discourages flowering.
Hibiscus spp. (hibiscus) Page 391	Evenly moist, humus-rich soil; full sun or light shade.	Take tip cuttings in July; sow seeds outdoors in fall or indoors in late winter.	—
Hosta spp. (hostas) Page 392	Evenly moist, humus-rich soil; light to full shade. Tough, versatile, and adaptable.	Divide in spring or fall.	Most species need protection from direct sunshine to prevent leaf browning. Slugs and snails often attack leaves.
Houttuynia spp. (houttuynias) Page 397	Constantly moist or wet, humus-rich soil; full sun or light shade. Will grow in standing water.	Divide in spring or fall; take stem cuttings in early summer.	Spreads rapidly and can become a nuisance.
Iberis spp. (candytufts) Page 398	Average, well-drained soil; full sun or light shade. Shear plants back by ⅓ after flowering.	Take tip cuttings in early summer; sow seeds outdoors in spring or fall.	—
Iris spp. (irises) Page 399	Evenly moist but well-drained, humus-rich soil; full sun to light shade. Bulbous species prefer rich soil that is moist in spring but dry in summer, with full sun.	Divide after flowering in summer or early fall; sow fresh seeds outdoors in summer or fall.	Rots and iris borers can attack plants.

Name and Page	Culture	Propagation	Problems
Kniphofia spp. (torch lilies) Page 405	Average to rich, well-drained soil; full sun. Good drainage is a necessity.	Divide by removing 1 or more crowns from the edge of the clump in fall; sow seeds indoors in winter (stratify for 6 weeks).	Excess water on the crowns, especially in winter, may kill the plants.
Lamiastrum spp. (yellow archangels) Page 406	Average to rich, well-drained soil; partial to full shade.	Divide in spring or fall; take tip cuttings in spring or summer.	Spreads rapidly; may be invasive. 'Herman's Pride' spreads more slowly than the species.
Lamium spp. (lamiums) Page 407	Moist, well-drained, humus-rich soil; light to partial shade.	Divide in spring or fall; take tip cuttings in spring or summer.	Spreads rapidly; may be invasive.
Lavandula spp. (lavenders) Page 407	Average to rich, well-drained soil; full sun. Can endure extremely dry conditions. A neutral or slightly alkaline soil is ideal.	Divide in spring or take tip cuttings from new growth in fall.	Good drainage is essential for survival; wet soils promote root rot.
Liatris spp. (gayfeathers) Page 408	Average to rich, moist but well-drained soil; full sun.	Divide corms in early fall; sow seeds outdoors in fall or indoors in late winter (stratify for 4–6 weeks).	Tall species may flop; 'Kobold' and other cultivars are compact.
Ligularia spp. (ligularias) Page 410	Constantly moist, fertile, humus-rich soil; light to partial shade.	Divide in spring or fall.	Leaves may turn brown if soil is dry; slugs may be a problem.
Lilium spp. (lilies) Page 411	Cultural needs vary according to species and hybrid group. Most require deep, loamy, well-drained, neutral to slightly acid soil; full sun or light shade.	Divide bulbs in late summer as they go dormant.	Plants are prone to viruses; aphids may spread the disease.
Limonium spp. (statice) Page 416	Average to rich, well-drained soil; full sun or light shade. Tolerates alkaline soil; adaptable to seaside conditions.	Sow seeds outdoors in fall.	Established plants are difficult to divide or transplant successfully.
Linum spp. (flax) Page 416	Average, sandy or loamy, well-drained soil; full sun or light shade.	Divide in spring or fall or take stem cuttings in early summer; sow fresh seeds outdoors in late summer or fall.	Plants are prone to rot if soil is too wet, especially in winter.
Liriope spp. (lilyturfs) Page 417	Average to rich, well-drained soil; full sun to full shade. These tough, adaptable plants endure extreme heat, high humidity, and drought.	Divide clumps in spring or fall.	—

(continued)

Name and Page	Culture	Propagation	Problems
Lobelia spp. (lobelias) Page 419	Rich, constantly moist soil; light to partial shade.	Divide in fall; sow seeds uncovered outdoors in fall or indoors in late winter.	Plants are often short-lived.
Lupinus spp. (lupines) Page 420	Rich, acidic, evenly moist but well-drained soil; full sun or light shade.	Remove sideshoots in fall; sow fresh seeds outdoors in late summer or indoors in winter. Before planting indoors, soak seeds overnight in warm water; sow in flats and chill 4–6 weeks, then move to a warm, bright place.	Plants may be short-lived, especially in warmer zones.
Lychnis spp. (campions) Page 421	Most need light, average to rich, moist but well-drained soil; full sun or light shade. *L.* × *haageana* needs consistent moisture for best growth.	Divide plants in spring; plants self-sow readily.	*L. coronaria* is prone to dying out if soil is too wet.
Lycoris spp. (spider lilies) Page 423	Rich, moist, well-drained soil; full sun or light shade. Plant in fall.	Divide bulbs after flowering.	Plants do not have foliage in summer.
Lysimachia spp. (loosestrifes) Page 423	Evenly moist, humus-rich soil; full sun or partial shade.	Divide in spring or fall.	Extended drought is fatal. Spreads rapidly; may become invasive.
Lythrum spp. (loosestrifes) Page 424	Moist, average to rich, humus-rich soil; full sun or light shade.	Divide in spring or take stem cuttings in summer.	Plants tend to spread aggressively and become invasive.
Malva spp. (mallows) Page 426	Average, near neutral, well-drained soil; full sun or light shade.	Sow seeds outdoors in spring or fall or indoors in late winter; take tip cuttings in early summer.	Plants are more susceptible to pests and foliar diseases in warm, humid areas.
Mertensia spp. (bluebells) Page 427	Consistently moist but well-drained, humus-rich soil; sun or shade.	Divide after flowering; plants will self-sow.	Plants go completely dormant after flowering.
Monarda spp. (bee balms) Page 428	*M. didyma:* moist, humusy soil; full sun or partial shade. *M. fistulosa* and *M. punctata:* average to rich soil; full sun to light shade.	Divide in early spring or fall.	Susceptible to powdery mildew.
Narcissus spp. (daffodils) Page 429	Moist, well-drained, humus-rich soil; full sun or light shade. Plant in fall.	Divide plants as foliage yellows in summer.	Plants go dormant by early summer.

Name and Page	Culture	Propagation	Problems
Nepeta spp. (catmint) Page 432	Average, sandy or loamy, well-drained soil; full sun or light shade. After flowering, shear plants back by $\frac{1}{2}$–$\frac{2}{3}$.	Divide in spring or fall or take tip cuttings in early summer.	—
Oenothera spp. (evening primroses) Page 433	Average to rich, well-drained soil; full sun or light shade. Tough and drought-tolerant.	Divide the rosettes in early spring or after flowering.	*O. speciosa* is invasive.
Opuntia spp. (prickly pears) Page 434	Average, sandy or loamy soil; full sun.	Remove pads anytime during the growing season and cover their bases with moist sand.	Leaves and debris caught within the clumps are quite difficult to remove.
Paeonia spp. (peonies) Page 435	Moist, loamy, humus-rich soil; full sun or light shade.	Divide in late summer.	Botrytis blight may cause buds to abort or may wilt and kill stems; thrips may be a problem on buds.
Papaver spp. (poppies) Page 438	Average to rich, well-drained soil; full sun.	Divide in late summer; take root cuttings in late summer or fall.	Plants go dormant after flowering.
Patrinia spp. (patrinias) Page 440	Average to rich, moist but well-drained soil; full sun or light shade.	Sow fresh seeds outdoors in fall; divide in spring.	May self-sow too prolifically.
Penstemon spp. (penstemons) Page 440	Sandy or loamy, humus-rich, well-drained soil; full sun or light shade. Good drainage is essential for most; *P. digitalis* tolerates moist or wet soils.	Divide in early spring or after flowering; sow seeds outdoors in fall or indoors in winter (stratify for 4–6 weeks).	Root rot may be a problem in waterlogged soils.
Perovskia spp. (Russian sages) Page 442	Well-drained, sandy or loamy soil; full sun.	Take stem cuttings in early summer.	Prone to rot if soil is too wet, especially in winter.
Phlox spp. (phlox) Page 443	Woodland species: evenly moist, humus-rich soil; light to full shade. Low, mounding species: average, sandy or loamy, well-drained soil; full sun. Border species: average to rich, moist but well-drained soil; full sun or light shade.	Divide woodland species after flowering, mounding species in fall, border species in spring; take stem cuttings in spring or early summer; take root cuttings in fall.	Powdery mildew often attacks leaves.
Physostegia spp. (obedient plants) Page 447	Evenly moist, average soil; full sun or partial shade. Tolerates considerable moisture.	Divide in spring or late fall.	Plants tend to flop in rich soil; select a compact cultivar.

(continued)

Name and Page	Culture	Propagation	Problems
Platycodon spp. (balloon flowers) Page 448	Average to rich, well-drained soil; full sun or light shade. Plants are tough and adaptable. New shoots are slow to emerge; take care not to dig into them.	Divide in spring or early fall; sow fresh seeds outdoors in late summer or fall.	—
Polemonium spp. (Jacob's ladders) Page 449	Evenly moist, humus-rich soil; full sun or partial shade.	Sow fresh seeds outdoors in fall; divide after flowering or in fall.	*P. caeruleum* does not thrive in areas with hot summers.
Polygonatum spp. (Solomon's seals) Page 449	Moist, humus-rich soil; partial to full shade.	Divide in spring or fall; sow cleaned fresh seeds outdoors in fall.	*P. commutatum* does not tolerate dry conditions.
Polygonum spp. (smartweed) Page 450	Moist, humus-rich soil; full sun or partial shade.	Divide in spring or fall.	Plants do not tolerate full sun in warmer zones.
Potentilla spp. (cinquefoils) Page 451	Well-drained, sandy or loamy, acidic soil; full sun or light shade. Extremely drought-tolerant once established.	Divide in spring or fall.	Plants grow poorly in areas with extreme high or low temperatures.
Primula spp. (primroses) Page 452	Moist, humus-rich soil; light to partial shade. *P. japonica* and *P. denticulata* require moist to boggy soil. In northern zones, winter mulch is essential; in the South, protect from hot sun.	Divide after flowering; sow fresh seeds outdoors in fall or indoors in early spring.	May go dormant if conditions get too hot or dry.
Pulmonaria spp. (lungworts) Page 454	Evenly moist, humus-rich soil; partial to full shade. Moderately drought-tolerant once established.	Divide after flowering in fall.	Plants may go dormant if conditions get too dry.
Ranunculus spp. (buttercups) Page 456	Evenly moist, humus-rich soil; full sun or light shade.	Divide after flowering or in fall; plants often self-sow.	Spreads rapidly; may become invasive.
Rodgersia spp. (rodgersias) Page 457	Constantly moist to wet, humus-rich soil; light to full shade.	Divide in fall.	Plants in warmer zones need shade to prevent leaf browning.
Rudbeckia spp. (coneflowers) Page 457	Moist but well-drained, average to rich soil; full sun or light shade.	Divide in spring; sow seeds indoors in winter or outdoors in spring or fall.	Taller species and cultivars may need staking.

Name and Page	Culture	Propagation	Problems
Ruta spp. (rue) Page 459	Sandy or loamy, moist but well-drained soil; full sun. Easy to establish and long-lived.	Take stem cuttings in late summer or early fall.	Working around these plants may cause a skin rash.
Salvia spp. (sages) Page 460	Well-drained, sandy or loamy soil; full sun or light shade. Most species are tough and extremely drought-tolerant.	Divide plants in spring or fall; take tip cuttings in early summer.	Overly rich or moist soils may encourage weak, floppy stems.
Santolina spp. (lavender cotton) Page 462	Well-drained, sandy or loamy soil; full sun. Easy to grow and quite drought-tolerant. Cut back hard after flowering.	Take cuttings anytime during the growing season.	Plants tend to fall open with age.
Saponaria spp. (soapworts) Page 462	Average, sandy or loamy, well-drained soil; full sun or light shade.	Divide plants in spring or fall; take tip or stem cuttings in summer.	May overgrow and flop in rich soil. Spreads rapidly; may be invasive.
Scabiosa spp. (scabious) Page 463	Well-drained, sandy or loamy, humus-rich, non-acidic soil; full sun or light shade. Dead-head to prolong flowering.	Divide in spring only if they become overcrowded; sow fresh seeds outdoors in fall or indoors in late winter.	Plants will rot in overly moist soils.
Sedum spp. (sedums) Page 464	Average to rich, well-drained soil; full sun to light shade. Easy to grow.	Divide in spring or fall or take tip cuttings in summer.	—
Senecio spp. (groundsels) Page 467	Average to rich, moist but well-drained soil; full sun to partial shade.	Divide after flowering or in fall; often self-sows.	Spreads readily by creeping roots and self-sown seedlings.
Sidalcea spp. (checker-blooms) Page 468	Average to rich, moist but well-drained soil; full sun or light shade. Cut plants to the ground after flowering to promote new foliage.	Divide in fall.	—
Silene spp. (catchflies) Page 468	Average, sandy or loamy soil; full sun or light shade.	Sow fresh seeds outdoors in fall.	May be short-lived in gardens but often self-sows.
Sisyrinchium spp. (blue-eyed grass) Page 469	Moist, average to rich soil; full sun or partial shade.	Divide after flowering.	—
Smilacina spp. (Solomon's plumes) Page 470	Moist, humus-rich, neutral or acid soil; light to full shade.	Divide in early spring or fall.	—

(continued)

Name and Page	Culture	Propagation	Problems
Solidago spp. (goldenrods) Page 470	Average, moist but well-drained soil; full sun or light shade. *S. caesia* and *S. flexicaulis* prefer humus-rich soil in partial shade.	Divide in spring or after flowering; self-sown seedlings often appear.	Rich soils encourage rampant spread and flopping.
Stachys spp. (lamb's-ears) Page 472	Well-drained, sandy or loamy soil; full sun or light shade.	Divide in fall.	Plants do not perform well in hot, humid areas or where there is frequent summer rain; woolly foliage traps water and is subject to rot.
Stokesia spp. (Stoke's asters) Page 473	Average to rich, moist but well-drained soil; full sun or light shade. Easy to grow; long-lived.	Divide in spring or fall; sow fresh seeds outdoors in fall or indoors in winter (stratify for 6 weeks).	—
Tanacetum spp. (tansies) Page 474	Average, moist soil; full sun.	Divide in spring or fall.	Plants spread rapidly by creeping roots and self-sown seedlings.
Thalictrum spp. (meadow rues) Page 475	Moist, humus-rich soil; full sun or light shade.	Divide in fall.	—
Thermopsis spp. (false lupines) Page 476	Average to rich, moist but well-drained, acidic soil; full sun or light shade.	Divide in spring; take stem cuttings in early summer from sideshoots; sow fresh seeds outdoors in late summer or indoors in winter after soaking for 12–24 hours in hot water.	Foliage may be unattractive after flowering.
Tiarella spp. (foamflowers) Page 476	Humus-rich, slightly acidic, evenly moist soil; partial to full shade.	Divide in spring or fall; remove rooted runners anytime during the growing season; sow seeds outdoors in spring and leave uncovered.	—
Tradescantia spp. (spiderworts) Page 477	Average to rich, moist but well-drained soil; full to light shade.	Divide plants as they are going dormant; self-sown seedlings are often abundant.	Plants get shabby or go dormant after flowering; cut to the ground.
Tricyrtis spp. (toad lilies) Page 478	Evenly moist, humus-rich soil; light to partial shade. Easy to grow; long-lived.	Divide in spring; plants often self-sow.	In northern zones, plants are often damaged by frost before they bloom.

Name and Page	Culture	Propagation	Problems
Trillium spp. (trilliums) Page 479	Moist, humus-rich soil; shade. *T. erectum* requires acid soil.	Sow fresh seeds outdoors in summer.	Germination is slow (1–2 years); plants take 5–7 years to bloom from seed. Most trilliums sold are wild-collected.
Trollius spp. (globeflowers) Page 480	Constantly moist to wet, humus-rich soil; light to partial shade.	Divide in early spring or fall; sow fresh seeds outdoors in summer.	Plants do not thrive in areas with hot summers.
Tulipa spp. (tulips) Page 481	Moist but well-drained, fertile, humus-rich soil; full sun. Dormant bulbs need dry soil in summer. Plant in fall.	Divide species tulips after flowering.	Some hybrids are short-lived.
Uvularia spp. (bellworts) Page 484	Moist, humus-rich soil; shade.	Divide in fall.	—
Verbascum spp. (mulleins) Page 485	Average, well-drained, sandy or loamy soil; full sun.	Take root cuttings in early spring; self-sown seedlings will often appear.	Plants will rot without good drainage.
Verbena spp. (verbenas) Page 486	Well-drained, sandy or loamy soil; full sun to light shade. Tough; heat- and drought-tolerant.	Take stem cuttings during the growing season; sow fresh seeds outdoors in late summer or fall or indoors in winter (stratify for 3–4 weeks).	—
Veronica spp. (speedwells) Page 487	Average to rich, moist but well-drained soil; full sun or light shade. *V. virginica* needs rich, moist soil.	Divide in spring or fall; take stem cuttings in early to mid-summer.	—
Vinca spp. (periwinkles) Page 489	Average to rich, moist but well-drained soil; light to full shade.	Divide in early spring or after flowering; take stem cuttings in summer.	Spreads rapidly; may become invasive.
Viola spp. (violets) Page 490	Moist, humus-rich soil; light to full shade.	Divide in spring or fall; transplant self-sown seedlings.	Spreads by creeping stems and self-sown seedlings; may become invasive.
Yucca spp. (yuccas) Page 492	Well-drained, sandy or loamy soil; full sun or light shade. Extremely drought-tolerant.	Divide offsets in spring or fall.	Most species are large. Place them carefully in small gardens.

Enjoying Your Perennials

Aperennial garden is a beautiful sight. And fortunately for the perennial gardener, it's possible to enjoy perennials indoors as well as out. That's because they can be used fresh in arrangements or dried in wreaths, bouquets, and potpourris for year-round color. In this chapter, you'll find out which perennials are best for cutting fresh, which are best for drying, and the simple techniques you need to make them into delightful arrangements and crafts.

CUT FLOWER GARDENING

Unless you have a cutting garden—a bed set aside for producing flowers especially for cutting and set up in rows or blocks something like a vegetable-garden bed—you'll pick your cut flowers from your perennial garden. Take time to evaluate the plants you have now: Will they make attractive fresh arrangements, or dry well for arrangements and crafts? Look at the lists of best perennials for cutting (page 270) and drying (page 274). How many of these flowers are you growing? How many would you like to grow? As you buy perennials to fill holes or make new beds, keep cut flowers in mind.

When you've noted which perennials in your garden are suitable for cut flowers, run through this checklist: Do you have a good variety of flowers for cutting? Do you have a good range of flower colors, heights, and shapes? Do you have lots of fragrant flowers? Does your garden have a selection of flowers for cutting from spring through fall? If your answer to any of these questions is no, reevaluate your garden design and see if you can add or substitute to fill in the gaps.

Cutting flowers can leave bare places in your borders if you have only one or two of each plant. (In a cutting garden, which isn't meant to be an ornamental feature in the landscape, it isn't a problem if you cut all the blooms.) This is another good argument for planting groups of each perennial to maximize impact instead of planting a collector's garden—

Successful Cutting Gardens

Setting off a special garden to grow cut flowers is a great way to produce all the flowers you love in the colors you want. The easiest and most efficient way to arrange a cutting garden is with all the plants of each species grown together in rows or blocks as in a vegetable garden. That way you can tend them efficiently. Paths between rows or blocks make it easy to get to the flowers for cutting, and it's a snap to work down the rows to add a layer of mulch or to chop down weeds with a hoe before they get out of hand. Raised beds are ideal, especially if your soil isn't perfect. You can even intersperse your cut flowers among the tomatoes, peppers, and other plants in your vegetable garden.

To grow cut flowers successfully, choose the planting site carefully and prepare the soil well. Most of your plants will thrive if you select a site with well-drained, humus-rich soil and full sun. Check the cultural requirements of the plants you want to grow; group plants with similar needs together.

Give your plants the care they need: adequate watering and fertilizing, diligent weeding and deadheading (removal of faded flowers), and winter protection and pest control when necessary. An organic mulch, such as compost or shredded leaves, conserves moisture, inhibits weeds, and keeps flowers and leaves clean and mud-free. Commonsense care and careful plant selection will give you a constant supply of beautiful cut flowers all season.

---

a mishmash of single plants without a unifying design. If you have three or five plants of each flower, you can cut as many blooms as you want without denuding your garden.

Pay particular attention to your favorite flowers as you evaluate your garden. If you love peonies or Siberian iris (*Iris sibirica*), plant a wide selection of cultivars. Choose cultivars in a range of colors, as well as plants that bloom at different times to extend the season.

Some perennials, like bearded iris, columbines (*Aquilegia* spp.), and chrysanthemums, come in such a wide range of colors and sizes that you could include them in practically any arrangement. If, on the other hand, you especially love a flower that is only available in yellow, such as Carolina thermopsis (*Thermopsis caroliniana*), think of including other plants in your garden that will bloom at the same time in harmonious colors.

If you have a favorite color or color scheme, plan to have a variety of perennials in your garden that bloom in that color (or those colors). Make sure you have other flowers in colors that look good with your favorite, too. No matter how much you love red, a solid red arrangement will never look as satisfying as a red arrangement with a little blue, purple, yellow, chartreuse, or orange added for sparkle. White flowers will make a blue or yellow arrangement glow. A few peach flowers in a pink arrangement—or pink flowers in a peach arrangement—add sophistication. Variegated foliage will really perk up an arrangement, too—try adding cream and white hosta leaves to a peach or orange arrangement.

Extending the Cutting Garden

When you've evaluated your perennial garden for suitable cutting flowers, look at the rest of your yard. Are you growing annuals to mix in your arrangements? Snapdragons, coleus, cosmos, marigolds, stock (*Matthiola incana*), and zinnias can round out an arrangement, adding missing colors and shapes. The intense color of many annuals can add much-needed pizzazz when the perennial garden offers a pastel palette. Ornamental grasses are also effective both fresh and dried; they add neutral colors and feathery spikes to all kinds of arrangements.

Bulbs make beautiful cut flowers, too. If you're not growing them in your perennial beds, look beside your walkways and around your shrubs and trees for clumps of daffodils, groups of hyacinths, tulips, and Dutch iris (*Iris Xiphium Hybrids*), and clusters of smaller bulbs like grape hyacinths (*Muscari* spp.) and lily-of-the-valley (*Convallaria majalis*). If your yard doesn't provide enough variety, it's never too late to add these delightful plants to your flower beds.

Don't overlook foliage when you're out cutting flowers for arrangements. Adding beautifully colored, textured, shaped, or variegated foliage can integrate the different shapes and colors of your flowers and give an arrangement added charm and sophistication. Shade-loving plants such as ferns, hostas, pachysandras, and bergenias (*Bergenia* spp.) are easy to grow and offer a range of texture and leaf shapes. In addition, some hostas and pachysandras have variegated foliage, which can add color and drama to any arrangement. Groundcovers like English ivy and common periwinkle (*Vinca minor*) and the foliage of perennials like ferns, lady's-mantles (*Alchemilla* spp.), lamb's-ears (*Stachys byzantina*), and *Heuchera* 'Palace Purple' add unifying greens, grays, and purples, tying the flower colors together.

Herb foliage can turn a bland arrangement into a sensory delight. Rosemary, lavender, thyme, scented geraniums, and the many mints will make a centerpiece a conversation

Best Perennials for Cutting

You may already be growing these familiar perennials in your garden. They are long-lasting in fresh arrangements, and they give you a wide selection of shapes and colors. They combine beautifully with annuals, roses, and ornamental grasses.

Achillea spp. (yarrows): showy flat flower heads in yellow, white, rose, cream, or salmon

Alchemilla spp. (lady's-mantles): airy clouds of chartreuse flowers and lovely geranium-like foliage

Allium spp. (alliums): flat or round heads of pink, white, lavender, or purple flowers

Aster spp. (asters): clusters of daisy flowers in blue, purple, lavender, rose, or pink

Chrysanthemum spp. (chrysanthemums): daisy or cushion flowers in every color but blue

Delphinium spp. (delphiniums): spires of cupped flowers in blue, purple, lavender, pink, or white

Echinacea purpurea (purple coneflower): white or purple daisy flowers with showy orange cones

Echinops spp. (globe thistles): blue or lavender globe-shaped flowers

Gypsophila paniculata (baby's-breath): clouds of tiny white flowers

Hosta spp. (hostas): spires of tubular flowers in lavender, purple, or white; striking green, blue-green, chartreuse, or variegated foliage

Liatris spp. (gayfeathers): fuzzy wands of purple, white, or lavender blooms

Lilium spp. (lilies): starry clusters of orange, red, white, yellow, or pink flowers

Lupinus spp. (lupines): large, showy spires in blue, yellow, red, white, or bicolors

Paeonia lactiflora cultivars (peonies): large, single, semidouble, or double, rounded flowers in white, pink, red, rose, coral, or salmon

Phlox spp. (phlox): showy rounded panicles in white, pink, salmon, red, or lavender

Platycodon grandiflorus (balloon flower): blue, white, or pink clusters of bell-shaped flowers

Rudbeckia spp. (coneflowers): yellow-orange daisies with showy black or green centers

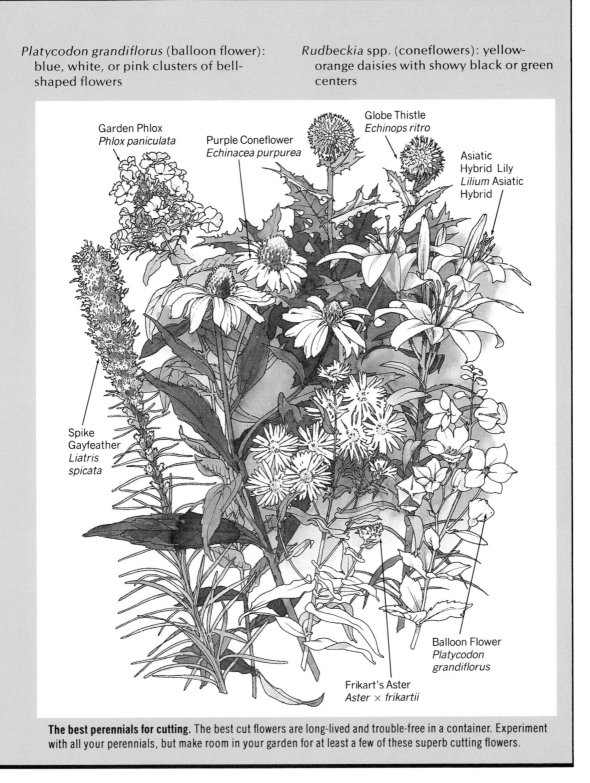

Garden Phlox
Phlox paniculata

Purple Coneflower
Echinacea purpurea

Globe Thistle
Echinops ritro

Asiatic Hybrid Lily
Lilium Asiatic Hybrid

Spike Gayfeather
Liatris spicata

Frikart's Aster
Aster × frikartii

Balloon Flower
Platycodon grandiflorus

The best perennials for cutting. The best cut flowers are long-lived and trouble-free in a container. Experiment with all your perennials, but make room in your garden for at least a few of these superb cutting flowers.

piece as friends and family run their fingers over the scented leaves. The colors of herb foliage are often interesting, too—the needle-like gray-green leaves of rosemary and lavender, ferny blue rue foliage, upright crinkly mint spikes, and soft, felted geranium leaves. Thymes and sages are available with beautiful variegations that add to their appeal. Next time you draw a blank when designing an arrangement, head for the herb garden.

Flowering shrubs and vines provide plenty of material for arrangements, and many of them are fragrant, too. Roses, in their many colors and shapes, will perk up any arrangement. Lilacs, butterfly bushes (*Buddleia* spp.), spireas (*Spiraea* spp.), honeysuckles, viburnums, trumpet vine (*Campsis radicans*), and hydrangeas are a few of the many possibilities. Spring arrangements can feature forsythias, witch hazels (*Hamamelis* spp.), and pussy willows with early bulbs and perennials. In the fall, the brightly colored leaves of oakleaf hydrangea (*Hydrangea quercifolia*), sumacs (*Rhus* spp.), Boston ivy (*Parthenocissus tricuspidata*), and

Tips for Long-Lasting Cut Flowers

Your flowers will last a lot longer if you use common sense when picking them. Here's a list of dos and don'ts that will keep your arrangements fresh:

▶ **Do** pick flowers early in the day. **Don't** wait until the heat of the day, when flowers are tired and wilted.

▶ **Do** choose flowers for cutting that aren't fully open. **Don't** pick the ones that look prettiest today, but will have dropped their petals tomorrow.

▶ **Do** cut flower stems cleanly with sharp scissors or pruners. **Don't** mash the stems with a dull blade or wrench them off the plants.

▶ **Do** carry a bucket of lukewarm water and plunge stems into it as soon as they're cut. The water should come at least halfway up the stems but shouldn't reach the blooms. **Don't** leave cut flowers lying on the ground or in a harvest basket until you go indoors.

▶ **Do** set the bucket in a cool, shady place. **Don't** leave cut flowers out in the hot sun.

▶ **Do** strip off all leaves and buds that would be underwater in your arrangement. **Don't** leave them on to foul the water.

▶ **Do** recut stems on a slant before adding them to an arrangement. **Don't** settle for the original cut; the stem end may have sealed and be unable to take up water.

▶ **Do** use lukewarm water for your arrangement. **Don't** shock your flowers with icy water.

▶ **Do** treat foliage like artemisias, ivy, and lamb's-ears the same way you treat flowers. **Don't** forget to include these and other foliage plants in your arrangements.

Some flowers need special treatments. Flowers that drip milky sap from their cut ends, including poppies, spurge (*Euphorbia* spp.), and buttercups (*Ranunculus* spp.), last longer if you sear the cuts in a flame for a second or dip them in boiling water for a minute. Flowers with hollow stems like daffodils, delphiniums, lupines (*Lupinus* spp.), and alliums (*Allium* spp.) last longer if you fill each stem with water, then plug the end with part of a cotton ball.

Virginia creeper (*P. quinquefolia*) blend beautifully with asters, boltonia (*Boltonia asteroides*), goldenrods (*Solidago* spp.), mums, and other late-blooming perennials.

Cutting Fresh Flowers

If you're cutting flowers for a fresh arrangement, your selection is limited only by flower availability. However, there are some commonsense rules to follow if you want to get the most from your cut flowers. You'll find these useful tips in "Tips for Long-Lasting Cut Flowers" on the opposite page.

Cutting Flowers for Drying

If you're cutting flowers or foliage for drying, there are a few special things to keep in mind. First, cut only dry flowers for drying, not flowers that are wet with dew or rain. Wet flowers will dry with discolored spots. Second, make sure you choose perfect flowers, with no holes or blackened areas. If you can see a defect in the fresh flower, you'll see it magnified when the flower has dried. Third, cut flowers that are slightly less open or mature than you actually want. They'll open more as they dry.

Tips for Fresh Arrangements

Some of the most inspired arrangements include vines, branches, stems of perennials that aren't in bloom, herbs, and even weeds. Don't limit yourself. And don't be afraid to liven up arrangements by mixing in some flowers from the florist to round out your garden flowers. A few carnations, roses, or mums may be just what your arrangement needs.

There are a few special tricks and plain commonsense measures you can use to keep fresh flowers looking good longer. Prolong vase life by changing water daily if it begins to color or smell, and topping it up daily if it's still fine. Other secrets of long-lasting arrangements include adding an aspirin or a drop of household bleach and a spoonful of sugar, or some Sprite or 7-Up, to the vase water. (The aspirin and bleach lower the pH of the water, discouraging bacterial growth, while the sugar encourages buds to develop and open; lemony sodas supply both sugar and acid.) You can also keep flowers looking fresher by keeping your arrangements out of direct sunlight and away from a heat source.

Tips for Dried Arrangements

Try these techniques for making the most of dried arrangements and keeping them looking good longer. First, don't forget that you're almost unlimited when it comes to containers for dried arrangements. Whether you choose a Shaker basket, Great-Grandmother's Victorian boot, or a piece of chrome pipe, let yourself go when you're planning a dried bouquet.

One tip that applies as well to dried as to fresh arrangements is to visit your local florist, herb shop, or craft shop if your collection of home-dried flowers is monotonous. It's easy to spice up a pale, washed-out, or drab assortment with some colorful dried flowers from the florist. Many florists carry a variety of dried flowers, and they're especially likely to have lovely colors of annual statice. (If they only have fresh statice, remember that it dries very easily at home.) You can also add variety and color to a dried arrangement by adding dried grains (like wheat), foliage, and vines (bittersweet is especially striking).

Two tricks will give more life to your dried arrangements: Keep them out of direct sun from bright windows, and blow off dust every day. Finally, you can perk up a tired arrangement by taking out ragged or faded flowers and adding new ones; work gently, but don't be afraid to rework a favorite composition.

DRYING FLOWERS

Drying flowers extends your garden season. With a selection of dried flowers, foliage, and pods or seed heads, you can create lovely dried arrangements to enjoy year-round. It also gives you a supply of plant materials for craft projects like wreaths, trimmed baskets, Christmas ornaments, sachets, and potpourris. Besides pressing flowers, there are three simple methods for foolproof flower drying—air drying, desiccant drying, and microwaving.

Air Drying Is Easy

Air drying flowers requires no special equipment—all you need are a warm, dry, dark room and your plant materials. The only limitation is that not all flowers air dry well. Sturdy flowers that tend to keep their shape in the garden after bloom—yarrows, ornamental grasses, alliums (*Allium* spp.), and sea lavender (*Limonium latifolium*), for example—are the ones that air dry best. Air drying is also an excellent technique for stems of showy seedpods like baptisias (*Baptisia* spp.), blackberry lily (*Belamcanda chinensis*), and Siberian iris (*Iris sibirica*).

The best way to air dry most perennials is to hang them upside down in bunches. Strip off the leaves first, unless you'd like to experiment and see how they look dried. Then gather six to ten stems together and bind them with a rubber band about 2 inches from the end of the stems. (Wrap the rubber band fairly tightly, since the stems will shrink as they dry.)

Hang the bunches in an attic, closet, or dry basement for one to three weeks. Flowers are

Best Perennials for Drying

It's a pleasure to discover that you don't have to plant a special garden just for drying. Many popular perennials dry beautifully. Round out your arrangements with dried roses, ornamental grasses, and a selection of annuals, including cockscomb (*Celosia cristata*), strawflower (*Helichrysum bracteatum*), annual statice (*Limonium sinuatum*), and seedpods of honesty (*Lunaria annua*) and love-in-a-mist (*Nigella damascena*). Here's a group of well-known perennials that air dry easily.

Achillea spp. (yarrows): showy flat flower heads in yellow, white, rose, cream, or salmon

Anaphalis spp. (pearly everlasting): clusters of small, rounded, white, strawflower-like blooms, some with yellow centers

Artemisia spp. (artemisias): gray, gray-green, or yellow-green foliage

Delphinium spp. (delphiniums): spires of cupped flowers in blue, purple, lavender, pink, or white

Echinacea purpurea (purple coneflower): strip off petals and use showy orange cones in arrangements

Echinops spp. (globe thistles): blue or lavender, globe-shaped flowers

Eryngium spp. (sea hollies): cone-shaped flowers in green, silver, blue, or lavender, with showy, thistle-like bracts at their bases

Gypsophila paniculata (baby's-breath): clouds of tiny white flowers

Lavandula angustifolia (lavender): slender spires in purple, lavender, pink, or white

Limonium latifolium (sea lavender): broad, airy, lavender-blue clusters of tiny flowers

Stachys byzantina (lamb's-ears): felty white or greenish white leaves

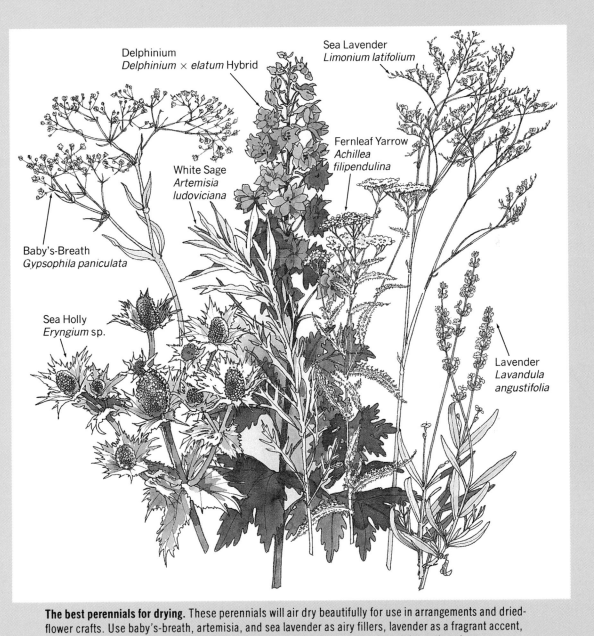

Delphinium
Delphinium × *elatum* Hybrid

Sea Lavender
Limonium latifolium

Fernleaf Yarrow
*Achillea
filipendulina*

White Sage
*Artemisia
ludoviciana*

Baby's-Breath
Gypsophila paniculata

Sea Holly
Eryngium sp.

Lavender
*Lavandula
angustifolia*

The best perennials for drying. These perennials will air dry beautifully for use in arrangements and dried-flower crafts. Use baby's-breath, artemisia, and sea lavender as airy fillers, lavender as a fragrant accent, and yarrow and delphinium to anchor arrangements with their bold shapes and dramatic colors.

completely dry when you can snap a stem crisply in two. Use this method for drying spike-blooming perennials like lavender, delphiniums, sages (*Salvia* spp.), goldenrods (*Solidago* spp.), and monkshoods (*Aconitum* spp.).

Some perennials dry better if they're stood upright in a vase, can, or jar. Use this technique for globe thistles (*Echinops* spp.) and baby's-breaths. You'll find that this method works better with some perennials if you stand them in ½ inch of water and let it evaporate as the flowers dry. Try this with yarrows and alliums.

When your flowers are dry, you can leave them hanging in bunches or standing in their cans or vases if you have room. If space and dust are concerns, store them loosely in shoe boxes or other covered boxes lined with tissue paper. Put the boxes where you can get to them easily for projects, and be sure to label each box with the names of the flowers inside and the date you dried them.

Desiccant Drying Is Versatile

Desiccant drying involves laying flowers in a bed of absorbent material that dries the flowers by removing water from the petals. It's a more complicated technique than air drying, but results in more lifelike flowers. You can try drying any perennial with desiccants—even delicate ones that won't air dry well. Double flowers like peonies dry beautifully with this technique, but if you're extremely gentle, you can even dry single flowers like poppies and cranesbills (*Geranium* spp.).

To dry flowers with desiccants, you need a desiccant and a container to hold it and the plant material. Silica gel—which looks like clear plastic sand, not gel—is the most popular desiccant. You can buy it at hobby and craft stores and at garden centers. You'll need to buy 5 to 10 pounds, but you can reuse it as often as you want. Re-dry the silica gel after

several uses because it gradually absorbs moisture from the flowers. Most silica gel contains colored crystals that change color when it's time to re-dry it. Re-dry it in an oven or microwave and follow the manufacturer's directions. Store silica gel in an airtight container like a plastic food-storage box or cookie tin.

It's especially important that the surfaces of flowers and foliage be perfectly dry before you set them in the silica gel—the gel will stick to wet spots on leaves or petals, discoloring them. When you've collected your plant material, you can layer it in an airtight box. Start with a ½- to 1-inch layer of silica gel in the bottom of the box. Lay leaves flat, making sure they don't touch. When you've filled the space, pour in another inch or two of silica gel, then start the next layer. Continue until the box is full.

Sort your flowers by shape, since each is handled differently. Cut all flower stems so they're only 1 to 2 inches long. Lay flower spikes like delphiniums lengthwise in the box. (To keep large spikes straight, support the stems with cardboard hurdles set every 2 inches under each spike.) For daisy flowers like single chrysanthemums or other fragile single flowers like poppies, make a small mound of silica gel and turn the flower upside down over the mound. Set double flowers like peonies upright in the gel and gently fill in around and between the petals. Again, make sure flowers aren't touching.

Desiccant drying can be faster than air drying. Flowers and leaves should be dry in as little as one to two weeks. Check your box by tilting it gently until the gel runs off to reveal a leaf or flower. Plant material will be dry when it's crisp and papery. Pour off the silica gel to remove the flowers, carefully brushing clinging gel from each flower with an artist's brush.

Make wire stems for your dried flowers by

placing a piece of floral wire alongside the stem stub of each flower and taping it on with floral tape. (Both tape and wire are available from craft shops and florists.) Wrap the wire stem by gently stretching and spiraling the floral tape down its length. When all the flowers have new "stems," store them upright in an airtight container with an inch of silica gel in the bottom.

Desiccant-dried flowers can "re-humidify" in the comparatively moist home atmosphere. You can spray them with hair spray or petal sealant to help keep them dry. Or, if they start looking a little soft or going limp, put them back in the desiccant for a few days to re-dry them.

Microwave Drying Is Fast

With a microwave oven, you can dry perennials almost as fast as you cook popcorn. You'll get the most lifelike flowers if you combine microwaving with desiccant drying. Put ½ inch of silica gel in the bottom of a microwave-safe container, arrange the flowers on the gel as you would for normal desiccant drying, and cover them with more gel. Set the dish in the microwave with a cup of water (the water protects the microwave from damage). Heat on high for 2 minutes, then check the flowers. If they're not crisply dry, heat again for 1 minute and recheck; if they're too dry, try the next batch for 1 minute. Since each microwave is different, you'll need to keep records on just how long it takes your oven to dry each type of flower.

You can also dry leaves in a microwave by folding them in a paper towel and placing the towel in the microwave with a microwave-safe plate on top to keep the leaves from curling as they dry. Put the cup of water in to protect the oven, then heat on high for 2 minutes. Adjust the drying time as needed. Keep a close watch on the foliage as it's drying—it burns easily.

CRAFTS FROM PERENNIALS

Dried perennials offer a wealth of wonderful options besides arrangements. You can make lovely wreaths, potpourris, trimmed hats and baskets, swags, and endless other projects from dried flowers. Remember these crafts when you're ordering new plants for your garden, as well as at cutting time.

Creative Wreathmaking

Like flower arrangements, wreaths can match your mood, the season, a holiday, or your decor. They can be simple, using just one kind of flower, or elaborate. Start your perennial wreath with a wreath base, which you can buy in a craft or hobby shop or at a florist. If you plan to cover the entire base with dried flowers, choose a Styrofoam, straw, or wire wreath base. If you want the base to show, use a grapevine wreath or a straw wreath base. (A straw base is solid enough to cover completely but decorative enough to show.)

For Styrofoam or straw wreath bases, you can use floral pins, floral picks (which look like large toothpicks with a wire on one end), or a hot glue gun to attach your materials. For wire or grapevine wreath bases, use a hot glue gun or short lengths of wire.

Floral pins look like giant hairpins and are very easy to use. Just hold the flowers in place and stab the wires into the Styrofoam or straw base. For floral picks, wrap the wire part of the pick around one or several stems to bind the dried flower(s) to the pick. Then stab the wooden end into the Styrofoam or straw to anchor it. It's a good idea to secure the flower stems to floral picks with a bit of floral tape. To use a hot glue gun, put a drop of glue on the back of the flower, then stick the flower on the wreath. Remember that you can use all three methods on the same wreath. A glue gun is perfect for attaching extra blooms to a wreath after it's nearly complete, without disturbing the flowers that are already in place.

If you're making a wreath with several kinds of flowers, start by attaching filler material to the wreath base as a background. Artemisia, baby's-breath, Tatarian statice (*Goniolimon tataricum*), and sea lavender (*Limonium latifolium*) are good background choices. Work from the inside of the wreath to the outer edge, moving in the same direction and overlapping stems as you go. Then add larger flowers, dried grasses, pods, rose hips, dried annuals, and other materials.

The Pleasures of Potpourri

Potpourri is the easiest dried-flower craft. It not only smells wonderful and makes a great gift, it's also fun to make and looks beautiful in bowls, baskets, and jars. All you really need to make potpourri is a selection of

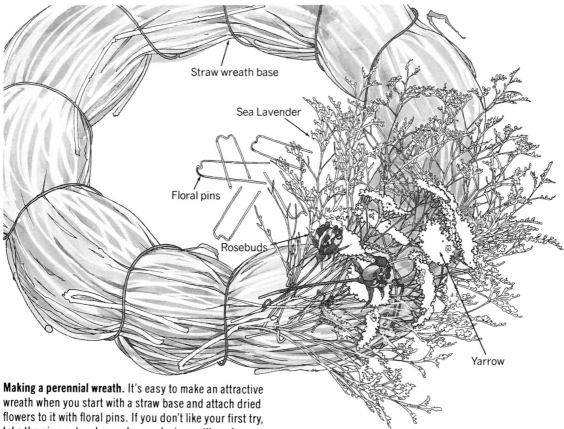

Making a perennial wreath. It's easy to make an attractive wreath when you start with a straw base and attach dried flowers to it with floral pins. If you don't like your first try, take the pins out and rework your design until you're pleased with it. A foolproof technique is to attach the background material — airy fillers like artemisia or sea lavender — first, then pin on showier flowers like yarrow. Try adding dried ornamental grasses, everlastings like annual statice (*Limonium sinuatum*), rosebuds, and pods for added color and texture. Make sure you leave 3 to 5 inches of stem on the dried material. Experiment with covering the entire wreath base with flowers, or leaving part of the base exposed and making a swag or bouquet of flowers on one side or the center.

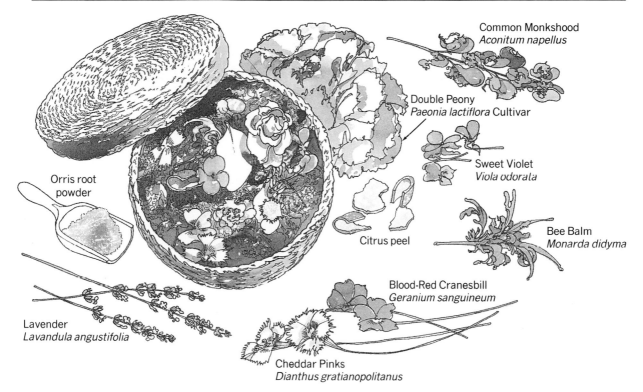

Common Monkshood
Aconitum napellus

Double Peony
Paeonia lactiflora Cultivar

Sweet Violet
Viola odorata

Bee Balm
Monarda didyma

Orris root
powder

Citrus peel

Blood-Red Cranesbill
Geranium sanguineum

Lavender
Lavandula angustifolia

Cheddar Pinks
Dianthus gratianopolitanus

Perennial potpourri. You can make a lovely potpourri with fragrant, colorful perennials like lavender, bee balm, cheddar pinks, and sweet violets. Dry these flowers carefully to preserve their shape and color. Add dried peonies for bulk, rosebuds and petals for extra color, orris root (available from craft and herb shops and craft supply catalogs) as a fixative to hold fragrance in the mix, and dried citrus peel for a fresh, bracing scent to contrast with the sweet perfume of the flowers. Other dried perennials like cranesbills, delphiniums, and yarrows can add color and texture to your potpourri.

different types of dried flowers.

Cut the stems of flowers you plan to use for potpourri very short. Make the bulk of your potpourri from neutral-colored filler material, like dried white or light-pink peony petals, artemisia, scented geranium leaves, and chamomile flowers. Add other fragrant flowers like lavender, as well as fragrant herbs like dried rosemary, mint, or thyme if you'd like a potpourri with a fresh scent. For a spicy scent, mix in some cinnamon sticks and cloves; for a citrusy fragrance, add dried lemon or orange peel, lemon balm, and lemon verbena.

Next, add showy dried flowers for color. Yarrow, bee balm (*Monarda didyma*), and

delphiniums add a range of colors and distinctive flower shapes to potpourri. Colorful annuals like cockscomb (*Celosia cristata*) can perk up a mixture that looks bland. Potpourris are a great place to use dried florist's flowers, too.

If you'd like a stronger fragrance in your potpourri, add a few drops of your favorite essential oil. Use just one type of essential oil per batch of potpourri. Ten to 20 drops of essential oil will scent 5 cups of potpourri. You can keep a potpourri's fragrance stronger by mixing in a fixative. The best are orris root, calamus root, and oak moss. Fixatives and essential oils are available from craft shops.

*Beautiful combinations like this one start with plants that need the same growing conditions and that flower together in compatible colors. Here, primrose-yellow 'Moonshine' yarrow (*Achillea × 'Moonshine'*), blue-violet 'Johnson's Blue' cranesbill (*Geranium × 'Johnson's Blue'*), and red valerian (*Centranthus ruber*) hold the spotlight. Look up perennials in this encyclopedia to check their bloom season, color, height, and preferred conditions.*

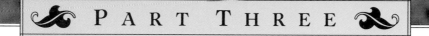

PART THREE

PERENNIAL ENCYCLOPEDIA

Acanthus Acanthaceae, Acanthus Family

uh-KAN-thus. Bear's-Breech. Late-spring and summer bloom. Full sun.

Spiny bear's-breech (*Acanthus spinosus*) is adaptable, long-lived, and practically indestructible. The bold spring foliage remains attractive throughout the growing season, and the lovely bicolor flowers are good for cutting.

Description: Bear's-breeches are robust plants with evergreen leaves. One-inch flowers with purple hoods and 3 white lower petals are borne in tall spikes in spring and summer.

Acanthus mollis (MAHL-iss), bear's-breech. Size: 2½'–4' tall; leaves 1½'–2' long. The broad leaves are lustrous dark-green, with deep lobes and teeth. Zones 8–10.

A. spinosus (spine-OH-sus), spiny bear's-breech. Size: 3'–4' tall; leaves 1'–2' long. Large, erect leaves bear stiff spines and are narrower and more deeply lobed than those of *A. mollis*. Plants form dense clumps. Zones 7–10.

How to Grow: Plant in moist, well-drained soil in full sun or partial shade. Remove brown leaves in early spring. Plants spread quickly by creeping roots. Propagate by dividing in spring or taking root cuttings in spring or late fall.

Landscape Uses: Use as a focal point in a formal garden, as a foundation planting, or as an accent in the shade garden. 🍂

Achillea   Compositae, Daisy Family

uh-KILL-ee-uh. Yarrow. Late-spring and summer bloom. Full sun.

Achillea 'The Beacon' bears a profusion of rich red flowers for a month or more in early summer. Remove spent flower heads to prolong the flowering season. 'The Beacon' is one of the new Galaxy series hybrids, which come in a rainbow of colors.

Description: Yarrows have showy, flattened flower heads composed of many tiny, tightly packed flowers of white, yellow, pink, rose, or red. The often ferny, green or gray foliage is usually aromatic.

Achillea filipendulina (fill-ih-pen-djew-LEE-nuh), fernleaf yarrow. Size: 3'–4' tall; leaves 8"–10" long. A stately yarrow with deeply cut, olive-green foliage. The tall, leafy stems are topped by 4"–5"-wide flattened flower heads with small, tightly packed, golden-yellow flowers. Plants may need staking when they are in full flower. The cultivar 'Gold Plate' is taller, to 5', with deep-yellow flower heads up to 6" across. 'Parker's Variety' grows 3'–4' tall, with golden-yellow flowers borne on stronger stems than the species. Zones 3–9.

The similar *A.* × 'Coronation Gold' is a hybrid between *A. filipendulina* and *A. clypeolata*. The plants are shorter (3' tall) and more robust and seldom need staking. The 5"-wide, mustard-yellow flower heads are set off beautifully by the gray-green foliage. This is one of the best yarrows for use in the garden and for cutting. It blooms throughout the summer months and is tolerant of a wide range of conditions. It is the best yellow yarrow for areas with hot, humid summers. Zones 3–9.

A. millefolium (mill-uh-FOE-lee-um), common yarrow. Size: 1'–2½' tall; leaves 6"–8" long.

Common yarrow is a popular old-fashioned perennial with delicate, fine-textured foliage. Most garden selections have ½"–1"-wide heads of pink or red flowers. They bloom throughout the summer months on stems 1½'–3' tall. The dense clumps spread rapidly and need dividing every 3 years to control their roaming. The cultivar 'Cerise Queen' is a strong grower, to 1½' tall. 'Fire King' is one of the most commonly available cultivars, with deep rose-red flowers on 2' stems. 'Rose Beauty' has pale rose-pink flowers. Zones 3–9.

The new Galaxy Series of *A. millefolium* × *A. taygetea* hybrids from Germany has expanded the color choice and rekindled interest in these hardy but underused plants. The Galaxy hybrids have larger (2"–3") flower heads on sturdy stems. Flower color ranges from brick-red to rose, pink, salmon, and pale-yellow. The flowers tend to fade as they age, giving the plants an interesting multi-colored effect. Zones 3–9.

Achillea × 'Moonshine' is an attractive, easy-to-grow yarrow prized for its compact growth, blue-gray foliage, and sulfur-yellow flowers. The flowers are long-lasting when cut and used fresh or dried. The seed heads are attractive left standing in the garden.

A. × 'Moonshine', moonshine yarrow. Size: 1'–2' tall; leaves 5"–6" long. The 3" sulfur-yellow flower heads are produced all summer on sturdy stems that seldom need staking. Its smaller stature makes this plant ideal for gardens with limited space. The pale-yellow flowers are easier to blend into the flower border than the harsh yellows of other yarrows. The ferny foliage is soft blue-gray and forms dense, wide clumps. The plants prefer a well-drained situation and do not tolerate extreme heat and high humidity. Zones 3–8.

A. ptarmica (TAR-mick-uh), sneezewort. Size: 1½'–2' tall; leaves 1"–4" long. This sprawling yarrow was called sneezewort because the dried root was used as a substitute for snuff. This species bears little resemblance to other yarrows, having lance-shaped leaves without the characteristic ferny appearance. The species is somewhat weedy, but the popular cultivar 'The Pearl' bears a profusion of ¾" creamy-white double flowers in early summer. Plants may easily escape cultivation and become invasive. Zones 2–9.

A. tomentosa (toe-men-TOE-suh), woolly yarrow. Size: 8"–12" tall; leaves 4"–6" long. This hairy plant is best in northern gardens; it is intolerant of extreme heat and humidity. The plant's compact form makes it excellent for rock gardens or the front of the border. The soft yellow flowers on ½"–1" heads resemble those of *A.* × 'Moonshine'. This European native flowers throughout the summer. Zones 3–7.

How to Grow: Yarrows are low-maintenance plants that thrive with little care. Plant them in full sun in average to poor soil that is well-drained. Rich soils encourage luxuriant growth that may require staking. Yarrows are quick to establish and spread to form dense clumps. Space plants 2'–3' apart to accommodate their spread.

Some species, especially *A. millefolium*, can be invasive. Plants need dividing every

3-5 years. Lift the clumps in early spring or fall and remove any dead stems from the center of the clump. Replant divisions in well-prepared soil. Propagate yarrows from tip cuttings in spring or early summer. Plants may develop powdery mildew or rust that disfigures the leaves. Stem rot can also be a problem. To treat all of these fungal diseases, remove affected parts and dust the remaining plants with sulfur to prevent further spread of the disease.

Landscape Uses: The versatile yarrows are at home in the formal border or in informal situations. They are good for the middle or back of the border, or for softening bold textures. These plants are excellent for cutting or drying. Pick yarrows for drying when they have good color but before they start to turn brown. 🌿

Aconitum   Ranunculaceae, Buttercup Family

ack-oh-NEYE-tum. Monkshood. Late-summer and fall bloom. Partial shade.

Description: Monkshoods are poisonous plants with tall, spiky flower heads and deeply lobed foliage. The 1″–1½″ flowers have a protruding helmetlike hood above 3 lower petals.

Aconitum × bicolor (BYE-color), bicolor monkshood. Size: 3′–4′ tall; leaves 2″–3″ long. A tall, showy perennial with blue, purple, or bicolor flowers borne in tall spikes in late summer. The leaves have 5–7 lobes. The cultivar 'Bicolor' grows 3′–4′ tall and has two-tone flowers. The hood is pale-blue with white streaks; the lower petals are intense blue. 'Bressingham Spire' is shorter, with 2½′–3′ stems that seldom need staking and blue-violet flowers. Zones 3–7.

A. carmichaelii (car-mih-KELL-ee-eye), azure monkshood. Size: 2′–3′ tall; leaves 3″–6″ long. A sturdy plant with thick, 3-lobed leaves and deep-blue, hooded flowers borne in spikes from late summer through fall. Zone 2 (with protection) or Zones 3–7.

A. napellus (nuh-PELL-us), common monkshood. Size: 3′–4′ tall; leaves 2″–4″ long. This old-fashioned flower is no longer as popular as its sturdier cousins, but it still deserves a place in the garden. It blooms in

Azure monkshood (*Aconitum carmichaelii*) bears tall spikes of helmet-shaped blue flowers in late summer. The lush, deeply lobed foliage is lovely all season long and turns pale-yellow after the flowers fade.

late summer, with dark blue-violet, hooded flowers borne in tall spikes. Zones 3–8.

How to Grow: Monkshoods have thick,

fleshy roots that dislike disturbance. Plant them in spring or fall in rich, moist but well-drained soil in full sun. Space the plants 2'–3' apart, and place the crowns just below the surface. The roots are brittle and easily damaged. Do not disturb the plants unless they become overcrowded. They prefer cool night temperatures. At the southern limit of their range, site them where they'll get afternoon shade. Propagate by division of the brittle roots in fall or early spring. The flower spikes of tall-growing monkshoods may need staking.

Landscape Uses: Monkshoods are tall, spiky plants that are best for the back of the border. Plant them with late-blooming perennials such as Joe-Pye weed (*Eupatorium purpureum*), Russian sage (*Perovskia atriplicifolia*), and asters. Create bright combinations of purple and yellow with common sneezeweed (*Helenium autumnale*), sunflower heliopsis (*Heliopsis helianthoides*), and black-eyed Susan (*Rudbeckia hirta*). For a softer combination, grow monkshoods with obedient plant (*Physostegia virginiana*) or pink turtlehead (*Chelone lyonii*). 🌿

Aegopodium Umbelliferae, Parsley Family

ee-go-POE-dee-um. Bishop's Weed. Foliage plant with summer flowers. Partial to full shade.

For a fast-growing groundcover in dry shade, you can't beat variegated bishop's weed (*Aegopodium podagraria* 'Variegatum'). The thrice-divided leaves with creamy-white edges brighten up even the darkest corners of the garden.

Description: *Aegopodium podagraria* (poe-duh-GRARE-ee-uh), bishop's weed. Size: 1'–1½' tall; leaves 4"–6" long. Plants bear twice-divided green leaves with rounded, lobed leaflets. Open 2"–3" clusters of whitish flowers appear in summer. Remove the flowers to prevent self-sowing. 'Variegatum' has leaves with a creamy-white border; it is less invasive and more ornamental than the species. Zones 4–9.

How to Grow: Bishop's weed is easy to establish in average, well-drained soil in partial to full shade. Weed out any plants that revert from variegated to green. Left unchecked, bishop's weed will quickly overtake less-vigorous plants. Divide in spring or fall.

Landscape Uses: Bishop's weed thrives under trees and shrubs despite intense root competition. Use in mixed plantings with other aggressive plants like daylilies, ivy, and pachysandra. The bright foliage of *A. podagraria* 'Variegatum' adds life to shaded corners. 🌿

Ajuga Labiatae, Mint Family

uh-JOO-guh. Ajuga, Bugleweed. Foliage plant with late-spring and early-summer bloom. Sun or shade.

Description: Ajugas are low, spreading groundcovers with glossy, spoon-shaped, spinachlike leaves and 3″–5″ spikes of ½″, 2-lipped, usually cobalt-blue flowers.

Ajuga genevensis (jen-eh-VEN-sis), Geneva bugleweed. Size: 6″–12″ tall; leaves 4″–5″ long. A dense, upright ajuga with broad, deep-green foliage and blue or pink flowers in whorled clusters on open spikes. Zones 4–9.

A. pyramidalis (peer-uh-mid-AL-iss), upright bugleweed. Size: 6″–9″ tall; leaves 3″–4″ long. A bushy, slow-creeping plant with glossy, puckered foliage and bright-blue flowers. 'Metallica Crispa' has very shiny foliage with crinkled margins. Zones 3–9.

A. reptans (REP-tanz), common bugleweed. Size: 4″–10″ tall; leaves 2″–3″ long. A fast-spreading groundcover with dark-green or bronze foliage and blue flowers. *A. reptans* var. *alba* has white flowers and green leaves. 'Atropurpurea' has deep bronze-purple leaves that color best in full sun. 'Burgundy Glow' has multicolored white, pink, and green foliage. 'Catlin's Giant' has bronze-green foliage. 'Cristata' is a small-leaved, tightly crinkled plant. 'Jungle Beauty' produces large, leathery, dark-green leaves. 'Pink Beauty' has deep-pink flowers and green leaves. 'Silver Beauty' has gray-green leaves edged in white. Zones 3–9.

How to Grow: Ajuga grows in average to rich, well-drained soil in sun or shade. Plant plugs or divisions in spring or fall. The plants establish and spread quickly; *A. reptans* can be invasive. Let the spent flower spikes wither away, or remove them to tidy up smaller plantings. Propagate by cuttings in spring or summer, or divide anytime during the

The tricolor foliage of 'Burgundy Glow' bugleweed (*Ajuga reptans* 'Burgundy Glow') makes a lovely groundcover. For an eye-catching combination, plant it with straplike iris foliage, blue-gray ornamental grasses, and blue, pink, or rose-colored flowers.

growing season. Crown rot may cause entire clumps of ajuga to wither and die. Provide good drainage and air circulation to help prevent problems. If the disease does strike, remove damaged portions and dust remaining plants with sulfur to prevent the spread of the disease.

Landscape Uses: Plant ajuga wherever you need a solid, weedproof groundcover. The dense mats of foliage exclude all but the most persistent weeds. Use ajuga in the dry shade of lawn trees where no grass will grow. It is also perfect for edging beds and for planting under downspouts and gutters, where water beats down at irregular intervals. Try clumps of

A. genevensis in a rock garden. Use upright bugleweed where you need a slower-growing groundcover. Plant fancy-leaved types at the front of perennial gardens or in combination with other foliage plants in a shade garden. 'Silver Beauty' bugleweed brightens up a planting of wildflowers and ferns. The lovely flowers of all ajugas are an added bonus. They transform a massed planting into a showy spectacle in spring and early summer. 🌿

Choose common bugleweed (*Ajuga reptans*) for a fast-growing, deep-green groundcover in sun or shade. As a bonus, the plants bear short, dense spikes of deep-blue flowers in spring.

Alcea Malvaceae, Mallow Family

AL-see-uh. Hollyhock. Summer and early-fall bloom. Full sun.

The lovely, saucer-shaped flowers of hollyhocks (*Alcea rosea*) command attention when planted with other perennials or used alone as specimens.

Description: *Alcea rosea* (ROSE-ee-uh), hollyhock. Size: 2'–8' tall; leaves 8"–12" long. An erect, showy biennial or short-lived perennial with coarse rounded or lobed foliage. The bold, 2"–4"-wide single or double flowers range in color from yellow through white and pink to deep-red. They open over a long period. 'Nigra' has chocolate-red flowers. Zones 2–9.

How to Grow: Hollyhocks thrive in average to rich, well-drained soils in full sun or partial shade. Sow seed in winter for summer bloom or outdoors in summer for bloom the second year. Rust and spider mites can be serious problems, causing orange spots or yellow stippling on leaves. Dust rust-infected plants with sulfur. Control mites with insecticidal soap spray.

Landscape Uses: Plant hollyhocks at the back of a perennial border, in a cottage garden, or along fences and walls. A stately clump makes an excellent accent. 🌿

Alchemilla Rosaceae, Rose Family

al-keh-MILL-uh. Lady's-Mantle. Spring and early-summer bloom. Sun or partial shade.

Description: Clump-forming perennials with soft, hairy foliage and mounded clusters of ¼" green or chartreuse flowers.

Alchemilla alpina (al-PIE-nuh), mountain mantle. Size: 6"–8" tall; leaves 2" long. A low, delicate plant with deeply lobed leaves edged with silver hairs. Very cold-hardy and intolerant of high heat. Zones 3–7.

A. mollis (MAHL-iss), lady's-mantle. Size: 1' tall; leaves 4"–6" long. A robust, mounding plant growing from slow-creeping roots. The pale-green, softly hairy foliage is round and deeply pleated; flowers are yellow-green. Zones 3–8.

How to Grow: Grow lady's-mantle in rich, moist soil in sun or shade. Where summer temperatures are high, grow plants in partial to full shade. Space plants 2'–2½' apart. Cut to the ground if the foliage becomes tattered—plants will quickly produce a new set of leaves. Divide overgrown clumps in spring or fall, or sow fresh seed outdoors in summer. These plants will often self-sow; remove spent flowers if this is a problem.

Landscape Uses: Enjoy lady's-mantle at the front of the perennial border, along a wall, or edging a walk. Try it with Siberian iris (*Iris sibirica*) and astilbes (*Astilbe* spp.). The small *A. alpina* is perfect for rock gardens and containers. 🌿

Lady's-mantle (*Alchemilla mollis*) rewards gardeners with lovely chartreuse flowers and lush clumps of soft, gray-green, fan-shaped foliage. Water beads up on the leaf hairs, creating an enchanting, jeweled display unequaled by any other perennial.

Allium Liliaceae, Lily Family

AL-ee-um. Allium, Ornamental Onion. Spring, summer, and fall bloom. Full sun.

Description: Alliums produce fleshy, straplike leaves from pungent bulbs. The clustered flowers come in a rainbow of colors including yellow, white, pink, purple, and blue.

Allium aflatunense (uh-flat-oon-EN-see), Persian onion. Size: 2'–3' tall; leaves 1'–1½' long, spreading. A showy allium with 4½" rounded clusters of red-violet flowers borne in spring or early summer. The leaves disappear after flowering. Zones 4–8.

A. cernuum (SIR-new-um), nodding onion.

Allium senescens is an ornamental onion that bears mauve flowers in midsummer. It looks great when combined with silver-leaved plants such as lamb's-ears (*Stachys byzantina*) and artemisias. The deep-green, straplike foliage remains attractive all season.

Size: 1½'–2' tall; leaves 1'–1½' long. The nodding, tear-shaped buds open to loose 1"–1½" clusters of pink flowers in summer. Zones 4–9.

A. christophii (kris-TOFF-ee-eye), star of Persia. Size: 1'–2' tall; leaves 1'–1½' long. Spectacular 10" rounded clusters of metallic-violet flowers are carried on stout stems above the coarse foliage. Showy seed heads follow summer bloom. Zones 4–8.

A. giganteum (jeye-GAN-tee-um), giant onion. Size: 3'–5' tall; leaves 1'–1½' long. Five-inch round heads of purple flowers are borne high above a basal rosette of broad leaves in spring or early summer. Zones 4–8.

A. karataviense (kah-ruh-tuh-vee-EN-see), Turkestan onion. Size: 6"–12" tall; leaves 8"–12" long, spreading. Two to 4 broad gray-green leaves curve outward from a short, stout stem bearing a 6"–8" rounded cluster of pale-pink flowers. Zones 4–9.

A. moly (MOLE-ee), lily leek. Size: 12"–15" tall; leaves 10"–12" long. The golden-yellow flowers of this attractive late-spring bulb are held in open 2" clusters between a pair of narrow, flat leaves. Zones 3–9.

A. neapolitanum (nee-uh-pahl-ih-TAN-um), Naples onion. Size: 8"–12" tall; leaves to 1' long. A deliciously fragrant spring-blooming onion with white flowers borne in 2"–3" open, flat-topped clusters. Zones 7–9.

A. schoenoprasum (show-no-PRAH-sum), common chives. Size: 10"–20" tall; leaves 8"–18" long. A popular edible onion with pungent hollow leaves borne in thick clumps with numerous 1"–2" pink to mauve flower clusters all summer. Zones 3–9.

A. senescens (sen-ESS-enz). Size: 10"–12"

tall; leaves 4"–8" long. Rounded 1" clusters of mauve flowers bloom above dull-green leaves in midsummer. 'Glaucum' is shorter (8"–10"), with a whorl of blue-gray foliage. Zones 3–9.

A. sphaerocephalum (sfay-row-SEFF-uh-lum), drumstick chives. Size: 1½'–3' tall; leaves 1'–1½' long. Small, red-violet flowers are tightly packed into 1"–2" diamond-shaped clusters in early summer. Zones 4–9.

A. tuberosum (too-ber-ROW-sum), garlic chives. Size: 1½'–2' tall; leaves 8"–12" long. Garlic chives bear edible, straplike leaves and erect stems with 2" clusters of starry white rose-scented flowers in late summer. The showy seed heads dry well. Zones 4–8.

How to Grow: Alliums thrive in average to rich, well-drained soils in full sun. Some need excellent drainage and almost-dry soil

The huge purple-flowered globes of giant onion (*Allium giganteum*) are showstoppers in the early-summer garden. The flower heads are perched atop slender, leafless stalks that tower above other perennials.

Garlic chives (*Allium tuberosum*) produce dozens of snow-white flower clusters held above the pungently scented, grasslike leaves. They bloom in late summer with asters and goldenrods and are lovely when planted as an edging or along a low fence.

after flowering, especially *A. moly.* Plant dormant bulbs in fall. Place the top of the bulb at a depth 3 times the height of the bulb. You may want to remove the spent flowers to avoid rampant self-sowing. Divide crowded clumps as they go dormant (generally after flowering). Most alliums are easy to grow from fresh seed sown outdoors in summer or fall.

Landscape Uses: Plant the taller alliums in the middle of the perennial border. They combine beautifully with mounded plants such as cranesbills (*Geranium* spp.), bee balms (*Monarda* spp.), and yarrows, as well as with ornamental grasses. Use the tallest species as exclamation points in groundcover plantings or among annuals. Combine spring- and early-summer-blooming species with herbs or other bushy plants that will hide the yellowing foliage; later-blooming alliums often remain attractive throughout the growing season. 🍃

Amsonia Apocynaceae, Dogbane Family

am-SOWN-ee-uh. Blue Star. Spring and early-summer bloom. Full sun to light shade.

Willow blue star (*Amsonia tabernaemontana* var. *salicifolia*) bears its starry, steel-blue flowers in spring. The bright-green willowlike foliage turns yellow and fiery orange in fall.

Description: Blue stars are adaptable plants with clusters of ½″ starry flowers and green leaves that turn yellow to orange in fall.

Amsonia ciliata (sill-ee-AH-tuh), downy blue star. Size: 1′–3′ tall; leaves 2″–4″ long. A fine-textured, bushy plant with pale-blue flowers and narrow, downy leaves that cluster toward the end of the stems. Zones 6–10.

A. tabernaemontana (tab-er-nay-mahn-TAN-uh), willow blue star. Size: 1′–3′ tall; leaves 4″–6″ long. A robust plant with lance-shaped leaves and blue flowers. The variety *salicifolia* has much narrower leaves. Zones 3–9.

How to Grow: Plant in average to rich, evenly moist soil in full sun or partial shade. For compact growth, prune shade-grown plants to 10″ after flowers fade. Divide in fall. Propagate by tip cuttings in early summer.

Landscape Uses: The dense clumps add structure to the perennial garden. Try a massed planting for a good hedge or low screen. ❦

Anaphalis Compositae, Daisy Family

uh-NAFF-uh-liss. Pearly Everlasting. Late-summer bloom. Full sun.

Description: Pearly everlastings are airy plants with gray-green foliage and clusters of papery white flowers with yellow centers.

Anaphalis cinnamomea (sin-uh-MOW-me-uh), pearly everlasting. Size: 2′–3′ tall; leaves 2″–4″ long. The ¼″–½″ flowers are borne above the grayish leaves. This plant is also known as *A. yedoensis*. It is native to India. Zones 3–8.

A. margaritacea (mar-gah-rih-TAY-see-uh), pearly everlasting. Size: 1′–3′ tall; leaves 3″–4″ long. The narrow leaves appear whorled beneath the ¼″–½″ flowers. This plant is quite similar to *A. cinnamomea* but is native to North America. Zones 3–8.

A. triplinervis (trih-plih-NER-viss), three-veined everlasting. Size: 1′–1½′ tall; leaves 4″–8″ long. Leaves are woolly and broader than those of other *Anaphalis* species. Zones 3–8.

How to Grow: Pearly everlastings thrive in average to rich, evenly moist soil in full sun or light shade. In dry soils, the plants lose their lower foliage. Plants spread by underground stems to form tight clumps with many upright stems. To keep the plants vigorous, divide every 3–4 years in early spring or after they go dormant in late fall. Propagate by cuttings taken in early summer or by seed sown outdoors in late summer or indoors in late winter.

Landscape Uses: Pearly everlastings are lovely in the late-summer garden. They are the best choice for adding gray foliage to a moist site. Use the strawflower-like blooms fresh or dried in arrangements. 🍂

Unlike most plants with gray foliage, *Anaphalis triplinervis* 'Summer Snow' prefers moist sites. Like the other species and cultivars in this genus, it has woolly leaves and papery flowers that are a welcome accent in the border.

Anchusa Boraginaceae, Borage Family

an-KOO-suh. Bugloss. Late-spring bloom. Full sun.

Description: *Anchusa azurea* (uh-ZURE-ee-uh), Italian bugloss. Size: 2'–5' tall; leaves 12"–16" long. An erect plant with large, oblong leaves clothed with stiff hairs. Bright-blue ¾" flowers are carried above the foliage in long, multibranched clusters. Plants are short-lived and have a tendency to self-sow too freely. 'Dropmore' is only 4' tall and has deep-blue flowers. 'Loddon Royalist' is 3' tall with gentian-blue flowers. Zones 3–8.

How to Grow: Plant bugloss in rich, well-drained soil in full sun or light shade. Choose a named cultivar for better form and longevity. Cut back after flowering to encourage rebloom. Divide clumps every 2–3 years. Propagate by root cuttings in early spring.

Landscape Uses: Combine bugloss with other bright flowers such as poppies, yarrows, and peonies. 🍂

Plant stately Italian bugloss (*Anchusa azurea*) at the back of the border. The brilliant blue flowers open for 3 to 4 weeks in late spring and early summer.

Anemone Ranunculaceae, Buttercup Family

uh-NEM-oh-nee. Anemone, Windflower. Spring, summer, or fall bloom. Sun to shade.

The bright-pink blooms of *Anemone × hybrida* 'Margarete' are a welcome sight as the flowers of summer begin to fade. They command attention at the middle or back of the perennial border and produce a profusion of blooms over a 3- to 4-week period.

Description: Anemones have fragile, 5-petaled flowers with fuzzy, bright-yellow stamens (male reproductive structures) and white, pink, red, purple, or blue petal-like sepals. Double flowers may have 6–14 sepals. Leaves are usually deeply lobed and appear in pairs or whorls below the flower clusters, as well as in loose rosettes from the crown. Some species have tuberous roots.

Anemone apennina (app-pen-NEE-nuh). Size: 6"–8" tall; leaves 1"–1½" long. A low, spring-blooming woodland plant with semi-double, 1½" sky-blue flowers and deeply lobed foliage. Plants go dormant after flowering. Zones 6–9.

A. blanda (BLAND-uh), Grecian windflower. Size: 6"–8" tall; leaves 1"–1½" long. Similar to *A. apennina*, but the dark-blue spring flowers are larger (to 2" across). Plants go dormant after flowering. 'Blue Star' has dark-blue 2½" flowers. 'Pink Star' has light-pink flowers of similar size. 'White Splendor' is a good pure-white. Zones 4–8.

A. canadensis (can-uh-DEN-sis), meadow anemone. Size: 1'–2' tall; leaves 6"–8" long. An exuberant grower with bright-white 2" flowers held on slender stems in spring above deeply cut leaves. Zones 3–7.

A. coronaria (core-oh-NAH-ree-uh), poppy anemone. Size: 8"–12" tall; leaves 1"–2" long. A showy spring-flowering plant with 2" pink, red, purple, or blue saucer-shaped flowers and finely divided leaves. 'De Caen' hybrids have single flowers in single or mixed colors. 'St. Brigid' hybrids have semidouble flowers in a range of single or mixed colors. Zones 6–9.

A. hupehensis (hue-pea-HEN-sis), Chinese anemone. Size: 2'–3' tall; leaves 10"–12" long. Slender stalks support fragile, 5-petaled, 2"–3" rose-pink flowers above mostly basal, 3-lobed leaves. Plants grow from thick, tuberous roots and bloom in late summer and fall. 'September Charm' has rose-colored flowers that fade toward the center. Zones 5–9.

A. × hybrida (HIGH-brid-uh), Japanese anemone. Size: 3'–5' tall; leaves 1'–1½' long. Plants are similar to *A. hupehensis* but taller. In late summer and fall, the single or double 2"–4" flowers range in color from white to pink and rose. 'Honorine Jobert' has pure-white single flowers with bright-yellow stamens on 3'–4' stems. 'Margarete' has semidouble deep-pink flowers on 3' stems. 'Max Vogel' has single 4" pink flowers on 4' stems. 'Queen Charlotte' has 3" semidouble pink flowers. 'Whirlwind' is 4'–5' tall with 4" semidouble flowers. Zone 4 (with winter protection) or Zones 5–8.

A. nemorosa (nem-or-OH-suh), wood anemone. Size: 4"–10" tall; leaves 1"–2" long. A low, spreading woodland plant with 3 deeply lobed leaves below 5–7-petaled, ½"–¾" flowers. Plants go dormant after spring flowering. The variety *allenii* has lavender-blue flowers; *rosea* has single pale-rose flowers. 'Flore Pleno' has double white flowers. Zones 4–8.

A. pulsatilla (pull-suh-TILl-uh), pasque flower. Size: 6"–10"; leaves 4"–6" long. This spring-blooming species bears 2" cupped flowers in shades of white, pink, reddish purple, and blue. The threadlike, fuzzy leaves vanish in summer after fluffy white seed heads appear. Pasque flowers are also sold as *Pulsatilla* spp. Zones 3–8.

A. sylvestris (sill-VES-tris), snowdrop anemone. Size: 1'–1½' tall; leaves 1"–2½" long. A lovely snow-white single-flowered anemone for the spring garden. The erect stems each bear one 2" flower above the deep-green divided foliage. Snowdrop anemones spread quickly by creeping rhizomes. Zones 3–8.

A. tomentosa 'Robustissima' (toe-men-TOE-suh), Japanese anemone, or grape-leaved anemone (also sold as *A. vitifolia*). Size: 2'–3' tall; leaves 10"–12" long. This cultivar is similar to other Japanese anemones but hardier, with 2" metallic-pink flowers in fall and attractive dark-green foliage all season. Zones 3–8.

How to Grow: Plant spring-flowering species *A. apennina, A. blanda, A. nemorosa,* and *A. sylvestris* in moist, humus-rich soil in partial shade. *A. pulsatilla* prefers full sun and well-drained soil. All but *A. sylvestris* will go

When the lovely spring-blooming wood anemone (*Anemone nemorosa*) is finished flowering, the plant goes dormant and disappears completely from the garden. Take care not to disturb these plants with summer planting. Disguise the bare spots they leave with delicate ferns or leafy hostas.

completely dormant after flowering. Plant in early spring or fall. To propagate or renew overgrown clumps, divide after flowering or when dormant. Sow fresh seed outdoors in summer.

A. coronaria is short-lived and best treated as an annual. Soak the dried tubers for at least 12 hours before planting in average, well-drained soil in sun to partial shade. Fall planting is recommended for best flowering.

Spring-flowering *A. canadensis* has the same cultural requirements as the summer- and fall-blooming species, *A. hupehensis, A. × hybrida,* and *A. tomentosa.* Give these beauties a rich, evenly moist soil in sun or light shade. They spread by creeping underground stems to form showy clumps. *A. canadensis* may become invasive and is best used in the wild garden. Divide clumps in spring or after flowering. Propagate from root cuttings taken after the plants are dormant or by sowing fresh seed outdoors in summer or fall.

Landscape Uses: Grow the woodland species in massed plantings under the shade of trees or in combination with spring bulbs, wildflowers, and ferns. Plant exuberant *A. canadensis* in a meadow or in the moist soil of a bog garden. It is an excellent groundcover and is perfect for planting under shrubs. *A. sylvestris* is also a delightful groundcover. The snow-white flowers add grace to spring combinations of bulbs, ferns, phlox, common bleeding heart (*Dicentra spectabilis*), and bellflowers (*Campanula* spp.). Choose *A. coronaria* for any garden spot where you need a colorful spring show. Combine it with spring bulbs and early perennials such as bleeding heart, Virginia bluebells (*Mertensia virginica*), primroses, and columbines (*Aquilegia* spp.).

Use the stunning fall-flowering anemones in massed plantings to enliven the late border. Their airy, swaying heads are perfect complements to asters, goldenrods (*Solidago* spp.), sunflowers (*Helianthus* spp.), ornamental grasses, monkshoods (*Aconitum* spp.), sages, and Kamchatka bugbane (*Cimicifuga simplex*). Plant the taller kinds in front of flowering shrubs or with large ferns such as ostrich fern (*Matteuccia struthiopteris*) or cinnamon fern (*Osmunda cinnamomea*). 🍂

Anthemis   Compositae, Daisy Family

AN-them-iss. Marguerite, Chamomile. Summer bloom. Full sun.

To brighten up a dry site, try golden marguerite (*Anthemis tinctoria*). The bright-yellow, daisylike flowers appear for up to 2 months in summer; regular deadheading may extend flowering into fall. The lovely gray-green foliage sets the flowers off to good advantage.

Description: *Anthemis tinctoria* (tink-TOE-ree-uh), golden marguerite. Size: 1'–3' tall; leaves 2"–3" long. An erect to sprawling plant with pungent, finely divided foliage and bright-yellow, 1½" daisy flowers. 'Moonlight' has light-yellow flowers. Zones 3–8.

How to Grow: Marguerites prefer lean soil and are quite drought-tolerant once established. Plant in a well-drained spot in full sun for best bloom and sturdy growth. Remove spent flowers regularly to promote bloom. To encourage new growth, cut plants back as flower production wanes. Divide every 2–3 years in spring or fall. Propagate by stem cuttings in spring or early summer or by seed sown indoors in late winter or outdoors in spring.

Landscape Uses: The mounds of summer flowers complement blue sages, cranesbills (*Geranium* spp.), and bee balms (*Monarda* spp.). Use marguerite on dry sites, in rock gardens, and in containers. 🍂

Aquilegia   Ranunculaceae, Buttercup Family

ack-wih-LEE-gee-uh. Columbine. Spring and early-summer bloom. Sun to partial shade.

Description: The curious flowers of columbines never fail to attract the attention of gardeners and hummingbirds alike. Five long-spurred petals and 5 petal-like sepals surround a central column of projecting yellow stamens (male reproductive structures). Lush mounds of compound foliage with fan-shaped leaflets arise from a thick taproot. Leaflets of most species are under 1″ long.

Aquilegia alpina (al-PIE-nuh), alpine columbine. Size: 1′–2′ tall. A blue-flowered species of exceptional garden merit. The abundant, short-spurred, 2″-wide flowers nod over dense clumps of blue-green foliage. *A.* × 'Hensol Harebell', a hybrid between *A. alpina* and *A. vulgaris,* bears deep-blue flowers through midsummer. It is longer-lived than other hybrids. Zones 3–8.

A. caerulea (sir-ROO-lee-uh), Rocky Mountain columbine. Size: 1′–2′ tall. This lovely columbine has upward-facing, 2″-wide flowers with white, long-spurred petals and pale- to deep-blue sepals. 'Blue Star' resembles the species, with deep blue-and-white flowers. It is heat- and drought-resistant. Zones 3–8.

A. canadensis (can-uh-DEN-sis), wild columbine. Size: 1′–3′ tall. A beloved Eastern wildflower with nodding 1½″-wide red-and-yellow flowers produced in profusion for 4–6 weeks. The graceful plants often grow from cracks in rocky ledges but are equally at home in garden soil. 'Corbett' has yellow flowers. Zones 3–8.

A. chrysantha (kris-AN-thuh), golden columbine. Size: 2′–3′ tall. A wide-spreading, open plant with 2″–3″-wide, long-spurred, golden-yellow flowers. 'Silver Queen' has white

Plant colorful hybrid columbines like the deep-blue *Aquilegia* × 'Hensol Harebell' as an accent among small-flowered groundcovers like forget-me-nots. Both plants are lovely beside the new red shoots of peonies.

flowers. 'Yellow Queen' has lemon-yellow flowers. Zones 3–9.

A. flabellata (flah-bell-AH-tuh), fan columbine. Size: 6″–16″ tall. Short-spurred 1″–1½″-wide blue or white flowers are held just above the thick blue-green foliage. This compact columbine is long-lived and comes true from seed. 'Blue Angel' is a dwarf deep-blue selection. 'Mini-Star' is a dwarf blue-and-white bicolor. 'Nana Alba' is 8″–10″ tall with white flowers. Zones 3–9.

A. formosa (for-MOW-suh), crimson columbine. Size: 2′–4′ tall. A tall, openly

For a bright accent in the spring shade garden, plant generous drifts of free-flowering wild columbine (*Aquilegia canadensis*). Let the plants go to seed, then cut the stems back and enjoy the delicate ferny foliage until hard frost.

Hybrid columbines (*Aquilegia × hybrida*) like this red-and-yellow-flowered one are stunning plants but can be short-lived. Plant in loose, well-drained soil and start new plants from seed every 2 or 3 years.

branching columbine with spreading 1½″–2″-wide deep red-and-yellow flowers. Zones 3–7.

A. × hybrida (HIGH-brid-uh), hybrid columbine. Size: 2′–3′ tall. This mixed group of hybrids includes 2″–3″-wide flowers that are variously colored and have short, medium, or long spurs. 'Biedermeier' hybrids are compact 1′ bicolors in a variety of colors. 'Crimson Star' is 2½′ tall with crimson-and-white flowers. 'Dragonfly' hybrids are under 2′ tall in mixed colors. 'McKana' strain is a series of large-flowered hybrids in white, red, yellow, and blue. 'Nora Barlow' has double flowers, each a mixture of red, pink, and green. 'Spring Song' hybrids are 3′ tall in mixed colors. Zones 3–9.

A. longissima (long-GISS-ih-muh), long-spur columbine. Size: 2′–3′ tall. The yellow flowers with 6″ spurs are showstoppers. Plants are short-lived in cultivation. 'Maxistar' is bright-yellow. Zones 4–9.

A. vulgaris (vul-GAH-riss), European columbine. Size: 1½′–3′ tall. A short-spurred blue to violet species most noted as a parent for popular hybrids. The variety *nivea* has white flowers on vigorous, 3′ plants. Zones 3–9.

How to Grow: Although many species of columbine are short-lived, seldom lasting more than 2–4 years, they are extremely easy to grow. They reward the gardener with a month or more of brightly colored flowers that sway with every breeze. Plant columbines in light, average to rich, moist but well-drained soil. They grow well in full sun or partial shade.

Plants self-sow freely, but only the true species produce attractive seedlings. Hybrid seedlings are often pale or grotesquely mis-shapen; uproot and discard them. To get high-quality plants, use purchased seed, or collect from species grown in isolation from other columbines. Sow seed outdoors; it germinates easily in fall or the following spring. Or sow seed indoors in winter after dry-storing it in a refrigerator for 4 weeks.

Leafminers often attack columbine leaves, creating pale-tan tunnels or blotches in the blades of the leaves. Check plants frequently, and remove and destroy infected leaves immediately. If the problem is severe, spray weekly with insecticidal soap. Borers can also be a problem. They cause the whole plant to collapse dramatically. Remove and destroy above- and below-ground portions of infected plants.

Landscape Uses: Plant columbines in groups of 3 or 5 or in large sweeps to complement spring perennials and late bulbs. They start blooming with the late tulips and continue through the early summer. Combine them with cranesbills (*Geranium* spp.), evening primroses (*Oenothera* spp.), irises, peonies, and lupines. Use columbines around the base of tall, shrubby perennials such as blue stars (*Amsonia* spp.), baptisias (*Baptisia* spp.), monkshoods (*Aconitum* spp.), and delphiniums. *Aquilegia canadensis* is lovely in drifts in the rock garden or woodland garden with Virginia bluebells (*Mertensia virginica*), trilliums (*Trillium* spp.), wild blue phlox (*Phlox divaricata*), and ferns. Use *A. caerulea* and *A. flabellata* in the rock garden or in the border. Accent a shrub planting with drifts of mixed hybrids or a single species. 🍂

Arabis   Cruciferae, Mustard Family

AR-uh-biss. Rock Cress. Early-spring bloom. Full sun.

Description: These evergreen plants are covered in spring with small white flowers.

Arabis caucasica (caw-KA-sih-kuh), wall rock cress. Size: 6"–10" tall; leaves ½"–1" long. A low, mat-forming perennial with toothed, woolly, gray leaves and upright clusters of 4-petaled white or pink flowers. Zones 3–7.

A. procurrens (pro-KER-enz), rock cress. Size: 6"–12" tall; leaves ¼"–½" long. A creeping groundcover with shiny green leaves and sprays of white flowers. Zones 4–7.

How to Grow: Plant in average to good, well-drained soil in full sun or light shade. They prefer cool temperatures and low humidity. In warm regions, site plants where they will get afternoon shade. Cut them back after flowering to keep them neat. Divide every 2–4 years after flowering. Propagate by cuttings in spring.

Landscape Uses: Plant rock cresses with spring bulbs, in a rock wall with ferns, or with spring-blooming wildflowers. 🍂

For the well-drained rock garden, choose a generous planting of early-blooming wall rock cress (*Arabis caucasica*). The evergreen foliage is all but smothered by the profusion of flowers produced for a month or more. White-flowered selections are also available.

Arenaria Caryophyllaceae, Pink Family

ah-ray-NAH-ree-uh. Sandwort. Spring and early-summer bloom. Full sun or partial shade.

Diminutive, mat-forming moss sandwort (*Arenaria verna*) is an excellent plant for the sunny rock garden. The needlelike leaves form dense carpets that are accented in spring by small, starry white flowers.

Description: Low, cushion-forming plants with narrow leaves and white, 5-petaled flowers.

Arenaria montana (mahn-TAN-ah), mountain sandwort. Size: 2″–4″ tall; leaves ⅛″–¼″ long. A mounding, softly hairy plant with flat ½″ flowers on 1′ stalks. Zones 4–8.

A. verna (VER-nuh), moss sandwort. Size: 2″ tall; leaves ¹⁄₁₆″–⅛″ long. A cushion-forming plant with ½″ white flowers. The variety *caespitosa,* Irish moss, forms small clumps; 'Aurea' is yellow-green. Zones 5–8.

How to Grow: Plant in average, sandy or loamy, well-drained soil in full sun. They prefer neutral to slightly acid soil. They spread slowly to form undulating mounds of dense foliage. Plants are shallow-rooted, so water regularly during dry spells. Divide in spring or fall, or sow seed indoors in spring or outdoors in fall.

Landscape Uses: Sandworts make excellent low groundcovers for rock gardens.

Arisaema Araceae, Arum Family

ar-iss-EE-muh. Jack-in-the-Pulpit. Spring or early-summer bloom. Full to partial shade.

Description: These plants bear unusually shaped 3″–5″-long flowers with a hood (known as the spathe) surrounding a thick central column (the spadix). Spring or early-summer blooms are followed by red berries in late summer.

Arisaema dracontium (drack-KON-tee-um), green dragon. Size: 1′–3½′ tall; leaves 1′–2′ long. A single leaf with 7–9 leaflets towers above the green spathe and long, tonguelike spadix. Zones 4–9.

A. sikokianum (see-koh-kee-AIN-um), Jack-in-the-pulpit. Size: 1½′ tall; leaves 8″–12″ long. Single or paired, 5-leaflet leaves are held above a squat, white-and-green striped spathe with a purple interior. Zones 6–9.

A. triphyllum (try-FILL-um), Jack-in-the-pulpit. Size: 1′–3′ tall; leaves 8″–12″ long. Single or paired, 3-lobed leaves frame the green and purple spathe, which droops at the tip to hide the short spadix. Zones 3–9.

How to Grow: Plant these woodland wildflowers in moist, humus-rich soil. *A. dracontium* needs sun for best growth; *A. triphyllum* tolerates very deep shade and poorly drained soil. Plant in spring or fall. Propagate by seed. Collect the red berries in fall, remove the pulp, and sow outdoors right away. Seedlings have only 1 short leaf the first year. Plants take several years to reach flowering size.

Landscape Uses: Use Jack-in-the-pulpits as specimens in the shade garden with wildflowers, hostas, groundcovers, and ferns. *A. dracontium* is a wonderful accent in front of shrubs or in a mixed foundation planting. 🍁

Jack-in-the-pulpit (*Arisaema triphyllum*) bears unusual green-and-purple flowers that are often obscured by a pair of bold, 3-lobed leaves. In fall, its red berries brighten up shaded recesses.

Armeria Plumbaginaceae, Plumbago Family

ar-MAIR-ee-uh. Thrift, Sea-Pink. Late-spring and summer bloom. Full sun.

Description: *Armeria maritima* (ma-RIH-tih-muh), common thrift. Size: 10″–14″ tall; leaves 2″–4″ long. Common thrift forms low tufts of gray-green grasslike evergreen foliage. Vibrant pink to rose flowers are borne in dense, 1″ rounded heads atop naked stems. 'Alba' has white flowers. 'Laucheana' has large, deep-pink flowers. 'Vindictive' is compact, to 6″, with abundant rosy red flowers. Zones 3–8.

How to Grow: Plant thrifts in average, well-drained, loamy or sandy soil in full sun. Plants prefer cool temperatures and low humidity. Provide afternoon shade where summers are hot. Thrifts tolerate seaside conditions. Divide in spring or fall, or sow seed in winter in a warm (70°F) seedbed.

Landscape Uses: Thrifts are lovely in rock and wall gardens. 🍁

Common thrift (*Armeria maritima*) bears tufted mounds of grassy foliage topped by dozens of flowering stems from early to midsummer.

Artemisia Compositae, Daisy Family

ar-teh-MEEZ-ee-uh. Artemisia, Wormwood. Foliage plant with summer and fall bloom. Full sun.

Description: Artemisias are shrubby, aromatic plants with showy green or gray foliage and terminal clusters of insignificant yellowish or grayish late-season flowers. Their foliage varies from deeply lobed or divided to broadly lance-shaped. This diverse genus contains a wide range of ornamental, culinary, and medicinal plants, many of which are commonly grown in herb gardens. Most species originated in arid regions or prairies.

Artemisia absinthium (ab-SIN-thee-um), common wormwood. Size: 2′–3′ tall; leaves 1″–2″ long. A robust perennial, common wormwood becomes somewhat woody with age. The deeply lobed aromatic foliage is clothed in silky hairs. Inconspicuous yellow flowers are borne in late summer. This plant was used to flavor the drink absinthe. 'Lambrook Silver' has lovely silver-gray foliage. Zones 3–9.

A. canescens (kah-NESS-senz). Size: 1′–1½′ tall; leaves ½″–1″ long. An open, mounding plant with finely divided silver-gray foliage. Zones 4–8.

A. dracunculus (drack-KUN-kew-luss), tarragon. Size: 2′–5′ tall; leaves 4″–6″ long. An aromatic culinary herb and garden ornamental, tarragon has an open habit and green, lance-shaped foliage. Zones 3–8.

A. lactiflora (lack-tih-FLOOR-uh), white mugwort. Size: 4′–6′ tall; leaves 6″–8″ long. White mugwort is the only artemisia grown for its flowers rather than its foliage. Plumes of small, creamy flowers are held high atop erect, leafy stalks in late summer. The broad, deeply divided leaves are bright-green. Plants prefer moist soil. Zones 4–9.

A. ludoviciana (loo-doe-vick-ee-AH-nuh), white sage. Size: 2′–4′ tall; leaves 4″–6″ long. A slightly aromatic plant with creeping roots and slender stems clothed in woolly, white lance-shaped leaves. 'Silver King' is upright and spreading; 'Silver Queen' has broader leaves and is slightly more compact. 'Valerie Finnis' is a lovely hybrid with broadly lance-shaped leaves and dense, upright stems. Zones 3–9.

A. × 'Powis Castle'. Size: 2′–3′ tall; leaves 1″–3″ long. This is a shrubby hybrid, with *A. absinthium* as a parent. The aromatic, silvery white foliage is deeply cut. Plants retain a compact form throughout the growing season. Zone 4 (with winter protection) or Zones 5–8.

A. schmidtiana (shmit-ee-AH-nuh), silvermound artemisia. Size: 1′–2′ tall; leaves

Silvermound artemisia (*Artemisia schmidtiana*) produces low, tightly mounded clumps of soft silver foliage that's perfect for edging beds or configuring knot gardens. Plant it in rock gardens with sedums (*Sedum* spp.) and other prostrate or dwarf plants.

Like other cultivars of white sage, drought-tolerant *Artemisia ludoviciana* 'Silver King' is a good weaver—a plant used to unify groupings of more dramatic perennials. A large clump makes a lovely specimen in the dry garden with perennials such as yarrows (*Achillea* spp.).

½″–1½″ long. A dense, mounded plant with finely divided silver-gray foliage. In warm regions, plants may flop, creating an open center and spoiling the mounded appearance. 'Nana' (also sold as 'Silver Mound'), similar to the species but shorter and more compact, is more common in cultivation than the species. Zones 3–7.

A. stelleriana (stel-lair-ee-AH-nuh), beach wormwood. Size: 10″–12″ tall; leaves 3″–4″ long. Beach wormwood is a low, spreading plant with lobed, silvery foliage. It is tolerant of seaside conditions. Zones 3–8.

How to Grow: Most artemisias thrive in average, well-drained soil in full sun. These plants need little care; once established, most of them are extremely drought-tolerant. Give *A. lactiflora* moist but well-drained soil for best growth. In warm, humid regions, the mounding species (especially *A. schmidtiana*) tend to

fall open from the center. Plant the upright and shrubby species instead of the mounding species if heat is a problem. Prune all species back hard if they start to lose their form. Proper siting and good culture will result in pest- and disease-free plants.

Propagate shrubby types such as *A. absinthium* and *A.* × 'Powis Castle' by taking cuttings from new shoots with a piece of old wood attached. A side branch works well for this technique. Such cuttings are called mallet cuttings and are best taken in late summer. Dust the bases of cuttings with rooting hormone to speed root production.

Fast-spreading species such as *A. lactiflora* and *A. ludoviciana* need dividing every 2–3 years to restrain their exuberant growth and to rejuvenate the old clumps. Lift the clumps in spring or fall and replant divisions into well-prepared soil. Take softwood cuttings in early summer or mallet cuttings as above. They root quickly in a mixture of equal parts peat and perlite. If you want to prevent these possibly invasive species from taking over your garden, plant them in a sunken barrel or bottomless pot to contain the spreading roots.

Landscape Uses: The showy, soft, silver-gray or white leaves of artemisias are a valuable asset in the garden. Use the foliage to brighten colors, especially hot pinks, reds, and oranges, or to create cool pictures with pastel pinks, purples, and blues. Combine the shrubby species with yuccas (*Yucca* spp.), ornamental grasses, groundcovers, and flowering shrubs.

Use the herbaceous species with annuals and perennials in beds, borders, and containers. The low-growing species are suitable for edging or for rock gardens. Most species, especially *A. stellerana*, are good plants for seaside gardens and other areas where salt is a problem. The tall, showy plumes of *A. lactiflora* are perfect for adding grace and motion to plantings of heavy-headed daisies and mums, or as a background for other plants. They are especially beautiful with Japanese anemone (*Anemone* × *hybrida*) and monkshoods (*Aconitum* spp.). Mix *Artemisia dracunculus* with other herbs or with perennials. ❦

Arum Araceae, Arum Family

AR-um. Arum. Foliage plant with spring bloom. Partial to full shade.

In winter and spring, Italian arum (*Arum italicum* 'Pictum') bears lush, arrowhead-shaped leaves. The spring flowers are followed by berries that ripen to bright-red in late summer.

Description: *Arum italicum* (ih-TAL-ih-kum), Italian arum. Size: 1'–1½' tall; leaves 10"–12" long. Arums have hooded 3"–4" flowers that emerge in spring from buttonlike tubers. The fleshy, deep-green, arrowhead-shaped leaves are often veined with yellow. They are produced in the fall, persist through the winter, and disappear after flowering the next summer. Clusters of orange-red berries appear in late summer before new leaves emerge. 'Pictum' has creamy-white leaf veins. Zones 6–9.

How to Grow: Italian arums grow best in moist, humus-rich soil in light shade. Plants tolerate dry soil in summer when they are leafless. Propagate by dividing clumps in summer as the leaves wither. Sow fresh seed outside in fall after removing pulp. Plants may self-sow.

Landscape Uses: Combine Italian arums with evergreen plants like heart-leaved bergenia (*Bergenia cordifolia*) and golden sedges (*Carex* spp.). ❦

Aruncus   Rosaceae, Rose Family

uh-RUN-kuss. Goat's Beard. Late-spring and early-summer bloom. Sun to partial shade.

Description: Goat's beards are large, showy perennials. They have thrice-divided leaves with broad leaflets and open, fuzzy white flower plumes. Goat's beards are dioecious: Male and female flowers are borne on separate plants. Male flowers are more showy due to their many fuzzy stamens, but the female flowers are also attractive. Nurseries do not sell the sexes separately. The species vary from tall, broad, shrubby plants to low, clumping types barely 8″ tall. All grow from stout, fibrous roots.

Aruncus aethusifolius (ay-THOOS-uh-foe-lee-us), dwarf goat's beard. Size: 8″–12″ high; leaves 3″–5″ long. This dwarf, clumping plant has branched cylindrical 3″–4″ clusters of tiny creamy-white flowers and shiny deep-green compound leaves. Zones 4–7.

A. dioicus (die-OH-ih-kuss), goat's beard. Size: 3′–6′ tall; leaves 1′–3′ long. A stately perennial of shrublike proportions, goat's beard has 1′–2′ open plumes of white flowers on stout stems and divided leaves. 'Child of Two Worlds' is more compact, reaching 3′–4′ in height. 'Kneiffii' is 3′ tall with deeply cut, ferny foliage. Zones 3–7.

How to Grow: Goat's beards are plants of open woodlands and woods edges. Plant them in moist, humus-rich soil in partial shade. In cooler areas, they will stand full sun if kept constantly moist. In deep shade, plants will bloom sparsely. Place them at least 4′ apart when planting in groups. Once established, the stout roots do not move easily. If division is necessary, lift clumps in spring and cut the roots with a sharp knife. Leave at least one eye (bud) per division. Sow fresh

Goat's beard (*Aruncus dioicus*) is a stately perennial that reaches shrublike proportions in the lightly shaded garden. The foliage remains attractive long after the early-summer flowers have faded.

seed indoors or outdoors in summer in a warm (70°F) seedbed. Seedlings will appear in 2–3 weeks.

Landscape Uses: Goat's beards are bold accent plants. Use them singly, or plant them in small groups at the edge of a woodland path or in front of flowering shrubs. Combine them with ferns, wildflowers, and groundcovers. In the perennial or mixed border, treat them like herbaceous shrubs. Give them plenty of room to spread—each plant may reach 4′ across. Where space is limited, plant one of the smaller cultivars. Choose *A. aethusifolius* for shaded rock gardens with small-leaved hostas and delicate wildflowers, for the front of the border, or for edging paths. 🍂

Asarum Aristolochiaceae, Birthwort Family

uh-SAH-rum. Wild Ginger. Foliage plant with spring bloom. Partial to full shade.

European wild ginger (*Asarum europaeum*) bears glossy evergreen leaves that create an attractive green groundcover to brighten up a shady area. The unusual reddish brown juglike flowers are hidden under the foliage.

Description: Wild gingers are lovely small foliage perennials with creeping aromatic rhizomes that smell like commercial ginger (*Zingiber officinalis*), from which they take their common name. The unusual ½"–¾" jug-shaped brown or red flowers appear in late spring. The inflated flowers are fleshy, with 3 flaring lobes. The lobes may be rounded or drawn out to long points. The flowers are gnat-pollinated. Each bloom rests on the soil and is borne between 2 leaves that are evergreen or deciduous, depending on the species. The evergreen species are often placed in the genus *Hexastylis.*

Asarum arifolium (air-uh-FOE-lee-um), arum wild ginger. Size: 6"–12" tall; leaves 4"–6" long. A showy evergreen species with arrow-shaped gray-green leaves mottled with silver. The inconspicuous light-brown flowers appear in spring. Zone 5 (with winter protection) or Zones 6–9.

A. canadense (can-uh-DEN-see), Canada wild ginger. Size: 6"–12" tall; leaves 4"–6" long. A fast-spreading groundcover with satiny, broadly heart-shaped deciduous leaves. The reddish brown flowers have long, pointed lobes. Zones 3–8.

A. caudatum (caw-DAH-tum), British Columbia wild ginger. Size: 6"–8" tall; leaves 2"–6" long. A creeping plant with semi-evergreen heart-shaped leaves and purple-brown flowers with long tails. Zones 4–7.

A. europaeum (your-oh-PEA-um), European wild ginger. Size: 6"–8" tall; leaves 2"–3" long. This species is a lovely groundcover with glossy evergreen kidney-shaped leaves that are often faintly mottled. The reddish brown flowers are insignificant. Zones 4–8.

A. shuttleworthii (shut-tull-WORTH-ee-eye), mottled wild ginger. Size: 6"–8" tall; leaves 2"–3" long. An open groundcover with dark, mottled evergreen leaves and attractive broad-lipped flowers. 'Callaway' is a fast-spreading small-leaved selection that makes an excellent groundcover. Zones 5–9.

How to Grow: Wild gingers are easy-care woodland inhabitants. Plant them in moist, humus-rich soil in partial to full shade. *A. canadense* tolerates alkaline conditions, but the other species prefer acid soils. *A. caudatum* grows best in the cooler conditions available north of Zone 7. *A. canadense, A. caudatum,* and *A. europaeum* spread rapidly to form dense, neat groundcovers of exceptional beauty.

Other species spread slowly from branching rhizomes to form tight clumps.

Division is seldom necessary for the slow-growing species. For propagation, however, you can lift and divide plants in fall. Divide *A. canadense, A. caudatum,* and *A. europaeum* in spring or fall. You can also propagate all types of wild ginger by mallet cuttings in late spring or early summer. To make mallet cuttings, remove a 1″–1½″ tip section of the rhizome with a pair of leaves attached. Stick the cuttings in a mix of equal parts of peat moss and perlite or sand. Cuttings will root in 4–6 weeks. Sow fresh seed inside or outside in midsummer. Seedlings germinate quickly, but plants develop slowly. *A. canadense* and *A. caudatum* will self-sow freely in the garden.

Landscape Uses: Wild gingers are unparalleled groundcovers. In the shade or rock garden, combine them with hostas, ferns, and wildflowers such as trilliums (*Trillium* spp.) and foamflowers (*Tiarella* spp.). Plant miniature bulbs such as crocus and squills (*Scilla* spp.) among clumps of the evergreen species for early spring show. To enjoy the subtle flowers of wild gingers, plant the clumps on a slope or at the edge of rock walls where the foliage does not obscure them. ❦

Asclepias Asclepiadaceae, Milkweed Family

as-KLEE-pea-us. Milkweed. Summer bloom. Full sun to light shade.

Description: Milkweeds are tough, showy plants of fields and prairies. They are named for the milky sap produced when plants are picked or damaged. The unusual waxy flowers have 5 backward-pointing petals with forward-protruding lobes. They are borne profusely in rounded clusters in the axils of the leaves or in flat-topped terminal clusters. Flower color varies among species from green to orange, yellow, pink, or purple. Stems may be borne singly or in dense clumps. In the fall, showy inflated seedpods split to release seeds that are carried away by the breeze on silken parachutes. Milkweed leaves are the sole food source for the caterpillars of the monarch butterfly. The flowers are important nectar sources for a wide variety of adult butterflies.

Asclepias incarnata (in-car-NAH-tuh), swamp milkweed. Size: 3′–5′ tall; leaves 4″–6″ long. A stately denizen of moist to wet soils, with flat terminal 2″–4″ clusters of pale-rose to deep rose-purple ¼″ flowers. Stems with

Butterflies are attracted to the bright-orange flowers of butterfly weed (*Asclepias tuberosa*) like magnets. The blooms appear in summer and are host to constant activity until the green, bean-shaped seedpods form.

opposite lance-shaped leaves arise in loose clumps from a creeping rhizome. Zones 3–8.

A. speciosa (spee-see-OH-suh), showy milkweed. Size: 1'–3' tall; leaves 4"–8" long. A compact plant with opposite pale-green leaves and axillary 2"–4" clusters of starry rose-purple ½" flowers. Zones 3–8.

A. tuberosa (too-ber-ROW-suh), butterfly weed. Size: 1'–3' tall; leaves 4"–5" long. Dense clumps of leafy stems are topped with broad, flat, 2"–5" clusters of fiery orange, red, or yellow ½" flowers. The plant grows from a brittle fleshy taproot. 'Gay Butterflies' is a seed-grown strain with mixed flower colors. Zones 3–9.

How to Grow: Milkweeds grow along roadsides, in meadows, and on prairies. Give them average, loamy or sandy soil in full sun. *A. incarnata* will succeed in dry soil, but prefers moist to wet, humus-rich soil. Most milkweeds spread by rhizomes and can be invasive, especially in rich soils. Remove unwanted shoots as they appear. *A. tuberosa* grows from a taproot, so do not disturb plants once they are established.

To propagate *A. tuberosa,* take tip cuttings in late spring or early summer; they root in 4–6 weeks. Propagate other species from root cuttings or pieces of rhizome removed in fall and placed in a sandy rooting mix. All milkweeds are easy to grow from fresh seed sown outdoors in fall. Indoors, sow fresh seed in winter in a warm (70°F) seedbed. Indoors or out, transplant seedlings of *A. tuberosa* as soon as the second set of true leaves has formed—transplanting after this stage may damage the taproot. Early transplanting is not critical for other species.

Landscape Uses: Try a generous planting of milkweeds in a meadow with native grasses and sun-loving wildflowers. Use butterfly weed and showy milkweed in restored grasslands or stylized prairie gardens. Containers of swamp milkweed are ideal for a bog or water garden. In formal perennial borders, choose *A. speciosa* and *A. tuberosa* for the front or middle of the border, combined with blanket flower (*Gaillardia aristata*), 'East Friesland' sage (*Salvia × superba* 'East Friesland'), and silver-leaved artemisias. Plant other milkweeds toward the back of the border with ornamental grasses, asters, Joe-Pye weed (*Eupatorium purpureum*) and bee balms (*Monarda* spp.). 🍁

Aster   Compositae, Daisy Family

AS-ter. Aster. Summer and fall bloom. Full sun to partial shade.

Description: A large genus of showy, floriferous perennials with mounds of daisylike blooms. The flowers consist of overlapping rows of thin petal-like ray flowers surrounding a round, yellow disk that consists of many tightly packed, petal-less flowers. The rays come in a rainbow of colors from purple to lavender, rose, pink, red, and white. Plants vary in size from 1'–8' tall. The stems may be densely clothed in clasping leaves or have sparsely arranged heart-shaped leaves on short stalks. Many species have basal leaf clusters in addition to the stem leaves. All species grow from creeping rhizomes.

Aster × alpellus 'Triumph' (al-PELL-us try-umph). A hybrid between *A. amellus* and *A. alpinus,* this aster bears violet-blue flowers with orange disks on 1½' stalks. Zones 4–8.

A. alpinus (al-PIE-nus), alpine aster. Size. 6″–12″ tall; leaves 1½″–2″ long. A low, mounding plant with many stems, each bearing a single bloom. The 2″ early-summer flowers are purple with yellow centers. The slender, oblong leaves are mostly clustered around the base; the stem leaves decrease in size toward the flower head. 'Albus' has pure-white flowers. 'Dark Beauty' has deep blue-violet flowers. 'Happy End' is rose-pink. Zones 2–7.

A. amellus (uh-MEL-us), Italian aster. Size: 2′–2½′ tall; leaves 4″–5″ long. Italian aster has 2½″ flowers with purple rays and a yellow center. Flowers are borne in dense clusters atop leafy stems arising from clumps of roughly hairy foliage. 'Pink Zenith' has deep-pink flowers on compact 2′ plants. 'Rudolph Goethe' has violet flowers on 2′–3′ stems. Zones 5–8.

A. divaricatus (dih-var-ih-KAH-tus), white wood aster. Size: 1′–1½′ tall; leaves 5″–7″ long. A shade-tolerant aster with loose clusters of ¾″ starry white flowers on wiry black stems. Zones 4–8.

A. ericoides (air-ih-COY-deez), heath aster. Size: 1′–3′ tall; leaves 1″–3″ long. A leafy, densely flowered aster with hundreds of tiny white or pale-blue flowers borne on stiff terminal and side branches. 'Blue Star' has sky-blue flowers. 'Cinderella' has white flowers with reddish centers. Zones 3–8.

A. × *frikartii* (frih-CART-ee-eye), Frikart's aster. Size: 2′–3′ tall; leaves 1″–2½″ long. These asters are a group of hybrids between *A. amellus* and *A. thomsonii*. The fuzzy-leafed plants have a loose habit. The 2½″ lavender-blue flowers are borne from midsummer through fall. 'Monch' has erect stems and deeper blue flowers than the similar 'Wonder of Staffa'. Zones 5–8.

A. laevis (LEE-vis), smooth aster. Size: 2′–3½′ tall; leaves 3″–5″ long. Smooth aster has 1″ pale lavender-blue flowers and attractive

In late summer, white wood asters (*Aster divaricatus*) light up shady gardens with their bright-white, daisylike flowers. They are lovely combined with the foliage of lungworts (*Pulmonaria* spp.) or begonias.

blue-green foliage. The basal leaves are shaped like narrow hearts. The stem leaves are much smaller than the basal leaves. Zones 2–7.

A. lateriflorus (lat-er-ih-FLOOR-us), calico aster. Size: 2′–4′ tall; leaves 4″–6″ long. A bushy aster with hundreds of tiny white flowers on branching leafy stems. 'Horizontalis' is more compact (to 2½′) with burgundy-red foliage and white flowers with reddish disks. Zones 3–8.

A. macrophyllus (mack-row-FILL-us), bigleaf aster. Size: 1′–2½′ tall; leaves 6″–8″ long. A woodland aster with large, heart-shaped leaves and leafy stems bearing broad, flat clusters of 1″ white to pale-blue flowers. Zones 3–7.

A. novae-angliae (NO-vay ANG-lee-eye), New England aster, Michaelmas daisy. Size: 3'–6' tall; leaves 3"–5" long. A tall, leafy-stemmed aster with clusters of showy 2" purple flowers with bright-yellow centers that appear in late summer. Many selections have been made for large flower size, flower color, and compact growth. 'Alma Potschke' has deep salmon-pink or cerise flowers on dense, 3' plants. 'Barr's Pink' bears semidouble rose-pink flowers on 4' plants. 'Harrington's Pink' is an older cultivar with late-blooming pale salmon-pink flowers on 3'–5' stems. 'Hella Lacy' bears royal purple flowers on dense, 3'–4' plants. 'Mt. Everest' has white flowers on 3' plants. 'Purple Dome' is a rounded, compact plant (to 2') with late-season royal purple flowers. 'September Ruby' has deep ruby-red flowers on floppy, 3'–5' plants. 'Treasure' bears lavender-blue flowers

Tartarian aster (*Aster tartaricus*) is the giant of the genus, growing as tall as 8'. Plant it with other stately plants of autumn such as sunflowers (*Helianthus* spp.), boltonia (*Boltonia asteroides*), and ornamental grasses.

on 4' stems. Zones 3–8.

A. novi-belgii (NO-vee BEL-jee-eye), New York aster, Michaelmas daisy. Size: 1'–6' tall; leaves 4"–7" long. A fall-blooming species with smooth, lance-shaped leaves and 1"–1½" flowers with wide, densely packed blue to white rays and yellow centers. This species has compact growth, rich flower color, and floriferous habit. 'Ada Ballard' bears double lavender-blue flowers on 3' stems. 'Audrey' has lilac flowers on 1' plants. 'Bonningdale White' has semidouble white flowers on 4' plants. 'Eventide' bears 2" semidouble lavender-blue flowers on 3'–4' stems. 'Jenny' bears red flowers on 1' stems. 'Marie Ballard' is an old cultivar with double powder-blue flowers on 4' stems. 'Professor Kippenburg' has semidouble lavender-blue flowers on compact 1' plants. Zones 3–8.

A. spectabilis (speck-TAH-bih-lis), showy or seaside aster. Size: 1'–2' tall; leaves 4"–5" long. A compact, leafy aster with 1" violet flowers in summer. Zones 4–8.

A. tataricus (tah-TAH-rih-kuss), Tartarian aster. Size: 5'–8' tall; leaves 1'–2' long. A late-blooming aster with tall, leafy stems and rounded clusters of 1¼", pale-blue to lavender flowers. Zones 2–8.

A. thomsonii (tom-SOWN-ee-eye), Thomson's aster. Size: 1'–3' tall; leaves 3"–4" long. A long-blooming aster with 1"–2" lilac-blue flowers on bushy plants. 'Nanus' is compact (less than 2' tall) with 1"–2" leaves. Zones 5–9.

A. tongolensis (ton-go-LEN-sis), East Indies aster. Size: 1'–2' tall; leaves 3"–4" long. A handsome, clumping groundcover with leafless stems, each bearing a single 2" pale-violet to lavender flower with drooping rays and a bright-orange center. Plants bloom in summer. 'Berggarten' has 2"–3" violet-blue flowers. 'Napsburg' has blue flowers. Zones 5–8.

A. umbellatus (um-bell-AH-tus), flat-topped aster. Size: 3'–6' tall; leaves 3"–6" long. A tall, leafy aster with neat foliage and broad, flat

Floriferous 'Hella Lacy' New England aster (*Aster novae-angliae* 'Hella Lacy') is a showstopper in the late summer and autumn garden. The plants are smothered with royal-purple flowers for up to 4 weeks. They are lovely as fresh-cut flowers.

clusters of ¾" white flowers borne in mid- to late summer. Zones 3–8.

How to Grow: Asters are a diverse group of plants with varying cultural requirements. They can be divided into 3 broad groups. It's important to keep these groups in mind and match the asters you buy to your cultural conditions: Many asters are moisture-sensitive, and stressed plants often lose their lower foliage or do not flower well.

The first group contains asters of mountains and seasides, including *A.* × *alpellus, A. alpinus, A. amellus, A.* × *frikartii, A. spectabilis,* and *A. tongolensis.* These plants require average to rich soil with excellent drainage in full sun; they cannot tolerate excess moisture or wet soil. Most also prefer cool night temperatures. These species form clumps and spread by slow-creeping stems. Divide plants in spring or fall as necessary or for propagation.

They may be short-lived in cultivation.

The second group contains meadow, prairie, marsh, and roadside species, most of which thrive in average to rich evenly moist soil. Some are more tolerant of dry soil than others. *A. ericoides, A. laevis, A. lateriflorus, A. tataricus,* and *A. thomsonii* tolerate the widest range of conditions. *A. novae-angliae, A. novi-belgii,* and *A. umbellatus* require even moisture for best growth. In the border, tall plants may need to be staked. Many of these plants spread rapidly and need frequent division to keep them attractive. Divide clumps in spring. Discard old, woody portions, and replant clumps into amended soil. Propagate by stem cuttings taken in late spring or early summer.

The third group contains the woodland species *A. divaricatus* and *A. macrophyllus.* They tolerate deep shade but bloom best in light to partial shade. These species prefer moist, humus-rich soil but tolerate dry soil. They spread to form attractive groundcovers. Divide overgrown clumps as needed.

All asters are easy to grow from seed, but germination can be uneven. Sow fresh seed outdoors in fall or indoors in winter. If sowing indoors, water the sown pots or flats and place them in the refrigerator for 4–6 weeks; then remove the pots or flats and place them in a sunny position.

Many asters are susceptible to an incurable wilt fungus that attacks their roots. Good drainage is the best prevention. Take tip cuttings from infected plants and destroy old plants. Powdery mildew may be a problem on some species, especially *A. novae-angliae* and *A. novi-belgii*. Promote good air circulation and avoid wetting the leaves. If mildew does attack, dust affected plants with sulfur to reduce the spread of the disease.

Landscape Uses: Use the low-growing mountain and seaside species in rock gardens, dryland gardens, and containers. Plant the woodland species in combination with ferns and wildflowers. The meadow, prairie, marsh, and roadside species sport low, mounding plants for the front or middle of the border and tall plants for the background. 🍂

Astilbe Saxifragaceae, Saxifrage Family

uh-STILL-bee. Astilbe, False Spirea. Late-spring and summer bloom. Full sun to full shade.

Feathery, light-pink plumes borne well above the foliage are the hallmark of *Astilbe japonica* 'Europa', an early-blooming selection.

Description: Astilbes are regal plants for consistently moist soils. Their airy plumes of densely packed, tiny flowers are showstoppers in the summer garden. Flower clusters vary in size from 6″–24″. Some are stiff and upright, others are open and plumelike; still others cascade outward like fireworks. Flower color varies from red through all shades of magenta, rose, and pink to lavender, lilac, cream, and white. The foliage is twice- to thrice-divided, with many small-toothed leaflets; leaves may be hairy or glossy. Some species, particularly red-flowered cultivars, have leaves and stems tinged with bronze or red. The smallest species are under 1′ tall, while the tallest may top 4′. All grow from thick, often woody, fibrous-rooted crowns and form clumps or slowly spreading patches.

Astilbe × arendsii (uh-REND-zee-eye), astilbe. Size: 2′–4′ tall; leaves 1″–1½″ long. This hybrid species was created by Georg Arends of

Germany by crossing *A. chinensis* var. *davidii* with *A. astilboides, A. japonica,* and *A. thunbergii.* These and other crosses have been repeated by several hybridizers, and many hybrids exist. Some of the best are listed here; plants are grouped by flowering time. Early (May in the South to June in the North): 'Amethyst' has lilac-purple flowers on 1½'–2' stems; 'Bridal Veil' has nodding snow-white flowers on 2' plants; 'Fanal' has deep cherry-red flowers and red foliage on 2' plants; 'Gloria' has dark-pink flowers on 2½' stems; 'Spinel' is a bushy plant with carmine-red flowers on 2½' stems. Midseason (June in the South to July or early August in the North): 'Anita Pfeifer' has salmon-pink flowers on 2'–2½' stems; 'Avalanche' has white flowers on 2½'–3' stems; 'Cattleya' is lilac-pink and reaches 3' in height; 'Hyacinth' has lilac-rose flowers on 2' stems; 'Irrlicht' is white-tinged pink on 2' stems. Late Season (July in the South to August in the North): 'Feuer' ('Fire') has fire-red flowers on 2½' stems; 'Glut' ('Glow') has light-red flowers on 1½' stems. Zones 3–9.

A. biternata (bye-ter-NAH-tuh), false goat's beard. Size: 3'–5' tall. A woodland plant with glossy leaves and tiny off-white flowers borne in open clusters. Zones 4–7.

A. chinensis (chy-NEN-sis), Chinese astilbe. Size: 1'–3' tall; leaves 4"–12" long. A floriferous, creeping plant with bright-green leaves and abundant rose-pink flowers in late summer and early fall. The variety *pumila* is a low groundcover plant with vibrant rose-pink flowers on 8"–24" stems. Several cultivars of this variety have been reclassified from *A. × arendsii.* 'Finale' has pale rose-pink flowers on 1'–1½' stalks; 'Intermezzo' is salmon-pink and under 1' tall; 'Serenade' is rose-red and 1' tall. Zones 3–8.

A. japonica (juh-PON-ih-kuh), Japanese astilbe. Size: 1'–2' tall; leaves 8"–12" long. An early-blooming astilbe with dense, pyramidal flower clusters, and glossy leaves often tinged with red. Hybrid cultivars include 'Deutschland', with spikes of white flowers on 1½' stems; 'Europa', with light-pink flowers on stems 2½' tall; 'Koblenz', with carmine-red flowers on 2' stems; and 'Red Sentinel', with bright-red flowers on 2' stems. Zones 4–8.

A. × rosea (ROSE-ee-uh), rose astilbe. Size: 2'–3' tall. Hybrids between *A. chinensis* and *A. japonica* with rose-pink flowers in midsummer. 'Peach Blossom' has salmon-pink flowers in large clusters. 'Queen Alexandra' is deep salmon-pink. Zones 4–8.

A. simplicifolia (sim-plih-sih-FOE-lee-uh), star astilbe. Size: 8"–12" tall; leaves 2½"–3" long. The glossy leaves of this dwarf species are lobed but not divided. The flowers are borne in open, often nodding clusters. Hybrids include 'Aphrodite', which has bronze foliage

The weeping pink plumes of *Astilbe thunbergii* 'Ostrich Plume' are showy both before and after the flowers fade. Resist the temptation to tidy up, and enjoy the decorative dried heads throughout the summer and fall.

and rosy-red flowers on 1½' stalks; 'Bronze Elegans' and 'Rosea', which have pink flowers; and 'Sprite', which has pale creamy-pink flowers. Zones 5–8 for the species; most hybrids seem to be hardy to Zone 4.

A. taquetii (tuh-KETT-ee-eye), fall astilbe. Size: 3½'–4' tall; leaves 4"–12" long. Fall astilbe is similar to *A. chinensis* but is quite tall and more tolerant of dry conditions. The inflorescence is upright and tightly packed. The cultivar 'Superba' is a tall, slender midseason bloomer with lavender-pink flowers; 'Purple Lance' has red-violet flowers. Zones 4–8.

A. thunbergii (thun-BERG-ee-eye), Thunberg's astilbe. Size: 2'–3' tall; leaves 10"–12" long. A showy plant with open, nodding flower clusters on tall stems above hairy foliage. Plants bloom July and August. 'Professor van der Weilen' has creamy-white flowers. Zones 4–8.

How to Grow: Astilbes are long-lived, easy-care perennials. They have one overriding requirement: moisture. Plant them in consistently moist, slightly acid, humus-rich soil in light shade to filtered sun. Dry soil can be fatal to astilbes, especially when they are in sunny situations. Crispy brown leaf edges are a sign that the soil is too dry. Wet or soggy soil is also detrimental, causing rot.

Astilbes tolerate a wide range of light levels. In northern gardens, a site in full sun with moist soil is acceptable. Provide shade from hot afternoon sun to prolong the attractive foliage display after flowering. In warmer regions, light to partial shade is mandatory. Plants will grow in deep shade but will not flower as prolifically.

Astilbes spread steadily from thick woody crowns to form broad clumps. Crowns often rise above the surrounding soil as they grow. Top-dress with rich, humusy soil, or lift and replant the clumps. Astilbes benefit from a

Like all astilbes, *Astilbe japonica* 'Cologne' is lovely in massed plantings in moist sites. The stiff, upright, deep-red flower clusters are set off to good advantage by the glossy, red-tinged foliage.

balanced organic fertilizer applied in spring. Removing the flower heads will not promote continued flowering, and the seed heads are attractive in their own right, so leave them standing for late-season interest.

Divide overgrown clumps every 3–4 years in spring or fall; replant into well-prepared soil. Propagate cultivars by division, as seeds do not come true to their parents. Seeds of true species are short-lived and difficult to germinate. Sow fresh seed outdoors in summer or early fall, as soon as you collect it.

Landscape Uses: The regal astilbes have a place in every garden that can satisfy their moisture requirements. Plant them along a stream or at the edge of a pond where their graceful plumes are reflected in the water. Combine them with ferns, irises, hostas, and other moisture-loving plants. In borders with evenly moist soil, astilbes combine attractively with lady's-mantle (*Alchemilla mollis*), lungworts (*Pulmonaria* spp.), and Siberian iris (*Iris sibirica*). In warmer areas, though, their crisping foliage can be a liability. Dwarf astilbes are suitable for edgings along walks or underplanting shrubs. *Astilbe chinensis* var. *pumila* tolerates dryer soils; try it in rock gardens or as a groundcover around the roots of trees. Mix taller astilbes with Solomon's seals (*Polygonatum* spp.) and ferns in an area with partial shade.

Aubrieta Cruciferae, Mustard Family

aw-bree-EH-tuh. Rock Cress. Spring bloom. Full sun to partial shade.

Description: *Aubrieta deltoidea* (dell-TOY-dee-uh), rock cress. Size: 6″–8″ tall; leaves 1″–1½″ long. Rock cress is a low, mat- or cushion-forming plant that spreads by thin rhizomes. In spring, the evergreen foliage is buried under ¾″–1″-wide 4-petaled white, rose, or purple flowers. Zones 4–8.

How to Grow: Plant in average, well-drained, neutral or alkaline soil in full sun or light shade. Plants grow best in areas with cool nights and low humidity. Shear after flowering to encourage reblooming and again in midsummer for compact growth. Divide in fall to rejuvenate clumps. Take cuttings after flowering.

Landscape Uses: Plant rock cresses in the crevices of unmortared walls or between pavers at the edge of walks. Try them in the rock garden with species bulbs. In the front of the border, combine them with cranesbills (*Geranium* spp.), crested iris (*Iris cristata*), and basket-of-gold (*Aurinia saxatilis*).

Early-flowering purple rock cress (*Aubrieta deltoidea*) provides loads of bright color in the early-spring rock garden. It will also grow in the vertical faces of rock walls, seemingly in no soil at all.

Aurinia Cruciferae, Mustard Family

aw-RIN-ee-uh. Basket-of-Gold. Spring bloom. Full sun.

Description: *Aurinia saxatilis* (sacks-uh-TILL-iss), basket-of-gold. Size: 10"–12" tall; leaves 4"–6" long. Basket-of-gold is also often sold as *Alyssum saxatile.* Its glowing yellow 4-petaled flowers are borne in slender, branching 4"–6" clusters above rosettes of fuzzy oblong gray-green foliage. The individual flowers of basket-of-gold are small, but the dense flower clusters and bright color create quite a show. 'Citrinum' has lemon-yellow flowers. 'Sunny Border Apricot' bears peach-yellow blooms. Zones 3–7.

How to Grow: Basket-of-gold demands a well-drained position with average soil in full sun. In rich and overly moist soils, the clumps flop and may rot; high temperatures and excessive humidity have a similar effect. Cut the clumps back by ⅓ after flowering to encourage compact growth. In hot areas, it's often best to treat these plants as annuals or biennials. Plant them in fall and remove them after flowering the next spring when they begin to look shabby. Propagate by division in fall, or take cuttings in spring or fall.

Landscape Uses: Basket-of-gold's cheerful yellow flowers are perfect for sunny rock and wall gardens. Position these plants along steps or walks or at the front of borders for a splash of bright spring color. Ideal companions for basket-of-gold include spring bulbs, perennial candytuft (*Iberis sempervirens*), and sedums. ❦

You can't beat basket-of-gold (*Aurinia saxatilis*), *right,* for bright spring color that captures the glow of the sun. For a striking effect, combine the species with the soft-yellow flowers of *A. saxatilis* 'Citrinum', *left.*

Baptisia   Leguminosae, Pea Family

bap-TEEZ-ee-uh. Baptisia, False Indigo. Late-spring and early-summer bloom. Full sun or light shade.

Description: Baptisias are handsome perennials with colorful spikes of pealike flowers in blue, yellow, cream, and white. Individual flowers look like those of lupines, but the habit is quite different. The plants ultimately reach shrublike proportions. They branch profusely to form rounded mounds. The 1″–3″ leaves have 3 rounded leaflets, usually gray-green or bluish in color. The gray or brown seed heads persist throughout the fall and are quite showy. The dried pods are also attractive for arrangements. Cut them after they darken and hang them upside down until they dry.

Baptisia alba (AL-buh), white wild indigo. Size: 2′–3′ tall; leaves 1″–2″ long. A compact plant with open, 1′-long spikes of ½″ white flowers. The flowers may be veined with purple. Zones 5–8.

B. australis (aw-STRAH-lis), blue false indigo. Size: 2′–4′ tall; leaves 1″–3″ long. The 1″

Blue false indigo (*Baptisia australis*) produces spikes of indigo-blue flowers in late spring and early summer. The gray-black seedpods are interesting in winter.

indigo-blue flowers are carried on open spikes up to 1' long held just above the soft blue-green foliage. Each clump produces many stems from a tough, gnarled, deep taproot. Zones 3–9.

  B. leucantha (lew-CAN-thuh), prairie wild indigo. Size: 3'–5' tall; leaves 2"–3" long. A tall plant with erect pointed 1'–2' spikes of 1" white flowers held well above the horizontal clump of foliage. Zones 4–8.

  B. leucophaea (lew-coe-FEE-uh), plains wild indigo, buffalo-pea. Size: 1'–2' tall; leaves 1"–2" long. A low, spreading plant with tightly packed, drooping clusters of creamy-yellow 1"–1½" flowers. Blooms in early spring before the other species. Zones 3–9.

  B. pendula (PEN-djew-luh), nodding wild indigo. Size: 3'–4' tall; leaves 2"–3" long. A showy species similar to *B. alba,* but with ¾" white flowers on erect 1' spikes, and nodding seedpods. Zones 5–8.

  B. perfoliata (per-foe-lee-AH-tuh), Georgia wild indigo. Size: 1'–2' tall; leaves 2"–3" long. A unique baptisia with disklike leaves pierced in the center by the stem. The plant resembles a sprawling eucalyptus and is grown more for its foliage than its flowers. A single ¼" yellow flower is produced in early summer above each point where the stem emerges from the leaf. Zones 7–9, or try it farther north with winter protection.

  B. viridis (VEER-ih-diss). Size: 2'–2½' tall; leaves 2"–3" long. Spikes of bright-yellow 1" flowers are borne above bushy clumps of blue-green leaves. Zones 7–9.

  How to Grow: Baptisias are tough, long-lived, low-maintenance perennials. Plant them in average to rich, moist but well-drained soil in full sun or light shade. All species are drought-tolerant once established. *B. alba, B. australis,* and *B. pendula* prefer rich, moist soils, while the other species will thrive on

Baptisia viridis produces upright spikes of yellow blooms and deep-green foliage. The flowers give way to showy seedpods. These shrublike plants are best used as specimens with shrubs or in perennial borders.

poor soil. Plants will bloom well in light shade, but they may need staking; use rounded peony hoops. Place them over the clumps as they emerge in early spring. Baptisias grow slowly at first but eventually spread to form huge clumps. The tough roots are massive on established plants. Start with young plants for best results. Space individual plants at least 3' apart. Leave them in place once they are established unless they overgrow their position.

  Divide in fall, if necessary, using a sharp knife or shears to cut through the tough clumps. Leave at least 1 eye (bud) per division. To propagate, take tip cuttings after flowering, or sow fresh seed outdoors or indoors in summer. The seeds have a hard seed coat; soak them overnight in hot water before planting. Germination will occur over a 2-to-4-week period. Keep seedlings on the dry side to prevent damping-off, a disease caused by fungi that attack seedlings at the soil line, causing them to topple over.

Landscape Uses: Baptisias are excellent border plants. Use them toward the back of the border in the company of bold flowers such as peonies, oriental poppies, and irises.

Plant airy plants such as columbines (*Aquilegia* spp.), bleeding hearts (*Dicentra* spp.), and cranesbills (*Geranium* spp.) around the bases of the clumps to hide the ugly "ankles" of the tall stalks. After flowering, the shrubby plants make an excellent background for late-blooming perennials. Contrast the blue-green foliage with fine-textured ornamental grasses. The showy seedpods add interest in the late-summer and fall garden. 🍁

Begonia Begoniaceae, Begonia Family

bih-GOAN-yuh. Begonia. Late-summer and fall bloom. Partial to full shade.

Description: *Begonia grandis* (GRANdis), hardy begonia. Size: 1′–2′ tall; leaves 6″–10″ long. Hardy begonia has succulent stems with large pointed leaves. Open clusters of 4-petaled pink flowers, followed by pink seedpods, are borne in the axils of the upper leaves. Plants grow from a small tuber. 'Alba' has white flowers. Zone 5 (with winter protection) or Zones 6–10.

How to Grow: Plant in evenly moist, humus-rich soil in partial to full shade. In cooler climates, plants tolerate considerable sun. They will spread to form open masses that seldom need division. Propagate by bulbils (found in the leaf axils); plant them outdoors in late summer.

Landscape Uses: The coarse, open texture of hardy begonias combines well with ferns, Japanese anemone (*Anemone* × *hybrida*), and hostas. Scatter clumps among flowering shrubs or low groundcovers to add late-season interest. The nodding flower clusters are attractive when reflected in the water of a shaded pool. 🍁

Delicate pink flowers and lush foliage make hardy begonia (*Begonia grandis*) a great choice for shade gardens. This easy-care plant grows in any moist spot and rewards gardeners every summer with its graceful flowers.

Belamcanda Iridaceae, Iris Family

bell-am-CAN-duh. Blackberry Lily. Summer bloom. Full sun to light shade.

Blackberry lily (*Belamcanda chinensis*) bears flat, irislike fans of foliage and bright-orange flowers that give way to green pods. In fall, the pods split to reveal seeds.

Description: *Belamcanda chinensis* (chy-NEN-sis), blackberry lily. Size: 2'–4' tall; leaves 2' tall and 1"–2" wide. Blackberry lilies have bright-orange flowers with darker speckles. They bloom through the summer in open, branching clusters. Each 1"–2"-wide flower has 3 petals and 3 petal-like sepals. Inflated seed capsules split to reveal rows of jet-black seeds. Plants have fans of lance-shaped leaves that grow from a creeping rhizome. Zones 4–10.

How to Grow: Plant in average to rich, well-drained soil in full sun. In hot regions, afternoon shade prolongs bloom. Divide overgrown clumps in spring or late summer. Plants often self-sow. Plant fresh seed outdoors in fall.

Landscape Uses: The small flowers of blackberry lily show up best when planted with fine-textured plants such as baby's-breaths or larger flowers such as daylilies. The showy capsules last well indoors if collected when they split open. 🍂

Bergenia Saxifragaceae, Saxifrage Family

ber-GEEN-ee-uh. Bergenia. Foliage plant with early-spring bloom. Full sun to partial shade.

Description: Bergenias are handsome clump-forming perennials with bold, leathery, usually evergreen foliage. They grow from thick, creeping roots that branch frequently. Dense 5"–6" clusters of fleshy, rose, pink, or white flowers rise from the center of each plant.

Bergenia ciliata (sill-ee-AH-tuh), winter begonia. Size: 1½'–2' tall; leaves to 14" long. A robust perennial with hairy, oval or rounded leaves that die back in the fall, unlike other bergenia species. The white or clear-pink flowers bloom in early spring. Zones 5–9.

B. cordifolia (core-dih-FOE-lee-uh), heart-leaved bergenia. Size: 12"–14" tall; leaves to 10" long. The bold, rounded or heart-shaped foliage is borne in dense rosettes that turn bronze or purple with the onset of cold weather. The rose or pink flowers are usually produced in spring, but occasional flower spikes may develop at any time throughout the growing season. 'Perfecta' has exceptional form and deep rose-red flowers on 20″ stems. 'Purpurea' has large, round foliage and magenta flowers. Zones 3–9.

B. purpurascens (purr-purr-AS-senz), bergenia. Size: 12″–15″ tall; leaves to 10″ long. The elliptic to oval leaves are blushed on the underside with deep-red. The purple or magenta flowers are produced on stout stalks in the spring. Zones 4–9.

Bergenia hybrids. Several hybrid bergenias are also available. 'Abendglut' ('Evening Glow') has broad oval leaves that turn bronze in the fall. The flowers are dark-red. 'Bressingham Bountiful' is a compact hybrid with rose-pink flowers. 'Bressingham White' has pure-white flowers. 'Morgenrote' ('Morning Red') has smaller round leaves and produces carmine-red flowers throughout the growing season. 'Silberlicht' ('Silver Light') is a strong grower with broad, heart-shaped leaves and white flowers that blush to pink. 'Sunningdale' has red flowers in spring, bright rose-red leaves in winter, and exceptional cold tolerance.

How to Grow: Plant bergenias in moist, humus-rich soil in full sun to light shade. These adaptable plants can tolerate alkaline soils and drought. In the North, grow them in full sun; in warm southern gardens, protect bergenias from hot afternoon sun to avoid leaf scald. Remove damaged leaves and spent flowerstalks as needed.

The cabbage-like clumps are very tough, but the leaves may brown and the growing point may be damaged in cold areas without consistent snow cover. Mulch with coarse leaves or marsh hay for winter protection.

The bold evergreen leaves of heart-leaved bergenia (*Bergenia cordifolia*) turn rich purple or bronze in the autumn and remain attractive all winter. Nodding clusters of pink or red flowers rise on fleshy stalks in the spring.

Remove the mulch when temperatures moderate to allow the early flowerstalks to emerge unhampered. In summer, slugs may damage leaves; exclude them with a barrier of diatomaceous earth around the plants. If this is not feasible, use beer traps or handpick them.

Divide plants when they become open in the center. Lift the clumps in spring and cut the thick stems with a sharp knife. Replant the divisions just deep enough to support the large rosettes. Sow ripe seed immediately and leave it uncovered (light may help speed germination). Seedlings develop quickly when kept at 68°–70°F. Reduce temperature slightly after germination. Transplant to the garden after 2–3 months.

Landscape Uses: You can use the bold foliage of bergenias to advantage in almost any garden situation. The rounded form and dark-green color complement rock walls and provide an excellent border for stone walks. Plant them with fine-textured shrubs to create contrast and excitement. They tolerate the dry shade of mature trees and make excellent groundcovers in combination with Solomon's seals (*Polygonatum* spp.), lungworts (*Pulmonaria* spp.), and ferns. Bergenias even perform well in containers. 🍂

Boltonia Compositae, Daisy Family

bowl-TOE-nee-uh. Boltonia. Late-summer and fall bloom. Sun or light shade.

'Snowbank' boltonia (*Boltonia asteroides* 'Snowbank') bears clouds of lacy, white, daisylike flowers that reflect light and give life to the garden in evening. These floriferous plants grow 3' to 4' tall and stay in bloom for 4 to 6 weeks in autumn.

Description: *Boltonia asteroides* (as-ter-OY-deez), boltonia. Size: 4'–6' tall; leaves 3"–5" long. A tall rounded plant with blue-green willowlike foliage and a profusion of 1" white daisylike flowers with yellow centers. The cultivars are superior to the species. 'Pink Beauty' offers pale-pink flowers in August and September. 'Snowbank' is more compact (3'–4') with stout upright stems and bright-white flowers in September and October. Zones 3–9.

How to Grow: Plant these easy-care perennials in moist, humus-rich soil in full sun or light shade. Established plants tolerate drought. On consistently dry soil, plants will grow but will be smaller in stature. Divide oversize clumps in spring. Cultivars do not come true from seed. Tip cuttings root easily when taken in May or June.

Landscape Uses: Create a charming combination with switchgrass (*Panicum virgatum*), pink Japanese anemone (*Anemone* × *hybrida*), asters, and goldenrods (*Solidago* spp.). Use 'Pink Beauty' with obedient plant (*Physostegia virginiana*), Joe-Pye weed (*Eupatorium purpureum*), and one of the white-variegated cultivars of Japanese silver grass (*Miscanthus sinensis*). Other late-blooming perennials that are suitable companions for boltonias include sunflowers (*Helianthus* spp.), 'Autumn Joy' sedum (*Sedum* × 'Autumn Joy'), common sneezeweed (*Helenium autumnale*), and monkshoods (*Aconitum* spp.). 🍂

Brunnera   Boraginaceae, Borage Family

BROON-er-uh. Brunnera. Spring bloom and bold summer foliage. Partial to full shade.

Description: *Brunnera macrophylla* (mack-row-FILL-uh), Siberian bugloss. Size: 1'–1½' tall; leaves 6"–8" long. A showy plant in flower and foliage, the ¼"-wide forget-me-not-like blue flowers emerge with the heart-shaped leaves in early spring. After flowering, the foliage expands to provide a showy display that lasts all summer. The stout crown produces fibrous black roots. 'Variegata' has leaves with a large irregular white border and requires constantly moist soil. Zones 3–8.

How to Grow: Give Siberian bugloss continually moist, humus-rich soil and light to full shade for best growth. Plants do well in drier soils, but the foliage will be smaller. If drought persists, the plants will go dormant to conserve energy. Division is seldom necessary. To propagate, you can divide plants in early spring or fall, or take 3"–4" root cuttings in fall or early winter. Self-sown seedlings will appear around the parent plants and are easy to transplant.

Landscape Uses: Use a generous planting of Siberian bugloss with bright-yellow daffodils, bleeding hearts (*Dicentra* spp.), and leopard's bane (*Doronicum orientale*). The showy heart-shaped leaves also combine well with other shade-loving foliage plants, such as epimediums (*Epimedium* spp.), lungworts (*Pulmonaria* spp.), hostas, and ferns. 🍂

Siberian bugloss (*Brunnera macrophylla*) combines bold foliage with attractive flowers, making it an invaluable addition to the lightly shaded garden. As the deep-blue spring flowers fade, the large, heart-shaped leaves expand and claim prominence for the remainder of the summer.

Caltha   Ranunculaceae, Buttercup Family.

KAL-thuh. Marsh Marigold. Spring bloom. Sun or partial shade.

The butter-yellow blooms of marsh marigold (*Caltha palustris*) are perfect for bog and water gardens. Glossy, bright-green, heart-shaped leaves set the flowers off to good advantage. By midsummer the plants disappear.

Description: *Caltha palustris* (pal-US-tris), marsh marigold, cowslip. Size: 1'–2' tall; leaves 4"–6" long. Marsh marigolds bear open clusters of 1½" butter-yellow flowers above rounded leaves. After flowering, the entire plant goes dormant. 'Flore Pleno' ('Multiplex') has double flowers. Zones 2–8.

How to Grow: Marsh marigolds demand constantly moist or wet soil and will even grow in standing water. They require humus-rich or loamy soils and full sun to light shade. Soil moisture is less critical after flowering, but don't let the soil become completely dry. Divide in summer. Sow fresh seeds outdoors in moist soil; they'll germinate the following spring. Double-flowered selections do not come true from seed.

Landscape Uses: Choose marsh marigolds for a stream or pond edge where the flowers are reflected in the water. Plant with primroses (*Primula* spp.), irises, astilbes, and ferns in a bog garden or moist, low spot. 🌿

Campanula Campanulaceae, Bellflower Family

kam-PAN-yew-luh. Bellflower, Harebell. Spring and summer bloom. Sun or partial shade.

Description: A variable genus of showy plants ranging from low, mat-forming creepers to tall, upright specimens for the back of the border. Flowers are bell-shaped or starry with 5 petals fused for varying portions of their length. Some flowers are borne singly, others in clusters; some face upward, while others are nodding. The taller species have larger basal leaves, with stem leaves that reduce in size as they ascend toward the flowers.

Campanula carpatica (car-PAT-ih-kuh), Carpathian harebell. Size: 8"–18" tall; leaves to 2" long. A mounding, floriferous species with 2" cup-shaped blue or white flowers from spring through summer. The triangular leaves form a tight clump, which complements the delicate flowers. 'Blue Clips' has 2" medium-blue flowers on compact plants and comes true from seed. 'China Doll' has azure-blue flowers. 'Wedgewood Blue' bears 2½" violet-blue flowers on 6" stems. 'White Clips' has 2½"–3" flowers on compact plants. Zones 3–8.

C. cochlearifolia (cock-lee-uh-rih-FOE-lee-uh), spiral bellflower. Size: 4"–6" tall; leaves to 1" long. A low, mat-forming plant with small, nearly round leaves and profuse ¾" blue-lilac, bell-shaped flowers in summer. Plants spread outward from underground runners. The variety *alba* is a vigorous grower with pure-white flowers. 'Miranda' has pale

Clumps of cheery, blue-flowered Carpathian harebell (*Campanula carpatica*) are perfect for rock gardens and walls and for edging beds. Regular deadheading will keep the plants in bloom for 4 to 6 weeks in spring and summer.

sky-blue flowers. Zone 4 (with winter protection) or Zones 5–8.

C. garganica (gar-GAH-nih-kuh), Gargano bellflower. Size: 5″–6″ tall; leaves 1″ long. A fast-spreading groundcover with fuzzy, heart- to kidney-shaped leaves and starry ½″ blue flowers with white centers. Zones 6–8.

C. glomerata (glahm-er-AH-tuh), clustered bellflower. Size: 1′–3′ tall; leaves to 5″ long. A stout, upright, summer-blooming plant bearing 1″ purple or violet flowers clustered at the nodes (leaf joints) and at the tips of the hairy stems. The plants spread by creeping underground stems to form open clumps. The variety *acaulis* is a dwarf plant (to 5″ tall) with violet-blue flowers in early summer. 'Alba' has white flowers. 'Crown of Snow' has white flowers on 2′ stems. 'Joan Elliot' has dense

Peach-leaved bellflower (*Campanula persicifolia*) carries its 1″- to 1½″-wide flowers on tall stalks. Plant it toward the middle or rear of the sunny border with peonies and irises.

Clustered bellflower (*Campanula glomerata*) bears royal-purple flowers in tiered whorls above the lance-shaped leaves. The plants are lovely combined with the foamy chartreuse flowers of lady's-mantle (*Alchemilla mollis*) in the early-summer garden.

clusters of deep blue-violet flowers on multiple 1½′ stems. 'Superba' is a vigorous grower with deep-violet flowers on 2½′ stems. Zones 3–8.

C. lactiflora (lack-tih-FLOOR-uh), milky bellflower. Size: 3′–4′ tall; leaves to 5″ long. A large, showy, summer-blooming species with tight clusters of 1″ blue or white bells. The variety *alba* has white flowers. 'Loddon Anna' has stout stems with pale-pink flowers. Zones 3–7.

C. latifolia (lat-ih-FOE-lee-uh), great bellflower. Size: 2′–5′ tall; leaves to 6″ long. A coarse bellflower with tall, spiky clusters of 2″–3″ purple-blue, upright, bell-shaped flowers in early summer. 'Brantwood' has violet flowers. Zones 3–7.

C. persicifolia (per-sick-ih-FOE-lee-uh), peach-leaved bellflower. Size: 1′–3′ tall; leaves 4″–8″ long. A lovely, graceful species with narrow leaves and a profusion of 1"–1½" open, bell-shaped, blue-violet flowers in summer. 'Alba' has white flowers. 'Telham Beauty' is 3'–4' tall with pale lavender-blue flowers. Zones 3–7.

C. portenschlagiana (pore-ten-schlahg-ee-AH-nuh), Dalmatian bellflower. Size: 4"–6" tall; leaves 1"–2" long. A creeping plant with tight rosettes of small, triangular leaves and a profusion of 1" blue-purple bell-shaped flowers in late spring and early summer. 'Resholt' has indigo-blue flowers. Zones 4–8.

C. poscharskyana (poss-shar-skee-AH-nuh), Serbian bellflower. Size: 6"–12" tall; leaves 1"–1½" long. A trailing, fast-spreading species with ½"–1" open starry blue flowers in spring and early summer. Zones 3–7.

C. rotundifolia (row-ton-dih-FOE-lee-uh), bluebell, harebell. Height: 4"–14" tall; leaves ½"–1" long. A delicate, clump-forming plant with nodding, ¾" sky-blue, bell-shaped flowers

borne on slender stems. Zones 2–7.

How to Grow: Bellflowers are easy-care perennials for borders and rock gardens. Cultural requirements vary among species. In general, the low, spreading species (*C. carpatica, C. cochleariifolia, C. garganica, C. portenschlagiana, C. poscharskyana,* and *C. rotundifolia*) require average to rich, well-drained soil in full sun or light shade. *C. portenschlagiana* tolerates more shade than other species.

Plant the larger bellflowers in moist, well-drained humus-rich soil in full sun or light shade. Most species are sensitive to high temperatures. Provide afternoon shade in warmer regions to prolong the life of the plants. *C. glomerata* prefers evenly moist alkaline soil and tolerates partial shade.

Divide plants as necessary in early spring or fall. *C. garganica* and *C. poscharskyana* are particularly rapid spreaders and may need division every 2–3 years. Propagate by tip

Plant Serbian bellflower (*Campanula poscharskyana*) in a dry wall or in a rock garden for an easy-care, fast-growing groundcover in sun or light shade. The plants bear starry blue flowers for a month or more in summer.

cuttings in early summer. Sow ripe seed indoors on a moist medium; do not cover because light can encourage germination. In warm (70°F) conditions, seedlings germinate in 3–6 weeks. Several species, especially *C. carpatica,* may self-sow.

Slugs are the only serious pest. Protect plants with a barrier strip of diatomaceous earth, or use a dish of beer as bait to drown the pests.

Landscape Uses: Choose the low-growing and creeping bellflowers for rock gardens and informal rock walls. The blue and purple flowers are lovely against the lush foliage, and contrast well with the rough surfaces of rocks. The plants will clamber over rocks and creep through crevices to soften even the harshest rock face. Try these low gems at the front of a border or spilling over the straight edges of walks. Plant medium-size clustered bellflower (*C. glomerata*) in a moist site with Siberian iris (*Iris sibirica*), leopard's bane (*Doronicum orientale*), and ferns. Use the taller bellflower species in beds and borders or along walls and fences. They are lovely in large drifts, as accents, or combined with goat's beard (*Aruncus dioicus*), yarrows, and baby's-breaths. ❧

Catananche Compositae, Daisy Family

cat-uh-NAN-chee. Cupid's Dart. Summer bloom. Full sun or light shade.

For a sunny garden with dry, sandy soil, try Cupid's dart (*Catananche caerulea*). The blue flowers are attractive and long-lasting when cut for fresh use or drying.

Description: *Catananche caerulea* (sir-ROO-lee-uh), Cupid's dart. Size: 1½'–2' tall; leaves to 1' long. The 2″ lilac-blue flowers are borne singly on wiry stems above clumps of hairy, linear foliage. The flowers dry well and are ideal for use in arrangements with other everlastings. 'Blue Giant' has deep-blue flowers on 2' stems. 'Major' stands 3' tall with lilac-blue flowers. Zones 4–9.

How to Grow: Grow Cupid's darts in humus-rich, sandy, well-drained soil in full sun or light shade. Plants may be short-lived, especially in heavy clay soils. Dividing the clumps annually helps maintain vigor. Propagate by root cuttings in fall or winter. Sow seeds indoors in late winter. They will bloom the first summer.

Landscape Uses: Plant Cupid's darts in masses to increase their visual impact. Use them toward the front of the border or in rock gardens or containers. To dry the flowers, cut them as soon as the rays (petals) expand. ❧

Centaurea Compositae, Daisy Family

sen-TOR-ee-uh. Centaurea, Cornflower, Knapweed. Late-spring and early-summer bloom. Full sun to light shade.

Description: Cornflowers are informal plants with fringed flowers. The flowers have a scaly base below the petal-like ray florets.

Centaurea hypoleuca (high-poe-LEW-kuh), knapweed (also sold as *C. dealbata*). Size: 1½′–2½′ tall; leaves to 1′ long. A bushy, fast-spreading perennial with showy 1½″ rose-pink flowers. 'John Coutts' bears 2″ flowers on compact plants. Zones 3–7.

C. macrocephala (mack-row-SEFF-uh-luh), globe centaurea, Armenian basket flower. Size: 3′–4′ tall; leaves to 10″ long. A coarse plant with 3″ yellow thistle-like blooms on 4′ stems. Zones 2–8.

C. montana (mahn-TAN-uh), mountain bluet. Size: 1½′–2′ tall; leaves to 8″ long. A lovely but weedy perennial with 2½″ cobalt-blue flowers. Spreads by rapidly creeping roots to form colonies. 'Alba' has white flowers. Zones 3–8.

How to Grow: Plant in average to rich, moist but well-drained soil in full sun or light shade. Divide clumps in spring or fall as necessary, usually every 2–3 years. Sow fresh seed outdoors in fall or indoors in late winter.

Landscape Uses: Cornflowers are well-suited to informal gardens. The flowers are excellent for cutting fresh or for drying. Harvest flowers for drying as soon as they are fully expanded. ❧

The stunning, electric-blue flowers of mountain bluet (*Centaurea montana*) are borne for 1 to 2 months in summer if the plants are regularly deadheaded. Plant them in masses in borders or in informal areas.

Centranthus Valerianaceae, Valerian Family

sen-TRAN-thus. Valerian, Jupiter's Beard, Centranth. Spring and early-summer bloom. Full sun.

Red valerian (*Centranthus ruber*) is so tough it can even grow from crevices in brick walls. In addition to the white *C. ruber* var. *albus* pictured here, there are red and pink selections.

Description: *Centranthus ruber* (ROO-ber), red valerian. Size: 1'–3' tall; leaves to 4" long. An attractive perennial with clusters of ½" pink, rose, coral-red, or white flowers on erect, branching stems. The smooth leaves are blue-green and quite attractive during and after flowering. The variety *coccineus* has deep-scarlet flowers; *roseus* has rose-red blooms; *albus* has white blooms. Zones 4–8.

How to Grow: Red valerian is easy to grow on average to sandy, neutral or alkaline soils in full sun. Shear plants after flowering if they become floppy. Plants may self-sow freely under favorable conditions.

Landscape Uses: This adaptable plant is ideal for rock gardens and stone walls. The coral-red flowers can be difficult to use in combination with other plants but are perfect with neutral rock surfaces. In the border, plant the softer colors with yarrows, asters, and coreopsis (*Coreopsis* spp.).

Cerastium Caryophyllaceae, Pink Family

sir-AS-tee-um. Mouse-Ear Chickweed, Snow-in-Summer. Late-spring and early-summer bloom. Full sun.

Description: These low-mounding, sub-alpine plants bear small, white-woolly leaves and clusters of ½"–1" white flowers. Each flower has 5 deeply notched petals, giving the illusion of double the true number.

Cerastium biebersteinii (bee-ber-STEIN-ee-eye), Taurus chickweed, snow-in-summer. Size: 6"–12" tall; leaves to 2" long. A woolly, white, mounding or mat-forming perennial with spreading stems and ¾" white flowers in sparse clusters. Zones 3–7.

C. tomentosum (toe-men-TOE-sum), snow-in-summer. Size: 6"–10" tall, leaves to 1" inch long. A woolly, mat-forming perennial with 1" white flowers in many-flowered clusters. 'YoYo' is more compact than the species. Zones 2–7.

How to Grow: Give these care-free perennials average, well-drained soil and full sun. Divide plants if they spread too aggressively. Poorly drained soil will encourage fungal rots that blacken the foliage; avoid problems by providing good drainage. High heat and humidity can cause similar problems in the South. Propagate by tip cuttings in summer or by division.

Landscape Uses: Mouse-ear chickweed is well-adapted to growing among rocks. Plant it in walls or with spring bulbs, saxifrages (*Saxifraga* spp.), primroses (*Primula* spp.), and bellflowers (*Campanula* spp.) in a sunny rock garden. The creeping mats are also attractive on dry or sandy banks. Mouse-ear chickweed will also grow in containers. 🍁

Plant carpet-forming snow-in-summer (*Cerastium tomentosum*) in rock gardens or along walks where you can enjoy the gray foliage and pretty white flowers in combination with other small plants.

Ceratostigma Plumbaginaceae, Plumbago Family

sir-at-oh-STIG-muh. Plumbago, Leadwort. Summer and fall bloom. Full sun to partial shade.

Description: *Ceratostigma plumbaginoides* (plum-bah-jih-NOY-deez), plumbago, leadwort. Size: 6″–12″ tall; leaves to 3½″ long. A creeping, semi-woody perennial with deep-green, diamond-shaped leaves and clusters of 5-petaled blue flowers nearly 1″ across. Zones 5–9.

How to Grow: Plant in average to rich, moist but well-drained soil in sun or partial shade. Prune out winter-killed stems before new growth expands in late spring. Flowering starts in early to mid-summer and often continues until fall. Leaves turn red or orange after frost. Divide in spring. Propagate by tip cuttings in summer.

Landscape Uses: Choose plumbago when you need a tough, fast-growing groundcover. Plants will succeed on dry, sunny banks or between rocks in a wall. 🍁

Choose plumbago (*Ceratostigma plumbaginoides*) for a tough and beautiful groundcover in sun or light shade. The bright-green foliage and deep-blue flowers are suitable for walls, rock gardens, and borders.

Chelone Scrophulariaceae, Figwort Family

chee-LOW-nee. Turtlehead. Late-summer and fall bloom. Full sun to partial shade.

Plant drifts of pink turtleheads (*Chelone lyonii*) in moist spots with full sun or partial shade. These plants are perfect for bog gardens or along the sides of ponds with ferns and irises.

Description: These robust, moisture-loving perennials produce coarse, lanceolate leaves along upright or arching stems. The unusual 1″ inflated, tubular flowers are borne in terminal and axillary clusters. They resemble the head of a turtle with its mouth agape. The dried seed heads are also attractive.

Chelone glabra (GLAY-bruh), white turtlehead. Size: 3′–5′ tall; leaves to 6″ long. A lovely, upright to vase-shaped plant with white flowers blushed with violet. The dark-green leaves are narrow and lance-shaped. Zones 3–8.

C. lyonii (lye-ON-ee-eye), pink turtlehead. Size: 1′–3′ tall; leaves 4″–7″ long. These compact plants offer bright rose-pink flowers and wide, lush foliage. Zones 3–8.

C. obliqua (oh-BLEE-kwah), rose turtlehead, red turtlehead. Size: 2′–3′ tall; leaves to 6″ long. A floriferous species with rose or red-violet flowers on upright stems. The leaves are narrower and shorter stalked than those of *C. lyonii*. 'Alba' has white blooms. Zones 4–9.

How to Grow: Turtleheads are plants of wet meadows, ditches, and other moist soils. They are quite adaptable to garden conditions. Give them rich, evenly moist soil in full sun or partial shade. In warmer zones, plants in full sun must have constant moisture. Early pinching will decrease height but may alter the natural form of the plant.

Divide the fleshy-rooted crowns in spring, or late fall after flowering. Propagate by stem cuttings in early summer. Sow seeds outdoors when ripe. Indoors, sow seeds in winter and place in the refrigerator for 4–6 weeks. Then move them to a bright location with a temperature of 60°F. Plants germinate in 2–3 weeks; transplant outdoors in summer.

Landscape Uses: Turtleheads are regal plants for the late-summer and fall garden as accents or specimens. In the perennial border, plant them with Joe-Pye weed (*Eupatorium purpureum*), asters, pearly everlasting (*Anaphalis* spp.), and Japanese anemone (*Anemone* × *hybrida*). In the informal garden or meadow, plant drifts of turtleheads with goldenrods (*Solidago* spp.), sunflowers (*Helianthus* spp.), asters, and grasses. At pond's edge, where the flowers are reflected in the still water, plant turtleheads with water irises (*Iris* spp.), great blue lobelia (*Lobelia siphilitica*), and ferns. ❦

Chrysanthemum Compositae, Daisy Family

kris-AN-thuh-mum. Chrysanthemum. Summer or fall bloom. Full sun.

Description: *Chrysanthemum* is a large, variable genus of colorful, daisy-flowered perennials. Botanists have recently re-evaluated the proper classification of the plants in this genus. As a result, most species have been reassigned to new genera. The new botanical names are included in parentheses following their more widely recognized names.

C. coccineum (cock-SIN-ee-um), painted daisy, pyrethrum (also sold as *Tanacetum coccineum*). Size: 1½'-2' tall; leaves to 4" long. An open, reclining plant with ferny foliage and 3" red, rose, or pale-pink flowers borne singly in early summer. The blooms are long-lasting as cut flowers. An extract of this plant is used as an organic insecticide to control aphids, whiteflies, and other pests. 'James Kelway' has scarlet to crimson flowers on 1½' stems. 'Robinson's Crimson' has crimson flowers on 2' stems. Zones 3-7.

C. corymbosum (core-im-BOH-sum), chrysanthemum (also sold as *Tanacetum corymbosum*). Size: 1'-4' tall; leaves to 6" long. A stiff, leafy perennial with mostly basal foliage and broad, open clusters of 1" white daisies in summer. Zones 4-8.

C. frutescens (frew-TESS-senz), marguerite (also sold as *Argyranthemum frutescens*). Size: 2'-3' tall; leaves 1"-2" long. A bushy, erect plant with stiff, dissected foliage and 2" white or sulfur-yellow flowers on sturdy stalks. Zones 9-11; grown as an annual in other zones.

C. leucanthemum (lew-CAN-thuh-mum), oxeye daisy (also sold as *Leucanthemum vulgare*). Size: 1'-3' tall; leaves to 6" long. The 2"-3" white flowers with bright-yellow centers wave above the deeply toothed, mostly basal foliage.

'May Queen' is an early- and long-blooming plant of exceptional merit. Zones 2-10.

C. × morifolium (more-ih-FOE-lee-um), garden mum, hardy mum, florist's chrysanthemum, mum (also sold as *Dendranthema × grandiflorum*). Size: 1½'-5' tall; leaves to 4" long. Garden mums have maintained unparalleled popularity for nearly 2,500 years. The Chinese first "domesticated" garden mums through extensive hybridization of several species native to China and Japan. Judicious selection was made based on size, form, and color to get the best plants. The first mums reached Europe in the seventeenth century

Hardy garden mums such as *Chrysanthemum × morifolium* 'Grandchild' are showstoppers. They bloom for weeks on end with the last of the season's perennials.

In cool climates, the hardy painted daisy (*Chrysanthemum coccineum*) rewards gardeners with lush, dissected foliage and bright-pink daisies up to 3'' across. This plant is also the source of a commonly used botanical insecticide called pyrethrins.

where they were an instant sensation. Hybridization continues today, especially to create new flower forms and for increased cold-hardiness—now over 5,000 cultivars are named. Some are suitable only for greenhouse cultivation for cut flowers or potted plants; others are quite hardy.

Flower colors range from white through pink, rose, red, burgundy, bronze, gold, yellow, and cream. The flower heads may be daisylike, pompon (with double, ball-like flowers), cushions (with flat, double flowers), decoratives (with large, semidouble or double flowers), buttons (with small, tightly packed, double flowers), and novelty types such as spiders and spoon-petaled cultivars. Flower size varies from under 1'' up to 6'' across.

C. × *morifolium* hybrids are short-day plants. Their bud set and flowering are triggered by decreasing day length, hence their fall blooming period. Forced florist's mums make poor garden plants in the North because they bloom late in the season. Planted outdoors, they often start to bloom when the weather is too harsh for them to develop properly. Pot- or field-grown plants sold at your local garden center should be hardy in your area.

Mums have deep-green, often hairy, lobed leaves that are attractive throughout the season. There are thousands of cultivars, all of which vary in hardiness. Check with your local garden center or nursery to obtain the best selections for your area. For northern gardens, look for plants with names beginning with 'Minn', such as 'Minnautumn'; these cultivars are particularly hardy. Zones 4–9.

C. nipponicum (nih-PON-ih-kum), Nippon daisy (also sold as *Nipponanthemum nipponicum*). Size: 1'–3' tall, leaves 3''–4'' long.

A mounding, semi-woody plant with glossy leaves and showy 3″ white daisies in late summer and fall. Nippon daisies respond well to cool seaside conditions. Zones 5–8.

C. pacificum (puh-SIFF-ih-kum), gold-and-silver chrysanthemum (also sold as *Ajania pacifica*). Size: 1′–1½′ tall; leaves 2″–3″ long. A mat-forming perennial with scalloped, gray-green, white-edged leaves. Clusters of button-like ½″ yellow flowers appear in October. Zones 5–9.

C. parthenium (par-THEEN-ee-um), fever-few (also sold as *Tanacetum parthenium*). Size: 2′–3′ tall; leaves to 3″ long. This popular, old-fashioned perennial is erect and bushy with bright-green lobed foliage and mounds of ¾″ white daisies with large centers. They bloom profusely from summer to fall. Zones 4–8.

C. × *superbum* (soo-PER-bum), Shasta daisy (also sold as *Leucanthemum* × *superbum*). Size: 1′–3′ tall; leaves to 10″ long. These cheerful summer-blooming chrysanthemums resemble oxeye daisies. Their 2″–3″ pure-white flowers with bright-yellow centers are held on stout stalks above the deep-green, oblong foliage. 'Alaska' is an older, extremely cold-hardy (to Zone 3) selection with 3″ flowers. 'Little Miss Muffet' is only 8″–12″ tall with 3″ off-white flowers. 'Majestic' has 3″–4″ flowers. 'Mount Shasta' has double flowers on 2′ stems. 'Polaris' is a giant with 5″–6″ somewhat-floppy flowers on 3′ stems. 'T. E. Killen' blooms in mid- to late summer on sturdy 3′ stems and has shorter ray florets (petals) than the other selections. Zones vary by cultivar, generally 4–8.

C. zawadskii var. *latilobum* (zah-WAD-ski-eye lat-ih-LOBE-um), hardy garden chrysanthemum (also sold as *C.* × *rubellum* and *Dendranthema zawadskii*). Size: 1′–3′ tall; leaves 1″–1½″ long. An extremely hardy, early-blooming mum with deeply lobed leaves, often edged in red, and 2″–3″ pink flowers. 'Clara Curtis' is 2′–2½′ tall with deep-pink

Shasta daisies such as *Chrysanthemum* × *superbum* 'Aglaya' are tough, easy-care perennials. They thrive in average, moist but well-drained soil and bloom for a month or more in summer.

flowers. 'Mary Stoker' has straw-yellow flowers. Zones 4–9.

How to Grow: Chrysanthemums are easy to grow. Plant them in average to rich, moist but well-drained soil in full sun. Mums generally thrive in neutral or alkaline soils. Waterlogging is sure death to most species, especially in winter. *C. nipponicum* and *C.* × *superbum* are tolerant of dry, sandy soils and seaside conditions. *C. pacificum* tolerates poor, dry soil and sun or partial shade.

Shearing *C. parthenium* and *C. coccineum* after flowering will improve their appearance and encourage reblooming. *C.* × *morifolium* and *C. zawadskii* var. *latilobum* respond well to pinching, to control their height and make the plants bushy. Start pinching when the plants have 6–8 well-formed leaves. Remove shoot tips with garden shears or your fingers, taking care to make a clean break. When sideshoots have developed, pinch them again to 2–4 leaves. You may need to give some

For a stunning, season-long foliage display, plant gold-and-silver chrysanthemum (*Chrysanthemum pacificum*) as a groundcover among rocks or at the front of the border. The buttonlike yellow flowers are borne in fall.

plants another pinch to get a nice shape. Stop pinching altogether before July 1; later pinching may reduce the flower display.

You can increase the size of individual mum flowers by disbudding (removing all but the largest and topmost flower bud on each stem). Do this when the buds are still in the button stage, before they show any color. When the flower opens, it will be larger and more full because it isn't competing with the others.

Many mums spread by creeping stems to form broad clumps. Because they grow so rapidly, the plants often die out in the center. Divide clumps in spring every 1–2 years to keep them healthy and attractive. Frequent division also prolongs the life of short-lived species such as *C. parthenium*, *C. coccineum*, and *C.* × *superbum*. *C. nipponicum* has a woody base, so it does not respond well to division. All mums are easy to grow from

cuttings taken in late spring or early summer. Most will bloom in the first year.

Aphids and spider mites can be problems, causing yellowed, curled leaves and stunted plants. Remove badly infested portions and discard. Spray plants with a strong jet of water to knock off aphids. To control either pest, spray with insecticidal soap or a botanical insecticide such as pyrethrins.

Landscape Uses: Mums are so varied in bloom time, color, size, and adaptability that they have a place in almost every garden. Use the brilliant fall flowers of hardy garden mums with asters, sedums, ornamental grasses, and shrubs. Plant *C. coccineum* and *C.* × *superbum* in borders with summer-blooming perennials such as irises, poppies, daylilies, and yarrows. Choose *C. parthenium* for a filler between bold flowers and foliage. *C. pacificum* is wonderful as a groundcover or container plant. 🍂

Chrysopsis Compositae, Daisy Family

krih-SOP-sis. Golden Aster. Summer and fall bloom. Full sun.

Description: *Chrysopsis mariana* (mar-ee-AH-nuh), Maryland golden aster (also sold as *Heterotheca mariana*). Size: 1'–3' tall; leaves to 9" long. A mounding plant with dark-green leaves clothed in gray hairs. Bright-yellow, ½" flowers cover the plant in late summer into fall. Zones 4–9.

C. villosa (vill-OH-suh), hairy golden aster (also sold as *Heterotheca villosa*). Size: 1'–5' tall; leaves to 2" long. 'Golden Sunshine' is 4'–5' tall with hairy foliage and 1½" golden-yellow flowers in late summer through fall. Zones 4–9.

How to Grow: Plant in average, well-drained soil and full sun. Divide in spring or take tip cuttings in early summer. Sow fresh seed outdoors in fall or indoors in winter. Place them in a refrigerator for 4–6 weeks before moving them to a warm, bright place.

Landscape Uses: Give *C. villosa* a position toward the back of a border where it has plenty of room to spread up and out. ❧

Maryland golden aster (*Chrysopsis mariana*) is a tough, drought-tolerant perennial for dry, sunny banks and well-drained gardens. After flowering, the fuzzy tan seed heads are quite attractive.

Cimicifuga Ranunculaceae, Buttercup Family

sim-ih-siff-YOU-guh. Bugbane, Black Cohosh, Snakeroot. Summer and fall bloom. Full sun to open shade.

Description: Dozens of ¼"–½" creamy-white petal-less flowers crowd together on branching stalks. The compound leaves emerge in early spring and remain attractive through frost.

Cimicifuga japonica (juh-PON-ih-kuh), bugbane. Size: 2'–3' tall; leaves to 1' long. Pure-white flowers bloom in upright or arch-ing flower spikes over finely divided, shiny leaves. The variety *acerina* has maplelike leaves. Both the species and variety bloom in late summer or early fall. Zones 3–8.

C. racemosa (ray-sih-MOW-suh), black snakeroot, black cohosh. Size: 4'–7' tall, leaves to 2' long. A regal plant with tall, branching spikes of white, ill-scented flowers in early

The blooms of black snakeroot (*Cimicifuga racemosa*) appear in woodlands in midsummer.

summer. The variety *cordifolia* has pale-amber flowers. Zones 3–8.

C. simplex (SIM-plecks), Kamchatka bugbane. Size: 3'–6' tall; leaves to 1' long. The sweetly scented, white flowers bloom in autumn on branched stalks. The variety *ramosa* has 5'–6' narrow, sparsely branching spikes. 'White Pearl' is shorter (to 3'). Zones 3–8.

How to Grow: Plant in moist, humus-rich soil in sun or shade. In warmer regions, choose a site with consistent moisture and shade from afternoon sun to keep foliage from browning. Plants grow slowly. Divide in fall (leave at least 1 bud per division), or sow fresh seed outdoors in fall.

Landscape Uses: In borders, contrast their vertical form with rounded plants such as phlox and cranesbills (*Geranium* spp.).

Clematis   Ranunculaceae, Buttercup Family

KLEM-uh-tiss. Clematis. Vines or subshrubs with late-spring, summer, or autumn bloom. Full sun or light shade.

The indigo bells of solitary clematis (*Clematis integrifolia*) appear in midsummer, followed by fuzzy seed heads.

Description: *Clematis* is a large genus of woody vines, subshrubs, and herbaceous plants. The subshrubs and herbaceous species discussed below are wonderful for use in a perennial garden. They are not as showy as some of the woody-vined large-flowered hybrids, but they have a subtle, restrained beauty. Their flowers have colorful sepals that resemble petals, usually 4 per flower. The starry or bell-shaped blooms appear singly or in clusters. The seeds have fuzzy tails that are tangled in a mass.

C. heracleifolia (hair-ack-lee-ih-FOE-lee-uh), tube clematis. Size: 1'–3' tall; leaves 5"–12" long. A subshrub with weakly upright stems and compound leaves. The 1" starry blue flowers cluster in the axils of the upper leaves. The variety *davidiana* is more upright with fragrant indigo-blue flowers. Zones 3–8.

C. integrifolia (in-teg-rih-FOE-lee-uh), solitary clematis. Size: 1½'–3' tall; leaves to 4" long. A weakly upright to sprawling plant with paired ovate leaves and solitary 1¼" wide-flaring indigo bells with recurved sepals. The variety *caerulea* has light-blue flowers. Zones 3–9.

C. recta (WRECK-tuh), ground clematis. Size: 2'–4' tall, leaves 2"–3" long. A weakly upright to open shrublike plant with compound leaves having 5–9 small leaflets. The starry, fragrant, ¾" white flowers are borne in dense terminal clusters in summer and fall. 'Purpurea' has red-violet foliage that sets off the flowers to good advantage. Zones 3–7.

C. texensis (tex-EN-sis), scarlet clematis, Texas clematis. Herbaceous climbing vine; leaves 2"–3" long. A rambling vine with compound blue-green leaves and ¾" nodding scarlet bells with pale-yellow insides. Zone 4 (with winter protection) or Zones 5–9.

C. virginiana (ver-jin-ee-AH-nuh), virgin's bower. Herbaceous climbing vine; leaves 3"–5" long. A fragrant autumn-blooming clematis with masses of ½"–1" starry white flowers that cover the 3-lobed leaves. Zones 4–9.

How to Grow: Plant clematis in humus-rich soil in full sun. Keep the plants mulched. A cool, evenly moist, fertile root run is as important as sun for good growth and bloom. Propagate by stem cuttings before flowering in spring or early summer. Sow fresh seed indoors or outdoors in summer or fall. 🍁

Convallaria Liliaceae, Lily Family

con-val-AIR-ee-uh. Lily-of-the-Valley. Spring bloom. Sun or shade.

Description: *Convallaria majalis* (may-JAL-iss), lily-of-the-valley. Size: 6"–8" tall, leaves to 8" long. A dense, fast-growing groundcover with 2–3 broad leaves arising from each bud or "pip" along the tough slender rhizome. In spring, erect stems carry fragrant nodding ¼"–½" white bells followed by glossy red berries in summer. 'Fortin's Giant' is 12"–15" tall with large (¾") bells. 'Rosea' has dusty-pink flowers. Zones 2–8.

How to Grow: Lily-of-the-valley thrives in a wide range of soil and moisture conditions in sun or shade. In warm regions, plants need more moisture and shade. Divide in summer or fall.

Landscape Uses: Plant lily-of-the-valley for a fast-spreading groundcover under shrubs or trees. Divide frequently to keep it from taking over less-vigorous perennials. 🍁

Beloved by gardeners everywhere, lily-of-the-valley (*Convallaria majalis*) bears delightfully fragrant, bell-shaped flowers. Their lush foliage forms an attractive groundcover in partial to full shade.

Coreopsis Compositae, Daisy Family

core-ee-OP-sis. Coreopsis, Tickseed. Late-spring and summer bloom. Full sun.

Description: A large genus of mostly summer-blooming perennials with profuse, cheerful yellow daisylike flowers. Plants range in height from under a foot to 6′ giants. These dependable, easy-care plants have a place in almost any perennial garden.

Coreopsis auriculata (aw-rick-you-LAH-tuh), mouse-ear coreopsis. Size: 1′–2′ tall; leaves 2″–5″ long. A low, spreading groundcover with fuzzy triangular leaves and 2″ yellow-orange flowers held well above the foliage in spring. Creeping stems advance steadily outward but are seldom invasive. 'Nana' is a compact cultivar, with cheery yellow-orange blooms held on 6″–8″ stems. Zones 4–9.

C. grandiflora (gran-dih-FLOOR-uh), large-flowered tickseed. Size: 1′–2′ tall; leaves 3″–6″ long. A popular, old-fashioned perennial with clumps of lance-shaped, entire or 3–5-lobed leaves on leafy stems. The 2½″ deep-yellow flowers are excellent for cutting. 'Early Sunrise' is compact (to about 1½′), with 2″ double flowers. This handsome plant won the 1989 All-America Selections award. It is easy to start from seed. 'Goldfink' is more compact (9″) with 2″–3″ single flowers. This cultivar is often listed under the closely related *C. lanceolata*. Zones 3 or 4–9.

Choose threadleaf coreopsis (*Coreopsis verticillata*) for up to 3 months of summer bloom. Here, bright-yellow 'Golden Showers' grows happily with pale-yellow 'Moonbeam'.

C. lanceolata (lan-see-oh-LAH-tuh), lance-leaved coreopsis. Size: 1'–2' tall; leaves 2"–6" long. Similar to *C. grandiflora,* this species is as floriferous but perhaps longer-lived. Listed cultivars may belong here or may be of hybrid origin from these 2 species. 'Sunburst' has 2" semidouble flowers on 2' stems. 'Sunray' is a popular, long-flowering cultivar with 2" double flowers on 2' plants. Zones 3–8.

C. rosea (ROSE-ee-uh), pink tickseed. Size: 1'–2' tall; leaves to 1" long. A low, mounding plant with 3-lobed needle-like leaves and dozens of 1" pink flowers with bright-yellow centers. Pink tickseed can tolerate partial shade and more moisture than other species. Zones 4–8.

C. tripteris (TRIP-ter-is), tall tickseed. Size: 3'–9' tall, leaves to 4". A stately plant with stout stems clothed in 3-lobed, lance-shaped leaves and topped with wide clusters of starry 2" yellow flowers. Zones 3–8.

C. verticillata (ver-tih-sill-AH-tuh), thread-leaf coreopsis. Size: 1'–3' tall; leaves 1"–3" long. An airy, mounding plant with 3-lobed needle-like leaves and dozens of 1"–2" yellow flowers borne throughout the summer. 'Golden Showers' is a 2' selection with 2½" golden-yellow flowers. 'Moonbeam' is 1'–2' tall with 1" soft-yellow flowers from early summer through frost. 'Zagreb', only 8"–18" tall, is a compact version of 'Golden Showers'. Zones 3–9.

How to Grow: Coreopsis are tough, easy-care perennials. Plant in average to rich, moist soil in full sun. They are quite drought-tolerant once established and thrive even under stress. Overly rich soils promote flopping. To prolong flowering, remove spent flowers regularly, especially on *C. grandiflora* and *C. lanceolata* types. Mouse-ear coreopsis grows well in partial or open shade and retains its attractive foliage all season if the soil remains moist.

Divide overgrown or declining plants in

Pink tickseed (*Coreopsis rosea*) is covered with a cloudlike mass of delicate daisylike flowers for a month or more in midsummer. These plants require more moisture than other coreopsis species.

spring or fall. Plants often self-sow if not deadheaded. Sow ripe seeds indoors under warm (70°F), moist conditions. They germinate in 2–4 weeks. Take stem cuttings in early summer. They root quickly and can be planted out in the same season.

Landscape Uses: Coreopsis are excellent border plants. Combine the golden-yellow flowers with white, blue, red, and purple for lively viewing. The soft-yellow flowers of *C. verticillata* 'Moonbeam' are nice with more restful colors, such as pink and lavender. Asters, iris, blanket flower (*Gaillardia pulchella*), purple coneflowers (*Echinacea* spp.), and phlox are comfortable companions. Use *C. auriculata* along walks or in an informal setting with groundcovers and ferns. Plant *C. tripteris* at the back of the border or in meadow and prairie plantings with native grasses, purple coneflowers, asters, bonesets (*Eupatorium* spp.), gayfeathers (*Liatris* spp.), and other yellow daisies. ❦

Crocosmia Iridaceae, Iris Family

kro-koss-ME-uh. Montbretia, Crocosmia. Summer and fall bloom. Full sun.

Crocosmias (*Crocosmia masoniorum*) are striking plants that grow from corms similar to those of gladiolus. In cold zones, lift the corms in fall and store them over the winter in a cool, dry place.

Description: Montbretias are fiery-colored perennials with lush green swordlike foliage. Their 1½" funnel-shaped flowers are carried on arching, zigzag stems that are good for cutting. They grow from buttonlike corms that spread to form tight clumps.

Crocosmia × *crocosmiiflora* (kro-koss-me-ih-FLOOR-uh), crocosmia. Size: 2'–3' tall; leaves to 3' long. A hybrid species from various free-flowering cultivars. First bred by the French hybridizer Lemoine in 1880, most modern cultivars are of English origin. The flowers are slightly nodding. 'Citronella' has 1" orange-yellow flowers. 'Emily McKenzie' has

2½" deep-orange flowers, each with a crimson throat. 'Solfatare' has 1½" golden-yellow flowers. Zones 6–9.

C. masoniorum (may-son-ee-OR-um), crocosmia. Size: 2½'–3' tall; leaves to 3' long. A tall plant with upward-facing 1½"-long flowers of fiery-orange. 'Firebird' has red-orange flowers with a yellow throat. Zones 5–9.

Crocosmia hybrids. Many showy crocosmia cultivars have been created through crosses between related genera as well as among different species. These hybrids vary in hardiness but are generally suited for Zones 5–9. *C.* × 'Emberglow' has burnt-orange flowers on 2'–3' plants. 'Lucifer' has deep-scarlet flowers and is an extremely popular selection. 'Spitfire' has large orange-red flowers with a yellow throat.

How to Grow: Plant montbretias in the spring in moist, humus-rich soil in full sun. They spread to form tight clumps of beautiful foliage. In Zones 5 and colder, lift bulbs in the fall and store indoors in a cool, dry spot. In warmer areas, divide clumps in the fall. Thrips or spider mites may attack, causing white stippling on the leaves. Spray with insecticidal soap as necessary or with a botanical insecticide such as pyrethrins. Cut badly infested foliage to the ground and destroy or discard it.

Landscape Uses: The spectacular flowers of montbretias are showstoppers. Plant them with other hot colors and deep purples for contrast. Choose coreopsis (*Coreopsis* spp.), garden phlox (*Phlox paniculata*), lavenders, goldenrods (*Solidago* spp.), and sages for border companions. Massed plantings are effective in front of walls or fences or with flowering shrubs. 🍂

Crocus Iridaceae, Iris Family

CROW-kuss. Crocus. Winter, spring, or fall bloom. Full sun or partial shade.

Description: The colorful crocuses are among the best-loved spring bulbs. To many gardeners, their delightful flowers signal the end of winter and the start of a new gardening season. However, there are also many species that bloom in the fall, and winter bloom is common in milder climates. Crocuses grow from squat, buttonlike corms. The flowers emerge just ahead of or with the grasslike foliage. Each flower has 3 petals and 3 petal-like sepals ranging in color from white, cream, and yellow to lilac and purple. The outside of the flowers is often blushed or striped with a contrasting darker color. As summer approaches, the plants go dormant and disappear from above ground.

Crocus ancyrensis (an-see-REN-sis), golden bunch crocus. Size: 4"–6" tall, leaves to 6" long. An early crocus with 1" bright-yellow flowers borne with the leaves. 'Golden Bunch' is an especially floriferous cultivar. Zones 3–9.

C. biflorus (bye-FLOOR-us), Scotch crocus. Size: 4"–6" tall, leaves to 8" long. An early 1½" white, yellow-throated crocus striped with purple on the outside of the petals. 'Adamii' has lilac flowers striped outside with brown. The variety *alexandri* ('Alexandri') has white flowers blushed with purple on the outside. 'Fairy' ('Waldenii Fairy') is silvery white with a blue-gray outer blush. Zones 5–9.

C. chrysanthus (kris-AN-thus), golden crocus. Size: 4"–6" tall, leaves to 6" long. An early yellow crocus with 1½" honey-scented flowers. Many hybrids are available. 'Advance' is lemon-yellow with a blue-violet outer blush. 'Cream Beauty' is creamy yellow. 'E. A. Bowles' has butter-yellow flowers blushed with brown.

Dutch hybrid crocuses such as *Crocus* 'Striped Beauty' are perfect for naturalizing in lawns and among open groundcovers. Their early-spring blooms signal the end of winter.

'Lady Killer' is pale-purple, darker on the outside. 'Snowbunting' is pure-white. Zones 4–9.

C. goulimyi (goo-LIM-ee-eye), crocus. Size: 4"–6" tall, leaves to 5" long. A fall crocus with 1½" starry lavender flowers held above the foliage. Zones 7–9.

C. kotschyanus (cot-she-AH-nus), Kotschy's crocus. Size: 4"–6" tall, leaves to 6" long. A fall bloomer with 1½" lilac to rose-lilac flowers borne before leaves appear. Zones 5–9.

C. minimus (MIN-ih-muss). Size: 3"–4" tall, leaves to 4" long. An early crocus with 1" bowl-shaped lilac flowers. Zones 6–9.

C. pulchellus (pull-CHELL-us). Size: 4"–6" tall, leaves to 6" long. A fall crocus with 1½" lilac-blue flowers. 'Zephyr' is white with outer gray blush. Zones 5–9.

C. sativus (suh-TYE-vus), saffron crocus. Size: 4″–6″ tall, leaves to 6″ long. An autumn crocus with 1½″–2″ deep-lilac flowers veined in purple. The dried stigmas (female reproductive structures) are the source of the pungent spice saffron. Zones 5–9.

C. sieberi (SEE-ber-eye). Size: 4″–6″ tall, leaves to 6″ long. A late-winter crocus with 1½″ lilac-blue flowers with purple veins. 'Firefly' is lilac-pink. 'Hubert Edelsten' is white inside and violet outside. 'Violet Queen' is deep-violet. Zones 5–9.

C. speciosus (spee-see-OH-sus), showy crocus. Size: 4″–6″ tall, leaves to 6″ long. Early-fall crocus with 2″ lavender-blue flowers. The variety *albus* has white flowers. 'Artabir' has light-blue flowers with darker veins. 'Cassiope'

has violet-blue flowers. Zones 5–9.

C. tomasinianus (tom-uh-sin-ee-AH-nus), Tomasini's crocus. Size: 4″–6″ tall, leaves to 10″ long. A spring crocus with 1½″ lilac flowers, paler on the outside. 'Ruby Giant' has large red-violet flowers. 'Whitewell Purple' has violet flowers. Zones 5–9.

C. vernus (VER-nus), Dutch crocus. Size: 4″–6″ tall, leaves to 1′ long. A large-flowered spring crocus with 2″–3″ white to pale-violet flowers with purple streaks. This is a popular species, often in the parentage of the large-flowered Dutch hybrid crocuses. 'Violet Vanguard' has violet flowers. 'Haarlem Gem' has lilac flowers with gray outsides. Zones 3–9.

How to Grow: Plant fall-blooming species as soon as they are available in late summer. If you order by mail, specify an early shipping date (late July or early August), especially if you live in the North. Spring-blooming crocuses can be planted in September and October. Crocuses prefer well-drained soil in sun or part shade.

Once established, crocuses need little care, and the species often spread by self-sown seeds. The corms also multiply, forming great clumps. Divide when flowering begins to wane or when clumps appear too crowded. Rodents can be a problem: Use a repellent or plant the corms in wire boxes or baskets.

Landscape Uses: Few experiences are more memorable than finding the first crocus in bloom as the winter snow is receding. Plant crocuses anywhere you want a bit of early color. Use them in rock gardens, massed in borders, or naturalized in the lawn. Combine early spring species and hybrids with hellebores (*Helleborus* spp.), cushion spurge (*Euphorbia epithymoides*), bergenias (*Bergenia* spp.), wildflowers, and other bulbs. Plant fall-blooming species among foliage plants such as ferns for late color. 🌿

Late-winter snows often dust the early blooms of species crocuses like *Crocus chrysanthus* 'Gypsy Girl'. Fortunately, they're seldom damaged. The flowers close during inclement weather and reopen when warm sunshine returns.

Delphinium Ranunculaceae, Buttercup Family

dell-FIN-ee-um. Delphinium, Larkspur. Late-spring and summer bloom, fall rebloom. Full sun.

Description: Delphiniums have tall sturdy stalks that are clothed in deeply lobed or divided maplelike leaves. The showy flowers are densely packed on open-branching spikes. Each flower has 5 petal-like sepals in shades of blue or purple, the top one bearing a long, recurved spur. At the center of the flower are 2 or 4 fuzzy true petals that give the flower a beard, or "bee." Although some wild species are attractive garden plants, the majority of cultivated delphiniums are hybrids with *Delphinium elatum* as an important parent. Delphiniums grow from thick, fleshy roots.

D. × belladonna (bell-uh-DON-uh), belladonna delphinium. Size: 3'–4' tall, leaves to 6" long. A group of hybrids with 1" summer and fall flowers carried on branching stems above deeply lobed leaves. 'Bellamosum' has deep-blue flowers on 4' plants. 'Casa Blanca' is pure-white. 'Clivedon Beauty' has large sky-blue flowers on 3' plants. Zones 3–7.

D. elatum (ee-LAY-tum), candle larkspur, bee delphinium. Size: 4½'–6' tall, leaves to 8" long. A stately perennial with deeply cut leaves and 1" blue-violet flowers. Zones 4–7.

D. exaltatum (ex-all-TAY-tum), tall larkspur. Size: 2'–6' tall; leaves to 5" long. An erect, sparsely branching plant with deeply divided leaves and ¾" spurred blue flowers. Zones 5–7.

D. grandiflorum (gran-dih-FLOOR-um), Chinese delphinium. Size: 1'–2½' tall, leaves 2"–3" long. A floriferous compact species that produces deeply divided leaves with threadlike segments and 1"–1½" deep-blue flowers. 'Album' has white flowers. 'Blue Dwarf' ('Blue Elf') is only 1' tall. 'Blue Mirror' has blue flowers on 2' stems. Zones 4–8.

D. nudicaule (new-dih-KAW-lee), Canon delphinium. Size: 1½'–2' tall; leaves 1"–4" long. An orange-flowered delphinium with spurred, ½" flowers in open, spiky clusters. Plants go dormant after flowering. Zones 5–7.

The towering spikes of hybrid delphiniums (*Delphinium × elatum*) are quite top-heavy. Plant them where they are protected from strong winds and stake each stem separately to keep them erect.

D. semibarbatum (sem-eye-bar-BAY-tum). Size: 1'–2' tall; leaves to 4" long. An erect plant with deeply lobed leaves and funnelform, spurred, ½" yellow flowers. Plants go dormant after flowering. Zones 6–7.

Delphinium hybrids. Besides *D. × bella-donna,* several other hybrid delphiniums are wonderful for the perennial border. The *D. × elatum* hybrids have showy, dense spikes of 1½" flowers in white, pink, blue, and purple on 4'–6' stems that usually need staking against wind and rain. Blackmore and Langdon Hybrids are a seed-grown series of mixed colors with 1½"–2" flowers. Mid-Century Hybrids are tall (4'–5'), sturdy, and mildew-resistant.

'Ivory Towers' is white. 'Moody Blues' has light-blue flowers. 'Rose Future' has pink flowers. 'Ultra Violet' is dark-blue. The Pacific Hybrids have huge, single to semidouble, 1½"–2" flowers on 4'–5' stems. 'Astolat' has lavender flowers with a dark center. 'Black Knight' has dark-purple flowers. 'Galahad' is a late-summer bloomer with white flowers. 'Guinevere' is a blue bicolor, darkest on the outside. 'King Arthur' has dark-blue flowers on 5' stems. 'Summer Skies' is light-blue with a darker center. The Connecticut Yankee Series delphiniums are similar to *D. × belladonna* hybrids. 'Blue Fountains' has 1½" flowers in the medium- to pale-blue range on 2' stems. It performs well in the heat of Zone 8.

How to Grow: Delphiniums are lovely old-fashioned perennials that are popular but often disappointing garden plants. They are extremely cold-hardy but do not tolerate hot summer nights or extended warm growing seasons. Delphiniums are often short-lived and are treated by some gardeners as annuals, especially in hot climates. The species forms of delphiniums are often longer-lived than the hybrids.

For best growth, plant in deep, moist, humus-rich soil in full sun. The soil should be alkaline or only slightly acidic. Delphiniums are heavy feeders, so apply a balanced organic fertilizer regularly during the growing season, or top-dress annually with rich compost or composted manure.

Plant in spring or fall, taking care not to damage the brittle roots. As plants emerge in spring, thin stems to promote vigor and reduce the chance of disease; leave 3–5 stems per mature clump. The stems are often succulent and susceptible to wind damage; to avoid broken stems, stake all hybrids over 2' tall. To promote reblooming, cut plants back to a point above the foliage but below the flower spikes. Remove spent shoots after new basal shoots have developed. The new shoots will flower as cool weather returns.

Divide overgrown clumps in spring and replant into amended soil. Delphiniums are easy to propagate by fresh seed sown in summer or fall. Take stem cuttings in early spring from newly emerging shoots.

Slugs are the most insidious pest of delphiniums, damaging the stems and causing large holes in the leaves. Protect plants with a barrier strip of diatomaceous earth, or trap the pests in a shallow pan of beer. Powdery mildew, which causes a dusty white coating on leaves and stems, can be a problem, especially in warmer zones. Avoid this fungal disease by planting resistant cultivars and by providing good air circulation. Dust affected plants with sulfur to reduce the spread of the disease.

Landscape Uses: Place hybrid delphiniums at the rear of the border, where their towering spikes can show off against a wall or hedge. Combine them with lilies, peonies, irises, poppies, and roses to create a charming cottage-garden effect. Use them for vertical accent with summer perennials such as yarrows. Plant them in bold masses of mixed colors as an accent along a wall or fence. Choose the shorter species and hybrid delphiniums for the middle of the border. 🌿

Dianthus Caryophyllaceae, Pink Family

dye-AN-thus. Pinks, Carnation. Spring and summer bloom. Full sun to light shade.

Description: Pinks are beloved for their old-fashioned charm and delightful fragrance. They produce low carpets or bushy rosettes of foliage crowned with showy 5-petaled flowers borne singly or in loose clusters on wiry stems. The petals are often fringed or deeply cut, giving an attractive ragged look to the blooms.

Dianthus × allwoodii (all-WOOD-ee-eye), Allwood pinks. Size: 1'–1½' tall, leaves to 5" long. A tufted plant with blue-green lance-shaped leaves and fringed white, pink, or purple 2" flowers often borne in pairs. Plants bloom for up to 8 weeks. 'Alpinus' has single flowers in mixed colors. 'Aqua' has double white flowers on 1' stems. 'Doris' has fragrant salmon-pink flowers, each with a dark eye. 'Mars' has double pink flowers on 3"–6" stems. Zones 4–8.

D. alpinus (al-PIE-nus), alpine pinks. Size: 3"–6" tall, leaves to 1" long. A clump-forming plant with bright-green rounded narrow leaves

Plant drought-tolerant maiden pinks (*Dianthus deltoides*) in the sunny rock garden where their bright summer flowers and mat-forming foliage show off to best advantage.

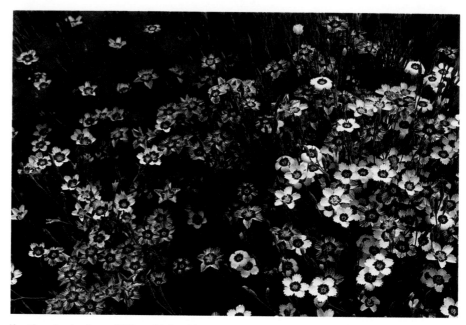

Use the mixed colors of 'Microchip' maiden pinks (*Dianthus deltoides* 'Microchip') to brighten up a container planting, a sunny rock garden, or the crevices of a rock wall. This cultivar can be grown from seed.

and 1½″ single pink flowers in spring. The variety *albus* has white flowers. Zones 3–7.

D. barbatus (bar-BAY-tus), sweet William. Size: 10″–18″ tall, leaves 2″–3″ long. A biennial or short-lived perennial with tufts of deep-green lance-shaped leaves and dense rounded heads of 1″–1½″ bicolored or "eyed" flowers. 'Indian Carpet' is a seed strain in various colors on 10″ stems. 'Newport Pink' has deep-pink flowers and is 10″–12″ tall. 'Pink Beauty' has salmon-pink flowers on 15″ stems. 'Scarlet Beauty' is deep-scarlet. Zones 3–9.

D. deltoides (dell-TOY-deez), maiden pinks. Size: 6″–12″ tall, leaves 3″–6″ long. Mat-forming plant with a profusion of single ¾″ pink or rose-colored flowers borne 1 to a stem. 'Albus' has white flowers. 'Brilliant' has scarlet-red flowers. 'Flashing Light' has ruby-red flowers. 'Zing Rose' has deep-red flowers. Zones 3–9.

D. gratianopolitanus (grah-tee-ah-nuh-poe-lih-TAH-nus), cheddar pinks. Size: 9″–12″ tall, leaves to 5″ long. A spring bloomer with 1″ fragrant rose-pink flowers carried singly or in pairs. The variety *grandiflorus* has 1½″ rose-pink flowers. 'Petite' is a true dwarf with 4″ cushions of foliage and small pink flowers. 'Splendens' has deep-red flowers. Zones 3–9.

D. plumarius (ploo-MAH-ree-us), cottage pinks. Size: 1½′–2′ tall, leaves to 3″ long. A cushion-forming plant with grasslike leaves and 1″ fragrant white or pink flowers borne 2–5 per stem. Cultivars sold under *D. plumarius* are often hybrids with *D. gratianopolitanus*. 'Mrs. Sinkins' has fragrant double white flowers. 'Spring Beauty' is a seed-grown strain of clove-scented semidouble to double flowers in white, pink, rose, and red. Zones 3–9.

D. superbus (soo-PER-bus), lilac pinks. Size: 1′–2′ tall, leaves to 4″ long. Open mounds of grasslike leaves and 1″ fragrant, deeply cut, ragged flowers in lilac, pink, or white. Zones 4–8.

How to Grow: Give pinks a sunny position with moist to dry, well-drained alkaline to slightly acid soil. They spread quickly and are often short-lived, so divide the clumps every 2–3 years to keep them vigorous. Removing spent flowers regularly will keep most species and cultivars in bloom for 6 weeks or more.

Propagate pinks from stem cuttings in summer. Take a 2″–3″ portion of the stem with a whorl of foliage and strip the leaves from the lower ⅓. Cuttings from the dwarf pinks may be 1″ long or less. Place the cuttings in a humid environment in a medium with excellent drainage. Roots will appear in 2–3 weeks. Sow seeds outdoors in spring or indoors in winter. Germination takes 15–20 days. Self-sown seedlings often appear around the garden.

The most serious pest is rust, a fungus that forms yellow-green spots on the upper leaf surface and orange spots below. If your plants have had rust in previous years, dust them in spring with sulfur to prevent damage in the current season. Good air circulation and drainage are the best precautions against problems.

Landscape Uses: Plant low-growing pinks at the front of beds and borders, where their mat-forming foliage makes an attractive groundcover. Combine them with lamb's-ears (*Stachys byzantina*), threadleaf coreopsis (*Coreopsis verticillata*), artemisias, and columbines (*Aquilegia* spp.). Use dwarf and cushion-forming species such as *D. alpinus* and *D. deltoides* in rock gardens or stone walls with bellflowers (*Campanula* spp.), thymes (*Thymus* spp.), sedums, and dwarf yarrows. Combine the larger species and hybrids of pinks with creeping baby's-breath (*Gypsophila repens*), cinquefoils (*Potentilla* spp.), creeping phlox (*Phlox bifida* and *P. subulata*), and low ornamental grasses such as fescues (*Festuca* spp.).

Allwood pinks (*Dianthus × allwoodii*) form dense mats of spiky gray foliage perfect for edging walks or at the front of beds. These hybrids come in a range of sizes and colors; some are fragrant.

Dicentra Fumariaceae, Fumitory Family

dye-SEN-truh. Bleeding Heart. Spring and summer bloom. Sun or shade.

Description: *Dicentra* is a genus of mostly woodland plants, many of which have been popular in gardens for centuries. The apt name of bleeding hearts describes the unique flowers, which resemble pink hearts with drops of blood dangling from their tips. The flowers have paired, inflated lobes that may be rounded (as in bleeding hearts) or extended into a pointed hollow tube (as in Dutchman's breeches). The compound foliage is deeply divided and often fernlike. *Dicentra* species grow from thick, brittle roots or tuberous rhizomes.

D. canadensis (can-uh-DEN-sis), squirrel corn. Size: 8"–12" tall, leaves to 10" long. A delicate woodland plant with hyacinth-scented, ½" white hearts crowded at the end of a weak stalk. The ferny foliage disappears as soon as the seeds ripen in early summer. Zones 4–7.

D. cucullaria (cue-cue-LAHR-ee-uh), Dutchman's breeches. Size: 10"–12" tall, leaves to 10" long. A dainty woodland plant with ferny leaves and ½" flowers resembling strings of inverted pantaloons hung out to dry in the spring breeze. The plant disappears soon after flowering. Zones 3–8.

D. eximia (ex-EE-me-uh), fringed bleeding heart, wild bleeding heart. Size: 10"–18" tall, leaves to 1' long. A bushy floriferous plant with mounds of clustered ¾" pink hearts

'Luxuriant' bleeding heart (*Dicentra* 'Luxuriant') earns high marks for both its ferny blue-green foliage and its red flowers. Give plants rich, moist soil and some sun and they will bloom continuously from spring until frost.

borne throughout spring and summer over the ferny blue-green foliage. 'Alba' has greenish white flowers. 'Boothman's Variety' has soft-pink flowers and blue-gray foliage. 'Snowdrift' has pure-white flowers. Zones 3–9.

D. formosa (for-MOW-suh), western bleeding heart, Pacific bleeding heart. Size: 8″–18″ tall, leaves to 1′ long. Similar to *D. eximia,* but the ½″ cherry-red flowers are more square and the foliage more blue-gray. The plants spread by creeping rhizomes. 'Adrian Bloom' has ruby-red flowers. 'Bountiful' has rose-pink flowers. 'Zestful' has large rose-red flowers. 'Luxuriant', a floriferous selection with cherry-red flowers, is thought to be a hybrid with *D. eximia.* Zones 3–9.

D. spectabilis (speck-TAH-bih-lis), common bleeding heart, old-fashioned bleeding heart. Size: 1′–2½′ tall, leaves to 1½′ long. A beloved spring perennial with strings of 1″ bright-pink hearts on tall arching stems. The leaves have wider leaflets than other species and persist through the cooler summers of more northern zones. 'Alba' has pure-white flowers. 'Pantaloons' is a more robust white selection. Zones 2–9.

How to Grow: Plant in evenly moist, humus-rich soil in light to full shade. In cooler climates, bleeding hearts can grow in full sun as long as the soil is consistently moist. Plant *D. canadensis* and *D. cucullaria* in the shade of deciduous trees. They need the spring sun and moist soil to bloom well, but once dormant, they can tolerate shade and dry soil. To keep *D. eximia* and *D. formosa* in continuous bloom, give them moisture and at least half a day of sun. In warmer zones, shade plants from hot afternoon sun. *D. spectabilis* will bloom for 4–6 weeks if temperatures are moderate and the soil is constantly moist. The foliage often remains attractive through most of the season. In warm climates or in dry soil, they go dormant by midsummer.

Divide overgrown clumps in fall or as they go dormant. Take care not to damage the brittle roots or rhizomes. Take root cuttings in fall, or propagate by sowing fresh seed outdoors in summer.

Landscape Uses: Combine *D. eximia* and *D. spectabilis* with daffodils, ferns, and hostas in the light shade of a woodland garden. The foliage and flowers of the 2 species, when grown together, create a wonderful contrast of size and shape. In a semishaded or sunny border, plant *D. spectabilis* with daffodils, tulips, peonies, irises, primroses, early phlox such as *Phlox divaricata,* columbines (*Aquilegia* spp.), and cranesbills (*Geranium* spp.). Use *D. eximia* in formal and informal plantings with garden perennials, ferns, wildflowers, and hostas. Plant *D. canadensis* and *D. cucullaria* with plants that expand to fill the blank spots left when they go dormant; lungworts (*Pulmonaria* spp.), Siberian bugloss (*Brunnera macrophylla*), wildflowers, and ferns are good companions. 🌿

Common bleeding heart (*Dicentra spectabilis*) blooms with lilacs and late tulips. After flowering, the plants go dormant. In the North, the foliage may remain attractive through midsummer.

Dictamnus Rutaceae, Rue Family

dik-TAM-nus. Gas Plant, Dittany. Late-spring and early-summer bloom. Full sun to light shade.

Description: *Dictamnus albus* (AL-bus), gas plant. Size: 1'–4' tall, leaves to 1' long. A stout, long-lived perennial growing from thick, almost woody roots. The erect stems are clothed in pinnately compound leaves with bright-green rounded leaflets. The 1" white flowers, borne in spiky terminal clusters, have 5 showy petals and 10 long, curled stamens (male reproductive structures) that give the flowers a frivolous look. The plant is so named because the flowers emit a flammable oil. All parts of the plant are strongly lemon-scented when bruised. 'Purpureus' has violet-purple flowers with dark veins. 'Ruber' has pale red-violet flowers with darker veins. Zones 3–8.

How to Grow: Plant gas plants on a well-drained site with average to rich soil in full sun or light shade. Established plants are difficult to transplant successfully, so site them carefully. Take care not to disturb the roots when planting container-grown stock in spring. Once established, they bloom tirelessly for many years with little care.

Gas plant is difficult to re-establish successfully after division, so the best way to propagate it is by seed. Sow fresh seed outdoors in late summer. Seedlings will appear the following spring but will take 3–4 years to bloom. Move seedlings to their permanent position the third spring after germination.

Root rot may be a problem in soggy soil and hot weather. Good drainage is the best preventative. Longer, deep-penetrating waterings are preferable to frequent, light waterings.

Landscape Uses: Combine gas plant with other perennials that demand good drainage. Oriental poppy (*Papaver orientale*), yarrows, sages, and asters are excellent companions. The flowers of gas plants are short-lived, but the foliage and starry seed capsules remain attractive all season. The purple- and reddish-flowered cultivars look lovely with a basal planting of color-coordinated cranesbills (*Geranium* spp.) spread about their feet. Small or fine-textured flowers such as baby's-breath also make good companions. ❧

Gas plants, including *Dictamnus albus* 'Purpureus' shown here, are hardy, long-lived perennials. Established plants reach shrublike proportions and bloom profusely in early summer.

Digitalis Scrophulariaceae, Figwort Family

dij-uh-TAL-lis. Foxglove. Summer bloom. Sun to partial shade.

Description: Foxgloves are erect, stout perennials with leafy stems and tall spikes of funnelform flowers in pink, rose, white, yellow, or brown. The insides of the flowers are often spotted. Plants form dense rosettes of broadly lance-shaped leaves. Many are biennial or short-lived perennials.

Digitalis ferruginea (fair-roo-JIN-ee-uh), rusty foxglove. Size: 4'–5' tall, leaves to 1' long. A stately plant with rusty brown 1½" flowers spotted in dark-red. Zones 4–7.

D. grandiflora (gran-dih-FLOOR-uh), yellow foxglove (also listed as *D. ambigua*). Size: 2'–3' tall, leaves to 10" long. A long-lived foxglove with graceful spikes of 2" soft-yellow flowers and rich, green foliage. Zones 3–8.

D. × mertonensis (mer-toe-NEN-sis), strawberry foxglove. Size: 3'–4' tall, leaves to 8" long. This hybrid foxglove bears 2½" spotted flowers in shades of rose, pink, and white. Zones 3–8.

D. purpurea (purr-PURR-ee-uh), common foxglove. Size: 2'–5' tall, leaves 8"–10" long. This foxglove commonly acts as a biennial or short-lived perennial. It bears long spikes of 2"–3" tubular flowers that are often spotted inside. 'Alba' has white flowers. 'Excelsior' bears dense flower spikes in a range of colors. 'Foxy' grows to only 2½' and can bloom the first year from seed sown indoors in winter. Zones 4–8.

How to Grow: Plant foxgloves in moist, humus-rich soil in full sun or partial shade. The perennial types need little attention. To keep the biennial and hybrid types vigorous, lift the plants after flowering and remove and replant the new rosettes. If this is not practical, cut the flower stalks back to the ground as the last blooms fade. Leave at least 1 stalk if you

Common foxglove (*Digitalis purpurea*) is short-lived but easy to grow. Lift the clumps after flowering and remove the spent bloom stalks. Replant the new rosettes for next year's bloom.

want self-sown seedlings. Sow seeds indoors in late winter or outdoors in late summer. Plants usually bloom the second year.

Landscape Uses: Combine the yellow species with clustered bellflower (*Campanula glomerata*), bleeding hearts (*Dicentra* spp.), hostas, and ferns. Plant the taller species with goat's beard (*Aruncus dioicus*), bugbanes (*Cimicifuga* spp.), yuccas, and snowdrop anemone (*Anemone sylvestris*). 🍁

Disporum Liliaceae, Lily Family

die-SPORE-um. Fairy-Bells, Mandarin. Spring bloom. Partial to full shade.

Yellow fairy-bells (*Disporum flavum*), like its white-flowered relative Japanese fairy-bells (*Disporum sessile*), is ideal for moist, shaded spots in woodland gardens.

Description: *Disporum sessile* (SES-ill-ee), Japanese fairy-bells, nodding mandarin. Size: 1′–2′ tall, leaves to 4″ long. A rhizomatous perennial forming open clumps of leafy stems with nodding 1″ white flowers paired at the tips of the stems. The broad, oval, pleated leaves alternate up the stems. 'Variegatum' is commonly grown for its white-variegated leaves; the species is seldom available. Zones 4–8.

How to Grow: Plant fairy-bells in moist, humus-rich soil in partial to full shade. The foliage remains neat throughout the season. Divide clumps if they spread or become crowded. Sow fresh seed outdoors in summer. Germination may take 1–2 years. Plants develop slowly.

Landscape Uses: Use the graceful fairy-bells in a woodland garden with hostas, astilbes, ferns, and wildflowers such as wild blue phlox (*Phlox divaricata*), creeping Jacob's ladder (*Polemonium reptans*), and Allegheny foamflower (*Tiarella cordifolia*). ❧

Dodecatheon Primulaceae, Primrose Family

doe-deh-KATH-ee-on. Shooting-Star. Spring bloom. Sun or shade.

Description: Shooting-stars produce basal rosettes of broadly lance-shaped foliage that usually disappear after flowering. The naked flower spikes are crowned with circles of gracefully arching white, pink, rose, or violet flowers with reflexed petals and dartlike points that protrude forward.

Dodecatheon clevelandii (kleev-LAND-ee-eye), Padres shooting-star. Size: 8″–16″ tall, leaves to 5″ long. Slender plant with spatulate leaves and tightly packed clusters of magenta to white 1″ flowers. Zones 6–7.

D. meadia (ME-dee-uh), shooting-star. Size: 1′–2′ tall, leaves to 1′ long. A stout woodland and prairie perennial with white or pale-pink 1″ flowers. Zones 4–8.

D. pulchellum (pul-CHELL-um), shooting-star. Size: 3″–20″ tall, leaves to 10″ long. Adapted to rock cliffs and banks, this species bears rose or magenta ¾″ flowers. Zones 4–7.

How to Grow: Plant shooting-stars in moist, humus-rich soil in sun or shade. Once plants are dormant, they tolerate dry soil and deep shade. Most species prefer a neutral or slightly acidic soil. Divide clumps in summer or fall. Take root cuttings in summer or fall. Sow fresh seed outdoors in summer. Plants develop slowly and take several years to bloom.

Landscape Uses: Interplant shooting-stars among leafy plants that will hide the spaces left during dormancy. In the shade garden, combine them with creeping Jacob's ladder (*Polemonium reptans*), wild ginger (*Asarum* spp.), and ferns. In a rock garden, plant them with primroses (*Primula* spp.), columbines (*Aquilegia* spp.), epimediums (*Epimedium* spp.), and mounding plants. ✿

Shooting-star (*Dodecatheon meadia*) quickly disappears after flowering in spring, leaving a cluster of seed heads.

Doronicum Compositae, Daisy Family

dur-ON-ih-kum. Leopard's Bane. Spring and early-summer bloom. Full sun or partial shade.

Description: *Doronicum orientale* (or-ee-en-TAL-ee), leopard's bane (also listed as *D. caucasicum* or erroneously as *D. cordatum*). Size: 1'–2' tall, leaves to 2″ long. Leopard's banes bear a profusion of yellow 1″–2″ daisy flowers over bright-green, triangular or heart-shaped leaves. Plants go dormant by mid-summer. 'Magnificum' has 2″ flowers. *D.* × 'Miss Mason' is a hybrid with persistent foliage. Zones 3–8.

How to Grow: Plant in consistently moist, humus-rich soil in sun or shade. Even soil moisture is important even when the plants are dormant, especially in warmer zones. Mulch the soil to keep the roots cool during the growing season. Divide plants every 2–3 years to keep them vigorous. Sow seeds indoors in late winter. ✿

For a bright splash of color in a moist spot, plant leopard's bane (*Doronicum orientale*). The yellow blooms appear in spring.

Echinacea Compositae, Daisy Family

eck-in-AY-see-uh. Purple Coneflower. Summer bloom. Full sun.

Description: Purple coneflowers are erect perennials with coarse lance-shaped to oval leaves and large daisylike flowers with mounded heads and showy rose or pink petal-like rays. The flower heads are usually borne singly on stout stems, well above the foliage. They bloom throughout the summer, and the seed heads are attractive throughout the fall and winter. Plants grow from thick fibrous taproots that are quite deep on mature plants.

Echinacea angustifolia (an-gus-tih-FOE-lee-uh), narrow-leaved coneflower. Size: 1'–2' tall, leaves to 8" long. A compact coneflower with spare, lance-shaped basal leaves with stiff hairs and mostly leafless stems topped by 2" flower heads with short (1"), drooping rose-pink rays. Zones 3 (possibly 2) –8.

E. pallida (PAL-ih-duh), pale coneflower, pale purple coneflower. Size: 3'–4' tall, leaves to 5" long. A sparsely branching plant with stout, nearly leafless stems topped with large flower heads of drooping, pale-rose, 1½"–3" rays. The basal leaves are lance-shaped and clothed in stiff hairs. Zones 4–8.

E. purpurea (purr-PURR-ee-uh), purple coneflower. Size: 2'–4' tall, rarely to 6', leaves to 1' long. A shrubby, well-branched plant with leafy stems and dozens of flowers with flat or drooping rose-pink to red-violet 1½"–2½" rays. 'Alba' has creamy-white flowers. 'Bright Star' is rose-pink with mostly flat flower heads. 'Magnus' has huge, flat flower heads. 'White Lustre' has larger, brighter white flowers than 'Alba'. Zones 3–8.

How to Grow: Purple coneflowers are plants of prairies and open woods. Give them average, loamy soil in full sun. Plants grow best with adequate moisture but are quite tolerant of extended drought. These tough plants have deep taproots that enable them to store some water for lean times.

Individual plants increase to form broad

clumps. Division is seldom necessary and not recommended. Once divided, plants tend to become bushy and produce fewer flowers. If you leave the seed heads for winter interest, plants may self-sow. Propagate by root cuttings in fall. Sow seed outdoors in fall or indoors in winter. If sowing indoors, you can encourage uniform germination by placing the sown pots or flats in a refrigerator for 4–6 weeks before moving them to a warm, bright place.

Landscape Uses: Purple coneflowers are effective additions to formal and informal landscapes alike. Plant them in borders with garden phlox (*Phlox paniculata*), gayfeathers (*Liatris* spp.), yarrows, and Shasta daisy (*Chrysanthemum × superbum*). Create a pastel combination with lamb's-ears (*Stachys byzantina*), verbenas (*Verbena* spp.), pink bee balms (*Monarda* spp.), and cranesbills (*Geranium* spp.) backed with ornamental grasses. In meadow and prairie gardens, plant purple coneflowers with native grasses, goldenrods (*Solidago* spp.), butterfly weed (*Asclepias tuberosa*), and coneflowers (*Rudbeckia* spp.). You can also grow purple coneflowers in deep containers. 🍂

Showy purple coneflower (*Echinacea purpurea*) is extremely heat- and drought-tolerant because of its thick, deep taproots, which store moisture for lean times. The large rose-pink flowers are an impressive addition to the summer garden.

Echinops   Compositae, Daisy Family

ECK-in-ops. Globe Thistle. Summer bloom. Full sun.

Description: *Echinops ritro* (RIH-troh), globe thistle. Size: 2'–4' tall, leaves to 8" long. Globe thistle is a coarse, erect perennial with lobed spiny leaves and spherical 1"–2" heads of tightly packed steel-blue flowers. These stately, long-lived plants produce several stout stems from a thick, branching taproot. 'Taplow Blue' has 2", medium-blue heads. 'Veitch's Blue' has darker blue heads on sturdier plants. Zones 3–8.

How to Grow: Plant globe thistles in average to rich, sandy or loamy soil in full sun. Once established, plants are quite drought-tolerant. Good drainage is essential for these tough plants, especially in winter. Globe thistles seldom need to be divided. For propagation, remove an auxiliary rosette from the plant without disturbing the entire clump. Or take root cuttings in spring or fall or sow seeds indoors in late winter. Globe thistles are seldom bothered by pests or diseases.

Landscape Uses: Plant globe thistles with other drought-tolerant perennials such as yarrows, oriental poppy (*Papaver orientale*), and ornamental grasses. Position them near the middle or back of the border with fine-textured plants that can act as a foil to their bold thistle-like foliage. Baby's-breaths, garden phlox (*Phlox paniculata*), 'Autumn Joy' sedum (*Sedum* × 'Autumn Joy'), and Russian sage (*Perovskia atriplicifolia*) are good companions. Globe thistles are also excellent in arrangements as cut or dried flowers. 🍂

Globe thistles, including *Echinops ritro* 'Veitch's Blue', thrive on benign neglect. Plant them in average, well-drained soil, and they'll reward you with spiky blue flowers in summer. The blooms are long-lasting as cut or dried flowers.

Epimedium   Berberidaceae, Barberry Family

ep-ih-MEE-dee-um. Epimedium, Barrenwort. Foliage plant with spring bloom. Partial to full shade.

Description: Epimediums are ground-covers that spread to form dense mats of evergreen or semi-evergreen foliage from wiry roots. The leaves are divided into small, glossy heart-shaped or triangular leaflets. The unusual flowers are carried in open clusters in early spring before the new leaves emerge. Each flower has 8 petal-like sepals and 4 often spurlike petals. Flower color ranges from white to yellow, bronze, red, and pink.

Epimedium alpinum (al-PIE-num), alpine epimedium. Size: 6"–9" tall, leaves to 8" long. A compact plant with triangular, pointed leaves and ½" crimson-red flowers. The foliage dies back in the fall. 'Rubrum' has red-and-yellow flowers. Zones 3–8.

E. grandiflorum (gran-dih-FLOOR-um),

long-spurred epimedium. Size: 8"–15" tall, leaves to 1' long. A large plant with rounded leaflets and showy, long-spurred 1"–1½" flowers. 'Rose Queen' has rose-pink flowers with white-tipped spurs. 'White Queen' has bright-white flowers. Zones 4–8.

E. perralderianum (per-all-der-ee-AH-num), epimedium. Size: 10"–12" tall, leaves to 1' long. Spikes of bright-yellow ¾" flowers are carried above the dense mounds of heart-shaped foliage. 'Frohnleiten' is a vigorous grower with showy yellow flowers and large dark-green leaflets. Zones 4 (with protection) or 5–8.

E. pinnatum (pih-NAY-tum), epimedium. Size: 8"–12" tall, leaves to 10" long. A leafy plant with bright-yellow ¾" flowers. Zones 4–8.

E. × *rubrum* (ROO-brum), red epimedium. Size: 8″–12″ tall, leaves to 10″ long. Similar to *E. alpinum* but more compact with ¾″–1″ bright-red flowers. Zones 4–8.

E. × *versicolor* (VER-suh-kuh-ler), Persian epimedium, bicolor barrenwort. Size: 10″–12″ tall, leaves to 1′ long. A popular plant with red-and-yellow 1″ flowers held above the foliage. 'Sulphureum' has yellow flowers. Zones 4–8.

E. × *warleyense* (war-lay-EN-see), Warley epimedium. Size: 8″–12″ tall, leaves to 10″ long. A deciduous species with brick-red to apricot ¾″ flowers borne in spring before the new leaves emerge. Zones 4–8.

E. × *youngianum* (yung-ee-AY-num), Young's barrenwort. Size: 6″–8″ tall, leaves to 8″ long. A compact, small-leaved plant with ¾″ flowers held above the foliage. 'Niveum' has snow-white flowers. 'Roseum' has rose to lilac flowers. Zones 4–8.

How to Grow: Plant epimediums in moist, average to humus-rich soil in partial to full shade and they will thrive. Once established, not even dry shade can discourage these versatile plants. They perform admirably under mature trees where little else will grow. Avoid waterlogged soil, and mulch the plants at the northern edge of their hardiness zones. In spring, cut the old foliage to the ground unless it has survived the winter undamaged. New leaves will emerge with or just after the flowers. Divide plants as necessary to control their spread or for propagation. Late summer is the best time to divide or move plants, but they can tolerate disturbance at any time.

Landscape Uses: Plant the adaptable epimediums in the shade garden with astilbes (*Astilbe* spp.), hostas, primroses, wildflowers, bulbs, and ferns. 🌿

Like all epimediums, red epimedium (*Epimedium* × *rubrum*) can tolerate even the most difficult of garden spots: dry shade. Although they bloom in spring, epimediums are primarily grown for their foliage, which is attractive all summer and turns bronze in winter.

Eremurus Liliaceae, Lily Family

air-ee-MURE-us. Foxtail Lily, Desert-Candle. Spring and summer bloom. Full sun to light shade.

Stately foxtail lilies, such as this *Eremurus* hybrid, are tough, drought-tolerant perennials for sunny, well-drained sites. Their spiky flower clusters combine well with airy plants such as sea lavender (*Limonium latifolium*).

Description: *Eremurus stenophyllus* (sten-oh-FILL-us), foxtail lily. Size: 2′–3′ tall, leaves to 1′ long. This breathtaking perennial bears stout wands of 1″ yellow, pink, or white flowers above clumps of pointed straplike leaves. The plants grow from a hard crown with brittle, spreading roots. 'Shelford Hybrids' are a hybrid group with white, yellow, or pink flowers. Zones 5–9.

How to Grow: Plant in summer or fall in moist but well-drained, humus-rich soil in full sun or light shade. Wet soil, especially in winter, promotes fatal root rot. Take care not to bury them more than 4″–6″ deep. Divide crowded clumps in fall. Sow fresh seed indoors or outdoors in fall. Germination may take 6 months. Seedlings develop slowly.

Landscape Uses: Combine stately foxtail lilies with small-flowered plants such as baby's-breath or with bold flowers such as peonies and oriental poppy (*Papaver orientale*). Use them as specimens in front of walls or in the company of flowering shrubs. 🌿

Erigeron Compositae, Daisy Family

ee-RIJ-er-on. Fleabane. Summer bloom. Full sun.

Description: A diverse group of floriferous summer-blooming asterlike plants. The clusters of white, orange, pink, rose, or purple flowers are held on leafy stems above basal rosettes of fuzzy lance-shaped or oval leaves.

Erigeron pulchellus (pull-CHELL-us), poor Robin's plantain. Size: 10″–18″ tall, leaves to 6″ long. A creeping groundcover plant with 1″ lilac to blue flowers held singly above the matlike foliage. Zones 4–8.

E. speciosus (spee-see-OH-sus), daisy fleabane. Size: 1½′–2½′ tall, leaves to 6″ long. A showy, floriferous species blooming throughout the summer. The leafy stems bear a profusion of 1½″ flowers for 4–6 weeks. Many hybrids of this species are available. 'Darkest of

All' has violet-blue flowers. 'Foerster's Darling' has pink double flowers. 'Pink Jewel' is a popular pink selection. 'Prosperity' is an older cultivar with lavender-blue flowers. 'Sincerity' has pink flowers. Zones 2–9.

How to Grow: Plant in moist but well-drained, rich soil in full sun or light shade. *E. pulchellus* also tolerates infertile soil. Flea-banes are long-lived but benefit from fall division every 2–3 years. Take tip cuttings in early summer, or propagate from seed sown outdoors in fall or indoors in winter. Outdoors, seedlings appear the spring after sowing; indoors, seedlings will germinate within 2 weeks of sowing.

Landscape Uses: Plant fleabanes in borders and beds with daisies, coneflowers (*Rudbeckia* spp.), phlox, evening primroses (*Oenothera* spp.), and ornamental grasses. 🍂

Try poor Robin's plantain (*Erigeron pulchellus*) on a dry, sunny or lightly shaded bank. The foliage rosettes form an attractive groundcover.

Eryngium Umbelliferae, Parsley Family

er-IN-gee-um. Sea Holly, Eryngo. Summer and fall bloom. Full sun.

Description: These taprooted biennial and perennial species produce globose heads of small, tightly packed flowers often sur-rounded by showy stiff bracts (modified leaves). It is these bracts that command attention in most species. They are silvery gray, blue, or purple and are often elaborately incised or lobed. The glossy heart-shaped or pinnately divided leaves form tufted rosettes at the base of the stiff flowerstalks.

Eryngium alpinum (al-PIE-num), alpine sea holly. Size: 1'–2' tall, leaves to 6" long. The 1¼"-long steel-blue flower heads are surrounded by leafy rings of upturned purple-blue bracts. The basal leaves are heart-shaped; the stem leaves are lobed and often tinged with blue.

'Amethyst' grows to 3' tall. 'Opal' is similar but only 2' tall. 'Superbum' has large deep-blue flowers. Zones 3–8.

E. amethystinum (am-uh-this-TIE-num), amethyst sea holly. Size: 1'–1½' tall, leaves to 10" long. A floriferous species with small ½"-long steel-blue heads surrounded by sparse, narrow blue bracts. The stems are also blue. The basal leaves are pinnately divided. Zones 2–8.

E. bourgatii (bour-GAT-ee-eye), Mediter-ranean sea holly. Size: 1'–2' tall, leaves to 6" long. A compact plant with pinnately divided leaves with prominent white veins. The silvery blue ¾" flowers are surrounded by long spiny bracts. Zones 5–8.

E. giganteum (jeye-GAN-tee-um), giant

The spiny leaflike bracts that surround the flower heads of Mediterranean sea holly (*Eryngium bourgatii*) retain their gray-blue color when dried. This species is also quite attractive in the garden, with white-veined leaves and silvery blue flowers.

sea holly. Size: 4'–6' tall, leaves to 1' long. A coarse plant with green 3"–4"-long flower heads and broad, spiny, gray-blue bracts. The basal leaves are heart-shaped. This species is a biennial or short-lived perennial. Zones 4–8.

E. planum (PLAN-um), flat sea holly. Size: 2'–3' tall, leaves to 8" long. This species is similar to *E. alpinum* and, although not as showy, is better for hot regions. The bracts are fewer and form a flattened ring around the mostly green ½"-long flower head. Zones 3–9.

E. yuccifolium (yuck-ih-FOE-lee-um), rattlesnake master. Size: 2'–3' tall, leaves to 14" long. A unique species with rosettes of lance-shaped gray-green leaves and tall stout stalks crowned by open clusters of pale-green 1"-long flower heads with inconspicuous bracts. Zones 4–9.

E. × zabelii (zuh-BEL-ee-eye), Zabel eryngo. Size: 1'–1½' tall, leaves to 8" long. A showy plant with bright-blue 1" flower heads and bracts carried in a mound atop branching stems. Zones 4–8.

How to Grow: Plant sea hollies in average, well-drained soil in full sun. They tolerate all manner of adversity, thriving in gravel and sand in the full summer sun. Plants seldom need division. Sow fresh seed outdoors in fall, or sow indoors in winter and place the pots or flats in a refrigerator for 4–6 weeks before moving them to a warm, bright place. Plants often self-sow. Move volunteers to their desired position while they are young; older plants may be difficult to reestablish after transplanting.

Landscape Uses: Sea hollies are bold architectural gems that command attention and add interest to the garden. Plant them in the company of floriferous perennials such as goldenrods (*Solidago* spp.). 🍂

Erythronium   Liliaceae, Lily Family

air-ih-THROW-nee-um. Trout Lily, Avalanche Lily, Adder's Tongue. Spring bloom. Sun or shade.

Description: Trout lilies are delicate spring flowers with paired, green or mottled leaves and single to triple nodding flowers with colorful reflexed petals and sepals and protruding stamens (male reproductive structures). The woodland wildflowers with mottled leaves are called trout lilies because their leaves resemble spotted trout. They spread by slender stolons that form bulbs at their ends. The plants go dormant immediately after flowering.

Erythronium albidum (AL-bih-dum), white trout lily. Size: 4"–8" tall, leaves to 6" long. This species has mottled leaves and 1"–2" white flowers with a purple or blue blush on the outside of the sepals. Zones 4–8.

E. americanum (uh-mare-ih-KAH-num), yellow trout lily. Size: 6"–10" tall, leaves to 8" long. A species with 1"–2" yellow flowers and mottled foliage. Zones 3–8.

E. dens-canis (denz-KAH-nis), dogtooth violet. Size: 4"–6" tall, leaves to 6" long. A short, floriferous plant with 1" rose-pink to deep-lilac flowers and mottled leaves. Zones 2–7.

E. grandiflorum (gran-dih-FLOOR-um), avalanche lily. Size: 6"–18" tall, leaves to 8" long. The tall flowering stems bear 1–3 bright-yellow 2" flowers above green leaves. Zones 3–7.

E. revolutum (rev-oh-LOO-tum), coast fawn lily. Size: 4"–12" tall; leaves to 8" long. A showy species with 1½" pink flowers and mottled leaves. 'Pagoda', of hybrid origin, has 1–3 clear-yellow flowers and mottled leaves. 'Pink Beauty' has pink flowers. 'White Beauty' has creamy-white flowers. Zones 5–8.

How to Grow: Plant trout lily bulbs in

Coast fawn lilies, including *Erythronium revolutum* 'White Beauty' shown here, are early-spring bulbs that disappear soon after flowering. Plant species and cultivars with leafy plants that will fill the gap left when they go dormant.

summer or fall in moist, humus-rich soil. Spring sun is essential, but the site can become quite shady once plants are dormant. Take care not to dig into the clumps during the dormant season. Divide plants in summer as the leaves are yellowing. Sow fresh seed outdoors in early summer. Seedlings develop slowly and may take 3–5 years to bloom.

Landscape Uses: Combine the graceful trout lilies with spring bulbs, wildflowers, and early perennials. Plant them among ferns and foliage plants such as lungworts (*Pulmonaria* spp.), wild bleeding hearts (*Dicentra eximia* and *D. formosa*), and hostas to cover the gaps left in summer. 🍂

Eupatorium Compositae, Daisy Family

you-puh-TOUR-ee-um. Boneset, Joe-Pye Weed. Summer and fall bloom. Full sun.

Description: Bold perennials of shrublike proportions with opposite or whorled leaves and clouds of small fuzzy flowers in terminal clusters. The plants form strong multi-stemmed clumps from stout crowns with tough fibrous roots. The name "Joe Pye" commemorates a native American medicine man who believed in the special powers of these plants. The common name boneset comes from the early use of this plant to aid in the soothing of aching bones.

The foamy, rose-purple-colored flowers of *Eupatorium* 'Atropurpureum' are lightly scented like vanilla. Like other Joe-Pye weeds, they are effective planted in formal borders or meadow gardens.

Eupatorium coelestinum (see-lease-TIE-num), hardy ageratum. Size: 2'–3' tall, leaves to 3" long. An open bushy plant resembling the popular annual ageratum, with 1" clusters of powder-blue flowers in late summer and fall. Zones 6–10.

E. fistulosum (fist-you-LOW-sum), Joe-Pye weed. Size: 5'–14' tall, leaves to 14" long. A stately giant with 4–5 whorled leaves and elongated 6"–9" domes of dusty-rose flowers in summer. Plants vary considerably in height according to soil fertility and moisture. Zones 4–9.

E. maculatum (mack-you-LAY-tum), spotted Joe-Pye weed. Size: 4'–6' tall, leaves to 1' long. Similar to *E. fistulosum* but shorter, with compact, flattened, 4"–6" clusters of cherry-red to rose-purple flowers. 'Atropurpureum' is a selection of either this species or *E. purpureum* with wine-red stems and darker purple, fragrant flowers. Zones 2–8.

E. perfoliatum (per-foe-lee-AY-tum), boneset. Size: 3'–5' tall, leaves to 6" long. A more delicate species with opposite, lance-shaped foliage joined in the middle and pierced by the sturdy stem. The airy 2"–3" clusters of white flowers are produced in mid- to late summer. Zones 3–8.

E. purpureum (purr-PURR-ee-um), Joe-Pye weed, sweet Joe-Pye weed. Size: 3'–6' tall, leaves to 1' long. Similar to *E. maculatum* but with only 4 leaves per whorl and 4"–6" mounded or domed clusters of pale-rose or light-purple sweet-scented flowers. *E.* × 'Gateway' is likely a hybrid between the 2 species. Zones 3–8.

E. rugosum (roo-GO-sum), white snakeroot. Size: 3'–4' tall, leaves to 4" long. An attractive late-summer bloomer with opposite triangular leaves and small white flowers in 3″–4″ clusters. The silver seed heads of this prolific spreader are also very showy. Zones 3–7.

How to Grow: Plant bonesets in moist, average to rich soil in full sun or light shade. They are of easy culture and need little care once established. It takes at least 2 years for new plants to reach their full size. They spread steadily outward to form dense bushy clumps of unparalleled beauty and stature.

Divide oversize clumps in spring or fall. Separate the tough crown into sections using a sharp knife or shears. Divide *E. coelestinum* and *E. rugosum* every 3–4 years. The other species need division only when they outgrow their position. Propagate by tip cuttings taken in early summer. Sow seeds outdoors in fall. Many species will self-sow freely in the garden. *E. rugosum* is very prolific. To keep these plants from becoming weeds in your garden, remove most of the heads before seeds form.

Landscape Uses: Bonesets are equally at home in formal and informal landscapes. Use them in borders for their bold form and soft cottony flowers. Combine them with common rose mallow (*Hibiscus moscheutos*), purple coneflowers (*Echinacea* spp.), garden phlox (*Phlox paniculata*), asters, daylilies, irises, and ornamental grasses. *E. rugosum* thrives in the dry shade of woodlands and enlivens dark recesses with its late-season white flowers. *E. coelestinum* is perfect for informal sites or along driveways. ❦

Euphorbia Euphorbiaceae, Spurge Family

you-FOR-bee-uh. Spurge, Euphorbia. Spring and summer bloom. Full sun to partial shade.

Description: Spurges are succulent perennials with leafy stems and milky sap that flows freely when the leaves or stems are picked or damaged. They are grown for their smooth, often blue-green foliage and their colorful bracts (modified leaves) that surround the inconspicuous yellow flowers. Most species spread by creeping underground stems.

Euphorbia amygdaloides var. *robbiae* (uh-mig-duh-LOY-deez ROB-ee-ee), wood spurge. Size: 1′–2′ tall, leaves to 4″ long. A creeping spurge with thick stems clothed in dark evergreen leaves and topped with open clusters of ½″ rounded light-green bracts. Zone 6 (with winter protection) or Zones 7–8.

E. characias (char-AH-kee-us), spurge. Size: 3′–4′ tall, leaves to 4″ long. A stout bushy perennial with stems densely clothed in long,

The chartreuse flowers of spurge (*Euphorbia characias*) reflect light and appear illuminated from within.

Cushion spurge (*Euphorbia epithymoides*) enlivens dry, sunny gardens with bright-yellow, flowerlike bracts in spring, followed by apricot to orange foliage in autumn.

narrow gray-blue leaves and 8″–10″ elongated clusters of ½″ chartreuse flowers with black eyes. The variety *wulfenii,* thought by some to be a separate species, is similar but has larger eyeless yellow flowers. Zones 7–9.

E. corollata (core-oh-LAY-tuh), flowering spurge. Size: 1′–3′ tall, leaves to 3″ long. A creeping plant with slender stems sparsely covered by pale-green leaves and topped with broad, airy clusters of ¼″ flowers with white, petal-like bracts. The plant resembles a stout baby's-breath. Zones 3–8.

E. epithymoides (eh-pith-ih-MOY-deez), cushion spurge (also sold as *E. polychroma*). Size: 1′–1½′ tall, leaves to 2″ long. This compact plant forms a mound of bright-yellow ¾″ flowers in early spring. In fall, the leaves turn red and orange. Zones 3–8.

E. griffithii (grih-FITH-ee-eye), Griffith's spurge. Size: 2′–3′ tall, leaves to 4″ long. A shrublike spurge with pale-green pointed leaves tinged pink in spring and turning red in

fall. Clusters of fiery ¾″–1″ orange-red flowers are borne in summer. 'Fireglow' has bright-orange bracts and red-veined leaves. 'Dixter' has darker orange flowers. Zones 4–8.

E. myrsinites (mur-sin-EYE-teez), myrtle euphorbia. Size: 6″–10″ tall, leaves to 1″ long. A prostrate plant with thick stems clothed in scaly blue-gray leaves and ¾″ yellow flowers in spring. Zones 5–9.

How to Grow: Spurges are easy-care, long-lived perennials. Plant in well-drained, average to rich soil in full sun or partial shade. Most species are quite drought-tolerant, except for *E. griffithii,* which prefers continually moist soil. *E. amygdaloides* var. *robbiae* tolerates full shade. Provide winter protection to prevent leaf burn and stem damage where cold temperatures persist for long periods without snow cover. Divide spreading clumps as necessary to control their advance or for propagation; *E. amygdaloides* is a particularly fast spreader. Propagate by tip cuttings taken in summer and stuck in well-drained soil before the stem end dries out.

Landscape Uses: Combine spurge with perennials or flowering shrubs. Plant the early-blooming species such as *E. epithymoides* and *E. characias* with spring bulbs, forget-me-nots (*Myosotis* spp.), and silver-leaved plants such as lamb's-ears (*Stachys byzantina*) and artemisias. Use *E. amygdaloides* var. *robbiae* around shrubs or in the dry shade of large trees with other tough groundcovers and shade perennials such as Solomon's seals (*Polygonatum* spp.), bergenias (*Bergenia* spp.), and epimediums (*Epimedium* spp.). *Euphorbia myrsinites* is perfect for the front of the border, along walks, or in a rockery with dwarf conifers and bright perennials such as pinks (*Dianthus* spp.), creeping phlox (*Phlox subulata* and *P. bifida*), rock cresses (*Arabis* spp.), and sedums. Choose *E. griffithii* for a moist site with irises, astilbes, and hostas. 🍁

Filipendula Rosaceae, Rose Family

fill-uh-PEN-djew-luh. Meadowsweet, Queen-of-the-Prairie. Late-spring and summer bloom. Full sun to partial shade.

Description: Meadowsweets are elegant perennials with frothy heads of tiny 5-petaled flowers. Flower color ranges from white through pink to rose. The plants spread by creeping stems to form broad clumps of deep-green, pinnately divided leaves.

Filipendula palmata (pal-MAY-tuh), Siberian meadowsweet. Size: 3′–4′ tall, leaves to 8″ long. A compact plant with open, 4″–5″ clusters of pink flowers and leaves with a distinctive broad terminal leaflet. 'Elegans' is more compact with white flowers. 'Nana' is very short, to 10″ tall, with pale-pink flowers. Zones 3–8.

F. rubra (ROO-bruh), queen-of-the-prairie. Size: 4′–6′ tall, leaves to 1′ long. A tall, stately plant with bold foliage and large (to 9″) clusters of pink or rose flowers. 'Venusta' has deep-rose flowers. 'Venusta Magnifica' has deep carmine-pink flowers. Zones 3–9.

F. ulmaria (ul-MAH-ree-uh), queen-of-

Choose queen-of-the-prairie (*Filipendula rubra*) for a moist or wet spot in full sun to light shade. The airy flowers and bold foliage are lovely combined with ferns.

the-meadow. Size: 3'–6' tall, leaves to 8" long. A medium-size plant with bold foliage and creamy-white flowers in 6" clusters. 'Aurea' has leaves mottled with golden-yellow; its flowers are insignificant. 'Flore-Plena' has showy double flowers. Zones 3–9.

F. vulgaris (vul-GAH-riss), dropwort (also sold as *F. hexapetala*). Size: 2'–3' tall, leaves to 10" long. A short plant with mostly basal, deeply dissected foliage and weakly upright stalks bearing flattened 4"–6" clusters of creamy-white flowers. 'Flore Pleno' is shorter (to 2') with showy double flowers. Zones 3–8.

How to Grow: Plant in evenly moist, humus-rich soil in full sun or light shade. All but *F. vulgaris* (which tolerates drier soil) thrive in highly moist soil, such as that found along creeks or the sides of ponds. Remove spent flower heads to encourage some reblooming, or leave them in place and enjoy the seed heads throughout the season. If foliage becomes tattered, cut meadowsweets to the ground and fresh leaves will emerge. As long as the soil stays moist, the new foliage will be attractive the rest of the season.

Clumps spread rapidly by creeping stems and need frequent division to keep them from crowding other plants. Lift and divide clumps in fall. Old clumps can be quite tough and may require a knife or shears to separate them.

Landscape Uses: Use meadowsweets in formal borders, with shrubs, or in meadow and pondside plantings. Combine their cotton-candy flowers with roses, irises, daylilies, phlox, and daisies. In untamed spots, plant them with ferns, bee balms (*Monarda* spp.), bellflowers (*Campanula* spp.), purple coneflower (*Echinacea purpurea*), and grasses. Use *F. vulgaris* to edge beds or to soften the harsh lines of walkways and paths. Combine it with the gray foliage and blue flowers of Persian nepeta (*Nepeta mussinii*). 🍂

For lacy texture in the summer garden, try double-flowered dropwort (*Filipendula vulgaris* 'Flore Pleno'). It bears masses of frothy white flowers and the shiny, green, fernlike leaves make an attractive edging long after the flowers have faded.

Fritillaria   Liliaceae, Lily Family

frih-tih-LAH-ree-uh. Fritillary, Checkered Lily. Spring bloom. Full sun or partial shade.

Description: Fritillaries are spring-blooming bulbs with nodding bell-shaped flowers borne in open clusters or in erect spikes. The foliage is often blue-green and dies back after the flowering season. All parts of the plants have a curious, pungent (some say musky) odor. There are many species, only a few of which are readily available as nursery-propagated plants. Bulbs are often collected from the wild. Do not buy them unless they are labeled "nursery propagated."

Fritillaria imperialis (im-peer-ee-AH-lis), crown imperial. Size: 2½'–3' tall, leaves to 6" long. A stout plant with leafy stems crowned by a tight cluster of nodding red, orange, or yellow 2" flowers with a topknot of leaves. 'Aurora' has orange-red flowers. 'Lutea Maxima' is a hardy yellow-flowered form. 'Rubra Maxima' has large fiery-orange flowers. Zones 5–8.

F. meleagris (mel-ee-AH-gris), checkered lily. Size: 10"–15", leaves to 6" long. A delicate plant with oversize inflated 1½" bells on slender stems and narrow blue-green leaves. Flower color varies from white to brown or purple; plants are usually sold as mixed colors. 'Alba' has creamy-white flowers. Zones 4–8.

F. persica (PER-sih-kuh), bells of Persia. Size: 2½'–3' tall, leaves to 5" long. Leaf stems are topped with elongated spiky clusters of nodding purple-brown ¾" bells. 'Adiyaman' is a vigorous cultivar with plum-colored flowers. Zones 5–7.

How to Grow: Plant fritillary bulbs 4"–6" deep in the fall into light but rich, well-drained soil in full sun or partial shade. Once established, they are long-lived (with the exception of *F. imperalis,* which is often treated as an annual in many parts of the eastern United States). *F. meleagris* will grow in quite moist soils in warmer regions, but in areas with severe winters, good drainage is essential to survival. Divide established clumps after flowering if they become overcrowded.

Landscape Uses: Plant drifts of *F. imperalis* in combination with flowering shrubs and foliage perennials. Use *F. persica* as an accent among early perennials and other bulbs. Choose smaller species for rock gardens, troughs, or containers. Plant alone or in combination with early-blooming plants. 🍂

Spring-blooming crown imperials (*Fritillaria imperialis*) bear striking bell-like flowers in yellow, orange, or red. If you dislike their strong musky scent, site them where they can be appreciated from a distance.

Gaillardia Compositae, Daisy Family

gah-LARD-ee-uh. Blanket Flower. Summer bloom. Full sun.

Plant blanket flowers such as *Gaillardia × grandiflora* 'Goblin' for a splash of brilliant summer color in a sunny site. They are ideal for seaside gardens or any other well-drained spot.

Description: Blanket flowers are showy summer perennials with daisylike flowers that have a single or double row of ragged petal-like rays surrounding broad buttonlike centers. These cheery plants are grown for the fiery-orange, yellow, and brown colors of their 4″ flowers. The wiry flowerstalks arise from a tight clump of lobed, hairy foliage. When the flowers fade, the spherical seed heads are clothed in stiff, tawny bristles.

Gaillardia aristata (air-ih-STAH-tuh), blanket flower. Size: 2′–2½′ tall; leaves to 10″ long. A plant of dry prairies with yellow ray florets (often blazed with brown) and a purple-brown disk. Zones 2–10.

G. × grandiflora (gran-dih-FLOOR-uh), blanket flower. Size: 2′–3′ tall; leaves to 10″ long. A showy hybrid between *G. aristata* and the annual *G. pulchella,* this popular plant is floriferous and hardy but may be short-lived. The flowers are orange-and-yellow, often with brick-red bands or eyes. 'Baby Cole' is a long-lived dwarf selection only 8″ tall. 'Bremen' has copper-red flowers tipped in yellow on 2′–3′ stems. 'Burgundy' is a lovely deep red. 'Dazzler' has yellow-centered flowers with red-tipped rays. 'Goblin' is a 1′ dwarf with red-and-yellow flowers. 'Golden Goblin' is of similar size to 'Goblin' and has all-yellow flowers. Zones 4–9.

How to Grow: Plant blanket flowers in average, well-drained soil in full sun. They seem to thrive on neglect and heat. They are perfect for seaside gardens because they are salt- and drought-tolerant. The only place they grow poorly is in rich, moist soil, which makes them floppy and shortens their life expectancy. Divide blanket flower every 2–3 years in early spring to keep the clumps thriving. Propagate by stem cuttings in early summer. Sow seeds outdoors in fall, or sow indoors in winter and place the pots or flats in a refrigerator for 4 weeks before moving them to a warm, bright place. Seedlings develop quickly and may bloom the first year.

Landscape Uses: Blanket flowers produce mounds of brilliant flowers from early summer through fall. Plant them with other warm-colored perennials such as coreopsis (*Coreopsis* spp.), butterfly weed (*Asclepias tuberosa*), and yarrows. Add interest and excitement with the spiky yellow leaves of Spanish bayonet (*Yucca filamentosa* 'Golden Sword') and purple flowers such as sage (*Salvia* × *superba* 'East Friesland'). 🌿

Galium Rubiaceae, Madder Family

GAL-ee-um. Sweet Woodruff, Bedstraw. Spring bloom. Sun or shade.

Description: *Galium odoratum* (oh-door-AH-tum), sweet woodruff. Size: 4″–10″ tall; leaves to 1½″ long. A showy groundcover with whorls of broadly lance-shaped leaves and tight clusters of starry white ¼″ flowers on erect stems. When dried, all parts of the plant have a spicy fragrance reminiscent of sweet hay. Zones 4–8.

How to Grow: Sweet woodruff requires even moisture and partial shade. It creeps steadily outward to form broad clumps. Divide in spring or fall to control its spread. Propagate by stem cuttings in early summer (remove any flowers or seed heads first).

Landscape Uses: Use sweet woodruff in large patches in the shade of trees and shrubs. Plant spring bulbs and wildflowers such as Virginia bluebells (*Mertensia virginica*) among the creeping stems. 🌿

Sweet woodruff (*Galium odoratum*) is an adaptable, easy-to-grow groundcover for a shady site. Plants thrive in either moist or dry soil. In spring, dainty white flowers appear.

Gaura Onagraceae, Evening Primrose Family

GAW-ruh. Gaura. Summer bloom. Full sun.

White gaura (*Gaura lindheimeri*) bears its delicate white flowers from June until frost if the spent bloom spikes are removed regularly. Plants thrive equally well in moist or dry soil.

Description: *Gaura lindheimeri* (lind-HIGH-mer-eye), white gaura. Size: 3′–4′ tall; leaves to 3″ long. An exuberant shrubby perennial with erect stems carrying spikes of 1″ white 4-petaled flowers well above the deep-green foliage. As the flowers age, they blush to pale-rose. Clumps grow from a thick, deep taproot. Zones 5–9.

How to Grow: Plant in any moist, well-drained soil in full sun. Once established, the plants are drought-tolerant, but they perform best with even moisture. Gauras tolerate heat and humidity and still bloom well. Plants seldom need division. Sow seed outside in fall. Self-sown seedlings will likely appear.

Landscape Uses: In borders or informal gardens, combine the airy spikes of gaura with ornamental grasses and small-flowered plants such as verbenas (*Verbena* spp.), sedums, red valerian (*Centranthus ruber*), and sea lavender (*Limonium latifolium*). 🌿

Gentiana Gentianaceae, Gentian Family

jen-SHE-ah-nuh. Gentian. Fall bloom. Sun or partial shade.

Description: The lovely autumn-flowering gentians have trumpet- or bottle-shaped flowers of an intense blue that has come to be called gentian blue. Plants vary in size and shape from low and sprawling to stiffly upright. The clumps grow from tough cordlike roots.

Gentiana asclepiadea (as-klep-ee-AH-dee-ah), willow gentian. Size: 1½′–2′ tall; leaves to 3″ long. A leafy gentian with weakly upright stems clothed in stiff lance-shaped leaves.

Clusters of late-summer blooms cover the upper half of the stems. Each flower is an inflated tube with tips reflexed to form a starry rim. Zones 5–7.

G. septemfida (sep-TEM-fih-duh), crested gentian. Size: 4″–8″ tall; leaves to 1½″ long. Bright-blue trumpet-shaped 1½″-long flowers appear in late summer over spreading mats of oval bright-green leaves. Zones 3–8.

How to Grow: Plant in evenly moist,

humus-rich soil in full sun or partial shade. Protect from afternoon sun, especially in warmer zones, to avoid browned foliage. Plants dislike disturbance and seldom need dividing. Propagate by lifting clumps in spring and carefully splitting the crowns. Sow fresh seed outside in late fall, or sow indoors in late winter and place the pots or flats in a refrigerator for 4–6 weeks before moving them to a warm, bright place. Plants bloom in 3 years.

Landscape Uses: Combine gentians with ferns and woodland asters in the shade garden. Their rich blue color is lovely with small-leaved hostas, variegated sedges (*Carex* spp.), and other lush foliage plants. Gentians are a good choice for fall color in a rock garden or border with ornamental grasses. 🦋

In late summer, crested gentian (*Gentiana septemfida*) bears clusters of exceptionally beautiful, brilliant-blue flowers.

Geranium Geraniaceae, Geranium Family

jer-ANE-ee-um. Cranesbill, Hardy Geranium. Spring and early-summer bloom. Full sun or partial shade.

Description: A large genus of mounding or bushy, long-lived perennials not to be confused with tender bedding or zonal "geraniums" of the genus *Pelargonium*. Most species have rounded, palmately lobed leaves, some quite elaborately incised. The showy, 5-petaled flowers are somewhat saucer-shaped or occasionally cupped. Flower colors range from white to blue, purple, rose, or pink, often with deeper colored veining. The common name cranesbill refers to the rigid, beak-shaped capsules that hold the seed until it's ripe and then split elastically and project the seeds outward from the plants. Plants grow from thickened rhizomes with wiry roots.

Geranium cinereum (sin-ee-REE-um), grayleaf cranesbill. Size: 6″–12″ tall; leaves to 1½″ long. A low, spreading plant with deeply

Soft-pink flowers in spring and early summer and lovely, finely cut foliage characterize Endres cranesbill (*Geranium endressii*).

incised leaves and 1″ saucer-shaped pink flowers lined with purple veining. 'Alba' has white flowers. 'Ballerina' is a hybrid with large lilac-pink flowers boldly veined and eyed with deep-purple borne throughout the summer. 'Giuseppii' has bright-magenta flowers with a dark eye. 'Splendens' has bright-pink flowers with a dark eye. Zone 4 (with winter protection) or Zones 5–8.

G. clarkei (klar-KEY-eye), Clark's geranium. Size: 15″–20″ tall; leaves 4″–6″ long. A floriferous species with ¾″ purple or white flowers over deeply cut leaves. This species was recently separated from *G. pratense*. 'Kashmir Purple' has deep purple-blue flowers. 'Kashmir White' has white flowers with pale-pink veins. Zones 4–8.

G. dalmaticum (dal-MAT-ih-kum), Dalmatian cranesbill. Size: 4″–6″ tall; leaves 1″–2″ tall. A low, mounding plant that spreads rapidly by creeping rhizomes but is never invasive. The 1″ soft-mauve flowers cover the tight rounded foliage in late spring and early summer. The variety *album* has white flowers. 'Biokovo' is a hybrid with *G. macrorrhizum* with pink flowers. Zones 4–8.

G. endressii (en-DRESS-ee-eye), Endres cranesbill, Pyrenean cranesbill. Size: 15″–18″ tall; leaves 3″–5″ long. A mounding to sprawling plant with starry leaves and dozens of 1″ soft-pink flowers. 'A.T. Johnson' has silvery pink flowers. 'Claridge Druce', a hybrid with *G. versicolor,* is a vigorous grower having lilac-pink flowers with darker veins. 'Wargrave Pink' has rich pink flowers. Zones 4–8.

G. himalayense (him-uh-lay-EN-see), lilac cranesbill (also sold as *G. grandiflorum*). Size: 12″–15″ tall; leaves to 3½″ long. A sprawling plant with deeply cut palmate leaves and 2″ violet-blue flowers borne throughout the summer. 'Birch Double' has small double lavender flowers. 'Gravetye' is more compact

Blood-red cranesbill (*Geranium sanguineum*) is one of the hardiest and most heat-tolerant of the geraniums. Blooms are carried above attractive foliage that turns wine-red in autumn.

than the species with 2″ bright-blue flowers. 'Johnson's Blue', a hybrid with *G. pratense*, has 2″ clear-blue flowers on bushy 16″–18″ plants. Zones 4–8.

G. ibericum (eye-BEER-ih-kum), Caucasus geranium. Size: 1½′–2′ tall; leaves 5″–6″ long. A robust dense mounding plant with round broad-lobed soft-hairy leaves with elongated leafstalks and violet flowers. Zones 3–8.

G. macrorrhizum (mack-row-RISE-um), bigroot cranesbill. Size: 15″–18″ tall; leaves 3″–4″ long. Clusters of bright-pink flowers are carried above the aromatic, palmately lobed leaves. The clumps spread easily by underground stems. 'Album' has white flowers surrounded by pink sepals. 'Breven's Variety' has magenta flowers and deep-red sepals. 'Ingwersen's Variety' has light-pink flowers and glossy leaves. 'Spessart' has white flowers and pale-pink sepals. Zones 3–8.

G. maculatum (mack-you-LAY-tum), wild cranesbill. Size: 1′–2′ tall; leaves to 4″ long. A tall plant with loose clusters of clear-pink or white flowers above open clumps of starry rounded leaves. Zones 4–8.

G. × *magnificum* (mag-NIFF-ih-kum), showy geranium. Size: 1½′–2′ tall; leaves to 6″ long. This robust, bushy hybrid between *G. ibericum* and *G. platypetalum* has large rounded velvety leaves with broad lobes and clusters of 1½″ blue-violet flowers. Zones 3–8.

G. platypetalum (plat-ee-PET-uh-lum), broad-petaled geranium. Size: 1½′–2′ tall; leaves 4″–6″ long. A rounded mounding plant with deep-purple flowers and round lobed hairy leaves with long petioles (leafstalks). Zones 3–8.

G. pratense (pray-TEN-see), meadow cranesbill. Size: 2′–3′ tall; leaves to 6″ long. A vigorous plant with deeply incised starry leaves and 1½″ purple flowers veined in red. 'Mrs. Kendall Clarke' has pale-blue flowers with rose stripes. Zones 3–8.

Geranium × 'Johnson's Blue' is a shrubby, floriferous plant for the front or middle of the border. The cup-shaped blue flowers are borne above the deeply cut leaves from summer into early autumn.

G. psilostemon (sigh-LOW-steh-mon), Armenian cranesbill. Size: 2′–4′ tall; leaves to 8″ long. A magnificent perennial with large starry evergreen leaves and 2″ deep-magenta flowers with black eyes. 'Bressingham Flair' grows only 2′. Zones 5–8.

G. sanguineum (san-GWIN-ee-um), blood-red cranesbill, bloody cranesbill. Size: 8″–12″ tall; leaves to 2″ long. A low, wide-spreading geranium with mounds of deeply incised spidery leaves and flat 1″ bright-pink flowers held just above the foliage. 'Album' grows to 1½′ and is more open, with white saucer-shaped flowers. 'Alpenglow' is a compact mounding plant with brilliant rose-red flowers. 'Shepherd's Warning' is only 6″ tall and has deep rose-pink flowers. The variety *striatum* (also sold as *lancastriense*) has pale-pink flowers with deep-rose veins. Zones 3–8.

G. sylvaticum (sill-VAT-ih-kum), wood cranesbill. Size: 2½′–3′ tall; leaves 6″–7″ long. An early-blooming geranium with 1″ violet-blue flowers on open bushy plants. The leaves are rounded with deep lobes. 'Mayflower' is a more compact cultivar. Zones 3–8.

How to Grow: Plant cranesbills in moist but well-drained, humus-rich soil in sun or partial shade. In warmer zones, shade from hot afternoon sun is essential. Some species, especially *G. macrorrhizum, G. sanguineum,* and *G. endressii,* are drought-tolerant. *G. dalmaticum, G. macrorrhizum, G. sanguineum,* and *G. sylvaticum* are quite shade-tolerant. Most species are slow-spreading and can grow for many years in the same spot without division. Others grow quickly to form broad clumps. Divide the most vigorous spreaders every 2–3 years. To increase your supply, lift plants in early spring or fall and pull the clumps apart. Many geraniums will self-sow. If you catch the seeds before they are catapulted toward the neighbor's yard, sow them outdoors or inside in a warm (70°F) seedbed. Seedlings develop in 3–5 weeks.

Landscape Uses: Cranesbills are versatile plants for the summer border. Combine them with bold flowers and spiky forms or use them as "weavers" to tie together different combinations. Siberian iris (*Iris sibirica*), garden phlox (*Phlox paniculata*), bellflowers (*Campanula* spp.), evening primroses (*Oenothera* spp.), and ornamental grasses are good companions. *G. cinereum* and other dwarf selections are good for the rock garden. Most species have lovely burgundy-red, scarlet, or orange fall foliage color. ❦

Geum Rosaceae, Rose Family

JEE-um. Avens. Spring and early-summer bloom. Full sun to light shade.

For bright summer color, plant a clump of scarlet-flowered *Geum quellyon* 'Mrs. Bradshaw'. Like other members of the genus, it prefers a cool, moist but well-drained spot.

Description: A genus of tough, hardy perennials for climates with cool summers. Basal rosettes of fuzzy, pinnately divided evergreen leaves are crowned by slender stalks bearing fiery-orange, red, or yellow flowers in spring and early summer. They grow from stout, slow-creeping roots.

Geum coccineum (cock-SIN-ee-um), scarlet avens (often sold as *G.* × *borisii*). Size: 9″–12″ tall; leaves 6″–8″ long. The showy 1½″–2″ brick-red flowers are held well above the basal, thrice-divided leaves. 'Borisii' has orange-red flowers on 10″ stems. 'Georgenberg' is a hybrid with bright yellow-orange flowers. Zones 4–7.

G. quellyon (quell-EE-on), Chilean avens (also sold as *G. chiloense*). Size: 1½′–2′ tall; leaves 8″–12″ long. This avens has 1½″–2″ scarlet flowers in early to mid-summer in loose clusters atop wiry stalks. 'Fire Opal' is a floriferous, deep-red semidouble selection. 'Lady Stratheden' has semidouble bright-yellow flowers. 'Mrs. Bradshaw' is an old cultivar with semidouble scarlet flowers. 'Red Wings' has orange-red semidouble flowers. Zones 4–7.

G. triflorum (try-FLOOR-um), long-plumed purple avens, prairie smoke. Size: 4"–12" tall, leaves 4"–6" long. A slow-creeping plant with ferny foliage and early-spring flowers in groups of 3. Each 2"-long flower has dusty-rose sepals and creamy-white petals and is capped by long, pointed purple bracts (modified leaves). The fuzzy tails of the seeds form plumes resembling puffs of smoke. Zones 2–8.

How to Grow: Plant in evenly moist but well-drained, humus-rich soil in full sun or light shade. *G. triflorum* fares well in drier soils. Most species are sensitive to high temperatures; provide shade from hot afternoon sun in warm zones. *C. coccineum* and *G. quellyon* can be short-lived; divide frequently (in spring or fall) to help prolong their lives. Sow fresh seed outdoors in fall.

Landscape Uses: Grow the fiery-colored avens with other bright flowers such as black-eyed Susans (*Rudbeckia hirta*) and tickseeds (*Coreopsis* spp.). Plant *G. triflorum* in the rock garden or along a walk with white creeping phlox (*Phlox subulata*), sedges (*Carex* spp.), and bloody cranesbill (*Geranium sanguineum*). 🌿

Gillenia Rosaceae, Rose Family

gih-LEN-ee-uh. Bowman's-Root, Indian Physic. Late-spring or early-summer bloom. Full sun to partial shade.

Description: *Gillenia trifoliata* (try-foe-lec-AH-tuh), bowman's-root (reclassified as *Porteranthus trifoliatus*). Size: 2'–4' tall; leaves to 4" long. An erect shrublike perennial with toothed trifoliate leaves and broad clusters of 1" 4-petaled starry white or pinkish flowers in late spring or early summer. The plants grow from thick, deep roots. Zones 4–8.

How to Grow: Plant in moist, rich soil in sun or partial shade. Once established, plants are quite drought-tolerant. They prefer shaded sites but will tolerate full sun in all but the hottest regions. Plants spread slowly and seldom need dividing. Take stem cuttings in spring or sow seed outdoors in summer.

Landscape Uses: In nature, bowman's-root grows on lightly shaded hillsides with red fire pink (*Silene virginica*), pink phlox (*Phlox carolina*), and grasses. Plant in borders with late tulips and large-flowered perennials. 🌿

Tough and adaptable bowman's-root (*Gillenia trifoliata*) grows to shrublike proportions in moist or dry soil. Plants may need staking in rich soil.

Gladiolus Iridaceae, Iris Family

glad-ee-OH-lus. Gladiolus, Glads. Summer bloom. Full sun.

Description: These stalwart harbingers of summer are grown for their tall spikes of brightly colored flowers. The irislike foliage emerges from a large buttonlike corm in early summer, followed by 1-sided spikes of open, funnelform flowers.

Gladiolus communis (kahm-YOU-nis), gladiolus. Size: 2'–3' tall; leaves to 2' long. This species bears swordlike leaves and uneven spikes of pink 1½" flowers. The subspecies *byzantinus* (also sold as *G. byzantinus*) has deep reddish purple flowers. 'Albus' has white

Colorful glads, such as *Gladiolus communis* subsp. *byzantinus*, are perfect for cutting or for summer display in a border.

flowers. Zones 6–10.

G. × *hortulanus* (hort-you-LAN-us), gladiolus. Size: 2'–4' tall; leaves to 3' long. These hybrids bear large, tightly packed flowers that come in all colors except blue. Hundreds of named cultivars are available. Most are hardy to Zone 7 with winter protection; in colder climates treat them as annuals, or dig the corms in fall and store indoors in a frost-free place.

How to Grow: Plant gladiolus corms 4"–8" deep in spring. Glads need moist but well-drained, light, humus-rich soil. Full sun is necessary to promote bloom the following year, especially for the hybrids. Glads need approximately 90 days from the time they are planted to root, grow, bloom, and store enough energy for the next year. Remove flowerstalks as soon as the flowers fade. Staking is usually necessary, especially for the large-flowered hybrids.

Thrips are a serious problem. They produce pale blotches or lines between the veins of the leaves. In serious cases, they may also deform the flowers. Early detection is critical. As soon as you see the first sign of damage, spray plants with insecticidal soap every 3 days for 2 weeks. Remove and destroy badly infested foliage. Aphids may also be a problem but are easy to control with insecticidal soap.

Landscape Uses: The unusual, often top-heavy gladiolus is difficult to work into garden situations. It is often relegated to the cutting garden or planted among annuals. Try combining glads with bushy perennials and ornamental grasses. Baby's-breath and other airy, floriferous plants are also good companions. For indoor use, cut the flower spikes as the lowest buds are showing color. 🍂

Gypsophila Caryophyllaceae, Pink Family

jipp-SOFF-ill-uh. Baby's-Breath. Summer bloom. Full sun or light shade.

Description: Baby's-breath is a beloved perennial with clouds of tiny white or pink flowers above the mostly basal leaves. The plants grow from thick, deep taproots.

Gypsophila paniculata (pan-ick-you-LAH-tuh), baby's-breath. Size: 3'–4' tall; leaves to 4" long. This airy plant attains shrublike proportions when in full bloom. Masses of ⅛" white flowers smother the rosettes of narrow blue-green leaves. 'Bristol Fairy' is compact (to 2') with double flowers. 'Perfecta' is robust with large double flowers. 'Pink Fairy' is a pink version of 'Bristol Fairy'. 'Pink Star' has bright-pink flowers. 'Red Sea' has double rose-pink flowers on 4' stems. Zones 3–9.

G. repens (REE-penz), creeping baby's-breath. Size: 4"–8" tall; leaves to 1" long. This low, creeping plant spreads to form leafy mats of gray-blue foliage. The ¼" flowers are carried in broad flat clusters. 'Alba' has white flowers. 'Rosea' has pale-pink flowers. Zones 3–8.

How to Grow: "Gypsophila" literally means lime loving, and both species thrive in rich, moist, neutral to slightly alkaline soils in full sun or light shade. *G. repens* tolerates acidic soils. Plant in the spring, and do not disturb the clumps once they are established. Some cultivars tend to be short-lived. Good drainage is essential for longevity. Taller cultivars (over 1½') need staking. Encourage reblooming by cutting old stalks to the ground as the last of the flowers fade. Many double selections are grafted onto rootstocks of seed-grown single forms; plant them deeply to encourage rooting of the stems. Propagation by cuttings in spring is possible but not easy at home without a greenhouse. Sow seeds of the single forms outdoors in spring or fall or sow

Gypsophila paniculata 'Pink Fairy' bears its tiny, pale-pink blooms in cloudlike profusion; the species has white flowers. Baby's-breaths are ideal when used to fill in gaps left by dormant perennials such as bulbs.

seeds indoors in late winter.

Landscape Uses: *Gypsophila* species are indispensable fillers for perennial gardens. Use them to hide the yellowing foliage of bulbs and other plants that go dormant in summer. The airy mounds of flowers are lovely in combination with spikes of gayfeathers (*Liatris* spp.) and speedwells (*Veronica* spp.) and with large flowers such as purple coneflower (*Echinacea purpurea*), Shasta daisy (*Chrysanthemum × superbum*), and asters. Use the diminutive *G. repens* as an edger for beds, along walks, or in rock and wall gardens. The flowers are long-lasting when cut and hung upside down to dry. 🍃

Helenium Compositae, Daisy Family

hel-EE-nee-um. Sneezeweed, Helen's Flower. Late-summer and fall bloom. Full sun.

Add a touch of bright-yellow to the autumn garden with *Helenium* 'Kugelsonne'. Like other sneezeweeds, it thrives in average, evenly moist soil.

Description: These showy late-season perennials produce abundant yellow or orange daisylike flowers with spherical centers atop erect winged stalks. The sparsely branching stems arise from stout roots.

Helenium autumnale (awe-tum-NAH-lee), common sneezeweed. Size: 3′–5′ tall; leaves 4″–6″ long. A tall plant with leafy stems topped by broad clusters of 2″ yellow or orange, yellow-centered flowers. The bright-green leaves are broadly lance-shaped with toothed margins. 'Brilliant' has orange-bronze dark-centered flowers on sturdy 3′ plants. 'Butterpat' has bright-yellow flowers on 3′–4′ plants. 'Crimson Beauty' has mahogany flowers. 'Riverton Beauty' has golden-yellow flowers with bronze-red centers. Zones 3–8.

H. flexuosum (flecks-you-OH-sum), sneezeweed. Size: 2′–3′ tall; leaves 4″–8″ long. A compact grower with leafy stems and broad clusters of 3″ flowers with drooping yellow petal-like rays and brownish purple spherical centers. Zones 5–9.

H. hoopesii (who-PESS-ee-eye), orange sneezeweed. Size: 2'–4' tall; leaves to 1' long. An open plant with basal rosettes of large oval leaves and stems clothed in small leaves and topped with sparse clusters of 3" flowers with narrow, drooping 3" golden-yellow rays. Zones 3–7.

Helenium hybrids. The American perennial market is seeing an influx of German sneezeweed hybrids of mixed parentage that are extremely floriferous and quite hardy. 'Baudirektor Linne' is a late-blooming selection bearing mahogany flowers with brown centers. 'Kugelsonne' has bright-yellow flowers on erect, usually self-supporting 4'–5' stems. 'Red-Gold Hybrid' has brick-red and golden-yellow flowers. 'Zimbelstern' is an early-flowering selection with gold rays and brown centers.

How to Grow: Heleniums are native to woods edges, low meadows, and moist prairies. They thrive in evenly moist, humus-rich soil in full sun. *H. hoopesii* is more tolerant of dry soil than the other species and hybrids. Choose *H. autumnale* for a moist or wet spot. In the warmer zones, plants tend to stretch and may require staking. Pinch stem tips once or twice in the spring to promote sturdy, compact growth, or choose cultivars that are naturally compact and self-supporting. Divide clumps every 3–4 years to keep them vigorous. Propagate by stem cuttings in early summer. The species can be grown from seed sown outside in fall, but the cultivars will not come true from seed.

Landscape Uses: Sneezeweeds are invaluable additions to late-season borders and informal meadow plantings. Contrary to their name, they do not make you sneeze because their pollen is carried by insects, not the wind. Plant them in the company of garden phlox (*Phlox paniculata*), bee balm (*Monarda didyma*), asters, coreopsis (*Coreopsis* spp.), goldenrods (*Solidago* spp.), and ornamental grasses. The leafy stems of *H. autumnale* are attractive during the early summer as the plant grows toward flowering; try it in informal plantings at the edge of a pond with ferns, grasses, and speedwells (*Veronica* spp.). Plant *H. hoopesii* in a dry spot with yarrows, sages, and sedums. ❧

Helianthus Compositae, Daisy Family

hee-lee-AN-thus. Sunflower. Summer and fall bloom. Full sun.

Description: A large genus of robust summer- or autumn-blooming plants with stout leafy stems from thick tough roots. The starry yellow daisylike flowers are carried in flat or elongated clusters.

Helianthus angustifolius (an-gus-tih-FOE-lee-us), swamp sunflower. Size: 4'–8' tall; leaves 8"–12" long. A commanding plant with thick stems clothed in deep-green lance-shaped leaves and crowned with elongated branching clusters of 3" bright-yellow flowers with purple centers in September and October. Zones 6–9.

H. decapetalus (deck-uh-PET-uh-lus), thin-leaved sunflower. Size: 4'–5' tall; leaves 4"–8" long. A clump-forming sunflower with mounded, open clusters of 2"–3" yellow flowers with yellow centers. 'Capenoch Star' has clear-yellow flowers and is quite floriferous. Zones 4–8.

H. divaricatus (dih-var-ih-KAH-tus), wood-

Woodland sunflower (*Helianthus divaricatus*) blooms well in the partial shade of a woodland garden or in a sunny meadow or perennial border.

low leaf sunflower. Size: 3'–4' tall; leaves to 8" long. A delicate sunflower with narrow drooping gray-green leaves and slender upright clusters of 2" flowers in autumn. Zones 4–8.

How to Grow: Plant sunflowers in moist, average to rich soil in full sun. They are all quite drought-tolerant once established. *H. angustifolius, H. decapetalus,* and *H. maximiliani* tolerate wet soil. They are easy to grow but need room to spread. Stems seldom need staking except in windy areas. Divide overgrown clumps every 3–4 years in the fall. Propagate by stem cuttings in early summer or by seed sown outdoors in late summer or fall.

Landscape Uses: Sunflowers are indispensable additions to the summer and fall garden. Combine them with airy and small-flowered plants such as garden phlox (*Phlox paniculata*), baby's-breath, asters, summer bulbs, and ornamental grasses. 🍁

land sunflower. Size: 2'–5' tall; leaves 3"–7" long. The 2" yellow flowers are borne on slender stems above rough, toothed, lance-shaped leaves. Zones 3–8.

H. maximiliani (max-ih-mill-ee-ANE-ee), Maximilian sunflower. Size: 4'–10' tall; leaves 6"–12" long. A stately sunflower with drooping lance-shaped gray-green leaves and elongated clusters of 2"–3" flowers in late summer and fall. Zones 3–8.

H. × multiflorus (mull-tee-FLOOR-us), perennial sunflower, many-flowered sunflower. Size: 3'–5' tall; leaves to 10" long. A coarse summer sunflower of hybrid origin from a cross between *H. decapetalus* and *H. annuus.* 'Flore-Plena' has double bright-yellow flowers on 5' stems. 'Loddon Gold' has huge 5"–6" double golden-yellow flowers on 5'–6' plants. Zones 4–8.

H. salicifolius (sal-iss-ih-FOE-lee-us), wil-

Perennial sunflower (*Helianthus × multiflorus*) produces dozens of bright-yellow flowers in midsummer. It thrives in average to poor soil.

Heliopsis Compositae, Daisy Family

hee-lee-OP-sis. Heliopsis, Oxeye. Summer bloom. Full sun or partial shade.

Description: *Heliopsis helianthoides* (hee-lee-an-THOY-deez), sunflower heliopsis, oxeye. Size: 3'–6' tall; leaves to 5" long. Heliopsis are bushy plants with triangular leaves and 2"–3" bright-yellow flowers with yellow centers. The subspecies *scabra* is stout and floriferous with large, rough foliage. 'Golden Plume' is a compact (3'–3½') double-flowered selection. 'Summer Sun' is compact (to 3') with 4" flowers. Zones 3–9.

How to Grow: Plant in moist or dry, average to rich soil in full sun (for best growth) or partial shade. Tall forms may need staking. Divide plants growing in rich soils every 2–3 years to promote longevity. Divide others when necessary to control their spread or rejuvenate the clumps. Propagate by stem cuttings in late spring. Sow seed outdoors in fall or spring.

Landscape Uses: Combine heliopsis with summer perennials and grasses in borders and meadows. Garden phlox (*Phlox paniculata*), gayfeathers (*Liatris* spp.), hardy mums, speedwells (*Veronica* spp.), and asters are excellent companions. 🍂

Sunflower heliopsis (*Heliopsis helianthoides*) is the first of summer's yellow daisies to bloom. Flowering begins in early June and continues through July. Try it in the wild garden with other perennials such as butterfly weed (*Asclepias tuberosa*) and gayfeathers (*Liatris* spp.).

Helleborus Ranunculaceae, Buttercup Family

hell-uh-BORE-us. Hellebore, Christmas Rose, Lenten Rose. Winter and spring bloom. Light to partial shade.

Description: Hellebores are aristocrats of the winter and early-spring garden. Their leathery foliage is attractive throughout the summer and, in mild regions, during the winter season as well. All parts of the plant are poisonous. Some species produce persistent aboveground stems; others grow from creeping underground rhizomes with short-lived flowering stems. Those with persistent stems produce flower buds at the top of the stems in the fall. The buds of the rhizomatous species emerge as temperatures moderate in early spring. The flowers consist of 5 showy petal-like sepals surrounded by leafy bracts (modified leaves). Flowers may be flat with many fuzzy stamens (male reproductive structures) or tubelike with the stamens concealed. The leathery sepals persist for over a month, well after the seed capsules begin to form.

Helleborus argutifolius (ar-goo-tih-FOE-lee-us), Corsican hellebore (also listed as *H. corsicus*). Size: 1½'-2' tall; leaves 10"-12" long. A coarse plant with thick erect stems and glossy toothed 3-lobed evergreen leaves. The buds form in autumn at the tip of the stem and open to nodding, bowl-shaped, 2½" green flowers in early spring. The sepals persist well after the seed capsules begin to develop. Zone 6 (with winter protection) or Zones 7-8.

H. foetidus (FET-ih-dus), stinking hellebore. Size: 1½'-2' tall; leaves 8"-10" long. A stemmed

Lenten rose (*Helleborus orientalis*) blooms in early spring just as the new leaves are emerging. The nodding bells are typically reddish purple to deep-rose. Unlike other hellebores, this species is fairly easy to divide if necessary. Plants often self-sow prolifically.

hellebore with bright-green spidery leaves, each with 7-9 narrow, toothed leaflets. The nodding tubelike 1½"-2" green flowers have a red-brown edge on each sepal. They are carried above the foliage in erect, branching clusters. Zone 5 (with winter protection) or Zones 6-9.

H. niger (NYE-jer), Christmas rose. Size: 1'-1½' tall; leaves to 1' long. A rhizomatous hellebore with deep-green leaves with 5-7 irregular palmate lobes and long petioles (leafstalks). The 2"-3" white flowers rise singly on succulent stalks from the center of the clump in winter or earliest spring. They fade to pink and are often quite persistent. Zones 3-8.

H. orientalis (or-ee-en-TAL-iss), Lenten rose. Size: 1'-1½'; leaves 10"-14" long. The showiest hellebore with clusters of white, pink, rose, or purple nodding 3" flowers borne on succulent stems from a creeping rhizome. The mostly evergreen palmately compound leaves have 5-7 broad, irregular leaflets. Zones 4-9.

H. viridis (VEER-ih-diss), green hellebore. Size: 10"-16" tall; leaves 6"-8" long. A dainty hellebore with clustered nodding, 1"-2" green flowers carried on leafy stems and deciduous deeply lobed leaves with 7-11 narrow leaflets. Zones 5-8.

How to Grow: Hellebores are long-lived, easy-care perennials for flower and foliage interest. Plant them in evenly moist but well-drained, sandy, humus-rich soil in light to partial shade. Most species will tolerate deep summer shade if given sun in spring before tree leaves emerge. Plants thrive in alkaline or slightly acidic soils. *H. argutifolius* is quite drought-tolerant once it is well-established. In early spring, remove any leaves damaged by winter cold. If the stemmed species loose vigor, cut them to the ground to encourage new stems.

Plants take 1-2 years to become established and dislike disturbance. Divide clumps in spring only for purposes of propagation. Self-sown seedlings may appear around the parent plants, especially *H. orientalis*. Sow fresh seed outdoors in spring or summer. Transplant seedlings to their permanent location as soon as they are large enough to move easily. They will flower in 2–5 years.

Landscape Uses: Hellebores bloom throughout the winter and spring, depending on the climate. Try combining them with flowering shrubs that have attractive bark and early flowers; red- and yellow-stemmed dogwoods (*Cornus* spp.), serviceberries (*Amelanchier* spp.), and purple-leaved shrubs are good choices. The smaller bulbs, such as early crocus, reticulated iris (*Iris reticulata*), and species forms of daffodils and tulips, are good companions. The mottled, heart-shaped foliage of spring- or fall-blooming hardy cyclamen (*Cyclamen* spp.) combines nicely with the dark green of the hellebore leaves. Take care not to plant large floppy perennials near hellebores—smothering by exuberant neighbors promotes fungal rot and blocks the sun. ❦

White-flowered Lenten rose (*Helleborus orientalis*) provides a bright accent when planted alone or mixed with the more-common red forms. Good companions include primroses and small bulbs.

Hemerocallis Liliaceae, Lily Family

hem-er-oh-CAL-iss. Daylily. Spring and summer bloom. Full sun to partial shade.

Description: Daylilies are popular garden perennials with a rich and colorful history. The handsome daylily has been cultivated in China for food, medicine, and ornament for over 2,500 years. The flowers, flower buds, and young leaves were eaten as vegetables, and the roots and leaves were used as a pain reliever and for other medicinal purposes.

Daylilies first came to Europe in the mid-sixteenth century. The lemon or yellow daylily (*Hemerocallis lilioasphodelus*) pre-sumably arrived first in Hungary via Mongolia, and the familiar tawny daylily (*H. fulva*) was brought to Venice by Arabs and to Lisbon by Portuguese merchants. Both species took well to their adopted homes and quickly naturalized. By the nineteenth century, new species and hybrids were exported to the United States and Europe from China and Japan.

In America, the tawny daylily is a common site along roadsides, in meadows, and around abandoned homesteads. The persis-

Hemerocallis 'Helen' is just one of the hundreds of daylilies available. As the plant's common name implies, individual flowers last only a day, but hybrids produce dozens of flowers on each stalk, extending the summer bloom season for weeks.

tence and durability of this plant made it an instant sensation for tough spots. It earned the name of "outhouse lily" because of its frequent use with phlox and hollyhocks around outhouse foundations. Tawny daylilies are also called "ditch lilies" because they are so often seen naturalized along roadsides.

Today, daylilies are one of the most popular and varied perennials. Their colorful flowers are composed of 3 broad petals and 3 narrow, petal-like sepals that overlap for a portion of their length. Each flower lasts only a day, but a profusion of new buds keeps plants in bloom for 2–4 weeks. Some cultivars are rebloomers that produce new stalks throughout the season.

Modern hybrids exploit every color in the rainbow except blue. Pure-white has also eluded hybridizers, but many pale-yellow or pink selections come very close. Bicolor and even tricolor forms boast bold stripes, eyes, and bands. Flower form is also variable, including tubular, saucer, and spider shapes with thick or thin petals and smooth, wavy, or frilly margins. Some hybrids have flowers fully 6" across while others have miniature 2" flowers. Height ranges from dwarf cultivars under 1' tall to well over 6', although most cultivars are 2'–3' tall.

Daylily foliage is long and straplike, with a central vein running the entire length, producing a keel in cross-section. The plants grow from stout crowns with thick tuberous roots radiating outward in a circle. Established clumps have multiple crowns and produce an abundance of flowering stalks each season.

H. altissima (al-TISS-ih-muh), tall daylily. Size: 5'–6' tall; leaves to 5' long. This lofty species has fragrant pale-yellow flowers throughout the summer and early fall and is an important plant for hybridizing. The species form is regrettably scarce in gardens. Zones 4–9.

H. aurantiaca (aw-rahn-tee-AH-kuh), orange daylily. Size: 2½′–3′ tall; leaves to 3′ long. A fast-spreading daylily with coarse, persistent foliage and tubular 3″–4″-long orange flowers blushed with purple on the outside. Zones 7–9.

H. citrina (sih-TRY-nuh), citron daylily. Size: 3½′–4′ tall; leaves to 3½′ long. A coarse-leaved species with nocturnal, fragrant, 6″-long lemon-yellow flowers. Zones 5–9.

H. dumortieri (dew-more-tee-ERR-ee), early daylily. Size: 1½′–2′ tall; leaves to 1½′ long. Early daylily is an early-blooming species with fragrant, 2½″-long funnelform brown-tinged yellow flowers held just above or among the foliage. Zones 2–9.

H. fulva (FUL-vuh), tawny daylily. Size: 3′–4′ tall; leaves to 2½′ long. This familiar species has 5″-long rusty orange flowers carried well above the foliage in many-flowered clusters. 'Europa' is a sterile triploid selection with bright-orange flowers. 'Kwanso' has fully double flowers and occasionally variegated foliage. Zones 2–9.

H. lilioasphodelus (lill-ee-oh-as-foe-DELL-us), lemon daylily, yellow daylily. Size: 2½′–3′ tall; leaves to 2′ long. Lemon daylily is a sturdy plant with fragrant 4″-long lemon-yellow flowers held well above the foliage. Zones 3–9.

H. middendorfii (mid-en-DORF-ee-eye), Middendorff daylily. Size: 2′–2½′ tall; leaves to 2′ long. This short species has fragrant 2½″-long yellow-orange flowers held among or just above the leaves. It reblooms throughout the summer. Zones 3–9.

H. minor (MY-nor). Size: 1′–1½′ tall; leaves to 1½′ long. This floriferous dwarf species has fragrant 4″-long yellow flowers held above dense clumps of grassy foliage. Zones 4–9.

H. thunbergii (thun-BERG-ee-eye). Size:

2′–3′ tall; leaves to 2½′ long. The fragrant 3″-long lemon-yellow flowers of this species are carried above the foliage on flattened stems. Zones 4–9.

Hemerocallis hybrids. Modern daylily cultivars are hybrids, arising from crosses between species and earlier cultivars. Today's hybrids fall into 2 main groups: the diploids (having a single complement of chromosomes) and the tetraploids (with an artificially doubled chromosome complement). In addition to their wide range of color, form, and bloom season, tetraploid daylilies offer larger flowers with exceptionally thick petals that help them resist heat and keep their color. In the frenzy to

Hemerocallis 'Hyperion' is an old-fashioned hybrid that has remained popular for decades. The lemon-yellow flowers have a delightful fragrance missing from many newer hybrids.

Daylilies, such as *Hemerocallis* 'Eric the Red', are tough garden plants. They thrive in average to rich soil and bloom for over a month in summer.

create cultivars with broad petals, bicolor bands and blazes, extra frills, and extended bloom, some of the grace of the species and older cultivars has been lost. In fact, many of these older plants are seldom available from nurseries and risk being displaced from American gardens altogether. When planning your perennial garden, consider adding a few of these lovely and useful species daylilies.

If you want to grow cultivars of daylilies, you have hundreds to choose from. To find the ones that are best adapted to your area, consult local nurseries or your state chapter of the American Hemerocallis Society. If you are looking for a specific color, it's best to see the plant before you buy to ensure you get what you want. Catalog descriptions and photographs are often inadequate or misleading.

How to Grow: Grow these tough and adaptable plants in average to rich, well-drained soil in full sun or light shade. Some older cultivars and species tolerate partial shade, but today's hybrids need considerable sun for optimum flowering. Buy containerized or bareroot plants in spring or fall, and set them out with the crown just below soil level. Once established, they spread quickly to form dense, broad clumps. Newer cultivars need daily deadheading to keep them looking their best; older selections drop spent flowers. Most daylilies have excellent foliage that stays tidy all season, but some cultivars may have leaves that yellow; remove these leaves as they appear by grasping them firmly and tugging quickly to snap them off at the base. Remove the entire flowerstalk after the last blossom is spent.

Plants can remain in place for many years, but some hybrids produce so many stalks that the flowers get too crowded if the clumps are not divided every 3 years or so. Lift the entire clump in late summer and pull or cut the thick tangled roots apart.

Daylilies are fairly pest- and disease-free, but aphids and thrips may be a problem on the bloom stalks and flower buds. Soft-bodied aphids are readily detected, but thrips often go unnoticed until the flowers are deformed. Spray with insecticidal soap or a botanical insecticide such as pyrethrins according to label instructions as soon as you notice any damage.

Landscape Uses: Daylilies are favored for large scale and massed plantings because of their adaptability, rapid spread, and extended bloom period. In the home landscape, species and older fast-growing selections are good for massed plantings in tough spots such as banks and swales, or in combination with shrubs and trees. Use daylilies as accent plantings around foundations or with groundcovers. The slower-spreading selections are excellent border plants.

Hesperis Cruciferae, Mustard Family

HESS-per-iss. Dame's Rocket. Spring bloom. Sun or partial shade.

Description: *Hesperis matronalis* (may-troh-NAH-liss), sweet rocket. Size 2′–3′ tall; leaves 2″–4″ long. A beloved spring plant with fragrant, 4-petaled flowers carried in branched, open clusters atop stout leafy stems. The individual flowers are only ½″ across, in bright magenta, pink, or white. The broadly lance-shaped leaves are rich green and somewhat hairy. The biennial or short-lived perennial plants grow from sparsely branching roots. Zones 3–8.

How to Grow: Plant in moist, average to rich soil in sun or partial shade. Self-sown seedlings are prolific and perpetuate the plants from season to season. If plants become too prolific, cut most of them to the ground before they disperse their seeds; let a few self-sow to ensure new plants each year.

Landscape Uses: Naturalize in open woods, meadows, and other open spaces. Grow in the border with tulips, peonies, and irises; include plants such as artemisia and yarrow to fill in as sweet rocket goes dormant. 🍃

The sweet-scented flowers of sweet rocket (*Hesperis matronalis*) open in early spring. Individual plants may be short-lived, but they self-sow freely and form lovely drifts in semishaded woodlands.

Heuchera Saxifragaceae, Saxifrage Family

HUE-ker-uh. Alumroot, Coral Bells. Foliage plant with spring and summer bloom. Full sun to full shade.

Description: *Heuchera* is a large genus of lovely foliage plants, many of which also have showy flowers. The evergreen leaves are rounded, heart-shaped, or triangular and have long slender petioles (leafstalks). The plants grow from a stout woody crown with thin fibrous roots. The ¼″–½″ flowers are borne on narrow, upright stalks.

H. americana (uh-mare-ih-KAH-nuh), American alumroot, rock geranium. Size: 1½′–3′ tall; leaves 8″–10″ long. An open, mounding plant with mottled silvery green heart-shaped leaves and insignificant ¼″ green flowers. The foliage turns ruby-red or purplish in the fall. 'Dale's Strain' has gray-green leaves with silver mottling. Zones 4–9.

Coral bells (*Heuchera sanguinea*) are perfect for edging beds and borders. In summer, the rounded evergreen foliage is topped by open, branched clusters of lovely white, pink, or red flowers.

H. × brizoides (briz-OY-deez), hybrid coral bells. Size: 1′–2½′ tall; leaves 4″–8″ long. This group of hybrids is a result of crosses between *H. sanguinea, H. micrantha,* and *H. americana.* The hybrids vary in size and flower color and are more heat-tolerant than *H. sanguinea* cultivars. 'Chatterbox' has large pink flowers. 'Coral Cloud' is a floriferous coral-pink-flowered selection. 'Fire Sprite' has broad, compact clusters of rose-red flowers. 'June Bride' is a large-flowered white selection. 'Mt. St. Helens' has brick-red flowers. 'Rain of Fire' ('Pluie de Feu') has bright cherry-red flowers. 'White Cloud' is an excellent white cultivar with hundreds of flowers on multiple stalks. Zones 3–8.

H. cylindrica (sill-IN-drih-kuh), poker alumroot. Size: 1′–2½′ tall; leaves 6″–8″ long. Poker alumroot has slender spikes of single ¼″ flowers surrounded by creamy-white inflated tubular petal-like bracts (modified leaves). The hairy, rich green, rounded leaves are arrayed in tight clusters. 'Green Ivory' has showy creamy-white flowers with green bases. Zones 3–8.

H. micrantha (my-KRAN-thuh), small-flowered alumroot. Size: 1′–2′ tall; leaves 8″–12″ long. The ¼″ greenish white flowers are carried in airy clusters above shiny maplelike leaves. 'Palace Purple' is a superior selection of *H. micrantha* var. *diversifolia* with purple-brown foliage. It comes fairly true to seed but is somewhat variable. In warm zones, the leaves fade to bronze by midsummer. Zones 4–8.

H. sanguinea (san-GWIN-ee-uh), coral bells. Size: 1′–1½′ tall; leaves 4″–6″ long. The showiest species of the genus, coral bells have bright-crimson ½″ flowers above gray-green, heart-shaped leaves. 'Alba' has white flowers. 'Bressingham Blaze' has scarlet flowers. 'Splendens' has carmine-red flowers. Zones 3–8.

How to Grow: Plant alumroots and coral bells in moist but well-drained, humus-rich soil in full sun or partial shade. In warm regions, provide shade from hot afternoon sun to keep the leaves from bleaching, especially for 'Palace Purple' heuchera. Plants in heavy shade produce leggy mounds of foliage and seldom flower. Encourage *H. × brizoides* to rebloom by removing spent flowerstalks. Cooler summer temperatures also promote continued bloom.

As the clumps grow, they rise above the ground on woody crowns. Lift clumps every 3 years, remove the oldest woody portions of the crowns, and replant the rosettes into well-prepared soil. Grow the species forms from seed sown inside or outside. Cover the tiny seeds lightly and keep them warm (70°F).

Landscape Uses: Alumroots offer impeccable foliage and airy, often subtle, flowers. Coral bells have similar foliage and showy colorful flowers. Use these versatile plants in rockeries, beds, and borders. 🌿

× Heucherella Saxifragaceae, Saxifrage Family

hue-ker-ELL-uh. Foamy Bells. Spring and summer bloom. Light to full shade.

Description: × *Heucherella tiarelloides* (tee-uh-rel-LOY-deez), foamy bells. Size: 1′–2′ tall; leaves 3″–4″ long. *Heucherella* is a hybrid genus produced from a cross between *Heuchera* and *Tiarella*. This lovely plant bears ½″ pink flowers over tight clumps of triangular evergreen foliage. 'Bridget Bloom' has shell-pink flowers. Zones 3–8.

How to Grow: Plant in moist, humus-rich soil in light to partial shade. In all but the northern zones, foamy bells require shade to keep the foliage from burning, but plants will not flower well in deep season-long shade. Divide every third year in fall or early spring. The flowers are sterile and do not set seed.

Landscape Uses: Combine with flowering shrubs or with spring bulbs, woodland wildflowers, and ferns. Plant in the filtered shade of serviceberries (*Amelanchier* spp.), silverbells (*Halesia* spp.), American yellowwood (*Cladrastis lutea*), and other flowering trees. 🍂

Foamy bells, such as × *Heucherella* 'Bridget Bloom', combine the triangular foliage of foamflowers (*Tiarella* spp.) with the pink flowers of coral bells (*Heuchera* spp.).

Hibiscus Malvaceae, Mallow Family

hy-BISS-kus. Hibiscus, Rose Mallow. Summer bloom. Full sun to light shade.

Description: The shrublike hibiscus bear thick erect stalks that arise from a woody crown with deep, spreading roots. The palmately lobed leaves are arrayed alternately on the stems. Some species have deeply cut, spidery leaves; others have broad, maplelike leaves. The stems are crowned with open clusters of huge 5-petaled flowers, each with a central bottlebrush that bears the male and female reproductive structures. Individual flowers last only 1 day but open in succession for 3–6 weeks. The seed capsules are attractive in fall and winter.

Hibiscus coccineus (cock-SIN-ee-us), scarlet rose mallow. Size: 5′–8′ tall; leaves 10″–12″ long. This stately plant has broad, deeply incised palmately lobed or divided leaves, often with red-tinged margins. The 6″ saucer-shaped flowers are bright-red. Zones 6–10.

H. militaris (mill-ih-TAR-iss), soldier rose

The flowers of 'Disco Belle' rose mallow (*Hibiscus moscheutos* 'Disco Belle') last only a day, but new buds keep the plants in flower throughout July and August.

mallow. Size: 4'–7' tall; leaves 4"–6" long. This plant has beautiful triangular or narrowly heart-shaped leaves with 2 shallow side lobes and a long central lobe. The 5"–6" flowers are white to pale-pink with a crimson eye. Zones 4–9.

    H. moscheutos (moss-SHOO-toes), com-mon rose mallow. Size: 4'–8' tall; leaves 6"–8" long. This popular perennial has broadly oval leaves with 3–5 shallow lobes and 6"–8" white flowers with red centers. The subspecies *palustris,* marsh mallow, has 3-lobed leaves and solid white, pink, or rose flowers. Many hybrids have been made combining the compact growth of this species and its color variants with the red flowers of *H. coccineus.* The hybrids have huge 8"–10" flowers in pure-white, white with a crimson eye, pink, rose, and bright-red. Zone 4 (with protection) or Zones 5–10.

    How to Grow: Grow hibiscus in evenly moist, humus-rich soil in full sun or light shade. Plant young plants in spring or fall, leaving 3'–4' between each to allow for their eventual spread. Established plants can be divided, but this requires a strong back and a sharp spade to cut the clumps apart. Propagate by tip cuttings in July; remove the flower buds and reduce the leaf size by half unless you have a mist bed. Sow seeds outdoors in fall or inside in late winter. Seedlings germinate in 1–2 weeks and may flower the same season.

    Landscape Uses: The bold hybrid hibiscus are best used alone as accent plants against walls or hedges or as eye-catching focal points in large perennial gardens. Treat them as shrubs. ❦

Hosta Liliaceae, Lily Family

HOSS-tuh. Hosta, Plantain Lily, Funkia. Foliage plant with summer and fall bloom. Light to full shade.

    Description: Hostas are bold, dramatic foliage plants for shaded gardens. The leafy clumps vary greatly in size from 6" to over 3' in height. The leaves arise directly from a stout crown with thick spidery white roots. Each leaf has a long furrowed or cupped petiole (leaf-stalk) and a broad heart- or lance-shaped blade with deep, distinctive venation. Leaf surfaces may be puckered between the veins, and the entire blade may cup upward or droop outward toward the tip. Leaf margins vary from smooth to wavy. The outstanding attribute of hostas is their leaf color, ranging from deep-green through chartreuse, yellow, and gold, to blue. Many have leaves variously edged, striped, or irregularly patterned with white, cream, yellow, or sea-green. The spike-like bloom stalks may be up to 3′ tall. The bell-shaped or funnelform, white, lilac, or purple flowers have 6 or more spreading lobes. The blooms of some species are delight-fully scented.

Hostas are native to Japan, China, and Korea, where they grow in moist woodlands, on open grasslands, and along stream banks and river courses. Many species, including *Hosta plantaginea* and *H. ventricosa,* have been in cultivation for hundreds of years. Other species, which may actually be hybrids, are known only from gardens and are not found in the wild. Because of this long history of cultivation in Asia, and more recently in Europe and North America, the nomenclature is confused, with some cultivars ascribed to 2 or more species. Many hostas have such uncertain parentage that they are not listed with any species name.

H. crispula (KRIS-pew-luh), curled leaf hosta. Size: 2′–3′ tall; leaves to 7″ long. A slow-growing species having dense clumps of elongated, white-edged, heart-shaped leaves with drooping tips and wavy margins. The 2″ flowers are deep-lilac, somewhat pendulous, and are borne in midsummer on open spikes. Zones 3–8.

H. decorata (deck-or-AH-tuh), blunt hosta. Size: 1½′–2′ tall; leaves to 8″ long. This rhizomatous hosta spreads rapidly to form wide clumps of broadly heart-shaped leaves with creamy-white edges and slightly wavy

Use yellow-variegated *Hosta montana* 'Aurea-marginata' to brighten up a shady spot along your foundation or under the canopy of large trees. The plants also produce spikes of pale-lilac flowers in late summer.

Bold, sun-tolerant August lily (*Hosta plantaginea*) produces dense spikes of sweet-smelling white flowers in late summer. Ornamental grasses and late-flowering perennials are good companions.

margins. The 2′ flower spikes bear 2″ violet flowers in mid- to late summer. Zones 3–8.

H. elata (ee-LAY-tuh). Size: 2½′–3′ tall; leaves to 10″ long. Long petioles support the elongated, heart-shaped leaves of this species. The leaf margins are quite wavy and the surface is a glossy deep-green. The flower spike bears 2½″ blue-violet, funnelform flowers with reflexed lobes in early summer. Zones 3–8.

H. fortunei (for-TOON-ee-eye), Fortune's hosta. Size: 1′–2′ tall; leaves to 9″ long. The elongated heart-shaped leaves are green to gray-green with long, deeply furrowed and winged petioles. The 1½″ pale-lilac flowers are gathered toward the top of the stout scapes. Below each flower is a shovel-shaped, deep-violet leafy bract (modified leaf). Many excellent cultivars are available. 'Albo-picta' (also sold as 'Aureo-maculata') has yellow blades with green margins. The leaves turn green as the season progresses. 'Aurea' ('Albo-picta Aurea') has bright-yellow leaves that fade to yellow-green in summer. 'Albo-marginata' ('Marginata-alba') has large leaves with broad irregular white margins. 'Aoki' has gray-green foliage similar to the species. 'Aureo-marginata' has large glaucous green leaves with yellow margins. 'Gold Standard' has light-gold leaves edged with green. 'Hyacinthina' has large gray-green leaves. Zones 3–8.

H. lancifolia (lan-sih-FOE-lee-uh), narrow-leaved hosta, lance-leaved hosta. Size: 1½′–2′ tall; leaves to 7″ long. An old venerable hosta with glossy green, broadly lance-shaped leaves and floriferous spikes of deep-lilac flowers in late summer. 'Kabitan' has bright-yellow leaves with narrow green edges; it seldom flowers. Zones 3–8.

H. montana (mahn-TAN-uh). Size: 2½′–3′ tall; leaves to 10″. This species is often considered to be synonymous with *H. elata* but may be distinct. Plants have broadly oval to heart-shaped leaves with puckered surfaces. 'Aurea-marginata' is a popular cultivar with wide green leaves with wavy gold margins. Zones 3–8.

H. plantaginea (plan-teh-jih-NEE-uh), August lily, fragrant hosta. Size: 2′–2½′ tall; leaves to 10″ long. The large broad heart-shaped leaves are bright, glossy green. They act as a lovely backdrop to the sparkling white, fragrant 5″ flowers that crowd toward the tips of the stout leafy flowerstalks. 'Aphrodite' has exquisite double flowers. 'Honeybells' has trumpetlike, pale-lavender flowers with spreading, twisted lobes. 'Royal Standard' is similar to the species with white flowers. Zones 3–8.

H. sieboldiana (see-bold-ee-AH-nuh), Siebold's hosta. Size: 2½′–3′ tall; leaves to 1½′ long. A large hosta with stiff heart-shaped blue-green leaves and 2″ pale-lilac flowers held in leafy clusters just above the foliage. 'Elegans' has broad heart-shaped blue-green leaves with a puckered surface. The flowers vary in color from light-violet to white. 'Frances Williams' (also sold as 'Aureo-marginata') bears huge gray-green leaves with wide dark-yellow margins; the plants are slow to reach their mature size. Zones 3–8.

H. sieboldii (see-BOLD-ee-eye), seersucker hosta. Size: 2'–2½' tall; leaves to 6" long. This species is similar to *H. lancifolia* with long, pointed green leaves edged in white. The late-summer 2" lilac-colored flowers are evenly spaced along the bloom stalk. 'Louisa' is a slow-growing cultivar with a broader white edge. Zones 3–8.

H. × tardiana (tar-dee-AH-nuh). Size: 1'–2½' tall; leaves to 1' long. This hybrid species was produced from crosses between *H. sieboldiana* 'Elegans' and *H. tardiflora*. Most cultivars have narrow heart-shaped or oval waxy blue-green leaves and lilac flowers crowded into dense clusters and held above the foliage. 'Halcyon' has deep blue-gray waxy spear-shaped leaves. 'Blue Wedgewood' has wedge-shaped deep blue-gray foliage. 'Hadspen Heron' is a small plant with narrow blue foliage. Zones 3–8.

H. tardiflora (tar-dih-FLOOR-uh). Size: 10"–12" tall; leaves to 6" long. A small hosta with lance-shaped dark-green leaves and 1½" pale-purple flowers in autumn. Zones 3–8.

H. undulata (un-djew-LAH-tuh), wavy-leaved hosta. Size: 1'–1½' tall; leaves to 6" long. A variable species known only in cultivation, this group of plants is probably of hybrid origin. The leaves are narrowly oval to lance-shaped, with wavy margins. The 2" light-purple flowers are held high above the foliage on leafy stalks. 'Albo-marginata' has leaves with a narrow creamy-white band around them. 'Erromena' has shiny green leaves.

'Undulata' has white and cream leaves with green margins. 'Univittata' is a vigorous grower with green leaves striped down the center with white. Zones 3–8.

H. ventricosa (ven-trih-KOH-suh), blue hosta. Size: 2'–3' tall; leaves to 9" long. Blue hosta is a popular species with broad, heart-shaped dark-green leaves and 2" blue-violet, funnelform flowers with wide-flaring lobes. 'Aureo-maculata' has creamy-yellow stripes and speckles on the leaves that fade to green in summer. 'Aureo-marginata' has leaves with a creamy-white border. Zones 3–9.

Hosta hybrids. A myriad of hostas of mixed or uncertain parentage is available from garden centers and mail-order nurseries. Cultivars vary in color and in stature from miniatures with leaves the size of a fingernail to those with leaves fully 2' long. All are extremely hardy, usually rated for Zones 3–8.

Use the huge blue-green leaves of *Hosta sieboldiana* 'Elegans' as accents in lightly shaded spots. These bold plants take 3 to 5 years to reach their mature size. They combine well with spring-blooming bulbs and wildflowers.

How to Grow: Hostas are tough, versatile, and adaptable plants. They perform best in evenly moist, humus-rich soil in light to full shade. Plants with thick and waxy leaves are better adapted to dry soil conditions than thin-leaved ones, but none of them are able to thrive or even survive with dry or thin soil. Filtered sun encourages the best leaf color, especially on gold- and blue-leaved forms. The green-leaved types are the most shade-tolerant. Most species need protection from too much direct sunshine, especially hot afternoon sun. This is most critical in areas with high summer temperatures. Variegated cultivars, especially those with a lot of white in the leaves, burn very easily. Blue-leaved types will bleach to green with too much direct sun.

Hostas emerge late in the season but quickly unfurl to fill their allotted space. They grow slowly and may take 2–4 years to attain their full size (and even longer for the largest species and cultivars). Allow plenty of room when you plant to accommodate for their mature size. Small selections spread 3 times as wide as they are tall. Medium-size hostas spread twice their height, and the larger ones are at least as wide as they are tall.

Hostas are disease-resistant, but their succulent leaves are no match for slugs and snails. Keep a watchful eye on the emerging leaves, and pick off the assailants as you find them. Use saucers of beer to trap the slugs, or surround plants with a ring of diatomaceous earth to exclude the pests.

Landscape Uses: Hostas are the mainstays of the shaded garden. Plant them with ferns, wildflowers, and shade-loving perennials on the north side of a house or under the canopy of large trees. If the soil is rich and moist, hostas will thrive in the darkest recesses between buildings, under carports, or in narrow passages. Use them as specimens or accents on the shaded side of a shrub border or under flowering trees. Combine their lovely foliage with sedges (*Carex* spp.), ferns such as ostrich fern (*Matteuccia struthiopteris*) and lady fern (*Athyrium filix-femina*), and foliage perennials such as lungworts (*Pulmonaria* spp.), Siberian bugloss (*Brunnera macrophylla*), and wild ginger (*Asarum* spp.). Use medium-size hostas as groundcovers in front of flowering shrubs or in massed plantings of mixed leaf colors and shapes under shade trees. Plant the small-leaved selections in rock gardens or in containers and trough gardens. Take advantage of the fact that hostas emerge late, and plant them with spring-flowering bulbs and ephemeral wildflowers such as toothworts (*Dentaria* spp.), spring beauties (*Claytonia* spp.), and trout lilies (*Erythronium* spp.). As the early bloomers are dying away and looking shabby, the newly emerging hosta leaves will hide them from sight. 🍂

The crisp, white-edged leaves of medium-size *Hosta* 'Francee' are perfect for planting on the edges of beds and along walkways. Or try them in masses as a groundcover under flowering trees.

Houttuynia   Sauraceae, Lizard's Tail Family

hoo-TIE-nee-uh. Houttuynia. Foliage plant with late-spring bloom. Full sun to partial shade.

Description: *Houttuynia cordata* (core-DAH-tuh), houttuynia. Size: 1½'–2' tall; leaves 2"–3" long. This fast-spreading rhizomatous perennial forms broad clumps of erect stems clothed in heart-shaped bright-green leaves. A thick dense spike of petal-less flowers with fuzzy yellow stamens (male reproductive structures) rises from the center of 4 white, petal-like bracts. The white flowers are ½" long and are borne as the leaves unfold. 'Chameleon' has attractive leaves irregularly banded with white, pink, and red. Zones 3–8.

How to Grow: Plant in constantly moist or wet, humus-rich soil in full sun or light shade. The plants will grow in standing water or moist garden soil with equal vigor. The clumps spread rapidly by creeping rhizomes; pull out or divide plants as necessary to avert a full-scale takeover. Containerized plants placed in 1½' of water with the crowns just below the water surface often remain under control. Thin pots every year or two and replenish the soil. Propagate by division or stem cuttings taken in early summer.

Landscape Uses: Choose houttuynia for moist soil or pondside gardens. Combine it with other vigorous plants such as ostrich fern (*Matteuccia struthiopteris*), water irises (*Iris pseudacorus* and other species), large-leaved hostas, and sedges (*Carex* spp.). 🌿

Houttuynia cordata 'Chameleon' is a vigorous perennial that is popular for its colorful leaves. It spreads rapidly in moist or wet soils and will grow in full sun or light shade. To control it, sink containers in a pool or pond so the roots are confined.

Iberis Cruciferae, Mustard Family

eye-BEER-iss. Candytuft. Early-spring bloom. Full sun to light shade.

Early-blooming perennial candytuft (*Iberis sempervirens*) is perfect for planting in a rock garden with spring bulbs or as an edging along walks or walls.

Description: Candytufts are lovely long-flowering perennials for the spring garden. These mounding to mat-forming subshrubs have fibrous roots and persistent woody stem bases. The stems are densely clothed with narrow evergreen leaves and crowned with flat clusters of 4-petaled white flowers.

Iberis saxatilis (sacks-uh-TILL-iss), rock candytuft. Size: 3″–6″ tall; leaves to ¾″ long. A low plant that forms broad round clumps with brittle stems clothed in needle-like leaves. The ½″-wide white late-winter or early-spring flowers often fade to purple. Zones 2–7.

I. sempervirens (sem-per-VY-renz), perennial candytuft. Size: 6″–12″ tall; leaves to 1½″ long. In early spring the mounded clumps are shrouded in a profusion of ¼″-wide white flowers in tight round clusters. The persistent stems bear deep-green leaves. 'Autumn Snow' is 8″–10″ tall with larger clear-white flowers in spring and again in fall. 'Little Gem' is a floriferous compact grower only 5"–8" tall. 'Pygmaea' is a low spreader with 4"–5" stems. 'Snowflake' is compact and floriferous with flat 2"–3" inflorescences. Zones 3–9.

How to Grow: Plant candytufts in average, well-drained soil in full sun or light shade. Space plants 1'–1½' apart in informal plantings to accommodate their eventual spread; place them 6" apart if you are using them as an edger or as a formal border planting. Compact cultivars are best for this purpose. Shear plants back by ⅓ after flowering to encourage compact growth and good foliage. Prune them hard, at least ⅔ back, every 2–3 years to encourage production of fresh stems and to promote flower production. Plants seldom need division. The prostrate stems may root as they spread and are easy to transplant. Take tip cuttings in early summer; they will root in 2–3 weeks. Or sow seeds outdoors in spring or fall.

Landscape Uses: Candytufts are consummate edging plants. Their low, compact growth, early flowers, and evergreen foliage make them perfect for planting along stairs or walks or in the front of beds and borders. They perform well in soil pockets between rocks in a wall or planted just behind a wall where they will spill over and soften the edge. In rock gardens, combine them with spring bulbs, bleeding hearts (*Dicentra* spp.), basket-of-gold (*Aurinia saxatilis*), rock cresses (*Arabis* spp.), and purple rock cress (*Aubrieta deltoidea*). In the border, plant candytufts with tulips, columbines (*Aquilegia* spp.), forget-me-nots (*Myosotis* spp.), and other spring plants. 🍂

Iris   Iridicaeae, Iris Family

EYE-ris. Iris. Spring and summer bloom. Full sun to open shade.

Description: Irises are some of the most beautiful and popular perennials available to gardeners. The genus takes its name from Iris of Greek mythology, who was the messenger to Juno, the goddess of marriage. Legend holds that Iris traveled over the rainbow to reach Earth, and from her footsteps sprang flowers arrayed in the colors of the rainbow. The iris has been revered since the sixth century, and it became an icon for nobility in the 1100s when King Louis VII of France adopted the iris as his Fleur-de-Louis, now known as fleur-de-lis.

The iris flower has an unusual construction. It is composed of 6 segments: 3 falls and 3 standards. The 3 segments known as the falls ring the outside of the flower. They are held flat or are reflexed downward. Each one has a white or yellow blaze at its base, or a fuzzy beard in place of the blaze. The inner ring of 3 segments, called the standards, is erect or just slightly elevated above the falls. Most species have very showy, colorful standards and falls, but in some the standards are reduced in size or absent. The final component of the complex flower is a triad of columns containing the male and female reproductive structures. These columns curve out of the center of the flower and lie directly above the falls. Iris flowers vary widely in color, including white, pink, red, purple, blue, yellow, and brown. Different species flower from winter through summer. Many are excellent for cutting.

Iris leaves are either grassy, flat, and straplike or curled and cylindrical. They vary in size,

Diminutive reticulated iris (*Iris reticulata*) blooms in earliest spring and disappears for another season by summer. Try it in a rock garden or with a groundcover such as common periwinkle (*Vinca minor*).

according to species, from 3″ to well over 3′ long and may be deciduous or evergreen. Plants grow from thick creeping rhizomes, fibrous roots, or bulbs. An iris exists for every garden situation: sun or shade, moist soil or dry soil, early bloom or late bloom. Hundreds of hybrids and cultivars are available, developed from over 100 species.

Iris bucharica (boo-KAH-ree-kuh), Bokhara iris. Size: 1′–1½′ tall; leaves 8″–12″ long. A bulbous iris with thick stalks and alternate leaves. The 2″-wide spring flowers have yellow falls and cream standards. Plants go completely dormant by midsummer. Zones 4–9.

I. cristata (kris-TAH-tuh), crested iris. Size: 4″–8″ tall; leaves to 8″ long. A rhizomatous iris with short broad leaves and 2″-wide flattened sky-blue spring flowers with a yellow-and-white blaze. The variety *alba* has white flowers. Zones 3–9.

I. danfordiae (dan-FOR-dee-eye), Danford iris. Size: 4″–6″ tall; leaves to 1′ long. A bulbous

iris with curled cylindrical leaves and 1½″-wide yellow late-winter flowers. The leaves elongate immediately after flowering and disappear by summer. Zones 5–9.

I. douglasiana (dug-less-ee-AH-nuh), Douglas' iris. Size: 2′–2½′ tall; leaves to 2′ long. A strap-leaved plant with 4″-wide blue, pink, or white flowers resembling a Siberian iris. Zones 6–8.

The Pacific hybrids were produced by crossing Douglas' iris with other western natives such as *I. tenax* and *I. innominata*. They are softly colored in shades of blue and purple and grow best in well-drained soils in Zones 4–9 (hardiness varies).

I. ensata (en-SAH-tuh), Japanese iris (includes plants listed as *I. kaempferi*). Size: 2′–2½′ tall; leaves to 2′ long. Wild forms have strap-shaped leaves and summer flowers with small standards and broad floppy falls in blue or violet. Exquisite hybrids have been produced through years of selection. They have round, flat flowers up to 8″ wide with broad, reflexed standards and wide falls in a rainbow of blues, purples, pinks, reds, white, and bicolors. 'Moonlight Waves' has single white blooms. 'Pink Lady' has double rose-pink flowers. 'Wine Ruffles' bears large wine-red flowers. Zones 4–9.

I. foetidissima (fet-ih-DIS-ih-muh), stinking iris. Size: 1½′–2′ tall; leaves to 1½′ long. This species has evergreen strap-shaped leaves that emit a foul odor when crushed. The 2½″-wide blue-gray flowers fade to large pods that split in fall to reveal showy scarlet seeds. Zones 6–9.

I. fulva (FUL-vuh), copper iris. Size: 3′–4′ tall; leaves to 4′ long. An early-summer iris with 3½″-wide red flowers and strap-shaped leaves. The Louisiana hybrids come in a wide range of blues and reds and are popular with southern gardeners who must contend with extreme heat. Zones 4 (with winter protection) or 5–10.

I. histrioides (his-tree-OY-deez), harput iris. Size: 6″–9″ tall; leaves to 9″ long. An early-spring bulbous iris similar to *I. reticulata* with 4″-wide bright-blue flowers. 'Major' has deep-blue flowers. Zones 5–9.

I. missouriensis (mih-zore-ee-EN-sis), Missouri iris, Rocky mountain iris. Size: 1′–2′ tall; leaves to 1½′ long. A delicate iris with strap-shaped leaves and 3″-wide white to blue flowers in summer with slender standards and falls. Zones 3–8.

I. pallida (PAL-ih-duh), sweet iris. Size: 2′–3′ tall; leaves to 2′ long. This iris has stiff fans of gray-green foliage and tall stalks bearing fragrant light-violet 2½″ flowers with broad standards and falls. 'Variegata' (also sold as 'Aurea-variegata' or 'Zebra') has cream-variegated foliage. Zones 4–8.

I. pseudacorus (sue-DACK-or-us), yellow flag, yellow flag iris. Size: 3′–4′ tall; leaves to 4′ long. A stout coarse iris with stiff straplike leaves and 2½″-wide bright-yellow flowers in spring. 'Flore-Pleno' has unusual double flowers. 'Variegata' has leaves striped with yellow. Zones 4–9.

I. pumila (PEW-mill-uh), dwarf bearded iris. Size: 4″–8″ tall; leaves to 8″ long. A small creeping iris with 2″-wide bearded flowers in shades of blue and purple. This species is an important parent of dwarf bearded hybrids. Zones 3–8.

I. reticulata (reh-tick-you-LAH-tuh), reticulated iris. Size: 4″–6″ tall; leaves 1′–1½′ long. This small bulbous iris blooms in late winter or early spring. After the fragrant 2″-wide blue to purple flowers fade, the cylindrical leaves elongate until the plant goes dormant in summer. 'Cantab' has pale-blue flowers. 'Harmony' has royal-blue flowers. 'Joyce' has sky-blue flowers. 'J.S. Dijt' has red-violet flowers. Zones 5–9.

I. sibirica (sigh-BEER-ih-kuh), Siberian iris. Size: 1′–3′ tall; leaves to 3′ long. Siberian

Combine tall bearded iris, such as yellow-flowered *Iris* 'Zeus', with bushy plants, such as Caucasus geranium (*Geranium ibericum*), that continue flowering after the irises finish their brief but glorious flower display.

irises are popular garden plants for their foliage and flowers. Tidy clumps of narrow, sword-shaped foliage stay attractive all season. The 2″–3″-wide flowers are borne in early summer. They have upright standards and broad flat or reflexed falls. Colors vary from blues and purples to yellow, white, and bicolors. Hundreds of cultivars are available. 'Ego' is an excellent blue bicolor with good foliage. 'Ewen' is a lovely wine-red tetraploid. 'My Love' is a deep sky-blue rebloomer. 'Summer Sky' has pale ice-blue flowers. 'White Swirl' is a good pure-white. Zones 2–9.

I. tectorum (teck-TOUR-um), roof iris. Height 1′–1½′ tall; leaves to 1½′ long. A rhizomatous iris with broad fans of wide strap-shaped foliage. The somewhat flattened 5″-wide flowers are deep lavender-blue with dark blotches and are borne in late spring. 'Alba' has white flowers. Zones 4–9.

I. unguicularis (un-gwik-you-LAH-ris), winter iris. Size: 10″–12″ tall; leaves to 1′ long. This early-blooming iris has 2″-wide violet, blue, or white flowers and dense tufts of grassy, evergreen foliage. Zones 7–9.

I. versicolor (VER-suh-kuh-ler), blue flag iris. Size: 1½′–3′ tall; leaves to 3′ long. Blue flags are stout, leafy irises with bold strap-shaped leaves and 3″-wide, bright blue-violet flowers in early summer. This northern species is similar to the southern blue flag *I. virginica*. Both are widely grown. Zones 2–8.

I. xiphium (ZIH-fee-um), Spanish iris. Size: 1′–1½′ tall; leaves to 2′ long. Spanish iris is a bulbous spring-blooming iris with 4″–5″-wide flowers that has been extensively hybridized to produce the popular hybrids known as "Dutch iris," often sold under the name *I.* × *hollandica.* Although the species are attractive in their own right, most American gardeners know only the colorful Dutch hybrids. Zones 6–9.

Iris bearded hybrids. The hybrid bearded irises are among the most popular and well-loved garden plants. They have been cultivated in Europe for centuries and are divided into 3 main groups based on their size and species composition.

Group 1 (the Barbata-Elatior Group) contains the tall bearded irises. These familiar garden irises originated from crosses between *I. germanica* (thought to be a natural or garden hybrid) with *I. pallida, I. variegata, I. mesopotamica,* and *I. trojana.* They are characterized by fans of broad, pointed leaves growing from thick rhizomes. The flowerstalks must be taller than 28″ to be classified as tall bearded. The late-spring and summer flowers

Crested irises, such as *Iris cristata* var. *alba,* make a dense spring-blooming groundcover in sun or partial shade. Moist soil encourages the foliage to remain neat all season long.

have broad, upright standards and broad, drooping bearded falls. They are intensely fragrant, quite showy, and come in a wide range of colors, including white, brown, pink, blue, purple, and yellow. 'Beverly Sills' has coral-pink ruffled flowers with orange beards. 'Gay Parasol' has white standards and rose-purple falls. 'Titan's Glory' bears large deep purple-blue blooms. 'Lacy Snowflake' has white flowers.

Group 2 (the Barbata-Media Group) contains the intermediate bearded irises. These plants are sometimes listed as *I.* × *intermedia*. They were produced from hybrids between *I. chamaeiris* and *I. germanica*. Their height must fall between 15″ and 28″ to be placed in this group; otherwise, they are similar to tall beardeds. This group is further divided into intermediate, table, and border irises. 'Raspberry Blush' has pink flowers with a raspberry-colored accent. 'Bold Print' has white flowers edged in purple. 'Solo' bears creamy-yellow flowers with yellow centers.

Group 3 (the Barbata-Nana Group) contains the dwarf bearded irises. These plants are miniature versions of the above groups produced by crossing taller hybrids with *I. pumila*. They must be less than 15″ tall to be placed in this group. This group is further divided into standard dwarf (10″–15″) and miniature dwarf (4″–10″) categories. 'Golden Eyelet' grows only 5″ tall and bears bright yellow-orange flowers. 'Ornament' grows to 13″, with ruffled blue flowers marked with purple. 'Rain Dance' reaches 11″ with clear-blue flowers.

How to Grow: Irises are as varied in their requirements for growth as they are in their size and form. Most species (including *I. douglasiana, I. pallida, I. pumila, I. tectorum,* and the Pacific and bearded hybrids) perform well in full sun to light shade in evenly moist but well-drained, humus-rich soil. Many irises

Tall bearded irises such as *Iris* 'Arctic Dawn' are beloved for their exquisite form and heady fragrance.

that are native to moist or wet soil environments will also grow well under the above conditions; *I. sibirica, I. pseudacorus, I. versicolor, I. missouriensis,* and the Louisiana hybrids fall into this group. *I. ensata* needs wet soil in spring and summer but needs drier soil in winter. Most of these species are widely adaptable to neutral or slightly acid soils. *I. ensata* and *I. versicolor* need acid soil. Woodland species such as *I. cristata* and *I. foetidissima* prefer rich, moist, slightly acidic soil in light to partial shade.

The bulbous species such as *I. bucharica, I. danfordiae, I. histrioides, I. reticulata, I. xiphium,* and Dutch hybrid irises prefer full sun for best bloom but are suitable for sites that get sun in the spring or shade in the

Siberian irises such as *Iris sibirica* 'My Love' produce beautiful blooms atop clumps of attractive, sword-shaped foliage. Some cultivars will rebloom if the bloom stalks are removed after the flowers fade.

summer after they have gone dormant. Give them moist, rich soil in spring but let them dry out in summer, especially *I. danfordiae.* In many areas of the country, it's best to grow the bulbous species as annuals or short-lived perennials because they do not rebloom well.

Irises are susceptible to a number of problems. Rhizome rot and bacterial soft rot are two bacterial diseases that destroy irises from the ground up. Good culture is the best way to avoid problems. Match the species with their optimum soil moisture—planting rhizomatous species, such as the bearded irises, in overly moist soil or burying the rhizome below the soil are sure ways to invite diseases. Leaf spot is another prevalent problem. Remove and discard leaves with brown or black spots as soon as you see them to reduce the chances of future outbreaks.

Iris borer is a common pest. The adult moth lays eggs on the foliage, and the resulting larvae travel down the leaves into the rhizome, where they eat until nothing is left but a hollow shell. They also spread bacterial infections from plant to plant. Good culture is again the best prevention. Remove spent foliage in fall or early spring. The young borers tunnel through the leaves leaving dark streaks in their wake—watch for signs of damage. Remove infested leaves and destroy them, or squash the borers in their tunnels with your fingers. Dig up infected plants and destroy the fat pink grubs by hand. Replant the unaffected portions.

Propagate irises by dividing them after flowering in summer or early fall. Replant immediately in well-prepared soil. Bearded iris hybrids need frequent division to keep them vigorous; remove and discard old portions of their thick rhizomes and replant with the top half of the rhizome above the soil line. Most other species need division only when they become crowded or they start producing fewer flowers. Sow fresh seed outdoors in summer or fall; germination will occur the following spring. Many hybrids will not produce viable seed.

Landscape Uses: Bearded irises, *I. sibirica,* and other irises with similar cultural requirements are well-suited to beds and borders with spring and early-summer perennials. Combine their strap-shaped foliage with rounded forms and bold flowers. Choose the moisture-loving species for planting on the sides of ponds with ferns, hostas, and other lush perennials. Plant the smaller bulbous species, dwarf bearded irises, and *I. cristata* in rock gardens or at the front of the border. ❦

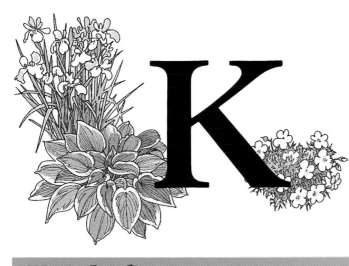

Kniphofia   Liliaceae, Lily Family

nee-FOFE-ee-uh. Torch Lily, Red-Hot Poker. Late-spring and summer bloom. Full sun.

Description: *Kniphofia uvaria* (you-VAH-ree-uh), common torch lily. Size: 3′–5′ tall; leaves to 3′ long. Dense 1′–2′ spikes of tubular 1″–2″ flowers bloom over evergreen tufts of stiff narrow gray-green leaves. The lowest flowers on the spikes are yellow; the upper ones are red. Hybrid cultivars include 'Little Maid' (2′ tall with salmon and white flowers) and 'Primrose Beauty' (3′ tall with light-yellow flowers). Zones 5–9.

How to Grow: Plant 2′ apart in average to rich, very well-drained soil in full sun. Established clumps are best left undisturbed. Propagate by removing a few crowns from the edge of an established clump in fall. Sow seed indoors in winter, and place the pots or flats in a refrigerator for 6 weeks before moving them to a warm, bright place. Seeds sprout in 3–6 weeks.

Landscape Uses: Torch lilies provide bold and colorful vertical forms for the late-spring and summer garden. 🍂

Kniphofia 'Royal Standard' and other hybrid torch lilies make an arresting late-summer show in sunny gardens. Try combining the softer coral- and yellow-flowered cultivars with baby's-breath, phlox, boltonia (*Boltonia asteroides*), and Persian nepeta (*Nepeta mussinii*).

Lamiastrum Labiatae, Mint Family

lay-me-AS-trum. Yellow Archangel. Foliage plant with spring bloom. Partial to full shade.

For a bright groundcover in dry shade, you can't beat variegated yellow archangel (*Lamiastrum galeobdolon* 'Variegatum'). Spring bulbs and early wildflowers emerge easily through the mass of stems to create a lovely combination.

Description: *Lamiastrum galeobdolon* (gay-lee-OB-doe-lon), yellow archangel. Size: 8″–14″ tall; leaves 1″–3″ long. Yellow archangel is a fast-creeping, stoloniferous groundcover with oval to triangular leaves spotted with silver. The ½″–1″ yellow flowers are borne in spring in whorls around the leaf axils. 'Herman's Pride' has striking silver variegation and is a less aggressive spreader. 'Variegatum' has a silver V in the middle of the leaf, while the edge and midvein are green. Zones 4–9.

How to Grow: Plant in average to rich, well-drained soil in partial to full shade. In northern zones, plants tolerate some direct sun. Divide clumps as they spread out of bounds, or pull plants from places where they don't belong. Take tip cuttings in spring or summer.

Landscape Uses: Yellow archangel is a tough fast-spreading groundcover for difficult spots, such as dry shade. Combine it with spring bulbs and early wildflowers, or with ferns on moist sites. 🍂

Lamium   Labiatae, Mint Family

LAY-mee-um. Lamium, Dead Nettle. Foliage plant with spring and summer bloom. Partial to full shade.

Description: *Lamium maculatum* (mack-you-LAY-tum), spotted lamium, spotted dead nettle. Size: 6″–12″ tall; leaves 1″–2″ long. Spotted dead nettle is a creeping, open groundcover with oval, silver-mottled or striped leaves and 1″ rose-pink flowers. 'Beacon Silver' has silver leaves with a thin green edge and rose-pink flowers; 'White Nancy' is similar but has white flowers. 'Shell Pink' has pink flowers. Zones 3–8.

How to Grow: Plant in moist, well-drained, humus-rich soil in partial shade. In warmer regions, shear plants after flowering to keep them compact. Propagate by division in spring or fall or by tip cuttings in spring and summer.

Landscape Uses: Choose spotted lamium for semishaded spots under flowering shrubs, evergreens, or high-canopied shade trees. Combine it with spring-flowering bulbs. 🍂

Choose a groundcover planting of 'White Nancy' spotted lamium (*Lamium maculatum* 'White Nancy') to brighten up a shaded spot under flowering shrubs or with hostas and ferns.

Lavandula   Labiatae, Mint Family

lav-AN-djew-luh. Lavender. Summer bloom. Full sun to light shade.

Description: *Lavandula angustifolia* (an-gus-tih-FOE-lee-uh), lavender. Size: 2′–3′ tall; leaves 2″–2½″ long. Besides being an important herb for perfumes and potpourri, lavender is a lovely garden ornamental. The woody stems are clothed in aromatic, gray-green, needle-like evergreen leaves. In summer, 5″-long spikes of ½″ lavender-blue flowers are held in profusion above the foliage. 'Dwarf Blue' is compact (1′ tall) with dark-blue

flowers. 'Hidcote' grows 15″ tall with very fragrant silver-gray leaves and deep blue-violet flowers. 'Jean Davis' is 1½′ tall with blue-green foliage and pink flowers. 'Munstead' is a long-blooming 1½′ cultivar with lavender-blue flowers. Zones 5–9.

How to Grow: Plant in average to rich, well-drained soil in full sun. Good drainage is essential for survival, especially in regions with wet or severe winters. Established plants can endure extremely dry conditions. A neutral or slightly alkaline soil is best. In spring, prune off any shoots damaged by winter cold, and reshape the plants. Every few years, give plants a hard shearing to encourage fresh growth and profuse flowering. Propagate by tip cuttings taken from new growth in fall, or divide in early spring.

Landscape Uses: Versatile lavender has many uses in ornamental and herb gardens. Plant the smaller, compact cultivars as edging for beds and borders or in knot gardens. Choose the taller cultivars for a low, fragrant, colorful hedge. Plant them in rock gardens with dwarf yarrows, rock cresses (*Arabis* spp.), and other dry-soil plants. In the border, combine lavender with sea hollies (*Eryngium* spp.), globe thistle (*Echinops ritro*), yarrows, pinks (*Dianthus* spp.), and sedums. 🌿

Lavender (*Lavandula angustifolia*) thrives in dry soil in full sun. The foliage is delightfully fragrant.

Liatris Compositae, Daisy Family

lee-AH-tris. Gayfeather, Blazing-Star. Summer bloom. Full sun.

Description: Gayfeathers are native American perennials of outstanding beauty. Tall spikes bear dozens of small red-violet to purple flowers carried in buttonlike clusters or in narrow, dense, compact clusters. The spikes open from the top down, unlike those of most other spike-flowering perennials. The grasslike leaves and flowering stems grow from a fat corm or a short rhizome. As the leaves ascend the stem, they reduce in size until they blend into the flowers. Gayfeathers are popular cut flowers. Many excellent species and cultivars are now available for garden and cut flower use.

Liatris aspera (AS-per-uh), rough gayfeather, button gayfeather. Height: 4'–6' tall; leaves up to 16" long. This stout species has tall spikes to 3' with 1" buttonlike clusters of flowers carried on short stalks, giving the inflorescence an open look. This species produces pale-purple or pink flowers in mid- to late summer. Zones 3–9.

L. cylindracea (sill-in-DRAY-see-uh), cylindric blazing-star. Size: 8"–24" tall; leaves to 10" long. This compact grower has large clusters of ½" pale-purple flowers in open spikes to 1' on leafy stems in late summer. Zones 3–9.

L. microcephala (my-crow-SEFF-uh-luh), small-headed blazing-star. Size: 1'–2' tall; leaves to 6" long. A slender plant bearing ⅛" heads of red-violet flowers in spikes to 10" in midsummer. Zones 4–9.

L. punctata (punk-TAH-tuh), dotted blazing-star. Size: 6"–14" tall; leaves to 6" long. A compact, densely clumping plant with small

⅛" heads packed tightly into dense, short 6" spikes. Plants bloom in late summer. Zones 2–8.

L. pycnostachya (pick-no-STAKE-ee-uh), Kansas gayfeather, prairie blazing-star. Size: 3'–5' tall; leaves to 1' long. This stately plant has tall (1'–2½') spikes of densely packed, red-violet to mauve ¼" flower heads on stiff, leafy stems. Plants bloom in midsummer and are extremely showy when grown in clumps. The variety *alba* has creamy-white flowers. Zones 3–9.

L. scariosa (scar-ee-OH-suh), tall gayfeather. Size: 2½'–3' tall; leaves to 1' long. This species is similar to *L. pycnostachya* but is smaller and a bit less showy, and it blooms a bit later. It is often compared to *L. aspera,* but the pale-purple flowers of *L. scariosa* are borne in dense spikes, not in buttonlike clusters. 'September Glory' has purple flowers in July or August. 'White Spire' has off-white flowers. Zones 4–9.

L. spicata (spih-KAH-tuh), spike gayfeather. Size: 2'–3' tall; leaves to 10" long. Spike gayfeather is the best garden plant in the genus. The compact (1'–2½') spikes are deep red-violet, and the leafy stems are stiff and seldom need support. 'August Glory' has blue-violet flowers on 3'–4' stems. 'Callilepis' is 4' tall with deep-purple flowers. 'Floristan White' has creamy-white flowers on 3' stems. 'Kobold' is the most popular cultivar, bearing dense spikes of mauve to violet flowers on stiff stems only 2'–2½' tall. Zones 3–9.

How to Grow: Gayfeathers are tough, long-lived, easy-care perennials. Plant them in average to rich, moist but well-drained soil in full sun. *L. aspera* and *L. punctata* naturally occur in dry, sandy soils and may overgrow and flop in rich, moist soil. *L. pycnostachya* will grow well in rich, moist soil but will need support from other plants or staking to keep the stems erect. Gayfeathers seldom need division. To propagate, divide the corms in

Liatris spicata 'Kobold' is one of the best spike gayfeathers for cutting. Each clump produces many bloom spikes, so you can remove a few without compromising the garden display.

early fall, or sow fresh seed outdoors for germination the next spring. You can also sow indoors in late winter. To encourage even germination, sow seed in pots or flats and place in a refrigerator for 4–6 weeks before moving them to a warm, bright place. Plants generally take 2–4 years to bloom.

Landscape Uses: Gayfeathers are lovely additions to formal gardens as well as informal meadow and prairie plantings. In a border, combine them with yarrows, purple coneflowers (*Echinacea* spp.), artemisias, Shasta daisy (*Chrysanthemum* × *superbum*), garden phlox (*Phlox paniculata*), and ornamental grasses. Choose *Liatris punctata* and *L. microcephala* for the rock garden. ❧

Ligularia Compositae, Daisy Family

lig-you-LAIR-ee-uh. Ligularia, Golden-Ray, Groundsel. Foliage plant with summer bloom. Light to partial shade.

Ligularia stenocephala 'The Rocket' creates a spectacular display with its yellow spikes of daisylike flowers. Plant it in moist or wet soil to keep the large leaves from wilting.

Description: Ligularias are variable in form and flower, but all possess lovely, lush foliage. The broad leaves have long petioles (leafstalks) and may be round or kidney-shaped to broadly triangular. Some have wavy margins, while others are toothed, lobed, or deeply cut. In midday sun, the leaves often go into a dramatic and alarming (but temporary) wilt; they will recover in the evening with no obvious harm to the plant. The daisylike flowers are yellow or orange, with reflexed petal-like rays and fuzzy central disks. They may be arrayed in tall slender spikes or grouped into domed or flat clusters. All grow from stout crowns with thick fleshy roots.

Ligularia dentata (den-TAH-tuh), bigleaf ligularia. Size: 3'–4' tall; leaves 1'–2' long. This bold species has broad kidney-shaped leaves to 20" long. In late summer, it produces 5"-wide bright-orange flowers in flat branched clusters. Each flower has 10–14 rays, which are 2½" long. 'Desdemona' has red leaves in spring that fade to deep-green on top but retain their reddish purple color on the underside. 'Othello' is similar to 'Desdemona' but has smaller foliage and flowers. 'Gregynog Gold' is a hybrid selection from crossing *L. dentata* with *L. veitchiana.* The plants are 4'–6' tall with bright-green leaves and bright-orange flowers. Zones 3–8.

L. przewalskii (seh-WALL-skee-eye), Shavalski's ligularia. Size: 4'–6' tall; leaves to 2' long. This handsome plant has deeply incised spidery leaves and tall 1'–1½' slender spikes of 1"-wide golden-yellow flowers. The flowerstalks and petioles are deep-purple to black. Zones 3–8.

L. stenocephala (sten-oh-SEFF-uh-luh), narrow-spiked ligularia. Size: 3'–4' tall; leaves to 2' long. This species is similar in flower to *L. przewalskii,* but the leaves are heart-shaped to triangular with toothlike lobes. The popular cultivar 'The Rocket' is listed by most American nurseries under this species but by European nurseries under *L. przewalskii. L. stenocephala* and *L. przewalskii* are similar in landscape effect, but the foliage of *L. przewalskii* holds up better in sun and dry conditions. Both of these species are excellent plants. Zones 4–8.

L. tussilaginea (tuss-sill-ag-in-EE-uh), leopard plant. Size: 1½′–2′ tall; leaves to 1′ long. The evergreen kidney-shaped leaves are the main prize of this somewhat tender species. The 1½″–2½″ yellow flowers are often removed by gardeners who grow leopard plant for its attractive leaves. The foliage of 'Argentea' has uneven white and pale-green variegation. 'Aureo-maculata' has leaves speckled with yellow. 'Crispata' has ruffled leaf margins. Zones 7–10.

How to Grow: Plant ligularias in constantly moist, fertile, humus-rich soil in light to partial shade. Avoid direct afternoon sun, especially in warmer zones, or plants will spend most of their day in a collapsed state. Consistent soil moisture is essential for success—plants will languish in dry soil and deteriorate beyond redemption. Ligularias seldom need division. For propagation, lift plants in spring or fall, and replant the divisions into enriched soil. Slugs may be a problem on leaves. Remove the pests by hand, or trap them in a shallow saucer of beer. You can also try excluding them by surrounding plants with a circle of diatomaceous earth.

Landscape Uses: The enormous foliage of ligularias makes a bold accent in the moist-soil garden. Ferns, monkshoods (*Aconitum* spp.), astilbes, hostas, meadowsweets (*Filipendula* spp.), and primroses are excellent companions. Plant ligularias along the edge of a pond or stream with irises, hostas, and royal fern (*Osmunda regalis*) where they will be reflected in the water.

Lilium Liliaceae, Lily Family

LILL-ee-um. Lily. Spring and summer bloom. Full sun to partial shade.

Description: The genus *Lilium* is a large and varied group of plants prized by gardeners for its range of sizes, colors, and flower forms. Lilies grow from bulbs with overlapping scales that lack the tunic (papery brown covering) of bulbs such as tulips and narcissus. A tall stalk rises from the center of the bulb, which is clothed in leaves that may be narrow and grasslike or wider and more swordlike.

The flowers are held in terminal clusters of 3–75 blooms, depending on the species. The trumpet-, star-, or bowl-shaped flowers may be nodding or upright. Colors vary from white and cream through all shades of yellow, orange, and red to pinks and purples; only black and blue are not represented. Many flowers have dark spots or streaks. Each bloom has 3 petals and 3 petal-like sepals that closely resemble the petals in shape and color. Seeds ripen in dry papery capsules that split when they ripen.

L. auratum (aw-RAH-tum), goldband lily. Size: 2′–6′ tall; leaves to 9″ long. Named "Queen of the Lilies," this lovely plant is crowned with as many as 35 broad, bowl-shaped flowers, each up to 1′ wide. The white flowers have bold yellow stripes down each petal and a generous sprinkling of crimson spots. The variety *platyphyllum* is a robust plant with larger flowers on 6′–8′ stems. Zones 4–9.

L. bulbiferum (buhl-BIFF-er-um), orange lily. Size: 3′–4′ tall; leaves to 4″ long. This species is an important plant for hybridization. Each flower cluster contains up to 40 upward-facing 4″-wide red-orange cup-shaped flowers. Zones 2–8.

L. canadense (can-uh-DEN-see), Canada

Lilium 'Enchantment' is just one of the Asiatic hybrid lilies that are perfect for adding a splash of color to a lightly shaded spot. For a real show, combine them with other summer-flowering perennials such as evening primroses (*Oenothera* spp.).

lily. Size: 4'–5' tall; leaves to 8" long. This tall slender lily has whorls of leaves and terminal clusters of up to 20 nodding 3"-wide bell-shaped yellow, red, or orange flowers. Plants grow from stoloniferous roots that produce new bulbs each year. Zones 3–7.

L. candidum (CAN-dih-dum), Madonna lily. Size: 2'–4' tall; leaves to 9" long. Ghostly white 3"–4"-long trumpet-shaped flowers are held in elongated clusters atop the leafy stems of this lovely species. Zones 4–9.

L. columbianum (koh-lum-bee-ANE-um), Columbia lily. Size: 3'–5' tall; leaves to 4" long. The tightly reflexed petals of this species make it resemble a small tiger lily. The 2"-wide orange flowers are spotted with maroon and are carried in open clusters above tiers of whorled foliage. Zones 4–7.

L. davidii (day-VID-ee-eye), David's lily. Size: 3'–4' tall; leaves to 4" long. Brilliant scarlet or orange, black-spotted, 3"-wide flowers with strongly reflexed petals hang in elongated clusters of up to 20 atop leafy stems. Zones 5–8.

L. formosanum (for-mow-SAN-um), Formosa lily. Size: 4'–7' tall; leaves to 8" long. This stately plant bears 3–10 white trumpets, 5"–8" long, at the summit of stout stems thickly clothed in slender leaves. Zones 5–8.

L. henryi (HEN-ree-eye), Henry lily. Size: 4'–6' tall; leaves to 6" long. This tall lily has broad foliage along the stem and open clusters of up to 20 spotted, orange, 4"-wide flowers with reflexed petals. Zones 4–8.

L. lancifolium (lan-sih-FOE-lee-um), tiger lily (also listed as *L. tigrinum*). Size: 4'–6' tall; leaves to 8" long. The familiar tiger lily has leafy stems topped with spotted, bright-orange 5"-wide flowers with strongly reflexed petals. Small purple-black bulbils form in the axils of the leaves and drop to the ground and produce new plants. Zones 3–9.

L. longiflorum (lon-gih-FLOOR-um), Easter lily. Size: 2½'–3' tall; leaves to 7" long. Three to 5, fragrant, white, 7"-long flowers crown each stout leafy stem. Easter lilies are commonly grown as potted plants for early-spring bloom. Zone 7 (with protection) or Zones 8–9.

L. martagon (MAR-tuh-gon), martagon lily, Turk's-cap. Size: 3'–5' tall; leaves to 7" long. This lovely species has airy clusters of as many as 50 waxy flowers 2" wide with reflexed petals crowning sturdy stalks with tiers of whorled foliage. The variety *album* has creamy-white flowers. 'Claude Shride' has dark-red flowers with ruffled petals on 5' stalks. 'Nepera' has rusty-orange flowers on 3' stems. Zones 3–8.

L. philadelphicum (fill-uh-DELL-fih-kum), wood lily. Size: 1'–4' tall; leaves to 4" long. An enchanting lily with 1–5 upward-facing cup-shaped 4"-wide flowers on delicate stems with whorled foliage. Zones 3–8.

L. regale (ray-GAH-lee), regal lily. Size: 4'–6' tall; leaves to 5" long. This exceptional lily has clusters of large 6"-long trumpet-shaped blooms with flaring throats atop tall leafy stems. The fragrant flowers are white on the inside and blushed with purple on the outside. Zones 3–8.

L. speciosum (spee-see-OH-sum), Japanese lily, showy lily. Size: 4'–5' tall; leaves to 7" long. A popular fragrant late-season lily having flattened 6"-wide flowers with wavy reflexed white petals striped with rose. The coarse foliage loosely clothes the stems. The variety *album* has white flowers with a green star in the throat; *rubrum* has deep purple-pink flowers with white margins around the petals. 'Uchida' is a virus-resistant cultivar with deep-pink flowers. Zones 4–8.

L. superbum (soo-PER-bum), Turk's-cap lily. Size: 4'–7' tall; leaves to 6" long. A tall, slender lily with tiered whorls of foliage and broad clusters of 4"-wide, spotted, bright-orange flowers with strongly reflexed petals. Zones 4–9.

Lilium hybrids. Hybrid lilies are separated into 8 divisions by the American Lily Society based on the shape and position of their flowers and on their hybrid origin.

Division I. Asiatic Hybrids. Asiatics are floriferous early-blooming lilies in bright yellows, oranges, and reds as well as more subtle pinks, purples, cream, and white. Most have upward-facing flowers, but a few have outward-facing or nodding blooms. They are produced from complex hybrids among many species, including *L. amabile, L. bulbiferum, L. lancifolium, L. pumilum,* and many others. Hundreds of cultivars are available. 'Connecticut King' has rich yellow upward-facing flowers. 'Connecticut Yankee' has salmon-orange upward-facing flowers. 'Enchantment' has glowing-orange upward-facing flowers. 'Mont Blanc' has white outward-facing flowers.

Division II. Martagon (Turk's-Cap) Hybrids. This hybrid group includes crosses of *L.*

The bold flowers of goldband lily (*Lilium auratum*) are delightfully fragrant. Plant the bulbs in well-drained, sandy soil.

Plant generous groupings of long-lived Asiatic lilies such as *Lilium* 'Corsica' in perennial gardens as accents or in informal plantings, or naturalize them with flowering shrubs. Ferns and hostas are excellent companions.

martagon with several similar species and is characterized by waxy, Turk's-cap flowers with strongly reflexed petals in yellows, oranges, reds, and whites. The Paisley hybrids and Marhan hybrids are typical of the group.

Division III. Candidum Hybrids. Crosses with the lovely trumpet-flowered Madonna Lily (*L. candidum*) have produced large-flowered fragrant hybrids.

Division IV. American Hybrids. Native American lilies, mostly from the West, have been hybridized to produce excellent plants for areas where summers are cool. Colors range from yellow to orange and red. Most have nodding spotted flowers with strongly recurved petals. Bellingham cultivars in mixed colors are typical of this group. 'Shuksan' has yellow-orange flowers in summer.

Division V. Longiflorum Hybrids. This hybrid group is characterized by long, flaring trumpets produced from crosses of the Easter lily (*L. longiforum*) with *L. formosianum* and other species.

Division VI. Trumpet Hybrids. This large and diverse group contains various hybrids divided into subgroups based on their parentage *Lilium regale, L. henryi,* and others. The group is characterized by outward-facing or nodding flared trumpets 6″–8″ long in pinks, reds, yellows, oranges, and white. The flowers are extremely fragrant. Many strains (seed-grown crosses that produce seedlings that are identical to their parents) and cultivars have been named. 'Black Dragon' strain has huge trumpets that are purple-brown outside and white inside. 'Golden Splendor' strain has golden-yellow flowers with reddish stripes on the outside. 'Pink Perfection' strain has bright rose-pink flowers.

Division VII. Oriental (Japanese) Hybrids. Some of the showiest late-summer lilies were produced from hybrids between *L. auratum,*

L. japonicum, L. speciosum, and other species. They are characterized by flattened or cupped flowers with broad, wavy, slightly reflexed petals. The various Imperial strains from Oregon are lovely plants in various shades of white, pink, rose, and red. 'Black Beauty' is a lovely deep-crimson with a green star in the throat.

Division VIII. Other Hybrids. A wide range of otherwise unclassified hybrids fall under this category. They vary in height and flower form and color.

How to Grow: Lilies are easy-care, long-lived bulbs if you meet their simple requirements for growth. Soil, moisture, pH, and light requirements vary according to species and hybrid group. Most species and hybrids require deep, loamy, well-drained, neutral to slightly acid soil in full sun or light shade. Lime-tolerant species include *L. bulbiferum, L. candidum, L. longiflorum, L. martagon,* and Aurelian hybrids. The American species and hybrids and most Japanese species, especially *L. auratum* and *L. speciosum,* need humus-rich, acid soils for success. Martagons, native American species, *L. henryi,* and *L. speciosum* tolerate partial shade as long as some direct sun is available. Good drainage is essential, especially in winter, to avoid rot.

Plant lily bulbs in the fall (September to November) or in early spring (March to April). If you order through the mail, get your orders in early and specify a delivery time that is suitable for your area—November shipments are useless to northern gardeners who already have frozen soil. Plant most lilies 2-3 times as deep as the bulbs are tall (if a bulb is 3″ tall, for instance, you'll plant it 6″-9″ deep). Some species such as *L. auratum, L. henryi, L. lancifolium, L. regale,* and *L. speciosum* root from the stem above the bulb as well as from the bulb. Plant these species 3-4 times as deep as the height of the bulb. An important

exception to these rules is *L. candidum:* Plant it just below the soil surface. Arrange bulbs in groups with 1′-1½′ between each bulb.

Protect the top-heavy plants from wind, which may cause whole plants to topple over or break off near the base. Tall species and cultivars generally need to be staked. Insert the stake near the stem, taking care not to spear the bulb. Attach the stem loosely to the stake. Remove flowers as they fade unless you specifically want to save seeds; seed production drains enormous amounts of energy from the bulb and may reduce the next year's bloom. In fall, cut the stalks back to at or just below the soil line.

Lilies are susceptible to a number of fungal and bacterial infections that damage or destroy the bulbs. Good cultural conditions are the best control. Keep water off the bulbs by planting in well-drained soil. Yellow mottling on the leaves generally indicates that the plants have an incurable virus. Dig and destroy all infected plants. Viral infections are spread by insects such as aphids. Apply insecticidal soap as directed on the label if aphids appear.

Propagate by dividing bulbs in late summer as they go dormant. Replant bulbs immediately, or store them in moist peat until you can replant—uncovered bulbs will dry out quickly. Some species produce bulbils in the leaf axils; remove these purple-black bulblike structures in late summer and plant them just under the soil surface. Sow fresh seed outdoors in summer or fall. Seeds need a combination of cool and warm treatments to germinate, so seedlings may not emerge for two seasons after sowing. Plants grown from seed may take 3-7 years to bloom.

Landscape Uses: Lilies are beloved for the grace, beauty, and fragrance they add to the garden. Use generous groupings with perennials, ornamental grasses, and vines. ❧

Limonium Plumbaginaceae, Plumbago Family

lih-MOAN-ee-um. Statice, Sea Lavender. Summer bloom. Full sun to light shade.

Sea lavender (*Limonium latifolium*) is a tough perennial that's salt-, heat-, and drought-tolerant. Better still, it produces both lush foliage and airy clusters of long-lasting flowers.

Description: *Limonium latifolium* (lat-ih-FOE-lee-um), sea lavender. Size: 2′–2½′ tall; leaves to 6″ long. Sea lavender produces broad, domed 2′-wide clusters of tiny pink flowers that form an airy haze above the basal rosettes of spatula-shaped leaves. Plants grow from stout woody crowns. Zones 3–9.

How to Grow: Plant in average to rich, well-drained soil in full sun or light shade. They prefer a slightly acid soil but tolerate lime and are extremely adaptable to seaside conditions and high salt levels. Plants take several years to settle in, so don't disturb established clumps. Propagate by removing young auxiliary crowns without disturbing the main clump. Sow seed outdoors in fall for spring germination. Seedlings are slow to reach blooming size.

Landscape Uses: Plant sea lavenders toward the front of the border, where their broad bright-green leaves are visible. Combine the airy flowers with irises and phlox. ❦

Linum Linaceae, Flax Family

LIE-num. Flax. Summer bloom. Full sun or light shade.

Description: Flax has a long history of cultivation for fiber and oil. High-quality flax fiber is used to make linen cloth and rope. The seed produces linseed oil, an ingredient in paints. In the garden, several species are grown for their electric-blue or yellow 5-petaled flowers. Wiry stems clothed with needle-like leaves grow from a stout woody crown.

Linum flavum (FLAY-vum), golden flax.

Size: 1′–1½′ tall; leaves to ¾″ long. Golden flax produces mounds of 1″-wide cup-shaped flowers in open clusters atop wiry stems with narrowly oval leaves. 'Compactum' grows only 6″–9″ tall but produces a mound of flowers. Zone 3 (with winter protection) or Zones 4–8.

L. narbonense (nar-bon-EN-see), Narbonne flax. Size: 1½′–2′ tall; leaves to ½″ long. The deep electric-blue, 1¼″-wide, saucer-shaped flowers of Narbonne flax have white centers. They are held in open, branching clusters that droop at their tips. The blue-green foliage is small and needle-like. 'Heavenly Blue' is more compact and has ultramarine flowers. Zone 4 (with winter protection) or Zones 5–9.

L. perenne (per-EN-ee), blue flax (also listed as *L. lewisii*). Size: 1′–1½′ tall; leaves to 1″ long. Blue flax is similar to *L. narbonense* but has 1″-wide steel-blue flowers. The American subspecies *lewisii*, often listed as a species, is hardier (Zone 3) than the European selections. 'White Diamond' has pure-white flowers on 1′ plants. Zones 4–9.

How to Grow: Flax are tough, long-lived perennials. Plant them in average, sandy or loamy, well-drained soil in full sun or light shade. Once established, they need little care and seldom require division; the clumps increase to form mounds of soft foliage and bright flowers. Propagate by stem cuttings in early summer. Sow fresh seed outdoors in late summer or fall.

Landscape Uses: Lovely, delicate flax are best displayed in groupings of 3–5 or more. For a bold combination, underplant brilliant-red or salmon-pink poppies with clouds of blue flax. Plant golden flax with deep-blue or

Blue flax and its cultivars, including *Linum perenne* 'Blue Sapphire', may look delicate, but they are actually quite tough and drought-tolerant. Grow flax in groups of 3 to 5.

purple flowers such as sages and great blue lobelia (*Lobelia siphilitica*). In a rock garden or dry meadow garden, plant flax with alliums (*Allium* spp.), lupines (*Lupinus* spp.), and wild cranesbill (*Geranium maculatum*). ❧

Liriope Liliaceae, Lily Family

lih-RYE-oh-pea. Lilyturf. Foliage plant with late summer bloom. Sun to full shade.

Description: Lilyturf produces tufted mounds of tough, leathery grasslike leaves from wiry creeping roots. Tiny pale-purple or white flowers are held in small clusters along spikelike flowerstalks in late summer. The flowers are followed by glossy black berries that persist into winter.

Liriope muscari (muh-SCARE-ee), blue lilyturf. Size: 1′–1½′ tall; leaves to 1½′ long. This lovely groundcover has straplike evergreen leaves 1″–1½″ wide. The erect 4″–6″ flower spikes of tiny, pale blue-violet or white flowers are held above the foliage. 'Christmas Tree' has lilac flowers arrayed in tapering spikes that resemble Christmas trees. 'Gold Banded' bears broad leaves with narrow,

Liriope muscari 'John Burch' boasts variegated leaves and blue-violet flowers that appear in late summer. It's a tough, evergreen plant that makes an ideal groundcover or edging plant.

golden-yellow margins and lilac flowers. 'John Burch' has broad leaves with central chartreuse stripes and dense flower spikes held well above the foliage. 'Lilac Beauty' has deep-lilac flowers held well above the dark-green foliage. 'Majestic' has deep lilac-purple flowers. 'Munroe's White' has showy elongated clusters of white flowers. 'Royal Purple' has deep-green leaves and purple flowers. 'Silvery Sunproof' is a sun-tolerant variegated form with regular creamy stripes on the leaves. The cultivar 'Variegata' bears leaves with creamy-white margins. Zones 6–9.

L. spicata (spih-KAH-tuh), creeping lilyturf. Size: 1'–1½' tall; leaves to 16" long. Creeping lilyturf differs from *L. muscari* in having narrow leaves only ¼" wide, less-showy, pale lavender flowers, and fast-creeping roots. Creeping lilyturf is also more cold-hardy. 'Franklin Mint' has large showy flowers similar to *L. muscari* but maintains the narrow foliage and rapid growth of *L. spicata*. Zones 5–9.

How to Grow: Plant in average to rich, well-drained soil in full sun to full shade. Lilyturfs are tough, adaptable plants able to endure extreme heat, high humidity, and dry soil conditions. They hold their ground under the canopy of mature trees and endure root competition no worse for the wear. If foliage gets ratty in winter, mow the plants to the ground. A new flush of growth will redeem the planting in spring. Divide clumps in spring or fall to control their spread or for propagation.

Landscape Uses: Lilyturfs are excellent for edging paths or planting at the front of beds and borders. Mix the variegated cultivars with brightly colored verbenas (*Verbena* spp.), or combine them with larger spiky plants such as blue oat grass (*Helictotrichon sempervirens*) or yuccas (*Yucca* spp.). Soften the planting with columbines (*Aquilegia* spp.) and sea lavender (*Limonium latifolium*). ❧

Lobelia   Campanulaceae, Bellflower Family

low-BEE-lee-uh. Lobelia. Summer and fall bloom. Full sun to partial shade.

Description: Lobelias produce erect spikes of irregularly shaped tubular flowers with 3 lower lobes and 2 upper ones. They form basal rosettes in fall from a fibrous-rooted crown and remain green throughout the winter except in the most rigorous climates. The brightly colored red or blue flowers open for 2–3 weeks in mid- to late summer, followed by button-shaped seed capsules.

Lobelia cardinalis (car-dih-NAH-lis), cardinal flower. Size: 2'–4' tall; leaves to 4" long. Dense 2' spikes of flaming scarlet 1½" flowers crown the leafy stems of this streamside plant. Each flower looks like a bird rising in flight. Lower, spent flowers may have ripened seed while the upper flowers are still opening. 'Royal Robe' has ruby-red flowers. Zones 2–9.

L. × *gerardii* (jer-ARD-ee-eye), purple lobelia (also sold as *L. vedrariensis*). Size: 3'–4' tall; leaves to 6" long. This showy plant resulted from crosses between *L. siphilitica* and one of the red-flowering species. The 1" flowers are royal-purple. Zones 4–8.

L. siphilitica (sih-fih-LIH-tih-kuh), great blue lobelia. Size: 2'–3' tall; leaves to 5" long. This species lacks the flaring "wings" of *L. cardinalis,* but the blue, buck-toothed, 1"-long flowers are desirable for their midsummer color. This species is important in hybridization. 'Alba' has white flowers. Zones 4–8.

L. × *speciosa* (spee-see-OH-suh), hybrid cardinal flower. Size: 2'–3'; leaves to 5" long. This group of hybrids was developed in Canada from several species and selections of lobelia. 'Brightness' has 1½" cherry-red flowers and bronze foliage. 'Hamilton Dwarf' has blood-red flowers on 2' stems. 'Oakes Ames' has deep-scarlet flowers and bronze leaves.

Hungry hummingbirds will seek out the brilliant-red blossoms of cardinal flower (*Lobelia cardinalis*), which is an ideal choice for wet sites such as along streams.

'Wisley' has light-red flowers and bronze leaves. Zones 3 or 4 (with winter protection) or Zones 5–9.

L. splendens (SPLEN-denz), Mexican lobelia (also listed as *L. fulgens*). Size: 2'–3' tall; leaves to 5" long. This species resembles *L. cardinalis* but has bronze leaves and stems and is less hardy. 'Queen Victoria' has bright-red 1" flowers and maroon foliage and may be a hybrid. Zones 7–9.

How to Grow: Lobelias are plants of low woods, streamsides, and ditches. Plant them in rich, constantly moist soil in light to partial shade. Plants will tolerate full sun in milder regions. Plants in warmer zones with

The sky-blue flowers of great blue lobelia (*Lobelia siphilitica*) are a welcome addition to late-summer gardens that all too often are dominated by golden-yellow flowers.

fluctuating winter temperatures often rot if mulched, but in colder zones a winter mulch is mandatory. To avoid smothering the rosettes, remove the mulch as soon as temperatures moderate. Plants are often short-lived and respond to frequent division to keep them vigorous. Lift clumps in early fall, and remove the new rosettes. Replant immediately in enriched soil. Plants self-sow prolifically where the soil is bare of heavy mulch in fall and winter. Sow seeds uncovered outdoors in fall or indoors in late winter. They are quick to germinate in spring and may bloom the first season.

Landscape Uses: Lobelias are best suited to moist-soil gardens, especially along ponds and streams. Plant them in the company of Siberian and Japanese iris (*Iris sibirica* and *I. ensata*), astilbes, ferns, and bold foliage plants such as bigleaf ligularia (*Ligularia dentata*) and hostas. Lobelias are good border plants if the soil does not dry out. Combine them with other moisture-tolerant border perennials such as daylilies (*Hemerocallis* spp.), spiderworts (*Tradescantia* spp.), garden phlox (*Phlox paniculata*), and sneezeweeds (*Helenium* spp.). 🍂

Lupinus Leguminosae, Pea Family

lew-PIE-nus. Lupine. Spring and summer bloom. Full sun to light shade.

Description: *Lupinus polyphyllus* (pahl-ee-FILL-us), Washington lupine, garden lupine. Size: 3′–5′ tall; leaves to 1′ long. Lupines produce dense conical flower spikes up to 2′ long over clusters of fan-shaped, palmately divided leaves on 6″–8″ petioles (leafstalks). The pea-shaped flowers come in white, pink, or blue. Plants grow from sparse, thick roots. Zones 3–7.

Lupinus hybrids. The popular Russell hybrid lupines were produced in England from crosses between different colors of *L. polyphyllus* with *L. arborescens* and other species. Although they tolerate Zone 3 winters with ease, they are not equally heat-tolerant and will not perform well in the eastern and central zones warmer than Zone 6. On the West Coast, they fare much better. Hybrids may have white, pink, rose, carmine, violet, or bicolor flowers. 'Minarette' series contains dwarf plants to 1½' in mixed colors. 'My Castle' is 2'-3' tall with brick-red flowers. 'Russell Hybrid' comes in mixed or individual colors. Plants are 2½'-3½' tall and flower in late spring.

How to Grow: Plant lupines in rich, acidic, evenly moist but well-drained soil in full sun or light shade. The hybrids will not tolerate dry or nutrient-poor soils and are best planted out of the path of warm, dry winds. Plants are best adapted to northern and West Coast gardens, which have cool summer temperatures.

Lupines may be short-lived, especially in warmer zones. To propagate them, you can remove sideshoots in fall without lifting the entire clump. Sow fresh seeds outdoors in late summer or indoors in winter. Before sowing indoors, soak seeds overnight in warm water and then sow them into pots or flats; place the pots or flats in a refrigerator for 4–6 weeks before moving them to a warm, bright place.

Landscape Uses: Lupines are colorful aristocrats of the spring and summer garden. Plant them as an accent with flowering shrubs or in the border with irises, peonies, bell-flowers (*Campanula* spp.), and annuals. 🍂

'Russell Hybrid' lupines reach their full potential in climates with warm, sunny days and cool nights. They bear dense spikes of pea-like flowers.

Lychnis Caryophyllaceae, Pink Family

LICK-nis. Campion, Catchfly. Spring and summer bloom. Full sun to partial shade.

Description: A large genus of short-lived showy plants with orange, red, rose, or white, 5-petaled flowers carried singly or in clusters. The bloom stalks appear in spring or summer over basal rosettes of foliage. The roots are fibrous and thin.

Lychnis × *arkwrightii* (ark-RIGHT-ee-eye), Arkwright's campion. Size: 1½'-2' tall; leaves 3"-4" long. This showy garden hybrid between *L. chalcedonica* and *L.* × *haageana* produces 1½"-wide orange-red flowers with notched petals. The stems bear pairs of elongated, oval dark-bronze leaves. Plants bloom in early summer. 'Vesuvius' has scarlet-orange flowers. Zones 3–8.

L. chalcedonica (chal-seh-DON-ih-kuh), Maltese cross. Size: 2'-3' tall; leaves 2"-4" long. Maltese cross is an old-fashioned garden favorite with ½"-1"-wide bright-scarlet flowers with 5 deeply notched petals. The flowers are held in tight rounded clusters atop sturdy stems with opposite, oval leaves in midsummer. 'Alba' has white flowers. Zones 3–9.

L. coronaria (core-oh-NAH-ree-uh), rose campion. Size: 2'–3' tall; leaves to 4" long. Rose campion is the showiest of the campions. Brilliant deep rose-pink 1"-wide flowers are held in broad, open, branching clusters above rosettes of hairy silver-gray leaves. Individual plants of this summer-bloomer are short-lived. 'Abbotswood Rose' has magenta flowers. 'Alba' has white flowers. 'Angel's Blush' has white flowers with a cerise eye. Zones 4–8.

L. × haageana (hah-jee-AH-nuh), Haage campion. Size: 10"–18" tall; leaves 2"–4" long. The showy 2"-wide flowers of Haage campion vary in color from deep red to crimson and are borne throughout the summer. This hybrid was produced from a cross between *L. fulgens* and *L. coronata,* two little-known species. Zones 3–9.

L. viscaria (vis-KAH-ree-uh), German

Maltese cross (*Lychnis chalcedonica*) is an old-fashioned garden favorite that produces clusters of brilliant-red flowers. Plant it in the middle or rear of the garden in moist, well-drained soil.

catchfly. Size: 1'–1½' tall; leaves to 5" long. This showy spring-blooming plant produces basal rosettes of long, slender leaves and open, elongated clusters of 1"-wide magenta flowers. 'Alba' has white flowers on 1' stalks. 'Fire' has bright rose-red flowers. 'Zulu' has deep-red flowers on maroon stems. Zones 3–8.

How to Grow: Campions vary in their requirements for growth. Give *L. × arkwrightii, L. chalcedonica,* and *L. coronaria* light, average to rich, moist but well-drained soil in full sun or light shade. In warmer areas, site plants where they will be shaded from afternoon sun to prevent leaf browning. *L. × haageana* needs consistent moisture for best growth. *L. viscaria* grows best in average, alkaline soil and is tolerant of dry conditions. *L. coronaria* is prone to dying out from the middle if soil is too wet, especially in winter. Divide plants every 2–3 years in spring to keep them vigorous. Regular deadheading may prolong the bloom season, but be sure to leave a few spent flowers if you want the plant to reseed. Plants self-sow readily, and the seedlings turn up in the oddest places.

Landscape Uses: The campions have strongly colored flowers that can be difficult to incorporate into the garden. All species look good when surrounded by green, and they combine well with shrubs. Plant the red- and orange-flowered species (*L. × arkwrightii, L. chalcedonica,* and *L. × haageana*) in combination with yellow and soft-blue flowers and foliage. Russian sage (*Perovskia atriplicifolia*), coneflowers (*Rudbeckia* spp.), yarrows, golden marguerite (*Anthemis tinctoria*), and delphiniums (*Delphinium* spp.) are good companions. The white-flowered form of *L. coronaria* is a lovely and easy-to-use plant enhanced by its gray foliage. Combine it with lavender, catmint (*Nepeta* spp.), and white or pale-pink lilies. Choose *L. viscaria* for the front of the border or in a sunny rockery. ❧

Lycoris   Amaryllidaceae, Amaryllis Family

lie-CORE-iss. Spider Lily, Lycoris. Summer and fall bloom. Full sun to partial shade.

Description: Spider lilies produce showy round clusters of 6-petaled flowers with long, upturned stamens (male reproductive structures). The flowerstalks emerge after the strap-shaped foliage dies down in midsummer.

Lycoris radiata (ray-dee-AH-tuh), red spider lily. Size: 1'–1½' tall; leaves to 8" long. This species bears clusters of 2" deep-red flowers. Leaves emerge in late fall. Zones 7–10.

L. squamigera (skwa-MIH-geh-ruh), magic lily. Size: 18"–30" tall; leaves to 1' long. Stout stalks bear 3" pink funnelform flowers in summer; leaves appear in early spring. Zones 4–9.

How to Grow: Plant bulbs 6" deep in fall in rich, moist but well-drained soil in full sun or partial shade. *L. squamigera* will bloom in partial shade. Lift and divide after flowering if flower production wanes or for propagation.

Landscape Uses: Plant in perennial gardens with late-summer bloomers such as asters, mums, phlox, and ornamental grasses. Combine with foliage plants for contrast. 🍂

Red spider lily (*Lycoris radiata*) explodes into a mass of color in autumn on naked flowerstalks. Combine it with low-growing perennials if you don't like the look of the bare stems.

Lysimachia   Primulaceae, Primrose Family

lie-sih-MAH-kee-uh. Loosestrife. Summer bloom. Full sun to light shade.

Description: Loosestrifes bear opposite or whorled leaves and 5–7-petaled yellow or white flowers. The flowers may be arrayed in dense, elongated terminal clusters or in whorls above the foliage. Plants spread from creeping stems with fibrous roots.

Lysimachia ciliata (sill-ee-AH-tuh), fringed loosestrife. Size: 1'–3' tall; leaves to 6" long.

This loosestrife has an open habit with opposite, oval leaves and pairs of 5-petaled fringed ¾"-wide yellow flowers at each node (leaf joint). An attractive purple-leaved form is available. Zones 3–9.

L. clethroides (kleth-ROY-deez), gooseneck loosestrife. Size: 2'–3' tall; leaves 3"–6" long. This lovely, fast-spreading plant has

Yellow loosestrife (*Lysimachia punctata*) thrives in full sun and moist to wet soil. Plants spread quickly to form dense, leafy clumps. Yellow loosestrife can be invasive.

opposite leaves and drooping terminal 8″–12″ spikes of 5–6-petaled, ½″-wide white flowers. In any one clump, all the flower spikes droop in the same direction, appearing like a flock of eager geese on the run. Zones 3–8.

L. nummularia (num-you-LAH-ree-uh), creeping Jenny. Size: 2″–4″ tall; leaves to 1″ long. This fast-growing, often invasive ground-cover spreads by creeping stems with opposite, rounded leaves and 5-petaled ¾″-wide yellow flowers. 'Aurea' has chartreuse leaves in spring that darken to lime-green in summer. Zones 3–8.

L. punctata (punk-TAH-tuh), yellow loosestrife. Size: 1′–2½′ tall; leaves 1″–3″ long. Yellow loosestrife bears wiry stems clothed in tiered whorls of hairy foliage and 1″-wide yellow flowers. Zones 4–8.

How to Grow: Plant loosestrifes in evenly moist, humus-rich soil in full sun or partial shade. Periods of dryness will slow growth; extended drought is fatal. Plants spread rapidly in moist soil and may become pests; they can quickly crowd out less-vigorous companions. Divide clumps in spring or fall as necessary to control their spread or for propagation.

Landscape Uses: Loosestrifes have an affinity for moist soil, which makes them perfect for use along streams or at poolside. Plant them in combination with Siberian iris (*Iris sibirica*), ligularias (*Ligularia dentata* or *L. stenocephala*), meadowsweets (*Filipendula* spp.), hostas, and ferns. ❦

Lythrum Lythraceae, Loosestrife Family

LITH-rum. Loosestrife, Lythrum. Summer bloom. Full sun to light shade.

Description: *Lythrum* is a genus of showy plants bearing candelabra-like spikes of pink or rose flowers throughout summer. The dense spikes bear hundreds of 5-petaled flowers on stout stems with opposite, lance-shaped leaves. Plants grow from woody crowns with dense, deep-penetrating fibrous roots.

L. salicaria (sal-ih-KAH-ree-uh), purple loosestrife. Size: 3′–5′ tall; leaves to 6″ long. Tall, 1′ showy spikes of ¾″-wide, pink, rose, or rose-purple flowers are produced throughout the summer. 'Firecandle' has rose-pink flowers. 'Robert' has deep-pink flowers on 2′ stems. 'The Beacon' has bright rose-red flowers on 3½′ stems. Zones 3–8.

L. virgatum (vir-GAH-tum), wand

loosestrife. Size: 2'–3' tall; leaves to 6" long. This species is very similar to *L. salicaria* but is smaller and has distinctly stalked ¾"-wide flowers. 'Dropmore Purple' has rose-purple flowers on 2½' stems. 'Morden Gleam' has rose flowers. 'Morden Pink' has bright pink flowers. 'Rose Queen' has light rose-pink flowers on 1½' stems. Zones 3–8.

How to Grow: Plant in moist, average to humus-rich soil in full sun or light shade. These plants are easy to grow in any but poor, dry soil. Many states have outlawed the sale and/or garden use of these plants because of their aggressive and destructive abilities. It was once thought that the cultivars did not produce seeds so they could be grown with impunity. Current research shows that although these plants are self-sterile (they cannot pollinate themselves), they can be pollinated by other cultivars, wild populations of *L. alatum,* and naturalized populations of *L. salicaria* and *L. virgatum.*

If you grow loosestrife, cut it down after flowering to reduce the chances of seeding. Also, stick to 1 cultivar so cross-pollination and seed production are not likely. Discard the stalks or compost them in a hot pile that will kill the seeds. Never plant the species or cultivars near any natural stream, river, lake, or pond—the risk of it escaping is too great, and these plants are very difficult to control. The seeds float remarkably well and are carried far and wide by any moving water.

To propagate these plants, lift and divide clumps in spring or take stem cuttings in summer. Handpick Japanese beetles from foliage.

Landscape Uses: *Lythrum* species are excellent for vertical accent at the middle or back of the border. Create a lovely garden scene by combining their tall spikes of pink or rose flowers with irises, peonies, poppies, phlox, daisies, and ornamental grasses. 🦋

Loosestrife thrives in moist soil but should never be planted near streams or ponds, where it becomes an invasive weed. Even cultivars that are self-sterile, such as *Lythrum virgatum* 'Morden Pink', can produce seed if planted near other species or cultivars.

Malva   Malvaceae, Mallow Family

MAL-vuh. Mallow. Summer bloom. Full sun or light shade.

Hollyhock mallow (*Malva alcea* 'Fastigiata') produces clumps of upright stems that are ideal for the back of the border. These tough plants are easy to grow in well-drained soil in full sun; they prefer areas with cool nights.

Description: The hibiscus-like mallows have saucer-shaped flowers, puckered leaves, and stout stems that rise from woody crowns with thick fibrous roots.

Malva alcea (AL-see-uh), hollyhock mallow. Size: 2'–3' tall; leaves to 6" long. The rose, pink, or white flowers are 1½"–2" wide. 'Fastigiata' has rose-pink flowers. Zones 4–8.

M. moschata (moss-SHA-tuh), musk mallow. Size: 2½'–3' tall; leaves to 6" long. This species has deeply divided leaves and 2"–2½"-wide rose-pink flowers. 'Alba' has white flowers and comes true from seed. Zones 3–7.

How to Grow: Plant in average, near neutral, well-drained soil in full sun or light shade. Mallows grow best in cooler zones. Take tip cuttings in early summer; sow seed indoors in late winter or outdoors in spring or fall.

Landscape Uses: Use mallows as accents in the border. They combine well with phlox, yarrows, gayfeathers (*Liatris* spp.), and artemisias.

Mertensia Boraginaceae, Borage Family

mer-TEN-see-uh. Bluebells, Cowslips. Spring bloom. Sun or shade.

Description: *Mertensia virginica* (ver-JIN-ih-kuh), Virginia bluebells. Size: 1′–2′ tall; leaves to 8″ long; flowers to 1″ long. Virginia bluebells are lovely spring wildflowers that grace woodlands, riverbanks, and meadows with pink buds that open to nodding clusters of sky-blue bells. Plants produce basal rosettes of leaves and stems from stout, thickened roots. The leaves are thin and delicate. The thick, succulent stems die down after flowering. 'Alba' has white flowers. Zones 3–9.

How to Grow: Plant bluebells in consistently moist but well-drained, humus-rich soil in sun or shade. Locate plants where you will not dig into the dormant clumps accidentally. Divide large clumps after flowering for propagation. Plants will self-sow readily on soil that is not heavily mulched. They bloom the third year from seed.

Landscape Uses: Bluebells are lovely alongside a shaded garden path in the company of spring bulbs, such as daffodils and species tulips, and wildflowers such as columbines (*Aquilegia* spp.), wild blue phlox (*Phlox divaricata*), Canada wild ginger (*Asarum canadense*), and trilliums (*Trillium* spp.). Interplant clumps of bluebells with ferns, hostas, and other foliage perennials to fill in the bare spots left when the bluebells go dormant. Do not plant directly over the clumps—allow a 1′ area around each clump so the bluebells can grow unimpeded. 🍂

Virginia bluebells (*Mertensia virginica*) are a natural choice for an informal shady border or a wild garden. Combine it with foliage plants such as ferns that will fill in the area after the bluebells go dormant.

Monarda　Labiatae, Mint Family

mow-NAR-duh. Bee Balm, Bergamot. Summer bloom. Full sun to light shade.

Put out the welcome mat for hummingbirds with generous clumps of summer-blooming bee balms, including *Monarda didyma* 'Cambridge Scarlet'.

Description: Bee balms bear aromatic foliage and round heads of tightly packed tubular flowers above a circle of colored leafy bracts (modified leaves). Bee balm has square stems and grows from fast-creeping runners with fibrous roots.

Monarda didyma (DID-uh-muh), bee balm, Oswego tea. Size: 2'–4' tall, leaves 4"–6" long. Bee balm has brilliant-scarlet 1"-long flowers in round 4" heads surrounded by deep-red bracts. The stout succulent stems have opposite, pointed leaves. 'Cambridge Scarlet' has brilliant-scarlet flowers. 'Croftway Pink' has soft-pink flowers. 'Mahogany' has dark ruby-red flowers. 'Marshall's Delight' is mildew-resistant, with pink flowers on 2' stems. 'Prairie Night' has red-violet flowers. 'Snow White' has creamy-white flowers on 3' stems. 'Violet Queen' has reddish purple flowers. Zones 4–8.

M. fistulosa (fist-you-LOW-suh), wild bergamot. Size: 2'–4' tall; leaves to 4" long. Bergamot has soft lavender-pink to pale-pink ¾"-long flowers and pink to white bracts. The flowers are carried in 3" heads atop wiry stems. Zones 3–9.

M. punctata (punk-TAH-tuh), spotted bee balm, spotted horsemint. Size: 1'–3' tall; leaves 1"–2" long. Wiry stems with long pointed leaves are crowned by tiered clusters of small, spotted, ½"–¾"-long yellow-green flowers above whorls of pink bracts. Zones 3–9.

How to Grow: Plant *M. didyma* in evenly moist, humus-rich soil in full sun or partial shade. Plants must never be allowed to dry out. *M. fistulosa* and *M. punctata* prefer average to rich soil in full sun to light shade; *M. punctata* tolerates seaside conditions. Lift and divide entire clumps every 2–3 years to keep bee balms vigorous. They are often affected by powdery mildew, which causes white blotches on leaves. *M. didyma* is the most susceptible; *M. punctata* is seldom affected. Avoid mildew by thinning stems and choosing a site with good air circulation.

Landscape Uses: Combine bee balms with other summer perennials like lilies, phlox, yarrows, cranesbills (*Geranium* spp.), and astilbes. In the moist wild garden, plant *M. didyma* with bonesets (*Eupatorium* spp.), queen-of-the-prairie (*Filipendula rubra*), hibiscus (*Hibiscus* spp.), and ferns. Plant *M. fistulosa* and *M. punctata* with meadow plants. 🍁

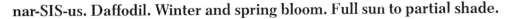

Narcissus   Amaryllidaceae, Amaryllis Family

nar-SIS-us. Daffodil. Winter and spring bloom. Full sun to partial shade.

Description: Daffodils are true harbingers of spring. Along with crocus and snowdrops (*Galanthus* spp.), they signal the start of a new growing season that is eagerly awaited by every gardener. The characteristic flower of the daffodil has a ring of 3 petals and 3 petal-like sepals, collectively called the perianth. In the center of the flower is a funnel-shaped cup of varying length called the corona. Together the perianth and corona form the cheery daffodil flowers that vary in size, shape, and color.

Narcissus species and hybrids are divided by the American Daffodil Society into 11 groups based on flower shape and species origin.

Division I. Trumpet Narcissus. Trumpets bear 1 flower per stem with perianth segments as long as or longer than the corona. Flowers may be yellow, white, or bicolored. 'Beersheba' has delicate white flowers. 'Cantatrice' has creamy-white flowers. 'King Alfred' has large

yellow flowers. 'Unsurpassable' has huge bright-yellow flowers with golden-yellow coronas.

Division II. Large-Cupped Narcissus. Large-cup daffodils have 1 flower per stem with the perianth segments more than ⅔ as long as, but still shorter than, the corona. Flowers are yellow, white, or bicolored. 'Carlton' has bright-yellow flowers. 'Ice Follies' has a white perianth and a yellow corona that fades to pale-yellow. 'Salome' has a white perianth and an apricot corona. 'Sun Chariot' is yellow with a yellow-and-orange corona.

Division III. Small-Cupped Narcissus. Small-cup daffodils have 1 flower per stem with the corona not more than ⅓ the length of the perianth segments. 'Barrett Browning' is white with an orange corona. 'Birma' is yellow with an orange corona.

Division IV. Double Narcissus. This group includes all double-flowered hybrids. 'Flower Drift' has a white perianth and a white, yellow,

One of the earliest daffodils to bloom in spring is *Narcissus* 'February Gold'. Plant it with a groundcover such as English ivy (*Hedera helix*), or create a more colorful combination with glory-of-the-snow (*Chionodoxa luciliae*).

and orange center. 'Golden Ducat' has bright golden-yellow flowers. 'Mary Copeland' is white with a white-and-red-orange center. 'White Lion' is white with a white-and-pale-yellow center.

Division V. Triandrus Narcissus. This hybrid group has the nodding clustered flowers of *N. triandrus* in white or yellow. 'April Tears' has 1″ yellow flowers. 'Hawera' has small yellow flowers. 'Liberty Bells' has 2″ yellow flowers. 'Silver Chimes' has small white flowers. 'Thalia' has starry 2″ white flowers.

Division VI. Cyclamineus Narcissus. This hybrid group has slightly nodding flowers with medium to long coronas and reflexed perianth segments reminiscent of *N. cyclamineus*. 'February Gold' has golden-yellow flowers. 'February Silver' is white with a pale-yellow corona. 'Jack Snipe' has a white perianth and a

short yellow corona. 'Peeping Tom' has a bright-yellow perianth and a long corona. 'Tête-à-Tête' has 1–3 small yellow flowers per stem.

Division VII. Jonquilla Narcissus. The rushlike foliage and clustered fragrant flat flowers of *N. jonquilla* are evident in these hybrids. 'Baby Moon' has small yellow flowers. 'Sundial' has pale-yellow flowers. 'Suzy' is golden-yellow with an orange corona. 'Trevithian' has lemon-yellow flowers.

Division VIII. Tazetta Narcissus. These hybrids have clustered, fragrant flowers with characteristics of *N. tazetta*. 'Geranium' is white with an orange corona. 'Minnow' has small lemon-yellow flowers with golden-yellow coronas. 'Scarlet Gem' is pale-yellow with an orange corona. Cultivars sold as "paperwhites" are hardy in Zones 8–10 only.

Division IX. Poeticus Narcissus. The poet's narcissus are fragrant hybrids with flat flowers and tiny coronas. 'Cantabile' has pale-green flowers with a red-edged corona.

Division X. Species and wild forms. There are over 50 naturally occurring species; the following are readily available as nursery-propagated bulbs.

N. bulbocodium (buhl-boh-KOH-dee-um), hoop-petticoat daffodil. Size: 6″–12″ tall; leaves to 12″ long. Hoop-petticoat daffodils have 1″-wide flowers with short, narrow perianth segments and wide, short coronas. They bloom early in the season. The leaves are narrow, rounded, and deep-green. The variety *conspicuosus* has deep-yellow flowers in late spring. Zones 6–9.

N. cantabricus (can-TAH-bree-kus), Cantabrian daffodils. Size: 6″–10″ tall; leaves to 1′ long. This daffodil is an early-season bloomer with 1″-wide white petticoat flowers and narrow leaves. Zones 6–9.

N. cyclamineus (SIGH-kluh-min-ee-us). Size: 3″–5″ tall; leaves to 6″ long. This whimsical daffodil has a 3″-long slender corona and narrow reflexed perianth segments. This species is an important parent for many popular hybrids. Zones 6–9.

N. jonquilla (john-KWILL-uh), jonquil. Size: 6″–12″ tall; leaves to 1′. This lovely, fragrant species has clusters of 3–6, 1½″-wide flowers with wide perianth segments and short coronas. The narrow leaves are deep-green. Zones 4–9.

N. minor (MY-nor), Size: 5″–6″ tall; leaves to 5″ long. A trumpet daffodil bearing 1″–1⅜″-long yellow blooms with deep-yellow coronas. The variety *pumilus plenus* ('Rip van Winkle') is a fully double form. Zones 5–9.

N. × *odorus* (oh-DOOR-us), Campernelle jonquil. Size: 10″-12″ tall; leaves to 1′ long. This delicate daffodil bears 2–4 fragrant 1½″-long flowers with wide perianth segments and a short corona. Zones 4–9.

N. poeticus (poh-ET-ih-kus), poet's narcissus. Size: 1′–1½′ tall; leaves to 1½′ long. This popular fragrant narcissus has single 1½″-wide flowers with wide, flat white perianth segments and a short soft-yellow corona rimmed in red. 'Actaea' has 2″ white flowers. Zones 4–9.

N. tazetta (ta-ZET-uh), polyanthus narcissus. Size: 1′–1½′ tall; leaves to 1½′ long. The fragrant creamy-white 1″-long flowers of this narcissus are carried in clusters of 4–8. The starry perianth surrounds the short pale-yellow corona. Zones 6–10.

N. triandrus (try-AN-drus), angel's-tears. Size: 5″–10″ long; leaves to 1′ long. The 1″-long nodding flowers of this lovely species have reflexed perianth segments and a bell-like corona. One to 5 white, cream, or yellow flowers are carried above the blue-green foliage. Zones 4–9.

Division XI. Miscellaneous Narcissus. This group includes hybrids that do not fit elsewhere. The Split Coronas have cups that are split and reflexed to resemble petals.

'Baccarat' has golden-yellow flowers. 'Parisienne' has a white perianth with an orange corona.

How to Grow: Plant daffodils in moist, well-drained, humusy soil in full sun or light shade. Enrich the soil at planting, and top-dress each spring with a low-nitrogen, high-phosphorus organic fertilizer such as bonemeal. Excess nitrogen encourages lush foliage at the expense of flowers. While the plants are actively growing, sun is essential to enable the bulbs to store enough energy for next year's growth and flowers. As the foliage yellows, sun is not important. Do not remove or mow over the foliage until it is fully yellowed.

Plant bulbs from August through November. Place the top of the bulb 4″–6″ below the soil surface, depending on the bulb size. Generally, plant them 2–3 times as deep as the bulbs are tall. Space the larger hybrids 3″–10″ apart (the wider spacing looks sparse

Combine cheerful daffodils such as *Narcissus* 'Flower Record' with perennials or early-flowering shrubs such as forsythias and lilacs.

the first few years but will eventually produce long-lived clumps). Bulbs increase to form tight clumps that may begin to lose vigor and cease flowering. Lift the bulbs as the foliage yellows, and store them in a dry, cool place for 3 months. Replant the largest bulbs in August or September into amended soil.

Some of the species daffodils need special treatment. *N. cyclamineus* needs moist, acid soil that bakes dry in the summer. Other species must also be allowed to become dry in the summer. Plant the small bulbs only 1″–4″ deep, depending on size. Order species bulbs early and plant them immediately. Do not buy species unless the dealer can assure you beyond a shadow of a doubt that the bulbs are nursery propagated. Many species, especially *N. triandrus*, are endangered because of over-collecting.

Landscape Uses: Use generous groups of daffodils with flowering shrubs or in mixed plantings with shrubs and perennials. Combine the larger hybrids with spring perennials such as hellebores (*Helleborus* spp.), tulips, and crocuses. Use the species and smaller hybrids of *Narcissus* in rock gardens or with early wildflowers such as Dutchman's breeches (*Dicentra cucullaria*). 🌿

Nepeta Labiatae, Mint Family

NEP-uh-tuh. Catmint, Nepeta. Spring and early-summer bloom. Full sun to light shade.

Blue catmint (*Nepeta* × *faassenii*) is perfect for planting along walks or walls in average, well-drained soil. It is also ideal at the front of perennial borders with other low plants.

Description: The soft gray-green leaves of catmint clothe wiry stems crowned with clusters of violet to lavender-blue tubular flowers.

Nepeta × *faassenii* (fah-SEN-ee-eye), catmint. Size: 1½′–2′ tall; leaves to 1½″ long. Catmint has erect stems and ½″ blue-violet flowers. 'Six Hills Giant' grows to 3′ with deep-violet flowers. Zones 3–8.

N. mussinii (mu-SIN-ee-eye), Persian nepeta, Persian catmint. Size: 1′–1½′ tall; leaves to 1″ long. This mounded plant has wiry stems and clusters of lavender-blue ½″ flowers. 'Blue Wonder' bears deep-blue flowers. Zones 3–8.

How to Grow: Plant in average, well-drained soil in full sun or light shade. Shear plants by ½–⅔ after flowering. Take tip cuttings in early summer or transplant rooted stems.

Landscape Uses: Catmints are lovely along walks or as edging for beds. Mix them with yarrows and verbenas (*Verbena* spp.). 🌿

Oenothera   Onagraceae, Evening Primrose Family

ee-no-THEE-ruh. Evening Primrose. Spring and summer bloom. Full sun.

Description: Evening primroses are plants of meadows, roadsides, and prairies. They have lovely saucer-shaped flowers with 4 wide, overlapping petals and a prominent stigma (female reproductive structure). The weakly upright, often succulent stems bear lance-shaped foliage and elongated terminal clusters of flowers. Plants grow from a thick taproot or fibrous roots.

Oenothera caespitosa (see-spih-TOE-suh), tufted evening primrose. Size: 4"–8" tall; leaves to 4" long. This low, tufted plant has spreading stems with deep-green lance-shaped leaves and 2"–3"-wide flowers that open white in the afternoon and fade to pink. Zones 4–7.

O. fruticosa (frew-tih-KOH-suh), sundrops. Size: 1½'–2' tall; leaves 1"–3" long. Sundrops are day-flowering plants with leafy, upright stems and bright-yellow 1½"–2"-wide flowers that open from red-tinged buds. Zones 4–8.

O. missouriensis (mih-zore-ee-EN-sis),

Oenothera fruticosa 'Youngii' will brighten up a dry, sunny spot with its bright-yellow flowers, which open during the day from tear-shaped red buds.

Ozark sundrops, Missouri primrose. Size: 6″–12″ tall; leaves 2″–4″ long. This showy species has large, 3″–4″-wide lemon-yellow flowers and narrow light-green leaves. 'Greencourt Lemon' has 2″–2½″ soft sulphur-yellow flowers. Zones 4–8.

O. speciosa (spee-see-OH-suh), showy evening primrose. Size: 1′–2′ tall; leaves 1″–3″ long. This sprawling plant produces a profusion of 2″-wide soft-pink flowers on wiry stems. Plants may be invasive. 'Rosea' has rose-pink flowers. Zones 5–8.

O. tetragona (teh-truh-GO-nuh), common sundrops. Size: 1′–3′ tall; leaves to 3″ long. Similar to *O. fruticosa* but with gland-tipped hairs on the flower buds and fewer flowers per stem. 'Fireworks' grows 1½′ tall with 2″ flowers and reddish stems. 'Yellow River' grows to 2′ tall and has 2″ bright-yellow flowers. Zones 3–8.

How to Grow: Grow these drought-tolerant plants in average to rich, well-drained soil in full sun or light shade. Most species spread by slow-creeping roots to form dense clumps; *O. speciosa* spreads rapidly in rich soil and may need to be divided or thinned out each season. Divide the rosettes in early spring or after flowering in late summer.

Landscape Uses: Plant smaller species with catmints (*Nepeta* spp.) and irises. Try *O. caespitosa* in a sunny rock garden. ❧

Opuntia Cactaceae, Cactus Family

oh-PUN-tee-uh. Prickly Pear. Early-summer bloom. Full sun.

For sandy seaside gardens or dry, sunny rock gardens, you can't beat the bright-yellow flowers of prickly pear (*Opuntia humifusa*).

Description: *Opuntia humifusa* (hew-mih-FEW-suh), prickly pear (also listed as *O. compressa*). Size: 4″–6″ tall; leaves absent. This temperate-climate cactus has oval, flattened stems called pads that are armed with fierce, short spines. The lovely, lemon-yellow, 3″–4″-wide flowers are carried in rows along the tops of the pads. Green or purple fruits form after flowering. The fibrous-rooted plants spread to form wide clumps. Zones 4–9.

How to Grow: Plant in average, sandy or loamy soil in full sun. Clumps spread steadily and need little care. Propagate by removing pads and covering their bases with moist sand.

Landscape Uses: Plant prickly pears with drought-tolerant perennials such as butterfly weed (*Asclepias tuberosa*), yarrows, sedums, and evening primroses (*Oenothera* spp.). In the wild garden or seaside garden, plant them with ornamental grasses. ❧

Paeonia Ranunculaceae, Buttercup Family

pay-OHN-ee-uh. Peony. Spring and early-summer bloom. Full sun or light shade.

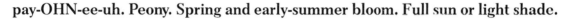

Description: Peonies are prized for their variety of form and color, their exceptional hardiness, and their ease of culture. Peonies have been in cultivation in China and Japan for centuries. Individual plants may live 100 years or longer. A few species are grown, but most garden peonies are hybrids of *Paeonia officinalis* and *P. lactiflora*. Colors range from white, cream, and yellow to pink, rose, and scarlet.

Plants are often classified by bloom time as early-May (April in the South) blooming, mid-May blooming, and late-May blooming. Plants can also be grouped into 4 categories by the shape of their flowers. Single peonies have a ring of 5 or more petals with a central ring of stamens (male reproductive structures). Japanese peonies have a ring of petals around a central cluster of modified stamens that are narrow and flat and bear no pollen. (Anemone-flowered peonies also fall into this group, but

Hybrid peonies take up to 3 years to reach their full flowering potential. Once established, they are long-lived and produce mounds of colorful flowers.

Stake double-flowered peonies such as *Paeonia* 'Cora Stubbs' to keep their heavy heads from lying facedown in the mud after a hard rain. Place a circular hoop over the plants in early spring, or support the growing stems with stakes and string.

their modified stamens are more petal-like.) Semidouble peonies have several rings of petals around visible stamens. Double peonies have many concentric rings of petals and no visible stamens.

P. lactiflora (lack-tih-FLOOR-uh), common garden peony, Chinese peony. Size: 1½'–3' tall; leaves to 1' long. This late-blooming species has single 3"–4"-wide, white or pink flowers. Many cultivars and hybrids have been named. 'Doreen' is a mid-season, rose-pink anemone. 'Duchess de Nemours' is an early white double. 'Festiva Maxima' is an early white double flecked with red. 'Gay Paree' is a mid-season cerise-and-white Japanese type. 'Karl Rosenfield' is a mid-season, dark-crimson double. 'Mons. Jules Elie' is an early rose-pink double. 'Nippon Beauty' is a late garnet-red Japanese type. 'Paula Fay' is an early pink semidouble. 'Red Charm' is an early red

double. 'Sara Bernhardt' is a mid-season, fragrant pink double. 'Sea Shell' is a mid-season pink single. Zones 2–8.

P. officinalis (oh-fiss-ih-NAH-lis), common peony. Size: 1½'–2' tall; leaves to 1' long. This peony is seen most often in gardens in its fully double, shell-pink form 'Rosea Superba', called the Memorial Day peony. The 3½"–5"-wide flowers may also be single, and several cultivars are readily available. 'Lobata' is a mid-season, salmon-orange single. 'Mutabilis Plena' is an early to mid-season rose-pink double with huge flowers. 'Rubra Plena' is an early-to mid-season red double also called a Memorial Day peony. Zones 3–8.

P. suffruticosa (suff-frew-tih-KOE-suh), tree peony. Size: 3'–5' tall; leaves to 1½' long. Tree peonies are actually shrubs with woody, sparsely branching stems that grow from thick roots. The leaves and flowers are produced each season on new growth. The 6″–8″-wide, crepe-paper-like flowers are white, rose-pink to red, or yellow. Many cultivars of exceptional garden merit have been developed. 'Age of Gold' has yellow fragrant semidouble flowers with visible stamens. 'Godaishu' ('Five Continents') has semidouble 10″ pure-white flowers. 'Hana-daijin' ('Minister of Flowers') has double deep-purple flowers. 'Kamada-nishiki' ('Kamada Brocade') is a fragrant semidouble with lilac-purple flowers. 'Kao' ('King of Flowers') has semidouble, brilliant-red flowers. Zones 3–8.

P. tenuifolia (ten-you-ih-FOE-lee-uh), fernleaf peony. Size: 1′–1½′ tall; leaves to 4″ long. This delicate peony has finely divided, fan-shaped leaves with narrow leaflets. The 2½″–3″-wide ruby-red spring flowers are perched on the top of the stems and surrounded by the leaves. 'Rubra Plena' has deep-red double flowers. Zones 3–8.

How to Grow: Peonies require moist, loamy, humus-rich soil in full sun or light shade. Plant the thick, fleshy roots of herbaceous peonies in September or October. Excavate a hole 8″–10″ deep in well-prepared soil. Place the eyes (buds) no more than 2″ below the soil surface. Plant each clump at least 3′ from other plants to allow for their mature spread. Mulch the first winter to protect from frost heaving. Protect plants with an annual winter mulch in areas where winter temperatures dip consistently below zero and snow cover is unpredictable.

Taller selections and most doubles usually need staking to keep their flowers out of the mud. In warmer zones, provide shade from afternoon sun to prolong flowering and help keep colors from fading. In fall, cut the stems to the ground.

Plants may grow undisturbed for years, but if roots get overcrowded or the soil gets impoverished, blooms may be sparse. Lift plants in late summer, wash off the soil, and cut the roots into sections with 4–5 eyes each. Use a sharp knife and make clean cuts. Replant divisions into enriched soil.

Occasionally peonies fail to bloom. The American Peony Society suggests the following reasons for poor garden performance:

▶ Plants are too small. Peonies may take several years to reach blooming size.

▶ Buds are more than 1″–2″ deep. Lift the clump and replant it at the correct level.

▶ Clump is crowded. Lift, divide, and replant.

▶ Buds were killed by winter cold. Provide a winter mulch to prevent damage next year.

▶ Buds were killed by disease. Botrytis, a fungal disease, may cause buds to abort. It can also kill stems or may even rot the roots. Destroy badly infected plants or spray leaves and stems with a fungicide. (See "Fungal Diseases" on page 227 for a list of organic fungicides.)

Single-flowered peonies such as *Paeonia* 'Prairie Moon' generally have self-supporting stems that stand up to wind and rain.

▶ Buds were killed by insects. Thrips, tiny insects that hide under the leaves and in bud scales, may cause deformed stems and buds. As soon as you see signs of damage, spray with insecticidal soap every 3 days for 2 weeks.

▶ Plants need fertilizer. Apply composted manure or high-potassium fertilizer such as greensand.

▶ The soil is too dry. Irrigate plants to supply evenly moist soil.

▶ Plants are not getting enough sun. Move them to a site where they will get 6–8 hours of full sun each day.

Tree peonies are equally easy to grow. Plant potted divisions in well-prepared, neutral to slightly acid, humus-rich soil in full sun or partial shade. Plants are often grafted. Plant them with the graft union 6″–12″ below the soil, especially in cooler zones where plants should be encouraged to form their own roots. Winter protection is important north of Zone 6 to ensure that the stems are not damaged. Prune plants as needed to encourage good form. If suckers arise from the rootstocks, remove them.

Landscape Uses: For early-spring color, combine their ruby-red shoots with minor bulbs and forget-me-nots (*Myosotis* spp.). The expanding peony foliage will shroud the declining bulb foliage. Plant peonies with spring and early-summer perennials such as Siberian iris (*Iris sibirica*) and foxgloves (*Digitalis* spp.). Choose tree peonies for a shrub border, or plant them with fine-textured and small-flowered plants. ❦

Papaver   Papaveraceae, Poppy Family

pa-PAH-ver. Poppy. Spring and early-summer bloom. Full sun.

Description: Poppies are delightful flowers with crepe-paper-like petals surrounding a ring of dark stamens (male reproductive structures) and a central knot that will ultimately become a seedpod. The flowers are carried singly atop stout stems and open from nodding buds. Plants produce clumps of broadly lance-shaped, oval, or lobed foliage from thick, deep taproots. The leaves have toothed margins and may be smooth and

For a dazzling flower display in early summer, plant oriental poppy (*Papaver orientale*). After flowering, plants quickly go dormant for the remainder of the season. Combine them with bushy plants that will fill the gap left when the leaves die down.

waxy or rough and hairy.

Papaver nudicaule (new-dih-KAW-lee), Iceland poppy. Size: 1'–1½' tall; leaves 4"–6" long. This short-lived perennial poppy has basal clumps of gray-green lobed leaves and blousy pink, salmon, orange, or white 2"–3"-wide flowers in spring. 'Wonderland' hybrids are available in mixed colors of 3" flowers. Zones 2–7.

P. orientale (or-ee-en-TAL-ee), oriental poppy. Size: 2'–3' tall; leaves to 1' long. Oriental poppies are one of the showiest perennials in the early-summer garden. The 3"–4"-wide flowers boast black spots at the bases of the petals and a central ring of fuzzy black stamens. The somewhat rank, hairy, lobed foliage disappears after flowering as the plants go dormant. The species has brilliant-orange flowers, but a number of cultivars with more easy-to-use colors are available. 'Allegro' is a compact (1½') grower with scarlet flowers. 'Beauty of Livermore' has deep-red flowers on tall (3') stems. 'Bonfire' is a widely sold cultivar with large brilliant-red flowers. 'Brilliant' has fiery-red flowers. 'Helen Elizabeth' has pale salmon-pink unspotted flowers. 'Princess Victoria Louise' has bright salmon-pink flowers. 'Snow Queen' is pure-white with prominent black spots. 'Watermelon' is watermelon-pink. Zones 2–7.

How to Grow: Iceland poppies grow best in rich, moist but well-drained soil in full sun; in the South, plants prefer partial shade. Direct-sow seed in late summer in the North or in fall in the South. Individual plants are short-lived, but they will self-sow if you allow some of the seedpods to mature. Oriental poppies are tough, long-lived plants. Give them average to rich, well-drained soil in full sun. In warmer zones, plants benefit from afternoon shade. Once established, the poppies grow to fill 2–3 square feet of garden space. The huge flowers are carried for several weeks, and then plants begin to fade and go dormant. Their disappearance leaves large gaps in the garden that must be filled by neighboring foliage and flowers.

When temperatures moderate in late summer, plants produce a new rosette of foliage. This is the time to divide overgrown clumps, a task usually required every 5–6 years. Lifted clumps invariably leave behind a few broken roots, which will form new plants. To propagate, take root cuttings while you are dividing the clumps and root them in moist sand. New plants develop quickly and can be planted out next spring.

Landscape Uses: Plant bold-flowered poppies with more-subtle perennials such as speedwells (*Veronica* spp.), bellflowers (*Campanula* spp.), baptisias (*Baptisia* spp.), and blue stars (*Amsonia* spp.). Use spreading plants such as baby's-breath to fill the inevitable border gaps. 🌿

Oriental poppies such as *Papaver orientale* 'China Boy' are extremely drought- and heat-tolerant. They grow from stout tap-roots that enable them to store water for dry periods.

Patrinia Valerianaceae, Valerian Family

puh-TRIN-ee-uh. Patrinia. Late-summer and fall bloom. Full sun or light shade.

Mature specimens of stately, autumn-flowering patrinia (*Patrinia scabiosifolia*) may reach 5′ to 6′ in height and are best planted at the rear of the border. Fresh-cut patrinia flowers last for weeks.

Description: *Patrinia scabiosifolia* (scab-ee-oh-sih-FOE-lee-uh), patrinia. Size: 3′–6′ tall; leaves 6″–10″ long. A tall, stately plant with basal rosettes of bold, pinnately divided leaves. The branching stems are crowned in a profusion of small, 2″-wide clusters of tiny yellow flowers. Plants grow from stout branching taproots. Zones 4–9.

How to Grow: Plant in average to rich, moist but well-drained soil in full sun or light shade. Once established, patrinias are long-lived and seldom need division. To avoid prolific self-seeding, remove flower heads as they fade, or cut stalks down when most of the flowers have bloomed. Propagate from seed sown outdoors in fall, or divide in spring or after flowering.

Landscape Uses: Plant patrinias in the middle or back of borders with tall asters (*Aster novae-angliae* or *A. tartaricus*) and ornamental grasses.

Penstemon Scrophulariaceae, Figwort Family

PEN-steh-mon. Penstemon, Beardtongue. Spring and summer bloom. Full sun or light shade.

Description: Penstemons produce slender unbranched spikes with tiers of inflated, irregularly shaped flowers with 2 upper and 3 lower lips. Flowers vary in color from white to pink, rose, lavender, and violet. Lush rosettes of evergreen leaves form wide patches that make attractive groundcovers when the plants are not in bloom. Clumps grow from fibrous roots. Success with penstemons depends on choosing the right species for your conditions. Species native to the western mountains often cook in the heat and rot in the humidity and dampness of midwestern and eastern gardens, but many excellent eastern natives and other adaptable species are available.

Penstemon albidus (AL-bih-dus), white-flowered penstemon. Size: 6″–14″ tall; leaves to 2½″ long. This prairie native has compact flowerstalks and ½"-long white flowers with flat faces. Zones 3–8.

P. australis (aw-STRAH-lis), southern penstemon. Size: 2½'–3' tall; leaves to 6" long. Southern penstemon has soft-hairy leaves and stems and white to pale-pink ¾"-long flowers with deep-rose stripes. Zones 5–9.

P. barbatus (bar-BAY-tus), common beardtongue. Size: 1½'–3' tall; leaves to 6" long. This stately plant has lance-shaped gray-green foliage and stout spikes of 1"–1½"-long pink to carmine flowers. 'Bashful' has salmon flowers on 12"–14" stems. 'Elfin Pink' has dark-green foliage and bright-pink flowers on 1' stems. 'Pink Beauty' has clear-pink flowers on 2'–2½' stems. Zones 3–8.

P. cobaea (koh-BE-uh), foxglove. Size: 1'–2½' tall; leaves to 2½" long. This handsome penstemon has 2"-long, inflated white flowers with violet stripes borne in tight clusters on the flowering stalks. Zones 5–9.

P. digitalis (dij-ih-TAL-iss), foxglove penstemon. Size: 2½'–5' tall; leaves to 8" long. This tall penstemon has shiny green leaves that form tufted rosettes. The flowerstalks bear open clusters of somewhat inflated 1"-long white flowers. 'Husker Red' has deep ruby-red foliage and stems and pink flowers. Zones 4–8.

P. hirsutus (her-SOO-tus), hairy beardtongue. Size: 2'–3' tall; leaves to 4" long. A fuzzy penstemon with purple to violet, narrow, tubular 1"-long flowers. 'Pygmaeus' has reddish foliage and lilac flowers on 8" stems. Zones 4–8.

P. laevigatus (lee-vih-GAH-tus), smooth beardtongue. Size: 2'–3' tall; leaves to 4" long. Similar to *P. digitalis,* but the 1"-long flowers are often pink and the plants are more compact. Zones 5–9.

P. pinifolius (pin-ih-FOE-lee-us). Size: 1'–2' tall; leaves to ¾" long. This shrubby penstemon has multibranched stems clothed

Tough, drought-tolerant hairy beardtongue (*Penstemon hirsutus*) is perfect for rock gardens or for planting on dry banks in full sun to light shade. The name "beardtongue" refers to the fuzzy mass of hairs on the sterile stamen (male reproductive structure).

in small, needle-like leaves and crowned with 1″–1½″-long tubular scarlet flowers. Zones 6–8.

P. smallii (SMALL-ee-eye), Small's beardtongue. Size: 2′–2½′ tall; leaves to 4″ long. This shrubby penstemon is clothed top to bottom in 1″-long rose-purple flowers for several weeks in early spring. Plants are short-lived. Zones 6–8.

Penstemon hybrids. Many hybrid penstemons of mixed parentage are available. Some of the most adaptable include the following: 'Firebird', with scarlet flowers in summer on 2′ stems; 'Mesa', with deep-violet flowers on 20″ stems; 'Prairie Dusk', with pendant, bell-shaped purple flowers on 1½′–2′ stems; and 'Prairie Fire', with orange-red flowers all summer on 2½′ stems.

How to Grow: Plant penstemons in sandy or loamy, humus-rich, well-drained soil in full sun or light shade. Good drainage is essential for all but *P. digitalis,* which tolerates moist or even wet soils. Plants increase by slow-creeping stems to form dense clumps; divide every 4–6 years to keep them vigorous. *P. smallii* and *P. cobaea* need a poor, sandy soil and excellent drainage; they decline after 3 years but self-sow profusely. Propagate by seed sown outdoors in fall or indoors in winter. If sowing indoors, place the seed flats in a refrigerator for 4–6 weeks before moving them to a warm, bright place. Seedlings may bloom the first year.

Landscape Uses: Combine penstemon with cranesbills (*Geranium* spp.), spiderworts (*Tradescantia* spp.), yarrows, evening primroses (*Oenothera* spp.), lamb's-ears (*Stachys* spp.), yuccas (*Yucca* spp.), and ornamental grasses. Use *P. smallii, P. pinifolius, P. hirsutus* 'Pygmaeus', and *P. cobaea* in the rock garden, where good drainage is assured. ❦

Perovskia Labiatae, Mint Family

per-OFF-skee-uh. Russian Sage. Summer bloom. Full sun.

Description: *Perovskia atriplicifolia* (ay-trih-pliss-ih-FOE-lee-uh), Russian sage. Size: 3′–5′ tall; leaves 1″–2½″ long. Russian sage is a shrubby, branching perennial with gray-green deeply toothed leaves and airy 12″–15″ sprays of tiny powder-blue flowers. The plants grow from woody crowns with dense fibrous roots. 'Blue Spire' is an upright selection with violet-blue flowers. 'Longin' has stout, erect stems and grows to 3′ or more. Zones 4–9.

Russian sage (*Perovskia atriplicifolia*) earns its keep in the garden by producing soft, gray-green shoots in spring, powder-blue flowers that bloom for over a month in summer, and silky gray, dried seed heads in autumn.

How to Grow: Plant in well-drained, sandy or loamy soil in full sun. Good drainage is essential. After hard frost, cut plants back to 1′. In the North, plants often die back to the soil but resprout from the roots. They seldom need dividing. Take stem cuttings in early summer.

Landscape Uses: The soft-blue flowers of Russian sage complement pink, yellow, deep blues, and purples. Plant it in the middle or back of the perennial border with yarrows, phlox, balloon flower (*Platycodon grandiflorus*), gayfeathers (*Liatris* spp.), and ornamental grasses. 🍂

Phlox   Polemoniaceae, Phlox Family

FLOCKS. Phlox. Spring and summer bloom. Full sun to shade.

Description: Phlox are garden favorites among wildflower fanciers and perennial enthusiasts alike. Their ease of culture, prolific bloom, and fragrance have endeared them to generations of gardeners. The 5-petaled flowers are tubular at the base and flare at the end to form a flat face. The flowers open from gracefully twisted buds. Flowers may be white, pink, rose, red, violet, blue, or bicolored. Some species form basal carpets of opposite, short-stalked leaves with ephemeral bloom stalks that wither away after seeds ripen. Others produce tall, persistent leafy stems crowned with dense, domed heads of flowers. Plants grow from crowns with dense, fibrous white roots.

Phlox bifida (BIH-fid-uh), sand phlox. Size: 6″–8″ tall; leaves to 2″ long. A creeping plant with needle-like leaves and loose clusters of ⅜″-wide spring flowers with deeply notched white to lavender petals. ‘Colvin’s White’ has pure-white flowers. Zones 4–8.

P. carolina (care-oh-LIE-nuh), thick leaf phlox. Size: 3′–4′ tall; leaves to 5″ long. This stout phlox has glossy oval leaves and elongated flower clusters. Flowers are ¾″-wide and pink to purple, or sometimes white. ‘Miss Lingard’ has white flowers with pale-yellow

The hybrid ‘Chattahoochee’ phlox resembles wild blue phlox (*Phlox divaricata*) but has a violet eye and requires full sun or light shade for best flowering.

eyes and is mildew-resistant. ‘Rosalinde’ has vibrant deep-pink flowers. Zones 4–9.

P. divaricata (dih-var-ih-KAH-tuh), wild blue phlox, woodland phlox. Size: 10″–15″ tall;

Floriferous wild blue phlox (*Phlox divaricata*) has fragrant sky-blue flowers that last for 2 weeks in shaded gardens. The plant's creeping stems form an attractive groundcover.

leaves to 2″ long. This woodland species forms erect, spreading clumps of glossy, evergreen, broadly lance-shaped leaves. The flowering stems are erect and hairy, topped by an open cluster of fragrant sky-blue ¾″-wide flowers. The stalk withers after flowering. 'Dirigo Ice' has pale-blue flowers. 'Fuller's White' is a sturdy, compact plant with pure-white flowers. The subspecies *laphamii* has periwinkle-blue flowers. *P.* 'Chattahoochee' (also known as 'Moody Blue') is a hybrid of contested origin with *P. divaricata* subsp. *laphamii* as one parent and probably *P. pilosa* as the other. The plants have linear leaves and prefer sun, but have lavender-blue flowers with violet eyes that bleed their color into the petals. Zones 3–9.

P. douglasii (DUG-less-ee-eye), Douglas's phlox. Size: 4″–8″ tall; leaves to ½″ long. The creeping stems form dense mats with needle-like leaves and lavender, pink, or white ½″-wide flowers in 1–3-flowered clusters. 'Cracker Jack' has carmine-red flowers. 'Waterloo' has violet-red flowers. Zones 3–8.

P. maculata (mack-you-LAH-tuh), wild sweet William, early phlox. Size: 2′–3′ tall; leaves to 4″ long. Early phlox is similar to *P. carolina* but with linear foliage and narrower clusters of ½″-wide flowers. 'Alpha' has rose-pink flowers with slightly darker eyes. 'Delta' has elongated, 1′ heads of white flowers with deep-pink eyes. 'Omega' has white flowers with lilac-pink eyes. Zones 3–9.

P. ovata (oh-VAH-tuh), mountain phlox. Size: 12″–20″ tall; leaves to 6″ long. This upright, spreading phlox has glossy, oval leaves and open clusters of white, pink, or magenta 1″-wide flowers in late spring. 'Spring Delight' has rose-pink flowers from late spring through early summer. Zones 4–8.

P. paniculata (pan-ick-you-LAH-tuh), garden phlox, summer phlox. Size: 3′–4′ tall; leaves 2″–5″ long. Garden phlox is a popular summer perennial with huge domed clusters of fragrant magenta, pink, or white 1″-wide flowers and broadly lance-shaped, dull-green leaves on erect, stiff stems. Hundreds of selections and hybrids have been made to increase the color range to violet, purple, rose, cerise, salmon, orange, and bicolors. Hybridizers have also endeavored to increase the mildew resistance of garden phlox by crossing them with glossy-leaved species, particularly *P. maculata*. Some of the most popular selections are listed below. 'Bright Eyes' has pink flowers with crimson eyes and is mildew-resistant. 'Caroline van den Berg' has purple flowers. 'David' has huge heads of pure-white flowers and shows excellent mildew resistance. 'Dodo Hanbury Forbes' has large heads of pure-pink rose-eyed flowers. 'Mt. Fujiyama' is a late-summer reblooming white with moderate mildew resistance. 'Orange Perfection' is a compact (2′) grower with orange-salmon flowers. 'Sandra' is a dwarf (1½′) grower with scarlet flowers. 'Sir John Falstaff' has deep salmon-pink flowers with purple eyes. 'Starfire' is an early, vibrant deep-red with red-tinged foliage. 'The King' has deep-purple flowers. Zones 3 or 4 (depending on the cultivar) –8.

P. stolonifera (stoh-lon-IF-er-uh), creeping phlox. Size: 6″–8″ tall; leaves to 1″ long. This lovely woodland phlox forms broad, dense clumps from creeping stems that root as they go. The ephemeral bloom stalks carry open clusters of ¾″-wide lavender to pink flowers in early to mid-spring. 'Blue Ridge' has lilac-blue flowers. 'Bruce's White' has white flowers with yellow eyes. 'Pink Ridge' has mauve-pink flowers. 'Sherwood Purple' has purple-blue, fragrant flowers. Zones 2–8.

P. subulata (sub-you-LAH-tuh), moss pink, moss phlox. Size: 4″–8″ tall; leaves to ¾″ long. The best-selling spring phlox, moss phlox is widely grown on slopes and banks and in rock gardens. The ¾″-wide, pink, magenta, blue, or white flowers cover the mounds of needle-like foliage and wiry stems. Plants bloom for several weeks. 'Emerald Cushion Blue' has blue flowers. 'Emerald Cushion Pink' has pink flowers and is long-blooming. 'Maiden's Blush' is pink-flushed white with a red eye and is a good rebloomer. 'Millstream Daphne', a hybrid with *P. stolonifera*, is vibrant-pink with a yellow eye. 'Scarlet Flame' has bright-scarlet flowers. 'White Delight' has pure-white flowers. Zones 2–9.

How to Grow: The cultivated phlox can be placed into 3 groups based on their

Like other cultivars of garden phlox, *Phlox paniculata* 'Starfire' has a heady fragrance familiar to generations of perennial gardeners. A myriad of colors is available for mixing with other summer-blooming perennials such as globe thistles (*Echinops* spp.).

Bright-pink *Phlox* 'Millstream Daphne' is ideal for planting in rock gardens or on dry, sunny banks.

their susceptibility to powdery mildew, which causes white patches on plant leaves. Choose a site with good air circulation, try resistant species and cultivars, and thin the stems of dense clumps to keep them in peak condition. Mildew is often the greatest threat at the end of the summer or during hot, dry spells. If you really want to avoid mildew, spray leaves with wettable sulfur 1–2 times per week when you notice the first signs of white mildew. (The woodland species are also mildly susceptible to mildew and can be treated similarly if infection develops.) Propagate plants by stem cuttings in spring and early summer. They also grow from root cuttings taken in the fall and laid horizontally in moist sand.

Landscape Uses: Choose the woodland phlox for early color in the shade or wild-flower garden. Plant them with spring bulbs, lungworts (*Pulmonaria* spp.), lilies-of-the-valley, bellflowers (*Campanula* spp.), leopard's bane (*Doronicum orientale*), bleeding hearts (*Dicentra* spp.), Solomon's seals (*Polygonatum* spp.), hostas, and ferns. Wildflowers such as wild columbine (*Aquilegia canadensis*), Virginia bluebells (*Mertensia virginica*), Canada wild ginger (*Asarum canadense*), and Allegheny foamflower (*Tiarella cordifolia*) are also good choices. The low, mounding phlox species are perfect for rock gardens, at the front of the border, or along walks. Plant them with basket-of-gold (*Aurinia saxatilis*), sedums, rock cresses (*Arabis* spp.), penstemons (*Penstemon* spp.), and yuccas (*Yucca* spp.). Border phlox are best placed in the middle or rear of the garden. Give them ample room to spread, and combine them with perennials such as bonesets (*Eupatorium* spp.), bee balms (*Monarda* spp.), Shasta daisy (*Chrysanthemum* × *superbum*), astilbes, meadow-sweets (*Filipendula* spp.), cranesbills (*Geranium* spp.), delphiniums, daylilies, and ornamental grasses. ❦

requirements for growth. The woodland species, including *P. divaricata* and *P. stolonifera*, require evenly moist, humus-rich soil in light to full shade. They form evergreen groundcovers that seldom need dividing unless they crowd other plants. Division is best done after flowering. Take cuttings in May and June. They root quickly and bloom the next season.

The low, mounding phlox include *P. bifida, P. douglasii, P.* × 'Chattahoochee', and *P. subulata.* Give them average, sandy or loamy, well-drained soil in full sun. Divide them in fall or take cuttings in spring or early summer.

The border phlox include *P. carolina, P. maculata, P. ovata,* and *P. paniculata.* Plant them in average to rich, moist but well-drained soil in full sun or light shade. Plants perform best where summers are cool and often bloom for weeks on end. By selecting cultivars carefully, you can have border phlox in bloom from June through September. They form multi-stemmed clumps that need division every 3–4 years in spring. Cultivars vary in

Physostegia Labiatae, Mint Family

fie-so-STEE-gee-uh. Obedient Plant. Late-summer bloom. Full sun to partial shade.

Description: *Physostegia virginiana* (ver-jin-ee-AH-nuh), obedient plant, Virginia false dragonhead. Size: 3′–4′ tall; leaves to 5″ long. Obedient plant is a fast spreader with creeping stems and fibrous roots. The flower spikes are 1′–1½′ tall, with coarsely-toothed, lance-shaped leaves and 4 vertical rows of 1″-long bilobed flowers. The name obedient plant arises from the tendency of the pale lilac-pink flowers to remain in any position to which they are shifted. 'Pink Bouquet' has bright-pink flowers on 3′–4′ stems. 'Summer Snow' is pure-white, compact (to 3′), and less rampant. It blooms several weeks earlier than the other cultivars. 'Variegata' has leaves edged in creamy-white and pale-pink flowers. 'Vivid' has vibrant rose-pink flowers on 2′–3′ stems. Zones 3–9.

How to Grow: Plant in evenly moist, average soil in full sun or partial shade. Plants tolerate considerable moisture. They tend to flop in rich soil, so select a compact cultivar if your soil is rich in humus; staking may still be necessary. Divide every 2–3 years to control their spread. Stem cuttings root easily in early summer.

Landscape Uses: Combine obedient plant with late-summer perennials such as asters, boltonia (*Boltonia asteroides*), phlox, meadow rues (*Thalictrum* spp.), bonesets (*Eupatorium* spp.), goldenrods (*Solidago* spp.), sunflowers (*Helianthus* spp.), and ornamental grasses. 🍂

The vivid pink flowers of 'Rosy Spire' obedient plant (*Physostegia virginiana* 'Rosy Spire') open for up to 3 weeks in late summer. Plants will bloom a month or more if you deadhead them regularly.

Platycodon Campanulaceae, Bellflower Family

plah-tee-KOE-don. Balloon Flower. Summer bloom. Full sun to light shade.

Balloon flower (*Platycodon grandiflorus*) comes in a wide range of sizes—from 6″ to 3′ in height. For a small garden, dwarf forms, such as the one pictured here, are ideal.

Description: *Platycodon grandiflorus* (gran-dih-FLOOR-us), balloon flower. Size: 2′–3′ tall; leaves 1″–3″ long. Balloon flower is a showstopper in the garden. The bright-blue 2″–3″-wide saucer-shaped flowers have 5 starry lobes that open from inflated round buds that resemble balloons. The flowers are borne singly on short branches off the main stems. Plants produce upright succulent stems clothed in toothed, triangular leaves from thick, fleshy roots. The variety *albus* has white flowers. 'Apoyama' produces blue-violet flowers on 6″ plants; many semidwarf plants are sold under this name. 'Double Blue' has bright-blue double flowers on 2′ plants. 'Fuji'

series is a seed-grown strain of mixed pink, white and blue selections on tall stems. 'Komachi' is clear-blue and 1′–2′ tall. The variety *mariesii* (also sold as 'Mariesii') has rich blue flowers on 1′–1½′ plants. 'Shell Pink' has soft pale-pink flowers on 2′ plants. Zones 3–8.

How to Grow: Plant balloon flowers in average to rich, well-drained soil in full sun or light shade. Plants are tough and adaptable. New shoots are slow to emerge in spring—take care not to dig into the clumps by mistake. Balloon flowers bloom for a month or more in early to mid-summer. Removing the spent flowers will encourage continued bloom and keep the plants tidy. They seldom need division once established. If you wish to divide for propagation or if you must transplant them, lift the clumps in spring or early fall. Dig deeply to avoid damaging the thick roots. Plants will self-sow in the garden. Sow fresh seeds outdoors in late summer or fall. Plants will bloom the second year from seed.

Landscape Uses: Combine balloon flowers with summer-blooming perennials such as yellow yarrows (*Achillea* × 'Moonshine' and *A. filipendulina*), alliums (*Allium* spp.), violet sage (*Salvia* × *superba*), bee balm (*Monarda didyma*), and garden phlox (*Phlox paniculata*). Use foliage to set off the bright-blue or pink flowers. Choose silvery lamb's-ears (*Stachys byzantina*) and artemisias, along with ornamental grasses. The compact varieties and dwarf cultivars are well-suited to growing in containers. Blooms last well as fresh-cut flowers—singe the stem ends with a match to stop the milky sap from flowing. ❦

Polemonium Polemoniaceae, Phlox Family

po-leh-MOW-nee-um. Jacob's Ladder. Spring and summer bloom. Full sun or partial shade.

Description: Jacob's ladders are noted for their distinctive divided leaves. Clusters of cup- or saucer-shaped flowers bloom atop succulent stems that emerge from fibrous-rooted crowns.

Polemonium caeruleum (sir-ROO-lee-um), Jacob's ladder. Size: 1½'–2' tall; leaves 3"–5" long. This summer-blooming species has erect stems and deep-blue ½"-wide flowers. The variety *album* has white flowers. Zones 3–7.

P. reptans (REP-tanz), creeping Jacob's ladder. Size: 8"–16" tall; leaves 4"–8" long. Mounds of foliage cover short, branching stems topped with deep sky-blue, ½"-wide flowers. Zones 2–8.

How to Grow: Plant in evenly moist, humus-rich soil in full sun or partial shade (especially in warm regions). Plants seldom need division. Sow seed outside in fall.

Landscape Uses: Plant in masses under shrubs or airy flowering trees. 🌿

After the charming, sky-blue flowers of creeping Jacob's ladder (*Polemonium reptans*) fade, the pinnately divided leaves make an attractive groundcover throughout the summer.

Polygonatum Liliaceae, Lily Family

poe-lig-oh-NAY-tum. Solomon's Seal. Foliage plant with spring bloom. Light to full shade.

Description: Solomon's seals are graceful plants with erect, arching stems clothed in alternating, broadly oval leaves that form stair steps along the stem. The clustered, bell-shaped greenish or white flowers hang below the foliage from the nodes (leaf joints). Waxy, blue-black berries are produced in summer. Plants grow from thick, slow-creeping rhizomes with spidery, fibrous roots.

Polygonatum biflorum (bye-FLOOR-um), Solomon's seal. Size: 1'–3' tall; leaves 4"–4½" long. This plant has narrowly oval, deep gray-green leaves spaced in close succession along the stem. The ½"-long greenish white flowers are carried in pairs. Zones 3–9.

P. commutatum (kahm-you-TAH-tum),

If you have dry shade, variegated fragrant Solomon's seal (*Polygonatum odoratum* var. *thunbergii* 'Variegatum') is a must. The arching stems clothed in white-edged leaves are elegant.

great Solomon's seal. Size: 3'–7' tall; leaves 3"–7" long. This giant has stout stems with well-spaced oval leaves and clusters of 3–8, ¾"-wide greenish white flowers. Zones 3–7.

P. multiflorum (mull-tee-FLOOR-um), Eurasian Solomon's seal. Size: 2'–3' tall; leaves 2"–6" long. This species resembles *P. biflorum*, but the leaves are broader and the ¾"-wide flowers are white. Zones 4–7.

P. odoratum (oh-door-AH-tum), fragrant Solomon's seal, Japanese Solomon's seal. Size: 1½'–2½' tall; leaves 4"–6" long. This species has fragrant 1"-long white flowers and is seen in cultivation as the cultivar 'Variegatum'. This cultivar is larger (to 3') and has broadly oval leaves striped with creamy-white. Zones 3–9.

How to Grow: Plant Solomon's seals in moist, humus-rich soil in partial to full shade. Plants tolerate sun in the North but must have shade from any but morning sun in the South. Most species tolerate dry conditions with the exception of *P. commutatum*, which requires moist soil. Plants spread by branching rhizomes; divide them whenever they overgrow their position. Lift clumps in spring or fall and replant into amended soil. To propagate, remove the seeds from the pulpy fruit in fall and sow immediately outdoors. They may take 2 years to germinate and will grow slowly.

Landscape Uses: Solomon's seals are prized for the strong architectural quality of their arching stems. Combine them with bold foliage plants such as hostas, ferns, alumroots (*Heuchera* spp.), and lady's-mantle (*Alchemilla mollis*). Most species tolerate the dry shade under mature shade trees.

Polygonum Polygonaceae, Smartweed Family

poh-LIG-oh-num. Smartweed, Knotweed. Summer and fall bloom. Full sun or partial shade.

Description: Smartweeds are creeping plants bearing oblong shiny leaves alternately up the jointed stems. The erect flower spikes, sometimes nodding at the tip, are composed of tiny, tightly packed pink flowers with no distinguishable petals. They grow from woody crowns with fibrous roots.

Polygonum affine (uh-FEE-nee) Himalayan fleeceflower. Size: 6"–10" tall; leaves to 4" long. This slow spreader has bright-green leaves with prominent midveins and tight, erect, 2"–3" spikes of tiny rose-red flowers.

'Border Jewel' has rose-pink flowers. 'Darjeeling Red' has deep crimson-pink flowers. 'Dimity' has lighter pink flowers. Zones 3–7.

P. bistorta (bis-TOUR-tuh), snakeweed. Size: 1½'–2½' tall; leaves to 6" long. This is a stout plant with broad paddle-like foliage and dense, 4"–5" spikes of tiny, bright-pink flowers held well above the foliage. 'Superbum' has huge flower spikes. Zones 3–8.

How to Grow: Plant in moist, humus-rich soil in full sun or partial shade. *P. bistorta* tolerates considerable moisture; both species languish in dry soil. They do not tolerate full sun in the warmer zones. Plants spread by creeping stems that root as they go. Divide clumps in spring or fall to control their spread.

Landscape Uses: Plant smartweed where you need a spreading groundcover with excellent foliage and spiky flowers. Use *P. affine* at the front of a border or along steps. ❦

Snakeweed (*Polygonum bistorta* 'Superbum') requires moist or wet soil for the lovely foliage and showy flowers to reach their full potential.

Potentilla Rosaceae, Rose Family

poh-ten-TILL-uh. Cinquefoil. Summer bloom. Full sun or light shade.

Description: Cinquefoils have tight rosettes of hairy, divided leaves growing from a weakly taprooted crown. The flowers have 5 petals arrayed around a ring of fuzzy stamens (male reproductive structures). The petals may be yellow, orange, red, or (occasionally) white. Flowers are grouped into open, branching clusters.

Potentilla atrosanguinea (at-row-san-GWIN-ee-uh), Himalayan cinquefoil. Size: 1'–2' tall; leaves to 8" long. Tufts of 3-parted leaves set off the open clusters of deep-red 1"-wide flowers. 'Firedance' has salmon-red flowers on 1' stems. 'Gibson's Scarlet' produces brilliant-red flowers all summer on 1½' stems. 'Vulcan' has deep-red double flowers on 1'

Use diminutive *Potentilla tabernaemontani* as a groundcover in well-drained rock gardens or in the crevices of stone walls.

stems. 'William Rollison' has large (1½″) deep-orange flowers with bright-yellow centers. Plants bloom all summer. Zones 4–8.

P. nepalensis (neh-pall-EN-sis), Nepal cinquefoil. Size: 1′–2′ tall; leaves to 1′ long. This bushy species has leaves with long petioles (leafstalks) and 3–5 leaflets. The 1″-wide crimson flowers are carried above the foliage in open, branching clusters. 'Miss Wilmot' is a compact grower to 1′ with carmine flowers. Zones 4–8.

P. recta (WRECK-tuh), sulphur cinquefoil. Size: 1′–2½′ tall; leaves to 6″ long. This weedy species has rounded tufts of leaves with 5–9 leaflets and erect, broad clusters of ½″-wide yellow flowers. The variety *warrenii* is floriferous and showy. Zones 3–7.

P. tabernaemontani (tab-er-nay-mahn-TAN-ee), (also sold as *P. verna*). Size: 1′–2½′ tall; leaves to 8″ long. The ½″-wide yellow flowers appear in spring above mats of palmately lobed evergreen leaves. The cultivar 'Nana' reaches only 1″–3″ tall. Zones 4–8.

P. tridentata (try-den-TAH-tuh), wine-leaf cinquefoil. Size: 6″–12″ tall; leaves to 3″ long. The shiny, 3-parted deep-green foliage and clustered ¼″-wide white flowers make this species desirable. The leaves turn deep wine-red and orange in the autumn. 'Minima' is only 4″–6″ tall. Zones 2–8.

How to Grow: Cinquefoils grow best in well-drained, sandy or loamy soils in full sun or light shade. All prefer areas where neither winter nor summer temperatures are extreme. Plants creep slowly to form dense clumps. Divide in spring or fall.

Landscape Uses: Plant cinquefoils in rock gardens, in rock walls, or at the front of perennial gardens. Combine them with sedums, flax (*Linum* spp.), and baby's-breaths. ❦

Primula   Primulaceae, Primrose Family

PRIM-you-luh. Primrose. Spring and early-summer bloom. Sun to partial shade.

Description: Primroses are beloved spring flowers that bloom with flowering bulbs when the earth is reawakening. The broad leaves rise directly from stout crowns with fibrous roots. The flowers are tubular with broad, flattened 5-petaled faces. They are carried in open, branched clusters or in whorled tiers on erect stems. Most are native to cool regions, and some do not perform well in heat and high humidity.

The soft-yellow flowers and bright-green leaves of the dainty English primrose (*Primula vulgaris*) make it a valuable addition to the spring garden. It is also an important parent of many showy hybrids known as polyantha primroses.

Primula auricula (aw-RICK-you-luh), auricula primrose. Size: 2″–8″ tall; leaves 2″–3″ long. This hardy primrose has thick, bright-green paddle-shaped leaves. The clustered bell-shaped bright-yellow 1″-wide flowers are produced in April and May. Zones 2–8.

P. denticulata (den-tick-you-LAH-tuh), drumstick primrose. Size: 8″–12″ tall; leaves 4″–6″ long. The sharply toothed spatula-shaped leaves surround a thick stalk crowned by a cluster of ½″-wide lilac or white flowers. The variety *alba* has white flowers. 'Cashmere Ruby' has wine-colored flowers. 'Ronsdorf Strain' is a seed-grown strain of white, rose, purple, or lavender flowers. Zones 3–8.

P. elatior (ee-LAY-tee-or), oxslip. Size: 10″–12″ tall; leaves to 8″ long. The broad leaves are puckered or crinkled. The open, nodding, 1″-wide flowers are soft-yellow. Zone 3 (with winter protection) or Zones 4–7.

P. japonica (juh-PON-ih-kuh), Japanese primrose. Size: 1′–2′ tall; leaves to 1′ long. The broad paddle-shaped leaves have sharply toothed margins. The tiered, whorled clusters of pink, rose, or white ½″-wide flowers are borne in late spring and early summer. 'Millar's Crimson' has bright rose-red flowers. Zones 5–8.

P. × *polyantha* (pahl-ee-AN-thuh), polyanthus primrose. Size: 8″–12″ tall; leaves 8″–10″ long. These hybrids have broad crinkled leaves and short stalks with sparse clusters of flat, broad-petaled, 1½″-wide flowers. Many selections are available in a range of solid and bicolor forms. Zones 3–8.

P. sieboldii (see-BOLD-ee-eye), Siebold's primrose. Size: 4″–8″ tall; leaves 2″–4″ long. Siebold's primrose has fuzzy heart-shaped leaves with rounded teeth and 1″–1½″-wide, flattened, white, lavender, pink, or rose flowers with notched petals. 'Barnhaven Hybrids' come in mixed colors. Zones 4–8.

For a wet site with rich soil, try planting Japanese primrose (*Primula japonica*). Its cheerful flowers appear in early summer atop paddle-shaped leaves. The blooms are carried in whorled tiers on tall stalks.

Cowslip primrose (*Primula veris*) is an easy-care plant for lightly shaded woodlands or rock gardens. The pendulous yellow flowers are delightfully fragrant.

P. veris (VEE-ris), cowslip primrose. Size: 8"–12" tall; leaves 6"–8" long. Lovely, nodding, fragrant, ½"-wide yellow flowers are held above the elongated oval leaves of this delicate early primrose. Zones 4–8.

P. vulgaris (vul-GAH-riss), English primrose. Size: 6"–9" tall; leaves 4"–6" long. The wild English primrose has wrinkled, elongated, oval foliage and broad pale-yellow 1"-wide flowers with darker centers borne singly on short stems. Zones 4–8.

How to Grow: Primroses are generally easy to grow if you meet their simple needs. Most grow best in moist, humus-rich soil in light to partial shade. *P. japonica* and *P. denticulata* require constantly moist to boggy, humusy soil. In northern zones, winter mulch is essential, especially if snowfall is erratic. In the South, provide constistent moisture and shade from hot afternoon sun; when plants get too hot or dry, they go dormant early (although usually without adverse results). Divide overgrown clumps after flowering and replant into amended soil. Sow seed outdoors in fall or inside in early spring.

Landscape Uses: Primroses have a place in every garden. Plant them in clumps or drifts with spring bulbs such as tulips, snowdrops, and daffodils. Combine the wet-soil-loving species with irises, hostas, ferns, and lady's-mantle (*Alchemilla mollis*). 🌿

Pulmonaria Boraginaceae, Borage Family

puhl-muhn-AIR-ee-uh. Lungwort, Bethlehem Sage. Spring bloom. Light to full shade.

Description: Lungworts are early-blooming perennials with short, weakly upright stems sporting open clusters of nodding 5-petaled flowers. Some species have flowers that open pink and turn to blue; others bear pink, red, or white blooms. The basal leaves emerge and expand as the flowers are fading. They may be lance-shaped or ovate with pointed tapering tips and long petioles (leafstalks). The foliage of some species is attractively spotted and blotched with silver, while others have solid-green leaves. Plants grow from stout crowns with thick fibrous roots.

Pulmonaria angustifolia (an-gus-tih-FOE-lee-uh), blue lungwort. Size: 9"–12" tall; leaves 6"–8" long. Blue lungwort has ⅜"-wide deep-blue flowers and narrowly oval, bristly leaves. The plants spread by underground stems to form open clumps. 'Azurea' has vibrant gentian-blue flowers. 'Johnson's Blue' has deep-blue flowers. Zones 2–8.

P. longifolia (lon-gih-FOE-lee-uh), long-leaved lungwort. Size: 9″–12″ tall; leaves 8″–18″ long. The strap-shaped pointed leaves of this species are speckled with silver gray. The ⅜″-long flowers open pink and change to rich blue. 'Bertram Anderson' has narrower leaves than the species. Zones 3–8.

P. rubra (ROO-bruh), red lungwort. Size: 1′–2′ tall; leaves 4″–6″ long. This tall species has weakly upright stems and pointed, oval green leaves. The ½″-wide coral-red flowers make this a popular plant. Zones 4–7.

P. saccharata (sah-kah-RAH-tuh), Bethlehem sage. Size: 9″–18″ tall; leaves 6″–12″ wide; flowers ½″ wide. This is the most well-known lungwort, grown for its pointed, oval foliage with silver spots and clusters of pink buds and ½″-wide blue flowers. 'Janet Fisk' has densely spotted leaves and lavender-pink flowers. 'Mrs. Moon' has large broad leaves and pink flowers that fade to blue. 'Sissinghurst White' has white flowers. Zones 3–8.

How to Grow: Lungworts are easy to grow in evenly moist, humus-rich soil in partial to full shade. Plants are moderately drought-tolerant once established, but they may go dormant early if conditions get too dry. Divide overgrown clumps after flowering or in fall, and replant into amended soil.

Landscape Uses: Lungworts are lovely spring perennials with colorful foliage and flowers. Combine them with daffodils and other spring bulbs in beds and borders or under flowering trees and shrubs. The tough and attractive summer foliage is outstanding as a groundcover. In the perennial garden, plant lungworts in drifts with hellebores (*Helleborus* spp.), anemones (*Anemone* spp.), bleeding hearts (*Dicentra* spp.), and irises. ❦

Pulmonaria saccharata 'Mrs. Moon' produces delicate spring flowers that are just the beginning of the plant's seasonal display. The flowers are followed by broad clumps of lush, silver-spotted foliage that persist until hard frost.

Ranunculus Ranunculaceae, Buttercup Family

ruh-NUN-cue-lus. Buttercup. Spring bloom. Partial shade.

For a fast-spreading groundcover in a moist spot, try double-flowered creeping buttercup (*Ranunculus repens* 'Flore Pleno'). The buttonlike double yellow flowers, borne in spring, make this plant irresistible.

Description: *Ranunculus repens* (REE-penz), creeping buttercup. Size: 1½'–2' tall; leaves to 6" long. Buttercups are bright spring plants of meadows and gardens. Their shiny yellow flowers have 5 petal-like sepals surrounding a ring of fuzzy stamens (male reproductive structures). The ¾"-wide flowers bloom in sparse clusters above basal rosettes of 3-lobed, palmately divided leaves. Plants grow from fast-creeping fibrous roots. 'Flore-pleno' has rounded double flowers. Zones 3–8.

How to Grow: Plant buttercups in evenly moist, humus-rich soil in full sun or light shade. Plants spread rapidly by roots and self-sown seedlings. For control or propagation, divide after flowering or in fall. Cut off bloom stalks as flowers fade to prevent self-seeding.

Landscape Uses: Use buttercups as groundcovers in moist soil and with hostas, ferns, and other plants that can hold their own. Plants are best kept out of the formal perennial garden. 🍂

Rodgersia Saxifragaceae, Saxifrage Family

row-JER-zee-uh. Rodgersia, Roger's-Flower. Foliage plant with late-spring to early-summer bloom. Partial to full shade.

Description: These bold plants have huge, palmately lobed leaves and tall, branched spikes of fuzzy flowers. They grow from thick, slow-creeping rhizomes with fibrous roots.

Rodgersia aesculifolia (ess-cue-lih-FOE-lee-uh), fingerleaf rodgersia. Size: 4'–6' tall; leaves 2' wide. A handsome plant with crinkled leaves and 2' clusters of creamy-white flowers. Zones 4–7; may be hardier farther north.

R. podophylla (poh-doe-FILL-uh), bronzeleaf rodgersia. Size: to 5' tall; leaves to 2' wide. One-foot clusters of yellowish white flowers bloom over coppery-green leaves. Zones 5–7.

How to Grow: Rodgersias must have constantly moist to wet, humus-rich soil in light to full shade. Plants in warmer zones need more shade. Propagate by division in fall.

Landscape Uses: Rodgersias are lovely plants for bog and water gardens. Plant them with water-loving irises, meadowsweets (*Filipendula* spp.), globeflowers (*Trollius* spp.), ligularias (*Ligularia* spp.), astilbes, and ferns. 🍂

In moist or wet soil along ponds or streams, the bold foliage and airy plumes of bronzeleaf rodgersia (*Rodgersia podophylla*) create an impression of tropical luxuriance.

Rudbeckia Compositae, Daisy Family

ruhd-BECK-ee-uh. Coneflower, Black-Eyed Susan. Summer bloom. Full sun to light shade.

Description: Coneflowers are bright summer flowers of meadows, woods, and roadsides. These hardy, adaptable plants are among the most widely grown perennials. Their daisylike flowers have golden-yellow petal-like rays and brown to green domed or buttonlike disks. Plants gradually form broad clumps from branched crowns with fibrous roots. The basal leaves are oval, occasionally lobed, and usually rough and hairy. The stem leaves are smaller than the basal leaves.

Rudbeckia fulgida (FULL-jih-duh), orange coneflower. Size: 1½'–3' tall; leaves to 8" long. This popular perennial has showy orange-yellow 2"–2½"-wide flowers with deep-brown centers. The rough, hairy leaves are oval to broadly lance-shaped. Orange coneflowers bloom profusely for nearly a month in mid- to late summer. Several varieties exist. The widely available variety *sullivantii* is a stout grower with leafy stems and larger flowers than the species. 'Goldsturm' belongs to this variety and is a compact, long-blooming, floriferous selection with 3″–4″ flowers. Many plants sold under this name are seed-grown and therefore variable, but all are good garden plants. The variety *speciosa* (also known as *R. neumanii*) is a floriferous plant with single yellow flowers. Zones 3–9.

R. laciniata (luh-sin-ee-AH-tuh), ragged coneflower, green-headed coneflower. Size: 2½′–6′ tall; leaves to 16″ long. This tall, stout plant has large 3–5-lobed basal leaves and leafy stems with 3-lobed leaves. The stems are crowned by branched clusters of clear-yellow 2″–3″-wide flowers with drooping rays and a conical green disk. 'Gold Drop' has fully double flowers on compact 2′–3′ stems. 'Golden Glow' has 3½″–4″ lemon-yellow flowers on 3′–5′ stems. Zones 3–9.

R. maxima (MAX-ih-muh). Size: 5′–6′ tall; leaves to 16″ long. Tall stems bearing 5″-wide golden, black-centered flowers rise above eye-catching rosettes of gray-green foliage. Zones 3–9.

R. nitida (NIT-ih-duh), shining coneflower. Size: 3′–4′ tall; leaves to 1′ long. This species is similar to *R. laciniata* but has oval leaves without lobes. Most plants grown as *R. nitida* actually belong to *R. laciniata*. 'Goldquelle' is a floriferous selection with shaggy double flowers on 3′ stems. 'Herbstsonne' (also known as 'Autumn Sun') grows 5′–7′ tall and blooms in mid- to late summer. It has single 2″–3″-wide flowers with broad yellow rays and green to light-brown disks. Zones 4–9.

How to Grow: Plant *Rudbeckia* species in moist but well-drained, average to rich soil

'Goldsturm' black-eyed Susan (*Rudbeckia fulgida* var. *sullivantii* 'Goldsturm') is a workhorse perennial. Plants thrive in ordinary garden soil, endure heat and humidity, and bloom for over a month in late summer.

in full sun or light shade. *R. fulgida* and *R. maxima* are generally self-supporting; *R. laciniata* and *R. nitida* may require staking. If plants are floppy, cut them to the ground after flowering. Some species need frequent division in spring to control their spread. Divide *R. fulgida* every 2–3 years, *R. laciniata* every 3–5 years, and *R. maxima* as needed. Sow seed indoors in winter or outdoors in spring or fall.

Landscape Uses: Coneflowers are perfect for adding bright, long-lasting color to perennial gardens. Plant them with other summer-blooming flowers such as purple coneflower (*Echinacea purpurea*), Russian sage (*Perovskia atriplicifolia*), garden phlox (*Phlox paniculata*), sedums, bee balms (*Monarda* spp.), and ornamental grasses. They are also nice in meadow gardens. 🍂

Shining coneflower (*Rudbeckia nitida*) bears daisylike flowers atop 3' to 4' stems. It thrives in moist soil.

Ruta Rutaceae, Rue Family

ROO-tuh. Rue. Foliage plant with summer bloom. Full sun.

Description: *Ruta graveolens* (grah-VEE-oh-lenz), rue. Size: 1'–3' tall; leaves to 6" long. Rue's aromatic blue-gray leaves are finely dissected into many small leaflets. The leafy flowerstalks are crowned by flattened, branched clusters of small yellow flowers. Plants grow from a persistent woody base with a twisted, branched taproot. Some people reportedly develop a skin rash when working around rue foliage. 'Blue Mound' is a wide-spreading selection with rich blue-green foliage. Zones 4–9.

How to Grow: Give rues sandy or loamy, moist but well-drained soil in full sun. Plants seldom need division. Propagate by stem cuttings in late summer and early fall.

Landscape Uses: Rues are good plants for bordering perennial beds and edging herb gardens. 🍂

Rue (*Ruta graveolens*) forms shrubby mounds of finely cut blue-green leaves that are stunning in the border.

Salvia Labiatae, Mint Family

SAL-vee-uh. Sage. Summer and fall bloom. Full sun to light shade.

Use clumps of violet sage (*Salvia × superba*) to add upright, spiky forms to the middle or front of the border. They bloom for up to 2 months if old flower spikes are removed.

Description: Sages are mounded to shrubby mints with tubular flowers and square stems. The flowers have inflated upper lips that project over the lower ones. They are borne in tiered whorls at the tips of the branching stems. Many sages have aromatic foliage. The leaves may be oval or broadly lance-shaped. Plants grow from woody crowns with fibrous roots.

Salvia argentea (ar-JEN-tee-uh), silver sage. Size: 2′–4′ tall; leaves to 6″ long. Silver sage is grown for its luscious, crinkled, soft silver-gray foliage. Remove the insignificant yellow ½″-long flowers before they open. Zones 5–9.

S. azurea (uh-ZURE-ee-uh), azure sage. Size: 3′–4′ tall; leaves to 3″ long. This upright bushy sage has lance-shaped basal leaves, leafy stems, and dense terminal spikes of ¾″-long azure-blue flowers. The variety *grandiflora* has larger flowers. Zones 5–9.

S. farinacea (far-ih-NAY-see-uh), mealycup sage. Size: 1½'–4' tall; leaves to 3" long. This open, loosely branching sage has narrowly oval leaves and terminal spikes of ¼"-long violet-blue flowers held above the foliage. 'Blue Bedder' has deep-blue flowers on 1½'–2' stems. 'Victoria' is similar but more compact (1½'). Zones 8–10.

S. guaranitica (gwar-uh-NIT-ih-kuh). Size: 3'–3½' tall; leaves 2"–5" long. This tender sage bears spikes of violet-blue flowers above aromatic foliage. Zones 7 or 8–10.

S. leucantha (lew-CAN-thuh), velvet sage, Mexican bush sage. Size: 3'–4' tall; leaves 2"–6" long. This shrubby sage has woolly stems and leaves and 10" spikes of ¾"-long lavender flowers all summer long. Zones 8–10.

S. officinalis (oh-fiss-ih-NAH-lis), garden sage. Size: 1½'–2' tall; leaves 1"–2½" long. This ornamental and culinary sage is a semiwoody shrub with wrinkled, oblong leaves and somewhat insignificant ½"-long blue-violet flowers. 'Compacta' is a compact grower (to 15") with smaller leaves. 'Icterina' has gold-and-green variegated foliage. 'Purpurascens' has grayviolet leaves. 'Tricolor' has pink, green, and white leaves. Zones 3–9.

S. pratensis (pray-TEN-sis), meadow sage. Size: 1'–3' tall; leaves 3"–6" long. This slender sage has bushy rosettes of oval leaves and branching stems tipped with 1"-long, showy violet-blue flowers. 'Indigo' has deep-blue flowers and may be a hybrid of *S. farinacea*. 'Rosea' has rose-purple flowers. Zones 3–9.

S. × superba (soo-PER-buh), violet sage. Size: 1½'–3½' tall; leaves 1"–3" long. This lovely hybrid is smothered in stiff spikes of ½"-long violet-blue flowers for 3–4 weeks in early to mid-summer. The triangular leaves are bright-green with soft hairs on their undersides. 'Blue Queen' has violet flowers and is 1½'–2' tall.

The open habit of violet-blue *Salvia guaranitica* makes it perfect for sprawling among flowering shrubs such as *Rosa* 'The Fairy'.

'East Friesland' has deep-purple flowers on compact 1'–1½'-tall plants. Zones 4–7.

How to Grow: Plant sages in well-drained, sandy or loamy soils in full sun or light shade. They will get leggy and flop in too much shade. Overly rich or moist soils also encourage flopping. Most species are tough and extremely drought-tolerant. Cut plants back to the ground in fall or early spring. Divide plants in spring or fall if they overgrow their position. Propagate hardy species by stem cuttings in early summer. The less hardy species can be treated as annuals in colder zones and grown each season from seed sown indoors in late winter or from overwintered cuttings.

Landscape Uses: Sages are excellent additions to well-drained perennial gardens. Combine them with yuccas (*Yucca* spp.), yarrows, sedums, coneflowers (*Rudbeckia* spp.), daylilies, coreopsis (*Coreopsis* spp.), daisies, mums, and ornamental grasses. Plant *S. officinalis* in herb gardens or with ornamentals. They also respond well to container culture. 🌿

Santolina Compositae, Daisy Family

san-toe-LEE-nuh. Lavender Cotton. Summer bloom. Full sun.

Lavender cotton (*Santolina chamaecyparissus*) is an evergreen plant that produces mounds of white-woolly foliage. The plants are perfect for edging beds or knot gardens and can be clipped into formal shapes.

Description: Lavender cottons form dense, thickly branched mounds from fibrous-rooted woody crowns. In summer, buttonlike clusters of yellow flowers appear.

Santolina chamaecyparissus (kam-ee-sip-uh-RISS-us), lavender cotton. Size: 1′–2′ tall; leaves 1″–1½″ long. This plant has white-woolly, pinnately divided leaves and tiny yellow flowers in ¾″ rounded heads. Zones 6–8.

S. virens (VEER-enz), green lavender cotton. Size: 1′–2′ tall; leaves 1″–2″ long. This species is similar to *S. chamaecyparissus* but has deep-green foliage. Zones 6–8.

How to Grow: These drought-resistant plants need well-drained, sandy or loamy soil in full sun. Provide winter protection in colder areas. Prune hard after flowering to keep plants bushy. Take tip cuttings during the growing season.

Landscape Uses: Lavender cottons are ideal for edging beds and walks. 🌿

Saponaria Caryophyllaceae, Pink Family

sap-oh-NAH-ree-uh. Soapwort. Summer bloom. Full sun or light shade.

Description: Soapworts produce masses of 5-petaled pink flowers for several weeks in summer. The flowers crown leafy stems clothed with opposite, oval leaves. Plants grow from fleshy white roots that produce new shoots as they creep. The floppy stems often root where they touch the ground.

Saponaria × *lempergii* (lem-PERG-ee-eye), soapwort. Size: 4″–6″ tall; leaves to 1″ long. This stellar hybrid forms sprawling, leafy clumps covered with 1″-wide deep-pink flowers in midsummer. 'Max Frei' is a compact grower with pink flowers. Zone 4 (with winter protection) or Zones 5–8.

S. ocymoides (oh-kim-OY-deez), rock soapwort. Size: 4″–6″ tall; leaves ½″ long. This sprawling plant is covered in small bright-pink ¼″-wide flowers for several weeks in early summer. 'Alba' has white flowers. 'Rubra Compacta' is more compact, with deep-pink to red flowers. 'Splendens' has rose-pink flowers. Zones 3–7.

S. officinalis (oh-fiss-ih-NAH-lis), bouncing bet. Size: 1'–2½' tall; leaves 2"–4" long. This tall, sprawling species has oval leaves and 1"-wide pale-pink flowers. 'Rosea-plena' has double rose-pink flowers. 'Rubra-plena' has deep-rose double flowers. Zones 2–8.

How to Grow: Soapworts grow in average, sandy or loamy, well-drained soil in full sun or light shade. Rich soil causes them to overgrow and flop. Plants spread enthusiastically to form broad clumps. *S. officinalis* self-sows prolifically; avoid problems by choosing double-flowered cultivars, which do not set seed. After flowering, cut plants back to encourage fresh growth; *S. ocymoides* may rebloom. Divide plants in spring or fall to control their spread. Propagate by division, or take cuttings any time during the summer.

Landscape Uses: Choose *S. ocymoides* for the rock garden or for edging along walks and steps. It also makes a good groundcover for a sunny, well-drained site. In the border,

The small flowers of *Saponaria ocymoides* 'Rubra Compacta' smother the creeping clumps of foliage in early summer. Use it and other rock soapworts as a groundcover in rock gardens or for cascading over stone walls.

combine soapworts with summer-blooming perennials such as artemisias, yarrows, daylilies, speedwells (*Veronica* spp.), and sedums. 🍃

Scabiosa Dipsacaceae, Teasel Family

scab-ee-OH-suh. Scabious, Pincushion Flower. Summer bloom. Full sun or light shade.

Description: *Scabiosa caucasica* (caw-KA-sih-kuh), pincushion flower. Size: 1½'–2' tall; leaves to 6" long. Pincushion flowers are old-fashioned perennials with broad flat flower heads. Each 2"–3" head is composed of many tiny, soft-blue flowers that increase in size as they near the margins of the heads. Each flower head is held on a slender naked stem above a sparsely branched clump. The basal leaves are lance-shaped, and the stem leaves often have 3 pointed leaflets. All foliage is

gray-green and fuzzy. Plants grow from a fibrous rooted crown. 'Alba' has white flowers. 'Blue Perfection' has lavender-blue flowers with fringed petals. 'Butterfly Blue' is of uncertain parentage, but its beautiful lilac-blue flowers and long blooming period certainly make it worth growing. 'Fama' has 4" deep lavender-blue flowers on 1½' stems. 'House Hybrids' ('Isaac House Hybrids') come in mixed blues and whites. Zones 3–7.

How to Grow: Plant scabious in well-

drained, sandy or loamy, humus-rich, neutral or alkaline soil in full sun or light shade. Plants form good-size clumps under ideal conditions but are sensitive to heat and excess soil moisture. In southern zones, site plants where they will get afternoon shade. Dead-head the plants regularly to prolong flowering. Divide clumps in spring only if they become overcrowded. Propagate by sowing fresh seed outdoors in fall or indoors in late winter.

Landscape Uses: Plant scabious in groups of 3 or more to produce a significant display. 🍂

Pincushion flower (*Scabiosa caucasica*) is an old-fashioned favorite that bears its lacy flowers on tall stems, making them perfect for cutting.

Sedum   Crassulaceae, Stonecrop Family

SEE-dum. Sedum, Stonecrop. Spring and summer bloom. Full sun to partial shade.

Description: Sedums are drought-tolerant plants with thick, succulent, waxy leaves and fleshy, often trailing stems. The small starry flowers are borne in domed or flat clusters in spring or summer. The seed heads of many species retain their color after flowering and hold their form when dried. Plants grow from fibrous-rooted crowns or trailing stems.

Sedum aizoon (EYE-zoon), Aizoon stonecrop. Size: 12″–15″ tall; leaves 2″ long. This sedum is an upright grower with oval, toothed leaves and flat, terminal, 3″–4″-wide

Sedums are perfect for drought-tolerant plantings. Here, showy stonecrop (*Sedum spectabile*), *top right,* and *Sedum* 'Rosy Glow', *bottom left,* are growing with blue fescue (*Festuca caesia*) and dwarf mugo pine (*Pinus mugo* var. *mugo*).

clusters of yellow flowers in early summer. Zones 4–9.

S. album (AL-bum), white stonecrop. Size: 4″–6″ tall; leaves to ⅝″ long. This creeping sedum has lance-shaped evergreen leaves and 1″–2″ clusters of white flowers in early summer. 'Chubby Fingers' has plump, succulent leaves. 'Coral Carpet' has dark-green leaves with orange highlights in spring. Zones 3–9.

S. kamtschaticum (kamt-SHAH-tih-kum), Kamschatka stonecrop. Size: 2″–6″ tall; leaves ½″–2″ long. This low, spreading sedum produces short, upright stems clothed in narrow, toothed green leaves and topped by open, 1″–2″-wide clusters of bright-yellow flowers. The variety middendorffianum has more-slender, toothed leaves. 'Variegatum' has leaves edged in creamy-white. Zones 3–8.

S. maximum (MAX-ih-mum), stonecrop. Size: 1½′–2′ tall; leaves 2″–5″ long. This upright sedum bears thick oval leaves and domed 1″–3″-wide clusters of creamy-rose flowers. The variety atropurpureum 'Honeysong' has deep rose-purple leaves and stems and rose-pink flowers. Zones 3–8.

S. sieboldii (see-BOLD-ee-eye), October daphne. Size: 6″–9″ tall; leaves to 1″ long. Pink ½″-wide flowers in tightly packed, domed clusters smother the rounded leaves of this spreading species in September and October. 'Variegatum' has white-variegated leaves. Zones 3–8.

S. spectabile (speck-TAH-bih-lee), showy stonecrop. Size: 1′–2′ tall; leaves to 3″ long. Showy stonecrop is one of the most popular sedums. The 4″–6″ domed heads of ½″-wide pink flowers crown erect stems clothed in broad, blue-green leaves. 'Atropurpureum' has deep rose-red flowers. 'Brilliant' has bright rose-pink flowers. 'Carmen' has dark carmine-pink flowers. 'Variegatum' (also known as S. alboroseum 'Medio-variegatus') has pink flow-

Variegated showy stonecrop (Sedum spectabile 'Variegatum') has broad blue-green leaves with creamy-yellow centers. Its succulent leaves and stems store enough water to enable the plants to endure prolonged periods of heat and drought.

ers in fall and leaves with creamy-yellow centers. Zones 3–9.

S. spurium (SPUR-ee-um), two-row sedum. Size: 2″–6″ tall; leaves ½″–1″ long. This sedum forms mats of wiry stems with rounded leaves crowded toward their tips. Open clusters of ½″-wide pink flowers are produced in summer. 'Dragon's Blood' has red-tinted foliage and rose-red flowers. 'Ruby Mantle' has red foliage and red flowers. The leaves of 'Tricolor' are variegated with pink, white, and green. Zones 3–8.

S. ternatum (ter-NAH-tum), whorled stonecrop. Size: 2″–6″ tall; leaves ¾″ long. This low, open spreader has disproportionately large, starry inflorescences with 3 long arms and ½″-wide flowers. 'White Waters' has larger flowers. Zones 4–8.

Sedum hybrids. Several popular sedums are of hybrid origin. 'Autumn Joy' is a stout perennial derived from crosses involving *S. spectabile.* It has thick 2′ stems densely clothed in rounded leaves and crowned with domed, 5″–6″ flower clusters of pink flowers. Flowers come in late summer. 'Ruby Glow' has weakly upright or sprawling 1′ stems with rounded purple-tinged leaves and ruby-red flowers. 'Vera Jameson' is similar but has waxy bluish or purple leaves.

How to Grow: All sedums are tough, easy-care perennials. Plant them in average to rich, well-drained soil in full sun to light shade. The low-growing species will grow in partial shade. *S. ternatum* tolerates moist, rich soil. Once they are established, plants generally require little care except for division in spring or fall to control their spread. Propagate by division, or take cuttings, which root readily throughout the summer.

Landscape Uses: Sedums are versatile plants for beds, borders, and rock gardens and as groundcovers under open trees. Use the low, spreading species along paths. 🍂

Plant two-row sedum (*Sedum spurium*) in the crevices of a stone wall where the creeping stems will cascade over the faces of the stones, or use it as a groundcover in rock gardens or on dry, sunny banks. 'Red Carpet' is the cultivar shown here.

Senecio Compositae, Daisy Family

seh-NEE-see-oh. Groundsel, Senecio. Spring or summer bloom. Full sun to partial shade.

Description: Groundsels have starry yellow flowers with straplike, petal-like rays and green or yellow centers. The flowers are borne in open clusters atop loose, branching stems. Basal rosettes of semi-evergreen to evergreen leaves grow from fibrous-rooted crowns.

Senecio adonidifolius (ay-don-ih-dih-FOE-lee-us), groundsel. Size: 1'–1½' tall; leaves 2"–4" long. This is a slender leafy plant with curly, pinnately divided leaves and open clusters of ½"-wide golden-yellow flowers, each with 4–5 rays. Zones 5–7.

S. aureus (AW-ree-us), golden ragwort. Size: 1½'–2½' tall; leaves 4"–6" long. Golden ragwort has basal rosettes of heart-shaped foliage and open clusters of ¾"-wide golden-yellow flowers. Zones 4–9.

S. cineraria (sin-uh-RARE-ee-uh), dusty miller. Size: 1'–2' tall; leaves 2"–4" long. Dusty miller is popular for its pinnately lobed, silver-gray leaves. Plants seldom bloom. Zones 8–10.

S. doria (DOOR-ee-uh), groundsel. Size: 3'–4' tall; leaves to 6" long. This tall, leafy species has upright stems with toothed, lance-shaped leaves and flat, broad (8"–10") clusters of ¾"-wide bright-yellow flowers. Zones 4–8.

S. smithii (SMITH-ee-eye), white groundsel. Size: 2'–4' tall; leaves to 1' long. This tall, coarse plant has large, wedge-shaped, hairy basal leaves and stout leafy stems with clustered 1"-wide white flowers. Zones 6–8.

How to Grow: Give groundsels average to rich, moist but well-drained soil in full sun to partial shade. *S. cineraria* needs average soil on the dry side. *S. smithii* needs rich, moist to wet soil. Both need full sun. *S. aureus* tolerates light shade. All species are easy to grow and

Golden ragwort (*Senecio aureus*) will light up the spring shade garden with its clusters of bright-yellow daisylike flowers. These plants thrive in moist soils and self-sow readily.

spread readily by creeping roots and self-sown seedlings. Divide after flowering or in fall; replant into amended soil. Grow *S. cineraria* as an annual north of Zone 8; take stem cuttings before frost to overwinter plants indoors.

Landscape Uses: Groundsels are good plants for beds and borders, or meadow and rock gardens. Plant *S. cineraria* to edge beds of annuals or with perennials that complement its silvery foliage. Choose *S. aureus* for the shade garden with wildflowers such as wild blue phlox (*Phlox divaricata*), Allegheny foamflower (*Tiarella cordifolia*), and wild columbine (*Aquilegia canadensis*). *S. smithii* is a good choice for the water garden. 🍂

Sidalcea Malvaceae, Mallow Family

see-DAL-see-uh. Checkerbloom. Summer bloom. Full sun to light shade.

Checkerbloom (*Sidalcea malviflora*) looks like a miniature hollyhock and is perfect for smaller gardens that can't accommodate the 6' stalks of hollyhocks.

Description: *Sidalcea malviflora* (mal-vee-FLOOR-uh), checkerbloom. Size: 2'–4' tall; leaves to 3" long. Checkerblooms resemble small, delicate hollyhocks. They have stout stems with palmately lobed leaves and 2"-wide mallowlike pink or rose flowers. Plants grow from woody crowns with fibrous roots. Cultivars of mixed parentage are available on 2' plants. 'Brilliant' has carmine-red flowers. 'Loveliness' has shell-pink flowers.

How to Grow: Plant in average to rich, moist but well-drained soil in full sun or light shade. Cut plants to the ground after flowering to promote fresh foliage. If plants overgrow their space or die out in the middle, lift the clumps in fall and discard the old portions. Replant vigorous divisions into amended soil.

Landscape Uses: Checkerblooms are good for the middle or rear of the border or for meadow gardens. Plant them with yarrows, baby's-breath, purple coneflower (*Echinacea purpurea*), and ornamental grasses. 🍃

Silene Caryophyllaceae, Pink Family

sigh-LEE-nee. Catchfly, Campion, Pink. Spring and early-summer bloom. Full sun to partial shade.

Description: Catchflies have basal rosettes of narrow foliage and wiry stalks bearing open clusters of tubular flowers with starry 5-petaled faces. Plants grow from thick, branched taproots.

Silene polypetala (pahl-ee-PET-uh-luh), fringed campion. Size: 4"–6" tall; leaves 2"–4" long. This tufted plant has open clusters of 1½"-wide pink flowers with deeply incised, ragged petals. Zones 6–8.

S. regia (REE-jee-uh), royal catchfly. Size: 2'–5' tall; leaves to 5" long. This tall catchfly has opposite, stalkless leaves and 6"–12" terminal clusters of 1"-wide, fiery-red flowers. Zones 5–8.

S. schafta (SHAFF-tuh), schafta pink. Size: 3"–6" tall; leaves ½" long. This pink forms dense cushions of oblong leaves and few-flowered clusters of ¾"-wide bright-pink flowers.

'Splendens' has rose-pink flowers. Zones 4–8.

    S. virginica (ver-JIN-ih-kuh), fire pink.
Size: 2'–3' tall; leaves 3"–4" long. Crimson
¾"-wide flowers with notched petals bloom
over low basal rosettes. Zones 3–9.

    How to Grow: Plant catchflies in average,
sandy or loamy soil in full sun or light shade.
All species need good drainage. Plants may be
short-lived in gardens, but self-sown seedlings
are common. To propagate, sow fresh seed
outdoors in fall. Seedlings develop slowly.

    Landscape Uses: Catchflies are good
plants for rock and wall gardens. *S. schafta*
grows readily at the front of the border with
other low perennials and small ornamental
grasses. *S. regia* is striking in the dry garden or
in meadow and prairie plantings. 🌿

Fire pink (*Silene virginica*) is best grown in the well-drained soil
of rock gardens or on dry banks in full to partial sun.

Sisyrinchium Iridaceae, Iris Family

**sis-ih-RING-key-um. Blue-Eyed Grass. Early-summer bloom. Full sun to partial
shade.**

    Description: Blue-eyed grass produces
tufts of flat, grasslike foliage and clusters of
starry blue flowers.

    Sisyrinchium angustifolium (an-gus-tih-
FOE-lee-um), blue-eyed grass. Size: 6"–10" tall;
leaves to 10" tall. This is a delicate species with
few-flowered clusters of ½"-wide, deep steel-
blue flowers. Zones 3–9.

    S. bermudiana (ber-mew-dee-AH-nuh).
Size: 1'–2' tall; leaves to 2' tall. This tender
species bears violet-blue, yellow-eyed, ¾"-wide
flowers. Zones 8–10.

    How to Grow: Plant in moist, average to
rich soil in full sun or partial shade. Divide
after flowering.

    Landscape Uses: Use groups of blue-
eyed grass in meadow plantings or as an
accent in perennial gardens. 🌿

Plant *Sisyrinchium bermudiana* where the delicate flowers and
fine-textured foliage can be viewed from close up.

Smilacina Liliaceae, Lily Family

smy-lah-SEE-nuh. Solomon's Plume, False Solomon's Seal. Late-spring bloom. Light to full shade.

Solomon's plume (*Smilacina racemosa*) is a shade-tolerant native wildflower perfect for woodland gardens or underplanting flowering shrubs.

Description: *Smilacina racemosa* (ray-sih-MOW-suh), Solomon's plume. Size: 2'–4' tall; leaves 5"–9" long; flowers small, in 6" clusters. Solomon's plume is a spectacular woodland wildflower with deep-green, satiny, pointed oval leaves. The graceful arching stems bear well-branched terminal plumes of small fuzzy white flowers, followed by red-and-white speckled fruit. The plants grow from fleshy, creeping rhizomes. Zones 3–8.

How to Grow: Plant in moist, humus-rich, neutral or acidic soil in light to full shade. Plants bloom more freely with some sun. Divide clumps in early spring or fall for propagation or to control their spread.

Landscape Uses: Use Solomon's plumes in informal plantings and woodland gardens or as a groundcover under trees and shrubs. Combine them with foliage plants such as hostas, ferns, lungworts (*Pulmonaria* spp.), and epimediums (*Epimedium* spp.). 🍂

Solidago Compositae, Daisy Family

sole-ih-DAY-go. Goldenrod. Summer and fall bloom. Full sun.

Description: Goldenrods are a welcome sight in the garden, blooming at a time when many other flowers are going dormant for the season. The lemon-yellow or golden flowers are carried in spikelike, flat-topped, or plumelike clusters. The leafy stems may be smooth or hairy. The leaves are lance-shaped or oval and often have jagged, toothed margins. Some plants are clump-formers; others grow from fast-creeping rhizomes.

Solidago caesia (SEE-zee-uh), wreath goldenrod. Size: 1'–3' tall; leaves 3"–5" long. This spiky goldenrod has loose clusters of ⅜"-wide yellow flowers and narrow blue-green leaves alternating up smooth wiry stems. Plants bloom in early fall. Zones 4–8.

S. canadensis (can-uh-DEN-sis), Canada goldenrod. Size: 2'–5' tall; leaves 4"–6" long. Canada goldenrod has showy 1-sided plume-shaped clusters of ⅜"-wide bright-yellow flowers atop fuzzy, leafy stems. The toothed, lance-shaped leaves are covered with tiny soft hairs on their undersides. Plants form colonies from creeping rhizomes. Zones 3–8.

S. flexicaulis (flecks-ih-CAW-lis), zigzag goldenrod. Size: 1'–3' tall; leaves 6" long. Zigzag goldenrod has thin, wiry stems that bend back and forth at the nodes (leaf joints) of alternate, rounded leaves. The ⅜"-wide flowers are carried along the upper ⅓ of the stem. Zones 3–8.

S. odora (oh-DOOR-uh), sweet goldenrod. Size: 2'–5' tall; leaves 4" long. This slender species has smooth, lance-shaped, anise-scented foliage and 1-sided clusters of ⅜"-wide flowers. Zones 3–9.

S. rigida (RIJ-ih-duh), stiff goldenrod. Size: 3'–5' tall; leaves up to 1' long. A tall, leafy goldenrod with broad flat clusters of ¼"-long flowers, fuzzy stems, and large-leaved basal rosettes. Zones 3–9.

S. sempervirens (sem-per-VY-renz), seaside goldenrod. Size: 2'–4' tall; leaves 1'–1½' long. A smooth goldenrod with large, spatula-shaped basal leaves. The lance-shaped stem leaves decrease in size as they ascend to the 1-sided, plumed inflorescence bearing ¼"-long flowers. Zones 4–9.

S. spathulata (spath-you-LAY-tuh), goldenrod. Size: 1'–2' tall; leaves 6" long. This creeping goldenrod has deep-green paddle-shaped leaves and ⅜"-wide flowers in branched inflorescences like exploding yellow fireworks. Zones 4–9.

S. sphacelata (sfay-sell-AH-tuh), dwarf goldenrod. Size: 1'–2' tall; leaves to 3" long. A tidy groundcover with rosettes of heart-shaped leaves and golden-yellow flowers in fall. 'Golden Fleece' is quite floriferous. Zones 4–9.

S. virgaurea (vir-GAR-ee-uh), European goldenrod. Size: to 3' tall; leaves 4"–6" long. This species is similar to *S. canadensis* but grows only 3' tall. Many garden hybrids have

Goldenrods, such as *Solidago* 'Crown of Rays', are often mistakenly blamed for hayfever. But goldenrod flowers are actually pollinated by insects, so the pollen is not released into the wind and does not aggravate allergies.

been produced from these 2 species. 'Baby Gold' is 2'–2½' tall with large flower clusters. 'Cloth of Gold' has pale-yellow flowers on 1½'–2' stems. 'Crown of Rays' has large flaring flower clusters. 'Goldenmosa' is 2½' tall with soft-yellow flowers in cascading clusters. Zones 3–9.

How to Grow: Goldenrods commonly grow on roadsides and in wasteplaces, meadows, and prairies; some species even grow in woodlands. Most species prefer average, moist but well-drained soil in full sun or light shade. Rich soils encourage rampant spread and flopping. *S. caesia* and *S. flexicaulis* grow in humusy woodland soil in light or partial shade; they bloom poorly in deep shade. *S. odora* and *S. sempervirens* grow in poor soil and are salt-tolerant. All species hold up well under droughty conditions. Most species in-

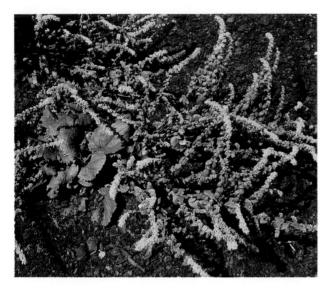

For a fast-growing, fall-blooming groundcover, choose *Solidago sphacelata* 'Golden Fleece'. Plants grow in full sun or light shade.

crease well under cultivation and need division every 2–3 years. *S. canadensis,* the *S. virgaurea* hybrids, and *S. spathulata* may need more frequent control. Divide in spring or after flowering. Self-sown seedlings often appear.

Landscape Uses: Goldenrods are at home in formal and informal landscapes. Plant them in meadows and prairies or in beds and borders. Combine them with coneflowers (*Echinacea* spp. and *Rudbeckia* spp.), balloon flower (*Platycodon grandiflorus*), gayfeathers (*Liatris* spp.), bonesets (*Eupatorium* spp.), lavender (*Lavandula angustifolia*), sages, asters, and ornamental grasses. Use *S. sempervirens* in coastal gardens with other salt-tolerant species such as blanket flowers (*Gaillardia* spp.) and sea lavender (*Limonium latifolium*). ❦

Stachys   Labiatae, Mint Family

STAY-kiss. Lamb's-Ears, Betony. Spring and summer bloom. Full sun to light shade.

The soft, woolly leaves of lamb's-ears (*Stachys byzantina*) create a pleasing edging for beds and borders with well-drained soil. They combine well with either pastels or brightly colored flowers.

Description: Like all members of the mint family, lamb's ears have 2-lipped flowers with 2 upper and 3 lower lobes. The flowers are carried in tiered whorls on erect stems. All species have hairy leaves and stems; on some, the hairs are dense, soft, and silvery. Plants grow from creeping stems with fibrous roots.

Stachys byzantina (bih-zan-TEEN-uh), lamb's-ears (also listed as *S. lanata*). Size: 6"–15" tall; leaves to 4" long. The densely white-woolly leaves form soft mats from which the equally fuzzy bloom stalks arise. Purple ½"-long flowers emerge from the tangle of hairs in late spring. 'Primrose Heron' has yellow spring foliage that turns to gray-green in summer. 'Silver Carpet' has silvery leaves and reputedly does not produce flowers. Zones 4–8.

S. grandiflora (gran-dih-FLOOR-uh), betony. Size: 1'–1½' tall; leaves to 2⅔" long. Basal rosettes of scalloped, heart-shaped leaves are punctuated with upright, leafy stalks crowned with spikelike clusters of 1"-long pink flowers. The variety *robusta* grows to 2' tall and is showier than the species. 'Alba' has white flowers. 'Rosea' has deep rose-pink flowers. Zones 2–8.

S. officinalis (oh-fiss-ih-NAH-lis), betony, wood betony. Size: 1½'–2' tall; leaves 4"–5" long. This species is similar to *S. grandiflora* but has denser clusters of smaller, ½"-long violet flowers. The variety *rosea* has soft rose-pink flowers. Zones 4–8.

How to Grow: Plant *S. grandiflora* and *S. officinalis* in average to rich, moist but well-drained soil in full sun or partial shade.

Grow *S. byzantina* in well-drained, sandy or loamy soil in full sun or light shade. It does not perform well in hot, humid areas or where there is frequent summer rain; the woolly foliage traps water and is subject to rot. Good drainage is essential to success. If rot occurs, cut plants back and wait for cooler weather— they resprout in fall, and the leaves often overwinter. Remove spent flowerstalks. All species spread well when grown in their ideal conditions. Divide overgrown clumps in fall to control their spread or for propagation.

Landscape Uses: Plant lamb's-ears in either formal or informal gardens with irises (*Iris* spp.), goat's beards (*Aruncus* spp.), alum-roots (*Heuchera* spp.), bergenias (*Bergenia* spp.), and lungworts (*Pulmonaria* spp.). *S. byzantina* is perfect for the front of the border. 🍂

Stokesia   Compositae, Daisy Family

STOKES-ee-uh. Stoke's Aster. Summer bloom. Full sun or light shade.

Description: *Stokesia laevis* (LEE-vis), Stoke's aster. Size: 1'–2' tall; leaves 6"–8" long. This species produces broad rosettes of shiny green lance-shaped leaves from white cordlike roots. Branched flowerstalks bear flat, 2"–3"-wide flower heads with blue petal-like rays and fuzzy white centers. 'Alba' has white flowers. 'Blue Danube' has 5" lavender-blue flowers. 'Klaus Jelitto' has 4" deep-blue flowers. Zones 5–9.

How to Grow: Plant in average to rich, moist but well-drained soil in full sun or light shade. Divide in spring or fall. Sow fresh seed outdoors in fall, or sow indoors in winter and place the flats in a refrigerator for 6 weeks before moving them to a warm, bright place.

Landscape Uses: Stoke's asters are dramatic in flower. Combine them with verbenas (*Verbena* spp.) and artemisias. 🍂

The thick, wiry roots of Stoke's aster (*Stokesia laevis*) enable it to endure periods of drought. It produces dozens of flowers and will rebloom if old stalks are removed at the base.

Tanacetum Compositae, Daisy Family

tan-uh-SEE-tum. Tansy. Summer bloom. Full sun.

For a colorful, easy-to-grow perennial, plant common tansy (*Tanacetum vulgare*) in average soil and full sun. The buttonlike flowers are good for fresh use or for drying.

Description: *Tanacetum vulgare* (vul-GAH-ree), common tansy. Size: 2′–3′ tall; leaves 3″–5″ long. This aromatic, rather weedy perennial has stout stems clothed in ferny, deep-green, pinnately divided leaves. The buttonlike heads are rich golden-yellow and have no rays (petal-like structures) but only the tiny central disk flowers. Plants grow from a stout crown with fibrous roots. The variety *crispum* is a selection with large, more finely cut divisions. It is superior to the species as a garden plant. Zones 3–8.

How to Grow: Tansy grows luxuriantly in all but the poorest soils. Plant in average, moist soil in full sun. Divide overgrown plants in spring or fall. Remove the spent flowers to eliminate self-sown seedlings.

Landscape Uses: Tansy is well-suited to meadows, herb gardens, or perennial plantings. Combine it with yarrows, artemisias, asters, sea lavender (*Limonium latifolium*), sages, and ornamental grasses.

Thalictrum Ranunculaceae, Buttercup Family

thuh-LICK-trum. Meadow Rue. Spring or summer bloom. Full sun to partial shade.

Description: Meadow rues are airy plants with large, dissected leaves, each with many small, gray-green, scalloped leaflets. The stems are crowned with domed clusters of fuzzy flowers. Plants grow from fibrous roots.

Thalictrum aquilegifolium (ack-wih-lee-jih-FOE-lee-um), columbine meadow rue. Size: 2'–3' tall; leaves 6"–10" long. The foliage of this meadow rue has blue-gray leaflets resembling those of columbines (*Aquilegia* spp.). Each showy ½"-wide flower is petal-less and consists of many stamens (male reproductive structures). The flower heads are 6"–8" wide. 'Album' has white flowers. 'Atropurpureum' has violet flowers. 'Thundercloud' has deep-purple flower heads. Zones 4–8.

T. delavayi (duh-LAH-vay-eye), Yunnan meadow rue. Size: 2'–4' tall; leaves 8"–12" long. This meadow rue has showy lilac sepals and creamy stamens in 1"-wide flowers. 'Hewitt's Double' has double flowers. Zones 4–7.

T. dioicum (die-OH-ih-kum), early meadow rue. Size: 1'–3' tall; leaves 6"–8" long; flowers ¼" wide. Early meadow rue has separate male and female plants. Male plants produce candelabra-like flower clusters significant for their pendant golden stamens. Female flowers are insignificant. Zones 3–8.

T. flavum (FLAY-vum), dusty meadow rue (also sold as *T. speciosissimum*). Size: 3'–5' tall; leaves 8"–10" long. Dusty meadow rue is the loveliest member of the genus. The luscious foliage is gray-green and the 4" upright flower clusters are pale sulphur-yellow. The variety *glaucum* has blue-gray foliage. Zones 4–8.

T. rochebrunianum (row-shuh-brew-nee-AY-num), lavender mist. Size: 3'–5' tall; leaves

Columbine meadow rue (*Thalictrum aquilegifolium*) has blue-green, columbine-like foliage and airy plumes of flowers. Plant it toward the rear of the border with bold flowers such as daylilies and irises.

6"–10" long. This species is similar in both foliage and flower to *T. delavayi* but has stouter stems. Zones 4–7.

How to Grow: Meadow rues are easy to grow in moist, humus-rich soil in full sun or light shade. Plants seldom need division but can be lifted in fall for propagation.

Landscape Uses: Plant meadow rues at the middle or rear of the border. Their airy flowers create a charming background for larger flowers and bold foliage. Combine them with daylilies, hibiscus (*Hibiscus* spp.), and phlox. Plant *T. dioicum* in the shade garden with wildflowers, ferns, and hostas. 🌿

Thermopsis Leguminosae, Pea Family

ther-MOP-sis. False Lupine. Late-spring bloom. Full sun to light shade.

Carolina lupine (*Thermopsis caroliniana*) is a versatile native perennial. It thrives in moist or dry soil and blooms well in sun or partial shade.

Description: *Thermopsis caroliniana* (care-oh-lin-ee-AH-nuh), Carolina lupine (also listed as *T. villosa*). Size: 3'–5' tall; leaves 3"–5" long. A stately species with stiff stalks, gray-green leaves, and 8"–12" dense clusters of ¾"-long, lemon-yellow flowers. Plants grow from woody, fibrous-rooted crowns. Zones 3–9.

How to Grow: Plant in average to rich, moist but well-drained, acidic soil in full sun or light shade (especially in warm zones). If foliage declines after bloom, cut it to the ground. Clumps seldom need division. Propagate by stem cuttings from sideshoots in early summer. Sow seed outdoors in late summer or inside in winter after soaking it for 12–24 hours in hot water.

Landscape Uses: Plant Carolina lupines where they will have plenty of room in the middle or back of the border. Combine them with peonies (*Paeonia* spp.) and bellflowers (*Campanula* spp.). Plants are also well-suited to meadows and sunny wild gardens. 🍂

Tiarella Saxifragaceae, Saxifrage Family

tee-uh-REL-uh. Foamflower. Spring bloom. Partial to full shade.

Description: *Tiarella cordifolia* (core-dih-FOE-lee-uh), Allegheny foamflower. Size: 6"–10" tall; leaves to 8" long. Foamflowers are spring-blooming, quick-spreading groundcovers with erect conical clusters of small, ¹⁄₁₆"-wide, fuzzy white to pale-pink flowers. The heart-shaped to triangular leaves are borne on 4" petioles (leafstalks). The plants grow from fibrous-rooted crowns with central foliage rosettes and long, leafy runners. Zones 3–8.

T. wherryi (WHERE-ee-eye), Wherry's foamflower (also listed as *T. cordifolia* var. *collina*). Size: 6"–10" tall; leaves to 8" long. This plant is similar to *T. cordifolia* but produces leafy clumps with no runners and a greater profusion of flowerstalks. The leaves are also glossy green. Zones 3–8.

How to Grow: Plant foamflowers in

humus-rich, slightly acidic, evenly moist soil in partial to full shade. *T. cordifolia* spreads quickly from runners to form leafy mats. *T. wherryi* produces broad clumps with age. Divide plants in spring or in fall, or remove and replant rooted runners anytime during the growing season. Sow seed outdoors in spring and leave it uncovered.

Landscape Uses: Foamflowers make exceptional groundcovers, with their lovely flowers and dense mats of weed-excluding foliage. Plant them under shrubs and trees, alone or in combination with other plants. In the shade garden, combine foamflowers with wild blue and creeping phlox (*Phlox divaricata* and *P. stolonifera*), wild columbine (*Aquilegia canadensis*), hostas, and ferns. 🍂

Allegheny foamflower (*Tiarella cordifolia*) is a lush, fast-spreading groundcover. It bears lovely spikes of foamy white flowers.

Tradescantia Commelinaceae, Spiderwort Family

trad-es-KANT-ee-uh. Spiderwort. Late-spring and early-summer bloom. Full sun to partial shade.

Description: Spiderworts are floriferous spring wildflowers with attractive, satiny, 3-petaled flowers carried in clusters atop succulent jointed stems. Flower color varies from purple, lavender, and blue to pink, rose-red, or white. Each flower lasts but half a day, closing by early afternoon. The bases of the long, narrow blue-green leaves encircle the joints at right angles to the stem. Plants go dormant after flowering but may re-emerge in fall. They grow from thick fleshy-rooted crowns.

Tradescantia × andersoniana (an-der-sown-ee-AH-nuh), common spiderwort. Size: 1'–2' tall; leaves to 1½' long. This floriferous hybrid is the product of several species including *T. virginiana*, with which it is often confused. The 1"–1½" flowers have wide triangular petals with bright-yellow stamens.

The flowers of common spiderwort (*Tradescantia × andersoniana*) open in the wee hours of morning and close by early afternoon.

Several outstanding cultivars are available. 'Blue Stone' has rich, medium-blue flowers. 'Innocence' is pure-white. 'Iris Pritchard' is white with a violet-blue blush. 'James C. Weguelin' has sky-blue flowers. 'Pauline' has orchid-pink flowers. 'Purple Dome' has rosy-purple flowers. 'Red Cloud' has maroon flowers. 'Zwanenberg Blue' has purple-blue flowers. Zones 3–9.

T. ohiensis (oh-HIGH-en-sis), Ohio spiderwort. Size: 1'–3' tall; leaves to 1' long. Ohio spiderwort has narrow blue-green leaves and ¾"-wide blue, rose, or white flowers with rounded petals. Zones 3–9.

T. virginiana (ver-jin-ee-AH-nuh), Virginia spiderwort. Size: 2'–3' tall; leaves to 1' long. Similar to *T. × andersoniana* but more deli-cate. The 1"-wide flowers are blue to purple. Zones 4–9.

How to Grow: Plant in average to rich, moist but well-drained soil in full to light shade. Plants grow well in partial shade but do not flower as long. Plants tend to get shabby, or even go dormant, after flowering; cut them to the ground. They will produce new foliage quickly where summers are cool, or by autumn in warmer zones. Plants spread quickly to form dense clumps. Divide them every 2–3 years, as they are going dormant. Self-sown seedings are often abundant.

Landscape Uses: Plant spiderworts with leafy plants that will fill the void left when they go dormant. Use them in combination with groundcovers to underplant shrubs. ❧

Tricyrtis   Liliaceae, Lily Family

try-SER-tis. Toad Lily. Late-summer and fall bloom. Light to partial shade.

Common toad lily (*Tricyrtis hirta*) is an unusual perennial for the shade garden. It blooms in autumn when few other woodland plants are flowering.

Description: *Tricyrtis hirta* (HER-tuh), common toad lily. Size: 2'–3' tall; leaves to 6" long. This species has broadly lance-shaped leaves and arching stems growing from fleshy roots. The 1"-wide, purple-spotted flowers are upward-facing and funnelform. Blooms are clustered in the leaf axils along the upper ⅔ of the stem and at the end of the stem. Plants flower late in the season and may be killed by early frost in the North. Zones 4–9.

How to Grow: Plant toad lilies in evenly moist, humus-rich soil in light to partial shade. They are long-lived and easy to grow. Divide clumps in spring for size control or propagation. Self-sown seedlings will appear if the season is long enough to allow the seeds to ripen.

Landscape Uses: Toad lilies have a subtle and unusual beauty that is best appreciated at close range. Plant them near a path. ❧

Trillium   Liliaceae, Lily Family

TRIL-ee-um. Trillium. Spring bloom. Light to full shade.

Our beautiful native trilliums, including white trillium (*Trillium grandiflorum*), are often collected from the wild for sale by nurseries. To be sure your plants do not come from the wild, purchase only nursery-propagated plants from reputable dealers.

Description: Trilliums are beloved spring wildflowers that grow from thick rhizomes with fleshy roots. The broadly oval leaves join together at the top of the stem beneath a single flower with 3 broad petals and 3 green sepals.

Trillium erectum (ee-WRECK-tum), red trillium, stinking Benjamin. Size: 1'–2' tall; leaves 6"–10" long. Red trillium has 2"-wide, unpleasantly scented flowers that are deep blood-red and nod slightly on 1"–4" stalks. Zones 4–9.

T. grandiflorum (gran-dih-FLOOR-um), white trillium. Size: 1½'–2' tall; leaves 4"–6" long. White trillium has 3"-wide, snow-white flowers held erect above a whorl of bright-green leaves. The flowers fade to pink as they age.

'Flore-pleno' has double flowers. Zones 3–9.

How to Grow: Plant trilliums in moist, humus-rich soil in shade. *T. erectum* requires acid soil, while *T. grandiflorum* is more adaptable. If the soil stays moist, the foliage persists through the summer. Plants may form offsets, which can eventually be divided. Propagation by seed is slow. Sow fresh seed outside in summer. Germination takes a year, and plants will bloom in 5–7 years. Most trilliums sold today are collected from the wild; buy only nursery-propagated plants from reputable dealers.

Landscape Uses: Plant trilliums in shade gardens with wildflowers, shade perennials, and ferns. They are lovely planted with spring-blooming shrubs and trees. 🍂

Trollius Ranunculaceae, Buttercup Family

TROW-lee-us. Globeflower. Spring bloom. Full sun to partial shade.

Plant *Trollius* 'Fireglobe' and other hybrid globeflowers in a cool spot with moist or evenly wet soil. Plants are intolerant of excessive heat.

Description: Globeflowers are showy spring perennials with waxy bowl-shaped single or double flowers. The flowers have no petals but instead have orange or yellow petal-like sepals. The palmately divided leaves have 5–7 incised leaflets and are carried on long stalks. Plants produce basal rosettes from thick, fleshy roots.

Trollius chinensis (chy-NEN-sis), Chinese globeflower. Size: 2'–3' tall; leaves 7" long. This globeflower has 5-parted leaves and tall stalks with golden-yellow flowers. The 1"–2"-wide flowers are more open than other species, with 1" erect and flattened stamens (male reproductive structures) projecting from the flowers. Plants sold as *T. ledebourii* belong here. Zones 3–6.

T. × cultorum (kul-TORE-um), hybrid globeflower. Size: 2'–3' tall; leaves 4"–6" long. This group of hybrids includes garden selections from a number of different species, especially *T. europaeus, T. asiaticus,* and *T. chinensis.* 'Earliest of All' has pale orange-yellow flowers early in the season. 'Fireglobe' has deep-orange blooms. 'Golden Queen' has 2" tangerine flowers; it is often listed as a cultivar of *T. chinensis.* 'Lemon Queen' has lemon-yellow flowers. 'Prichard's Giant' grows 3' tall with bright-yellow flowers. Zones 3–6.

T. europaeus (your-oh-PEA-us), common globeflower. Size: 1½'–2' tall; leaves 4"–6" long. Common globeflower has tufts of 5-lobed leaves and erect stalks bearing 1–2 lemon-yellow, 1"–2"-wide flowers. 'Superbus' is more robust and flowers more profusely. Zones 4–7.

How to Grow: Plant globeflowers in constantly moist to wet, humus-rich soil in partial shade. Plants prefer cool weather and perform best in northern zones. Clumps increase from slow-creeping roots. Divide plants in early spring or fall. Sow fresh seed outdoors in summer; stored seed germinates poorly.

Landscape Uses: Globeflowers produce bright spots of color in the spring garden. Plant them in a moist-soil garden or near the water's edge with water-loving irises (*Iris pseudacorus* and other species), lady's-mantle (*Alchemilla mollis*), forget-me-nots (*Myosotis* spp.), primroses, meadowsweets (*Fillipendula* spp.), ligularias (*Ligularia* spp.), rodgersias (*Rodgersia* spp.), hostas, and ferns. ✤

Tulipa Liliaceae, Lily Family

TEW-lih-puh. Tulip. Spring bloom. Full sun or light shade.

Tulipa 'Rosy Wings' and other single late hybrid tulips bloom after most of the spring bulbs have passed. With careful planning, you can have tulips in bloom for 2 months in the spring. Grecian windflower (*Anemone blanda*) is a charming companion for tulips.

Description: Tulips are classic spring bulbs. The 3 petals and 3 petal-like sepals form lovely flowers that are borne singly or in groups atop the naked stems. Flowers come in every color except true-blue. Shades of white, pink, red, and yellow are most common. The long, broad leaves often have wavy margins; they may be blue-green, dark-spotted, or striped. Several species are available, but most of the tulips grown today are hybrids.

Tulips are grouped according to their flowering time, flower shape, and hybrid origin. The Royal Horticultural Society recognizes 15 classes.

1. Single Early Tulips. Size: 12″–14″ tall. Fragrant flowers in mid- to late spring. Good for bedding or forcing. Cultivars include 'Bellona' (golden-yellow), 'Diana' (white), 'General De Wet' (orange), and 'Princess Irene' (salmon and orange).

2. Double Early Tulips. Size: 10″–12″ tall. Flower in mid-spring; good for bedding or forcing. Cultivars include 'Electra' (magenta), 'Mr. van der Hoef' (lemon-yellow), 'Peach Blossom' (soft-pink), 'Triumphator' (bright-pink).

3. Triumph Tulips. Size: 1½′–2′ tall. Large flowers in late spring on strong stems; good for bedding or forcing. Cultivars include 'Apricot Beauty' (apricot), 'Dreaming Maid' (lavender-and-white), and 'Golden Melody' (golden-yellow).

4. Darwin Hybrid Tulips. Size: 2′–2½′ tall.

Tulipa tarda is a diminutive, early-blooming rock-garden tulip that self-sows readily to form broad, handsome clumps.

Flower in late spring. Cultivars include 'Daydream' (apricot), 'Elizabeth Arden' (salmon-pink), 'Jewel of Spring' (lemon-yellow), and 'President Kennedy' (deep-yellow).

5. Single Late Tulips. Size: 1½'–3' tall. Flower in late spring; good for bedding or cutting. This popular group of tulips includes the cottage and Darwin tulips. Cultivars include 'Aristocrat' (warm-pink), 'Halcro' (bright-red), 'Maureen' (ivory), 'Pink Supreme' (deep-pink), and 'Temple of Beauty' (salmon-orange).

6. Lily-Flowered Tulips: Size: 2' tall. Flower in late spring. Good garden tulips with reflexed, pointed petals. Cultivars include 'Ballade' (violet with a white edge), 'Queen of Sheba' (red), 'West Point' (yellow), and 'White Triumphator' (white).

7. Fringed Tulips. Size: 2' tall. Flowers have fringed margins. Cultivars include 'Blue Heron' (lilac-purple), 'Burgundy Lace' (deep-red), and 'Fringed Elegance' (soft-yellow).

8. Viridiflora Tulips. Size: 20"–22" tall. Flowers have green flares or stripes. Cultivars include 'Esperanto' (green-and-red), 'Greenland' (green-and-pink), 'Hummingbird' (green-and-yellow), and 'Spring Green' (green-and-cream).

9. Rembrandt Tulips. Size: 18"–20" tall. Flowers with multicolored streaks; often called "broken" tulips. Cultivars include the 'Rembrandt Hybrids' in mixed colors.

10. Parrot Tulips: Size: 14"–20" tall. Large flowers with wavy or incised petals on supple stalks. Cultivars include 'Black Parrot' (deep brown-purple), 'Blue Parrot' (blue-purple), 'Estella Rijnveld' (red-and-white), and 'White Parrot' (white).

11. Double Late Tulips (Peony-Flowered). Size: 12"–16" tall. Stout tulips with large double flowers. Cultivars include 'Angelique' (pale rose-pink), 'Gold Medal' (pure-yellow), and 'Mount Tacoma' (creamy-white).

12. Kaufmanniana Tulips. Size: 4"–8" tall. These flowers are striped or flushed on the outside and pale and solid-colored on the inside. The leaves are striped with brown. *Tulipa kaufmanniana* has creamy-white blooms flamed with rose-red. Cultivars include 'Heart's Delight' (rose on pale-pink), 'Shakespeare' (carmine on salmon), and 'The First' (carmine on white).

13. Fosteriana Tulips. Size: 10"–20" tall. The elongated flowers are borne on leafy stems with broad leaves often banded in brown. *T. fosteriana* is scarlet with black spots inside. Cultivars include 'Pink Emperor' (deep-pink edged with yellow), 'Red Emperor' (vermillion with black spots), 'Sweetheart' (pale-yellow with a white edge), and 'White Emperor' (white).

14. Greigii Tulips. Size: 8"–12" tall. Starry flowers are borne over leaves often lined with brown. *T. greigii* is orange-scarlet with black spots inside. Cultivars include 'Corsage' (rose), 'Golden Tango' (buttercup-yellow), and 'Red Riding Hood' (scarlet).

15. Wild Species. Descriptions of the most commonly available species are listed below.

T. acuminata (ack-you-min-AH-tuh), horned tulip. Size: 16″–20″ tall; leaves to 6″ long. This tulip has long, narrow-pointed, 4″-long yellow petals and slender leaves. Zones 5–8.

T. clusiana (klooz-ee-AH-nuh), lady tulip. Size: 10″–12″ tall; leaves to 10″ long. Lady tulips have 2″-long starry white flowers with rose-red stripes on the outside. The leaves are long and slender. Zones 4–8.

T. praestans (PRE-stanz). Size: 10″–12″ tall; leaves to 10″ long. This small tulip bears long, slender leaves and 1–4 bright-red 2½″-long flowers on each stem. Zones 4–8.

T. pulchella (pull-CHELL-uh), (also listed as *T. humilis*). Size: 4″–5″ tall; leaves to 6″ long. This squat tulip has 1¼″-long, round violet flowers and strap-shaped leaves. 'Humilis' has violet-pink flowers. 'Violacea' has deep violet-purple flowers. Zones 5–8.

T. tarda (TAR-duh). Size: 3″–4″ tall; leaves to 9″ long. This little tulip has 2″-long, starry yellow flowers with white centers and straplike leaves. Zones 4–8.

How to Grow: Tulips are easy to flower the first season because they are planted with the buds already developed. Many hybrids decline after the second year, so gardeners often treat them as annuals and replace them each year. Darwin Hybrid Tulips and Single Late Tulips are the longest-lived and most dependable. Species tulips are also reliably perennial, often persisting and even increasing for many years.

Tulips need ample water and food when actively growing and a reasonably dry, summer dormant period. Plant them in full sun in well-drained, fertile, humus-rich soil that is moist in spring and fall but dry in summer. Plant new bulbs in the fall at a depth of 8″ from the soil surface to bottom of the bulb. If you are planting tulips for a bedding display, be sure to plant them all at the same depth or they will bloom unevenly. Space bulbs 2″–6″ apart, depending on the size of the plants. Do not remove the foliage until it is fully yellow, no matter how strong the temptation, unless you are discarding the bulbs. Next year's flower production depends on the previous year's foliage.

Landscape Uses: Tulips are lovely in massed bedding schemes in single or mixed colors, combined with other spring bulbs, or planted with perennials and shrubs. Choose the species and wild tulips for rock gardens and gardens with daffodils and early perennials such as lungworts (*Pulmonaria* spp.), Siberian bugloss (*Brunnera macrophylla*), bleeding hearts (*Dicentra* spp.), and columbines (*Aquilegia* spp.). 🌿

Tulipa 'Heart's Delight' is one of the early-blooming Kaufmanniana tulips, which close their starry flowers each night to protect them from rain and cold.

Uvularia Liliaceae, Lily Family

you-view-LAH-ree-uh. Bellwort, Merrybells. Early-spring bloom. Partial to full shade.

After the flowers of great merrybells (*Uvularia grandiflora*) fade, the blue-green foliage forms a lush groundcover that tolerates shade and dry soil.

Description: *Uvularia grandiflora* (grandih-FLOOR-uh), great merrybells. Size: 1'–1½' tall; leaves to 5" long. Bellworts are woodland wildflowers with slender stems and oblong gray-green leaves. The 2"-long, nodding lemon-yellow flowers have 3 petals and 3 showy sepals, each of which is twisted and curled. The foliage is somewhat limp while the plants are in bloom, giving the flowers prominence; as they fade, the leaves spread out to form excellent foliage plants. Plants grow from slender creeping rhizomes to form tight clumps. Zones 3–8.

How to Grow: Bellworts are easy to grow in moist, humus-rich soil in shade. Propagate by dividing the clumps in fall.

Landscape Uses: Bellworts are lovely in the shade garden with wildflowers, hostas, and ferns. Combine their upright form with spreading plants such as Allegheny foamflower (*Tiarella cordifolia*) and wild gingers (*Asarum* spp.). ❦

Verbascum Scrophulariaceae, Figwort Family

ver-BASS-kum. Mullein. Summer bloom. Full sun.

Description: Mulleins produce tight rosettes of soft, hairy foliage and stout, leafy stalks topped with small, 5-petaled yellow or white flowers. Plants grow from stout roots.

Verbascum chaixii (SHAY-zee-eye), nettle-leaved mullein. Size: 2'–3' tall; leaves 3"–6" long. This mullein has gray-green leaves and ¾"-wide yellow flowers. The cultivar 'Album' has white flowers with purple centers. Zones 4–8.

V. olympicum (oh-LIM-pih-kum), olympic mullein. Size: 3'–5' tall; leaves 6"–8" long. A bold plant with 3'-wide rosettes of silver-gray leaves and 1"-wide yellow flowers. Zones 6–8.

How to Grow: Plant in average, very well-drained, sandy or loamy soil in full sun. Plants seldom need division but are easily propagated from root cuttings in early spring. They often self-sow.

Landscape Uses: Choose mulleins for wild gardens and meadows or the middle or rear of perennial gardens. Plant with catmints (*Nepeta* spp.) and ornamental grasses. 🌿

Nettle-leaved mullein (*Verbascum chaixii*) is just one of the mulleins that make an attractive addition to the dry garden. Mulleins produce lush foliage and striking flower spikes.

Verbena Verbenaceae, Vervain Family

ver-BEAN-uh. Verbena, Vervain. Summer bloom. Full sun to light shade.

Rose verbena (*Verbena canadensis*) is a tough, drought- and salt-tolerant species that blooms for several months in spring and summer if regularly deadheaded or pruned back after flowering.

Description: Verbenas are colorful, floriferous perennials that bloom throughout the summer. The tubular flowers have flat, 5-petaled faces and are carried in flat or spiky terminal clusters on wiry stems. The oblong leaves are usually lobed or deeply incised and dissected. Plants grow from fibrous-rooted crowns.

Verbena bonariensis (boh-nah-ree-EN-sis), Brazilian vervain (also known as *V. patagonica*). Size: 3′–4′ tall; leaves 4″ long. This tall verbena has open, branching stalks with sparse foliage and terminal, rounded clusters of ³⁄₁₆″-wide violet flowers. Zones 7–9.

V. canadensis (can-uh-DEN-sis), rose verbena. Size: 8″–18″ tall; leaves 1″–3″ long. Rose verbena has trailing wiry stems and flat terminal flower clusters that elongate into short spikes as the ⅜″-wide purple, rose, or white flowers open. Zones 4–10.

V. hastata (has-TAH-tuh), blue vervain. Size: 3′–5′ tall; leaves to 6″ long; flowers ⅛″ wide. This graceful, erect verbena has long, narrow leaves and branched, candelabra-like spikes of blue flowers. Zones 3–8.

V. rigida (RIJ-ih-duh), rigid verbena. Size: 1′–2′ tall; leaves 2″–4″ long. This upright verbena has rounded terminal clusters of ⅜″-wide purple flowers. Zones 8–10.

V. tenuisecta (ten-you-ih-SEK-tuh), moss verbena. Size: 4″–8″ tall; leaves 1″–1½″ long. This floriferous trailing verbena has thin, wiry stems and terminal clusters of ¼″-wide deep-lavender flowers that elongate to short spikes. Zones 7–10.

How to Grow: Verbenas are tough, heat- and drought-tolerant perennials that bloom tirelessly during the summer. Plant them in well-drained, sandy or loamy soil in full sun to light shade. The creeping species spread quickly to form showy groundcovers. The clumping species increase slowly. *V. hastata* is the only verbena to grow in moist or even wet soil, but it is very adaptable to garden conditions. Plants are easy to grow from stem cuttings taken anytime during the growing season. Sow fresh seeds outdoors in late summer or fall, or sow indoors in winter and place the flats in a refrigerator for 3–4 weeks before moving them to a warm, bright place. Seedlings develop quickly.

Landscape Uses: The trailing verbenas are excellent weavers—plants used to tie mixed plantings together. Let them creep among foliage plants such as yuccas (*Yucca* spp.), artemisias, mulleins (*Verbascum* spp.), and ornamental grasses. They also serve to bridge gaps between flowering perennials such as coneflowers (*Echinacea* spp. and *Rudbeckia* spp.), butterfly weed (*Asclepias tuberosa*), yarrows, and others. Plant the upright species in the middle of the border for their spiky form. Try the airy species such as *Verbena bonariensis* and *V. hastata* at the front of the border, where you can view other colors through their open stems. 🍂

Plant Brazilian vervain (*Verbena bonariensis*) near the front of the border where you can view other plants through its tall, airy flower stems.

Veronica Scrophulariaceae, Figwort Family

ver-ON-ih-kuh. Speedwell, Veronica. Spring or summer bloom. Full sun or light shade.

Description: *Veronica* is a genus of colorful perennials with both upright and creeping species. The upright species have long terminal, spikelike flower clusters. The trailing species have smaller spikes or terminal clusters. The flowers are tubular, with flat 4–5-petaled faces. Color varies from white to pink, rose, purple, and blue. The alternate or whorled leaves may be narrow and lance-shaped, oblong, oval, or wedge-shaped. Plants grow from woody crowns with fleshy or fibrous roots.

V. alpina (al-PIE-nuh), Alpine speedwell. Size: 4"–8" tall; leaves 1"–1½" long. This evergreen creeper has shiny oval leaves and terminal spikelike clusters of ¼"-wide, dark-blue flowers. 'Alba' has white flowers. 'Goodness Grows' is a hybrid with upright showy spikes of blue flowers. Zones 3–8.

V. gentianoides (jen-shee-uh-NOY-deez), gentian speedwell. Size: 6"–20" tall; leaves 1"–3" long. This upright species has leafy stems and pyramidal spikes of ½"-wide, pale sky-blue flowers. 'Variegata' has leaves marked with white. Zones 4–8.

V. grandis (GRAN-dis). Size: 1½'–2' tall; leaves 3" long. This species is similar to *V. spicata*, but the leaves are broader and are shiny green. The variety *holophylla* has broad heart-shaped leaves. 'Blue Charm' (also sold as 'Lavender Charm') is a bushy plant with 6" spikes of ¼"-wide lavender-blue flowers. 'Sunny Border Blue' is similar with deep navy-blue flowers. Zones 4–8.

V. incana (in-KAH-nuh), woolly speedwell.

Plant low, spreading clumps of spike speedwell, such as *Veronica spicata* 'Minuet', toward the front of the border or as an edging along walks. Plants are heat- and drought-tolerant.

Size: 1'–2' tall; leaves 1"–3" long. Woolly speedwell has soft-hairy, gray or silvery oblong leaves and 3"–6" terminal spikes of ¼"-wide blue, pink, or white flowers on 1'–1½' stems. 'Rosea' has pink-tinged flowers. 'Wendy' has lavender-blue flowers. Zones 3–8.

V. longifolia (lon-gih-FOE-lee-uh), longleaf speedwell. Size: 2'–4' tall; leaves 2"–3" long. This strongly upright speedwell has opposite or whorled, lance-shaped leaves and dense 10"–12" spikes of ¼"-wide, pale-blue to lavender flowers. 'Icicle' is a good white, possibly of hybrid origin. 'Romilley Purple' has deep violet-blue flowers on 2' stems. Zones 3–8.

V. prostrata (prose-TRAH-tuh), harebell speedwell. Size: 3"–8" tall; leaves ½"–1" long. This creeping veronica has oval to oblong leaves and axillary clusters of ⅓"-wide blue flowers. 'Heavenly Blue' has sapphire-blue flowers. 'Loddon Blue' is deep-blue. Zones 5–8.

V. spicata (spih-KAH-tuh), spike speedwell.

Size: 1'–3' tall; leaves 1"–3" long. This popular speedwell bears 1' spikes of ¼"-wide pink, blue, or white flowers. 'Barcarolle' has rose-pink flowers and gray-green leaves on 12"–15" stems. 'Blue Fox' has lavender-blue flowers on 15"–20" stems. 'Blue Peter' has dark-blue flowers on 2' stems. 'Minuet' is 1'–1½' tall with silvery leaves and rose-pink flowers. 'Red Fox' has deep rose-red flowers. 'Snow White' has branching inflorescences of white flowers on 1½' stems. Zones 3–8.

V. teucrium (TEWK-ree-um), Hungarian speedwell (also listed as *V. latifolia*). Size: 6"–20" tall; leaves 1½" long. This spreading species has spikes of ¼"-wide, bright-blue flowers and oblong, toothed leaves. The stems are weakly upright to sprawling. 'Crater Lake Blue' has ultramarine flowers on 12"–15" stems. 'Royal Blue' has deep-blue flowers and is 12"–15" tall. 'Trehane' is more spreading with deep-blue flowers. Zones 3–8.

V. virginica (ver-JIN-ih-kuh), Culver's root (also listed as *Veronicastrum virginicum*). Size: 2'–6' tall; leaves to 6" long. This tall plant has tiered whorls of 5 leaves that ascend the stem to a branched 9" inflorescence of ⅛"-wide white flowers. Zones 3–8.

How to Grow: Plant in average to rich, moist but well-drained soil in full sun or light shade. *Veronica virginica* needs rich, evenly moist soil for best growth. Divide plants in spring or fall for propagation or to control their spread. Take stem cuttings in early to mid-summer.

Landscape Uses: Combine the colorful spiky flowers of speedwells with rounded plants such as coreopsis (*Coreopsis* spp.), butterfly weed (*Asclepias tuberosa*), yarrows, cranesbills (*Geranium* spp.), daylilies, and ornamental grasses. Plant creepers such as *V. alpina* and *V. repens* and smaller *V. spicata* cultivars at the front of a border or in rock and wall gardens. 🍁

When planted in moist soil, the tall stalks of *Veronica grandis* 'Blue Charm' need staking to keep them from flopping. In dry soil, however, plants don't grow as tall.

Vinca   Apocynaceae, Dogbane Family

VING-kuh. Periwinkle, Vinca. Spring bloom. Sun or shade.

Description: Periwinkles are trailing plants with wiry stems that root at the nodes (leaf joints) as they spread. The shiny, deep-green, oval or rounded leaves are paired along the stems. In spring, short upright stems bear open clusters of sky-blue, funnel-shaped flowers with 5 square petals. Plants have fibrous-rooted crowns.

Vinca major (MAY-jor), large periwinkle. Size: 6"–10" tall; leaves 3" long. This periwinkle has large rounded leaves and an open habit. The 1"–1½"-wide, deep sky-blue flowers are borne in early spring. 'Variegata' has leaves with creamy-white margins. Zones 7–9.

V. minor (MY-nor), common periwinkle. Size: 4"–6" tall; leaves 1½" long. This species is similar to *V. major* but is much smaller and is hardier. It has oval leaves and ¾"–1"-wide lavender-blue flowers. 'Alba' has white flowers. 'Atropurpurea' has red-violet flowers. 'Bowles' Variety' has light-blue flowers. 'Miss Jekyll's White' has pure-white flowers. 'Sterling Silver' has lavender-blue flowers and deep-green leaves edged in creamy-white. Zones 4–9.

How to Grow: Periwinkles are easy to grow in average to rich, moist but well-drained

soil in partial to full shade. They bloom and grow best in partial shade. Plants spread far and wide and usually need control. Cut runners back to keep *V. major* looking full. Propagate by division or stem cuttings, or transplant rooted stems.

Landscape Uses: Vincas make good groundcovers under shrubs and trees. They are excellent for filling odd spaces or creating a luxuriant evergreen carpet. *V. major* is prized for use as a trailing plant in containers with annuals or perennials. ❦

Periwinkles, such as *Vinca minor* 'Alba', are fast-growing, evergreen groundcovers. The white or sky-blue spring flowers are an added bonus.

Viola Violaceae, Violet Family

vy-OH-luh. Violet. Spring bloom. Sun or shade.

Description: Violets are well-loved spring flowers with distinctive, colorful blooms. The irregular flowers have 2 upper and 3 lower petals that are joined into a short spur. The insides of the lower petals may have fuzzy beards or bright-yellow markings. There are 2 groups of violets, which differ in their growth habit. Stemless violets have leaves and flowers that arise in a clump from a creeping rhizome. Stemmed violets produce sparse basal leaves and upright stalks that bear both leaves and flowers; they also grow from a creeping rhizome.

For early-spring color in a shady spot or wildflower garden, plant woolly blue violet (*Viola sororia*), shown here with *V.* 'Priceana', *top right,* which produces white flowers with purple centers.

The cheery flowers of horned violet (*Viola cornuta*) come in a variety of colors, including blue, purple, orange, yellow, and white. Plants bloom for several weeks in spring.

Viola canadensis (can-uh-DEN-sis), Canada violet. Size: 6″–12″ tall; leaves 2″–3″ long. This tall violet has heart-shaped leaves and ½″–¾″-wide creamy-white flowers with yellow eyes and a purple blush on the back of the petals. Zones 3–8.

V. cornuta (core-NEW-tuh), horned violet. Size: 4″–12″ tall; leaves 1″–2″ long. Horned violets have evergreen rosettes and sprawling, leafy stems. The 1″–1½″-wide flowers resemble pansies. 'Arkwright Ruby' has cherry-red flowers. 'Blue Perfection' has sky-blue flowers. 'Chantreyland' is deep-apricot. 'White Perfection' has white flowers. Zones 6–9.

V. labradorica (lab-ruh-DOOR-ih-kuh), Labrador violet. Size: 1″–4″ tall; leaves 1″ long; flowers ¾″ wide. This diminutive stemmed violet has deep-green, heart-shaped leaves and deep-purple flowers. The variety *purpurea* has purple-tinged leaves. Zones 3–8.

V. odorata (oh-door-AH-tuh), sweet violet. Size: 2″–8″ tall; leaves 2″–3″ long. This stemless violet has rounded, heart- or kidney-shaped leaves. The ¾″-wide, deep-purple or blue flowers are deliciously fragrant. 'Deloris' has deep-purple flowers. 'White Queen' has small white flowers. 'White Czar' has white flowers with a yellow eye. Zones 6–9.

V. sororia (sore-OR-ee-uh), woolly blue violet. Size: 3″–6″ tall; leaves 4″–6″ long. The commonly grown blue violet has ½″–1″-wide bearded flowers and heart-shaped leaves. Selections of *V. cucullata* and *V. papilionaceae* are often listed under this species or under *V. odorata*. 'Freckles' has light-blue flowers speckled with purple. 'Priceana' has purple-centered white flowers. 'Red Giant' has rose-red flowers. Zones 3–9.

How to Grow: Plant violets in moist, humus-rich soil in light to full shade. They can spread by creeping stems and self-sown seedlings and may become invasive. Divide in spring or fall. Transplant self-sown seedlings.

Landscape Uses: Violets are lovely foliage plants for yearlong groundcover effect under trees and shrubs. 🍁

Yucca Liliaceae, Lily Family

YUK-uh. Yucca, Adam's-Needle, Spanish Bayonet. Summer bloom. Full sun to light shade.

Grow drought- and heat-tolerant *Yucca flaccida* 'Ivory' in well-drained, sandy or loamy soil. Use it as a specimen plant or combine it with other drought-tolerant perennials.

Description: Yuccas produce huge clusters of bell-shaped flowers over upright, leathery, swordlike leaves in large evergreen rosettes. They grow from a branched taproot.

Yucca filamentosa (fill-uh-men-TOE-suh), Adam's-needle. Size: 5'–15' tall; leaves 2½' long. A graceful plant with 2"-long white flowers and broad blue-green leaves with curling filaments along their margins. 'Bright Edge' has yellow-variegated leaves. Zones 3–10.

Y. flaccida (flah-SID-uh). Size: 4'–7' tall; leaves 2½' long. This species is very similar to *Y. filamentosa* but has less-rigid leaves. 'Ivory' has outward-facing white flowers. Zones 4–10.

How to Grow: Plant yuccas in well-drained, sandy or loamy soil in full sun or light shade. Divide offsets (called pups) in spring or fall.

Landscape Uses: Yuccas are bold in foliage and in flower. Plant them alone for accent or in combination with perennials. Contrast the stiff foliage with soft leaves. 🍂

Basic Botany
and Nomenclature

We've tried to keep botanical jargon to a minimum in this encyclopedia, but it's still helpful to familiarize yourself with some basic terms so plant descriptions make sense. The illustrations of parts of a plant (below), leaf forms (page 494), and flower forms (page 495) will give you a good start. For more terms, see "Key Words" on page 498.

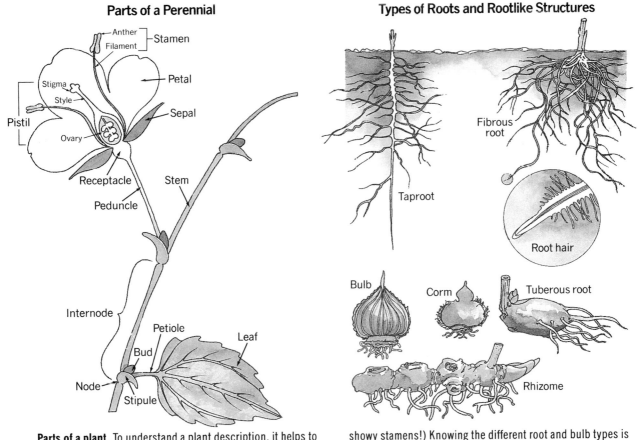

Parts of a Perennial

Types of Roots and Rootlike Structures

Parts of a plant. To understand a plant description, it helps to know basic plant parts. (You have to know what a stamen is to know what a catalog means when it says a perennial has showy stamens!) Knowing the different root and bulb types is useful at planting time, and later if you want to move or divide a plant.

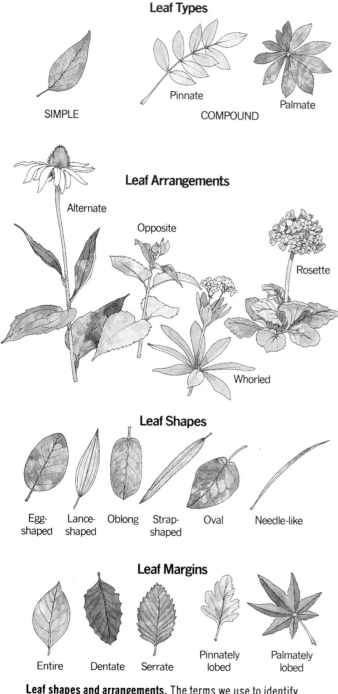

Leaf Types

SIMPLE

Pinnate

COMPOUND

Palmate

Leaf Arrangements

Alternate

Opposite

Rosette

Whorled

Leaf Shapes

Egg-shaped Lance-shaped Oblong Strap-shaped Oval Needle-like

Leaf Margins

Entire Dentate Serrate Pinnately lobed Palmately lobed

Leaf shapes and arrangements. The terms we use to identify leaf shapes and arrangements give us a common language for describing plants.

LEAF AND FLOWER FORMS

When you're reading a plant description or trying to describe a plant to someone else, where do you start? Plant height (for perennials, this includes the flowers) is self-explanatory; usually leaf and flower colors are, too. Width is straightforward: Rounded or mounding plants are usually as wide as they are tall, while tall or narrow plants are usually two to three times as tall as they are wide. But when you look at shapes and textures, botanical key words will help you understand exactly what the plant looks like.

Looking at Leaves

When you look at a leaf, make a mental checklist. First, look at leaf color and size. Is the color of the underside of the leaf different from the color on top? Is the leaf small, medium, or large? What about texture? Is the leaf smooth or rough to the touch? Is it glossy like pachysandra, waxy like sedum, or hairy like black-eyed Susan?

Leaf Types

Once you've checked off size, color, and texture, see how the leaf is growing on the plant. Is each leaf attached separately to the stem, or is it divided into smaller leaflets? Here are a few key words that are often used to describe leaf types:

Simple. Leaves that aren't divided into leaflets are called simple.

Compound. Leaves that have leaflets are compound.

Pinnate. When the leaflets of compound leaves run down either side of the leaf stem, they're called pinnate.

Palmate. When the leaflets of compound leaves are borne in a fan- or finger-like pattern, they're called palmate.

Leaf Arrangements

Next, see how the leaves attach to the stem. Here are four different ways a leaf and stem can connect:

Alternate. If the leaves are staggered up the sides of the stem, with one leaf at each node, they're alternate.

Opposite. If pairs of leaves are borne at the same place or node on the stem, they're opposite.

Whorled. If three or more leaves are borne at the same place, on the stem they're whorled.

Rosette. If the leaves seem to form a circle or crown directly on the ground, they're called a rosette.

Leaf Shapes

Look at the leaf shape. Is the leaf (or leaflet) egg-shaped, lance-shaped, oblong, strap-shaped, oval, or needle-like? What about the margins of the leaf? If the leaf margin is smooth, it's called entire. If it's toothed, it's dentate, but if the margin is cut like saw teeth, it's serrate. Leaf margins may be more deeply cut, resulting in fingerlike projections called lobes. These may run evenly up the sides of the leaf, like an oak leaf (called pinnately lobed). Or they may be arranged in a fingerlike pattern, like a maple leaf (called palmately lobed).

Facts about Flowers

Look at flowers the same way you look at leaves. Are the flowers borne singly, like

Flower cluster types. The perennial flowers shown here represent basic flower cluster types. When you come across descriptions of unfamiliar flowers, remember these plants for an instant mental picture.

columbine, or in clusters, like yarrow? The shape of a flower cluster can help you identify it. Here are typical cluster shapes:

Spike. If the flowers are closely attached (not on stalks) along an unbranched stem (like torch lily), it's a spike.

Raceme. If the flowers have individual stalks and are attached along an unbranched stem (like a lupine), it's a raceme.

Panicle. If the flowers have individual stalks and are attached along a branched stem (like an astilbe), it's a panicle.

Umbel. If the flowers all have stalks that are the same length, and all emerge from the same place on the stem, they form a flat-topped cluster (like Queen-Anne's-lace) called an umbel.

Individual Flower Shapes

Individual flowers have distinctive shapes as well. They may be daisy-shaped, like aster; star-shaped, like sedum; tubular, like hosta; bell-shaped, like campanula; pealike, like baptisia; cup-shaped, like poppy; or spurred, like delphinium or columbine.

Some flower shapes are characteristic of their genus, like iris and narcissus. Others, like the daisy shape, are characteristic of whole plant families: You can recognize plants in the aster family, Asteraceae, including chrysanthemums, coneflowers, coreopsis, and many other perennials, by their daisy flowers.

ALL ABOUT PLANT NAMES

Being able to understand a plant description—or to describe a plant accurately to a nursery owner—will make your life as a perennial gardener a lot easier. But to talk about, read about, or buy plants with confidence, you still need to know the plant's name.

So often, descriptions of plants are vague and confusing. When your neighbor says her great-aunt used to grow a plant that had pink flowers and was short and fragrant, you may have a hard time picturing the plant she means. Even if a plant springs to mind, it's probably the wrong one. Imagine trying to find someone in New York City who'd been described to you as a short woman with dark hair!

Botanical Nomenclature

The popular names we use for plants, technically called common names, usually evolved locally to describe either a characteristic of the plant or one of its uses. Many of these names are colorful and delightful—black-eyed Susan, goat's beard, painted daisy, cupid's dart. The trouble starts when the same plant has several common names, each aquired in a different place. Do you plant hostas, funkias, or plantain lilies? Red hot pokers or torch lilies? Gayfeathers or blazing-stars? In each case, you have the same plant, "disguised" under several names.

Another problem with common names is that they're sometimes applied to several plants. Are your geraniums annuals with big, round flower heads and fancy foliage (*Pelargonium* spp.), or perennials that make great groundcovers (*Geranium* spp.)? Do your coneflowers have purple petals (*Echinacea* spp.) or yellow petals with orange, black, brown, or green centers (*Rudbeckia* spp.)? When you're recommending a plant to a friend in another state or trying to find a plant you've read about, this kind of confusion can be disappointing.

Genus and Species

Botanical names are based on the binomial system of nomenclature, developed by Carolus Linnaeus, which assigns all plants and

Family Ties

When you turn to the individual entries in the encyclopedia section, you'll see the family name of each perennial listed with its botanical name. Families are groups of related genera that share broad characteristics. Family names usually end in "-aceae," like the rose family, Rosaceae. Knowing what family a perennial belongs to can give you some clues about its traits, behavior, susceptibilities, and preferred conditions.

For example, if you want to light up your garden in late summer and fall, you'll find that most favorite late-blooming perennials are in the aster family, Asteraceae, including *Aster, Boltonia, Chrysanthemum, Coreopsis, Dahlia, Echinacea* (purple coneflower), and *Rudbeckia* (coneflower). If you'd like to grow a sun-loving, trouble-free succulent perennial like *Sedum* or *Sempervivum* (hens-and-chickens) in your garden or on a rock wall, you'll find them in the Crassulaceae, the family of the familiar jade plant.

animals two Latinized names known as the generic name and specific epithet. Together these two names make up the species name. Here's how it works:

Genus. Closely related plants are grouped together under a single name, known as the genus.

Species. Plants within a genus can be separated from each other by recognizable, individual characteristics. Each different plant is assigned a specific epithet. Taken together, the genus and specific epithet form the species name.

Varieties, Cultivars, and Hybrids

Further groupings make a plant's identity even clearer. Here's how horticulturists define words you often find in garden books, magazines, and catalogs—variety, cultivar, and hybrid:

Variety. If a plant develops a characteristic in nature that makes it different from the rest of its species—say, white flowers in a species that normally has red flowers—it's set apart as a variety. For example, *Ajuga reptans* var. *alba* is a white-flowered variety of ajuga.

Cultivar. On the other hand, plant breeders work hard to create special characteristics like variegated foliage, new colors, and double flowers. Their plants are "cultivated varieties," called cultivars for short. Cultivar names are set in single quotes and can be used with the botanical or common name of a plant—for example, *Achillea filipendulina* 'Gold Plate' or 'Gold Plate' yarrow.

Hybrid. Breeders can also cross different species to develop plants that combine some characteristics of both parent species. These hybrids are indicated with an "×" in their botanical name—*Aconitum* × *bicolor*, for example. Rarely, plant breeders cross plants from two different genera. In those cases, the × precedes the botanical name.

Key Words

Acid soil.   A soil with a pH value less than 7.

Alkaline soil.   A soil with a pH value higher than 7.

Alternate.   The arrangement of leaves singly along a stem. Leaves occur on different sides of the stem, one leaf per node.

Annual.   A plant that completes its life cycle in one growing season and then dies.

Anther.   The tip or pollen-bearing portion of a stamen.

Axil.   The space or angle above the junction of a petiole and a stem.

Basal leaf.   A leaf that grows at the base of a plant, emerging directly from the crown.

Berry.   A fleshy fruit that contains many seeds and is formed from one ovary, such as blueberry or tomato.

Biennial.   A plant that completes its life cycle in two years and then dies.

Blade.   The flattened, enlarged portion of a leaf.

Bract.   A modified, often showy leaf located at the base of a flower or group of flowers; the "petals" of poinsettias are actually bracts.

Bulb.   An underground stem that stores energy in modified leaves, as in the bulbs of daffodils or tulips.

Calyx.   The collective group of sepals of a flower.

Capsule.   A dry fruit with two or more cells that splits open to release seeds.

Clone.   A group of plants all derived from one individual by vegetative (asexual) propagation such as cuttings or division.

Compound leaf.   A leaf with the blade divided into two or more distinct leaflets.

Corm.   An underground stem that stores energy in modified stem tissue, as in a crocus corm.

Corolla.   The collective group of petals of a flower.

Corona.   The crown-shaped central tube found on flowers such as daffodils.

Crown.   The part of a plant where the stem meets the roots, usually at or just below the soil line.

Cultivar.   A group of cultivated plants, selected and named for desirable characteristics such as flower size, color, or variegated foliage. The plants will keep their distinctive characteristics when propagated (sexually or asexually).

Cutting.   A piece of stem or root that is removed from a plant and induced to develop into a new plant with stems, leaves, and roots.

Deadheading.   Removing spent flowers.

Deciduous.   Losing leaves at the end of the growing season; not evergreen; used to describe trees that shed their leaves in fall.

Disbudding.   Removing some of a plant's buds to encourage the remaining buds to grow larger.

Disk flowers.   The small, tube-shaped flowers located in the center of flower heads of plants such as asters and daisies.

Division.   A plant separated or split apart from a clump of plants for the purpose of propagation; also the splitting of one clump of plants for the purpose of propagation.

Evergreen.   Retaining green foliage through the winter.

Filament.   The stalk of a stamen. The filament supports the anther.

Fruit.   A ripened ovary.

Herbaceous.   Dying back to the ground each year; not woody.

Inflorescence.   A cluster of flowers.

Irregular flower. A flower with an unevenly shaped corolla, sometimes having an upper and lower lip.

Leaflet. One of the divisions of a compound leaf.

Life cycle. The germination, growth, flowering, seed production and death of a plant.

Lobe. A segment of a divided leaf or petal.

Multiple fruit. A fruit like the pineapple, formed when the fruits of several closely-spaced flowers join together.

Neutral soil. Soil with a pH value equal to 7, neither acid nor alkaline.

Node. The point of attachment of a leaf to a stem.

Offset. A lateral shoot at the base of a plant that is easily removed to form a new plant.

Opposite. The arrangement of leaves in pairs on a stem. Leaves are located directly across from each other, on opposite sides of the stem, two leaves per node.

Ovary. The basal portion of a pistil, which develops into a fruit containing one or more seeds.

Palmate. Lobed or divided like the shape of a hand, with all of the divisions originating from the same point.

Perennial. A plant that lives for three or more seasons.

Petal. One of the showy, often colorful portions of a flower.

Petiole. The stalk of a leaf.

pH. The representation of the hydrogen ion concentration of soils. Used to measure the acidity or alkalinity of a soil.

Pinnate. Veins or leaflets emerging from a central midvein or leaf stem, arranged in rows like a feather.

Pistil. The female reproductive structure of a plant, found in the flower.

Pod. A dry fruit that splits open to release seeds.

Pollen. Minute grains that carry the male reproductive cells, borne on anthers.

Ray flowers. Strap-shaped flowers that surround the central disc flowers in flower heads of plants like asters and daisies.

Rhizome. A horizontal, underground stem modified and often enlarged for food storage.

Rootstock. A rhizome or underground stem. In grafting, the underground portion or stock of a plant onto which another plant is grafted.

Rosette. A basal cluster of leaves that arises from the crown.

Runner (stolon). A shoot or stem that usually creeps along the ground and roots at the nodes. It may produce a new plant at a node or the growing tip.

Seed. A fertilized, ripened ovule (egg) that can grow into a new plant.

Sepal. One part of a whorl of green, leafy structures, located on the flower stem just below the petals.

Sessile. Without a petiole or flowerstalk.

Simple leaf. A leaf with an undivided blade.

Spike. Generally a narrow, upright inflorescence; specifically, an upright inflorescence with sessile flowers.

Stamen. The male reproductive organ of a plant, found in the flower.

Stigma. The surface of a pistil that receives pollen.

Style. The stalk supporting the stigma.

Succulent. Having thick, fleshy, water-holding leaves or stems.

Taproot. The central, often thickened root of a plant, such as a carrot.

Terminal bud. The bud borne at the tip of a stem.

Tuber. A swollen, underground stem modified to store large quantities of food.

Variegated. Striped, spotted, or otherwise marked with a color other than green; often used to describe leaves.

Whorled. The arrangement of leaves or flowers in circular clusters around a stem.

Resources

Arranged by subject, here's a list of mail-order sources for seeds, plants, tools, and information. Although some catalogs are free, be sure to write and inquire since some do charge a fee and prices may change yearly. Plant societies and smaller companies would appreciate a self-addressed, stamped business envelope enclosed with your inquiry.

Some nurseries offer plants that have been collected from the wild, which may contribute to the near or total extinction of a species. Make sure bulbs, wildflowers, and native plants are nursery-propagated before you buy them.

Perennials and Ornamental Grasses

Andre Viette Farm and Nursery
Route 1, Box 16
Fishersville, VA 22939

Bluestone Perennials
7211 Middle Ridge Rd.
Madison, OH 44057

Busse Gardens
Route 2, Box 238
Cakato, MN 55321

Carroll Gardens
P.O. Box 310
444 E. Main St.
Westminster, MD 21158

Gilbert H. Wild and Son, Inc.
P.O. Box 338
1112 Joplin St.
Sarcoxie, MO 64862-0338

Henry Field Seed & Nursery Co.
415 N. Burnett St.
Shenandoah, IA 51602

Holbrook Farm and Nursery
P.O. Box 368
115 Lance Rd.
Fletcher, NC 28732

Klehm Nursery
Box 197
Penny Rd., Route 5
South Barrington, IL 60010

Kurt Bluemel, Inc.
2740 Greene Ln.
Baldwin, MD 21013

Milaeger's Gardens
4838 Douglas Ave.
Racine, WI 53402-2498

Montrose Nursery
P.O. Box 957
Hillsborough, NC 27278

Park Seed Co.
P.O. Box 31
Cokesbury Rd.
Greenwood, SC 29647

Schreiner's Gardens
3625 Quinaby Rd. NE
Salem, OR 97303

Siskiyou Rare Plant Nursery
2825 Cummings Rd.
Medford, OR 97501

Thompson & Morgan, Inc.
P.O. Box 1308
Jackson, NJ 08527

W. Atlee Burpee & Co.
300 Park Ave.
Warminister, PA 18974

Wayside Gardens
1 Garden Ln.
Hodges, SC 29695

We-Du Nurseries
Route 5, Box 724
Marion, NC 28752

White Flower Farm
P.O. Box 50
Route 63
Litchfield, CT 06759-0050

Bulbs

The Daffodil Mart
Route 3, Box 794
Gloucester, VA 23061

Dutch Gardens
P.O. Box 200
Adelphia, NJ 07710

John Scheepers, Inc.
P.O. Box 700
Bantam, CT 06750

McClure & Zimmerman
P.O. Box 368
108 W. Winnebago St.
Friesland, WI 53935

Van Bourgondien Bros., Inc.
P.O. Box A
245 Farmingdale Rd.
Babylon, NY 11702

Vandenberg
1 Black Meadow Rd.
Chester, NY 10918

Wildflowers and Native Plants

Applewood Seed Co.
5380 Vivian St.
Arvada, CO 80002

Clyde Robin Seed Co.
3670 Enterprise Ave.
Hayward, CA 94545

Fancy Fronds
1911 4th Ave. W.
Seattle, WA 98119

Native Seeds, Inc.
14590 Triadelphia Mill Rd.
Dayton, MD 21306

Niche Gardens
1111 Dawson Rd.
Chapel Hill, NC 27516

Plants of the Southwest
Route 6, Box 11-A
Santa Fe, NM 87501

Prairie Nursery
P.O. Box 306
Westfield, WI 53964

Woodlanders, Inc.
1128 Colleton Ave.
Aiken, SC 29801

Herbs

Caprilands Herb Farm
534 Silver St.
Coventry, CT 06238

Fox Hill Farm
P.O. Box 9
443 W. Michigan Ave.
Parma, MI 49269

Nichols Garden Nursery
1190 N. Pacific Hwy.
Albany, OR 97321

Sandy Mush Herb Nursery
Route 2
Surrett Cove Rd.
Leicester, NC 28748

Well-Sweep Herb Farm
317 Mt. Bethel Rd.
Port Murray, NJ 07865

Tools, Supplies, and Garden Accessories

Gardener's Eden
P.O. Box 7307
San Francisco, CA 94120-7307

Gardener's Supply Co.
128 Intervale Rd.
Burlington, VT 05401

Gardens Alive!
5100 Schenley Place
Lawrenceburg, IN 47025

Harmony Farm Supply
P.O. Box 460
Graton, CA 95444

The Kinsman Company, Inc.
River Rd.
Point Pleasant, PA 18950

The Natural Gardening Co.
217 San Anselmo Ave.
San Anselmo, CA 94960

Necessary Trading Co.
P.O. Box 305
422 Salem Ave.
New Castle, VA 24127

Peaceful Valley Farm Supply
P.O. Box 2209
Grass Valley, CA 95945

Smith & Hawken
25 Corte Madera
Mill Valley, CA 94941

The Urban Farmer Store
2833 Vicente St.
San Francisco, CA 94116

Walt Nicke Co.
P.O. Box 433
36 McLeod Ln.
Topsfield, MA 01983

Plant Societies

American Horticultural Society
7931 E. Boulevard Dr.
Alexandria, VA 22308

American Rock Garden Society
Jacques Mommens
P.O. Box 67
Millwood, NY 10546

The Hardy Plant Society—
   MidAtlantic Group
Betty Mackey
440 Louella Ave.
Wayne, PA 19087

Hardy Plant Society of Oregon
P.O. Box 609
Beaverton, OR 97005

National Wildflower
   Research Center
2600 FM 973 North
Austin, TX 78725-4201

New England Wild Flower Society
Membership
180 Hemenway Rd.
Framingham, MA 01701-2699

Perennial Plant Association
Attn: Dr. Steven M. Still
3383 Schirtzinger Rd.
Hilliard, OH 43026

Suggested Reading

Landscaping

Brookes, John. *The Book of Garden Design.* New York: Macmillan Publishing Co., 1991.

Favretti, Rudy and Joy P. *For Every House a Garden: A Guide for Reproducing Period Gardens.* 2d ed. Hanover, N.H.: University Press of New England, 1990.

Frey, Susan Rademacher, and Barbara W. Ellis. *Outdoor Living Spaces.* Emmaus, Pa.: Rodale Press, 1992.

Harper, Pamela J. *Designing with Perennials.* New York: Macmillan Publishing Co., 1991.

Hobhouse, Penelope. *Color in Your Garden.* Boston: Little, Brown & Co., 1985.

Schenk, George. *The Complete Shade Gardener.* Boston: Houghton Mifflin Co., 1985.

Squire, David. *The Complete Guide to Using Color in Your Garden.* Emmaus, Pa.: Rodale Press, 1991.

Taylor's Guide Staff. *Taylor's Guide to Garden Design.* Boston: Houghton Mifflin Co., 1988.

General Gardening

Ball, Jeff and Liz. *Rodale's Flower Garden Problem Solver.* Emmaus, Pa.: Rodale Press, 1990.

Daughtrey, Margery L., and Maurie Semel. *Herbaceous Perennials: Diseases and Insect Pests.* Information Bulletin 207. Ithaca, NY: Cornell Cooperative Extension, 1987.

Ellis, Barbara W., and Fern Marshall Bradley, eds. *The Organic Gardener's Handbook of Natural Insect and Disease Control.* Emmaus, Pa.: Rodale Press, 1992.

————. *Rodale's All-New Encyclopedia of Organic Gardening.* Emmaus, Pa.: Rodale Press, 1992.

Everett, Thomas H. *The New York Botanical Garden Illustrated Encyclopedia of Horticulture.* New York: Garland Publishing, 1981.

Liberty Hyde Bailey Hortorium Staff. *Hortus Third: A Concise Dictionary of Plants Cultivated in the United States and Canada.* New York: Macmillan Publishing Co., 1976.

Smith, Miranda, and Anna Carr. *Rodale's Insect, Disease & Weed Identification Guide.* Emmaus, Pa.: Rodale Press, 1988.

Perennials

Armitage, Allan M. *Herbaceous Perennial Plants.* Athens, Ga.: Varsity Press, 1989.

Clausen, Ruth Rogers, and Nicolas H. Ekstrom. *Perennials for American Gardens.* New York: Random House, 1989.

Harper, Pamela, and Frederick McGourty. *Perennials: How to Select, Grow, and Enjoy.* Los Angeles: Price Stern Sloan, 1985.

Keen, Mary. *The Garden Border Book.* Deer Park, Wis.: Capability's Books, 1987.

Lima, Patrick. *The Harrowsmith Perennial Garden.* Charlotte, Vt.: Camden House Publishing, 1987.

Lloyd, Christopher. *The Well-Tempered Garden.* New York: Penguin Books, 1985.

McGourty, Frederick. *The Perennial Gardener.* Boston: Houghton Mifflin Co., 1989.

Phillips, Roger, and Martyn Rix. *The Random House Book of Perennials.* 2 vols. New York: Random House, 1991.

Sheldon, Elisabeth. *A Proper Garden: On Perennials in the Garden.* Harrisburg, Pa.: Stackpole Books, 1989.

Still, Steven M. *Manual of Herbaceous Ornamental Plants.* 3d ed. Champaign, Ill.: Stipes Publishing Co., 1988.

Taylor's Guide Staff. *Taylor's Guide to Perennials.* Rev. ed. Boston: Houghton Mifflin Co., 1986.

Thomas, Graham Stuart. *Perennial Garden Plants.* 3d ed. Millwood, N.Y.: SagaPress Press, 1990.

Woods, Christopher. *Encyclopedia of Perennials: A Gardener's Guide.* New York: Facts on File, 1992.

Herbaceous Plants for Mixed Borders

Gardner, Jo Ann. *The Heirloom Garden: Selecting & Growing Over 300 Old-Fashioned Ornamentals.* Pownal, Vt.: Storey Communications, 1992.

Glattstein, Judy. *Garden Design with Foliage.* Pownal, Vt.: Storey Communications, 1991.

Greenlee, John. *The Encyclopedia of Ornamental Grasses.* Emmaus, Pa.: Rodale Press, 1992.

Johnson, Lady Bird, and Carlton B. Lees. *Wildflowers across America.* New York: Abbeville Press, 1988.

Proctor, Rob. *Country Flowers.* New York: Harper-Collins Publishers, 1991.

Reddell, Rayford Clayton, and Robert Galyean. *Growing Fragrant Plants.* New York: Harper & Row, 1989.

Taylor's Guide Staff. *Taylor's Guide to Annuals.* rev. ed. Boston: Houghton Mifflin Co., 1986.

———. *Taylor's Guide to Bulbs.* Rev. ed. Boston: Houghton Mifflin Co., 1986.

———. *Taylor's Guide to Ground Covers, Vines, and Grasses.* Boston: Houghton Mifflin Co., 1987.

Trees and Shrubs for Mixed Borders

Dirr, Michael A. *Manual of Woody Landscape Plants.* 4th ed. Champaign, Ill.: Stipes Publishing Co., 1990.

Reddell, Rayford Clayton. *Growing Good Roses.* New York: Harper & Row, 1988.

Taylor's Guide Staff. *Taylor's Guide to Roses.* Rev. ed. Boston: Houghton Mifflin Co., 1986.

———. *Taylor's Guide to Shrubs.* Boston: Houghton Mifflin Co., 1987.

———. *Taylor's Guide to Trees.* Boston: Houghton Mifflin Co., 1988.

Whitcomb, Carl E. *Know It and Grow It II: A Guide to the Identification and Use of Landscape Plants.* Stillwater, Okla.: Lacebark Publications, 1985.

Wyman, Donald. *Shrubs and Vines for American Gardens.* Enl. rev. ed. New York: Macmillan Publishing Co., 1969.

———. *Trees for American Gardens.* Enl. rev. ed. New York: Macmillan Publishing Co., 1969.

Regional Gardening

DeFreitas, Stan. *Complete Guide to Florida Gardening.* Rev. ed. Dallas, Tex.: Taylor Publishing Co., 1984.

Gundell, Herb. *Complete Guide to Rocky Mountain Gardening.* Fort Wayne, Ind.: Windless Orchard Series, 1991.

Hill, Lewis. *Cold-Climate Gardening.* Pownal, Vt.: Storey Communications, 1987.

Hunt, William Lanier. *Southern Gardens, Southern Gardening.* Durham, N.C.: Duke University Press, 1992.

McKeown, Denny. *Complete Guide to Midwest Gardening.* Dallas, Tex.: Taylor Publishing Co., 1985.

Rushing, Felder. *Gardening Southern Style.* Jackson, Miss.: University Press of Mississippi, 1987.

Smaus, Robert. *The Los Angeles Times Planning and Planting the Garden.* New York: Harry N. Abrams, 1989.

Sunset Magazine and Book Editors. *Sunset Western Garden Book.* 5th ed. Menlo Park, Calif.: Lane Publishing Co., 1988.

Taylor's Guide Staff. *Taylor's Guide to Gardening in the South.* Boston: Houghton Mifflin Co., 1992.

———. *Taylor's Guide to Gardening in the Southwest.* Boston: Houghton Mifflin Co., 1992.

Vick, Roger. *Gardening on the Prairies: A Guide to Canadian Home Gardening.* Saskatoon, Saskatchewan: Western Producer Prairie Books, 1987.

Index

Note: Page references in *italic* indicate tables.
Boldface references indicate illustrations and photographs.

505